The North Star State

The
North Star
State

A MINNESOTA HISTORY READER

EDITED BY
Anne J. Aby

FOREWORD BY
Paul Gruchow

MINNESOTA HISTORICAL SOCIETY PRESS

All images used in this book are in the collections of the Minnesota Historical Society. Front cover, top to bottom: Joseph R. Meeker, "Minnesota Harvest Field" (oil, 1877); Henry Inman, "Esh-Tan-Hum-Leah (Sleepy Eye)" (oil, c. 1835); Nicholas R. Brewer, "View of St. Paul (Wabasha Steetscape)" (oil, c. 1908); Syd Fossum, "The Meeting" (oil, 1937); Anonymous, "Samuel D. Badger (Drummer Boy)" (pastel, c. 1870). Spine and back cover, top to bottom: Anonymous, Crazy quilt (1880); Tim Rummelhoff, Stone Arch Bridge (1995, MHS Public Relations Office); Lee Radzak, Split Rock Lighthouse; Anonymous, Ojibwe bandolier bag (beaded cotton, late 19th/early 20th century); Newel C. Wyeth, "News from Home" (oil, c. 1915).

www.mnhs.org/mhspress

Printed in Canada.
10 9 8 7 6 5 4 3 2 1

International Standard Book Number
ISBN 0-87351-443-2 (cloth)
ISBN 0-87351-444-0 (paper)

⊛ The paper used in this publication meets the minimum requirements of the American National Standard for Information Sciences—Permanence for Printed Library Materials, ANSI Z39.48-1984.

Library of Congress Cataloging-in-Publication Data

The North Star State : a Minnesota history reader /
edited by Anne J. Aby ; foreword by Paul Gruchow.
     p.   cm.
Includes bibliographical references and index.
ISBN 0-87351-443-2 (alk. paper)
ISBN 0-87351-444-0 (pbk. : alk. paper)
     1. Minnesota—History.
     I. Aby, Anne J., 1945–
F606.5 .N67 2002
977.6—dc21   2002010099

The North Star State was designed by Will Powers at the Minnesota Historical Society Press. It was set in the Clifford family of typefaces by Allan Johnson at Phoenix Type, Inc., Milan, Minnesota. *The North Star State* was printed by Friesens, Altona, Manitoba, Canada.

The North Star State

Labor

Race and Ethnicity

Making History

Preface

Anne J. Aby

Minnesota is my adopted home. I grew up in New Jersey and Massachusetts, but in the 1960s I went to Carleton College in Northfield to major in mathematics. Instead I graduated as a history major. The history classes I took in college, especially those taught by Carlton Qualey and those in a Carleton-sponsored summer in Japan program after my sophomore year, gave me a life-long love of history. In 1976 I returned to the state to teach at Worthington Community College, now Minnesota West Community and Technical College, where I was asked to teach Minnesota history.

The very concept of teaching a single state's history was new to me; I never took New Jersey history or Massachusetts history when I was growing up, nor had I taught Virginia history when I was at Northern Virginia Community College. Those states assumed their state's history was *American* history. As a westward expansion state, Minnesota could not make such claims. The question I faced: what makes Minnesota unique? What is unusual or representative about its landscape, its industry, its people, and how have these factors shaped Minnesota's history? The essays I have selected for this collection form a partial answer, a compendium that can serve students and general readers equally well.

I began with geography, because landscape is a major factor in any state's early development. In Minnesota, we have glaciers to thank for vast areas of fertile soil in the Minnesota River and Red River valleys and for the unique flow of our waterways, running south by the Mississippi to the Gulf of Mexico, eastward to Lake Superior and the Gulf of St. Lawrence, and north by the Red River to Hudson's Bay.

Since water represented the only means of travel for centuries, Minnesota's abundant water routes helped extend and define its history. Eastern tribes like the Ojibwe, Dakota, and Assiniboine moved westward by way of the lakes in response to the arrival of Europeans along the eastern coast of North America. The French followed, seeking the riches of the fur trade as well as a Northwest Passage to the Pacific, and brought the French language—still evidenced in Minnesota place names like Lac Qui Parle and Mille Lacs. The fur trade brought together European traders, their culture, and their trade goods, with Native Americans, their culture, and their resources. Grand Portage in northern Minnesota, as discussed in Solon J. Buck's essay, was the center of the fur trade for nearly a century and the beginning of generations of difficult relations between Native American and white cultures.

The rivers that brought voyageurs would later carry steamboats filled with easterners and immigrants eager to settle lands made available by treaties relentlessly negotiated with the Ojibwe and Dakota. Soon they would transport logs from logging camps, power the mills in Minneapolis. From the headwaters at Lake Itasca south through the Twin Cities, the Mississippi became Minnesota's direct line to the rest of the growing nation. For this collection, I have selected articles approaching these changes from a diversity of perspectives— from Bruce M. White's examinations of early interactions between whites and Indians to Alison Watts's essay on the early milling industry.

Geography would also play a role in determining Minnesota's future as it emerged from the territorial period and state boundaries were drawn. Rhoda Gilman explains how an "east-west" Minnesota would mean a largely agricultural economy; a "north-south" state would ultimately mean a more diverse economy as the riches of lumber and iron ore were later realized. Placement of railroads and later the interstate highway system helped set commercial patterns and could even determine the survival of towns as Richard V. Francaviglia shows in his essay. Today over half the population of Minnesota is located in the metropolitan Twin Cities area. The rest of the state is often referred to as "outstate" or "greater" Minnesota. With the 2002 congressional redistricting map, Luverne and Worthington in the southwest corner of the state are in the same "I-90" district as Rochester and Winona, perhaps the revenge of those 1858 politicians who wanted an east-west state.

Geography played a key role in much of Minnesota's history, but it has always been the people—with their ambitions and schemes—that have shaped that landscape into a community. Since the 1960s, teaching the history of any people has become increasingly challenging and complicated. Not only does that "history" become a year longer with the beginning of each fall semester, but the discussion of whose history and whose voices will be included has assumed increasing importance. Minnesota has also been greatly enriched by the incredible and ever-increasing diversity of its population. Every group that "chose Minnesota" has made significant contributions to the state's culture, economy, politics, and history. These contributions, often made in the face of adversity, discrimination, and prejudice, were overlooked or disregarded for too long. I have selected essays that explore this difficult transition, including articles on racial segregation in early schools, anti-Semitic hiring practices, the immigration question, women's suffrage, and St. Paul's early Chinese community. Minnesota's willingness to reconsider its past and welcome new groups today serves as a model for an increasingly diverse United States.

For my Minnesota history students, the complexities of human history are often made most meaningful, most understandable by the personal voice of someone from that time period. The assignment they have most enjoyed over the years has been their interviewing an older Minnesotan, often a grandparent or other relative. It gives them a first-person understanding of the depression, World War II, or farming in earlier times. More than one hundred fifty of these audiocassette tapes are now deposited at the Nobles County Historical Society and continue to be a gift both for the families who have participated and the community as well. To re create this experience over a greater expanse of time, I have selected a number of journal entries, letters, and reminiscences from people who lived our history when it was still vital and uncertain, including Jasper Searles's letters home from the Battle of Bull Run and Wenzel Petran's diary of early business on the frontier.

It's remarkable enough that such a diversity of essays existed on all of these subjects, but, even more amazingly, all of them came from a single magazine: *Minnesota History*. A quarterly since its inception in 1915, *Minnesota History* always has sought to provide a mix of articles on various subjects and historical periods specific to Minnesota's past. While the journal's format has changed several times, the basic mission to present readable and well-researched articles on subjects found in *Minnesota History* has remained constant since the quarterly was established under the leadership of Solon J. Buck.

Thus *Minnesota History* has produced over nine hundred well-researched and interesting articles dealing with Minnesota's past. However, these articles do represent the past as defined by the interests and the topics of the authors who submit them—the journal has never paid for contributions or specific articles—so gaps in certain subjects are in some cases gaps in authors' submissions. Some topics have continued to be extremely popular; for example, articles dealing with the fur trade, Indians, and labor history have been numerous in every decade of the journal's existence.

Another challenge to fulfilling the journal's mission of presenting Minnesota's past and heritage is how long it may take for a historical period or subject to "safely" become a part of the past. For example, while the journal was started in 1915, in-depth articles dealing with Minnesota and World War I have largely only been published in the last thirty years—nearly sixty years after the war ended. La Vern Rippley's article, "Anti-Germanism in Minnesota Schools, 1917-1919," is an example of this flowering of scholarship.

There are still no articles, however, concerning Minnesotans and the Vietnam War, although Minnesota's participation in the Civil War has been a frequent topic in every decade of publication. The fur trade has been a much more studied "industry" than more recent Minnesota businesses like 3M or Honeywell. While courses on the Sixties have become popular on college campuses, articles dealing with such a recent period are rare.

Sometimes "classic subjects" are re-examined in light of changing approaches or perspectives of historians. For example, while Indians, the fur trade, and pioneer life have been classic staples in terms of articles appearing in *Minnesota History* through nine decades of publication, more recent scholarship has provided new needed insights in deepening understanding of even "classic" topics. Priscilla K. Buffalohead's "Farmers, Warriors, Traders: A Fresh Look at Ojibwe Women" provides such a voice for the Ojibwe, just as Glenda Riley's "In or Out of the Historical Kitchen?: Minnesota Rural Women" does much the same for the pioneer experience. Earlier pieces dealing with women were rare or incomplete.

I have gathered these essential essays under subject headings for ready use as a reference and a way of highlighting some of the central concerns of our history. Inevitably these categories blur or intersect in interesting ways. The essays on labor struggles provide a fascinating counterbalance to the articles on the growth of industry. Last of all, I have included three essays about the new and ongoing ways that historians are reconsidering and reconstructing our past. Personal in their approach, these articles reveal the new challenges our state's historians face.

Minnesota's history is long and rich. It includes the still vibrant Native American cultures, especially Ojibwe and Dakota; the years of settlement and the developing agricultural economy; the Civil War, which for Minnesotans was both the war in the East with the sacrifices of the First Minnesota and the other regiments as well as the Dakota War in the Minnesota River valley; the impact of Big Business and industrialization on the state's economy; the Progressive Era; World War I, which for Minnesotans was both the war overseas as well as strident persecution of dissent at home; the Great Depression and World War II. Through their history, Minnesotans have come to accept diversity in population and in politics, maverick politicians and third parties. How is Minnesota unique? Where else could one assemble a hypothetical political panel that included Little Crow, Joe Rolette, Knute Nelson, Clara Ueland, Nellie Stone Johnson, Hubert Humphrey, and Jesse Ventura?

ACKNOWLEDGMENTS

This book was the product of a 2001 fall semester sabbatical from my teaching responsibilities at Minnesota West Community and Technical College, Worthington campus. The original intent was to produce a reader using *Minnesota History* articles for college students. However, a survey of college history faculty in Minnesota indicated Minnesota history is no longer taught in many state colleges and universities. Thus the audience was redefined to be more general. This redefinition has permitted a broader range of subjects and hopefully made the collection in fact an introduction to Minnesota history as well as a serious representation of scholarship.

I wish to thank the Minnesota Historical Society and the Minnesota Historical Society Press, and more specifically Gregory Britton, director; Deborah L. Miller, research supervisor; Anne R. Kaplan, managing editor of *Minnesota History;* Ann Regan, managing editor; and Ted Genoways, my editor, for all their support and assistance.

Finally, I thank my family, Bob, Meredith, and Martha, for their continued support, encouragement, and understanding through a challenging year.

Foreword
Discovering the Universe of Home

Paul Gruchow

I believe that history is the primary act of the human imagination. Let me try to explain what I mean by telling you a story, a bit of my own history:

What if one's life were not a commodity, not something to be bartered to the highest bidder, or made to order? What if one's life were governed by needs more fundamental than acceptance or admiration? What if one were simply to go home and plant some manner of garden?

To plant a garden is to enter the continuum of time. Each seed carries in its genome the history that will propel it into the future, and in planting it we stretch one of the long threads of our culture into tomorrow.

A home, like a garden, exists as much in time as in space. A home is the place in the present where one's past and one's future come together, the crossroads between history and heaven. I learned this truth the day we buried my mother.

In the previous month I had felt often like a man without an anchor. We were living in St. Paul and expecting our first child. For my wife it was a difficult and somewhat dangerous pregnancy. Christmas passed and the days turned toward the new year. The baby was overdue. In those same days, Mother was lying in a hospital bed in Montevideo, Minnesota, emaciated and in pain. She had already lost a brave battle against cancer but was unwilling, just yet, to concede defeat, for reasons that were, to me, mysterious. She was long past delusion about her prospects. My own heart resided in both places, full of fear and hope at the same time. I did not know where my body should be.

On the penultimate day of the old year, the baby, after a stubborn resistance of her own, finally came. She was big and beautiful and healthy. She gave one lusty cry as she entered the world and then lay quietly while she was bathed and dressed, looking about the room in wide-eyed wonder.

I telephoned Mother with the news. She said with surprising energy that she hoped she might see the baby before she died. But that day a fierce cold front settled over Minnesota. For more than a week, daytime temperatures did not rise above zero. We were terrified, as I suppose first-time parents always are, of our responsibilities. The baby seemed so helpless and fragile. We dared not risk the three-hour drive to the hospital.

One cloudy morning in mid-January the weather at last broke. We bundled up the baby and made a dash for Montevideo. In the darkened hospital room, we introduced grandmother and granddaughter. The baby slept against the rails of the bed while Mother fondled her with eyes too big for their bony sockets. They joined hands, the baby's soft, fat, and warm, Mother's cold, gaunt, and hard. With tremendous effort, Mother whispered three words barely audible above the hum of the humidifier.

"Is she healthy?" she asked. We wept because she was.

When we arrived back home, the telephone was ringing. A nurse was on the line with the word, hardly news, that Mother had died.

The weather was still bitter and gray the day we buried her in the little cemetery at St. John's Lutheran Church. After the ceremony we three children—Kathy, Paulette, and I—who felt strangely like children again that day, vulnerable and bewildered in an impossibly big world, took refuge one last time in the farmhouse where we had laughed and cried, together and alone, so many times.

We had meant to see to the household goods. There would be few other opportunities for it; we lived at a distance from one another and seldom found ourselves together. But almost the first albums we came across were the photo albums.

We sat in the living room then, not bothering to light the lamp, looking at the pictures and talking until the day died.

"Do you remember when Mother turned toward the backseat of the car and said, 'Where's your sister?' and Paul said, 'Oh, she fell out a long time ago,' and she *had*?"

"Do you remember the day Mother told the neighbor she couldn't go to the Women's Christian Temperance Union meeting because her wine was ready for bottling?"

"Do you remember the day Grandmother sat down to play the piano for the pastor, and the moment she hit the first chord the dog began to yowl?"

"Do you remember the morning we floated a pound of butter in Mother's hot laundry starch?"

"Do you remember the time you threw a stick at Cousin Lyle and it stuck in the top of his head and twanged back and forth like an arrow and he had to go to the doctor to have it removed?"

Do you remember?

Do you remember?

The stories tumbled as if out of an overstuffed closet. Sometimes we had three of them going at once. We laughed until we ached. I remember it now as one of the happiest afternoons of my life, the metamorphosis of a friendship deepening as the years pass and we three face our own mortalities. I think that I have never been more exactly at home, more tenaciously alive, than that afternoon, when old joy and new sorrow and present love reverberated together inside me.

All history is ultimately local and personal. To tell what we remember and to keep on telling it is to keep the past alive in the present. Should we not do so, we could not know, in the deepest sense, how to inhabit a place. To inhabit a place means literally to have made it a habit, to have made it the custom and ordinary practice of our lives, to have learned how to wear a place like a familiar garment, like the garments of sanctity that nuns once wore. The word habit, in its now dim original form, meant *to own*. We own places not because we possess the deeds to them, but because they have entered the continuum of our lives. What is strange to us—unfamiliar—can never be home.

It is the fashion just now to disparage nostalgia. Nostalgia, we believe, is a cheap emotion. But we forget what it means. In its Greek roots it means, literally, the return to home. It came into currency as a medical word in nineteenth-century Germany to describe the failure to thrive of the displaced persons—including my own ancestors—who had crowded into that country from the east. Nostalgia is the clinical term for homesickness, for the desire to be rooted in a place—to know clearly, that is, what time it is. This desire need not imply the impulse to turn back the clock, which, of course, we cannot do. It recognizes, rather, the truth—if home is a place in time—that we cannot know where we are now unless we can remember where we have come from. The real romantics are those who believe that history is the story of the triumphal march of progress, that change is indiscriminately for the better. Those who would demythologize the past seem to forget that we also construct the present as a myth, that there is nothing in the wide universe so vast as our own ignorance. Knowing that is our one real hope.

Now, one might raise two obvious questions about this story, or about any story like it: first, is it true; and second, even supposing it is true, why does it matter?

To the question of truthfulness, I might reply that the story is as honest and accurate as I know how to make it. So far as I am concerned, it is a faithful and dependable record of a series of events that really did happen. Were you to press me, however, I would be obliged to concede that many others who were involved in these same events would answer much differently. I know this because I published the story and then listened to the responses.

My younger sister said, "You know, I was eight years younger than you when all of this happened, just a kid really, and still living at home. I'm happy to have your story because it's not at all like the one I remember, so it causes me to think about those events in an entirely new way."

My twin sister said, "You know I was the one who fell out of that car, and what you don't tell is that we were on the way to the hospital so I could have the bandages removed from my legs after I had burned them in that bonfire, and because of the damage that fall did, I had to wear those bandages for another six weeks. Why did you leave that part out?" And I had to say I had left those details out because I had completely forgotten them.

I had a letter from my mother's doctor, who didn't need to say anything at all to remind me that Mother did not survive to see our first child solely out of her own grit but also because of the remarkably compassionate and dedicated care of a young family practitioner who in the end didn't even charge a fee for his services. Surely I ought to have mentioned that, but it, too, had escaped my memory.

I saw an old neighbor who said, "You know, the week before your mother went into the hospital for the last time, we went over to visit her and she was down to her last stick of firewood. We had to bring her wood for the furnace or she might have frozen to death." Those words stung as much as they were meant to sting. That was something I hadn't known, a measure of my own neglectfulness which I had failed to confront.

And then, not long after the book in which I told this story was published, I happened upon a file I didn't know existed containing the weekly letters my mother wrote to me while I was in college. As I read them, I realized that I had allowed the image of my mother as a woman dying in her mid-forties to overshadow, even to obliterate, the woman I had known while she was still healthy, a woman who took a rural pride in working hard, who teased constantly and laughed loudly, who was frank to a fault, and who humiliated me when I was a young man trying to get on as a sophisticate in the strange new world of the city by sending me back to the college campus after weekend visits home with grocery sacks full of unwashed garden produce and then writing to my roommates seeking assurance that I was eating the good farm vegetables she had sent instead of the pig feed they sold at the grocery stores. "And is he sharing his vegetables like I asked?" she would inquire. "I bet he isn't, ha ha." There were a lot of ha-has in her letters; she never trusted written words to convey their real meaning, which in her case was often two-edged.

I realized when I read those letters that there is an important woman in my past whom I'll have to try to get to know all over again, a woman considerably more complicated and interesting than the one I had remembered despite a good deal of effort at the remembrance.

Still, I find myself saying when I go back to the story I did write about the woman I did remember that however incomplete it may be, however narrow in its point of view, it nevertheless expresses something I believe to be true about her, about me, and about us.

Does it matter whether my story is true? That's not for me to judge, except in this respect: it matters deeply if mine is to be the only story that survives about my mother. If mine is the only story that survives, no matter how conscientious and thorough I have been about writing it, the memory that endures of my mother will be in some important way untrue, not because anything in particular about my story is false, but because it is a story, and like all stories, like all versions of history, it is necessarily selective.

It seems likely, when our present time has passed into history, that this will come to be characterized as the moment in western culture when we first fully realized and appreciated the importance of diversity, how our lives both in biology and in culture are strengthened, extended, and enriched by variations of all kinds, and, on the other hand, how perilous our lives become when we tie them to single points of view, however meritorious those points of view may be in themselves.

Here is a story about that:

Only a little more than a century ago, there lived on the prairies a people who had staked their lives and fortunes upon the buffalo. The buffalo once existed in seemingly inexhaustible numbers. There were, perhaps, 60,000,000 of them. When Coronado, the first European to see the prairies, traveled to Kansas from Mexico in 1541, a journey of several months, he reported that he was never once beyond sight of them.

If you were born into plains culture in those days, you were wrapped in swaddling clothes made from the soft skin of a buffalo calf and carried about until you could walk in a cradle lined with the pulverized dung of the buffalo, which served as a diaper. You grew into an adult life dependent in every particular upon the buffalo. It supplied you with food, with raiment, with shelter, with tools, with household furnishings, with paints and dyes, with cosmetics, with fuel.

And when you died, you were buried or raised upon a platform in a coffin made of buffalo hide. The buffalo was literally the beginning and the ending of your existence. You would have believed that the buffalo was eternal.

And then came the Europeans, whose railroad lines and fences and plows and relentless hunting reduced the buffalo nearly to extinction. This decimation threatened the survival of plains culture, as Americans knew. The United States Congress passed a bill in the 1860s to protect the few hundred buffalo that still survived, out of the tens of millions. President Grant vetoed it on the advice of his secretary of war, who said that to get rid of the buffalo was to get rid of the Indian problem.

There arose, then, among the desperate Native Americans, a shaman who said that the buffalo had not died, that they had merely gone down into the safety of the underworld. If the people, the shaman preached, would say the right prayers and perform the right dances, the buffalo would return and their way of life would be saved. So all across the prairies, the people danced and prayed. But Americans, despite their Constitution, outlawed this new aspect of native religions, the Ghost Dance.

In South Dakota, in December of 1890, a group of Lakotas danced in defiance of the ban. When ordered to quit, they left their reservation and headed for the Badlands, where they might dance and pray in peace. Along the way they were set upon by American cavalry and slaughtered, men, women, and children alike. The few survivors were carried to a nearby mission and laid out on the sanctuary floor to be treated for their wounds. Above the altar, hung for the Christmas season, was a banner reading, "Peace on Earth, Good Will Toward Men." The place was Wounded Knee.

This was the last battle of a long war. The buffalo were not, after all, eternal.

Today we have made in the same places a culture as dependent upon corn as the Dakota culture was upon buffalo. A person born in our time will be clothed as an infant in a diaper made in part of corn and fed a formula based upon corn syrup. That person will grow into adult life sustained in thousands of ways by products made from, packaged in, or manufactured with derivatives of corn, from every kind of food except fresh fish to plastics, textiles, building materials, machine parts, soaps, and cosmetics, even highways. And when that person dies, some laws require that the body should be embalmed—in a fluid made in part from corn.

We have not begun to imagine a life without corn. We have assumed, by the default of failing to think about it, that corn is eternal. But it is not any more eternal than the buffalo. In fact, because the corn we cultivate shares a common cytoplasm, it would take exactly one persistent pathogen to devastate our culture as we know it.

Just as too narrow a dependence upon the physical sources of our sustenance is dangerous, so a culture that relies upon too narrow a set of ideas can be imperiled in the long run, and so, within that culture, the usefulness of memory, of history, can be fatally weakened when there are too few stories about what really happened. A culture with only one version of its past is as untenable in the long run as a prairie with only one species of grass, and for the same reason: that it is too poor in resources to meet the challenges of change.

Still, one might ask, of what use is the past? What's done is done and cannot be undone; we can't go back and live in the past; and, despite the old bromide about being condemned to repeat the history we can't remember, we seem to make the same mistakes over and over again, no matter how keen our memories.

I'd say that the past is vital because it is primarily through the agency of thinking about history that we come to a sense of the ideal. In remembering what has gone before, we are inevitably reminded of what we have especially hated or cherished, and this information equips us to imagine a world better than the one we currently inhabit. History gives us the imagination, in other words, to plan for the future.

But let me remind you what happens all the time when we use history in just this way.

Suppose I said, "Do you remember the time when the lake here at the edge of our town was a clear-water lake with a hard bottom, when it teemed with ducks in the fall and produced lunker northerns in the summer? Do you remember how practically everybody in town used to go down to the lake on Sunday afternoons in the summer to picnic and swim and loll about in the shade afterwards? Do you remember that there was even a resort on our lake not so many decades ago, and that people used to come on the train all the way from Chicago to vacation here? I don't suppose we'll ever attract tourists from Chicago again, or even great flocks of ducks in the fall, but don't you think it would be terrific if we could make a clean lake again, one we didn't mind swimming in, one that produced fish the Health Department thought it was safe to eat? What do you suppose it would take to bring our lake back to health?"

Or suppose I said, "Do you remember what it was like at harvest time in the countryside during the days of the big steam threshing rigs? Do you remember how all the neighbors got together and went from farm to farm, the whole community pitching in to get the work done in time. Oh, it was hard, hot work, both in the fields pitching those big bundles of wheat, and in the kitchens where the women labored to produce two big lunches and a noontime feast every day. But you know, the work somehow seemed to go easier when it was done in that kind of company, and there was always wonderful food and time for talk and laughter.

"Oh, the stories that flew when we were making the threshing rounds! Everybody was always glad enough to see the hard labor come to an end, but the days afterwards always seemed uncomfortably lonely and quiet, too. What do you suppose would happen if we found ways now and then to do some of our work together as a community again? Don't you think that would be a good thing?"

Or suppose I said, "Do you remember what this town was like when it still had a school? I think our community was a little more lively in those days, don't you? It seemed like there was always something going on at the school—a band concert, or a basketball game, or a Halloween spook house, or a play. I think the school and the achievements of our children gave us all something to take pride in, a sense of community that we don't seem to have anymore. I know there are too few children here these days to hope that we'll have our school back anytime soon, but I wonder if there aren't some things we can do to put the children here in town back at the center of our lives again. Don't you think that would be good for our town?"

If I said any such thing in most of the midwestern communities I have known, this is the response I would inevitably get: "Well, thanks for mentioning that idea, Paul. We appreciate your sharing that. But you know, you've got to get a grip. Those good old days you're talking about? I tell you, I wouldn't trade my electric lights and my running water for those good old days of yours for all the tea in China. That's just nostalgia you're talking about there, Paul."

"I'm talking about community values and you're talking about personal conveniences, and those are not at all equivalents," I might protest, or, "I like plumbing and electricity, too, but maybe material progress and social progress are different objectives, achieved in different ways." But it would be no use. We have been taught to use the cudgel of nostalgia to beat the imagination out of history.

Here is another way in which we deprive our children of the power of history. We do it by failing to teach them about the places in which they have been raised.

The schools in which I myself was educated were by most standards first-rate. But they were, as our schools often have been, largely indifferent to the place and the culture in which they operated.

Among my science courses I took two full years of biology, but I never learned that the beautiful meadow at the bottom of my family's pasture was remnant virgin prairie. We did not spend, so far as I can remember, a single hour on prairies—the landscape in which we were immersed—in two years of biological study.

I took history courses for years, but I never learned that one of the founders of my town and for decades its leading banker—the man who platted the town and organized its school system, its library, its parks, and its fire department— was also the author of the first comprehensive treatise on Minnesota's prairie botany. I can only imagine now what it might have meant to me—a studious boy with a love of nature—to know that a great scholar of natural history had made a full and satisfying life in my town. I did not know until long after I left the place that it afforded the possibility of an intellectual life.

I read, in the course of 12 years of English instruction, many useful and stimulating books, but I never learned that someone who had won a National Book Award for poetry—Robert Bly—lived and worked on a farm only 30 miles from my house. The countryside was full of writers, I would later discover, but I did not meet anybody who had written a book until I went away to college. I had not imagined, or been encouraged to imagine, that it was possible to live in the country and to write books, too. Nor did I suspect it was possible to write books about our countryside. We read Sir Walter Scott, John Steinbeck, and Robert Frost, but not O. E. Rolvaag or Black Elk, Lois Hudson or Thomas McGrath, Meridel LeSeuer or Frederick Manfred. We did not read them at the University of Minnesota, either. I was left to unearth by my own devices, years later, the whole fine literature of my place.

I studied industrial arts with a man who taught me how to make a wooden nightstand and an electrical motor; I did not learn until many years later that on his own time he made wonderful lithographs and woodblock prints of the prairie landscape. I grew up believing that scenery consisted of mountains and waterfalls and deer, rendered on black velvet, and that there was nothing worth seeing in our own tedious flatlands.

I studied vocational agriculture. I learned how to identify 30 common weeds and how to formulate a good pig ration but nothing of the history of farming and nothing that might have encouraged me to think critically or creatively about how we farm. My father was an organic farmer. What I mainly learned from my vocational agriculture classes was that he was a nut.

Nothing in my education prepared me to believe, or encouraged me to expect, that there was any reason to be interested in my own place. If I hoped to amount to anything, I understood, I had better take the first road east out of town as fast as I could. And, like so many of my classmates, I did.

When we fail to teach our children how to inhabit the places where they have been raised—when we don't teach them the stories, the customs, the practices, the nature of those places—then we also fail to teach them how to be at home anywhere.

But suppose local history, culture, and natural history were at the center of our teaching. Wouldn't that, you might well ask, just encourage parochialism and xenophobia, and don't we already have those attributes in more than adequate supply?

I would argue, on the contrary, that parochialism and xenophobia are fed by the suspicion that all the really important things happen somewhere else. One of the magical effects of freeing the imagination to go to work in the place where it finds itself is how this enlarges the world.

One might say about country places, about midwestern places, about Minnesota places, what is said all the time with such assurance and authority that even the people who live in them often accept them as true: that such places are mediocre, that they are sleepy, that they are places in which ambition is either absent or irrelevant—there is not, for example, in Lake Woebegon a single person with a shred of ambition—that they are simple, whatever that means.

Such perceptions, believed, have a way of becoming self-fulfilling.

But the fact is that the same dramas and miracles of life occur in Windom as in Tokyo. People are born, they struggle to live worthy and productive lives, they are challenged by fate, buffeted by setbacks and disappointments, heartened in unexpected hours, visited by evil and grace alike, and come to sudden and premature or to lingering and overdue deaths everywhere in the world.

The great spectacles of nature, of fire and wind, of rain and ice, of heat and cold, of metamorphosis, of birth and death, of struggle and decay, of quiet and beauty visit alike the prairies of southwestern Minnesota and the burroughs of New York City.

Ankara or Timbuktu can be reached as certainly from the hills of southeastern Minnesota as from Amsterdam or Buenos Aires. Everywhere, as the native Minnesotans said, is the center of the world.

What happens when you apply the imagination of history to the events of any place, however small, is that its connections with all the rest of the universe then come into view. I came to this sense of the interconnectedness of all things through the land that I knew intimately as a boy. Land is, after all, before anything else, a historical document.

I lived, when I was a boy, by the blue light of the moon along country lanes so quiet I could hear the town traffic miles away, visible only as a burst of mysterious light on the distant horizon. Fireflies flashed in the road ditches, and long leaves of corn sighed in the evening breezes. Here and there a dog barked in a farmyard. The sound of dogs barking in the night, of their barks echoing across the vast, empty countryside, was the surfacing sound of the wildness in them. I could hear in their voices the ancient cries of gray wolves in the days when great herds of bison roamed the plains and the moonlight danced in the endless waves of grass. I could feel then the wildness in my own bones.

And I lived in a woodpile, in a plum thicket, in the striped shade of an August cornfield where the whirligigs raced across the sweltering landscape, showering dust like rain. And in a prairie meadow, among overgrazed river bluffs, on a granite island in a widening of the river, along a grassy fenceline where a lone green ash grew.

But mainly I dwelled along the river under the spell of its mysterious waters, which ran to the Minnesota River, then into the Mississippi River, then down the central nervous cord of the continent, over the plains of Iowa, through the hills of Missouri and Arkansas, across the bayous of Louisiana, and into the Gulf of Mexico.

In my house there were many mansions.

When I sat on the overhanging limb of a willow tree dangling my bare feet into the brown Chippewa River, feeling the slow, steady tug of its unfailing current against my toes, I became connected to the great body of the continent. I was linked not merely with a small river in western Minnesota but swept up into the gigantic stream of life. I lived then in the piney waters of the North Woods, in the thundering waters of St. Anthony Falls, in the icy rush of mountain streams, in the stagnant backwaters of southern marshes, in the oceanic brine. I shared then a mansion with my little bullheads, yes, but also with ancient paddlefishes and cutthroat trout and sharks and catfishes as big as logs. I lived then among bald eagles and alligators and panthers. I lived where it always snows and where it never snows, high in the mountains and at the edge of the sea.

As a high-school biology student, I once traced the cardiovascular system of a domestic cat whose blood vessels had been injected with a rubbery substance, blue for the veins, red for the arteries. Beginning at the heart, I traced the vessels up into its skull and down into its toes and out along its tail, following them as they branched into smaller and smaller streams. It was an ecstatic experience; I carried my half-excavated specimen home in a clear plastic bag, unable to bear the suspense of waiting until the next day's class to discover where all the vessels ran. No one would sit in the same bus seat with me, but I was too excited to mind. There in the body of the cat lay a map of the world as I perceived it from my vantage point along the Chippewa River. I might be one tiny red corpuscle swimming in the slenderest of the tail arteries, but I was an undeniable part of something big and alive, a constituent particle of the whole organism. I had seen the universe in a two-dollar laboratory specimen.

The work that these writers have set upon here, the work of bringing the history of this state and of its many places alive, of making that history available to the imaginations of Minnesotans, both opens the future of Minnesota to intelligent choices and establishes the connections between this state and all the rest of the universe. It is work that makes Minnesota, quite literally, a bigger, and richer, and stronger place, and for that all of us owe them a debt of thanks and praise.

The North Star State

THE FUR TRADE

The Story of the Grand Portage

SOLON J. BUCK

In the 1600s, several European countries were regularly sending ships across the Atlantic for trade purposes. While the Spanish were looking for gold, the French further north were seeking "soft gold"—furs, especially beaver. Clothing made or trimmed with beaver fur became high fashion in Europe. In the wilderness, beaver skins served as currency for guns, kettles, blankets, and other articles of trade.

Champlain founded Quebec in 1608 and the French continued to move westward, following the St. Lawrence River and then exploring the Great Lakes. In 1731 Pierre Gaultier de Varennes, Sieur de la Verendrye, is thought to be the first white man to reach Grand Portage, "the great carrying place." Located on Lake Superior, Grand Portage was the starting point for nine-mile portage to the Pigeon River bypassing the falls.

Solon J. Buck discusses the significance of Grand Portage during its most important century. Under French control until the French and Indian War in 1763, Grand Portage fell under the control of the British partnered with joint stock companies like North West (NW) or XY, and finally came under control of the United States, which received the territory in the 1783 treaty that ended the Revolutionary War.

Modern mapmakers have the disagreeable habit, in the interest of economy, of dismembering the state of Minnesota and depicting the northeastern corner separately on a little inset map. Few people today realize that this little triangle of land, so cavalierly treated by our draughtsmen, was during many years the scene of more human activities than took place in all the rest of the state; that more than thirty years before the founding of Fort Snelling, which we are wont to look upon as the real beginning of Minnesota history, upwards of a thousand white men were assembled year after year at a post within this area; and that here occurred the only military operations of the American Revolution within the borders of the state.[1]

The explanation of the importance of this region is to be sought in the realm of geography. The Pigeon River, which now forms the international boundary at Lake Superior, was, in the days of water transportation, the best natural highway between the Great Lakes or the St. Lawrence system and the great northwestern section of the continent, with its thousands of lakes and streams draining into the Hudson Bay or the Arctic Ocean. But the Pigeon River, through the last twenty miles of its course before it flows into Lake Superior, is so obstructed by falls and by cascades in rocky canyons as to be impossible of navigation. On the Canadian side the land is too mountainous and the distance too great for portaging to be practicable; but on the American side the line of the lake shore is roughly parallel to the river, and about seven or eight miles from the mouth of the river a little bay forms a natural harbor from which a portage of about nine miles over not too difficult country can be made to the Pigeon River above the cascades.

That this *Grand Portage* or great carrying place, as it was early designated by the French, was used by the Indians for generations before the advent of white men in the region is almost a certainty, although apparently not susceptible of proof. When and under what circumstances the first white man crossed the portage and who he was are questions which cannot now be answered. Nor do we know who was the first white man to visit the little bay at the eastern end of the trail, which takes its name from the portage. Radisson and Groseilliers are believed to have reached the north shore of Lake Superior in 1660, but it is not likely that they went as far east as Grand Portage.[2] Du Luth coasted along the north shore in 1679 and established there a fort or trading post, the location of which is generally believed to have been near what is now Fort William, about thirty miles northeast of Grand Portage. Some writers assert that this post was located at Grand Portage and was thus the first establishment of white men in Minnesota, but the evidence in the main is against this interpretation. It is highly probable, however, that Du Luth or some of his men entered the bay at Grand Portage, and they may have traversed the portage itself. Fort Kaministiquia, as Du Luth's post was called, was maintained for several years, then was abandoned, and was reestablished in 1717. That the traders who made this their headquarters failed to discover and make use of the Grand Portage is unbelievable.[3]

The first white man to leave a record of the use of the portage, however, is the Sieur de la Vérendrye, who crossed it on his famous expedition along the boundary waters in 1731. In his account he called it the Grand Portage and refers to it in such a way as to lead to the inference that it was already well known by that name.[4] From this time until the French and Indian War, French traders were pushing constantly farther and farther into the great Northwest, and the indications are that practically all the traffic passed over the Grand Portage route. A post was undoubtedly established at the eastern end of the trail, where the goods destined for the trade were landed from the large canoes used on the lake and prepared for the nine-mile carry to the Pigeon River.[5] At the western end of the trail, where the goods were loaded into smaller canoes suitable for river transportation, some sort of shelter probably was erected during the French period, but of this no information has been found. During the last conflict between the French and the English in America, which terminated with the surrender of Canada in 1760, the trade on Lake Superior and westward appears to have been abandoned, and the Indians were forced to resort to the posts of the Hudson's Bay Company far to the north or to get along without white man's goods.[6]

In November, 1761, a British garrison took possession of the post at Michilimackinac or Mackinac between Lakes Michigan and Huron. Shortly before this, however, one Alexander Henry, who had outfitted at Albany, New York, arrived at the post prepared to engage in the Indian trade on the upper lakes, and soon after other English traders made their appearance in the vicinity. If a narrative written nearly sixty years afterward is reliable, a party of these traders, accompanied by a military escort, made its way through Lake Superior to Grand Portage in May, 1762, this being the first voyage through Lake Superior under the British flag. This, if true, would indicate that Grand Portage was recognized at this time as the most important place in the western part of Lake Superior. The Indians of the Northwest, however, did not welcome the substitution of the English for the French; in 1763 the post of Mackinac was surprised, the garrison was massacred, one of the traders was killed, and the others were taken captive. This outbreak, which was a part of the conspiracy of Pontiac, put an end to British attempts at trade in the Northwest until the close of the Indian war in 1765.[7]

In that year Alexander Henry began trading operations at Chequamegon Bay, on the southern shore of Lake Superior, whence he dispatched an agent with some Indians to Fond du Lac; and in a year or two traders were established at various places around the lake and were making their way over the Grand Portage to the old French posts in the interior.[8] When Jonathan Carver, in 1767, found himself stranded on the upper Mississippi for lack of supplies, which he had expected to get from traders at Prairie du Chien, he determined to go to Lake Superior "in hopes of meeting at the Grand Portage . . . the traders that annually go from Michilimackinac to the northwest; of whom I doubted not but that I should be able to procure goods enough to answer my purpose." Arriving at Grand Portage in July, Carver found about three hundred Indians assembled there "to meet the traders from Michilimackinac, who make this their road to the Northwest." The Indians received him kindly, gave him much information about the lakes and streams of the interior, and entertained him with a marvelous incantation and a prophecy, which was promptly fulfilled. Finally the traders arrived, but Carver was unable to procure from them the supplies which he needed for the continuance of his explorations and so he made his way eastward through Lake Superior. Carver makes no mention of any post at Grand Portage and from his narrative it is evident that at that time the place was occupied only intermittently.[9]

Alexander Henry made his first trip to the country west of Lake Superior in 1775. Arriving at Grand Portage on June 28, he "found the traders in a state of extreme reciprocal hostility, each pursuing his interests in such a manner as might most injure his neighbour. The consequences were very hurtful to the morals of the Indians." The transportation of Henry's goods across the portage was "a work of seven days of severe and dangerous exertion."[10]

The rapid increase in the trade by way of Grand Portage is indicated by a memorandum drawn up by General Haldimand in January 1778. At that time it amounted annually to forty thousand pounds and employed five hundred persons, who, "for about a month in the summer season, have a general rendezvous at the Portage, and for the refreshing and comforting those who are employed in the more distant voyages the Traders from hence have built tolerable Houses; and in order to cover them from any insult from the numerous savage Tribes, who resort there during that time, have made stockades around them." The memorandum goes on to state that there was some jarring of interests at Grand Portage and that from the lack of officers representing the government in the region the traders had found it necessary to provide some show and parade such as the firing of cannon to signalize the arrival of the brigades and the distribution of medals—the purpose of this being to impress the Indians.[11]

The antagonisms among traders representing separate interests, possible dangers from the Indians, and above all the fear that disaffected persons at the portage might send supplies to the American troops then operating in the Illinois country were the reasons for the sending of a military expedition from Mackinac to Grand Portage about June 1, 1778. On May 18 John Askin, the commissary at Mackinac, wrote to M. Beausoleille, the clerk of the Northwest traders at Grand Portage, to inform him that he would have "an officer and several soldiers to pass the summer" there, and to direct him to have a house, equipped with a chimney, ready to receive them. The letter concludes with the following remarkable sentences, of which no explanation will be attempted: "I need two pretty Slave girls from 9 to 16 years old. Have the goodness to ask the Gentlemen to procure two for me." The officer detailed for duty at this northwesternmost point of British military operations during the Revolution was Lieutenant Thomas Bennett of the Eighth Regiment of Foot, and his detachment consisted of about twelve soldiers. Their operations at Grand Portage included the construction of a small fort, at the expense of the traders, and possibly the laying out of a road across the portage. Apparently they left in the fall, for the next year the traders petitioned for another detachment. Major De Peyster, in command at Mackinac, protested that, in view of the imminent danger of his being attacked by the rebels, he could not spare the troops; and no evidence has been found as to whether or not they were sent.[12]

By this time the Northwest trade had grown to such proportions and the competition between different interests was resulting in so many abuses that movements were under way for consolidation; and, after several preliminary "joint stocks," the famous North West Company was organized in 1783.[13] The next twenty years comprise the greatest period in the history of the Grand Portage. The North West Company had a fort or stockade on the bay, which consisted of an enclosure of palisades twenty-four by thirty rods in size. The buildings within the fort, according to a contemporary description, were "sixteen in number made with cedar and white spruce fir split with whip saws after being squared, the Roofs are covered with Shingles of Cedar and Pine, most of their posts, Doors and windows, are painted with Spanish brown. Six of these buildings are Store Houses for the company's Merchandise and Furs, &c., the rest are dwelling houses shops compting house and Mess House—they have also a wharf or quay for their vessels to unload and Load."[14] The company had a vessel of ninety-five tons burden which made four or five trips to Grand Portage each summer. In the bay was a large canoe yard where seventy canoes were constructed annually for use in the trade.[15]

During July and August, Grand Portage was a very busy place. Here the brigades from Montreal, with goods for the trade of the ensuing winter, accompanied by two of the Montreal partners, met the wintering partners and other traders coming in from their posts scattered throughout the Northwest from the upper Red River to Lake Athabasca. Here was held the annual meeting of the company, at which arrangements were made and agreements entered into for the ensuing year. Here the employees received, and largely spent, their annual wages. The partners, traders, clerks, and guides, to the number of two or three hundred, lived in the fort and ate in the great dining hall, and outside were the camps of the pork-eaters and the winterers, as the canoemen from Montreal and the interior respectively were called. These *engages* subsisted principally upon pork and hominy, with plentiful supplies of liquor and tobacco; but the food served in the dining hall included bread, salt pork, beef, ham, fish, venison, butter, peas, corn, potatoes, tea, and wine. There was even plenty of milk, for a herd of cows was kept at Grand Portage. In the evenings the great hall was often the scene of much merriment, and interesting accounts may be read of festive balls at which the dusky maidens of the forest are reported to have danced very well and to have conducted themselves with much propriety. Besides the resident Indians, many others congregated about the fort during the summer.[16]

The task of transporting the packs of supplies and furs across the portage was a long and arduous one and required the services of a hundred men for several weeks. Parts of the trail were often in very bad condition being "knee-deep in mud and clay, and so slippery as to make walking tedious." The packs weighed ninety pounds each and two or more were carried by the men on their backs, the round trip of eighteen miles requiring about six hours. How many thousands of trips back and forth across this trail were made during the entire period, it is impossible to estimate, but it is small wonder that the soil still shows evidences of the trampling of many feet. In 1788 the company requested a grant of land along the route to enable it to construct a wagon road over the trail. The request was denied by the council at Quebec, probably because it would have given the company a monopoly of the route, but later on the trail was improved so that ox-carts could be used on it.[17]

At the western end of the portage, where it met the Pigeon River, was another stockade enclosing several buildings, which was known as Fort Charlotte. Here the goods were stored until the traders were ready to load them into their canoes and start for the wintering grounds. Of the history of this fort little has been ascertained as yet, but it evidently was a place of considerable importance for many years.[18]

The North West Company was not able to maintain a complete monopoly over the trade that passed across the Grand Portage. Rival companies were established from time to time, usually to flourish a few years and then amalgamate with "the Great Company." One of these companies, the XY Company, which operated from 1797 to 1804, had a separate establishment at Grand Portage and also, probably, at Fort Charlotte, for the map drawn by the surveyors for the boundary commission in 1824 indicates the outlines of two stockades at the western end of the portage.[19]

At the very beginning of this period of the greatest activity on the Grand Portage, the land over which it ran became, by virtue of the treaty of 1783, a part of the United States. The boundary, as laid down in the treaty, was somewhat indefinite, but it was generally understood by the traders that it had been fixed at the Pigeon River. So long as the military posts on the American side of the line in the Great Lakes region remained in the hands of the British, there was little likelihood that the traders would be disturbed; and those posts, for reasons which need not be considered here, were not surrendered until 1796. Soon after the occupation of Mackinac by an American garrison, however, intimations were given to the traders that a revenue officer might be sent to Grand Portage to collect duty on the great quantity of goods being imported there into the United States. As a result of this threat, and also, perhaps, of a desire to avoid the difficulties of the long carrying place, the North West Company began casting about for another route to the interior. In 1798 the Kaministiquia route, by way of Dog Lake to the boundary waters, was discovered, or rediscovered, for it had been known to the French; and in 1801 the company commenced the erection of a new headquarters at the mouth of the Kaministiquia River. To this, subsequently, was given the name of Fort William.[20]

Apparently the XY Company retained its headquarters at Grand Portage until the union of the two companies in 1804,[21] but thereafter the greatness of the place was a thing of the past. A local trading post was maintained by the company at Grand Portage until after the War of 1812, but the portage itself was little used, and apparently Fort Charlotte was allowed to fall into decay.[22] During this war a British trader is said to have visited Grand Portage for the purpose of endeavoring to enlist the Chippewa (Ojibwe) Indians there resident against the Americans.[23] At the close of the War of 1812, Congress passed an act excluding foreigners from the fur trade in American territory, and Astor's American Fur Company purchased the posts of the North West Company south of the line. Lewis Cass, governor of Michigan Territory, in 1815 recommended the establishment of a United States military post at Grand Portage for the collection of duties and the enforcement of trade regulations. The recommendation was not followed, however; and, as the American Fur Company confined its operations on Lake Superior to the southern shore for several years, the Grand Portage band of Indians continued to be supplied from Fort William. "In the winter of 1824," according to Henry R. Schoolcraft, "persons in the service of the Hudson Bay Company [*which had absorbed the North West Company in 1820*] carried off in trains the band of Chippewa's, living near old Grand Portage ... after the arrival of an American trader."[24]

In 1831 a single trader was licensed for Grand Portage, but the principal activities at the place during the thirties centered on the fishing industry conducted by the American Fur Company. Grand Portage was a central station for these operations, and large quantities of Lake Superior fish were there assembled from various stations along the north shore and packed in barrels for the export trade. In 1839 the establishment there consisted of two family dwelling houses, a "new store," two "mens houses, 1 Coopers Shop, 1 Fish Store, Stable Barn, Root house, &c below or near the beach, placed here and there without order or symmetry." About three acres were under cultivation and produced over two hundred bushels of potatoes. The fishing business was unprofitable, however, and seems to have been abandoned when the American Fur Company sold out in the forties.[25]

The village of Ojibwe Indians, which had been located near Grand Portage Bay apparently before the coming of the first traders, remained after the glories of the place had departed. For these Indians a Catholic mission was established at Grand Portage about 1838 by the Reverend Francis X. Pierz; and a few years later the Right Reverend Frederic Baraga, the famous missionary bishop, visited the place and held confirmation services. Sometime during the forties the Jesuits are said to have erected a mission on the American side of the Pigeon River about a mile from its mouth and half a mile below the falls.[26]

Perhaps the most interesting feature of the history of the Grand Portage in the nineteenth century is its connection with the boundary controversy. The region was carefully explored and mapped in 1822 by the surveyors of the commission provided for in the treaty of Ghent. When the commissioners held their final meeting in 1827, the representative of Great Britain offered to accept the Pigeon River route as the boundary, provided the line should be drawn through the portages, including the Grand Portage. When this was rejected he offered to accept the river as the boundary, providing the portages should be free and open to the use of both parties. This offer also was rejected; but, when the boundary controversy was finally settled by the Webster-Ashburton treaty in 1842, it was on exactly these terms. This treaty is still in force, and presumably British citizens would be entitled today to demand the unobstructed use of the ancient trail over the Grand Portage.[27]

In 1854 the United States purchased the triangle north of Lake Superior from the Chippewa, but a tract extending from the lake to the Pigeon River and including the entire line of the portage was set aside as a reservation for the Indians. In the later years of the nineteenth century, this reservation was broken up, allotments were given to the Indians, and the remainder of the land, with the exception of reservations for possible hydroelectric development, was sold for lumbering purposes or opened up to homesteading.[28]

NOTES
From Minnesota History 5 *(February, 1923)*

1. Read at the state historical convention under the auspices of the Minnesota Historical Society at Duluth, July 28, 1922. The writer desires to acknowledge the assistance of Miss Mary E. Wheelhouse and Miss Livia Appel of the staff of the Minnesota Historical Society in the assembling of the materials on which this paper is based.

2. Warren Upham, "Groseilliers and Radisson," in *Minnesota Historical Collections,* 10:506, 513 (part 2). Reuben G. Thwaites in *Wisconsin Historical Collections,* 11:96, n., interprets a sentence in Radisson's narrative as a reference to the Grand Portage. See also Lawrence J. Burpee, *The Search for the Western Sea,* lvi, 212, 307, n. (Toronto, 1908).

3. William W. Folwell, *A History of Minnesota,* 1:23, 44 (St. Paul, 1921). A statement in a letter of a French officer written in 1722 with reference to the best route from Kaministiquia to the site of a proposed post in the interior is probably a reference to the Pigeon River route. See Pierre Margry, ed., *Découvertes et établissements des Français,* 6:516 (Paris 1886); Warren Upham, in *Minnesota in Three Centuries,* 1:276 (New York, 1908); and Burpee, *Search for the Western Sea,* 202.

4. Margry, *Découvertes,* 6:586, 591.

5. Sir Alexander Mackenzie, in his *Voyages from Montreal through the Continent of North America,* viii (Philadelphia, 1802), refers to "the Grande Portage, where the French had a principal establishment, and was the line of their communication with the interior country. It was once destroyed by fire." Benjamin Sulte, in an article on "Early Forts in the North-West," dated 1919 and published in his *Mélanges historiques,* 10:139 (Montreal, 1922), says that "between 1718 and 1720 La Noue erected a fort at Grand Portage," but gives no indication of the evidence on which the statement is based.

6. Mackenzie, *Voyages,* vi; Louis F. Masson, "Esquisse Historique," in his *Les bourgeois de la compagnie du nord-ouest,* 1: 9 (Quebec, 1889); Alexander Henry, *Travels and Adventures in Canada and the Indian Territories,* 195 (New York, 1809); Gordon C. Davidson, *The*

North West Company, 33 (University of California, *Publications in History,* vol. 7—Berkeley, 1918); Folwell, *Minnesota,* 1:53.

7. Henry, *Travels and Adventures,* part 1; "Thompson Maxwell's Narrative—1760–1763," in *Wisconsin Historical Collections,* 11:215.

8. Henry, *Travels and Adventures,* 192–196; Mackenzie, *Voyages,* viii; Davidson, *North West Company,* 34.

9. Jonathan Carver, *Travels through the Interior Parts of North America in the Years* 1766, 1767, and 1768, 93, 106 (London, 1778).

10. Henry, *Travels and Adventures,* 238.

11. *Michigan Pioneer and Historical Collections,* 19:337–339.

12. *Wisconsin Historical Collections,* 11:142, 19:237, 239, 243; *Michigan Pioneer and Historical Collections,* 9:358; 19:345, 372; Davidson, *North West Company,* 28. Davidson states that a detachment was stationed at Grand Portage "in 1777 and succeeding years."

13. Davidson, *North West Company,* 8–14.

14. Anonymous journal of 1793 in the Masson Papers in the library of McGill University, Montreal, quoted in Davidson, *North West Company,* 237. A somewhat different version of parts of this document is in Burpee, *Search for the Western Sea,* 306. For other descriptions of the post, see Mackenzie, *Voyages,* xliii; Daniel W. Harmon, *A Journal of Voyages and Travels,* 40 (Andover, 1820); and George Heriot, *Travels through the Canadas,* 203 (London, 1807).

15. Heriot, *Travels,* 204.

16. Masson, *Bourgeois,* 2:466, 480; Mackenzie, *Voyages,* xliii–xlv; Harmon, *Voyages and Travels,* 41–43; Heriot, *Travels,* 204; Davidson, *North West Company,* 22, 204, 230; William W. Warren, "History of the Ojibways," in *Minnesota Historical Collections,* 5:379. See also the "Accounts of the Fur-trade, extracted from the journal of Count Andriani of Milan, who traveled in the interior parts of America in the year 1791," in the Duke de la Rochefoucault Liancourt, *Travels through the United States of North America, the Country of the Iroquois, and Upper Canada, in the Years 1795, 1796, and 1797,* 1:325–334 (London, 1799). The statements are here made that "a fort . . . garrisoned with fifty men" was maintained at Grand Portage and that "in this place there is frequently a concourse of one thousand people and upward."

17. Alexander Henry, the younger, in Elliott Coues, ed., *New Light on the Early History of the Greater Northwest,* 1:6 (New York, 1897); Mackenzie, *Voyages,* xlii; Henry Y. Hind, *Narrative of the Canadian Red River Exploring Expedition of 1857,* 1:74 (London, 1860); George Bryce, *Mackenzie, Selkirk, Simpson,* 12 (*The Makers of Canada,* vol. 8, Parkman edition—Toronto, 1909); Davidson, *North West Company,* 23, 49, n., 204, 211, 231. For an account of the method of carrying over portages see John Johnston in Masson, *Bourgeois,* 2:165.

18. Harmon, *Voyages and Travels,* 43; Henry, in Coues, *New Light,* 1:6; Heriot, *Travels,* 205.

19. Harmon, *Voyages and Travels,* 40; Coues, *New Light,* 7, n.; John B. Moore, *History and Digest of the International Arbitrations to Which the United States Has Been a Party,* 6: map 57 (Washington, 1898). Since the above was written, the outlines of the two stockades have been located on the ground. See *post,* n. 29.

20. Roderic McKenzie, "Reminiscences," in Masson, *Bourgeois,* 1:46–48; Warren in *Minnesota Historical Collections,* 5:292; Coues, *New Light,* 220, n.; Davidson, *North West Company,* 48, 105. David Thompson says that a United States collector landed at Grand Portage in 1800 and declared his intention of levying duties. See quotation in Burpee,

"Highways of the Fur Trade," in royal Society of Canada, *Transactions*, series 3, vol. 8, section 2, p. 188 (September, 1914).

21. Henry, in Coues, *New Light*, 1:218; François V. Malhiot, "A Wisconsin Fur-Trader's Journal, 1804–05," in *Wisconsin Historical Collections*, 19:169; Davidson, *North West Company*, 90.

22. A map in the British Museum, which is reproduced in Davidson, *North West Company*, 144, indicates that there was a North West Company post at Grand Portage as late as 1818. Hind apparently thought that Fort Charlotte was in an important post after the headquarters were moved from Grand Portage. He states that "Fort Charlotte was connected with Point des Meurons [*near Fort Williams*] by a traveled road in the time of the North-West Company." See his *Narrative*, 1:14, 74. General James H. Baker, on the other hand, in his "History of Transportation in Minnesota," in *Minnesota Historical Collections*, 9:9, says that a road thirty-six miles long was built in the earliest years of the nineteenth century between Grand Portage and Fort William and claims to have seen the remains of some of the bridges. Newton H. Winchell, in the Geological and Natural History Survey of Minnesota, *Final Report*, 4:502, describes the remains of the dock at Fort Charlotte as they were in 1893. He makes the mistake, however, of assigning the name "Fort Charlotte" to the post at Grand Portage.

23. Thwaites, in *Wisconsin Historical Collections*, 19:190, n.

24. *Wisconsin Historical Collections*, 19:378, 430; 22 Congress, 1 session, *Senate Documents*, no. 90, p. 43, 46 (serial 213); Warren, in *Minnesota Historical Collections*, 5:382; Folwell, *Minnesota*, 1:132. The American trader referred to may have been Bela Chapman, who wintered on the north shore of Lake Superior in 1823–24 and visited Grand Portage in the spring. In his journal, which is in the Sibley Papers in the possession of the Minnesota Historical Society, he tells of his unsuccessful efforts to prevent Indians from taking their furs to the British, who had given them "credits."

25. Table in 22 Congress, 2 session, *Senate Documents*, no. 90, p. 50; Gabriel Franchere's "Remarks made on a visit from Lapointe to the Fishing Stations of Grand Portage, Isle Royal and Ance Quiwinan—August 1839"; account of the fur trade around Lake Superior, written probably by Clement H. Beaulieu about 1880. The last two items are manuscripts in the possession of the Minnesota Historical Society. Hind found an American trading post at Grand Portage in 1857. See his *Narrative*, 1:75.

26. P. Chrysostomus Verwyst, *Life and Labors of Rt. Rev. Frederic Baraga*, 284, 384, 386 (Milwaukee, 1900); *Catholic Encyclopedia*, 13:487 (New York, 1912); Joseph G. Norwood, "Geological Report of a Survey of Portions of Wisconsin and Minnesota, made during the Years 1847, '48, '49, and '50," in David Dale Owen, *Report of a Geological Survey of Wisconsin, Iowa, and Minnesota*, 397, 398, 405 (Philadelphia, 1852). The location of the mission on Pigeon River is indicated on a map, plate N, at the back of Owen, *Geological Survey*.

27. Folwell, *Minnesota*, 1:500–502.

28. United States, *Statutes at Large*, 10:1109; 25:642; reports of the commissioner of Indian affairs, in Department of the Interior, *Reports*, 1896, vol. 2, p. 330; 1897, vol. 2, p. 312; 1906, vol. 2, p. 397; 1917, vol. 2, p. 93; report of the commissioner of the general land office, in Department of the Interior, *Reports*, 1916, vol. 1, p. 163; A. H. Sawyer to Minnesota Historical Society, April 26, 1922.

George Nelson's Fur Trade Reminiscences, 1802–1803

EDITED BY RICHARD BARDON AND GRACE LEE NUTE

The son of an English schoolmaster, George Nelson grew up in a small village outside Montreal. Each spring boys would depart for the west and a life of danger and challenges in the wilderness; they returned in the fall with the jauntiness and self-assurance of men. Nelson was only fifteen in spring 1802 when he visited the office of Sir Alexander Mackenzie's XY Company with a voyageur friend and signed up as an apprentice clerk for five years. Within a year he was promoted to manage a fur trade post on his own.

He recounts his experiences, his observations, his homesickness, and his fears. He made careful notes on the Ojibwe he encountered and their culture. An early November snowstorm caused him and his companion to be nearly hopelessly lost, wandering in circles for hours. With British authority in London and Montreal, rival companies like North West, XY, and Hudson's Bay fought for profits, increasing the dangers in the wilderness as each sought to secure a stronger relationship with the local Indians who would be bringing the furs. That led to supplying the Indians with abundant rum and spreading false stories about the other traders, often with disastrous consequences.

The next day (I do not remember the date, in June) we reached the, to the inhabitants of Canada; the famed, "Grand Portage." It is located, about the middle, of a bay, with a very handsome island before, the only *obstruction* to an immense & boundless view. The establishment of the N.W. C°, tho' there was nothing superfluous or unnecessary, but was of an extent to prove at once the great trade they carried on, their judgement & taste in the regularity & position of their numerous buildings. The neatness & order of things was not [the] least part of it.

Our company had a few buildings, a few hundred yards to the East of the N.W C° *below* the hill; but were busy building a very fine "fort" upon the hill.[1]

We were here several days before any one arrived either from Montreal or from the interior of the Country. I was placed in one of the Stores to Serve the people. At last they began to come in, all was business. Receiving Goods, corn,

flour, port &c &c from Montreal & Mackinac, & furs from the different wintering posts—Gambling, feasting, dancing, drinking & fighting. After a coupl[e] of
weeks to rest, for the Winterers to give in their returns & accounts, & to make
up their outfits, they began to return again, to run over the same ground, toils,
labors, and dangers.

But in this country took, where every step was beset with difficulties of themselves sufficient to exert every faculty & try the nerve, even here, the Demon of
Ambition followed us, blinded our better judgement, & sharpned our wits only
to oppose, annoy & injure each other. One of our brigades, fitted out I believe,
for Fort des Prairies, slept as usual at Portage la Perdrix, only a few hundred
yards from our Stores at the north end of the Grand portage,[2] where they
feasted & got drunk upon the "regale" that was always given them when they
arrived from, or departed for, their winter quarters. When they arose the next
morning they found thirty Kegs of High Wines (containing 9 Galls. ea.) had all
run out! Upon examination it was found they had been bored with two gim-
lets holes each! The consternation & injury this occasioned may be imagined.
Enquiries were set on foot & affidavits given in. No bible was to be found to
swear upon. I lent mine, for the purpose, but never saw it after though I en-
quired diligently. These were called *witty tricks.* Rumor gave out that it was
Benjamin Frobisher & [*blank in MS*] who bored the Kegs.[3] It created an exces-
sive bad feeling & led to retaliations some of which would have ended tragi-
cally but for providence, but nothing further ever followed.

I was the last that left, of the "Winterers." There two Canoes fitted out, one
to supply "Leach Lake" where M[r] [John] M[c] Bean had charge.[4] The other, to
the "Folle avoine."[5] In these two Canoes were three men, W[m] Smith, Frs: Savoyard & Pre: Sanfacon who had only this year left the N. W. Cos. Service.[6] As it
was a "maxim" carefully impressed upon all of us, indirectly indeed, but so as
not to be misunderstood, to do all we could to get *returns* & *oppose* our neighbors, no means were to trivial, nor method too base—Yes! I say *base,* so that we
could succeed. This occasion then, of these 3 men was too good a one to be let
pass without a trial. M[r] Duncan M[c] Gillivray one of the Agents of the N. W. C[o]
walked round the Canoes the men were arranging,—a quarrel ensued. We were
at dinner. The men came running up saying M[r] M[c] Gillivray was going to carry
off the men by main force. "The Knight" ran down, we all followed. And no
small affair it was, all in words, menaces & gestures indeed, but those are often
the fore-runners of blood. We at last embarked fully determined to defend ourselves, fight, & kill, if driven too it; & armed for the purpose. M[r] M[c] Gillivray
got into a boat with a *couple* of men, he hailed their vessel that was then anchored in the bay,—the Captain sent out the Jolly boat, But they at last gave up
the chace, assuring us however, that they would come upon us at *night;* and for
several days we were in great fear. As yet, such things were new to me:—the
men dreaded it, & I tho't they were right.

It was of a Wednesday, the 13ᵗʰ Septʳ 1802, I was shipped off on board a Ca-noe, with Three men, to winter & trade amongst a tribe of Indians remarkable for their courage, being at perpetual war with the Sioux, insolence & brutality. It was an "adventure"; in the "Invoice" it was merely said "Invoice of Goods sent to Folle-avoine"! Smith said *he* had the Charge; Savoyard maintained it was he and this was the cause of interminable quarrels the whole year.

We were, the above Wᵐ Smith, the Son of an old Scotch Soldier with a Canadian woman. Frs Savoyard, & Jos: Boisverd.[7] The two first had been about 14 years among the Indians; Boisverd, this was his second year!

On the 15ᵗʰ Smith shot a duck. I was very glad, because I was already tired of corn; for *they* had "made no allowances" for me. But when I saw the man-ner he was dressing it! He plucked, Singed, scraped of the ashes that had ad-hered to the bird in singing it on the coals, pulled out a few of the longest of the *stumps,* split it open, & *threw* it into kettle, wherein the *Indian corn,* for our supper, was boiling. He did not even rince it in the lake. This procedure shocked me terribly. He then broiled the entrails of the duck on the coals eat them him-self! "O, what a barbarian! what a hog! Am I to become like that!—is it for this I have left my father's house, the affectionate care of the *best* of mothers, de-prived of the society of my brothers & sisters!"—My heart swelled almost to bursting point with disgust, indignation, horror & grief. "But *I* shall *not* remain long here. I will save my earnings, return to the "civilized" (!) world, buy a farm & pass my life quietly & comfortably." How easily is the mind consoled & the heart relieved, with reflections that are not, can never be realized, very often from the influence of the very cause that gave rise to them! Alas! poor human nature! The duck was soon cooked, for in those countries "all things are pretty much of a piece." Smith offered me a very reasonable share,—I refused, thank-ing him; he rightly guessed the cause, "What? said he, because forsooth I did not wash it! oh, lah!—that squeamishness of yours will vanish. Why did you re-main hooked to your mothers apron? This, accompanied with many oaths & ribraldry, called with there, only served to increase my pain & cause me more to feel my wretchedness.

A few days after, we came to a place where were two families of indians. They had killed a moose dear & the men went out with them to help carrying it home. They at last returned, cooked some & we sate down to eat. I found it excellent though it had only been *passed* thro' the water. But, at this spot, the beach happened to be covered with those round, flat grayish stones, bearing a striking resemblance to Sea biscuit. I took up one as a biscuit & gave it a bite!— I was woefully, but effectually undeceived:—I made no more such mistakes.

Finding the people were rather a long time absent, I took their "road." It is a good road, but as you are not accustomed to these things yet, you had per-haps better not go. However, I went. The road was *discoverable* by the falling leaves being "here & there" disturbed, from the feet hooking into a root or rotten stick, *turning them up* & every 2 or 300 yards a branch broken. I made out however to follow it well for perhaps half or ¾ of a mile; but lest I might get astray, I though it most prudent to return. Such are Indian roads, & many hundred miles have I traveled upon them, with no other indications; but custom & a little attention to the *course* or direction of the route, render traveling upon them, comparatively sure. We at last reached "Fon du Lac," i. e. the furthest extremity, West end of the lake.[8] Here it is about six miles broad: the northern shore rocky, the mountains constantly near the beach; on the South, the mountains were much farther off, the shore flat & Sandy. The river St Louis which is properly speaking the Source of the St Lawrence, enters at the South side of the lake, takes an immediate bend, and follows the lake to the North Shore, leaving a narrow strip very much like an ox's tongue, tapering so gradually & so very regularly.[9] This strip of land is beautifully studded with the handsomest red & white pine trees, in all the magnificence & grandeur of unpolluted nature. I was mightily charmed with the view, & it is one of those that has riveted itself most firmly in my mind.

The River is about a mile wide. The western side is a Swamp. The N. West C°
had a trading post here: we had none.[10]

There were one or two indian families on this strip of land and though they were a considerable distance from us, I was terribly uneasy at night; *for our men said* they were great rascals, bad indians. I was very much afraid: this was the 2^d chapter of my fears. The men slept round the goods, lest the indians might have been employed by the N. W Co to "play off some trick" upon us, and the boring of our Kegs at the *Patridge* & Duncan Mc Gillivrays threats at our departure from the "Grand portage," with a multitude of other similar gentilities were all fresh in our mind.

I *barricaded* my tent & secured myself the best I could. I was surely in great dread. How "home," at this great distance, reflected beautiful thoughts in my mind! I was young,—had not been instructed *how* to *think,* nor how to apply the Scanty education I had—my thoughts were vague & confused. I could only think of my father, my mother, my brothers & sisters; their Security, peace & comforts; my duty to my creator again called upon him to defend & protect me: shivering with apprehensions, at last fell asleep. In the morning, all was right; nothing, even the indians, had not been near us.

In the afternoon we reached "Riviere Brulée" which we were to take to get to our "Wintering Grounds."[11] It is Seven leagues east of "fon du lac," Small but deep & takes its rise in a small lake or Swampy pond, nearly in a direct South direction. It is also the Source of the Ste Croix river, falling into the Mississippi a little above the "Falls of St Anthony."[12] They both (the Ste Croix & Brulée) take their rise in this Small lake, & the men told me that the indians with Small canoes, paddle in, and out of it, as some others I have known.[13]

We here found an old indian with his wife & Son. He told us that the N. W.

people had passed up long since & had no doubt bought up all the wild rice &c. He was employed to make us a canoe, to lighten the one we had, on account of the shallow waters above.

Two things here Surprised my inexperienced mind a great deal. Smith had bro't him a lancet, for which he seemed extremely thankful. To try it, he bound up his arm & made the puncture—after allowing it to bleed freely for a little while, on the ground he removed the bandage, took a leaf, moistened it with his saliva[,] applied to the orifice & resumed his work. I wondered & wondered at such Simplicity.—The other thing was, his Son had Killed a crow, they plucked, cooked & ate it!—"Carrion, barbarians, to eat carrion!" I thought it horrid.

At last our Canoe was ready; we took a reasonable proportion of the lading & pushed off, Savoyard & Boisverd in the "big" canoe, Smith & I in the other. I steered! but such zig zags! how many times I crossed & recrossed the river! Smith, with all his petulance & irrascibility, was certainly very patient & indulgent.

On our way up this river, one evening, they gave the old man rum. They all three enjoyed it very quietly & comfortably together untill next morning, when some words ensued, the Son, a chap about my own age, fell upon his mother & beat her, striking with his fist & Kicking her in the face & body! How I was astonished! a Son striking his mother! *kicking* her in the face & body!!! I was enraged, & finding the men, nor even the father would interfere, I was proceeding to give him a Sound drubbing But the men would not allow me; "for if you do they will all three get upon you: besides, it is among themselves—we dare not interfere." I tho't it an excessively hard and disgraceful act. I had an aversion to the wretch ever after & could not bear the sight of him. We soon, however, Seperated & I never Saw him after. Surely, thought I, the curse of God will fall on these people.

We soon go to the "Portage Ste Croix," about half a mile long, on a fine dry rising ground well wooded with beautiful pine. Here we left Savoyard & Boisverd to go in search of the indians & collect what we could of rice from them. At the South end of the Portage is a handsome lake, between 2 & 3 miles circumference, & at very short distance from the one where the river takes its rise.[14] The Portage is, I dare say 100 miles from the lake (Superior) & 80, or 90, from the Mississippi where it discharges itself.

We soon entered into the Ste Croix & glided gently down its placid bosom, but little obstructed with rapids. I do not remember if we were two or 3 days. But we arrived in the afternoon opposite the mouth of the "Riviere Jaune," where we landed [on] a most beautiful iland.[15]

The indians, the moment they saw us gave the whoop. They were all drunk, the N. W Co. had a little before given liquor. They came rushing upon us like devils, dragged our Canoe to land, threw the lading ashore, ripped up the bale cloths, cut the cords & Sprinkled the goods about at a fine rate. Such a noise, yelling & chattering! "Rum, Rum, what are you come to do here without rum?"— after a while, when they saw we had no rum, they gradually dispersed. A few of the more quite [sic] remained; they entered into friendly intercourse with Smith whom they knew for many years; & it is but bare justice to say that he acquitted himself like a man, both as regards prudence & courage on this critical and trying occasion. It was enough to test the nerve of any man. I soon became the object of their attention. They gathered round me, spoke kindly, laughed with me & tapped me friendly on the Shoulders & head. But I understood nothing of what they said. Smith done all the needful in this business for me. I never felt the least fear, as if the bouts I had experienced at the Long Sault & the last night in *Fon du lac,* had been "for all time to come," and indeed I did quake, and shake and tremble enough on those two occasions. On my side, though I was not fit to make any philosophical remarks nor draw deductions from what I did see, yet their appearance, manners & ways, struck me powerfully. They were the first I had seen in numbers & at their homes. Men of the common Stature, most of them besmeared (painted) black, with bruised charcoal & grease, being most of them mourning for some of their relations, killed the year before in a drunken quarrel on this very spot. There were five killed out-right & six very severly & dangerously wounded, with knives, only with a Capot & brich clout on, their Tommyhaw-pipes & k[n]ives in their hands. They look fierce, & were so. Strait as arrows, their motions & their eyes showed plainly, how frequently these faculties must have been bro't to the test.

Savoyard came the next day. We had to make our presents of liquor also. Singing, dancing, & yelling, & fighting too; but no stabbing,—they had had enough of it the year before, and besides, the worst of them were off for River au Serpent, some distance below.[16] But I got tired of it. I felt I wanted something. I resorted to my Prayer book, & by chance fell upon the 120th psalm— "Woe is me, indeed! that I am constrained to dwell with Mesheck & have my habitation among the tents of Kedar!" I thought this wonderfully appropriate to my present situation; "it was my lot, but I must not despond" for there seemed to me as a ray of promise that I was not altogether "cast off." This, & some of the 119th afforded me great comfort. I became more naturalized and gradually, (in the course of years) I became quite reconciled. The indians took great pity upon me. One of them adopted me as his Son, & told his own Son, a lad of about my age, to consider me as his Brother & to treat me so, and he did indeed the very few times we happened to meet after this.

We remained here three or four days, getting what little rice we could from them & giving out our "fall credits." We at last set off & went up the "Yellow river" being one continued rapid, for six or Seven miles. We encamped on a very handsome lake.[17] We passed the N. W. people at their encampment. They had some deer meat hanging upon the trees. It looked so much like mutton I

longed for some—it also gave me a longing for *home*. The next day we encamped on a beautiful low point on the border of "Yellow Lake." The indian
name is "Yellow water lake" from the yellow sand in the bottom. It is quite
round, about 2, or 2½ miles diameter. At the S. E. side it is flat & miry; & an immense quantity of rice grows there; and in their Season, ducks of various Sorts,
Geese & Swans in multitudes. There is also plenty of fish, Carp of several sorts,
some of monstrous size, pikeral, pike, &c. &c.

Their method of *making* the rice is this. Two persons get into a canoe, setting face to face; they each have two sticks of about 4 feet long. The one behind
thrusts his sticks one on each side into the standing rice, & bend it over into
the canoe, the other one with his two sticks beats it off. They soon fill a canoe,
& carry it to land, where others place it on a rack exactly similar to those our
habitans use for their flax. When it is sufficiently heated it is put in a skin, a
hole about the size of a half bushel being made in the ground, where another
one treads off the husks—it is then fanned out in a bark dish. Some families I
have been told make as much as 40 & even 50 bushels in some seasons, and I
do believe it. They also roast some in old copper Kettles, as they take it out of
the Canoe, & then tread & fan it. This is eaten so, or melting grease till *very* hot,
the rice thrown in & stirred smartly, swells & bursts; becomes very crisp & is
very good; but it requires teeth & good gums, for there are always many grains
that only harden, not getting enough of the grease, & these frequently plant
themselves in the gums & make them bleed.

The allowance is one quart, with two ounces of grease, (when we have it) to
season it, to each man. It is pleasant & good, but is not very nourishing, I should
have said strengthening. When boiled very leisurely, between three & four
hours, so slowly as not to replenishing with water, it has a strong resemblance
to boiled milk. The grain resembles the rye but much longer.

We remained here several days before they could decide upon the place
where to build; for, where the wood or locality Suited, there was no clay, & we
required this article to build our chimneys & plaster our houses. At last they
fixed upon a place, in a "pinery" on a beautiful small river below us, about half
a mile. While here, I got a great diarrhea. The men said it was from eating met
without bread; all new hands were thus attacked; but it would wear off. Indeed
it had to "wear off," for we had not particle of any discription of medicine with
us: neither tea nor Sugar; & the little flour we had was nearly all consumed.
The Company certainly treated me very ill. add to this, we had several days of
rain & the ground was low & wet. The poor fellows felt uneasy. After a few
days, thank God, I recovered.

At long last, we proceeded to our winter quarters & began to build, the N. W.
about 60 yards from us. Here, as the Sioux [came] every Spring in war excur-
sions, we had several proposals from the N. W. to build nearer to them, so that
we might assist each other in case of being attacked. The arguments they gave

were good & Sound; but we were traders "consequently opponents" This being our first year, strangers & weak, no indian could come to us that was not
more or less indebted to them virtually or impliedly, they would not therefore
dare to deal with [us] in the presence of their old traders & friends: and we
could not steal out to go after the indians. Besides we were afraid of incurring
blame from our employers. So there the matter rested, & each built his own way.

We did not make *palaces*,—ours was about 16 or 18 feet long, made thus:—
We build up the two sides, to the height required, say five & a half, or perhaps
six feet. These are secured by two stakes at each end, as a common rail fence,
& braced by a good strong stick, the whole breadth of the house, & notched at
each end, to lay on the two sides, to prevent their moving. Then two trenches
wherein to plant of set the *ends* upright, & of the same size as the sides. Two
strong posts in the middle, to receive a ridge pole, two & a half or 3 feet higher
than the sides, so that the roof, which consists of straight poles or split slabs,
when the timber admits, may have sufficient slope for the water to run off. An
opening is left at one end; that part *below* the cross stick or beam, for a *door*, &
that *above* for a *window*. The ends, being upright are secured by a pole, bound
with good strong withs, to prevent their falling. The whole is well plastered,
the *Shop* only out-side, as some of it will fall & dirty our furs or spoil our grease,
meat, &c. but the house is plastered on both sides, inside & out. The joints between the roofing is also plastered; carefully covered about a foot thick with
grass which we cut with our knives, & four or five inches of ground thrown on
to prevent its being blown off, also as a preservative against the fire. The window is made of the thinnest parchment skin we can procure. The chimney in
one side of the house, part of stone, when handy, but most commonly of earth
made into mortar & wrapped in grass. The doors of slabs, split with the axe &
then Squared down. The floors, when good wood to rive, cannot be had, is
squared from trees & then dubbed off with an adze, when we have one, if none,
then with the hoe, which we sharpen with the files, for we cannot take in grind
stones. Our beds, two posts, at the head & foot with a stick fixed one in the post
& the other in an auger hole (when we happen to have such article) or forced
into one of the chinks of the house. The door is secured by a wooden latch, &
a leather thong to raise it from the outside. Thus the house is finished, & surely
simple enough it is. The wood is cut 2½ feet long, & set upright in the chimney,
it burns much better & gives more heat. Tho' thus roughly & rudely constructed, we soon get accustomed, & when we have enough to eat we feel comfortable; for, here as every where else, we live in anticipation of better times &
never, at least very few of us know to enjoy what we possess. When the indians
come in we give them a few beaver or bear skins & they ly on the floor.

From the simplicity of the construction, & the season of the year, we always
haste to put ourselves under Shelter. The N W C° also soon finished theirs,
which they surrounded with stockades, about ten feet out of ground, with two

Bastions, loop holes &c. in case of an attack from the Sioux, whose visit we had more than ordinary reasons to apprehend.

We had two widows, one very old, to pass the winter by us in a wretched hut. They had two daughters & two boys, between 12 & 14 years of age. I [was] surprised to remark the boys frequently with black faces, upon enquiring, I found they were *fasting*. They sometimes *dreamed* of their departed friends,— "on those occasions, when they awake in the morning, they bruise soft charcoal in their hands, with which they rub their faces so as not to leave one spot of the natural color, take their guns or bow & arrows & go into the woods a hunting, and to mourn & weep where they may not be seen nor heard." They return at even & eat *after* Sun Sett The old woman would frequently go out to the foot of the hill some distance off, & weep & mourn & moan, addressing her departed husband & friends in accents & a tone of voice not to be misunderstood even by me, young, thoughtless & boistrous as I was.

What is this? is it Barbarism? if so, what signify the "Irish Wakes"? our own wailings on the departure of those dear to us? after a few months, & not unfrequently only some days, & we return to the busy occupations of life, & finally become quite reconciled & oblivious:—here, children after several years, go into the woods & bewail their departed friends in quiet & solitude, fasting the whole day. And [sic] old woman, many years after the melancholy events, goes & hides herself at the foot of a tree & holds a "talk" with them; complaining of her bereavement & asking forgiveness if she had ever injured, offended, or hurt their feelings! On their return, they would generally be cheerful, as if it had not been them who but a moment before were making such wailing, or, as if they had just been pouring off *all* their grief—I have very often witnessed such scenes: I was very young & reckless, but being a *Christian*, & *civilized*, these superstitious barbarities were beneath the attention of my superior knowledge; but they have left an indelible impression, which, with my years increases & furnish subject for reflection.

We had frequent visits from our indians, & though they bro't in but little to *us*, we had always to give them liquor, so that at one time we had perpetual drunken songs & noise for, I think, it was ten days. On one of these occasions, two young men of 20 to 22 years of age, plotted to kill *us* all. I mean we four. The widows put us on our guard. Laprairie, the master at the N. W. Cº house also warned us, and one night he overheard them say—"we will watch at the door, & when one comes we will shoot *him*, the report will cause another or perhaps all to rush out to see, we will shoot them also & rush in & dispatch the rest."[18] Laprairie called out to them "and have you forgotten that I shoot deer running thro' the woods? touch them if you dare & I will shoot you like dogs as you are." Finding they were discovered they dropped the idea, pretended to be *very drunk*; & coming to sleep at the house as they usually did, Smith scolded them very much, took their k[n]ives from them & gave them to me to put by.

Laprairie had secured their guns. They slept upon the floor. I also slept after sometime. In the morning they asked for their knives, & returned they [*sic*] very reluctantly, & after jabbering a good deal in french at them, which they no more understood than I did the indian; & I saw with indignation & wrath, seeing Smith did not keep the promise he had made the night before—"to give them a sound whailing." But Smith was experienced & prudent—I was without discer[n]ment, boistrous & very foolish.

We could never divine the reason why they wanted to murder us; for we had always been extremely kind to them. Had this occurred in the "North," where, not a few of the white have no such "qualms of conscience: *every soul of us would have been murdered.* I say this wittingly; for I there saw too much, & heard too much to have the least shadow of a doubt. But here, *opposition* was carried on in a more rational manner; the traders had always indeed had seperate interests, & the turbulent & warlike character of these indians who were still very numerous, proud, haughty & fierce, often compelled them, (the traders) to unite for their mutual safety: hence they were vastly more sociable & humane. But in the "North," it was "neck or nothing." *They* did not "stickle at trifles." In the course of this Journal, it will be too often sadly proved, & if I am permitted (with health & leisure) I will assign some of the causes.

We saw these indians once or twice after, but they were quite altered. One evening, after this, we heard an owl ooing in the woods, his notes & tones were so different from the others that we feared it might be a Scouter of the Scioux giving information of his "whereabouts" to some of his friends. These two chaps went off to see—they were with us, & tho' we kept a strict look as we thought, they *disappeared*, & shortly after we heard a Shot and one crying out "there dog, go, & make your noise elsewhere." It was indeed an owl, perched in a lofty pine tree. He flew off.

Some time about the latter end of October I went out with Boisverd & one of the indian lads to two families four or five miles off, towards the Mississippi. I was surprised to find them in a dense cedar Swamp, so that it was with difficulty we got to them At other times they would have encamped on a beautiful spot, quite near them; but the apprehension they were in of the Sioux induced them to select this spot. They gave us what little they had & bid us be off immediately "for the men have discovered suspicious appearances." We accordingly returned, being very late in the day we had to sleep upon the ground under some pines in a beautiful dry spot: the heavens for a blanket & the earth for a bed. We were excessively thirsty & no water to be had. In the night, I dreamed it was raining & I thought I opened my mouth to receive the little that might fall in. I thought I did catch a very [few] drops, & I awoke quite refreshed. The next morning we got home for breakfast.

After this, about the middle of November, Smith took me with him "en derouine," up "Rivier la Chaudiere," a river several leagues from the place

where we found the indians last fall (See p 21) falling in the S: Croix from the
N. W. side.[19] The next day we found the indians, Two or three "lodges." The
men were out a hunting & returned towards evening. They were all highly
pleased to see us. They had some furs & plenty of meat. They cooked a large
Kettle full for us & helped us generously but Smith eat very little being disgusted with the woman. One of her children had a "looseness," & the little
black devil was running about the lodge squattering out yellow stuff like mus-
tard; she scolded & laying the bratt on her lap opened the *cheeks* & with the
back of her knife Scraped off the Stuff, scolded him again for a dirty little dog,
wiped her knife upon the brush, scooped water with her right hand out of the
Kettle in which our meat was, to wash both, & finished cutting up, with the
same knife, a piece of beautiful fat meat, as a relish to what she had put on before. I was sadly disappointed, for I was hungry & always had a very strong ap-
petite. I kept my eyes upon her during the whole performance, which certainly
was dirty enough. But the knife was *cleaned*. There was nothing on her hands.
We gave them rum;—they got drunk, sang, danced, quarreled & fought; trampling, treading, & falling upon me in their Scuffles. I was annoyed, but "my
brother," who happened to be there with his father was very Kind indeed to
me; as well as the others. At last, after a great deal of talking, which neither of
us could understand, they made room for me to lye down. I soon fell into a
sound sleep; & tho' awoke several times in the night by their falling upon me
in their scuffles & in their dances tripping up each other, yet I awoke in the
morning quite refres[h]ed. We took our breakfast, & re-embarking in our canoe, we returned.

The weather, the day before, was very cold & Snowy. There was ice in many
places, & it formed also on our paddles; But this day it was more pleasant.

When we had reached a certain part of the Ste Croix, on our return, Smith
proposed we should leave our Canoe & cut thro' the angle to the house which
he said was not above 6 or 7 miles distant.[20] If you are Sure you will not lose
yourself I am willing enough. We accordingly carried our canoe into the woods,
bundles up our things & off we went. He was a Smart walker, but extremely impatient & rough, as he complained a great deal of the weight of his load & his
[gun], tho' I had one too, & within a few pounds my load was as heavy as his,
to pacify him, I took his gun too, which was extremely cumbersome. But the
country was level & but little "under brush." The Sun shone beautifully. We
halted two or three times after long walks, to rest a little; finally as it was getting dark, we had to encamp. We were lost! We had nothing to eat, for the little meat we had we left at the canoe: "it is not worth while to embarrass ourselves with it, as we would soon get home."

The next morning we awoke with four or five inches of Snow upon the
ground, & of course a good share on our blankets. We shook it off, bundled up
& away we went. Shortly after we fell upon a low grassy flat, through which

meandered a fine little brook covered with ice and Snow. In true military "neck or nothing" style we plunged in, nearly up to our breasts, Scrambled up the opposite bank, & walked on. After about an hour, we fell upon two tracks *quite fresh!* we followed Smartly to *overtake* them. In a few minutes we came to our fire we had so lately left! Smith was furious. Off we set again, & at furthest half an hour after we again came to our fire! Smith was humbled. "Stay here, and wait for me, said he. I will go out in an other [direction] "see if I can fall upon anything whereby I may recognise our position."

I was so extremely Simple that the serious predicament we were in never once struck me! Smith being gone sometime longer than I anticipated, I then *did* begin to think. Of the many distressing cases where sometimes poor creatures had to draw lots. Others expiring of hunger only a few hundred yards from home where they had lingered for days not knowing where they were. Some imputing their misfortunes to each other destroyed themselves in their rage. Some too, possessed with an evil spirit, would leave a weak or lame companion to perish. We were not very far from the Grounds where the Scioux used to hunt about this Season. These, & I dont know how many other stories passed in my mind rapidly. I knew the violence & irritability of Smith's temper. I thought of my mother, got on my knees, with tears in my eyes! We had not eaten since noon before; but I was neither hungry nor faint. I lamented & Sighed. He was about half an hour absent. O, how glad I was when I saw him return! "Let us go. I know now where we are: we took quite a wrong course." Off we set again, & walked, & walked, & walked. We came upon a high sand bank. "What is this? where are we?" All of a Sudden as one just awoke from his sleep, "oh I know now where we are: this is river La Coquille, & we have been quite near home.[21] We turned back & for some time actually retraced our steps. We soon after got home. My joy was full indeed, but I doubt if I thanked God, so extremely thoughtless was I.

NOTES

From Minnesota History 28 *(June, 1947).*

1. The XY Company's post at Grand Portage is described in Grace Lee Nute's "A British Legal Case and Old Grand Portage," *ante,* 21:117–148. A replica of the North West Company's stockade and post at Grand Portage was erected on the original site in 1938–40. See *ante,* 21:206. This part of Nelson's reminiscences is very valuable to the historian and the archaeologist because the exact sites and relationships of some of the numerous posts at Grand Portage, despite detailed research and extensive excavations, have never been clear.

2. Fort des Prairies was a post on the Saskatchewan River. See Gates, ed., *Five Fur Traders,* 98n. Portage la Perdrix is still called Partridge Portage. It is near the site of old Fort Charlotte at the western end of the Grand Portage, where the XY Company also had a fort. See Grace Lee Nute, "Posts in the Minnesota Fur-Trading Area, 1660–1855," *ante,* 11:358.

3. Benjamin Frobisher was the son of one of the most famous of the Nor'westers,

Joseph Frobisher, and was himself in the service of the North West Company from 1799 to 1804 as well as for several years prior to his untimely death in 1819 during the bitter struggle between his own company and the Hudson's Bay Company. For both Frobishers see Wallace, *Documents Relating to the North West Company,* 446.

4. The Leech Lake fort, on the large lake of that name near the source of the Mississippi River, was an important post in Nelson's day. McBean is mentioned in Curot's diary, in *Wisconsin Historical Collections,* 20:398.

5. "Folle Avoine" was a term used to designate the region about the upper stretches of the St. Croix River. The Indians of that region were often termed the Folle Avoine Saulteurs. See *Wisconsin Historical Collections,* 20:396n.

6. Smith's first name, which is given correctly here, is through an error of translation given as Gardant Smith in *Wisconsin Historical Collections,* 20:399n. See the same volume, pages 396 and 397, for mention of Toussaint Savoyard, who may or may not be the man who was with Nelson.

7. Joseph Boisverd was with Curot for the winter of 1803–04 at the Yellow River post. See *Wisconsin Historical Collections,* 20:397.

8. The term Fond du Lac, as used here by Nelson, must be distinguished from a later settlement of the same name, which is now a suburb of Duluth. The older term was much more comprehensive, including the areas now occupied by Superior, Wisconsin, and Duluth and Fond du Lac, Minnesota, as well as some adjacent territory.

9. Minnesota Point is the "ox's tongue." It extends into the bay of Duluth.

10. The Fond du Lac post of the North West Company was nearly ten years old when Nelson was there. A trader named Dufaut of that company had a wintering house there, probably on the site of Superior, when Jean Baptiste Perrault passed in 1784. In 1793, when Perrault went to "fond du Lac with 16 men in order to build there a fort which would be a depot for the fond du Lac region," he established Fort St. Louis on Minnesota Point. See Jean Baptiste Perrault, "Narrative of the Travels and Adventures of a Merchant Voyageur," in *Michigan Pioneer and Historical Collections,* 37:519, 568.

11. Brule River is the uneuphonious modern corruption of this famous stream's original French name. Famed in modern days for its trout and for the homes of wealthy summer residents, it was equally renowned among fur traders as a major canoe route of the continent.

12. The author is, of course, in error here. The St. Croix enters the Mississippi some miles below the Falls of St. Anthony.

13. The two rivers have their sources in a swampy area close to each other, but certainly not in the same "lake."

14. This is Upper Lake St. Croix. Solon Springs, Wisconsin, is on its shores.

15. Rivière Jaune becomes Yellow River on modern maps. There, at the junction with the St. Croix, is an Indian hamlet to this day, overlooking the "most beautiful" island and at the foot of a hill topped with Indian mounds. Danbury, Wisconsin, is the closest town, some eight miles to the south.

16. Snake River is the modern rendition of Rivière au Serpent of the French explorers and voyageurs. It enters the St. Croix from the Minnesota side not many miles below the mouth of the Yellow River.

17. Yellow Lake in Burnett County, Wisconsin, empties into the St. Croix through a twisting river that widens in spots into so-called lakes. It is obvious from later entries that the North West Company post, sixty yards from its rival, was located between the first and second "lakes," a half mile from the "beautiful low point on the border of 'Yellow Lake,'" to quote Nelson in the same paragraph.

18. Laprairie's first name has not been found, though references to him occur frequently in Nelson's reminiscences and Curot's diary.

19. *En derouine* was a voyageur's expression, meaning that the traders visited the Indians instead of letting them take their furs to the fort or trading post. Rivière la Chaudière is Kettle River, a beautiful stream rising in Carlton County almost on a parallel with the western end of Lake Superior. It empties into the St. Croix a little above the mouth of Snake River, after passing through an interesting gorge and forming many rapids. Nelson's reference, "See p 21," is to the portion of his manuscript in which he describes the meeting of the white men with the Indians at the mouth of the Yellow River; it is printed *ante,* p. 149.

20. Tradition in the vicinity of Danbury, Wisconsin, tells of a Sioux (Dakota) trail between the St. Croix and Yellow Lake, which began below the present Danbury bridge. This would have been about where Smith and Nelson apparently left the river.

21. "La Coquille" means "shell," but the modern translation of the river's name is Clam. Shell Lake, a little farther east, is the source of the Yellow River. The Clam River, after draining Clam Lake in its course, empties into the St. Croix a little above the mouth of the Kettle River.

Gift Giving in the Lake Superior Fur Trade

BRUCE M. WHITE

The fur trade represented complex commercial activities involving Europeans and Indians coming from very different societies and cultures, as well as products and markets separated by thousands of miles. The Europeans were involved in commerce with "business partners" who were unable to read, unfamiliar with contracts, and in a wilderness with neither laws nor courts. Trust was needed on both sides and the giving of gifts seemed to represent a solution. Bruce White focuses on the Indian side of gift giving, using the social and cultural meanings for the Ojibwe Indians. Gift giving was set in the context of family patterns like brother-brother or parent-child. Wampum, tobacco, and rum ("mother's milk") had special significance in these transactions.

White studies gift patterns between the Ojibwe and Dakota and then between Ojibwe and Europeans in both diplomatic and trade contexts. The particular family relationship could become problematic as Europeans felt they were the "parents" and yet they might need "brothers" more than "children" to secure the best furs. This ambiguity was sometimes resolved by the trader marrying a chief's daughter and thus establishing a very visible familial tie.

Gift giving was an essential custom followed by both Indians and Europeans to pursue trade and diplomatic relations in North America during the eighteenth and nineteenth centuries. Historical studies of this custom, however, have concentrated on European motives and machinations: historians have equated it with bribery and have suggested that it was introduced by Europeans. But why did fur traders give gifts at all? How did this expensive social act creep into what has usually been portrayed as merely an exercise in capitalism? One plausible explanation for the widespread use of gift giving lies in its social and cultural meanings for American Indians. A promising area in which to seek answers is the Lake Superior region, where the Ojibwe Indians were the focus of important and long-lasting relations with the French, British, and Americans.[1]

What was it about the meanings of gifts in Ojibwe culture that made their use important in trade and diplomacy? First, a trader arriving in the Lake Superior country to set himself up in business was one of only a few Europeans living far away from home in that foreign land. To his intended producers and customers, the Ojibwe, he was a stranger, potentially either an enemy or a friend. In order to do business, the trader had to prove to the Indians that he was trustworthy; he also had to make sure that he could trust these people with whom he wanted to trade. He needed to establish a reciprocal confidence that would minimize the risks on both sides.

The trader could not use European methods to do this. He could not, for example, take the Indians before a notary to sign legal contracts, for there were no written laws and no courts to enforce them. Rather, the trader had to make an agreement with the Ojibwe on their own terms, using Indian techniques to establish a binding relationship. The most common way was gift giving.

On the simplest level the Ojibwe, like many other cultural groups, believed that tangible objects could be used to signify feelings. The traveler Johann Georg Kohl, who visited Lake Superior in the 1850s, recorded a fur trader's belief that for the Ojibwe giving gifts was a necessary way of demonstrating one person's esteem for another: "If you say to one of them 'I love thee,'" wrote Kohl, "have a present ready to hand, to prove your love clearly. You will lose in their sight if a present, or some tangible politeness, does not follow on such an assurance. But it is often sufficient to hand them the plate from which you have been eating, and on which you have left a fragment for them."[2]

Gifts also aided in establishing and affirming more elaborate relationships. Depending on the situations in which they were given and on the words and ceremonies that accompanied them, gifts communicated something about what each partner to the relationship wanted.

Among the Ojibwe the family or kin group served as the basic producer and distributor of goods and services. The parents did not exert the same kind of authoritarian power over their children that European parents might have, and in a very real sense family members' roles were defined less by authority than by the ways in which they cared for, or were cared for by, others in the family. Infants were fed at their mother's breast. When they were weaned the father or elder brothers provided them with meat and clothing by hunting and fishing, and the mother or elder sisters might also fish and trap, harvest agricultural products, prepare the food, and make the clothing. The parents' role when the offspring were young was reversed when the grown children took care of old and feeble parents.[3]

The flow of goods and services along family lines was not limited to the nuclear family, although the extent of participation by cousins, uncles, aunts, grandfathers, and grandmothers in the family's material life might vary. Once an individual had grown up and married, many new patterns of exchange would be established, and these also might vary. In any case, marriage would probably broaden a person's economic possibilities and obligations.[4]

Another extension of material relationships was the *dodem* or totem. Every child inherited his father's totem through which he was related to a wide variety of individuals in his own and other Ojibwe communities around Lake Superior. These people, whom he would address as "brother" and "sister," were an important set of relatives to whom he could appeal when in need and to whom he himself would be obligated should they be without closer kin nearby.[5]

What then did this social pattern have to do with the dealings between Ojibwe who were not related, as well as with the society-wide institutions of trade and diplomacy in which the Ojibwe confronted non-Indian societies? Since the exchange of goods and services was basically a function of kinship, it appeared that the flow of these goods and services taking place outside the bonds of kinship was structured in kinship terms.

In such nonfamilial circumstances the bond would be invented, not inherited. The power and extent of these new relationships were based on the degree in which they could be made to resemble the social and economic relations that existed among family members. To have relationships with someone in a material sense was to be related in a metaphorical sense. John Tanner, a white man adopted by an Ottawa family, found this to be true when he and his adoptive kin were in need west of Lake Superior in the early 1800s. An Ojibwe family took them into its lodge, offering to care for and feed them during the winter. Later on, said Tanner, whenever he or his Ottawa family saw any member of the other family, they would call them "brothers" and treat them like relatives.[6]

On the other hand, if one person wished to establish with another a close relationship that encompassed all those rights and obligations found most clearly in the family, he would turn to a tangible definition of such bonds and give gifts. In recent times, anthropologist Ruth Landes noted that, among the Ojibwe of western Ontario, if a person wanted to adopt someone else, the relationship would be partly affirmed by gift giving. One of Landes's female informants told of being adopted by an older woman: "She took me for her daughter after her daughter's death, and she called me by her daughter's name. She asked me if she could not have me for a daughter. I said it was alright and I called her 'mother.' She gave me things and I gave her things as I would to my own mother." When the woman's husband died, her adopted mother helped provide gifts to her husband's family in a practice known as "paying off the mourning."[7]

Gifts made for a close relationship, just as a close relationship would result in gifts being given. If you wished to receive or to present goods to someone, you would address the other person as your brother, sister, father, or mother.

A mixed-blood named William Johnston, who traded near Leech Lake in 1833, offered an example of this in the hospitality shown him by several Ojibwe. "The Indians claimed relationship with me, from some remarks that I made, and that since I had the same totem I should partake of what they had; They gave me a bag of Rice." It was Johnston's mother who was Ojibwe; since the totem was usually inherited through the father, the Indians may have invented the relationship with Johnston to explain their kindness.[8]

Crucial to certain kinds of gift giving and their meaning in the idiom of kinship was a concept that has been translated as "pity" or "charity." These words occur not only in transcripts of Ojibwe meetings with traders and European diplomats but also in more modern ethnographic texts. Landes wrote that "In Ojibwa idiom, to 'pity' another is to adopt him and care for him as a parent or grandparent cares for a child." To give someone a gift with no thought of an immediate return was to "pity" him and thus in a sense to adopt him. This idea was applied not only to relationships between persons but also to those between humans and supernatural beings. A child fasting in search of a vision, for example, sought to evoke the interest of a supernatural spirit. By fasting he made himself "pitiful," hoping to obtain a long-term relationship with a spirit being. Later on, if he were in need, perhaps because of poor luck in hunting, he could call upon his spiritual "grandfather" or "grandmother" for help. One old man described his vision quest to John Tanner: "When I was yet a little boy, the Great Spirit came to me, after I had been fasting for 3 days, and told me he had heard me crying, and had come to tell me that he did not wish to hear me cry and complain so often, but that if ever I was reduced to the danger of immediately perishing of hunger, then I should call upon him, and he would hear and give me somethings."[9]

The Ojibwe endowed the animals they hunted with human qualities, frequently addressing them in terms of kinship. The trader Alexander Henry, the elder, who lived with the Ojibwe family of Wawatam near Michilimackinac in the winter of 1763–64, discovered that the killing of a bear was an occasion for elaborate ceremony and feasting. As soon as Henry had shot the bear, some of the Ojibwe took its head "in their hands, stroking and kissing it several times; begging a thousand pardons for taking away her life; calling her their relation and grandmother; and requesting her not to lay the fault upon them, since it was truly an Englishman that had put her to death."[10]

Back at their lodge, the Ojibwe took part in ceremonial gift giving designed to allay the bear's anger. "As soon as we reached the lodge," wrote Henry, "the bear's head was adorned with all the trinkets in the possession of the family, such as silver arm-bands and wrist-bands, and belts of wampum; and then laid upon a scaffold. . . . Near the nose, was placed a large quantity of tobacco.

"The next morning . . . preparations were made for a feast to the manes [*bear spirits*]. The lodge was cleaned and swept; and the head of the bear lifted up, and a new stroud blanket . . . spread under it. The pipes were now lit; and Wawatam blew tobacco-smoke into the nostrils of the bear, telling me to do the same, and thus appease the anger of the bear, on account of my having killed her."

As this description indicates, one gift given in such exchanges was tobacco. The importance of tobacco as a way of reconciling people and spiritual beings was evident in Ojibwe society into the twentieth century. Ethnographer Inez Hilger, after interviewing Ojibwe on a variety of reservations in Wisconsin and Minnesota, compared the role of smoking to praying. She quoted an interpreter discussing a Lac Courte Oreille man's spiritual guardian: "Lighting a pipe is the same as praying, for when he lights his pipe he asks his helper to help him." Hilger also cited the words of an Ojibwe woman who, taking a root cutting from a plant for medicinal use, placed a small amount of tobacco with the remaining roots, saying, "I'll take just a little for my use, and here is some tobacco for you!"[11]

This use of tobacco reflected the fundamental role of smoking in mediation among individuals in Ojibwe society. Peezhikee (Buffalo), an early nineteenth-century leader at La Pointe, Wisconsin, described clearly the importance of tobacco at an 1826 treaty meeting with United States government treaty commissioners. He compared his own authority with that of the government agents: "You are strong [enough] to make your young men obey you. But we have no way, *Fathers,* to make our young men listen, but by the pipe."[12]

Gift giving, as shown in these examples, was an important factor in Ojibwe life. Linked specifically to the idiom of kinship, it was used in a variety of human, animal, and spiritual relationships. It remains to show how it extended to the Indians' associations with people outside their society.

Many examples can be found in their dealings with their neighbors, the Dakota. Although warfare between the two groups often occurred, there were also occasions when they made peace. In a society with no central authority and where chieftainship was the result of winning public support through persuasion, the process of peacemaking often consisted of individual Ojibwe making friends with individual Dakota.[13]

When groups of Ojibwe hunters traveled into territory occupied by the Dakota, they might turn their potential enemies into friends by an exchange of goods as well as a mutual smoking of tobacco in a calumet. One special kind of exchange involved clothing. A well-known painting of the Ojibwe leader Okeemakeequid in Thomas L. McKenney's and James Hall's Indian portrait collection shows the result of such an exchange. He is dressed not in Ojibwe costume but in the garb of a Dakota warrior obtained during negotiations at the United States-sponsored treaty of 1825 held at Prairie du Chien. Okeemakeequid and a Dakota exchanged their clothing, and the Dakota called him "brother."[14]

Eight years later William Johnston, trading at Leech Lake, reported: "Ten canoes arrived[.] While hunting they met the Sioux, who came up, and extended the hand of friendship; and to ratify it, as is their custom they exchanged all there [*sic*] articles of clothing." The two incidents show that by making this even trade the two individuals established a relationship, however little binding on other members of their societies, in which each renounced his own self-interest. In the process they ceased being enemies and became brothers and friends.[15]

Another, possibly more permanent, kind of exchange by which the Ojibwe and Dakota made peace with each other was intermarriage. As anthropologist Claude Lévi-Strauss has clearly shown, intermarriage can be an important way for two societies, by joining their kin groups, to establish a reciprocity of trust and allow many other peaceful exchanges to take place. Describing a period in the early 1700s, historian William Warren noted: "On the St. Croix the two tribes intermingled freely. . . . They encamped together, and intermarriages took place between them." Warren told of one case where the daughter and only child of a leader of the Rice Lake, Wisconsin, band of Ojibwe married a Dakota chief who belonged to the wolf totem of his tribe. "He resided among the Ojibways at Rice Lake during the whole course of the peace, and begat by his Ojibway wife, two sons who afterward became chiefs, and who of course inherited their father's totem of wolf. In this manner this badge became grafted among the Ojibway list of clans." Another example Warren used was that of two celebrated Indian leaders, Ma-mong-e-se-da, an Ojibwe, and Wabasha I, a Dakota. They were half-brothers, sons of an Ojibwe woman who married twice.[16]

Diplomatic relations between the Ojibwe and representatives of European governments had many of the formal characteristics of the Indians' friendly relationships with each other. Tobacco, food, and hospitality were shared, and goods such as clothing, guns, and household equipment were also given. One special item transcended kinship diplomacy: it was wampum, belts or strings of shell beads, and it served as a record of transactions in diplomatic exchanges between tribes as well as with Europeans. Wampum represented in an enduring way the words spoken in an encounter. When two parties had not met face to face, wampum, accompanied by a speech delivered by a messenger, could initiate a transaction. The speech came to be called by the French word *parole*, and the wampun was the tangible, physical manifestation of the message. It was preserved and honored just as were the written treaties that Europeans professed to respect so much. If someone were not interested in making an agreement or did not accept the substance of the *parole*, he would refuse the wampum and any other gifts, just as European governments might refuse to sign treaties or accept diplomatic notes.[17]

Another feature of Ojibwe-European diplomacy, however, was somewhat different from the Ojibwe-Dakota relations discussed above. While the kinship of brother to brother may have come to typify certain peacemaking efforts of the two Indian groups, it was the relationship of parent to child that often embodied diplomatic relations between European governments and the Ojibwe.

It is part of traditional knowledge of Indian-white relations throughout North America that Indians would sometimes refer to a European king, an American president, or a diplomatic agent as "father" and that Europeans similarly called the Indians their "children." Who initially established this metaphor is not known, but the diplomatic idiom fits with what is known about the paternalism of European authority structure just as it coincides with the Ojibwe tendency to project the family metaphor onto a multitude of other situations. The key questions are: how did this idiomatic language reflect the aims of the treaty meetings between Europeans and American Indians? How were these purposes reflected in the objects used in accompanying gift exchanges? In the nineteenth century these meetings usually had to do with land purchase. Looking further back into the seventeenth and eighteenth centuries, however, it is clear that European powers in the area of the Great Lakes vied with each other mainly to win Indian loyalty to their military causes.[18]

Although it has yet to be shown in a quantified way, the Europeans apparently did the bulk of the gift giving in many of these diplomatic transactions, just as in the family group it was initially the father who gave to the child. In effect, then, such gifts became an expression of the role Europeans sought to play in relation to the Indians. Indians gave many gifts of furs and ceremonial presents during these exchanges. But they did not necessarily give tangible, equal presents in an economic sense, as in the peace talks between Ojibwe and Dakota. Their gift was something more profound—the loyalty that a child feels toward the parent, a long-term tie that was expressed by a defense of the parent against insult and violence and a willingness to avenge an attack. The result was a military alliance cast in kinship terms.

The meaning that this metaphorical kinship had for the Ojibwe is evident in the rich and significant speech given by one leader, Minavavana, to Alexander Henry at Michilimackinac shortly after the fall of Quebec in 1761: "Englishman, it is you that have made war with this our father. You are his enemy; and how, then, could you have the boldness to venture among us, his children?—You know that his enemies are ours. . . .[19]

"Englishman, our father, the king of France, employed our young men to make war upon your nation. In this warfare, many of them have been killed; and it is our custom to retaliate, until such time as the spirits of the slain are satisfied. But, the spirits of the slain are to be satisfied in either of two ways; the first is by the spilling of the blood of the nation by which they fell; the other, by *covering the bodies of the dead [in new clothing and ornaments before burial]*, and thus allaying the resentment of their relations. This is done by making presents.

"Englishman, your king has never sent us any presents, nor entered into any treaty with us, wherefore he and we are still at war; and, until he does these things, we must consider that we have no other father, nor friend, among the white men, than the king of France; but, for you, we have taken into consideration, that you have ventured your life among us, in the expectation that we should not molest you. You do not come armed, with an intention to make war; you come in peace, to trade with us, and supply us with necessaries, of which we are in much want. We shall regard you, therefore, as a brother; and you may sleep tranquilly, without fear of the Chipeways.—As a token of our friendship we present you with this pipe, to smoke."

For the Ojibwe this parent-child idiom was the function of a particular type of diplomatic contact with European governments. The Ojibwe might reject the use of the metaphor when whites attempted to impose it on a relationship that did not fit it. In 1832 Eschkebugecoshe (Flat Mouth) of Leech Lake objected when Indian agent Henry R. Schoolcraft in a speech to the assembled warriors of his band called them "children." "You call us children. We are not children, but men," he insisted. He criticized the American government for failing to enforce the agreement it had brought about between the Ojibwe and Dakota at Prairie du Chien in 1825.[20]

"Our great father promised us, when we smoked the pipe with the Sioux at Prairie du Chien in 1825, and at Fond du Lac in 1826, that the first party who crossed the line, and broke the treaty, should be punished. This promise has not been fulfilled. . . . I do not think the Great Spirit ever made us to sit still and see our young men, our wives, and our children murdered.

"Since we have listened to the Long Knives [*American soldiers*], we have not prospered. They are not willing we should go ourselves, and flog our enemies, nor do they fulfill their promise and do it for us."

Laying at Schoolcraft's feet the medals of all the Leech Lake leaders and a string of wampum given to him previously by the Americans, Eschkebugecoshe went on: "These and all your letters are stained with blood. I return them all to you to make them bright. None of us wish to receive them back until you have wiped off the blood. . . .

"The words of the Long Knives have passed through our forests as a rushing wind, but they have been words merely. They have only shaken the trees, but have not stopped to break them down, nor even to make the rough places smooth."

Eschkebugecoshe's objection to the term "children" appeared to have had little to do with resentment at being treated like children. Instead he seemed to resent being called "children" by a representative of the "Great Father," who had not kept the obligations of this metaphorical parenthood defined in the treaty at Prairie du Chien. Eschkebugecoshe rejected not only the term of address but also the representations of the government's words, the medals, and the strings of wampum. Were the government to validate its words through actions, perhaps someone like Schoolcraft would again be able to call the Indians "children," for then the words would not be empty or hypocritical.

Sir William Johnson, a member of the British Indian department in the early 1760s, recognized better than most Europeans the importance of gift giving. The year after the Ojibwe-led attack on Michilimackinac in 1763, Johnson sent a messenger to the western Great Lakes with a wampum belt and a speech inviting the Indians to a feast at Fort Niagara and promising them presents that would establish the tangible concern of the British government.[21]

Alexander Henry, who was at Sault Ste. Marie when Johnson's messenger arrived, helped to persuade the Ojibwe to accept the spirit of Johnson's words and accompanied a group eastward. Henry described an incident that took place en route which graphically showed what the Ojibwe expected of Johnson and helped to place this act of diplomacy in the context of other types of exchanges that occurred in Ojibwe society. One day Henry discovered a rattlesnake not more than two feet from his naked legs. He ran to get his gun.

"The Indians, on their part, surrounded it, all addressing it by turns, and calling it their *grandfather;* but yet keeping at some distance," wrote Henry. "During this part of the ceremony, they filled their pipes; and now each blew the smoke toward the snake, who, as it appeared to me, really received it with pleasure. In a word, after remaining coiled, and receiving incense, for the space of half an hour, it stretched itself along the ground, in visible good humour. . . . At last it moved slowly away, the Indians following it, and still addressing it by the title of grand-father, beseeching it to take care of their families during their absence, and to be pleased to open the heart of Sir William Johnson, so that he might *show them charity,* and fill their canoe with rum."

It is significant that these Ojibwe should have associated rum with "charity," for in diplomatic dealings between the Ojibwe and the Europeans rum, brandy, whisky, or other forms of alcohol seem to have crystallized the idiom of kinship more than any of the other gifts. The names given alcohol are important. Although it was known in nondiplomatic situations by a term translated as "firewater," when it was given away by European government agents in a ceremonial way, the Ojibwe referred to it as "milk," meaning mother's milk.[22]

One could postulate various psychological explanations for this metaphor. For example, under the influence of alcohol, a drinker might revert to childish behavior. What also of the possible associations between sucking from glass bottles—in which rum was sometimes given to the Ojibwe—and sucking from a breast?

There are also possible ironies in the use of the term, "milk." One can imagine the thoughts of the military officers at Drummond Island in 1816 when a noted leader of the Sandy Lake Ojibwe, Katawaubetai (Broken Tooth), stood before them and said: "Father—I come from a great distance and have waited patiently in hopes of getting some of your milk to drink but I find you do not seem inclined to let me draw near your breast." What did Thomas McKenney and his fellow commissioners at the treaty of Fond du Lac ten years later think when Peezhikee said: "*Fathers,*—you have many children. But your breasts drop yet. Give us a little milk, *Fathers,* that we may wet our lips.[23]

There probably was no better way for the Ojibwe leaders to insult the Europeans while at the same time getting what they wanted. In effect, they could be saying: "You call us your children. We do not think so much of you. You are women. Are you our mothers? Then feed us as a mother should." This rich, suggestive image contains many contradictory facets of relations between Europeans and Indians. But the image probably derives from the cultural meanings of mother's milk.

Milk is the first gift that a child receives when he is born. It is no exaggeration to suggest, as Marshall Sahlins has, that it is a prime example of the pure gift. It is the quintessence of all gifts that a parent gives to a child, because it flows freely from the mother to the infant and is given with absolutely no thought of a return gift. The obvious exchange for mother's milk is the loyalty of child to parent, perhaps one of the strongest manifestations of kinship.[24]

The strength of this image must have been especially powerful for Ojibwe society in which mothers nursed their children as long as four years, so that breast feeding might well be a strong memory for all. The geographer and ethnologist Joseph N. Nicollet, who traveled among the Ojibwe of the upper Mississippi in 1837, remarked that "One often sees a little boy leave the playground with his bow and arrow, find and unveil his mother's breast, suckle a few moments, then return to his game with his little friends." It is also interesting to note that it was only while she was still nursing the child that an Ojibwe mother had any authority over her sons and, in fact, she then had as much authority as the father later had.[25]

Rum, that valuable European liquid, came to represent mother's milk, the gift that more than any other signified the concern of a parent for her child and the loyalty of a child for his mother. Rum, given in diplomatic dealings, symbolized the seriousness with which the Ojibwe and other Indian groups treated these diplomatic transactions; it also demonstrated how the Ojibwe could give a foreign product unique meanings far from its original European context. The adoption of European material objects did not, therefore, necessarily endanger the Indians' own cultural values.[26]

Because rum held this symbolic meaning in diplomatic exchanges with the Ojibwe, it would be inaccurate to think that its full significance resided simply in its intoxicating qualities. Who would say the same of the wine which, in Christian communion, becomes the "blood of Christ"?

What evidence associates the metaphorical meanings of rum and other diplomatic gifts with those same gifts used in the fur trade? Is it valid to suggest that they served the same purposes in trade that they did in diplomacy? There was a similarity between the traders' requests of the Indians and those of governments. On the simplest level, the trader was a stranger seeking material exchange with the Indians. To succeed, he had to make an agreement, to establish relationships that resembled family ties. He also wanted to obtain loyalty that would bind the Indians to him and not to another trader. But in this respect the trader did not want to do all the giving; he did not want to be a "father" or "mother" to the Indians. Rather, he wanted reciprocity—the Indians providing furs equal in value to the trade goods he offered. Like the Dakota who exchanged clothing with his "brother" Ojibwe, the trader wanted to give clothing, blankets, and tools and receive in return the Indian's clothing, the beaver robes that he had worn, as well as all the other furs that he did not wear.

In some ways the fur trade relationship could exactly parallel that between the Indian agent and his "children." Sometimes a large fur company took on the characteristics that one would expect only a government to have had. The Ojibwe of Lac du Flambeau, Wisconsin, were in the habit of referring to William McGillivray, one of the chief partners of the North West Company, as their "father." When François Victoire Malhiot arrived there in the winter of 1804-05 as North West trader, his men circulated the rumor that he was McGillivray's brother. The Indians thereupon began addressing him as "father."[27]

McGillivray, a distant figure who did not come to visit the Ojibwe, performed in effect the function of a king or president. It was in McGillivray's name that presents were given at the beginning of the trading year. The actual exchanges of goods took place with a trader who more nearly represented a brother to them. Perhaps for this reason Malhiot undertook to represent himself not as their father but as an equal to the Ojibwe, calling them either his comrades or his relatives. In other ways he sought to capitalize on McGillivray's parental position. For example, Malhiot gave some presents to a chief named l'Outarde (Bustard), saying, "My Relation. The coat which I have just placed upon you is sent by the Great Trader [*McGillivray*]. It is with this clothing that he honors the most eminent of a nation. This flag is [also] a real mark of a leader with which you must feel honored, since we do not give them to just any Indian. You must be what you are to get one, that is to say, you must love the French [*the mostly French-Canadian traders who represented the company in the area*] the way you do and protect them and help make packs of furs for them. . . . Look at me, all of you, see before you the trader sent to you. I am the one you asked for. I received this summer three *paroles* from the chiefs on the prairies to go back to winter in their land. But I refused them in order to live up to what the Great Trader told you. He sent me here to be charitable toward you but not to be scorned. . . . Be devoted to our fort, protect its doors, and I will carry good news about you all to your Father in the spring."

The smaller companies and independent traders, who were more typical of the Europeans trading among the Ojibwe, had little chance to win their loyalty by giving gifts in the name of a Great Trader. Often they merely represented themselves. Yet they used many of the same gifts as North West Company traders. The account of John Long, an independent trader among a group of Ojibwe northeast of Lake Nipigon in Ontario in the 1760s, demonstrated the process by which inexperienced traders could be initiated into gift giving by the Ojibwe themselves.[28]

On arrival at his wintering place, Long was greeted by a large band of people and their leader Kesconeek (Broken Arm), who gave him skins, dried meat, fish, and wild rice. In return Long gave them some gifts, but he did not report what they were. Then the Indians went into Long's house. Kesconeek, "standing upright with great dignity in the centre of the tribe," delivered a speech that the trader recorded in both Ojibwe and English: "It is true, Father, I and my young men are happy to see you:—as the great Master of Life has sent a trader to take pity on us Savages [*the Ojibwe version of this speech gives this word as "Nishinnorbay," or Anishinabe, meaning simply people or Indians*], we shall use our best endeavours to hunt and bring you wherewithal to satisfy you in furs, skins, and animal food."

In Long's opinion the speech was as an attempt to "induce me to make them further presents; I indulged them in their expectations, by giving them two kegs of rum of eight gallons each, lowered with a small proportion of water, according to the usual custom adopted by all traders, five carrots of tobacco, fifty scalping knives, gun-flints, power, shot, ball, &c. To the women I gave beads, trinkets, &c and to eight chiefs who were in the band, each a North-west gun, a callico [*sic*] shirt, a scalping knife of the best sort, and an additional quantity of ammunition. These were received with a full yo-hah, or demonstration of joy."

In the metaphorical relationship of parent to child, the parent is seen, at least initially, as giving the greater quantity of goods. Thus, when an Ojibwe wanted to receive gifts from rather than give gifts to someone, he would, like Kesconeek, address the other as "father" and appeal to his "pity." The Ojibwe also sought to evoke the pity of spiritual beings by fasting—a way of showing that he was truly in need of any aid that being might offer. Long may very well have been correct in assuming that Kesconeek wanted the trader to give more presents. But did it necessarily follow that ceremonial demonstrations were made strictly with immediate material return in mind? If an Indian told a trader or a government agent that he was "destitute" and in great need, did this mean that he was simply acquisitive? Was it not also possible that he was interested in establishing a social and political tie with the trader or government agent?[29]

Such a possibility might put into perspective many accounts of diplomatic and trade meetings between the Ojibwe and Europeans in which the latter reported their distinct impression that the Indians were suffering, starving, and greatly dependent on them—perhaps far more than was actually the case. The Europeans may have been confusing objects and what they represented, ignoring the important contextual factors.[30]

An incident recorded by Alexander Henry, embarking on his first trading voyage west of Lake Superior in 1775, suggests that occasionally the Ojibwe claimed to be in need when they were really well off. His description of a typical transaction at Lake of the Woods contained many of the elements found in other such trades, but in this case the trader was just as much in need as the Indians claimed to be.[31]

"From this village," wrote Henry, "we received ceremonious presents. The mode with the Indians is, first to collect all the provisions they can spare, and place them in a heap; after which they send for the trader, and address him in a formal speech. They tell him, that the Indians are happy in seeing him return into their country; that they have been long in expectation of his arrival; that their wives have deprived themselves of their provisions, in order to afford him a supply; that they are in great want, being destitute of every thing, and particularly of ammunition and clothing; and that what they most long for, is a taste of his rum, which they uniformly denominate *milk*.

"The present, in return, consisted in one keg of gunpowder, of sixty pounds weight; a bag of shot and another of powder, of eighty pounds each; a few smaller articles, and a keg of rum. The last appeared to be the chief treasure, though on the former depended the greater part of their winter's subsistence.

"In a short time, the men began to drink, while the women brought a further and very valuable present, of twenty bags of rice. This I returned with goods and rum, and at the same time offered more, for an additional quantity of rice. A trade was opened, the women bartering rice, while the men were drinking. Before morning, I had purchased a hundred bags, of nearly a bushel measure each. Without a large quantity of rice, the voyage could not have been prosecuted to its completion."

Were the Indians in this ceremonial exchange saying that without the European's aid they would not be able to survive? Or were they simply following the etiquette of such encounters as they saw it?

The possible ambiguities in the metaphorical kinship ties that the Ojibwe used to establish friendship with strangers are evident. In terms of gift giving, for instance, a trader might function as a "father" or "mother"; in terms of direct trade, the relationship might be that of a "brother." Certainly such contradictions in the relationship might cause some confusion in regard to what each party expected from the other. But the trader might make another more durable bond, possibly assuring more clarity in his relations with the Ojibwe, by changing a metaphorical tie into a "real" one. He might marry an Indian woman.

Frequently, the influence and success that a trader had with the Indians corresponded to the strength and renown of his father-in-law. Leading traders often married the daughters of leading Ojibwe; in marrying a chief's daughter, the trader gained a powerful ally among his Indian customers. Since the authority of a chief was sometimes the result of extended kinship ties, the trader may have formed actual ties with a larger number of people. The chief's influence over kin and nonkin alike depended largely upon his persuasive abilities—especially his oratory. Thus, through marriage, the trader gained an alliance with a man of demonstrated ability to influence his fellows. The father-in-law became in a sense a diplomatic agent for the trader, useful in persuading his people to be friends and customers.[32]

For the chief there were comparable advantages. Allying with a trader could bolster his own influence and power with his people, since the chief would often distribute the gifts that his son-in-law brought each year to trade. In so doing, the leader gave material demonstration of concern for the welfare of the other Indians within his family or within the larger group, showing that he was worthy, generous, and unselfish. These attributes might strengthen his ties to nonkin.

In any case, gift giving was of continuing importance to the fur trader. Marrying into an Indian family did not lessen his obligation to give gifts; it simply provided him with a previously defined kinship network in which to carry on his gift giving. Only by continuing this was the trader's position in this kinship system validated.

Far from being bribery, gift giving—whether in personal relationships, trade, or diplomacy—was an important social act among the Ojibwe. Without participating in the process a foreigner, whether he be a diplomat or a trader, could not hope to arrive at his political or economic ends. By their participation, fur traders and diplomats demonstrated more than a superficial understanding of Ojibwe culture.[33]

NOTES

From Minnesota History 48 (Summer, 1982).

1. The author thanks Deborah L. Miller, Roger Buffalohead, Donald F. Bibeau, and Trevor Barnes for their valuable advice and criticism during the writing of this article.

Gift giving in diplomacy is described in Wilbur R. Jacobs, *Wilderness Politics and Indian Gifts: The Northern Colonial Frontier, 1748–1763* (Lincoln, Neb., 1967). Fur-trade gift giving is mentioned in Wilcomb E. Washburn, "Symbol, Utility, and Aesthetics in the Indian Fur Trade," in Dale L. Morgan, et al., *Aspects of the Fur Trade: Selected Papers of the 1965 North American Fur Trade Conference,* 50 (St. Paul, 1967). On the supposed European origins of gift giving, see Ida Amanda Johnson, *The Michigan Fur Trade,* 65 (Lansing, Mich., 1919).

2. Johann Georg Kohl, *Kitchi-Gami: Wanderings round Lake Superior,* 133 (Reprint ed., Minneapolis, 1956). To allow someone to eat from your plate is an intimate gesture characteristic of family life. The implications of this are discussed below.

3. This is neither an argument for nor against theories of the "atomistic" social organization of the Ojibwe discussed in Harold Hickerson, *The Southwestern Chippewa: An Ethnohistorical Study,* 9–11 (American Anthropological Association, *Memoir* 92—Menasha, Wis., 1962); Victor Barnouw, *Wisconsin Chippewa Myths & Tales and Their Relation to Chippewa Life,* 5–8 (Madison, Wis., 1977). To argue that the family was the basic unit of organization among the Ojibwe is not to suggest that there were not other important institutions of society. What is proposed here is that the family provided a metaphor for other more extensive links between individuals in Ojibwe life. On parental authority see Peter Jones, *History of the Ojebway Indians,* 67 (London, 1861).

4. Ruth Landes, *Ojibwa Sociology,* 27 (New York, 1937).

5. Landes, *Ojibwa Sociology,* 43; Sister M. Inez Hilger, *Chippewa Child Life and Its Cultural Background,* 155 (Bureau of American Ethnology, *Bulletin* 146—Washington, C., 1951).

6. Edwin James, ed., *A Narrative of the Captivity and Adventures of John Tanner,* 24 (Reprint ed., Minneapolis, 1956).

7. Landes, *Ojibwa Sociology,* 16, 17. See also Hilger, *Child Life,* 34.

8. William Johnston, "Letters on the Fur Trade 1833," in *Michigan Pioneer and Historical Collections,* 37:177 (Lansing, 1909, 1910).

9. Ruth Landes, *The Ojibwa Woman,* 6 (New York, 1938). See also Johnston, in *Michigan Pioneer and Historical Collections,* 37:182; James, ed., *John Tanner,* 143.

Here and throughout this article, English translations of Ojibwe words and speeches are used; unfortunately there are no Indian versions of most of these documents. In using these translations, the author assumes that there is a fair accuracy on the part of the translator and that the consistencies found in many of these translations are not accidental but are a reflection of real consistencies in the original Ojibwe terminology and the ideas in back of them. Work with modern Ojibwe informants by researchers skilled in the Ojibwe language may be the only way to deal linguistically with the issues presented here.

10. Here and two paragraphs below, see Alexander Henry, *Travels and Adventures in Canada and the Indian Territories,* 73, 143, 144 (Reprint ed., New York, 1976). See also Landes, *Ojibwa Woman,* 15. Wawatam was an Ojibwe whom Henry had first met at Michilimackinac and who adopted the trader as a brother soon after.

11. Hilger, *Child Life,* 47, 92.

12. Thomas L. McKenney, *Sketches of a Tour to the Lakes,* 462 (Reprint ed., Minneapolis, 1959). The spelling of Ojibwe names throughout this article follows that in the cited source; variations may be found in Newton H. Winchell, *The Aborigines of Minnesota: A Report,* 707–731 (St. Paul, 1911).

13. For a discussion of the roots of traditional Ojibwe authority, see James G. E. Smith, *Leadership among the Southwestern Ojibwa,* 17 (National Museums of Canada; National Museum of Man, *Publications in Ethnology,* no. 7—Ottawa, 1973). The words "chief" and "leader" are used interchangeably here to mean a person of influence rather than an individual with coercive power.

14. Thomas L. McKenney and James Hall, *The Indian Tribes of North America,* 256 (Edinburgh, 1933).

15. Johnston, in *Michigan Pioneer Collections,* 37:186. See also William W. Warren, "History of the Ojibways, Based Upon Traditions and Oral Statements," in *Minnesota Historical*

Collections, 5:268 (St. Paul, 1885); Marshall Sahlins, *Stone Age Economics,* 220 (Hawthorne, N.Y., 1976). Sahlins's work, especially his essay "On the Sociology of Primitive Exchange" (185–275), is a very useful guide to understanding the cultural meanings of gift giving.

16.   Claude Lévi-Strauss, *The Elementary Structures of Kinship,* 63–68 (Boston, 1969); Sahlins, *Stone Age Economics,* 222; Warren, in *Collections,* 5:164, 219.

17.   J[ohn] Long, *Voyages and Travels of an Indian Interpreter and Trader,* 47 (Reprint ed., Toronto, 1974).

18.   See Jacobs, *Wilderness Politics,* 11. Michael Paul Rogin examines the diplomatic parent-child metaphor and its role in United States Indian policy in his work *Fathers and Children: Andrew Jackson and the Subjugation of the American Indian* (New York, 1976). His discussion of the paternalism of European and American authority is useful (19–26), but his statement that the family metaphor "was not an Indian conceit but a white one" (209) is based on little evidence.

19.   Here and three paragraphs below, see Henry, *Travels and Adventures,* 43–45.

20.   Here and four paragraphs below, see Edward D. Neill, "History of the Ojibways and Their Connection with Fur Traders," in *Minnesota Historical Collections,* 5:480.

21.   Here and two paragraphs below, see Arthur Pound, *Johnson of the Mohawks, A Biography,* 404–409 (New York, 1930); Henry, *Travels and Adventures,* 176.

22.   Friedrich Baraga, *A Dictionary of the Otchipwe Language,* 1:216, 2:158 (Reprint ed., Minneapolis, 1969); Alexander Henry, *New Light on the Early History of the Greater Northwest,* 203 (Reprint ed., Minneapolis, 1965).

23.   Minutes of Councils (bound volume), July 22, 1816, p. 16, in William McKay Papers, McCord Museum, Montreal; McKenney, *Tour to the Lakes,* 462.

24.   Sahlins, *Stone Age Economics,* 194. For some the material exchange between mother and child symbolized the relations between all people in a "primitive tribal community." Karl Marx, for example, sees the primitive individual as "man . . . who has not yet severed the umbilical cord that unites him with his fellowmen." Marx, *Capital,* 1:79 (New York, 1977).

25.   Martha Coleman Bray, ed., *The Journals of Joseph N. Nicollet: A Scientist on the Mississippi Headwaters, with Notes on Indian Life,* 188 (St. Paul, 1970)

26.   The variety of works which suggest this last possibility is discussed in Donald F. Bibeau's valuable paper, "The Fur Trade from a Tribal Point of View: A Critique," given at the 1981 North American Fur Trade Conference.

27.   Here and below, see author's translation from François Victoire Malhiot, Journal, 1804–05, September 3, 1804, p. 13, in Rare Books and Special Collections, McGill University Libraries, Montreal.

28.   Here and two paragraphs below, see Long, *Voyages and Travels,* 55.

29.   Among the Australian Bushmen, for example, to ask someone for something was to show your love for him; Sahlins, *Stone Age Economics,* 232.

30.   See McKenney, *Tour to the Lakes,* 460.

31.   Here and three paragraphs below, see Henry, *Travels and Adventures,* 243.

32.   The behavior of the Ojibwe chief Keeshkemun (La Pierre à Affiler) toward his son-in-law, XY trader Simon Chaurette, suggests, however, that ambiguities might still be present in the relationship between father-in-law and son-in-law. Keeshkemun seemed to be Chaurette's ally as long as Chaurette was present. When he was gone, Keeshkemun dealt with Chaurette's rival, Malhiot. See Malhiot, Journal, August 5, 1804, p. 6, February 4, 1805, p. 27. Even more distant Indian-trader kinship was useful; trader Michael Cadot, at Lac du Flambeau in the 1780s, derived benefits from the intercession of his wife's uncle; Warren, in *Collections,* 5:302.

33. For more about cultural communication and understanding as important by-products of the fur-trade process, see Bruce M. White, "Parisian Women's Dogs: A Bibliographical Essay on Cross-Cultural Communication and Trade," in Carolyn Gilman, *Where Two Worlds Meet: The Great Lakes Fur Trade,* 120–126 (St. Paul, 1982). There are of course many unanswered questions having to do with the economic impact of gift giving on fur trade rates of exchange and traders' profits. At what point did metaphorical and real kinship become an impossible economic burden? The author is engaged in a study of these problems in relation to the Lake Superior fur trade.

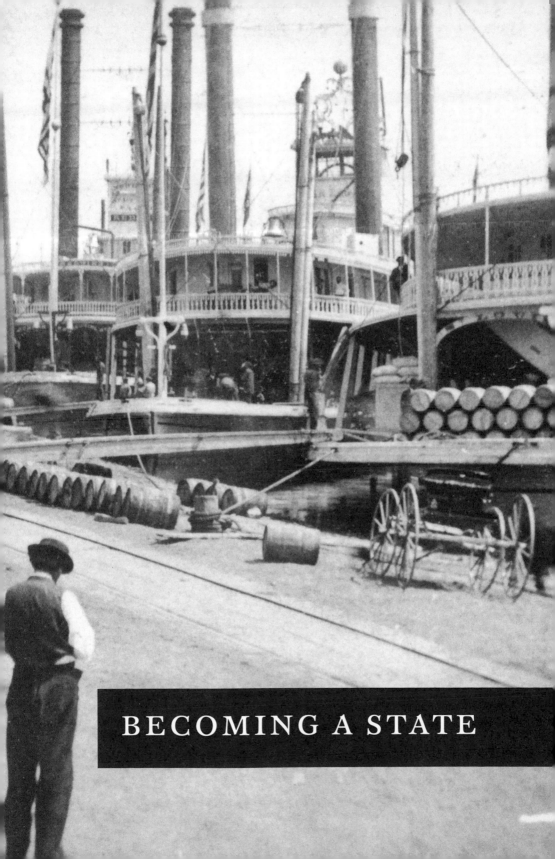

BECOMING A STATE

Territorial Imperative
How Minnesota Became the 32nd State

RHODA R. GILMAN

In 1857, only eight years after becoming a territory, Minnesota sought to become a state, in part because statehood would guarantee Minnesota's political participation in federal railroad projects. Timing of statehood also became important as the Democrats in Minnesota sensed the new Republican Party was rapidly gaining adherents. Rhoda R. Gilman reveals how Democratic and Republican party rivalries colored statehood politics in many ways, particularly as state boundaries were being debated and drawn. An east-west state would favor the growing Republican base in the southeast and also promote moving the capital to St. Peter since St. Paul would now be on the "border." A north-south state would favor the Democrats by including the Red River Valley and retain St. Paul as the new state's capital. Gilman provides a fascinating glimpse of how these arguments and compromises led to the founding of the thirty-second state in 1858.

The prairies and forests, the lakes and watersheds that surround the upper reaches of the Mississippi and Red Rivers, and the head of Lake Superior have been known and occupied by men and women for more than 10,000 years. During that span, the human and natural landscapes have been reworked several times by waves of climatic and cultural change. But none was swifter than the change that went into high gear as boundaries were drawn on a map and the region was named "Minnesota." That event occurred in March 1849, when a bill creating the new territory was passed by the U.S. Senate and signed by President James K. Polk.[1]

For most Americans, whether their sense of history stems from the classroom or from Disneyland, 1849 is associated with the California gold rush. The fact that Minnesota came into being at the same time is not entirely unconnected. Both events were expressions of the burst of expansion that transformed the United States in the 1840s. As late as 1842, the Senate had seriously considered but ultimately rejected a treaty with the Dakota nation that would have created a permanent island of Indian residence and government in the

region that was later to become southern Minnesota. The treaty promised the
Dakota and other northern tribes that white immigrants would be excluded
from the territory and that, after a short period of settled living, Indian people
there would be granted United States citizenship along with their own territorial and, ultimately, state government. The measure was urged by the war department, recommended by the president, and vigorously supported by Henry
H. Sibley, the local representative of the American Fur Company.[2] Yet less than
a decade later, Sibley was lobbying just as hard to organize the same region as
a territory for Euro-American settlers instead. What had happened?

The seven years between 1842 and 1849 saw the United States assume con-
tinent-wide dominance as its "manifest destiny." A war upon Mexico was concluded in February 1848 with the taking of that country's northern frontier
from Texas to California. Later in the same year, Oregon Territory was formed
from a region that until 1844 had been jointly occupied with Britain. Thus, the
entire configuration of the nation had changed, both on maps and in the minds
of its citizens. No longer was the Mississippi River some sort of ultimate boundary. Linking the East Coast to the Far West had become a national priority, and
the idea of placing between them a state that might differ in race and culture
from others in the American republic—an idea never accepted by Congress—
became unthinkable.

The 1840s had also seen the creation of two new states bordering the upper
Mississippi region—Iowa in 1846 and Wisconsin in 1848. What was left of the
two territories from which they had been carved straddled the headwaters of
the great river and reached west to the Missouri River and north to the British
possessions. Most of the land still belonged to the Dakota and Ojibwe tribes,
and the scattered white population of traders, missionaries, government agents,
and a few lumberjacks was far from the minimum of 5,000 required for territorial status—but the logic of national expansion called for the area to be organized immediately.

No one understood that fact more clearly than Senator Stephen A. Douglas.
The "Little Giant" of Illinois was already stepping into the large shoes being
vacated by the aging champions of national unity, Henry Clay of Kentucky and
Lewis Cass of Michigan. Cass, who as governor of Michigan Territory had
presided over the upper Mississippi country for 17 years, had visited the river's
headwaters, and had left his name on one of its lakes, was the Democratic candidate for president in 1848. During the campaign he addressed the divisive issue of whether slavery would be extended across the continent by advocating
local option, or "popular sovereignty." Although Cass's loss to the Whig candidate, Zachary Taylor, was sealed in part by the upstart Free Soilers, whose
antislavery platform foreshadowed the tensions that lay ahead, his doctrine of
popular sovereignty was adopted by the more charismatic Douglas. The Illinois

senator looked to the swelling population of the West along with the powerful forces of economic growth, corporate organization, and outward expansion to counteract the conflict over human slavery.[3]

Like some other western statesmen, Douglas read destiny in the geography of the upper Mississippi region. The river already provided the country with a thousand-mile channel uniting North and South. At the head of steamboat navigation, the tiny hamlet of St. Paul was nourished by a growing commerce that rolled over oxcart trails from the isolated British settlements on the Red River. From there it was not hard to chart the course of American empire across the far-flung private domain of the Hudson's Bay Company to the 54th parallel, where Russian claims began.[4] Moreover, the head of Lake Superior, little more than 100 miles from St. Paul, would eventually give deep-water access to the heart of the continent and be the logical terminus for a transcontinental railroad.

As early as 1846, Douglas, then a congressman, had prevented Iowa from extending its state line north to include the Fort Snelling area and the Falls of St. Anthony. Again in 1847, while Wisconsin struggled toward statehood, he reined in efforts from politicians in Madison to take in St. Paul and the falls by supporting a bill for the organization of "Minasota" Territory. It was tabled, but he revived it again in 1848, for he could see that if the small nucleus of American population growing at the head of river navigation were to be annexed by another state, the remaining northern reaches of the country extending to the British boundary would have little hope of organized government for years to come.[5]

For the time being, economic control on the upper Mississippi lay with a network of traders that was anchored during the 1840s by the firm of Pierre Chouteau Jr. and Company of St. Louis. They included Hercules L. Dousman at Prairie du Chien, his associate, a mercurial newcomer to the Indian trade named Henry M. Rice, and Sibley at Mendota. Formerly Dousman's partner, Sibley by 1846 was working independently with Chouteau, both as trader and land agent. His polish, education, and impeccable social and political connections gave him a recognized claim to leadership. Through a post operated by Norman W. Kittson at Pembina on the British border, he was fast developing a business in buffalo hides from the western plains and smuggled furs from the Hudson's Bay Company preserve.[6]

The late 1840s saw this group alternately challenged and supported by lumbermen moving from Maine and New Hampshire into the rich pine stands of the St. Croix Valley, which had been ceded in 1837 by the Ojibwe and Dakota. With financial backing from the northeastern states, these New Englanders began rafting logs down the Mississippi and building sawmills at places like Marine Mills and Stillwater. A personal link between the two groups was

Franklin Steele, brother-in-law and business associate of Sibley. Steele owned the key waterpower site at the Falls of St. Anthony, where he built the first sawmill and started producing lumber in September 1848.

Both traders and lumbermen were eager for the jobs, patronage, and wider influence that would accompany a new territory. With the support of Douglas, the Wisconsin boundary was eventually placed at the St. Croix River. Again in 1849 the Illinois senator played a key role at the last moment, saving the bill creating Minnesota Territory from a congressional deadlock over whether the outgoing Democratic or incoming Whig administration would appoint the territorial officers.

Those officers were ultimately named by the new president. Chief among them was the governor, Alexander Ramsey, a former Whig congressman from Pennsylvania. Sibley had already been sent to Washington by a quasi-legal election held in 1848 and was confirmed as the territory's congressional delegate in August 1849. Legislators, elected at the same time, held their first session at a St. Paul hotel early in September.

With the territory of 166,000 square miles organized, the prime issues became land and people. A census taken in the summer of 1849 recorded the resident Euro-American population as 4,535. Probably as many as one-third of those were of mixed Indian and European ancestry, including nearly everyone in the widely scattered settlement formed by the descendants of French traders and voyageurs around Pembina. Census takers listed these métis people as white, provided they dressed and lived in European fashion. The Indian population can only be guessed at. Ramsey's estimate was some 25,000—none, of course, considered citizens or voters.

While nearly half the population counted in the census was concentrated in the three towns of St. Paul, Stillwater, and St. Anthony, Indian people were spread widely. On the banks of the Missouri at the far western edge of the territory, more than 400 miles from St. Paul, the Mandan and Hidatsa tribes lived together in an earth-lodge village, Like-a-Fishhook, that was without much question the largest in the territory. Its estimated population of about 700 outnumbered Stillwater and probably surpassed St. Paul.[7]

Not for long, however, was this true. Creation of the new territory turned St. Paul into a feverish little boomtown. The population more than doubled within a year, four newspapers appeared, and shanties sprouted like mushrooms along the Mississippi River bluff. Nevertheless, all of the huge territory— except the narrow triangle of land between the St. Croix and the Mississippi Rivers and south of a line running through Lake Mille Lacs—was still Indian country. No treaties of purchase for the rest of the territory had yet been signed. Facing St. Paul across and just down the Mississippi lay the Dakota town of

Kaposia, a daily reminder of the fundamental barrier that stood in the way of new immigration.

The human face of that barrier was represented by three tribes: the Dakota or Sioux of southern Minnesota, the Ojibwe or Chippewa to the north, and the Ho-Chunk or Winnebago, who had been removed from their original homes in central Wisconsin and sent to northern Iowa, then promised a home in central Minnesota on land purchased in 1847 from the Ojibwe. All three groups were acquainted with European ways through traders who had lived and married among them for a century. More recently they had dealt with Christian missionaries and the U.S. Army. All three had experienced the fickleness of the Great Father in Washington and the unreliability of his many agents. Their principal leaders—Little Crow and Wabasha of the Dakota, Hole-in-the-Day and Flat Mouth among the Ojibwe, and Winneshiek of the Ho-Chunk—were canny and wary, yet keenly conscious of the power behind the migrating hordes that were poised to overrun their land.

In his inaugural address to the first legislature, Governor Ramsey targeted purchase of southern Minnesota from the Dakota tribe as the prime need of the new territory. A memorial on the subject was duly sent to Congress, and for the next three years that goal was the central preoccupation of Minnesota citizens. The key to achieving it peacefully was the trading establishment led by Sibley, who had lived and worked for nearly 20 years among the Dakota. Allied with him were powerful mixed-blood families like the Faribaults and Renvilles. Without support from these people and their widespread networks of kin among the four bands of the tribe, there was little hope for getting agreement to a treaty.

It was in July 1851 that Ramsey and Commissioner of Indian Affairs Luke Lea, acting as federal treaty negotiators, met with the Sisseton and Wahpeton bands at Traverse des Sioux, near present-day St. Peter. On the same spot, just 10 years earlier, these Dakota groups had agreed immediately to the treaty that would have created an all-Indian territory. But the Great Father had changed his mind, and in 1851 they were faced with something far different. In the meantime there had been lean years, and some of the people were close to starvation while others had survived only on credit from traders.[8]

The United States now proposed to take all their land as far west as Lake Traverse and the Big Sioux River for its own citizens. When the bargaining was finished, the two bands found themselves confined to a strip of country extending 10 miles on each side of the Minnesota River above the Yellow Medicine River. Below that, another 20-mile-wide strip was reserved for the Mdewakanton and Wahpekute bands, with whom a separate treaty would be made.

For their land they were to be paid about 7.5 cents an acre. Most of the sum would be invested and its interest would yield an annuity for 50 years. Some

$30,000 was to be spent immediately on schools, mills, blacksmith shops, and other government services, while the remaining $275,000 would be given to the chiefs, who might then pay the debts members of the tribe owed the traders. This was a feature of nearly every Indian treaty, despite mandates to the contrary often made by Congress in an effort to prevent fraudulent claims. To ensure collection, traders represented at Traverse des Sioux drew up a document listing the debts and secured the signature of each Indian headman as he left the treaty table.

Debate raged later as to whether the Dakota understood the traders' paper, and the procedure gave rise to complaints of fraud and favoritism from other traders. Those charges led to a congressional investigation that probed the close working relationship between Ramsey and Sibley but found no malfeasance. Most of the small traders who received money as a result of the treaty were deeply in debt to Sibley, who in turn owed nearly all of what he collected to the Chouteau company. Thus, little of the payment stayed in Minnesota.

Meanwhile a separate treaty had been signed at Mendota in August 1851 with the Mdewakanton and Wahpekute. Having already received some treaty money from ceding their land east of the Mississippi, the Mdewakanton were less hungry and desperate than the others. They were also more determined and suspicious, since they had learned from experience that government payments were always late and that many promises were never kept—facts that Little Crow repeatedly pointed out. But there was nothing they could do except protest. They were trapped by the fact that the western bands had already given in.

Lobbying the treaties through Congress was again the work of Sibley, this time in his role as territorial delegate. It was a bitter struggle. Southern diehards who opposed national expansion to the north succeeded in amending the documents in a way that they hoped the Indians would reject. One major change was to strike out the provision for a reservation along the Minnesota River and to leave the Dakota with nowhere to go except some unnamed place that the president might designate. The Dakota were indeed angered. But Ramsey assured them that the president would name the valley of the Minnesota River as their permanent home, and the revised treaties were reluctantly accepted in the fall of 1852.

During the same years the Indian barrier to the north was also under attack. Ironically, this began with an effort to move more Ojibwe into Minnesota Territory. In 1837 and 1842 they had ceded all of their land in northern Wisconsin, but in both cases treaty negotiators had assured the people that they would not have to move for several generations, if ever. What the United States wanted was only access to timber and minerals. By February 1850, however, the Great Father had changed his mind, and all of them were told to relocate west of the Mississippi. Governor Ramsey of Minnesota was to take charge of the process.[9]

Ramsey planned to put most of them in the neighborhood of Leech Lake, still far from the edge of settlement and away from increasing commerce on Lake Superior. The U.S. Indian agency would be moved from La Pointe, in northern Wisconsin, and the most immediate change he foresaw would be more government business, jobs, and money flowing through St. Paul to northern Minnesota. He took no steps, however, to get agreement from the Ojibwe bands already living around the Mississippi headwaters, and when they objected, the new location was changed to Big Sandy Lake. Forcing the Wisconsin bands to move was thought to be simple: their annuities, including both money and supplies, would be paid only at Big Sandy, and any who refused to travel there would receive none.

During the next three years a tangled and tragic tale, marked by incompetence, lies, and callousness to human suffering on the part of both Ramsey and Indian agent John M. Watrous, ended in the death of between two and four hundred Ojibwe. They were saved further loss from starvation, exposure, and disease when the election of 1852 sent Democrat Franklin Pierce to the White House. The new administration replaced Ramsey and Watrous with Democratic appointees. Possibly influenced by appeals from the Ojibwe leader Buffalo who with a few others traveled illegally to Washington, the president also cancelled the policy of removal.

Relieved and thankful, the Ojibwe bands around Lake Superior willingly signed a new treaty in 1854. In return for permanent, designated reservations in their own country they gave up the Minnesota Arrowhead, the northeasternmost region of the territory, which was already suspected to contain important mineral wealth. Also included in this treaty was the north bank of the St. Louis River at its mouth, where a sheltered deep-water port provided the key to transportation and commercial expansion at the head of Lake Superior. In 1855 still another section of the barrier against American occupation fell, when the Ojibwe bands around the Mississippi headwaters agreed to a similar arrangement and ceded most of north-central Minnesota. The same year saw the Ho-Chunk again moved, this time to a small reservation in the Blue Earth Valley of southern Minnesota.

With the signing of these treaties a subtle but profound change had already taken place. Prairie and oak openings had become acres; forests had become timber stands; tumbling rivers had become water rights. A world of natural features once invested with mystery and power of their own had become resources for human manipulation. Unlike the Dakota, the Ojibwe had a generation yet ahead of them to accommodate to this transformation. In southern Minnesota, change came more quickly.

To nineteenth-century Americans, too, land had an almost holy quality. The sacred element they saw was not the land itself, with its ancient layers of interwoven plant and animal life, but the dream of what human labor could produce from it. In the words of one anonymous mid-century poet:

> *The land is the gift of bounteous God,*
> *And to labor his word commands;*
> *Yet millions of hands want acres,*
> *And millions of acres want hands.* [10]

Even more alluring and powerful than the natural bounty of land was the meteoric rise in its value as population poured into an area. A tract bought from Indian people for 7.5 cents and resold by the government to its own citizens for $1.25 might be worth hundreds if platted as a town lot or even thousands if it became the business block of a rising city. Successive waves of land speculation built great fortunes and fueled the U.S. economy through much of the nineteenth century, and one of them was cresting just at the time Minnesota became a territory.

Not until February 1853 did the purchase of southern Minnesota from the Dakota become official, and settlement was not legal there until a year and a half later. But the tide would not be held back. As soon as the signing of the treaties was announced late in 1852, a flood of trespassers surged onto Indian land. As at Red Wing in the spring of 1853, the new owners hastened the departure of lingering Dakota neighbors by torching bark houses that stood in their way.

They came on overcrowded steamboats or they walked across Illinois and Wisconsin beside covered wagons—men, women, and children, cattle, pigs, and other livestock. Many were newcomers from Sweden, Germany, Ireland, and other north European countries. Some came as extended families and others accompanied neighbors from the Old Country. Along with their domestic animals they brought seed to replace the native prairie grasses with crops that had fed their ancestors in Europe. Thus, not only the human face but also the underlying biological patterns of Minnesota began to change immediately. By 1854 the Euro-American population of the territory was more than 30,000, and just three years later it topped 150,000. Among people over 15 years of age counted in the U.S. census of 1850, white men had outnumbered white women by more than two to one, but by 1860 the ratio was almost one to one. [11]

A sizable number of these people congregated in the new towns that sprang up along the Minnesota and Mississippi Rivers: Carver, Henderson, Mankato, Winona, Wabasha, Read's Landing, Red Wing, Hastings, St. Anthony Falls, and eventually Minneapolis, after the Fort Snelling military reservation was opened to land claims in 1855. The mainstays of this urban frontier were sawmills and river commerce. Farms in the country behind them were still small, producing little more than subsistence crops, and roads to market were few. So throughout the territorial years Minnesota imported food from downriver. Its principal exports remained lumber, hides, and furs.

During these years there was constant agitation for relaxing federal land law, which required that land be surveyed before it could be claimed. In 1854 this was changed for Minnesota to allow pre-emption (registering of a claim) on unsurveyed land. Such claims could be "proved up" later. The great fear of many settlers was that a land auction would be declared before they had the money to buy their claims, and politicians were kept busy working to have such sales postponed. In 1862 the Homestead Act ended this system, but during Minnesota's territorial years grassroots claim associations, which were prepared to defend the rights of vulnerable settlers, were common. So also were scores of "paper towns" platted and promoted in hopes of ballooning land values that were never realized. Along with these came land speculators and loan sharks like Jason C. Easton of Chatfield, who advertised that he made and brokered loans, collected on bad debts, paid taxes, examined titles, and above all located and dealt in military-bounty land warrants. Those certificates for the purchase of government land became a bonanza for speculators after 1855, when Congress gave them as a bonus to Mexican War veterans.[12]

Despite growing ethnic diversity, the economic, cultural, and political leadership of the territory was held firmly by Anglo-Americans, and the influence of those from northeastern states earned Minnesota the nickname "New England of the West." Laws and institutions embodied that influence. At its first session in 1849, the legislature passed an expansive common-school act, and nine years later 72 school districts offered free education to anyone between the ages of four and twenty-one. The same legislators chartered a university and proclaimed their keen sense of destiny by creating a historical society. While the university remained a dream for many years, church bodies moved ahead at once to supply the growing need for training schoolteachers and ministers. On the town square of Red Wing in 1856 Hamline University laid stone foundations for the first four-year college west of the Mississippi. The next year it opened its doors, admitting women as well as men. Other than elementary teaching, there was little paid employment for women in the territory, but they undertook social service and nursing when the Sisters of St. Joseph founded St. Paul's first hospital after a cholera epidemic in 1854.[13]

A literate population demanded newspapers, and by 1858 more than 80 had been started in the territory. From their print shops early editors like James M. Goodhue of the *Minnesota Pioneer* and David Olmsted of the *Minnesota Democrat,* both in St. Paul, and Charles G. Ames of the St. Anthony Falls *Minnesota Republican* acted as territorial boosters and opinion makers. In 1857 the first

woman's voice was heard, when Jane Grey Swisshelm issued the controversial
St. Cloud Visiter to champion abolition and women's rights.

In politics it was a time when party lines were shifting all across the nation in
response to rising sectional tensions. This was reflected in Minnesota, where
parties existed in name only through most of the territorial years. Although
replaced by Democrat Willis A. Gorman in 1853, Whig Governor Ramsey remained a power, far outweighing the influence of the few local Whigs. As his
party began to disintegrate he played a waiting game, refusing to commit to the
new Minnesota Republican Party, organized in 1855, until it gained unmistak-
able momentum. Sibley, a moderate Democrat, had strong personal and political ties to Cass and Douglas but, following the nonpartisan model set by Cass
in Michigan Territory, he maintained local allies in all camps. Sibley's chief
rival, Henry M. Rice, with whom he had quarreled in business and continued
to quarrel in politics, was nonpartisan in his own way. As the national Democratic Party threatened to split between northern and southern wings, Rice, a
skilled lobbyist and office-seeker, remained a friend of whoever was in power.
With unfailing charm and cheerful cynicism, he brought the spoils from Washington back to Minnesota.

A year after Minnesota emerged as a political entity, Cass, from his position
as senior statesman and senator from Michigan, stitched together the patch-
work of agreements known as the Compromise of 1850. It was made possible
by the pressure of economic interests from both North and South. With an immediate confrontation over slavery postponed, Douglas and others turned to
an emerging network of corporate enterprise that they hoped would support
a political coalition powerful enough to hold the nation back from war.

This new force rode on the steel rails that were even then transforming the
country by shrinking time and distance. Douglas himself had performed a political coup in 1850 when he secured to the state of Illinois the first major grant
of federal land for purposes of railroad building. He envisioned an expanding
web, knitting the country together, with the Illinois Central system at its heart.
Southern extensions would reach into Texas, and its northern anchor would
be a new city named Superior at the head of the big lake.[14]

That city, platted in 1853 on the Wisconsin side of the St. Louis River, further expressed the continental dreams that had gone into the making of Minnesota Territory. A possible route for a transcontinental railroad west from
Lake Superior was even then being explored by the U.S. Army. The Sault Canal,
already under construction, would bring shipping from the lower lakes to the
head of Lake Superior within two years. But the most immediate step would
be building a rail line that would link the lake with St. Paul and extend on
through Minnesota and Iowa where it would connect with a branch of the Illinois Central.

Then, as now, money ruled politics. In accord with Douglas's vision, shares in the far northern boom town were distributed to a host of influential Democratic politicians from both the southern and northern wings of the party, while much of the capital for its development came from the deep pockets of William W. Corcoran, a Washington-based financier with strong southern sympathies. In Minnesota, where the charter and a land grant for the proposed railroad link had to originate, all political factions were brought to the table, including Sibley, Ramsey, Gorman, and others less prominent. Henry Rice was among the first and most closely involved. After trying to make his own claims on the site of Superior, he had come to terms with the agents of Douglas and was actively promoting the scheme.

Rice had succeeded Sibley as Minnesota's territorial delegate in 1853, and a temporary truce prevailed between them. Then, early in 1854, lobbyists from the Illinois Central strong-armed the territorial legislature into passing the charter of the new Minnesota and North Western Railroad Company, with a provision that any land grant made to Minnesota for railroad building would automatically go to that company. Sibley became increasingly cool, and Congress also proved skittish about such a restrictive arrangement. One land-grant bill introduced by Rice was defeated.

As the price of his support for a second attempt, Sibley demanded the right to draw up the bill himself. In doing so, he worded it carefully so that the Minnesota and North Western would not be eligible to receive the grant. That version was successful in Congress, but jubilation in Minnesota came to a screeching halt when it was found that the law's wording had been altered to favor the company some time between its passage by the House of Representatives and its signing by the president. The resulting scandal sunk both the land grant and the Minnesota and North Western.

The steel rails that might have stretched from St. Paul to Superior in 1855 were not laid until 1870, and the whole railroad era in Minnesota was delayed beyond the end of the territorial years. Although Minnesota's isolation during the months when the Mississippi was frozen had been partially overcome by government roads and stagecoach lines established in the territorial years, the need for all-weather transportation remained, and the political scheming and burning desire for a share in the economic bonanza promised by railroads played an important role in the rush toward statehood.

Time was running out for the promoters of Superior and the Illinois Central, for in 1857 the wave of prosperity that had supported the northwest region's phenomenal growth crashed on the rocks of financial panic. Money became tight throughout the country and almost nonexistent in Minnesota; land values collapsed, and western settlement slowed. Superior shrank into a frontier outpost, and even exuberant St. Paul was thrown into the doldrums for several years.

For the political vision of Illinois's Little Giant, time had also run out. Far from defusing the slavery issue, the doctrine of popular sovereignty, embodied in the Kansas-Nebraska Act of 1854, had brought outright warfare to the territory of Kansas. The forces of corporate empire-building and interlocking material interests had not proved strong enough to contain those of moral outrage and cultural conflict. Thus, when Minnesota delegates gathered in the summer of 1857 to draw up a state constitution, the shadow of "Bleeding Kansas" hung over them. The flaming issues that divided them were the status of black people, both free and slave, and the new relationships implied by a recent decision of the U.S. Supreme Court, which held that Harriet and Dred Scott were still slaves, although they had lived for years at Fort Snelling in free territory. So hot were tempers that Minnesota's Democrats and Republicans met separately and drew up different constitutions.

Local self-interest remained alive and well, nevertheless. Statehood promised not only influence in debates at the national level but control over local borrowing and taxation. A crucial incentive was the continuing fever to subsidize and promote railroads, including the prospect of a transcontinental line running through Minnesota to the Pacific. Compromise was therefore reached outside the meeting rooms, and a single constitution was at last agreed upon.

In anticipation of statehood, elections were held that pitted Sibley, who campaigned as an antislavery Democrat, in a race for governor against Ramsey, the new champion of Minnesota Republicans. Margins were narrow but Sibley prevailed, and Democrats won most of the offices. The elected legislators agreed to send Henry Rice to the U.S. Senate. Candidates for the other Senate seat were deadlocked, and the choice went to a dark horse named James Shields, a former Illinois senator and friend of Douglas. With Congress immobilized over Kansas, Minnesota's admission was held up for months, but at last, on May 11, 1858, the territory became a state.

Its shape had been hotly debated. Some had argued that Minnesota should extend west to the Missouri and north only to the 46th parallel (the latitude of present-day Little Falls). Less compelling alternatives set the northern boundary at 45°30', 45°15', or even farther south. Such a state would have included most of Minnesota's immigrant farmers and a majority of Republican voters. The influence of Democrats Rice and Douglas in Washington, however, had ensured that an elongated north-south shape was specified in the enabling act passed by Congress, and this ultimately prevailed. In reaching to the British line and including the envisioned railroad route from Lake Superior westward, it reflected the continuing strength of expansionist ambitions.

As early as 1851 Ramsey had ridden to Pembina to negotiate with the Ojibwe a treaty of purchase for part of the Red River Valley. Congress had failed to ratify it, but throughout the territorial years trade with the British colony to the north had steadily increased. The first three years of statehood saw an even stronger push in that direction, with the building of a stage and wagon road to supplement the meandering oxcart trails that had served since the 1830s. A move was also made to open steamboat navigation on the Red River. These efforts were temporarily suspended, however, by the Civil and Dakota wars.[15]

In the interval thus created, Britain began the slow process of consolidating civil government in its sprawling North American territories and reached out to establish control over the Red River settlement and the restive *gens libres*, or métis, of the northern plains. With this, the vision of American territorial expansion began to fade, although in Minnesota it flickered a short time longer, encouraged by the U.S. purchase of Alaska in 1867 and the Riel Rebellion of 1870 in Manitoba. But although the 49th parallel remained the international line, bioregions, human communities, and economic interests continued to ignore it. Before the first railroad was opened from Minnesota to Puget Sound, Canadian citizen James J. Hill's St. Paul, Minneapolis, and Manitoba Railroad, financed by the Bank of Montreal, was carrying grain from Manitoba to the mills of Minneapolis.

The nine territorial years had set the stage for transforming the natural and cultural landscapes of the upper Mississippi country into those of a "civilized" Euro-American community. The undisturbed systems of plant and animal life that Americans called "wilderness" were converted into commodities subject to ownership and exchange. A way of life that regarded them as eternal and necessary for human existence was ruthlessly eliminated. As a result, the scene was also prepared for the tragic drama that drenched Minnesota's western prairies in blood when the Dakota made a last desperate effort to take back their country in 1862.

Still in the future during the territorial years was the time when the forests would be slashed and the curves of prairie land would be regimented into rectangular fields fenced with barbed wire and deeds. Even further in the future was the time when Minnesota could boast of being the world's breadbasket and its iron mines would build the steel infrastructure of an industrial society. And undreamed-of yet was the swelling metropolitan area that would leap even state lines to become the transportation, economic, and cultural hub of the whole region between the upper Great Lakes and the Rocky Mountains. The script, however, was already in place.

NOTES

From Minnesota History 56 *(Winter, 1998–99).*

1. Unless otherwise noted, factual material for this article can be found in standard sources on Minnesota history, especially volume 1 of William W. Folwell's *A History of Minnesota* (St. Paul: Minnesota Historical Society, 1956) and Theodore C. Blegen, *Minnesota: A History of the State* (Minneapolis: University of Minnesota Press, 1963).

2. For an account of this treaty, negotiated by Wisconsin Governor James D. Doty, see Rhoda R. Gilman, "A Northwestern Indian Territory—The Last Voice," paper delivered at the annual meeting of the Western History Association, Oct. 1997, forthcoming in *Journal of the West*.

3. The most recent biography of Cass emphasizes his role as a negotiator and compromiser; see Willard C. Klunder, *Lewis Cass and the Politics of Moderation* (Kent, Oh.: Kent State University Press, 1996). On Douglas, see Robert W. Johannsen, *Stephen A. Douglas* (New York: Oxford University Press, 1973).

4. The southern limit of Russian claims was 54°40'. As early as the election of 1844, Polk's supporters had coined the campaign slogan "54-40 or Fight," but destiny soon manifested to the south, and the U.S. and Great Britain compromised to set the northern border of Oregon at the 49th parallel.

5. For a full discussion of the controversy over the Wisconsin state boundary and the creation of Minnesota Territory, see William E. Lass, "Minnesota's Separation from Wisconsin: Boundary Making on the Upper Mississippi Frontier," *Minnesota History* 50 (Winter 1987): 309-20, and "The Birth of Minnesota," *Minnesota History* 55 (Summer 1997): 267-79.

6. Rhoda R. Gilman, "Last Days of the Upper Mississippi Fur Trade," *Minnesota History* 42 (Winter 1970): 122-40.

7. Folwell, *History of Minnesota*, 1: 351-52; Roy W. Meyer, *The Village Indians of the Upper Missouri: The Mandans, Hidatsas, and Arikaras* (Lincoln: University of Nebraska Press, 1977), 104.

8. For full accounts of the 1851 treaty, see Folwell, *History of Minnesota*, 1: 266-304; Lucile M. Kane, "The Sioux Treaties and the Traders," *Minnesota History* 32 (June 1951): 65-80.

9. On the Ojibwe removal effort, see James A. Clifton, "Wisconsin Death March: Explaining the Extremes in the Old Northwest Indian Removal," *Transactions of the Wisconsin Academy of Sciences. Arts and Letters* 75 (1987): 1-39; Ronald N. Satz, "Chippewa Treaty Rights: The Reserved Rights of Wisconsin's Chippewa Indians in Historical Perspective," *Transactions of the Wisconsin Academy of Sciences, Arts and Letters* 79 (1991): 51-59.

10. "The Acres and the Hands," *Daily Minnesotian* (St. Paul), Dec. 18, 1860.

11. See United States Historical Census Data Browser, with data from 1790 to 1970, http://fisher.lib.virginia.edu/census/.

12. Rodney C. Loehr, "Jason C. Easton, Territorial Banker," *Minnesota History* 29 (Sept. 1948): 223-30.

13. Sister Helen Angela Hurley, "The Sisters of St. Joseph and the Minnesota Frontier," *Minnesota History* 30 (Mar. 1949): 9.

14. For development of Superior and the political dreams and railroad schemes surrounding it, see Henry Cohen, *Business and Politics in America from the Age of Jackson to the Civil War: The Career Biography of W. W. Corcoran* (Westport, Conn.: Greenwood Press, 1971), 159-201. See also Johannsen, *Douglas*, 304-21, 435-37.

15. See Rhoda R. Gilman, Carolyn Gilman, and Deborah M. Stultz, *The Red River Trails: Oxcart Routes Between St. Paul and the Selkirk Settlement 1820-1870* (St. Paul: Minnesota Historical Society, 1979).

The Sioux Sign a Treaty in Washington in 1858

BARBARA T. NEWCOMBE

If James Buchanan is remembered at all, he is remembered as the president who did nothing as seven southern states left the Union before Lincoln took office in March 1861. Such inaction characterized his presidency. While the economic depression known as the Panic of 1857 deepened and sectional crises such as Bleeding Kansas and the Dred Scott case threatened to divide the country, Buchanan stood idly by.

This was the president that Little Crow had pinned his hopes on when his Dakota delegation went to Washington, D. C., in 1858. As Barbara T. Newcombe explains, Little Crow hoped broken treaties would be corrected, while the government wanted the Indians to surrender the northern and eastern half of their "permanent" reservation. Newcombe reveals the frustrations that Little Crow felt as he realized that Indian concerns were low priority for a government consumed by expansion and on the brink of civil war.

The eastern or Santee Dakota were known as Sioux until well into the twentieth century.

In the bitter cold of February, 1858, Indian Agent Joseph Renshaw Brown set out in a sleigh from his home town of Henderson in Sibley County on a long trip westward. He was following instructions he had evidently received on February 17 from William J. Cullen, superintendent of Indian affairs of the northern superintendency in St. Paul. Cullen in turn had been given orders by Charles E. Mix, acting commissioner of Indian affairs in Washington. Brown was to select a deputation of chiefs and headmen of the Upper Sioux or Dakota (Wahpeton and Sisseton) and take them to Washington, D.C. The object was to sign treaties that would untangle the question of Indian title to their land and, though the Dakota did not know it yet, would see them give up half of the reservation left them by the 1851 treaties of Traverse des Sioux and Mendota—the rich, ten-mile-wide strip on the north side of the Minnesota River. The Lower Sioux, tempted by the prospect of increased annuity payments, had long wanted to visit Washington and find out what happened to funds promised them in earlier treaties.[1]

Brown crossed the snowy prairie to the Lower Sioux (Redwood) Agency on the south side of the Minnesota near present-day Redwood Falls and Morton. There he arranged for some eighteen chiefs and headmen to be selected and authorized to act for their people. They were to be ready in ten days when they would be joined by the Upper Sioux delegation.

Andrew Robertson, the agency's assistant interpreter, was to be in charge of conducting the Upper Sioux delegation of ten chiefs and headmen. He accompanied Brown up the Minnesota River Valley to Lac qui Parle where Wahpeton chiefs were selected from Yellow Medicine bands and instructed regarding the upcoming trip. Robertson stayed at Lac qui Parle while Brown continued on to Big Stone Lake to round up chiefs there. By the time he returned to the Lower Agency on Saturday, February 27, to meet Robertson, the assembled Indians, and others, Brown had driven an exhausting 430 miles since leaving Henderson.[2] Now the party was ready to leave for Washington. Robertson and most of the others would not return to the agency until July 15— five months and 3,500 miles later. Brown would stay longer and travel farther carrying out instructions for Mix.

Brown must have felt at home on his trip to gather the delegation. His long, colorful career in Minnesota had begun in 1819 as a fourteen-year-old drummer boy with troops assigned to build Fort Snelling. Out of the army at twenty, Brown became one of Minnesota's best-known pioneers as a leading trader among the Dakota, lumberman, founder of cities, land speculator, legislator, Democratic politician, inventor, editor, and Indian agent. He was second editor of Minnesota's first newspaper, the *Minnesota Pioneer* (St. Paul), and founded and edited the *Henderson Democrat*. He served in seven sessions of the Minnesota territorial legislature and was an important member of the constitutional convention in 1857.[3]

After he was replaced as agent in 1861 by a Republican politician, Thomas J. Galbraith, Brown built an imposing, nineteen-room mansion for his Sisseton wife and twelve children on the north side of the Minnesota some seven miles downriver from the Upper Sioux Agency. It became a social center in the sparsely settled region but was burned during the Sioux Uprising of 1862. At that time Brown was in New York on business regarding his most famous invention, a steam wagon. His wife and children were captured and held by the Indians until freed on September 26, 1862, by a relief army led by Colonel Henry H. Sibley. Meanwhile, Brown joined Sibley's force and after the war served as commander of scouts on the Minnesota-Dakota border. He died at Browns Valley in 1870. In all his enterprises Brown was an able, articulate, perceptive, and energetic man. He needed all these qualities to handle the Indian delegation he took to Washington and back in 1858.[4]

The role that gave him this task, of course, was that of Indian agent. He had been appointed to the job the previous September. His predecessor, Charles E.

Flandrau, had suggested, as a means of accelerating the assimilation process, granting individual farms to the Lower Sioux. Flandrau perceived that the old tribal ways made some of the Indians uneasy. Why not take the older and more reliable ones to Washington where they would be free of the "influence of their young men" and could see for themselves the wealth and the might of the white man. Flandrau was appointed to the Minnesota Supreme Court, so his ideas were carried out by Brown. He, in fact, was a strong advocate of "civilizing" the Dakota and turning them into farmers. More than most agents, who were part of the political spoils system, Brown understood his charges and wanted to do right by them—according to his perceptions. He could speak their language and had married a woman of their tribe. This must have contributed to a feeling for her people. He would do the best he could in the circumstances in which he found himself.[5]

The full delegation, which arrived on March 9, 1858, at McGregor, Iowa, had some interesting members. Antoine J. {"Joe"} Campbell, head interpreter, was the son of a Dakota interpreter and grandson of an early trader who had married into the tribe. Joseph Brown's brother, Nathaniel, earned his way as assistant conductor of the Lower Sioux. Andrew Robertson was officially assistant conductor for the Upper Sioux. They lived with the Indians at the hotels, kept track of petty day-to-day expenses, and eventually conducted the Indians home. Among the ten Upper Sioux were three already involved with farming and closely identified with missionary stations. They were Little Paul, John Other Day, and Pa-pa. The sixteen to nineteen Lower Sioux (the number given varies) were nominally led by Wabasha, but Little Crow was the real leader and spokesman. His restless mind was open to new ideas. He was willing to try farming—or have his wives try it—and he preferred to live in a frame house during the winter months. His avid interest in the strange world of the whites convinced him that his people would have to adapt, but he could also sense the avaricious motives of the whites he knew best—the traders. At Washington he was to prove an able speaker and a formidable adversary even in a situation where he was illiterate in the working language.[6]

At McGregor, Brown found that his team of horses was too sick to undertake the return journey to Henderson. He thus paid off the teamster and entrusted the horses to a local farmer. After ferrying across the Mississippi, the entire group entrained at Prairie du Chien, Wisconsin, for Chicago. This new rail connection saved them twenty hours' travel time and also saved the government subsistence money for the entire delegation, which amounted to $2.50 per day per person. Already Andrew Robertson had had to purchase buffalo robes at $7.00 each for the Upper Sioux and other necessities such as "mockinsans" for $2.00 a pair, innumerable pairs of socks and "mitts," one comb each, blankets, and shawls. A pair of spectacles cost one dollar. After arriving in Washington he purchased each Indian a coat, two shirts, a handkerchief, and cloth for leggings.[7]

The Lower Sioux had begun to agitate for permission to visit Washington in 1853. Little Crow had been in Washington in 1854 to try to iron out unclear aspects of the treaties of 1851 and realized that the 1858 delegation would need fine hunting shirts, decent leggings, money for the hotel, candles, fires, and food. The Lower Sioux had the foresight to prepare for an expensive trip and so were able to lend $1,240 to the Upper Sioux. Payment of this loan was demanded by Little Crow before he consented to sign the treaty in June.[8]

The train took the delegation through an ever more heavily settled land where thorny problems affected everyday life. Economic depression gripped the East and Midwest and sent unemployed people marching in Buffalo, New York, and other cities. Congressional debate daily grew more bitter on the question of whether Kansas would become a free or slaveholding state. Statehood for Minnesota was tied to the Kansas issue. Mormons in Utah tied down elements of the United States cavalry sent to force them to obey federal laws. British cruisers stopped and searched American vessels suspected of engaging in the African slave trade. In 1858 the affairs of the nation were complicated enough for a brilliant statesman, which President James Buchanan was not.

In addition to the official delegation, there were at least seven others who felt it to their interest to make the trip from Minnesota to Washington. This meant paying for twelve days' travel and approximately 100 days in the capital. Their motives varied. One came with a benign, if ulterior, design. He was the Reverend Thomas S. Williamson, who was intent on saving souls and securing the future of his tiny mission (Pajutazee) and school near the Yellow Medicine (Upper Sioux) Agency. There also was Charles R. Crawford, Brown's brother-in-law and a son of Akepa, a Wahpeton chief who was a delegation member. On hand, too, were traders like Andrew J. Myrick, William H. Forbes, Friedrich Schmidt, and Madison Sweetser with fortunes to gain or lose from the negotiations. Superintendent Cullen and his wife also traveled to Washington.[9]

Many of the Indians on the train had already proved willing to try farming IF they could depend on protection from unsympathetic "blanket" Indians, IF they were furnished equipment and help, IF the money due them was not siphoned off to traders and others, and IF white settlers were kept off their land. Past experience in these matters did little to encourage them. It was not easy to ignore the taunts of other Indians who jeered at them for wearing breeches instead of blankets and cutting their hair, who stole and killed their stock, who trampled their crops, and who threatened the children they sent to the missionary schools. Then, too, their warlike cousins to the West, the Yankton, developed the annoying habit of showing up at annuity time and downgrading the Santee (Upper and Lower Sioux) for signing treaties with the white man.[10]

In many ways Joseph Brown and Little Crow were poles apart in spite of being in the same group on the same train bound for the same destination. But they shared some personal characteristics. Both were proud, lively, inquiring, and ambitious. Brown needed to succeed for the greater glory of Minnesota and himself. Little Crow needed to succeed for survival, both his own and that of his people. The Santee Sioux must not again give up much for little or nothing.

At Baltimore the entourage had to change to a Baltimore and Ohio train for Washington. Already there had been some illness, for which medicines were purchased in Harrisburg, Pennsylvania. After arriving in Washington on Saturday, March 13, 1858, the "26 [*sic*] fine and stalwart Santee" felt more like twenty-six worn and wasted men, objects of curiosity and some ridicule. Hard enough to bear under the best of circumstances, the situation called for the greatest exercise of dignity and restraint when their spirits were low. Only a small fraction of their trip was over. Little did they know they had to endure 125 more days away from home.[11]

The entire party was sorted into W. P. Chandler's coaches and conveyed to Mrs. Maher's Union Hotel.[12] On Monday, March 15, at 2:00 P.M., the full delegation with a large and mixed supporting cast met with Acting Commissioner Charles E. Mix in his office. Each delegate was introduced by a dramatized personal story. Mix in turn warned his "red children" against fire water, promised visits with Secretary of the Interior Jacob Thompson and President Buchanan, and reminded them that they should not conduct tribal warfare with the Pawnee who were also in town for treaty making.

Little Crow said he had come a long way and intended "while in your village, to walk your streets as a proud man." He pointed out that his people were obedient to the Great Father even to the point of hunting down renegade Indians—a dangerous and frustrating errand for which they had never been paid. He was referring to the unwelcome job of trying to capture Inkpaduta (Scarlet Point), an outlawed Wahpekute chief who led the so-called "Spirit Lake Massacre" in 1857 in which more than thirty settlers were killed. When the Indian office in Washington notified the Dakota that they would be held responsible for apprehending Inkpaduta, and that annuities would be withheld until they did, Little Crow, John Other Day, and others volunteered to go after the renegade. He eluded them as he had military pursuers earlier, but some women captives were eventually freed. The pressure put upon the Indians to capture Inkpaduta caused bad feelings not only toward the whites but also between various factions of the eastern Dakota themselves. The March 15 interview ended, and the delegation left for the hotel. A reporter noticed that one of the Indians shook hands "with a handsome young lady that he selected . . . for her beauty." She blushed properly, and the other laughed.[13]

The second interview with Commissioner Mix took place on March 27 and was again attended by both Upper and Lower Sioux members of the delegation. They were splendidly dressed; some wore feathers and paint. Little Crow had added a circle of blue paint around one eye. Mix asked an interpreter if Little Crow spoke for all. The answer was, "Yes, for all," and that situation continued throughout the negotiations. Little Crow came right to the point. He reminded the commissioner that, because of the treaties of 1851 in which the Dakota gave up vast lands for monetary and other considerations, "our people ought never be poor." He added that "our Great Father has plenty of funds belonging to us in his hands, and it takes plenty to enable a person to act like a man and not like a beggar." This was his way of bringing up the question of what happened to the money. Mix said a decision would soon be made in this regard and provisions sent for "their comfort and support."[14]

Mix insisted on knowing how the Indians planned to spend the money given them while in Washington. Little Crow pointed out: "My Father, a great many of the white people have money in their pockets, and you never ask them what they are going to do with it, and they spend it as they please." Mix understandably was still nervous about the problem of whisky. Little Crow rose and shook hands with the commissioner—his way of making a particular point— and said: "My Father, I speak for all the men present. They are all men of sense, and not fools, and when they say anything they intend to do it. You have mentioned that [whisky] to us two or three times, and I hope you will never mention it again. We don't want to hear it."

Superintendent Cullen broke in. He tried to smooth over the situation by asking interpreter Campbell to explain about perverse Indians who *would* go begging for money on the streets. Such was not and never would be the case with the dependable Santee. "They are too proud for that," said Campbell.

On March 29 the Dakota were taken on an outing that had an ulterior motive. They rode in the ubiquitous Mr. Chandler's carriages to see the new extension for the United States Arsenal being built at Greenleaf's Point. Undoubtedly the commissioner hoped to impress his "red children" with the military might of the United States. The new works, situated at present-day Fort McNair, were very much in the news in Washington in 1858. Visiting the arsenal at the same time as the Indians were some officials of the Turkish navy. After all had watched the firing of various types of guns, the Dakota entertained the other guests with songs and a war dance, "brandishing their pipes and tomahawks, and giving the war-whoop." Little Crow then gave a speech, translated by Major Brown, about the Inkpaduta chase of 1857 and the rescue of some of the prisoners. The visitors from Turkey "expressed themselves highly pleased with what they had witnessed."[15]

The next day the Dakota were part of a "long and striking funeral procession" for a Pawnee brave that went to the Congressional Cemetery. The Pawnee was Tuck-a-lix-tah, who had been staying at the same rooming house as the Dakota and had died after a long illness. He was buried with his buffalo robe, tomahawk, war club, moccasins, and trinkets. Reverend Williamson translated into Dakota the simple speech made by the Loup Pawnee, Sword Chief, who said that the Indians were tired now and wanted to go home. "We hope our Great Father will settle our business and let us go to our villages," he said.[16]

Little Crow echoed these thoughts on April 9 when the Lower Sioux met Mix for another interview: "I hope you will not keep us long, because if you do we will be too late to attend our planting, and our people will suffer again from the same cause." (He was referring to the fact that having to chase Inkpaduta in 1857 had forced the Dakota to neglect their corn crop.) He then listed some sixteen separate and precise complaints of promises not kept, naming names and citing sums of money due. It was a source of great dissatisfaction to the Dakota that one year the government withheld money if they fought their traditional enemies, the Ojibwe, and the following year threatened to withhold annuities if they did not fight Inkpaduta, one of their own tribe.[17]

Mix replied with the usual soothing words—their Great Father will redress every wrong, the money is to be used for their benefit or is stored in the treasury, the matter will be looked into, and so forth—but Little Crow would not be put off. He again shook hands with Mix. Then he pointed to the reporter, John Dowling, and said: "Four years ago you had also writing taken down. . . . If I were to give you an account of all the money that was spilled—of all that you sent but which never reached us—it would take all night to tell it."

He complained of a government farmer who ignored Little Crow but did whatever the Indian women asked; he asked for stoves to put into their houses and for cattle and horses every four years; and he inquired why Dutchmen (Germans) settled on land promised the Indians. Little Crow pointed out that he could not speak, read, or write English and had to accept on faith that the commissioner was telling him the truth. The only possible interpretation for unkept promises was that the Great Father's words got weak before they reached his agents in the field.[18]

The Indian Office wanted the Santee Sioux to model themselves after the Choctaw and Chickasaw who had set up their own police force. Indians everywhere were urged endlessly to imitate the white man, too. Many of them, familiar with whites and their whisky, resisted. The Dakota truly believed that, by giving President Buchanan a list of their needs and grievances, all problems would be solved as if by magic. They could not understand why other Indian delegations were invited to the White House, but not they.

Just three days prior to the April 9 meeting of the Lower Sioux with Mix, the Mount Vernon Ladies Association of the Union gained title to George Washington's home. About this time the Pawnee Indians left town, followed later by a delegation of the Yankton Sioux who signed a treaty. Some shopkeepers and numerous ordinary citizens heaved a sigh of relief. Although there was repeated and serious trouble with street gangs and ruffians, some people liked to exaggerate an occasional confrontation with the Indians. Commissioner

Mix, however, emphasized that the Indians "behaved with remarkable propriety. Their curiosity and unsophisticated ideas tend at times to make them somewhat indiscreet, but this . . . should not be . . . a ground of complaint. Their kindness towards each other of different tribes, and towards all with whom they have been brought into contact, [is] praiseworthy. It affords truly a most humiliating contrast with the outrageous proceedings of the civilized savages in our midst. . . ."[19]

The Dakota finally had their interview with the president on April 26 and, wrote Brown, "were much gratified with their kind reception. The president heard their 'little speeches' and replied in a tone of friendship and kindness highly pleasing and at the same time encouraging to the Indians."[20]

The Dakota delegation always met the commissioner at Seventeenth and Pennsylvania Avenue where the old Executive Office Building now stands. The Dakota stayed at Maher's boardinghouse, the Union Hotel, known in its palmier days as the Globe Hotel. It stood just behind the present United States Treasury Building. Jimmy Maher, the original owner, had quite a reputation as a hotelkeeper who could "talk to the Indians in their native language with his Irish brogue flavoring the whole conversations." He made them feel at least partially at home by encouraging them to sit on the porch, play drums, and sing songs. These harmless pastimes always attracted a crowd, which was good for business. Bed (such as it was) and board for each Indian cost $2.00 a day. Fires, candles, and laundry were extra. Little Crow resented that they were treated like uncivilized aborigines. Having saved money to pay for the trip, he said, "we thought we would come here and live like white men, and sleep in beds, but we had to sleep on the floor.[21]

The spring days turned warmer, but little progress was made toward signing of a treaty because the debate over the admission of Kansas monopolized the time of Congress and the president. It also held back statehood for Minnesota. Like a virus the Kansas question invaded the national political body, and as temperatures rose, energy dissipated. As a newspaperman and one of Minnesota's leading Democrats who took part in the convention to form a state constitution, Brown could not resist writing political dispatches from Washington for the *Henderson Democrat*. When Brown, frustrated over the delay in the Minnesota bill, blamed Senator Stephen A. Douglas for putting Kansas ahead of Minnesota, the *St. Paul Pioneer and Democrat* took vigorous issue with Brown on this point. The St. Paul paper also turned on him for advocating the Lecompton (proslavery) constitution for Kansas.[22]

Joseph R. Brown was a complex man. Williamson had initially distrusted him: "I have known the agent ever since I first came to [*the Minnesota area*] in 1834, when he was engaged as he had been for several years previous, in selling whiskey to the Indians. He is a man of little education, handsome talents, much kind feeling, and very little principle; probably more thoroughly acquainted with the Dakotas than any other man living . . . he feels a strong sympathy for the people, though owing to his lack of principle they greatly dislike him."[23]

Impatient with the glacial progress made on the treaty, Williamson decided he might as well go home to Yellow Medicine and get some crops in the ground. He left on April 6, convinced it would be useless to oppose the cession of land by which too many men stood to profit. In two months his opinion of Brown had changed some: "They [*Brown and Cullen*] seem to take considerable interest in the welfare of the Indians and have pretty correct views of what is necessary thereto, but they are destitute of religious principle and so not fully reliable especially as they are here constantly in contact with men at least as wise or shrewd as themselves who think their pecuniary interest may be much advanced by measures detrimental to the Indians."[24]

Of course, Williamson and other Santee reserve missionaries were not entirely disinterested spectators. Current negotiation involved the education funds, which, if diverted to pay traders' debts or used for some other purpose, would be a blow to the missionaries. They had built schoolhouses, churches, and homes for themselves and the Christian Indians. It was important to them to have clear land title.

Not only did Williamson depart, but so also did Superintendent and Mrs. Cullen, both of whom took sick and left in late April "to return to the pure air of Minnesota." The Cullens' illness, however, forced them to stay in Philadelphia for some time to recuperate. "This is a matter of regret," wrote Brown, "as his services would have been of great value in the negotiations between the department and the Indians. There are but few government appointees who stand fairer with the department with which they are connected than does Col. Cullen." This statement stands in marked contrast with Brown's estimate of Cullen the previous July when the superintendent, then a rank novice from Indiana, was attempting to deal with the Inkpaduta crisis. Brown doubted then that Cullen could "give a succinct, logical and intelligent description of the difference between the habits, manners, customs and peculiarities of a Sioux Indian and a snapping turtle."[25]

On May 11, 1858, Congress finally passed the admission bill, and Minnesota became a state. Its new constitution required Indians and mixed-bloods to pass a court test in addition to adopting the language and customs of civilization in order to enjoy "the rights of citizenship within the State."[26]

The sights, sounds, and smells of Washington in May would inspire many people to leave—if they could. In fact, "the Indians are inclined to think that visits to Washington are not so desirable as they were formerly," Brown wrote in a dispatch to the *Henderson Democrat*. Streets were unpaved. There was no municipal water supply with which to wet them down. By day's end the air was heavily polluted with dust. "Washington is probably the dustiest city in the Union," a correspondent wrote for the *New York Times*. If heaven donated a natural supply of water, another kind of pollution developed: "The sewerage of the entire city, high and low, was fearfully and conspicuously defective."[27]

However, the Potomac was relatively clean, and the movement of air over the water lifted the Indians' sinking spirits on April 30. That day they rode on a steamer to Alexandria on an outing that was well worth the twenty-six cents each ticket cost. It was a pleasure for them to leave Washington's "ant heap" of lobbyists and office seekers behind. The Dakota liked floating down the river to the bustling, exciting port and even announced that they would put on a drum-and-dance performance at Arlington Spring a month later. As demonstrated at the arsenal earlier, they enjoyed playing for their own pleasure and loved to see others dance and sway to the drumbeat, too.[28]

In spite of all the shopping, attending theatrical performances, and visiting churches, office buildings, and other places, the Dakota were bored by long stretches of inactivity. Some of the more curious among them even tried elixirs and compounds advertised in the newspapers—anything to take their minds off their long wait and the bad news that began arriving from home.

At annuity time the year before, the Santees' relatives, the Yankton and Yanktonai, had traveled from Dakota Territory to protest the 1851 treaties by burning buildings and driving out some settlers. Now they reportedly were converging on Yellow Medicine, and it looked to be the same all over again. Brown sent Mix a letter along with a *Henderson Democrat* news clipping in which the Reverend Stephen R. Riggs reported the Yankton and Yanktonai threat. Joe Campbell also wrote a letter for the Lower Sioux, telling Mix: "We do not like so many strangers to be near our homes and feel anxious for the safety of our wives and children." Secretary of the Interior Jacob Thompson and Senator Henry M. Rice of Minnesota also received letters they forwarded to Mix.[29]

On May 24, 1858, the Upper Sioux conferred with Mix, who at once asked them to live on lands to be allotted in severalty to the heads of families on the south and west side of the Minnesota River and to give up their lands on the north and east side. This was about half of the reservation left them by the 1851 treaty. The amount the Indians would receive for the land would be determined by the "Great Council" (the United States Senate). The proposal shocked the Wahpeton and Sisseton leaders. Now they could see why they had been kept waiting for forty-six days. When they visited President Buchanan on April 26, he seemed to be sympathetic to their problems. Now, however, their "Great Father" ignored their demands for an accounting of their money and, instead, asked for their land. Their fields, woods, and river valleys suddenly appeared to be more than they needed. Counting on the Indians' fatigue and frustration, Mix and the other ubiquitous negotiators were hoping to grind down Dakota resistance.

For the Upper Sioux, like the Lower, it was to be a losing battle, but they did not give up easily in spite of their concern, too, about the possible threat to their families and homes posed by other Sioux tribes to the west and also by the

Ojibwe. Red Eagle Feather and Iron Walker said they would have to confer with their people about the matters the commissioner brought up. Shoots-Iron-as-He-Walks told Mix that the new proposals would deprive his people of prime timber north of the river, put whisky-selling whites closer to the Indians than before, and still not repay them for what they had yielded in 1851. Iron Walker spoke eloquently for the others, saying: "Since we made the treaty of 1851 with our Great Father we call ourselves American citizens and feel that we are a portion of the American people and therefore determined to do right towards them in our dealing. . . . Since we made the treaty . . . we have lost a good deal of money which we ought to have got; and when we came here to inquire about it, we did not think we would have had to stay so long. We wanted to get through quick and go back and plant." The session ended without a decision.[30]

Forewarned by the Upper Sioux, the Lower Sioux met with Mix the next day, May 25, at "2½ P.M." in a stormy session. The general treaty terms that Mix laid out were much the same as for the Upper Sioux. The Mdewankanton and Wahpekute should relinquish their lands north of the Minnesota and farm on lands allotted to heads of families on the south side. Continuing to be spokesman, Little Crow tried to head off the inevitable with passionate and eloquent arguments. He again reminded Mix and others of broken promises in earlier treaties and then said:

> That is the way you all do. You use very good and pleasant language, but we never receive half what is promised or which we ought to get. I came here about the Reserve in 1854; I recollect you [*meaning the recorder*] very distinctly; and you were then writing at the table as you are now, surrounded by papers. You then promised us that we should have this same land forever; and yet, notwithstanding this, you now want to take half of it away. We ought, when we need to do business, talk like men and not like children. . . . When we came here, I thought we would do business . . . at once . . . but it appears you are getting papers all around me, so that, after a while, I will have nothing left. I am going to see that paper which you gave the Agent, and if, after examining it, I shall find anything good in it, I will come and see you again; and when I do, you will hear me talk like a man, and not like a child.

At this juncture, Little Crow shook hands with Mix, and the Indians left for their hotel.[31]

Both groups of Dakota now tried to rescue something from the negotiations by preparing documents with suggested treaty provisions of their own. On June 1 the Upper Sioux presented theirs, drafted with Brown's help. It asked for a definite written sum of money for their lands—not a blank to be filled in by the Great Council (Senate). The money was to be paid to the chiefs, not the traders. The Indians also indicated they would no longer hunt down their own criminals, and they wanted their timberland to be protected from the whites.[32]

On June 24 the Lower Sioux, aided by Robertson, also gave Mix a paper in which one proposal was to donate to Minnesota some reserve land in return for tax exemption as a hedge against the ending of money payments. During this interview Little Crow was careful to let Wabasha take more of a part than earlier since he was the principal chief. But when it came to polemics, Little Crow continued to hold the stage. He had read, as he said he would, the proposed treaty Mix had handed the Indians at the previous meeting. The chief complained that the paper "made me ashamed" because it in effect said "the Sioux Indians own nothing." He added that "we were promised a great many things . . . but it now appears that the wind blows it all off and that we got good words and nothing else. The Great Spirit has made his red children on the land which they own and their Great Father, when he wants it, buys it of them." Later on, Little Crow said he thought the Sioux ought to have more land than the treaty offered—"in 1854, I was promised a large tract." Here was the crux of the difficulty. The promises of 1854, or any year, were not the realities of a few years later. When it became inconvenient or expensive (politically or financially) to fulfill an obligation, the United States saw no hindrance to taking the cheap way out.[33]

The matter of what the Indians owed traders also came up at the June 4 meeting. Little Crow said he wanted to do what was right. "Living in a country where game is scarce, and we can't hunt," he said, "we are compelled to go in debt for provisions; and I am willing to give those who let us have them something by way of remuneration." When Mix pushed for an accounting, Little Crow indicated that the Lower Sioux owed a total of some $40,000 to such traders as Myrick, Campbell, Brown (before he became agent), Forbes, and Louis Robert.

Events now moved mercifully to a climax, and none too soon, for the weather was getting so warm that government officials and others were fleeing Washington. The last parties and "galas" were taking place. Harriet Lane, the president's niece and hostess, had left the capital for the fresher air of Wheatland, the Buchanan home in Lancaster, Pennsylvania. On oppressive nights Buchanan drove four miles up to the Soldiers Home where it was cool enough for a good night's sleep.[34]

As June dragged on, no real attempt was made to dignify the treaty farce being played by actually negotiating with the Indians. Mix, now a full commissioner, left no doubt that he expected a treaty to be signed when he summoned the upper bands to his office at 2:00 P.M. on June 19. First, though, the lengthy discussions resembled those of other meetings between Mix and both groups of Dakota. When Red Iron, head chief of the upper bands, tried to ask questions about the money, houses, and other promises in the 1851 treaty, Mix put him off, as he did Little Crow, by calling him a child. The commissioner tired of arguments and threatened to let the Upper Sioux return home without a treaty. Then they could see what conditions they could get out of the new state of Minnesota.[35]

The question of Indian title to their holdings came up, and Brown indicated he thought the Dakota were secure on their lands south of the river. He was relying on the terms of the July, 1854, agreement, in which the president was authorized "to confirm to the Sioux of Minnesota, forever, the reserve on the Minnesota River now occupied by them, upon such conditions as he may deem just." The president never took formal action, thereby leaving it (in the words of one historian) "an open question whether they had anything better than a tenancy at will."[36]

Mix, obviously trying to frighten the delegation into signing, expressed no doubt on the point of title: "They have no right whatever to the land they now occupy, and, which is held by sufferance." The United States wanted the land north of the river, and the alternative to taking it by force was to perform a treaty charade. The traders, of course, would be protected in their entrenched position by having "just" debts deducted from payments. The army would receive permission to establish posts and build roads. As for the lands still being held by the Dakota on the south side of the Minnesota, eighty acres would be allotted in severalty to heads of families (and to minors when they became heads of families) and the remainder of the reserve would be held in common. The Indians would pay survey costs, forego annuities when drunk, hand over all lawbreakers, and trust to the Senate to arrive at a fair price for the land ceded on the north side. Even without foreknowledge of the Civil War, Brown was misguided in his trust of the Senate and his belief that he could influence later events and persons. In fairness to Brown, however, it should be underscored that he doubtless was the one who pushed for civilization clauses like the eight-acre allotments and other provisions leading to Indians' cultivation of the soil. Late in the afternoon of June 19 the Upper Sioux at last signed the treaty.[37]

With one treaty out of the way, Mix probably was sorry he put off meeting with the Lower Sioux until 7:00 P.M. the same day. At any rate, the exhausting and bitter session dragged on until midnight, following the same script as the earlier one. Patience grew thin on both sides as fatigue set in. Little Crow again asked about past promises of payments never made. Mix threatened the lower bands as he had the upper and again referred to Little Crow as a child. This cut the chief, who answered: "You say I am a child! This time I am determined not to act as a child in signing a paper I do not understand."[38]

In frustration over Indian resistance, Mix warned against the "sinister councils of white men." Twice he appeared to question, openly, the validity of the translation being done by Joe Campbell. Mix's stock reply when asked about past promises was that everything was done for the good of the Great Father's red children. At last, depressed and unresponsive to the commissioner's tense questions, the Lower Sioux leaders also signed their "X's" to the paper. By then the reasons to sign appeared as great as those not to sign. Virtually nothing they wanted had been granted except a promise to keep whites out of the reserve and a chance, with the eighty-acre allotments, to farm individually. Any longer time away from home would be wasted, so the Lower Sioux signed.[39]

The treaties differed mainly in two respects. First, Little Crow insisted on deleting the article permitting tribal members to live off the reservation. He knew that "Our young men, if permitted to . . . run about among the whites . . . will pull down fences, and do mischief, and create bad feeling." Second, Campbell was reimbursed for land and payments promised his father, Scott Campbell, in 1837 but negated by Senate action.[40]

A farewell interview on June 21 between Mix and the Upper Sioux went quietly. Each Indian leader was presented a medal of their Great Father and promised "a good Northwest gun," a good conduct papery, and further presents of cloth and goods to be bought in New York City.[41]

At a later interview with Mix the same day, the Lower Sioux were deeply suspicious and only partly mollified by Brown's assurances that they would receive $1.25 an acre for their lands north of the Minnesota. Little Crow refused to be put off so easily. He mentioned that he had wanted to go to Washington "a good many years ago." He added, "There seemed to be a big fence around us, but Inkpaduta pulled it down[.] [I]f it had not been for that scrape, we would not be here." Little Crow realized that his previous efforts to keep settlers out of the reserve, account for the annuity payments, and regulate relations with the marauding Ojibwe had been hopeless. Only when the Spirit Lake murders scared the settlers had he been in a position to pressure the Indian Office to allow the visit to Washington.

Now the submerged antagonism between Little Crow and Brown surfaced, apparently over the sum of money the Lower Sioux lent the upper bands at the beginning of the trip. "I have a great many things to say against my agent," Little Crow said rather cryptically, "but do not wish to say them now." Brown replied: "I am not afraid to have him say what he knows of my conduct. He has been a great drawback to a faithful discharge of my duties as Agent. That is all I have to say to him."

Mix told Little Crow that he did Brown an injustice, adding: "If he has any thing to say against his Agent, he must say it here to his face, or else hereafter hold his tongue." Then Mix asked who their chief was "and if he is a man why does he not speak out." He repeated the question. After a long pause, the delegation finally took leave of Mix "and retired in apparent bad humor without replying to the question." Words were worthless.[42]

Chandler's carriages waited to take the Indians directly to the train for Baltimore—the first stop on the way home to families and farms they had left too long ago. John Other Day had acquired a bride—or, more accurately, a white woman, a waitress at the Indians' hotel, who would become his wife. The Dakota all had new clothes, medals, and memories. They no longer had almost one million acres of prime Minnesota land and, fortunately, did not yet know how little they would be paid for it.[43]

Brown joined the Indians at their Baltimore hotel, the Howard House, on June 23, having stayed behind to receive Mix's letter of instruction. While the Indians rode omnibuses on a sight-seeing tour of Baltimore, Brown went to Poltney's, hardware merchants, where he ordered $5,000 worth of farm equipment for the Dakota, as Mix had directed. In spite of pestering crowds of war-whooping rowdies, the Indians ascended the Washington Monument for a look at Baltimore below. They also visited a ship, and, dressed in "war costume," took in the last show of the season, the comedy "Wild Oats," at the Holliday Street Theatre. They always liked the lights and bright costumes of the theater and were fully aware of the impact they had on women.[44]

Heading for New York on June 24, the group stopped overnight in Lancaster, Pennsylvania, to receive their guns and powder horns at H. E. Leman's. The Amish and Mennonite farmers reportedly were less of a novelty to the Indians than vice versa, and it was a relief to be out of the crushing humidity of the coastal cities even for a few hours.

Record heat of nearly 100 degrees greeted the delegation when it reached New York. The Dakota were to have enjoyed a great shopping spree and rounds of sight-seeing and entertainment not possible in the limited resources of Washington. Mix instructed Brown to invest $5,000 in dry goods at Cronin, Hurxthal and Sears and advised the secretaries of the army and navy to arrange a welcome for the Indians at their New York installations. But there was no strength or enthusiasm for the least movement outside Hungerford's Hotel other than for a gasp of torrid air in the late evening.[45]

By June 28 Brown realized that health and tempers were deteriorating rapidly as each day set a new record for both thermometer and coroner. On June 30 nineteen persons died of sun stroke in New York. The Indians found a visit to see Wood's Minstrels slightly bearable because each was given a fan. The visitors were not slow to realize the power of the press and began giving reporters strictly personal and highly biased accounts of the Inkpaduta episode. Mix had asked Brown to stay over in order to obtain more medals but gave permission for the Dakota groups and their conductors to go on ahead. On July 2 the Dakota left for Niagara Falls and St. Paul. It was none too soon. In Minnesota on that same day the Lower Sioux broke into and plundered the government warehouses at both agencies. Among those arrested, while his father and other chiefs were returning home from Washington and New York, was the son of Shakopee.[46]

It did not take long for the effect of the well-meant phrases of the treaties to be all blown off, as Little Crow put it. By August 24, 1858, Superintendent Cullen

reported to Mix that the Indians gathered at Yellow Medicine were sullen, rebellious, and insulting, especially to Brown. Cullen suspected conspiracy "which
is of an ominous character and will require extreme watchfulness." The missionaries were concerned that they might have to abandon their buildings, farms,
schools, and churches without compensation if the treaty terms were strictly
interpreted. By November one of the most faithful of the "breeches" Indians,
Little Paul, was asking the Reverend Stephen Return Riggs to assist in preventing ratification of the treaties.[47]

Bitterness caused by the 1858 treaties, and especially by the way some of the
provisions were implemented, helped bring on the Dakota War in Minnesota
in 1862. Senator Henry M. Rice reported both treaties on March 9, 1859, and
the Senate ratified them without amendment. It took its time, however, settling
the question of Indian title and of just compensation for the land. Meanwhile,
in his 1859 report, Agent Brown claimed good progress in civilizing the Indians
and getting them to farm and asked for fair treatment of "a deeply wronged
portion of the human family." He thought the proceeds of the sale of one-half
of each of their reservations should place the Lower and Upper Sioux "beyond
the fear of future want." The excellent land being sold was worth $5.00 an acre,
he thought, but he preferred the plan of opening the lands to pre-emption at
$1.25 per acre, the established price. Allowing for proper deductions, he said
the Indians should receive at least $1.00 per acre. That appeared to be the feel-
ing, too, of the Senate committee on Indian affairs during deliberations in the
spring of 1860. But, inexplicably, the amount voted on June 27, 1860, as the session of Congress neared its end, was a mere thirty cents an acre. Asked historian Folwell: "Patient reader, do you wonder that Indian blood boiled?"[48]

An Indian appropriation bill was finally passed on March 2, 1861, that allowed the Lower Sioux $96,000 for 320,000 acres of land and the Upper
Sioux $170,880 for 569,000 acres. Wrote Folwell: "The total of $266,880 looks
small beside the sum of $889,600 which would have resulted from the price
of one dollar per acre . . . and still more insignificant when compared with the
sum of $4,448,000, the fair value of the land at five dollars per acre, in Brown's
opinion."[49]

The disposition of these inadequate sums greatly heightened the Indians'
exasperation. The traders got practically all of the $96,000 paid the Lower
Sioux for their land and almost half the sum allotted the upper bands. The
Lower Sioux treaty had stipulated that no more than $70,000, minus the cost
of purchases the delegation took home, could be used to pay debts acknowledged by the Indians in open council. The additional $26,000, however, even-
tually went to pay debts after a meeting—hardly an "open council"—at the Episcopal mission school at the Lower Agency on December 3, 1860. Afterwards,
Bishop Henry B. Whipple wrote: "What took place I do not know, but the following day Little Crow had a new wagon." The suspicion that the chief had

been bribed to give in to the traders led to his being replaced by Traveling Hail as principal speaker of his people. However, when it came time in August, 1862, to name a military leader against the whites, the Lower Sioux turned again to Little Crow. He reluctantly agreed to lead what he knew would be futile attacks at least in part to restore his reputation.[50]

And so increased frustration accompanied the understanding among the Dakota that their hope of becoming a "portion of the American people" was encouraged in Washington in 1858 and denied in Minnesota in the months following. They understood the difference between a promise of 1.00 an acre for their prime land and eventually receiving little or nothing for it. The 1862 war that cost hundreds of lives, untold property damage, and Indian banishment was telling testimony to the idiocy of Indian policy.

NOTES

From Minnesota History 45 *(Fall, 1976).*

1. An account of "Major" Brown's winter trip appeared in the *Henderson Democrat,* March 3, 1858 [p. 2], and was reprinted in the *St. Paul Pioneer and Democrat,* March 9, 1858, [p. 2] (all citations to this paper are to the daily edition); Charles E. Mix to William J. Cullen, February 5, 1858, Office of Indian Affairs (hereafter cited OIA), letters sent, National Archives Record Group (NARG) 75, National Archives microfilm publication M21, roll 58, p. 284.

2. *Henderson Democrat,* March 3, 1858, [p. 2].

3. For sketches of Brown, see Daniel S. B. Johnston, "Minnesota Journalism in the Territorial Period," in *Minnesota Historical Collections,* vol. 10, part 2:267 (1905); William W. Folwell, *A History of Minnesota,* vols. 1 (especially 231–238) and 2 (numerous references) (St. Paul, revised editions, 1956 and 1961); George S. Hage, *Newspapers on the Minnesota Frontier,* 1849–1860, 39–40, 155, 157 (St. Paul, 1967).

4. June D. Holmquist and Jean A. Brookins, *Minnesota's Major Historic Sites: A Guide,* 130–132 (St. Paul, 1972).

5. Mix to Brown, September 11, 1857, OIA, letters sent, NARG 75, M21, roll 57, p. 366–367; *St. Paul Pioneer and Democrat,* September 15, 1857, [p. 2]; Charles E. Flandrau to Cullen, September 24, 1857, in Indian Office, *Reports,* 1857, p. 60. Reverend Thomas S. Williamson wrote of his relief and hope because of Brown's appointment as agent: "Whatever faults he may have, I believe that his sympathies are such that his feelings will incite him to labor for their welfare, and to allay or prevent any unkind feelings between them and their white neighbors." See *New York Times,* August 13, 1857, p. 5 (reprint of letters to *St. Paul Times,* August 24, 1857).

6. For various views of Little Crow, see Dr. Asa W. Daniels, "Reminiscences of Little Crow," in *Minnesota Historical Collections,* 12:513–530 (1908); Thomas Hughes, *Indian Chiefs of Southern Minnesota,* 52–58 (Mankato, 1927; revised edition, Minneapolis, 1969); Isaac V. D. Heard, *History of the Sioux War and Massacres of 1862 and 1863,* 146, other pages (New York, 1863); Daniel Buck, *Indian Outbreaks,* 42–56 (Mankato, 1904; reprint edition, Minneapolis, 1965).

7. General Accounting Office, Second Auditor's Accounts, Joseph R. Brown, account no. 8499 (hereafter all cited GAO), James H. Brisbois, March 9, 1858, D. W. Freeman, July 17, 1858, Andrew Robertson, voucher 9, abstract B, July 21, 1858, and voucher 7, abstract

B, July 20, 1858; railroad advertisement in *St. Paul Pioneer and Democrat,* September 3, 1857.

8. In his excellent *History of the Santee Sioux* (Lincoln, 1967), Roy W. Meyer states on page 94 that Governor Willis A. Gorman and Little Crow "went to Washington in the spring of 1855. . . ." This is unlikely since Little Crow was definitely there in 1854. For instance, Gorman wrote Indian Commissioner George W. Manypenny on March 27, 1855: "I am requested by Henri Belland [,] the person who accompanied 'Little Crow' to Washington last year, to forward the enclosed claim for $200 against the Sioux," OIA, letters received, NARG 75, microfilm publication M234, roll 762.

9. Williamson to S. B. Treat, February 22, 1858, in Grace Lee Nute, comp., Manuscripts Relating to Northwest Missions, in the Minnesota Historical Society. For information on Crawford and Akepa, see Hughes, *Indian Chiefs,* 87–92.

10. Brown to Cullen, December 4, 1857, enclosed in Cullen to Mix, December 24, 1857, OIA, letters received, NARG 75, microfilm publication M234, roll 762; *St. Paul Pioneer and Democrat,* August 28, 1858, [p. 2]. Williamson said that "the Sioux have had to wait a month in a state of starvation for their annuities. The goods furnished them—$5,000 worth a year, being a little of everything and not enough of anything for general distribution—have caused much ill-will among themselves, and an opinion almost amounting to belief that they are cheated out of three-fourths of the goods due them." See *New York Times,* August 24, 1857, p. 5.

11. GAO, Robertson, voucher 7; *Washington Evening Star,* March 15, 1858, [p. 2]. The *National Intelligencer* (Washington) carried the same story of the Indians' arrival on the same date. There is no way to account for the discrepancies in numbers in the various sources.

12. GAO, W. P. Chandler, June 21, 1858. This same voucher includes all official trips of the Dakota delegation, which always made use of Chandler's carriage service in Washington. All other references to use of Chandler's carriages are based on this source.

13. "Sioux Delegation from Minnesota in the Indian Office," March 15, 1858, in Documents Relating to the Negotiations of Ratified and Unratified Treaties with Various Indian Tribes, 1801–1869 (hereafter cited DRN), OIA, NARG 75, microfilm publication T494, roll 6, frames 0214–0220. All references to this meeting are from the same source.

14. "The Sioux Indians from Brown County, Minnesota, 2d. Interview," March 27, 1858, DRN, OIA, NARG 75, microfilm T494, roll 6, frames 0233–0236. All references to this meeting are from the same source.

15. *Henderson Democrat,* April 13, 1858, [p. 2], quoting a story on the arsenal visit from the *Washington Union; Washington Evening Star,* April 2, 1858, [p. 3].

16. *Washington Evening Star,* March 30, 1858, [p. 3.] (first quote), March 31, 1858, [p. 3] (second quote).

17. "[Lower] Sioux from Brown County, Minnesota, in Indian Office," April 9, 1858, DRN, OIA, NARG 75, microfilm T494, roll 6, frames 0245–0261; Brown dispatch in *Henderson Democrat,* July 16, 1857, [p. 2], with parts reprinted in *St. Paul Pioneer and Democrat,* July 18, 1857, [p. 2].

18. "[Lower] Sioux from Brown County, Minnesota, in Indian Office," April 9, 1858, DRN, OIA, NARG 75, microfilm T494, roll 6. All references to this meeting are from the same source.

19. *Washington Evening Star,* April 7, 1858, [p. 2] (quotes), April 27, 1858, [p. 2].

20. *Henderson Democrat,* May 12, 1858, [p. 2].

21. Clifford Lewis, "Hotels of Washington from Past and Present," in John Clagett

Procter, ed., *Washington, Past and Present,* 2:782 (Maher quote); *Washington Evening Star,* May 3, 27, 1858, [both p. 3]; GAO, Maher, June 21, 1858; "Delegation of Lower Sioux: Final Meeting," June 21, 1858, DRN, OIA, NARG 75, microfilm T494, roll 6, frame 323 (Little Crow quote).

22. *Henderson Democrat,* April 13, July 21, 1858, [both p. 2]; *St. Paul Pioneer and Democrat,* April 22, July 17, 1858, [both p. 2].

23. Williamson to S. B. Treat, January 18, 1858, in Grace Lee Nute, comp., Manuscripts Relating to Northwest Missions.

24. Williamson to Treat, March 18, 1858 (quote), June 23, 1858, in Nute, comp., Manuscripts Relating to Northwest Missions.

25. *Henderson Democrat,* May 12, [p. 2.] (first quotes), May 26, [p. 2], 1858; July 16, 1857, [p. 2] (last quote).

26. For the story of Minnesota's admission to the Union, see Folwell, *Minnesota,* 2:9–18, and Theodore C. Blegen, *Minnesota: A History of the State,* especially 228–230 (Minneapolis, 1963; second edition, 1975).

27. *Henderson Democrat,* May 26, 1858, [p. 2]; *New York Times,* June 22, 1858, p. 1; John A. Porter, *The City of Washington,* in Herbert B. Adams, ed., Johns Hopkins University Studies in Historical and Political Science, Third Series, XI–XII, 24–25 (last quote) (Baltimore, November and December, 1885).

28. *Washington Evening Star,* March 27, May 29, 1858, [p. 3].

29. Brown to Mix, May 23, 1858, enclosed in letter, Mix to Secretary of Interior, June 4, 1858, Report Books of OIA, 1838–1885, NARG 75, National Archives microfilm publication 348, roll 11, p. 3–6; Secretary of Interior to Mix, June 1, 1858, Secretary of Interior, Indian Division, letters sent, NARG 48, microfilm 606, roll 3; *Henderson Democrat,* May 12, 1858, [p. 2].

30. Report of Upper Sioux meeting, May 24, 1858, DRN, OIA, NARG 75, microfilm T494, roll 6, frames 0340–0349. Translations and spellings of Indian names vary in treaty negotiations, and so do identifications of who said what. The recorder of the May 24 meeting said that the eloquent speech was made by the Man Walking in Iron, who often is called Iron Walker, or Walking Iron.

31. Report of Lower Sioux meeting, May 25, 1858, DRN, OIA, NARG 75, microfilm T494, roll 6, frames 0262–0267.

32. "Upper Sioux Delegation at Indian Office," June 1, 1858, DRN, OIA, NARG 75, microfilm T494, roll 6, frames 0350–0354.

33. "Lower Sioux Indians in the Indian Office," June 4, 1858, DRN, OIA, NARG 75, microfilm T494, roll 6, frames 0268–0280.

34. James J. Buchanan to Harriet Lane, October 15, 1858, Buchanan Papers, Manuscript Division, Library of Congress.

35. "Upper Sioux—Treaty Meeting," June 19, 1858, DRN, OIA, NARG 75, microfilm T494, roll 6, frames 0355–0367 (another copy in different handwriting, fames 0368–0388).

36. United States, *Statutes at Large,* 10:326; Folwell, *Minnesota,* 2:217.

37. "Upper Sioux—Treaty Meeting," June 19, 1858, DRN, OIA, NARG 75, microfilm T494, roll 6. Brown's evident self-confidence may have led him to some mistakes in judgment. The *St. Paul Pioneer and Democrat* commented on June 25, 1858: "We are glad to learn from Washington, that on the nineteenth treaties were concluded . . . with the . . . Sioux under the charge of 'Major' Brown—as the Henderson magician is styled."

38. "Lower Sioux—Treaty Meeting," June 19, 1858, DRN, OIA, NARG 75, microfilm T494, roll 6, frames 0281–0301; *St. Paul Pioneer and Democrat,* July 8, 1858, [p. 2] (Little

Crow quote). The St. Paul paper published an account of the treaty signing from the *St. Louis Republican* because its own story was burned with the mail in a fire that destroyed the steamboat "Galena" at Red Wing landing on July 1, 1858.

39. There is evidence that others, too, did not always accept Campbell's "official" translation. Trader Henry Forbes did some voluntary translating during the first two interviews of March 15 and March 27, and Williamson wrote Treat on January 18, 1858: "My presence would at least prevent the interpreter from willfully misinterpreting" (Nute, comp., Manuscripts Relating to Northwest Missions).

40. For the treaty, see Charles J. Kappler, comp. and ed., *Indian Affairs. Laws and Treaties*, 2:785–789 (Washington, D.C., 1904) and United States, *Statutes at Large*, 12:1031–1041 (pagination differs in other bindings). The Little Crow quote is in "Lower Sioux—Treaty Meeting," June 19, 1858, DRN, OIA, NARG 75, microfilm T494, roll 6, frame 0293.

41. "Delegation, Upper Sioux—Final Interview," June 21, 1858, DRN, OIA, NARG 75, microfilm T494, roll 6, frames 0406-0408.

42. "Delegation of Lower Sioux—Final Interview," June 21, 1858, DRN, OIA, NARG 75, microfilm T494, roll 6, frames 0320-0324. On the title page of the record of this interview, someone wrote: "Little Crow is bluffed!"

43. For Other Day's marriage, see Hughes, *Indian Chiefs*, 75, and Katharine C. Turner, *Red Men Calling on the Great White Father*, 151 Norman, Oklahoma, 1951). Thomas A. Robertson said in his reminiscences, written in the winter of 1918-19 (the Minnesota Historical Society has a copy): "On our return from Washington he [*Other Day*] brought back with him a white woman that he took out of a house of ill-fame, whom he married after he got back to the reservation." Other Day, who later helped many whites escape during the Sioux Uprising, was "a desperate character among his own people," (said Robertson) before his conversion to Christianity. The author of this article found no record of the marriage at the District of Columbia Marriage Records Office.

44. Mix to Brown, June 23, 1858, OIA, letters sent, M21, roll 59, p. 116; GAO, Howard House, Baltimore, June 24, 1858; *Baltimore Sun*, June 23, 24, 25, 1858, all p. 1.

45. Mix to Brown, June 23, 1858, OIA, letters sent, M21, roll 59, p. 116; Mix to Thompson, June 21, 1858, Secretary of Interior, letters received, NARG 48.

46. Mix to Brown, June 25, June 30, July 2, 1858, Mix to Cullen, July 3, 1858, OIA, letters sent, M21, roll 50, p. 126, 140, 147, 161-162, respectively; Brown to Mix, June 28, 1858, OIA, letters received, M234, roll 762; *New York Times*, June 29, 30, 1858; *New York Herald*, June 28, 1858; *New York Tribune*, June 29, 1858; *St. Paul Pioneer and Democrat*, June 30, 1858, [p. 1]. Mix expressed fear and anger to Cullen that the annuity goods due in St. Paul on May 23 had only just arrived.

47. Cullen to Mix, August 24, 1858, enclosed with Mix to Thompson, September 24, 1858, Secretary of Interior, letters received, NARG 48; Riggs to Treat, November 2, 1858, and Williamson to Treat, August 24, 1858, in Nute, comp., Manuscripts Relating to Northwest Missions.

48. Brown to Cullen, September 10, 1859, in Indian Office, *Reports*, 1859, 79–92 (quotes 82–83); Folwell, *Minnesota*, 2:398. Folwell has an excellent short account of "The Treaties of 1858" in an appendix to his second volume.

49. Folwell, *Minnesota*, 2:398.

50. Folwell, *Minnesota*, 2:399-400; Henry B. Whipple, *Lights and Shadows of a Long Episcopate*, 138 (New York, 1900). For Little Crow's acceptance of leadership in the war, see Folwell, *Minnesota*, 2:240-241, and Kenneth Carley, *The Sioux Uprising of 1862*, 10-12 (St. Paul, revised edition, 1976).

The Power of Whiteness
Or, the Life and Times of Joseph Rolette Jr.

BRUCE M. WHITE

The final article in this section focuses on the life and times of Joe Rolette and his role in literally shaping the new state. After an analysis of population changes in the territory based on the census of 1850 and 1860 and a discussion of the enormous boost to the territory's economy in its early years based on the annual Indian indemnity payments from the federal government, Bruce White deftly examines Joseph Rolette as both person and legend, demonstrating Rolette's usefulness to other more "statesman-like" politicians like Sibley and Ramsey, both future governors, as well as his position as a transitional figure from a culture composed of Indians, métis, and whites that was in the process of disappearing. In White's words, "the legend of Joe Rolette is about culture, politics, race, and power."

In March 1857 a short, merry, prank-loving member of the Minnesota territorial legislature made away with a recently passed bill in order to prevent it from going into law. For several days he stayed holed up in a local hotel where he ate sumptuous meals, drank fine wines and whiskies, played poker, and partied with his male and female friends. On the last day of the legislative session, just as the final gavel fell, he appeared, ready to report the bill, to the laughter of supporters and opponents alike. The following day he was paraded by torchlight through the streets of St. Paul. Within 15 years he died a pauper. Decades later a fellow territorial politician commemorated the events of 1857 by presenting two portraits of him in métis garb, one to the prestigious Minnesota Club, the other to the Minnesota Historical Society. For generations since, his exploits have been described in loving detail in books and magazines intended for adults and impressionable young people.[1]

The tale of Joseph Rolette Jr. is one of the key stories that Minnesotans of generations past have remembered about the territorial years. It was Rolette, also known as Jolly Joe, who "stole" the bill that would have moved the capital of Minnesota from St. Paul to St. Peter. It was also Joe Rolette—sometimes described as a "half breed"—who brought his dogs into the halls of the capitol, and about whom, when "a commotion was heard down the street," early residents of St. Paul said: "Well, it is either a big fire or else Joe Rolette is in town."[2]

What explains the popularity of Rolette—the character—and the endurance of the legend about the capital bill, an unusual one for a state that prides itself on clean politics? Perhaps it is simply a colorful, romantic legend, helpful in enlivening otherwise dry accounts of bills written, debated, and passed. Or perhaps the story provides a much-needed example of an individual making a difference in a world where committees and quorums govern. It could be that the legend of Joe Rolette is like the trickster stories found in the literature of many cultures, designed to amuse and to provide children with examples of otherwise unacceptable behavior.[3]

Whether or not these factors help explain the legend's endurance, the often-described incidents of Rolette's life—many of which appear to have occurred—are succinct records of important themes in the early history of Minnesota. The capital bill itself was the product of the conflict between political factions and economic interests in the territory, played out, in part, in terms of race. The events depend in part on Rolette's perceived status as a half breed, a category that many in the territory considered emblematic of the social, cultural, and political system they sought to remove or replace. Altogether, the legend of Joe Rolette is about culture, politics, race, and power. For these reasons it is worth remembering and reconsidering.

Studying the preterritorial period of Minnesota's history is a little like doing archaeology. Each generation creates a structure of belief and experience that covers up or reinterprets past experiences and past views of the world. This is especially true for generations that undergo great communal experiences such as mass movements, wars, and depressions. Such groups often reinvent the past as a tool for achieving social, political, and cultural change. In doing so, they make it difficult for later generations to understand the lives and experiences of people before the period of massive change. To imagine what life was like in the Minnesota region before 1849 and appreciate the nature of the drastic changes that took place in the 1850s, it is necessary to dig through the deposits of interpretation left by territorial Minnesotans.

In 1853 John Wesley Bond began his classic guidebook, *Minnesota and Its Resources,* with a description designed to reinterpret the region's culture and history: "A very few years ago and the present territory of Minnesota was a waste of woodland and of prairie, uninhabited save by the different hordes of savage tribes from time immemorial scattered through its expanse, with of later years a few white traders only intermingled. At intervals a zealous missionary of the cross, or adventurous traveler, by turns found their way to the Great Falls of St. Anthony."[4]

Found here are some of the basic themes of post-territorial Minnesota history: the region was inhabited by savage, uncivilized, wandering peoples who made wasteful use of the land and were occasionally visited by a few traders, missionaries, and daring adventurers. An early Minnesota politician, William P. Murray, provided an example of the way that these themes came to be copied and embellished. In a 1904 speech to the executive council of the Minnesota Historical Society, he described the territory in 1849 as "little more than a wilderness, a vast waste of prairie and pine lands," a region that was "more remote from settlement and civilization than the most distant part of our country today."[5]

A key concept in Murray's speech was "settlement," the term usually used to describe the process through which European Americans came to inhabit vast regions of the United States. Though the word can be used simply to mean a place where people live and the process by which people move from one region to another, nineteenth-century European Americans used it to describe a culturally specific set of beliefs about proper land use and, more generally, what constituted civilization.[6]

Thus, settlement was not merely the presence of people but the introduction of various features that symbolized Euro-American society and provided the basis for an ordered way of life. Essential to the concept was agriculture, defined as planting crops on a large scale or raising domestic animals. The so-called settlers of the 1850s were, in their terms, engaged in imposing agriculture and the agricultural way of life on an orderless region that they believed to be wasted on its inhabitants.

These beliefs would later provide the basis for the frontier thesis of historian Frederick Jackson Turner. For Turner, settlement was a process of social evolution, of "progress from primitive industrial society without division of labor, up to manufacturing civilization." The frontier was "the meeting point between savagery and civilization," the place where an oncoming movement of people of mainly European origin encountered what was seen as a wilderness, an area of "free land"—that is, land occupied only by Indian people.[7]

While the characteristics used to describe settlement were essentially cultural, race was becoming increasingly important in defining American civilization. More and more Americans in the mid-nineteenth century believed that human beings could be categorized according to racial groups, not all of which had the same intelligence and capabilities. Those considered superior were described as Anglo-Saxon, Germanic, Caucasian—or, simply, white. Indian people and blacks, as well as, on occasion, Irish, Italians, and others were thought to be inferior and without a part to play in the making of American society. In keeping with these new attitudes, settlement and civilization came to be described as the accomplishments of white people, even if other groups might live an orderly, cultured existence. From this point of view, the history of settlement in the Minnesota region, as described by post-territorial historians, was essentially the story of how Minnesota came to be white.[8]

Murray showed this perspective in his speech when he sought to define which early non-Indian residents of the region were white and which were not. He noted that early in 1849 the "entire white population scarcely exceeded one thousand persons." Later that year, when more immigrants had arrived, a census recorded 4,680 whites, but he stated that many of these individuals were not really white. For example, St. Paul "had a population of some two hundred, a majority of whom were Indian traders, French, and half breeds" and, of the 637 people of Pembina recorded in the 1849 territorial census, "only a small fraction ... were white." Murray wished to make clear that the people of European ancestry living in Minnesota in 1849—who had been in the region all of their lives and by many definitions would be called settlers—were not white, not part of the great movement of white settlers into the region. They were part of Minnesota's past, not its future.[9]

For almost 200 years before 1849 the Minnesota region was the scene of a complex economic endeavor, the fur trade, that supported an interdependent social system in which Indian people and mostly French traders lived peacefully together, trading and intermarrying.[10] This system—which benefited both Indian people and the European trade—persisted through British and American control, mainly due to the social and cultural continuity in communities of people of French, Indian, and mixed ancestry, later augmented by some British and American traders.

The evolution of the social system through generations of the trade was equally complex. Far from being a homogeneous group, the children of intermarriage between European traders and Indian people exhibited a range of cultural possibilities, often related to economic class. Some children were fully incorporated into Indian communities. Others—particularly those of prominent traders—were sent east to be educated and continue in a trading role. Culturally, they were European.

Still other people of mixed ancestry created new identities apart from the context of the trading post or the Indian village. Impetus for this creation came from the amalgamations of the XY and North West Companies in 1805 and the North West and Hudson's Bay Companies in 1821. These consolidations put many people out of work, forcing them and their families to survive through hunting, gathering, and trading, following both European and Indian patterns. In places such as Prairie du Chien, St. Paul, Mendota, Pembina, and the Red River settlement of Manitoba, as well as in areas surrounding trading-post villages throughout the region, people of mixed ancestry and culture created autonomous, diverse communities.[11]

In the mid-nineteenth century a variety of terms described the new identities of these people of mixed ancestry and cultures. The German ethnographer and geographer Johann G. Kohl noted that the people of Ojibwe-French heritage on Lake Superior referred to themselves with a jesting term, *chicot*—a French-Canadian word for half-burnt stumps. Other phrases were *bois brulé* or *bois grillé* (burned wood or grilled wood), "in reference to the shades of colour that bronze the face of a mixed breed." A newer term, originally used for specific groups of French-Indian people living on the northern plains and supported by the large herds of buffalo, was *métis*, which simply means mixed or mixed race in French.[12]

In contrast, the names that English-speaking Americans used for these people—"half breed," "half blood," and "mixed blood"—had racial implications. In some cases these words merely described the fact or degree of intermarriage. William W. Warren, an educated man of mixed ancestry himself, wrote a fictional tale in the early 1850s of a fur trader among the Blackfeet, a "halfblood" with a Scottish father and Indian mother.[13] Increasingly, however, these terms, particularly "half breed," were used as slurs, designed to suggest an alleged tainted nature.

The specific meaning of these various designations depended largely on context. The census of Minnesota Territory taken in 1850 provides an opportunity to examine the definitions of the terms "half breed" and "white." Like the census of 1849, the 1850 count was designed to measure the population of non-Indian people. It yielded a total of 6,077 residents. If one accepts the U.S. Department of Indian Affairs' estimates of 31,700 Indian people living in and near the territory in the early 1850s, these 6,077 represented only about 16 percent of the area's total population.[14]

In addition to recording names, sexes, and birthplaces, census enumerators could also note what would now be called racial classifications such as white, black, mulatto, half breed, and Indian (although no Indians were recorded). Some enumerators, such as the fur trader Alexis Bailly, who recorded Wabashaw County, and William Warren, who did Mahkahta and Wahnahta, listed no one as a half breed. In fact, the only racial categories they used were "black" and "mulatto," which meant that they classified all others as white. On the other hand, Jonathan McKusick, a 38-year-old lumberman who had arrived only the year before from Maine, listed a number of families as half breeds in his census of Washington and Itasca Counties. Probably few of the individuals he identified by this term varied in degree of Indian ancestry from many of the individuals Bailly and Warren recorded as white. In the end, the published 1850 census used only two categories: "whites"—including all those specifically described by enumerators as half breeds—and "free colored."[15]

Clearly, at the time of the 1850 census, the federal government was not concerned with identifying people of European-Indian ancestry. How many were living in the territory? Without a detailed look at the genealogies of those recorded, an actual measure is not possible. Nonetheless, a majority of those listed as being born in Minnesota and the British Red River region may have been of Dakota, Ojibwe, or other Indian ancestry. The sum of these categories suggests that people of Indian-European ancestry may have numbered as many as 2,237, or 37 percent of the territory's population. This figure includes the children of new arrivals and missionaries who had been in the region for some time, but it leaves out residents of mixed ancestry who had been born in Wisconsin, Michigan, Missouri, and other locations. In fact, statistician Joseph A. Wheelock wrote that in 1860 there were 3,475 people of mixed-Indian ancestry in the state. Since the area of the new state was smaller than that of the earlier territory, his larger figure may be the most accurate for 1850. In that case, more than 57 percent of the non-Indian population of Minnesota Territory would have been of mixed-Indian ancestry.[16]

The ways that different enumerators categorized the population of Minnesota Territory shows the contextual nature of the terms "white" and "half breed" and the way in which they evolved. Beginning in 1849, population figures were used to argue for recognition as a territory and, later, as a state. Categorizing people of mixed ancestry as white helped make the case for the territory.

Later on, however, in describing how far Minnesota had come, people like Murray minimized the white population before 1849 in order to emphasize the vast strides made by later settlers. At the same time, it was useful to stress the wild, unusual, foreign quality of the place before large numbers of whites arrived. Territorial Governor Ramsey in an 1853 speech provided an early example of this retrospective view, describing what he had seen when he first came to St. Paul four years before: "the motley humanity partially filling these streets—the blankets and painted faces of Indians, and the red sashes and moccasins of French voyageurs and half-breeds, greatly predominating over the less picturesque costume of the Anglo-American race."[17]

The early histories of Minnesota's settlement described the many "firsts" accomplished by white people—the first town, church, school, and child born— allegedly producing an orderly region of uniform whiteness in which no racial mixing took place. In these accounts, the presence or accomplishments of people of mixed background were seldom considered relevant.[18]

In reference to such accounts of firsts, George Bonga, a fur trader at Leech Lake and the grandson of a black slave at Mackinac Island who had married an Ojibwe woman, explained how he fit into the world of people who were either white or not white. Bonga "would frequently paralyze his hearers," according to territorial legislator Charles E. Flandrau, "when reminiscing by saying, 'Gentlemen, I assure you that John Banfil [an early St. Paul businessman] and myself were the first two white men that ever came into this country.'" Bonga's witty remark suggests that the term "white" was a relative one, often contrasted with either "black" or "red." In the Minnesota context, where the contrast between white and red was of prime importance, Bonga, a fur trader and, therefore, culturally non-Indian, had to be white.[19]

Other preterritorial residents of the region made other choices. Ethnographer Kohl noted that even "pure-blooded French Voyageurs" who had lived their entire lives among the Indians and intermarried with them sometimes identified themselves as *chicot* or *bois brulé*. Further, he noted, they "identified themselves with the Indians against the Anglo-Saxons," giving the example of one man who spoke nostalgically about what life was like before *les blancs,* the whites—meaning British, Scottish, Irish, and Yankees—had appeared among them. He missed most, he told Kohl, the songs that people in these communities had known and sung. It was sad, he said, that few people knew them any more.[20]

For this French Canadian, being nonwhite represented a specific society of European and Indian background, one that depended on an interactive social and economic relationship, one that was becoming less and less possible with the changes taking place in the region. Perhaps most significantly, the fur trade itself, which had given birth to this society, was ceasing to exist in its traditional form.

By the time Minnesota became a territory, native Americans were under pressure from the movement to colonize the Great Lakes country. With colonization, Indian people, who had held real power in the fur-trade era, were marginalized, no longer crucial to the survival or profit of Europeans who entered the area.

This process of marginalizing was gradual, and it began with the signing of treaties turning over title to vast areas of land to the U.S. government. Essential to the process was the participation of fur traders and other opportunistic entrepreneurs who created a new form of economic enterprise. In what historian Robert A. Trennert called the "Indian business," Indian people were still the source of profit but received little long-term benefit in return.[21]

The link between the Indian-based fur trade and the Indian business was the traditional credit system wherein Indian people were advanced a variety of trade goods in the fall to be repaid in furs throughout the fall and winter. Short-term variations in climate and in animal populations meant that it was sometimes difficult to repay debts fully. On the other hand, traders had allowed for a certain amount of unpaid credit in the rates of exchange they negotiated. Traders often forgave Indian debts because they were seldom real debts. Nonetheless, in treaties for land signed with Indian people beginning in the 1830s, large trading companies were able to persuade the federal government to allow for repayment of a variety of these often-illusory debts.[22]

For traders—including some of mixed ancestry—these payments were a windfall, an indemnity for losing their business, and the basis of a new kind of endeavor. For the government these payments were essentially a bribe or kick-back, a price that had to be paid for the cooperation of traders in negotiating the treaties. Some of the payments may have been justified, but the system spawned new kinds of traders who advanced goods to Indian people in antic-ipation of treaty signings for the sole purpose of later filing claims for inflated debts.[23]

Claims for debts were not the only ways in which traders profited from the government's system of paying Indian people for their land. Yearly disburse-ments of goods and money—called annuity payments—provided entrepreneurs with the opportunity to sell items to Indians. Being at the annuity payments also allowed traders to coerce Indian people into repaying debts. In addition, some traders and former trade employees were paid to be interpreters, farm-ers, or blacksmiths. Others were involved in government contracts to help re-settle Indian people on new lands, as required by some of the treaties.

In Minnesota Territory, the Indian business was an industry that not only profited individual companies and entrepreneurs but also fueled the fledgling economy. It was for this reason that the new territorial assembly passed, dur-ing its first session in 1849, a resolution asking the government in Washington to remove all Ojibwe living in areas that had been ceded under the treaties of 1837 and 1842. The ostensible reason for this request was to "ensure the secu-rity and tranquillity of the white settlements in an extensive and valuable dis-trict of this Territory," but the vast majority of these Ojibwe were actually liv-ing across the border in the new state of Wisconsin. Their removal would put them entirely within Minnesota Territory, up the Mississippi River from the commercial center of St. Paul.[24]

Comments by prominent participants in the Indian business make clear the hopes attached to this resolution. Former fur trader Henry M. Rice, who had made money in the late 1840s arranging for the removal of the Ho-Chunk (Winnebago) to a reservation they disliked in central Minnesota, told Gover-nor Ramsey in December 1849 that the Ojibwe who lived in Wisconsin and re-ceived their annuities at their agency at La Pointe

> should be removed from the ceded lands. They should receive their an-nuities on the Mississippi River, say at or near Sandy Lake, at which place an Agency for the whole tribe should be established. This would better ac-commodate the whole tribe and Minnesota would reap the benefit whereas now their annuities pass via Detroit and not one dollar do our inhabitants get altho' we are subject to all the annoyance given by those Indians.[25]

President Zachary Taylor ordered the removal of the Wisconsin Ojibwe into the Upper Mississippi region on February 6, 1850. A participant in the affair, Charles H. Oakes, a former American Fur Company trader on Lake Superior who was then setting up operations in St. Paul, wrote to business ally Henry H. Sibley: "I have received the appointment of removal agent for the Chippeways and hope to be able to make it profitable to the company as the employing of men, furnishing provisions and canoes &c. will necessarily be done through me."[26]

Subsequently, the whole removal effort fell apart from mismanagement and corruption on the part of government officials, not to mention the fact that many Ojibwe died from starvation and disease because of late annuity payments. Finally, the Wisconsin Ojibwe simply refused to remain in Minnesota Territory. Even then, charges made back and forth referred to the loss of potential profit. William Warren, who lived in Benton County, Minnesota Territory, and had been hired to help in the removal, stated that had it been successful, the "money would naturally have found its way down the Mississippi (the natural channel) and instead of hard times we should have had easy times, and money would have been plenty."[27]

In economic terms, what Warren referred to was the multiplier effect, the widespread result of a government expenditure on the economy. Businessmen who contracted with the government or who dealt directly with Indian people used their money to invest in real estate, to build buildings and houses, to buy, sell, and hire. Each person they paid spread the money around to others, helping to create a Minnesota economy, though little long-term benefit accrued to Indian people themselves.

Understanding of this multiplier effect is evident in a local saying from the early 1850s. As the *Minnesota Pioneer* reported on August 8, 1850: "One would suppose by the promises about town, that the Indian payment would square every debt in Minnesota, but the 'debt of Nature.' Every reply to a dun is, 'after the payment.' "

Alexander Ramsey, in an address to the 1851 legislature, put the matter succinctly: "The payments of the Indian annuities supply much the larger portion of our current currency, and through the various channels of trade contribute greatly to our prosperity." Five years later the *St. Paul Advertiser* provided more detail:

A few years ago the Indian Payments were the great event of the year in Minnesota. Everything in financial matters dated from and was referred to the Indian Payments; almost our whole specie currency was derived from this source. Notes fell due and Grocer's bills matured at the Indian Payment. The persistent dun, the wife's new dress, the ball, the workman, and the new hat, were put off till "after payment."

The article stated that annuity payments—regardless of the welfare of the Indian people who were supposed to benefit from them—were "one of the grand resources of Minnesota," discussed along with "vague hints of exhaustless coal fields and rich lead mines on the Minnesota, and perennial supplies of imaginary pumpkins, two feet in diameter."[28]

Statistics for the 1850s show the importance of Indian expenditures. In his 1860 compilation, J. A. Wheelock stated that from 1849 to 1859 the federal government expended $4.2 million to "fulfill Treaty obligations with Indian tribes." This amounted to more than $380,000 per year, although particular treaties affected the amount each year in different ways. By comparison, expenditures supporting the territorial government, building military roads, and erecting lighthouses and military posts amounted to only $1.2 million, or an average of $120,000 per year, for the same period. No private enterprise in the Minnesota region at the beginning of the 1850s could match the value obtained yearly from Indian expenditures. In 1849 one of the largest of the new businesses, lumbering in the St. Croix River Valley, produced logs worth an estimated $150,000. It was not until 1855 that the annual production exceeded $380,000 per year.[29]

By 1856, when other industries had come to rival Indian-related government expenditures, the *St. Paul Advertiser* noted that the expenditures had been important in a population of no more than 30,000 "nibbling for the most part on the edges of the Indian trade." But now that the region's population was 150,000 people involved in "agriculture, manufactures and commerce," no one cared when or where the Indians were paid. According to the newspaper, a single week's business in St. Paul exceeded the yearly payment in cash of $90,000 to the Dakota.[30]

It is clear from this evidence that Indian people, through the money due them for their land, were key in providing an early boost for the Minnesota economy. Without them, economic development would have been greatly slowed. Besides this boost, Indian expenditures shaped Minnesota politics in the territory's initial years. Its key figures—people like Sibley and Rice—owed their economic standing to the profits they made in the Indian business and their political power to their ability to deliver the Indian expenditures to the larger community. Most of the men involved in the Indian business and the political power connected to it were Democrats, as were most Indian traders, a result of the party's long-term control of Indian policy in Washington.[31]

In the early 1850s in Minnesota the major political contests were between Democratic factions eager to have the largest share of the pie. An example was the recurrent competition between Sibley and Rice who, essentially, sought the same political results but differed as to who would receive the economic benefits. The *Minnesota Chronicle and Register* once commented that a controversy over Rice's contract for the removal of the Ho-Chunk in 1850 did not warrant making political capital, since it was simply a "personal quarrel between two rival parties of Indian traders. . . . One party *wanted* the contract—the other *got* it."[32]

Even non-Democrats such as Ramsey, the Whig-appointed territorial governor and superintendent of Indian affairs, participated tacitly, if not always eagerly, in this profitable relationship between politics and the Indian business. In January 1853 the *St. Paul Democrat* condemned the "conclave" of Ramsey and Sibley in the "Sioux Frauds," the wholesale distribution of Indian money from the Dakota treaties of 1851 to a variety of traders.[33] Only with the appointment of Ramsey's replacement did successful opposition develop not only to the letting of particular contracts and the distribution of treaty money in certain ways but to the more general, widespread practice of mixing business and Indian policy.

The 1853 election of a new Democratic president, Franklin Pierce, brought reform to many policies of previous administrations. Instrumental in carrying out these changes in Minnesota Territory was the new governor, Willis A. Gorman, a lawyer, former and future military officer, and congressman, who was appointed in March. From the beginning, Gorman made it clear that he was unhappy with the way in which Indian policy had been carried out in Minnesota. He sought to cut off the access by businessmen of his own party to federal Indian money.

In the summer of 1853 Gorman took part in a congressional investigation of Ramsey's actions in negotiating the Dakota treaties of 1851. On August 8, 1853, Gorman negotiated a new treaty with the Ho-Chunk that shifted their reservation to a location more to their liking and left out payments to traders for past debts. That fall he took steps to terminate remnants of the policy of forcing Wisconsin Ojibwe to move to Minnesota.[34]

Needless to say, by the end of 1853 Gorman had earned many enemies in his own party, particularly Rice, who had been elected in October to replace Sibley as territorial delegate in Congress.[35] Rice was able to block ratification of the Ho-Chunk treaty, and rumors were circulating in Washington that Gorman's power over Indian matters would be curtailed by a separation of the duties of territorial governor and superintendent of Indian affairs, something that had been accomplished in other territories.

Gorman wrote to an official in Washington explaining the difficulties he had encountered in Minnesota due to his opposition to the people who had "fattened for 25 years upon the Indians and the U.S. Treasury." He stated: "These men are evidently in hopes of getting some one here who can be used by them. Now I need not tell you that there is or has been more fraud and cheating in the Indian trade in the Territory than it has been my lot to see or know of any where else on earth." This "interest," he explained, was represented by

Rice. When he first arrived in the territory, Gorman had supported Rice's election as territorial delegate because they were fellow Democrats. But Rice had claims against the Ho-Chunk that he sought to have included in the treaty, and Gorman had not backed him. Gorman stated: "I don't suit him. I have declined his overtures in Indian matters."[36]

Changes in the territory's population provided more backing for Gorman's positions. Between 1855 and 1857 the population grew from 40,000 to 150,000. These new settlers came primarily from the Middle Atlantic states, New England, and the Midwest. While figures from the pre-statehood census of 1857 have not been compiled, the influx from these regions is apparent in the 1860 federal census, taken after an additional 22,000 people had arrived in Minnesota. At that date, individuals from the three regions (excluding Minnesota) totaled 75,499, or 44 percent of the state's population. These individuals settled in large numbers in southeastern Minnesota and became the base for the new Republican Party, begun in the state in 1855. Despite being a Democrat, Gorman aligned himself with the Republicans in a major debate of the time concerning the ultimate borders of Minnesota, the state-to-be.[37]

The impressive growth in Minnesota's population created an impetus for statehood. In pushing for it, congressional delegate Rice favored a new western boundary roughly like the current one. In the territory, however, there was a strong sentiment, especially among southern Minnesotans, in favor of dividing it along an east-west line around the 45th (just north of the Twin Cities) or 46th parallels (just north of Little Falls).[38]

Economic interests shaped the opposing positions. For businessmen based in St. Paul with backgrounds in the Indian trade, like Rice and his supporters, the north-south state would include a vast northern region where the trade that had brought them money and power could continue. To keep profiting from the intersection of business and Indian money, Rice himself needed to have political power in the same governmental entity in which he carried on trade.

The many newcomers and Republicans in southern Minnesota, who believed the future lay in agriculture, saw that a horizontally shaped state would isolate St. Paul near the northern border and strengthen the hand of agricultural interests. Governor Gorman aligned himself with the Republicans on this issue, a logical extension of his opposition to the corruption endemic in the Indian business.

These new political interests did not seek to eliminate any role for federal government in fostering private enterprise. Rather, they sought their subsidies in different ways such as railroad grants, another important issue at the time. The capital-removal bill that Rolette confiscated was still another example. Not content to wait for action in Washington, Gorman and the Republicans sought to further their position by moving the capital of the territory to a town more centrally located in the state they hoped to create: St. Peter, on the Minnesota River. Gorman himself invested in the company hoping to develop the new capital—a form of graft and a conflict of interest or simply an indication of the depth of his feeling, depending on how one looked at it. Gorman was quoted in the *Daily Minnesotian* as saying that he hoped to see "grass grow in the business streets of St. Paul in two years."[39] The bill passed both houses of the assembly and seemed poised for signing. It was then, according to the legend of Joe Rolette, that the "jolly half breed" performed his heroic acts.

The many and varied versions of Rolette's adventures bear the mark of continuous telling and retelling during the late-nineteenth century. There are so many versions of the story that it is difficult to know what actually happened in 1857 and what was embroidered by later storytellers. It is also not always clear whose purposes were served by the various versions and emphases on particular aspects of the legend. It is worthwhile examining some of the patterns to see what was included as well as what was left out.

A major feature of some accounts is the suggestion that Rolette was a rough frontiersman. This is hard to match with the actual experiences of his life. His father was a successful and well-educated trader from French Canada, responsible for the American Fur Company's entire upper Mississippi region in the 1820s. As a boy, Joseph had been educated at a private school in New York City, under the protection of American Fur Company president Ramsay Crooks. Whatever the details of his experience in New York, it is hard to believe the accuracy of the legend that describes Rolette arriving there dressed in a full suit of buckskin and carrying a rifle over his shoulder.[40]

An equally misleading part of the Rolette legend is the suggestion that he was a half breed or mixed blood. Political journalist and historian Harlan P. Hall noted that, though he was "commonly supposed to be a half or quarter breed Frenchman," he was instead a "full-blooded French Canadian." More recently, historian Rhoda R. Gilman wrote that Rolette's heritage was almost entirely French and British, his "only traceable Indian ancestor being an Ottawa great-great-great-grandmother."[41]

Rolette's association with the Pembina community began in the 1840s, following the completion of his education, when he went to work for Sibley in the crucial northern border region along the Red River where the American Fur Company competed with the British Hudson's Bay Company. Rolette appears to have done his job well and was instrumental in initiating the commerce involving Red River oxcart trains bringing furs and buffalo skins from the northern plains to St. Paul. It was this commerce that essentially made St. Paul the key commercial center of the region.[42]

Rolette's tie to the Pembina community came about in part through his marriage to a métis woman, Angélique Jerome, following a pattern traditional for traders interested in carrying on business with native communities.[43] Associated in business with Sibley, Rolette was in a good position to be a broker, delivering benefits from Sibley to the métis and political support from the large métis community to Sibley.

The 1850 census gives some indication of the size of the métis population, showing 1,134 people living in Pembina County—almost 19 percent of the territory's entire population. Not all county residents were métis; while some were listed as being born at Pembina, many others were natives of the British Red River colony or eastern Canada. One way or another, by the standards of Johann Kohl's Lake Superior informants, they appear to have identified culturally and politically with the interests that Joseph Rolette represented.[44]

From the beginning of the territory, the métis sought to influence the new government. A petition from the "Half-Breeds of Pembina," sent sometime in 1849 and signed by a number of people including Rolette, asked Governor Ramsey to use his influence to establish courts and civil officials in the region, to exclude British subjects from hunting there, to erect a fort to protect the border, and to arrange for the sale of land from Indians to the métis so that residents could obtain clear title to their land.[45]

Despite their interest in government, not all of the people of the Pembina region were able to participate in the initial elections of territorial legislators. The congressional act providing for the organization of the territory stated that voters in the first election were limited to "free white male inhabitants" over the age of 21 who had lived in the territory when the act was passed and were citizens of the United States. The territorial legislature was empowered to determine voter qualifications in later elections. In the fall of 1849 a bill passed that provided that "all persons [men] of a mixture of white and Indian blood and who shall have adopted the habits and customs of civilized men, are hereby declared to be entitled to all the rights and privileges" of voting.[46]

If not immediately represented among the white voters of the territory, the métis were also not categorized as Indian people able to participate in treaty-making. As a result of the prompting in the métis petition, the federal government, in 1851, authorized Ramsey to negotiate the purchase of land in the Pembina region. When he arrived there he discovered that the métis wished to be signatories of the treaty, alleging, according to Ramsey, "that it was they who possessed the Country really, and who had long defended and maintained it against the encroachments of enemies." Ramsey wrote that "on the policy of the government and the impracticability of its treating with its own quasi citizens being explained to them, they were satisfied that their demands could not be complied with." Nonetheless, Ramsey saw that the treaty included a provision allowing this "interesting and peculiar people" in a "peculiar situation" to receive $30,000. Unfortunately for the métis, the Pembina treaty failed to pass Congress in 1852.[47]

Ramsey's dealings with these "peculiar" "quasi citizens" is in keeping with the general inability of other European Americans to know what to make of the métis but to make use of them when needed. This may explain why the law was passed in 1849 allowing people of mixed ancestry to vote. The Pembina district, represented by Joseph Rolette and his fellow trader Norman Kittson beginning in 1852, provided support to Sibley's "conclave" in the territorial legislature. In 1853, for example, Rolette took pleasure in reporting to Sibley's brother Frederick that he had prevented Rice from receiving many votes in Pembina.[48]

Rolette's legislative career between 1852 and 1857 has never been explored in much detail. One memorable anecdote is Murray's account of Kittson's and Rolette's first trip to the legislature in January 1852, an 18-day journey by dogsled. "For the first few days of the session it was hard to tell whether it was the dogs or the honorable members who represented Pembina, as the dogs were the first in the legislative halls and the last to leave, and it was only when the sergeant at arms was ordered to put the dogs out and keep them out, as Pembina was not entitled to double representation, that the two houses were relieved of their presence."[49]

In contrast to this light-hearted story, some of Rolette's actions as a territorial legislator suggest that he tried to further the interests of people of Indian ancestry in the region. On January 18, 1856, for example, Rolette introduced a memorial to Congress calling for changes in federal laws in order to extend citizenship to Indian people who had altered their "habits and mode of life." Written in the rhetoric of the time, which equated patterns of subsistence and types of clothing with civilization, the resolution stated, "By granting the right of citizenship . . . a great step would be gained in the progress of the tribes around us, in the path of civilization." The memorial noted that although an Indian person "assumed the dress of the white man, and by his industry has opened himself a farm," as he might have been urged by missionaries and other whites, he could not under current law own the land on which he farmed or "enjoy any of the many franchises [*sic*] and privileges which his mode of life and knowledge of our institutions should secure to him." It is not known how much of the resolution Rolette actually wrote, but the memorial, which passed both bodies of the territorial legislature, clearly reflected the belief common among people of mixed ancestry that cultural attributes were more important than so-called racial background.[50]

In addition, Rolette did not initially agree with Rice's 1856 proposal for the north-south shape of the state-to-be. His reaction was based on his relationship with the community he represented. At the beginning of 1856 he introduced a resolution calling for a division of the territory on an east-west line, apparently on the theory, as chronicler Arthur J. Larsen wrote, that this "would place his district in a commanding position in the northern half." The measure was defeated.[51]

Exactly how or in what way Rolette came to change his position on the borders is not clear. His motivation for carrying off the capital bill is left vague in most accounts. This ambiguity is a necessary part of the legend.

Contrary to many versions of the story, Rolette did not actually steal the bill, since, as chairman of the Territorial Council's Committee on Enrolled Bills, he had rightful possession of it after it passed. His duty was simply to certify the text so that it could be sent to the governor for signing. When the bill came into his hands on or before Saturday, February 28, 1857, Rolette simply stayed away from the proceedings. While he was gone, a call of the Council was issued, requiring the presence of all members. Since Rolette could not be found, the Council was prevented from taking further action unless a two-thirds vote dispensed with the call. Since this vote fell one short, the Council was required to remain in session during the call, day and night, until 1:00 P.M. Thursday, March 5—a total of 123 hours. The journal of the final session on March 7 contains a report stating that the Committee on Enrolled Bills had been unable to report back the bill "owing to the absence of the Chairman," that is, Rolette, who was one of the report's signers. Further, the committee related that "numerous errors" were found in comparing copies of the bill. The committee therefore retained the bill in its possession "subject to the order of the Council."[52]

Some variations in the versions of the legend concern minor details, such as which hotel and in which room Rolette stayed during the 123 hours. More significant were the disagreements about the degree of planning and purpose he exhibited and whether or not other powerful people in St. Paul were involved in his actions. Usually this part of the story is murky.

Clearly, what Rolette did was in the interests of St. Paul. During the time he was missing, a duplicate copy of the bill was passed and signed by the governor. Later on in the year, a St. Paul judge ruled that the bill had not properly passed. It is probable that, had it passed in the normal manner, grounds would have been found to overrule it for other reasons.[53]

Nonetheless, most versions of the legend insist that Rolette acted spontaneously. Hall stated, "It is due both Rolette and the citizens of St. Paul to say that no previous or corrupt arrangement was made with him to perform the role which was enacted." Charles Flandrau—despite his description of Rolette's "free and easy, half-savage characteristics"—made clear that he acted in his own interests as well as those of the business community of which he was a part: "It was at this point in the fight that Rolette proved himself a bold and successful strategist. He was a friend of St. Paul, and was determined that the plan should not succeed if it was possible for him to prevent it." J. Fletcher Williams suggested that for Rolette, who had seen the opposition to the bill in St. Paul, "a wink was as good to him as a nod." Historian William Watts Folwell, on the other hand, implied that Rolette was put up to his actions by influential people: "Of a romantic and jovial disposition, he was not at all averse to playing the part assigned him in this little drama." It is unclear whether Folwell was writing in a flowery manner or meant that the events had been scripted by someone else. In any case, although the accounts differ as to the degree of planning or participation, it is clear that many people in St. Paul knew what Rolette was doing while he was doing it.[54]

One way or another, the emphasis in all these stories is that Rolette was an unreflective, humorous, fun-loving, carousing, rough frontiersman—occasionally a half breed or mixed blood. These are the crucial details that help explain the Rolette legend and its hold on post-territorial Minnesota history.

Writing of classical legends, Henry David Thoreau stated, "To some extent mythology is only the most ancient history and biography. So far from being false or fabulous in the common sense, it contains only enduring and essential truth, the I and you, the here and there, the now and then, being omitted."[55]

For each generation, legends based on real and invented historical figures serve particular truths and memorialize particular views of the world. More than simply the story of a trickster, the Rolette legend describes a culture hero of the kind found in the literature of many societies: one who performs significant deeds out of hunger, curiosity, or recklessness; a primitive entrepreneur who makes possible the world as it is known and then obligingly disappears.[56]

The truths that Rolette serves come out of the historical context of territorial Minnesota: the replacement of one cultural system by another, rival politicians seeking to capture Indian payments for the local economy, attempts by later reformers to close off this mixture of money and politics (in order to replace it with other forms of business-government collusion), and debates about the shape of the state-to-be. The Rolette legend is, largely, nonpartisan. It serves the purposes of both sides, providing each with a vehicle to record its own views of the world and the nature of territorial Minnesota.

For legislators and St. Paulites who wanted the city to remain the commercial center of the state and who owed their success to the Indian business, the legend's characterization of Rolette is a useful one. Perhaps most significantly, it absolves influential and ordinary people from any accountability for a reckless, illegal action that deprived a democratic majority in both legislative houses of the right to pass a bill that the governor was ready to sign. While it would have been better for the drama had Rolette actually been a half breed, it was enough for him to play the part. This identification provided a cultural or racial cover for the actions that Rolette took, in the same way that a group of English colonists in Boston in 1775 dressed as Indians to protest the stamp tax while throwing tea into Boston Harbor.

It was equally useful for those who opposed the role of the Indian traders in Minnesota Territory to categorize Rolette as a reckless half breed. Half breeds symbolized the society that had existed before 1849, as well as the power of the businessmen associated with the Indian trade. One opponent of this power structure later wrote: "Such was the mixed character of the population at the time that a large proportion of the citizens were either by ties of consanguinity, or trading interest, allied to the Indians and their interests; and these were known and designated as the 'Moccasin Democracy or Indian Dynasty.'" Thus, opposition to a certain set of political positions became associated with race and an assertion of white identity. It was easy to blame "half breeds" like Rolette, even though his action benefited mixed bloods less than it did powerful figures in the community, people like Rice and Sibley whose corruption was anything but fun-loving and who would go on to become revered founding fathers in the story of Minnesota.[57]

Another event of 1857 shows how the so-called half breeds were both used to further the assertion of white identity and blamed for actions that, in fact, benefited the territory's elite. In October 1857 Sibley, running against Ramsey, was elected the first state governor. Commentator Hall noted that the election was extremely close; the many contested ballots in the southern part of the state, as they were counted, put the result in doubt though suggesting strongly that Ramsey would win. When the election results were received from the Cass and Pembina districts, "where Joe Rolette reigned supreme," the tally was "very unanimous for Sibley, giving him in Pembina 316 votes and in Cass 228, while Ramsey did not receive a vote in either county." This helped provide the final majority of 240 for Sibley.[58]

Hall implied that these results were fraudulent, not because they were tampered with, as the unanimous result might suggest. Rather, he explained, the territorial election law, providing that people of mixed white and Indian ancestry "who shall have adopted the habits and customs of civilized men" would be allowed to vote "practically conferred the right of suffrage upon all the [male] half-breeds in the territory." Hall alleged that this provision was interpreted by election judges to mean that "half-breeds wearing pantaloons filled the requirement. A tradition has come down to later generations to the effect that one pair of pants would do service for a swarm of half-breeds. One would don the trousers and go out and vote, and, soon coming back, passed the garment over to the next man, while he resumed his breech clout and blanket."[59]

Despite his intended slur on people of mixed ancestry, Hall suggested that allowing them to vote was a necessity: "But what else could you do? We had to have a governor, and inhabitants of Scandinavian countries had not then moved into Minnesota. Consequently, somebody had to do the voting, and in the emergency the half-breed, if he could borrow a pair of pants, was as good as anybody else." Hall's implication was that, by 1904 when he was writing, the emergency was past. Scandinavians were achieving political power. Minnesota had become "white," a region with a reinvented past that did not include Indian people or the Europeans who had lived with them in an era of interdependence. Race had become all-important. In this new Minnesota there was little room for the complex identity of people of mixed ancestry. Instead, the half breed would become a historical character, a transitional figure in the evolution of the frontier, a creature of legend, a symbol of a time when Minnesota had not attained its later state of whiteness.

Rolette personally shared the fate of the preterritorial Minnesota he symbolized. Having served the purposes of the rich and powerful, he died in 1871 without political power, in obscure but colorful celebrity. From the revisionist point of view of those who have written much of Minnesota's history in the last 150 years, Joe Rolette, like Indians, half breeds, fur traders, voyageurs, and other beings of the mythic prehistory of Minnesota, lives forever, but only in stereotype and legend.[60]

NOTES
From Minnesota History *56 (Winter, 1998–99).*

1. The author would like to thank Alan Woolworth for help in researching this topic, Rhoda Gilman for her help and encouragement, and Ken Mitchell, Brian Horrigan, Andrea Cutting, and David Hacker for their help in compiling the statistics.
    Major versions of the Rolette legend based on the memories of his contemporaries include Manton Marble, "To the Red River and Beyond," *Harper's New Monthly Magazine* 21 (Oct. 1860): 582; T. M. Newson, *Pen Pictures of St. Paul, Minnesota* (St. Paul: the author, 1886), 683–85; "Joseph Rolette," *Northwest Magazine*, Feb. 1888, p. 22; "Jolly Jo Rolette," *St. Paul Dispatch*, Feb. 10, 1894; H. P. Hall, "Observations," *Minneapolis Journal*, Apr. 13, 1896, and *Observations: Being More or Less a History of Political Contests in Minnesota from 1849 to 1904* (St. Paul: n.p., 1904), 28–36; Charles E. Flandrau, *The History of Minnesota and Tales of the Frontier* (St. Paul: E. W. Porter, 1900), 358–64; William B. Dean, "A History of the Capitol Buildings of Minnesota, with Some Account of the Struggles for Their Location," in *Minnesota Historical Society Collections* 12 (St. Paul, 1908): 9–15; "Bill for Removal of Capital," *St. Paul Dispatch*, May 3, 1911. One version for young people is Roy P. Johnson, "Joe Rolette and the Capital Scandal," in *Gopher Reader*, ed. A. Hermina Poatgieter and James T. Dunn (St. Paul: Minnesota Historical Society [MHS], 1966), 263–65. Newspaperman Merle Potter included the Rolette legend as the first in his well-known *101 Best Stories of Minnesota* (Minneapolis: Harrison and Smith Co., 1931), 1–3.

2. *St. Paul Dispatch*, Feb. 10, 1894.

3. On the educational functions of such stories, see Thomas W. Overholt and J. Baird Callicott, *Clothed-in-Fur: An Introduction to an Ojibwa World View* (Washington, D.C.: University Press of America, 1982), 25–26, 145–46; Stith Thompson, *The Folktale* (Berkeley: University of California Press, 1977), 319, 386.

4. John Wesley Bond, *Minnesota and Its Resources* (New York: Redfield, 1853), 1.

5. William P. Murray, "Recollections of Early Territorial Days and Legislation," in *Minnesota Historical Society Collections* 12 (St. Paul, 1908): 103. Many travelers' accounts emphasized the dangers posed by Indian people, often greatly exaggerated. See Bruce M. White, "Encounters with Spirits: Ojibwa and Dakota Theories about the French and Their Merchandise," *Ethnohistory* 41 (Summer 1994): 387–89.

6. Alexander Ramsey, in an 1853 speech to the legislature, made the common assumption that settlers were farmers: "The whole country . . . has the deepest interest in increasing the amount of this cultivation; and the most effectual way of doing this would seem to be by gratuitous grants of land in limited quantities to actual settlers"; Minnesota Territory, *Journal of the House*, 1853, p. 70.

7. Frederick Jackson Turner, *The Frontier in American History* (New York: Henry Holt and Co., 1920), 3.

8. On the cultural attributes of the term "white" and its meaning in nineteenth-century America, see David R. Roediger, *The Wages of Whiteness: Race and the Making of the American Working Class* (London: Verso, 1991); Reginald Horsman, *Race and Manifest Destiny: The Origins of American Racial Anglo-Saxonism* (Cambridge, Mass.: Harvard University Press, 1981), 154–55, 189.

9. Murray, "Recollections," 12: 103–04. Murray's claim of 4,680 whites does not match the commonly accepted total of 4,535; see William W. Folwell, *A History of Minnesota* (St. Paul: MHS, 1956), 1:351–52.

10. On such intermarriage, see Jennifer S. H. Brown, *Strangers in Blood: Fur Trade Company Families in Indian Country* (Vancouver: University of British Columbia Press, 1980), 51–110; Sylvia Van Kirk, *"Many Tender Ties": Women in Fur-Trade Society, 1670–1870* (Norman: University of Oklahoma Press, 1983), 74–94; Bruce M. White, "The Woman Who Married a Beaver: Trade Patterns and Gender Roles in the Ojibwa Fur Trade," forthcoming in *Ethnohistory*. For the history and origins of the mixed Indian-European society in the Great Lakes, see Jacqueline Peterson, "The People In Between: Indian-White Marriage and the Genesis of a Métis Society and Culture in the Great Lakes Region, 1680–1830" (Ph.D. diss., University of Illinois, 1981).

11. The term "freemen" was used to describe former fur-trade employees not under contract to large companies who continued to reside in Indian country; see Jacqueline Peterson and Jennifer S. H. Brown, eds., *The New Peoples: Being and Becoming Métis in North America* (Winnipeg: University of Manitoba Press, 1985), 81, 176.

12. Johann G. Kohl, *Kitchi-Gami: Life Among the Lake Superior Ojibwe* (1860; reprint, St. Paul: MHS Press, 1985), 260. For one of the earliest uses of "métis" in this context, see Edmund C. Bray and Martha C. Bray, eds., *Joseph Nicollet on the Plains and Prairies: The Expeditions of 1838–39 With Journals, Letters, and Notes on the Dakota Indians* (St. Paul: MHS Press, 1976), 187–89. See also John Francis McDermott, *A Glossary of Mississippi Valley French, 1673–1850*, Washington University Studies, New Series, No. 12 (St. Louis, 1941), 103. "Métis" is now sometimes used to refer to all people of mixed Indian-European ancestry.

13. William Warren, "Adventures among the Blackfeet Indians," *Minnesota Chronicle and Register* (St. Paul), Feb. 23, 1850.

14. For estimates of Indian population, see Table 1, originally published with this article in *Minnesota History* 56 (Winter 1998–99), 182. For the non-Indian census, see Patricia C. Harpole and Mary D. Nagle, eds., *Minnesota Territorial Census, 1850* (St. Paul: MHS, 1972), viii–ix. In 1862 statistician Joseph A. Wheelock explained, "The United States census does not regard the Indian tribes as a social constituent of the nation, and therefore takes no account of them in their tribal or savage state"; Minnesota Bureau of Statistics, *Minnesota: Its Progress and Capabilities* (St. Paul: William R. Marshall, 1862), 106–07.

15. Harpole and Nagle, eds., *Minnesota Territorial Census*, viii, 71–99; *United States Census, 1850*, p. 993, 996.

16. Minnesota Bureau of Statistics, *Minnesota*, 107. On birthplaces of non-Indian Minnesotans, see Table 2, *Minnesota History* 56:183.

17. Minnesota Territory, *Journal of the House*, 1853, p. 74.

18. See, for example, Edward D. Neill, *History of Washington County and the St. Croix Valley* (Minneapolis: North Star Publishing Co., 1881), 255. Neill also describes a "settlement of half-breeds," all unnamed, at Lakeland.

19. Charles E. Flandrau, "Reminiscences of Minnesota during the Territorial Period," in *Minnesota Historical Society Collections* 9 (St. Paul, 1901): 199, which states that Bonga was unaware of any categories except white and Indian, suggesting that his statement was naive. It is hard to imagine this to be the case. Bonga was not an ignorant man; like other children of North West Company traders, he was educated in Montreal. As a trader, he sought to imitate the lifestyle of a North West Company bourgeois.

20. Kohl, *Kitchi-Gami*, 260–61.

21. Robert A. Trennert Jr., *Indian Traders on the Middle Border: The House of Ewing, 1827–54* (Lincoln: University of Nebraska Press, 1981), 205–10.

22. Royce Kurtz, "Looking at the Ledgers: Sauk and Mesquakie Trade Debts," in Jennifer S. H. Brown, W. J. Eccles, and Donald P. Heldman, eds., *The Fur Trade Revisited: Selected Papers of the Sixth North American Fur Trade Conference, Mackinac Island, Michigan, 1991* (East Lansing: Michigan State University Press, 1994), 143–59; Trennert, *Indian Traders*, 110. Under the 1837 treaty with the Ojibwe, $70,000 and "other just demands" for claims were included to be paid to traders William A. Aitkin and Lyman M. Warren. A schedule of 55 claims totaling $75,000 was included in the 1842 treaty, some $24,000 of this for John Jacob Astor and another $13,000 for the American Fur Company; Charles J. Kappler, comp., *Indian Affairs. Laws and Treaties* (Washington, D.C.: Government Printing Office, 1904), 2: 482–85, 542–45.

23. For commentary about the newer traders, see, for example, Samuel W. Pond, *The Dakota or Sioux in Minnesota As They Were in 1834* (1908; reprint, St. Paul: MHS Press, 1986), 173.

24. Minnesota Territorial Assembly, Resolution, Oct. 11, 1849, in Office of Indian Affairs, Letters Received, Minnesota Superintendency, National Archives microfilm M234, Roll 428, Frames 124–28, copy in MHS; Bruce M. White, "The Regional Context of the Removal Order of 1850," report prepared for the Mille Lacs Band of Ojibwe for *Mille Lacs v. Minnesota*, Dec. 1993, forthcoming in James McClurken, comp., *Fish in the Lakes, Wild Rice, and Game in Abundance: Testimony on Behalf of Mille Lacs Ojibwe Hunting and Fishing Rights*.

25. At the same time, Rice was campaigning to remove the Menominee as well; Rice to Ramsey, Dec. 1, 1849, in Alexander Ramsey Papers, microfilm edition, Roll 4, Frame 284, MHS.

26. White, "Removal Order"; Kappler, comp., *Indian Affairs, Laws and Treaties* (1941), 5:663; Charles Oakes to Henry H. Sibley, June 14, 1850, in Henry H. Sibley Papers, microfilm edition, Roll 7, Frame 379, MHS.

27. *Minnesota Democrat* (St. Paul), Dec. 9, 1851.

28. *St. Paul Advertiser*, Dec. 6, 1856.

29. Minnesota Bureau of Statistics, *Minnesota: Its Place Among the States* (Hartford: Case, Lockwood, and Co., 1860), 168. These values are based on William H. C. Folsom's estimate that timber cut in the St. Croix Valley was worth $3 per thousand feet of logs; see Folsom, "Lumbering in the St. Croix Valley, with Biographic Sketches," in *Minnesota Historical Society Collections* 9 (St. Paul, 1901): 321–23.

30. *St. Paul Advertiser*, Dec. 6, 1856.

31. Charles D. Gilfillan, "The Early Political History of Minnesota," in *Minnesota Historical Society Collections* 9: 177.

32. *Minnesota Chronicle and Register*, June 10, 1850.

33. *St. Paul Democrat,* Jan. 12, 1853.

34. Folwell, *History of Minnesota,* 1:462–70, 478–82.

35. Folwell, *History of Minnesota,* 1: 373.

36. Gorman to unnamed, Dec. 17, 1853, in Willis A. Gorman and Family Papers, MHS.

37. Folwell, *History of Minnesota,* 1: 360, 375; Arthur J. Larsen, "Admission to the Union," *Minnesota History* 14 (June 1933): 159; John G. Rice, "The Old-Stock Americans," in *They Chose Minnesota: A Survey of the State's Ethnic Groups,* ed. June D. Holmquist (St. Paul: MHS Press, 1981), 59, 62. On racial makeup and birthplaces of Minnesotans in 1860, see Tables 4 and 5, *Minnesota History* 56:188.

38. Here and two paragraphs below, Larsen, "Admission," 157.

39. *Daily Minnesotian* (St. Paul), Mar. 3, 1857.

40. Rhoda R. Gilman, Carolyn Gilman, and Deborah M. Stultz, *The Red River Trails: Oxcart Routes Between St. Paul and the Selkirk Settlement, 1820–1870* (St. Paul: MHS, 1979), 18; *St. Paul Dispatch,* Feb. 10, 1894.

41. Hall, *Observations,* 28; Gilman et al., *Red River Trails,* 18. For a description of Rolette as a mixed blood, see Folwell, *History of Minnesota,* 1: 386.

42. Gilman et al., *Red River Trails,* 11; *St. Paul Dispatch,* Feb. 10, 1894; J. Fletcher Williams, *A History of the City of Saint Paul to 1875* (1876; reprint, St. Paul: MHS Press, 1983), 160.

43. Although her obituary, *Kittson County Enterprise,* Feb. 16, 1906, and many other sources list her name as Angelie, the parish register of Assumption Church, Pembina, N.D., (original in possession of church) consistently spells it Angélique. See, for example, the entry for the baptism of her son Henry, Sept. 19, 1857. A note on her photograph, donated to MHS in 1909, states that her first name was Angeline and that she was of Cree and French blood.

44. *U.S. Census,* 1850, p. 993.

45. Minnesota Territory, *Journal of the Council,* 1849, p. 197–99.

46. Minnesota Territory, *Acts, Joint Resolutions, and Memorials,* 1849, p. 6. For the act creating the territory, see Minnesota Territory, *Journal of the House,* 1849, p. 188–93.

47. Alexander Ramsey to A. H. Stuart, Nov. 7, 1851, in Office of Indian Affairs, Letters Received, Minnesota Superintendency microfilm M234, Roll 428, Frames 371–80; Folwell, *History of Minnesota,* 1: 290–91, 305.

48. Gilman et al., *Red River Trails,* 18; Joseph Rolette Jr. to F. B. Sibley, Sept. 20, 1853, Sibley papers.

49. Murray, "Recollections," 118–19.

50. Minnesota Territory, *Journal of the Council,* 1856, p. 72, and *Session Laws,* 1856, p. 354.

51. Larsen, "Admission," 158. The title or text of Rolette's resolution has not been found.

52. Minnesota Territory, *Journal of the Council,* 1857, p. 176–84.

53. Folwell, *History of Minnesota,* 1: 386–87.

54. Hall, *Minneapolis Journal,* Apr. 13, 1896; Flandrau, *Minnesota and Tales of Frontier,* 359–60; Williams, *History of St. Paul,* 370; Folwell, *History of Minnesota,* 1: 384, 386.

55. Henry David Thoreau, *A Week on the Concord and Merrimack Rivers* (New York: Signet Classic, 1961), 60.

56. On culture heroes and their roles in Indian creation myths, see Thompson, *Folktale,* 305, 307–08, 310–18.

57. [James A. Starkey], "Reminiscences of Indian Depredations: The Sunrise Expedition," *North-Western Chronotype* (St. Paul), 1 (July 1873): 50. A statue of Henry M. Rice was

enshrined in Statuary Hall at the capitol in Washington, D.C., on Feb. 8, 1916; see *Minnesota History Bulletin* 1 (May 1916): 339–40.

58. Hall, *Observations,* 50; Bruce M. White et al., comps., *Minnesota Votes: Election Returns by County for Presidents, Senators, Congressmen, and Governors,* 1857–1977 (St. Paul: MHS, 1977), 153.

59. Here and below, Hall, *Observations,* 51–52.

60. On Rolette's celebrity status after 1857, see *St. Paul Pioneer and Democrat,* Oct. 4, 1859; Marble, "Red River," 582. His death date is reported in *St. Paul Dispatch,* Feb. 10, 1894.

WAR

"Indeed We Did Fight":
A Soldier's Letters from the First Battle of Bull Run

EDITED BY EDWARD G. LONGACRE

As the Civil War broke out in April 1861, Minnesota Governor Alexander Ramsey was in Washington, D. C., and immediately offered Minnesota troops for the Union side. Within two weeks the First Minnesota was created, and more than nine hundred men eventually joined the regiment. These three letters were written by Jasper Searles of Hastings at the start of the First's three-year term of duty. The letters portray the enthusiasm, ideals, and innocence of the twenty-year-old Searles as he sets off to Washington with his regiment. The first battle of Bull Run on July 21, 1861, quickly ended that innocence. Union forces panicked and chaotically retreated to Washington, overrunning the civilians who had been picnicking on the surrounding hillsides watching the fray. The illusion the war would be short was gone and the country was hurled into our greatest national crisis.

INTRODUCTION

In the spring and summer of 1861, when the North went to war at least in part to preserve the Union, the First Minnesota Volunteer Infantry went with it— and with the First Minnesota went Jasper N. Searles of Hastings. An intelligent and precocious twenty-year-old when the Civil War broke out, Searles parlayed some rudimentary medical training into a brief stint as a hospital steward. Before the war was a year old, however, he assumed the duties of a line officer and by the time he was mustered out in May, 1864, had advanced from a private to the rank of captain in the First.

He carried his military prominence into postwar private life, where he forged a prosperous law career, first at Hastings and then for some thirty-five years at Stillwater. Searles served one term (1881–83 in the Minnesota House of Representatives and seven years 1917–24) as a judge of the district court. He died in Stillwater on April 25, 1927, at the age of eight-six.

A careful, observant recorder of the scenes that attended his military service, and blessed with a keen facility with a pen, young Searles left a graphic contemporary account of the early career of his regiment in the form of correspondence with his family and friends back in Dakota County. In three lengthy letters that follow, dated June 27, July 2, and July 27, 1861, he presents an especially vivid picture of the First Minnesota's formative days in military life—its long and arduous trip to the seat of war in the East, its training period in Washington, D.C., and its first exposure to warfare in northern Virginia which culminated in the battle of First Bull Run (or First Manassas) on Sunday, July 21, the first large-scale land engagement of the Civil War.

Though it brought defeat and gloom to the Union army as a whole, Bull Run covered the First Minnesota with great distinction. Not only had the regiment traveled farther to reach the fighting than any other unit, Federal or Confederate, but saw the most extensive participation and suffered the greatest number of losses of all the Union outfits engaged. The regiment, too, was one of the last to leave the field and most of it retired in reasonably good order unlike other outfits. In spite of its losses, as Searles points up, the First's spirit of combativeness, which prompted the regiment to resist retreating despite thrice being ordered to do so, remained intact at the battle's close. That spirit would carry the First through almost three more years of unparalleled carnage, which would climax on July 2, 1863, at Gettysburg, Pennsylvania. On that date the regiment made a sacrificial charge which, according to the most widely accepted account of Judge William Lochren, saw it suffer 82 per cent losses—the greatest casualty rate, in proportion to numbers engaged, sustained by any outfit in American history.[1]

The three Searles letters published here are among twenty-five he wrote to his family during the Civil War. They were donated to the Minnesota Historical Society in 1930 by Searles's widow and are now in the division of archives and manuscripts. Subjects covered after Bull Run include troop movements, the "Monitor" and the "Merrimac," General George B. McClellan's last review of the troops following his dismissal as commander of the Army of the Potomac, criticism of President Lincoln's conduct of the war and of his removal of McClellan, and a long description of the execution of a Union deserter. Earlier, in 1920, a fragment of Searles's Civil War diary was presented to the society by Mrs. R. E. Morris of Dunkirk, New York.[2]

The three letters are reproduced substantially as written. A few eccentric forms of punctuation have been standardized (Searles himself lamented that he did not have time to make corrections), and extra paragraphing has been added. The first letter takes the regiment to Washington, D.C., by way of Chicago, Harrisburg, and Baltimore.

District [of] Columbia
Capitol Hill June 27ᵗʰ 1861
Dear Friends at Home:
For the first time since we left Hastings have I had opportunity to write you, and I now undertake to fullfill my promise.

After leaving Has[tings] we landed at Red Wing, Lake City, Wabashaw, and Winona, at which places great scenes were enacted: the shaking of hands, sheding of tears, the hearty "God Bless You's" were so intermingled as to render it necessary to remain but a few minutes at either [each] place. yet the good steamer Northern Belle kept us upon the *"Father of Waters"* untill eleven o'clock that night, when we were transferred to a train of cars immediately, and started for Chicago direct, about one o'clock in the morning, arrived there about seven o'clock, on Sunday evening, June 23d. Was then transferred to another train, immediately, and was fortunate enough to obtain (as on the previous night) a sleeping car for the benefit of my patients—ergo—myself.

From Chicago we took the Chicago Ft Wayne and Pittsburgh R R, arrived at Ft Wayne, Indiana, seven o'clock in the morning of the 24th inst; passed through Ohio and [a] portion of Penn; during the day found the crops looking well, corn from twelve to eighteen inches high. Arrived in Pitts. about twelve o'clock P.M. 24th inst; changed cars immediately and started for Harrisburgh, passed the Allegahney [*sic*] Mountains about seven in the morning. There was a very perceptible change of temperature while crossing the mountains and splendid scenery—lofty cliffs; tall pines; deep ravines; heavy excavations, two Tunells and roaming streams.

We arrived at Harris. at about two o'clock P.M. 25th inst. We went into camp and had just posted our tents when it was rumored that we were ordered to Wash. We had Dress Parade in the evening, and an order was read ordering the Capt's to have their respective commands ready for marching at 3 o'clock the next morning[.] So in accordance with that order we were routed out in the morning by the tatto at two o'clock, struck our tents[,] packed [them] in boxes, loaded them into the cars, and settled ourselves as quietly as possible in our respective positions in the train and awaited the moment of our departure which came about five o'clock. We travelled all that day and till ten o'clock that night before we reached Was.—a distance of 188 miles. Arrived at Was. We found that Col. Aldrich[3] had prepared for us by securing the "Assembly Rooms" and the "First Cong[regational] Church" for our use during the night. The next day (today) we [are] occupied in running about town looking at the public buildings, and eating our salt pork and hard biscuits.

Taking it all together we got along very well considering the distance and time—over 2,000 miles in five day[s], a thing unparalled [*sic*] in the whole history of war. Sunday the boys were entirely without food excepting a slice of raw salt pork[;] indeed that was the rub and anything more [to eat was] the exception but through all that the boys kept up their spirits well so that when we marched into the depot at this place last night they looked and walked as sprightly as ever, and I heard it remarked among the bystanders that they were the best looking Regt. that had come to Was.

This morning it was rumored that we were to pass in review before the

President and probably would be his *body guard,* the post of honor. I think we stand a good chance if not the best [chance], for our men are all (as a general thing) large[,] energetic, well drilled men, just such men as is wanted in that place. At all events the 1st Min. will be placed in an important position; by the date of this letter you will discover that we are on capitol hill, about a half mile from the capitol building, right in the city—*the Capital of the Great Republic of America.*

All along the road through Wis. Ill. Ind. Ohio. Pa. Md. we were cheered from almost every house. The boys tired themselves more yelling, than from any thing they had to perform. In Pitts. we were treated to a supply of warm coffee and I succeeded with the officers in getting a supper, and a sleeping car to Harris. At every station we found old men and women ready to greet us as we passed, and in one instance an old lady, gray headed and trembling, sat in her door[way] as we passed, and blessed us in words and actions so fervently that she resembled a *spiritual medium* passing through her gyrations.

While stopping at Harris. I found my old friend and preceptor Proff. Allen a Lieut. in a Pen. Regt. and with him visited Camp Curtin.[4] He wished me to send his respects to his friends at H[astings], a duty which I hereby perform. In passing through Balt. we marched by Co., some with guns loaded, some not; with one or two exceptions there was no demonstration. Some one tried to give three cheers for Jeff Davis, but no one supported it, and he *dried up.* In a window three story high, a man was seen with a loaded pistol in his hand, but he was sensible enough to keep quiet. It was only the numbers, however, that kept down any disturbance. If a shot had been fired from any house, the Co's would have divided into squads, and riddled it, and all other of the same character, from top to bottom. We found the 12th Pen. Reg't stationed in squads all along the RR track from the Mary[land] border to Was. at the bridge. I noticed several bridge[s] that had been burnt.

Capt. [Alexander] Wilkin[5] and command arrived today (29th), passed through Balt. with loaded guns—no outbreak. The 71st Regt N.Y. captured 61 secessionists to-day, and brought them in prisoners. Four escaped, it was done close by our camp. . . .

The 1st Minn. makes a very favorable impression in Was. The Col. [Willis A. Gorman] is very strict now. I attended the medical dept today with the Surgeon. I have recd. no appointment yet, although [I] have got a sure thing in one or the other. Expect to be paid in a few days. Shall then get my uniform, and shall then send you my ambrotype. I am writing on a camp chest and tatto is sounding, so you will *excuse* me till next time, when I will give you a more systematic account of what I saw in Wash.
J.N.S.

*   *   *

In the second letter Searles tells of the First's leaving Washington to encamp on Arlington Heights near Alexandria, Virginia, and of association with the famed New York Fire Zouaves.

Virginia
Arlington July 2nd 1861
Dear Friends at Home:

We are on the "sacred soil of the Old Dominion," as you will see by the date.

To show you how it was done I will give you "verbatim et literatum" as I have it in my journal which was roughly taken as circumstances permitted.

Wash. D.C. July 1st 1861—. Occupied this morning in several minor surgical operations—such as extracting teeth, operating for corns &c. I then went down town with Assist Surg Le Boutulier [Dr. Charles W. Le Boutillier], and returned with a bag full of lettuce, cabbage, and crabs—look like fury—are to have them for dinner, but none of us know how to cook them—awfull fix—. Visited the Wash. Navy Yard this afternoon. Well pleased with its appearance[;] found the [warships] Pawnee and Pensacola lying there at the dock, the former under sailing orders, the latter undergoing repairs.

Wash. July 2nd—. No drill today. Secret and confidential orders by Col. Gorman this morning, and we are ordered to hold ourselves in readiness to march at ten minutes notice, and strike tents at the sound of the Bugle.

July 3rd—. All packed and tents struck; leave camp to ship on board a boat for Alexandria; leave the N[avy] Yard at just twelve o'clock, and arrive at Alex at just one o'clock eight miles below Wash; detrained three hours for transportation to carry us to camp—on Arlington Heights one mile from town. We are joined to B[rigadier] General {Irvin] McDowell's brigade, an old Mex[ican War] soldier and graduate of W[est] Point. Co "H" is detailed to advance in the morning and take[?] and guard a bridge. Arlington July 4th—. I awoke about three o'clock this morning, and heard firing somewhere about a mile from camp and waited quietly supposing it to be a picket fight as usual, and in about half an hour the *long roll* (beat to arms) was sounded by the drum, and in a minute I was up and loading my gun, and getting the Ambulance in readiness for action; and no less than ten minutes from the call, the whole battalion had formed in line of battle, awaiting orders from [the] Brig Genr; but after an hour [of] constant marching the battalion was dismissed, and the companies repaired to their respective posts. After breakfast Co "H" proceeded to their post—when it was ascertained that the firing occurred—caused by the picket guards ushering in the *Glorious Fourth* with a salute.

Occupied all day in arranging Hos. Stew[ard's supplies], &c. Four secessionists were brought into camp today by our guard; supposed to be spies, and sent to Alex. They were found outside the camp pitching quoits, and riding up and down the road alternately, directing most of their attention to us; so much so at least that the Lieut of the Guard considered them as suspicious persons, and arrested them. All were fine looking, smart young men. They denied the charge of being spies—of course—but will be tried, I understand; what will be done with them I do not know.

We are in camp with the Ells[worth] Zouaves [Eleventh New York Volunteer Infantry], 4th Mass. [actually, the Fifth Massachusetts Volunteers], 4th Penn., 10th Mich. [actually the First Michigan Volunteers, later brigaded elsewhere], all forming a brigade under Brig. Gen. McDowell.[6]

I was greatly disappointed in the looks of the city of Washington. With the exception of the Public Buildings it is a second or third class city. The building[s] all present a dirty, dilapidated, and common appearance. The city is full of soldiers; it was estimated that just before we left, there were about 100,000 soldiers in and about it. The 1st Min. produced a very favorable impression with the Pres. and all. The Col. tells us that "*Old Abe*" has confidence in us; and *we shall not betray it.*

As we passed through Alex. the town looked deserted almost, not a man to be seen scarcely, and but few women, and they (the women) whom we did see look[ed] daggers at us. But it was of no use. They know they are in a trap that the more they pull the tighter it draws, untill . . . it will choke them finally. Alex is under the guard of a Mass. Reg. and the Zouaves. I saw the building in which Ells[worth] was shot. It is almost in ruins, the soldiers chipping it off as relics.[7]

To show you how the Zouaves operate on picket guard at night I will tell you a little incident. One night the picket[,] instead of remaining upon dry land as usual, where they would [be] sought by their enemies, they (or one especially) waded out into a swamp, where a man *could not be coaxed* to go(?), and waited and watched [the Rebel lines]. Very soon he heard some approaching and listened attentively, when soon a lighted turpentine bull['s-eye lantern] was thrown into the air for the purpose of discovering his position. He remained quiet however and soon they lighted a fire, when he very quietly dropped his man, and proceeded to give chase to the fugitives who took good care to get out of the way as soon as possible. [B]ut unfortunately for three of them, they ran to the railroad where the[y] met some more pickets who dropped them also.

The Zouaves are regarded with a great deal of confidence. All agree that they will fight like devils if they get a chance. The reports that they loose [*sic*] two or three picket guards every night is false; only one I understand has yet been killed.

A report is rife in camp to night (brought by an officer) that Co "H" killed ten secessionists and took four horses. I think it is true. It is also reported that we move as the advance column of the brigade for Fairfax C[ourt] House to-morrow night. The order has not yet come, but the Col. expects it. While I write the camp is all alive with fun, mock Indian dances, bonfires, music, and everything that can contribute to noise and happiness.

The whole Reg. is in very good health. I have been well all the time.

It is late, and you must excuse me for I have yet to post up the Hos[pital] Register.

Please write and direct to the "1ˢᵗ Reg Minn. Vols". Give my respects to all, and tell my friends that I shall write to them as soon as I can get a chance, and time.

Yours

J.N. Searles

[P.S.] I do not discover but a very little differance in the temperatures here, the nights are cool. I you can read this you will do well. J.N.S.

No pay yet; make out our pay rolls this week.

J.N. Searles

*   *   *

The third letter is a full account of the First Minnesota's heavy involvement in the battle of First Bull Run.

Washington DC July 25ᵗʰ 1861

Friends at Home

I received a letter from Julius today, after a very tiresome march.

On the 16ᵗʰ inst. our division started on its forward movement towards Manassas, and encamped that evening at a point twelve miles distant. In the morning started forward, and encamped that night on the R R at Sengers [Sangster's] station; we calculated to intercept the retreating forces from Fairfax but was one hour too late.

The next day at about three o'clock in the afternoon we took up our line of march for Centreville; arrived about nine o'clock that night in a rain storm, but went into camp with other Regt's making in all about 33,000 men; with Rikers [Captain James B. Ricketts'] & [Colonel William T.] Sherman's Artillery, and two companies of Cavalry. Next morning killed some beef for rations, and made ourselves as comfortable as possible during the day. Next day we were ordered to pack up and be ready for a start at an hours notice—waited all day, and retired with the expectation of being routed [out of bed] during the night.

Bugles sounded about one oclock in the morning [of Sunday, July 21], and at two we took up our line of march to fight the enemy. By a circuitous route we gained the enemy about eleven o'clock, tired, hungry, thirsty, and worn down with marching; but no time was given them to recruit [their energy] but they were marched at "double quick" time up a long ravine to an open field where they were halted a few moments to await orders; here we could hear the discharge of the batteries, and anxiously awaited the command to *move forward,* and in the mean time I was assisting Surgeon Le Boutillier to dress two wounded men who had been brought from the field.

Soon the order came!! The battalion moved forward on the *double quick* and were again halted before reaching the field. In the mean time Le B. and I were going ahead, into the field, witnessing the battle.

What a sight About a mile and a quarter on our left, as we emerged from the woods, were the enemy in their entrenchments, playing upon us with their artillery, but their shots all went to[o] far over us. Within about a mile of the enemys batteries I saw a [Union] battalion lying down flat on their faces, firing with their muskets on the foe who had not yet all retreated into their fortifications. Soon, Shermans battery opened on them, and his shots *seemed to tell!!* Then the 1st Minn. came onto the field, and passed down in front to the left of their batteries and with the F[ire] Zouaves advanced to attack them on their left. We advanced rapidly, they turning their batteries on us all the time but doing nothing until we had reached the bottom of a hill [Henry House Hill] close on their left flank—when all of a sudden a new masked battery opened on us in the distance. But that also did no good, for we gave them no time to play, but moved rapidly up to the enemy fortifications which were on a hill, on the opposite side of which they had dug down about four feet so that they could fire at us kneeling and could stoop to load, and thus be out of sight, while we were directly before them within about thirty feet.

Well we moved up into position and beheld directly in front a large body of men who were dressed very nearly like some of our men—gray clothes[8]—and as we halted and brought ourselves into line they waved their hands in token of friendship, and exclaimed "Don't fire! We are friends." And we did not fire, although the men all knew they were our enemies, and the Adjutant, Lieut Col., Maj & Serg. Maj all exclaimed to the Col. that they were our enemies.

But he was soon undeceived for they suddenly gave us such a volley that had they not fired to[o] high, would have brought down two thirds of the Regt. But the boys dropped immediately, and when their volley had ceased the boys arose & returned it with a good will, and immediately dropped to reload. But soon there was such a force charged upon us that we were compelled to retire a few rods and then we rallied and charged in return driving our enemies before us to their batteries, and taking a Lieut Col prisoner.[9]

After firing five volleys and being broken up by our own cavalry[,] we were compelled to retreat down the hill and collect our forces. We did not again storm the batteries for it was absolutely impossible to accomplish any thing, and it would only be murdering the men. During the action I was directly behind the men dressing their wounds and sending them off the field, and when they retreated I allowed them to pass and then followed slowly behind to pick up any wounded. During the action I lost Doct Le Boutillier and the other steward; and have not seen them since.[10]

The 1st Minn. and N Y Zouaves were placed in the most dangerous position on the field and stood the fire *better than any of the other Regts*. We were commanded to retreat *three times* before we obeyed and then Gen'l McDowell's aid[e] was compelled to drive us off by such expressions as "Retreat"!! "God damn you"! "Retreat"! "What do you stand there for"!! "I never saw such men to fight!!" AND INDEED WE DID FIGHT![11] The regulars even retreated before we did.

The battery which we attacked was commanded by Gen. [Pierre Gustave Toutant] Beaur[e]gard—the battery in front by Jeff Davis & the battery on the right by Gen [Joseph E.] Johns[t]on. There were about one hundred and fifteen thousand rebels. They were retreating when we marched upon them, and they immediately occupied their masked batteries, and ordered reinforcements from Manassas Junction (5 miles distant) per R R. We had only about 17,000 men engaged during the engagement—some Reg'ts did not fire a gun. We were allowed no reserve to support us but were marched up like sheep to the slaughter—one two three—as it were.[12]

The whole conduct of the General I understand was against the orders of Gen [-in-Chief Winfield] Scott. Instead of attacking them when we did it was intended to wait till the next day when [General George B.] Mc[C]lellan would have arrived with another division and attacked them in the rear—when we should undoubtedly have defeated them. I understand that it was the plan of Gen Scott to halt the division this side of the enemy batteries and open on them, and under cover of the guns advance to another position, throw up reinforcements, and plant more batteries and thus draw the fire of the enemy and thus discover their position. But as it is the advance has been defeated, and has returned to its former position.

The conduct of McDowell brands him as either a fool or a traitor, so much so that he has been suspended and Gen Mc[C]lellan placed in his position. Col Gorman is no longer popular with the boys. His conduct on the field did not characterize him as a *very* brave man—not *his* conduct, but that of his horse which he could not keep on the field; not even by sinking his spurs into his sides & pulling with a will (!) Well it is a young horse (!) but it is to be regretted very much. There is a good deal of feeling against him (Gorman) all through the camp.[13]

Both Surgeons & the assist[ant] Steward is gone—the Surgeon . . . is probably taken prisoner; but the others I think are dead. Co H had 9 killed, 10 wounded & 3 missing, I transmit a list. The [regiment] suffered more than any other, about 196 killed & missing.[14]

We shall be paid soon & then I will transmit my ambrotype. I came off un-scathed although I was in the thickest of the fight. I went in conscious of per-fect safety, and the sequel proved my expectation to be correct.

On the whole I consider & so do old Mexican [War] soldiers, that it was *the* hardest battle ever fought in America. Capt Wilkin, an old Mexican soldier, says he never saw or rather heard bullets whistle so in his life, and his testimony is corroborated by all other experienced men.

I do not know that we can consider it in a discouraging light, because *now* all ideas of having a short & easy conflict is past, and the people must prepare to meet the issue of events as they occur.

I cannot write any more at present, and I have occupied a portion of two days in accomplishing this much. You may be assured that I shall take good care of myself at all times, both with regard to diet & bullets. The surgeons and Chapl[a]in mess with us, and as a natural consequence we have a little better fare than soldiers' rations.

I am in good spirits and have been all the while, and am anxious to follow the Minn 1st through this war,—and I am almost conscious that I shall succeed. I should have written before but was not allowed. Give my respects to all Friends and tell them to not wait for me to write for I am more engaged than ever; but [to] write if they want to hear from me.

Yours as ever

Jasper

[P.S.] Excuse penmanship & punctuation for I cannot stop to correct it.

NOTES

From Minnesota History *47 (Summer, 1980).*

1. William Lochren, "Narrative of the First Regiment," in Board of Commissioners, *Minnesota in the Civil and Indian Wars*, 1:32 (St. Paul, 1890). The First's part in the Bull Run battle is treated on p. 8–13. See also William Watts Folwell, *A History of Minnesota*, 2:84–85, 310–311 (St. Paul, Reprint ed., 1961). For another account of Bull Run by the au-thor of these letters, see Captain J. N. Searles, "The First Minnesota Volunteer Infantry," in *Glimpses of the Nation's Struggle*, second series, 84–87 (St. Paul, 1890).

2. See *Minnesota History*, 11:95–96 (March, 1930), and *Minnesota History Bulletin*, 4:71 (Feb.–May, 1921).

3. Cyrus Aldrich was a congressman from Minnesota and an officer in the militia.

4. This camp at Harrisburg was organized in April, 1861, by Governor Andrew G. Curtin of Pennsylvania and was said to be the "first regular camp organized north of the Potomac in the loyal States." See George P. Donehoo, ed., *Pennsylvania—A History*, 3:1438–1439 (New York, 1926).

5. Alexander Wilkin served as captain of the First Minnesota's Company A through the Bull Run battle, after which he was named major of the Second Minnesota and, later, colonel of the Ninth Minnesota. He was killed on July 14, 1864, at Tupelo, Mississippi,

Minnesota's highest-ranking casualty of the Civil War. See Ronald M. Hubbs, "The Civil War and Alexander Wilkin," in *Minnesota History*, 39:173–190 (Spring, 1965).

6. More specifically, the First Minnesota was part of Colonel William B. Franklin's First Brigade of Colonel Samuel P. Heintzelman's Third Division of the Union Army of Northeastern Virginia. Brigaded with the First at Bull Run were the Fifth and Eleventh Massachusetts regiments and Company I of the First U.S. Artillery (Ricketts' battery). See United States War Department, *War of the Rebellion: Compilation of the Official Records of the Union and Confederate Armies* (hereafter cited as *Official Records*), series 1, vol. 2, p. 405.

7. Ephraim Elmer Ellsworth, organizer and head of the New York Fire Zouaves (Eleventh New York) and a special friend of Abraham Lincoln's, was killed by the proprietor of the Marshall House Tavern in Alexandria on May 24, 1861, after he removed a Confederate flag from the roof of the building. This aroused war sentiment in the North. The Zouaves, who modeled themselves after the original ones of the French colonial armies, wore gaudy uniforms and could fire and reload muskets from a prone position. See Mark M. Boatner III, *The Civil War Dictionary*, 263, 954 (New York, 1959).

8. Adding to the confusion at First Bull Run was the fact that the First Minnesota, among other units, was not yet wearing regular army uniforms. Company K had been presented neat gray outfits by the citizens of Winona, and the state had furnished the rest of the regiment with black felt hats, black pantaloons, and red flannel shirts. See Lochren, in *Minnesota in the Civil and Indian Wars*, 1:4.

9. In his report of the battle, Colonel Gorman identified the prisoner as Lieutenant Colonel Boone (no first name given) of the Second Mississippi regiment. See Board of Commissioners, *Minnesota in the Civil and Indian Wars*, 2:23.

10. Both Dr. Jacob H. Stewart and Dr. Charles W. Le Boutillier, surgeon and assistant surgeon respectively, were captured at Bull Run (Le Boutillier was at first listed as killed) and taken to Richmond, Virginia. For a discussion of their replacements and the difficulties caused by the later refusal of both Stewart and Le Boutillier to resign their commissions when paroled, see John Q. Imholte, *The First Volunteers: History of the First Minnesota Volunteer Regiment, 1861–1865*, 43–46 (Minneapolis, 1963).

11. Capital letters are the editor's.

12. Searles's 115,000 figure for Confederate strength is a gross exaggeration. The figures often given are slightly more than 32,000 for the Confederates and 35,000 for the Federals at First Bull Run. Searles's figure of 17,000 Northerners actually engaged, however, may not be far off. See Francis F. Wilshin, *Manassas (Bull Run) National Battlefield Park, Virginia*, 17 (Washington, D.C., 1955)—No. 15 in the National Park Service Historical Handbook Series.

13. For a discussion of Gorman's unpopularity, see Imholte, *The First Volunteers*, 56–62.

14. While it is true that the First Minnesota suffered more losses than any other Union regiment, the figures usually given are somewhat less than Searles's. The *Official Records* (series 1, vol. 51, part 1, p. 22), for example, list the First's losses as 46 killed, 109 wounded, and 30 missing—a total of 185. Both Heintzelman and Franklin, the First's division and brigade commanders, praised the regiment's conduct at Bull Run.

Myrick's Insult:
A Fresh Look at Myth and Reality

GARY CLAYTON ANDERSON

*The Civil War was in its second year, and any illusions the war would
be easily won were gone. While Minnesotans were continuing to volunteer for the Union, another war broke out at home that August. Bad feelings had been brewing between white settlers and the Dakota people
for several years, as crop failures and poor hunting on the increasingly
crowded reservations brought the Dakota near starvation. As these
problems worsened in 1862, the white government stalled on promised
payments and food, and when an Indian council voiced their grievances, trader Andrew J. Myrick is said to have commented, "Let them
eat grass." Gary Clayton Anderson focuses on Myrick's alleged statement
and deftly researches the facts surrounding those words from a distance
of more than a century, in the hopes of gaining a better understanding
of the circumstances that led to the outbreak of the conflict.*

Historians of the western frontier are generally familiar with the established
causes of the tumultuous Dakota War, or Sioux Uprising, of August, 1862. Discontented with the treaties that forfeited lands in Minnesota and tired of the
corruption inherent in the Indian bureau's distribution of annuities, in retrospect the eastern Dakota, or Sioux, people seemed ripe for rebellion. In addition, the chances for trouble increased after the Civil War broke out; promised
money annuities were delayed, and white males on the frontier departed to
fight in the East and South. The long-range problems, however, sometimes are
given less attention than the actions of one Andrew J. Myrick, a trader on the
Dakota reservations in 1862. It was Myrick who supposedly refused food to the
Indians and replied to their entreaties by saying: "So far as I am concerned, if
they are hungry, let them eat grass."[1]

This heartless paraphrase of Marie Antoinette is frequently seen as the catalyst that spurred Dakota leader Little Crow and several hundred Mdewakanton warriors into rebellion. Clearly recent historians of Indian-white relations
see Myrick's role as crucial. In *The Long Death: The Last Days of the Plains
Indians,* Ralph Andrist subtitles his discussion of the war: "Let Them Eat

120

Grass." After Myrick apparently made his fateful comments, Andrist concludes, his words "were repeated among the Sioux—with sullen satisfaction by the most ardently anti-white factions." Dee Brown, on the other hand, notes that Little Crow was the most affected by Myrick's comments, the trader's words hitting the chief as "hot blasts upon his already seared emotions." Just two days after the supposed council with Myrick, Little Crow received word of the killings of five white settlers near Acton, Minnesota, by hunters from his tribe. After an all-night debate he finally decided to join in a war against the whites. The first assault took place on the morning of August 18 at the Lower, or Redwood, Agency near present-day Redwood Falls.[2]

The above sequence of events has been repeated so often by so many authorities that challenging its accuracy seems tantamount to debating the very outcome of the destruction that followed. Yet several chronological difficulties not known to earlier historians strongly suggest that Myrick's insult did not occur at the Lower Agency, nor is it likely that the council could have taken place immediately before the war. This is not to say that Myrick's insult did not occur at the Lower Agency, nor is it likely that the council could have taken place immediately before the war. This is not to say that Myrick's insult did not take place; rather, that discrepancies in the traditional interpretation of the event make it necessary to take a closer look at the impact of the comment. In addition, such an assessment leads to a better understanding of the origins of the war by offering a different vantage point from which to re-examine those crucial days in early August when the lives of so many people on Minnesota's frontier were affected by a brutal confrontation between Indians and whites.

Scholars know very little about Andrew J. Myrick. Along with his brother, Nathan, he kept stores at the Lower and Upper agencies, which were opened for the eastern Dakota along the upper Minnesota River in 1853 after they had sold their claims to Minnesota lands in treaties negotiated two years before. Like other traders, the Myricks spent most of their time at the Lower Agency, closer to St. Paul, rather than at the Upper Agency, 30 miles northwest of Redwood Falls near Yellow Medicine. Traders had become essential to the existence of the Dakota people by the eighteenth century. Their role as suppliers of manufactured goods, especially arms, increased during the first half of the nineteenth century. By the 1850s, men like the Myricks made a substantial profit on the two Dakota reservations by selling goods to Indians on credit and then claiming the cash received by individuals at the time the government distributed money annuities.[3]

By spring, 1862, this commerce had taken on added importance because of the growing difficulty that the government experienced in meeting its obligations to the Indians. The Civil War directed attention away from Indian matters, and Congress and the Bureau of Indian Affairs delayed in providing the necessary funds. Conversely, the Dakota had gradually reached a point where they felt that traders were taking advantage of them, demanding all of their annuity funds in exchange for relatively few goods. A clash seemed inevitable. It began at the Upper, or Yellow Medicine, Agency, when a native soldiers' lodge, or military society, resolved to stop the payment normally given to traders. The Sisseton and Wahpeton at Yellow Medicine made known their complaints in a council held with Lieutenant Timothy J. Sheehan, commander of a part of the Fifth Minnesota Volunteer Regiment sent to Yellow Medicine to keep order during the annuity distribution.[4]

Sheehan had arrived at the Upper Agency on July 2, 1862, with 101 men. Shortly thereafter he realized that the cash annuities had not yet arrived and that the normally peaceful Indians were demanding food. On August 4 a crisis ensued after Dakota warriors raided a government warehouse. Sheehan immediately sought and received reinforcements from Fort Ridgely. Four days of intense discussions followed. Government officials, including army officers and Indian Agent Thomas J. Galbraith, finally convinced the 6,000 Dakota people involved to leave peacefully for a buffalo hunt. By August 8 all seemed quiet again, and both Galbraith and the militia at Yellow Medicine left for the Lower Agency. Galbraith reached Redwood on August 13 and spoke with Little Crow two days later.[5] According to the standard interpretation of events, it was during this brief discussion that the Dakota chief conferred with the traders led by Myrick. The insult supposedly took place as the Dakota pleaded for assistance.

Unfortunately, Galbraith failed to leave a description of the council in his extensive account of events preceding the outbreak. This seems surprising in light of the emphasis that is placed upon the Myrick insult by some historians. Even more unusual is the description offered by the notes that Galbraith took on his meeting with Little Crow on August 15. "I had an interview with Little Crow," the agent said, "and he seemed to be well pleased and satisfied. Little, indeed, did I suspect at that time that he would be the leader of the terrible outbreak of the 18th." An "interview" is definitely not a council, and Galbraith failed to mention the traders or Myrick. In addition, the agent indicated that by August 15 corn and vegetable crops had matured and the Indians were harvesting them, providing some explanation for Little Crow's apparent friendliness. Possibly Galbraith was trying to absolve himself from responsibility for the subsequent violence by mentioning the abundance of food, but most observers agreed that the crops of 1862 were the most substantial ever produced on the agency lands, and they would have fed the Lower Sioux Indians throughout the coming winter.[6] The fact is that Little Crow and the majority of the Mdewakanton were not destitute on August 15.

A close inspection of primary sources reveals no contemporary mention of a council occurring on or near August 15. Not until the 1919 publication of Winifred Barton's biography of her missionary father, John P. Williamson, was

Myrick's insult put into the context of such a meeting. Barton gave a detailed description of the event, repeating the story as it had been handed down. But she failed to give a date, indicating only that the council occurred just before the outbreak. As for the participants, Barton noted that "hundreds" of Indians were present, along with the "storekeepers," traders, the agent, and her father. After the Indians haggled with the agent over the distribution of food, Galbraith finally turned to Myrick, who was acting as spokesman for the other merchants. When Myrick told the Dakota to "eat grass," the regular interpreter refused to repeat it. Then Galbraith apparently asked Williamson, who had grown up with the Dakota, to give an accurate translation. After he did so, the Indians stood silent for a moment and then "broke into weird and savage war-whoops."[7]

Despite her failure to date the event or to indicate where it occurred, Barton's story gained the attention of William Watts Folwell, who later wrote a definitive history of Minnesota. Folwell noted the omissions in 1919 when he began collecting materials for his chapters on the Dakota War. Other scholars would borrow and enlarge Folwell's discussion of the events surrounding the Myrick insult, but it was he who first sought to ferret out the truth surrounding the trader's role. The detective work could not have been in better hands, for Folwell was a thorough and concise scholar who worked by the strict principles of classical "scientific" history.[8]

From the start, Folwell had strong suspicions regarding the verbal exchange. He had access to Galbraith's report, where there was no mention of a council—just an "interview" with Little Crow. Hoping to find further evidence of the insult, Folwell began a writing campaign, seeking some verification of Barton's account. Since Williamson had died in 1917, the historian could only write Barton, explaining diplomatically that while he believed her summation of the event, "It is a rule among historians to make no positive assertions of past events unless upon the strength of at least two independent written accounts." Folwell then attached a sheet of questions regarding the Myrick incident. He asked Barton how many times she had heard the story, who else was present, and if she knew exactly when the council occurred. Folwell never thought to question her about the location, however, apparently assuming that the council had been held at the Lower Agency. Barton responded that she had heard her father repeat the account more than once, but that he did so mainly in his later years when "his mind seemed to revert to the past." The answer was less than gratifying to Folwell, and a year later he once again queried Barton. This time Williamson's daughter seemed annoyed that he would doubt her accuracy. If Folwell thought the evidence insufficient for use in his book, she wrote, "don't put it in."[9]

Meanwhile, Folwell questioned nearly everyone he could find who had been near the reservations in 1862 and had survived the war. The most likely individual in this category was Thomas A. Robertson, an interpreter who had lived a few miles from Redwood in August, 1862. Surprisingly, Robertson responded that he knew nothing, "not even that a council was held." Robertson admitted that at that time he "had very little to do with agency matters." Nevertheless, he could not understand why Galbraith did not mention it in his thorough report, and since Robertson appeared to recall that he had spent Sunday, August 17, at the agency, it seemed strange to him that he had not heard of such a dramatic event.[10]

Others Folwell wrote to for information included George G. Allanson, grandson of Joseph R. Brown, an early Indian agent, and Asa W. Daniels, an early agency physician. Allanson's mother, Ellen Brown, had been held captive by the Dakota during the war, but she had no information regarding Myrick's insult. She could not understand why Philander Prescott, the interpreter at the Lower Agency, would have been unwilling to interpret Myrick's comment. Even so, she did not exclude the possibility that such a council could have occurred. Daniels, on the other hand, was more forthright. He had spent many years with the Dakota and, when queried by Folwell, said simply: "Barton is mistaken in her statement, the council could not have taken place."[11]

At this point, Folwell turned to other members of the Williamson family, receiving responses from the old missionary's sons, John B., Jesse P., and Thomas C. Williamson. They strongly supported their sister's account, and even noted that their mother, still alive and living with them, had also heard her husband relate the event. Faced with many contradictions but convinced that the Williamsons were reliable sources, Folwell decided to use the material in his book. His decision seems to have been made by December 12, 1922, when he wrote Allanson that it was a *"fact"* that Williamson told the story as Barton reported it, but that certain minor details were faulty. In substance, Folwell had concluded that the council occurred at the Lower Agency on August 14 or 15, the day on which Galbraith had an "interview" with Little Crow, but that only small numbers of Indians, rather than hundreds, were present. Nonetheless, when he finally wrote up the description for his book, he noted that Little Crow spoke for "hundreds of Indians present" and emphasized the impact that Myrick's insult had upon the emotions of the Dakota. Barton's account and the letters of confirmation that Folwell had received from the other Williamson children served as the evidence for his footnote.[12]

As other scholars searching for the causes of the Dakota War would soon realize, the story of Myrick's insult was too sensational to be ignored. It made good reading and represented what some historians perceived as the "match" necessary to ignite the conflagration that followed. Indeed, Folwell set a trend when he elected to end his discussion of the major causes of the war with a two-page, emotional description of the inhumanity of Andrew Myrick, concluding that his "heartless and insolent statement... must have deeply incensed the Indians."[13]

Folwell's search for the truth undoubtedly would have been aided had he had access to John P. Williamson's personal papers. Among them is a letter written from Cincinnati in which Williamson stated, "suspecting no danger I left the Lower Sioux Agency ... on Monday [August 11] two weeks ago today." On the 12th he met his father, Thomas S. Williamson, near St. Peter, well east of the Lower Agency. In other words, John P. Williamson, Barton's father, was not at the Lower Agency on either August 14 or 15 to interpret Myrick's "heartless" response. When one considers further that Galbraith does not mention such a dramatic event in his report, it seems clear that it simply could not have occurred as Folwell and others who follow him have reported.[14]

The very existence of this letter leads to one of two conclusions: either the council never occurred, a suspicion that Folwell originally held, or it took place before August 11. If the latter is true, then the council could not have been held at the Lower Agency, since Galbraith did not arrive there until August 13. Yet the circumstances surrounding the affair are further confused by a vague and brief note that Williamson scribbled a short time before his death to Minneapolis journalist Marion P. Satterlee, claiming to have been at the "last council" with Little Crow.[15]

Although Williamson indicated that this discussion took place "two or three days" before the outbreak—an impossibility—it does suggest that a "council" did actually occur. It seems possible that in later years the missionary forgot the chronology of the outbreak. But if any credence can be given to this note, it more than likely meant that the council occurred "two or three days" before Williamson departed for Ohio, perhaps dating the meeting on or about August 8. In order to consider this theory more carefully, it is necessary to digress to the events at the Upper Agency during the early days of August. A close examination of the circumstances reveals that most of the actors in Barton's scenario were present at Yellow Medicine during the first week in August. Moreover, Indians at the Upper Agency were starving, providing the necessary conditions for the insult to have occurred.

Two major and sometimes contradictory descriptions by white participants have survived of the events at the Upper Agency during early August. Lieutenant Sheehan kept a journal, and Galbraith later gave a day-by-day account in his official report. Both agree that the Dakota at Yellow Medicine were suffering because game was scarce or nonexistent, Galbraith had only a small supply of food, most of which was intended to feed the large number of white government workers at the agency, and the traders had generally refused the Indians credit as long as they threatened not to pay for goods out of their annuities. Most of these Indians, in contrast to those at Lower Sioux, did not farm. Within a week or two after Sheehan arrived on July 2, members of the Dakota soldiers' lodge approached him and asked for food. They also restated their intention to stop traders from seizing their annuity cash once the distribution of goods, food, and money scheduled for July took place. Sheehan sent them to Galbraith, and the agent did hand out a few provisions, mostly soda crackers, at the annuity enrollment on July 25. The sight of Dakota men scurrying for crackers scattered on the ground from barrels attested to their destitution.[16]

By August 4, when no further provisions were forthcoming, these same Indians (almost entirely from the Sisseton and Wahpeton bands) surprised Sheehan's command and broke into the agency warehouse, carrying off several dozen barrels of flour and sugar. In all, Sheehan counted 1,500 Dakota men involved in the raid, perhaps an exaggeration. The lieutenant halted the pillaging by aiming a cannon at the door of the building and threatening to set it off. While Galbraith cowered inside his residence, Sheehan convinced the discontented Indians to join in a council. They demanded food, pointed out that the provisions in the warehouse were rightfully theirs, and threatened further violence if they were not satisfied. Sheehan carried the ultimatum to Galbraith, who first asked the lieutenant to retrieve the lost food but soon realized the futility of this request and issued a few provisions.[17]

The next day, August 5, the crisis heightened. After Galbraith instructed Sheehan to arrest the men involved in the warehouse raid, he made a cowardly attempt to escape to the Lower Agency with his family. The Dakota drove him back and then struck their tents, obviously making preparations for war. Galbraith next asked Sheehan to arrest Peter Quinn, who acted as army interpreter, and remove him to Fort Ridgely. Galbraith suspected that Quinn had encouraged the Indians to raid the warehouse; others would later dispute this charge. Sheehan wisely concluded that he could no longer control the situation and sent the old interpreter to the fort to ask the commanding officer to send reinforcements.[18]

Meanwhile, Galbraith requested aid from the Protestants whose mission was located a few miles north of the agency. Thomas S. Williamson, John's father, was then returning from the East, but missionary Stephen Return Riggs did respond to the request. Welcoming him to the agency on August 5, Galbraith asked Riggs whether there was "anything between the lids of the Bible" that would solve the problem. Riggs thereafter had several meetings with Dakota leaders, many of whom he had known for years. In a later newspaper account, Riggs indicated that Galbraith attended these councils, and it seems likely that, if the agent were in on the discussions, the traders or their clerks were also there. Unfortunately, Sheehan was busy guarding the warehouse and never attended, and Riggs only implied that through his mediation, which may have lasted several days, the difficulties were eventually resolved.[19]

At 1:30 P.M. on August 6 Captain John Marsh arrived from Fort Ridgely with reinforcements. After huddling with Sheehan, he promptly ordered Galbraith to issue "blankets and stuff" to the Indians. According to Sheehan, Marsh also threatened to "arrest the traders if they appeared to cause dissatisfaction amongst the Indians." Galbraith acquiesced to this and on August 7 and 8 held several more councils with the Dakota, after which the storehouses were opened. In exchange for the distribution of provisions, the vast majority of Indians left to hunt buffalo northwest of their agency. But August 11 Galbraith heard that the Indians of the Upper Agency were beyond Big Stone Lake; this dissipated concern about a war. Galbraith busied himself by recruiting for a militia unit called the Renville Rangers designed to fight in the Civil War. He left Yellow Medicine on August 13 for the Lower Agency, meeting Little Crow there two days later. On the eve of the outbreak, both agencies were quiet.[20]

In light of the foregoing testimony, the only time when conditions were right for the type of comment attributed to Myrick was during the early days of the month, specifically between August 5 and 8. Other circumstantial evidence supports this conclusion. For example, it now seems clear that most of the key actors in the event can be placed at the Upper Agency during this period. According to Sheehan, Little Crow arrived on either August 5 or 6. "He was there with two or three of his men at the time of the council," Sheehan noted, "when it was understood that provisions were to be issued to the Indians at Yellow Medicine." Barton's later description of Little Crow's role during the council with Myrick, Galbraith, and Williamson is probably a reference to this discussion. She said the chief told the assemblage that when Indians get hungry, "they help themselves."[21] What Barton failed to understand is that this statement must have been a reference to the Sisseton-Wahpeton raid on the warehouse at the Upper Agency.

Placing young Williamson at the Upper Agency is more difficult, since his normal residence was at the Lower Agency, where he had a mission church. But like Little Crow, Williamson had family connections at the Upper Agency and, after hearing news of the troubles, he could have ridden the 30 miles north to see if he could be of some assistance. Later, when he learned of the outbreak on August 25, he quickly returned from Ohio to learn what had become of his parents.

Trying to locate the traders also provides fuel for speculation. Why, for example, would other men involved in the trade and competing for business rely on Myrick to speak for them? An explanation could be that most traders resided at the Lower Agency and left clerks in charge of their houses at Yellow Medicine. Thus, if Myrick were at the Upper Agency, he would probably be consulted by the clerks. Although concrete evidence placing Myrick at the Upper Agency in early August does not exist, Galbraith does give the impression that the trader and his brother Nathan were behind the crisis. While the councils were going on, probably on August 6, Galbraith wrote a letter to a friend at Shakopee in which he complained vociferously of the "combination of N. Myrick & old [Indian commissioner Charles] Mix" to oust him.[22] One must wonder why the agent would single out Nathan Myrick, ignoring other traders, and make such a charge unless Nathan and, by proxy, his brother Andrew, were at that moment a thorn in his side. Possibly Galbraith felt that Andrew Myrick had somehow undermined his position, perhaps by adding to the discontent in the Indian camps. This would tend to be supported by Captain Marsh's threat to imprison "traders" on August 6. At the very least it is interesting that Galbraith's letter should focus on the actions of one trader at a time when he was facing a native rebellion.

Galbraith's letter left Yellow Medicine about the same time (perhaps August 6) that a group of women and children were successfully evacuated to the Lower Agency. Perhaps one of them posted it at Redwood. In 1863, one of these evacuees, Sarah Wakefield, wife of the agency physician, penned a description of the troubles at the Upper Agency, written from firsthand observation as well as information collected from friends. Wakefield recalled the rush on the warehouse and took pains to point out that the upper Indians were in a state of extreme need when it occurred. She also remembered the series of councils that took place shortly thereafter, saying that the traders told the Indians that they would get no more money from the government and that "they would have to eat grass like cattle, etc."[23] Like Barton's story, Wakefield's account is undated. On the other hand, it is far less dramatic and fails to mention a formal council, or Myrick, or the reaction that ensued in the Indian camp after the message became common knowledge. Although it is difficult to speculate about the significance of Wakefield's story, her chronology carries conviction that the comment occurred at Yellow Medicine during the early days of August.

Besides Wakefield, one other important person mentioned the "eat grass" insult. Little Crow, in a letter to Henry Sibley dictated during the fighting that followed, specifically charged Myrick with telling the Dakota that they could "eat grass or their own dung." Myrick was not the only trader mentioned; Little Crow singled out others who had become obnoxious to his people. Yet the chief's comments again make clear that Myrick had threatened the Dakota with starvation. Years later Chief Big Eagle would claim that after killing the traders at the Lower Agency on August 18, warriors stuffed Myrick's mouth full of grass. Big Eagle did not indicate, however, that he attended the council where Myrick made his remark and seemed to suggest that all was quiet at the Lower Agency just before the war broke out.[24]

In summary, the evidence that has survived indicates that at least two weeks before the war Andrew Myrick did insult a group of eastern Dakota, telling them they might as well "eat grass," or words to that effect. Folwell and other historians made the mistake of assuming that this discussion took place at the Lower Agency and provided the catalyst for the Mdewakanton to start the war. We know that a handful of Lower Agency Mdewakanton joined Little Crow in his trip to the Upper Agency in early August and were on hand during the councils that followed. But most of the lower Indians were not in attendance at such a council and did not hear Myrick's comments. Furthermore, there is no reason to believe that on the eve of the rebellion the majority of them were suffering like their western, buffalo-hunting relatives. Indeed, half of the Lower Agency Indians were, at least nominally, farmers by 1862, and they had a bumper crop to gather.

What this new information implies about the causes of the war is difficult to assess. It does question the belief that a charged emotional atmosphere existed in Mdewakanton camps before the attack on the Lower Agency. It follows that the war was less a tragic accident, brought on by unusual circumstances, than has previously been argued. If we de-emphasize the sense of provocation that Myrick's insult might have offered, it seems clear that historians may want to reassess the causes of the war, beginning with a more thorough consideration of the evidence. At least two Dakota informants later strongly implied that elements among the Mdewakanton had been dissatisfied with the governmental acculturation program, the increased occupation of neighboring hunting grounds by white pioneers, and an annuity distribution system that favored farmer Indians in order to discourage traditional occupations. A soldiers' lodge, formed at the Lower Agency well before the outbreak, discussed various options, including war. Furthermore, Little Crow had been promised some provisions for his role in mediating the troubles at Yellow Medicine on August 6–7. Those goods were apparently not delivered. More traditional, nonfarmer Indians living near the Lower Agency seem to have concluded that resistance to white rule was a solution for these inequities.[25]

In other words, the rationale for the rebellion was more complex than has been previously perceived; Myrick's statement has distorted the nature of the war by placing a much stronger emphasis on the emotionalism of the moment than on the dynamics of Dakota society in 1862. When this latter subject is scrutinized, no doubt the factionalism that was rampant on both Dakota reservations and the impact that government acculturation programs had upon the various factions will gain significance. But until then, as long as we continue to repeat the errors made by past scholars and fail to look carefully at new sources or new interpretations of old sources, the myths of that past will continue to distort our perception of the Dakota War of 1862.

NOTES

From Minnesota History 48 *(Spring, 1983)*.

1. Winifred W. Barton, *John P. Williamson: A Brother to the Sioux,* 49 (New York, 1919). The best contemporary discussion of the war's immediate causes is in Stephen Return Riggs to S. B. Treat, September 15, 1862, in American Board of Commissioners for Foreign Missions (ABCFM) Papers, Houghton Library, Harvard University, copies in Minnesota

Historical Society (MHS) and the Newberry Library, Chicago. Scholarly accounts of merit include William Watts Folwell, *History of Minnesota*, 2:212-241 (Revised ed., St. Paul, 1961); Roy W. Meyer, *History of the Santee Sioux: United States Indian Policy on Trial*, 109-132 (Lincoln, Neb., 1967); Kenneth Carley, *The Sioux Uprising of 1862*, 1-6 (Revised ed., St. Paul, 1976); Priscilla Ann Russo, "The Time to Speak Is Over: The Onset of the Sioux Uprising," in *Minnesota History*, 45:97-106 (Fall, 1976).

The author thanks Alan R. Woolworth and the staff in the archives and manuscripts division at the MHS for invaluable assistance in the preparation of this article.

2. Andrist, *The Long Death*, 31 (New York, 1964); Brown, *Bury My Heart at Wounded Knee: An Indian History of the American West*, 40 (New York, 1970). For an oral account of the logic behind Little Crow's decision, see "Taoyateduta Is Not a Coward," in *Minnesota History*, 38:115 (September, 1962). The Mdewakanton were a subdivision of the Dakota who lived in Minnesota west and south of Fort Snelling; the other eastern tribes were the Wahpekute, the Wahpeton, and the Sisseton. Except in quotations, place names, and titles, the preferred name of Dakota is used in this article.

3. For an analysis of the 1851 treaties, see Lucile M. Kane, "The Sioux Treaties and the Traders," in *Minnesota History*, 32:65-80 (June, 1951). See also "The Indian Payments," in *North-Western Democrat* (Minneapolis), March 22, 1856; Sarah F. Wakefield, *Six Weeks in the Sioux Tepees: A Narrative of Indian Captivity*, 7 (2nd ed., Shakopee, 1864).

4. Timothy J. Sheehan, Diary, July 8, 1862, Sheehan Papers, MHS. On the money issue, see Folwell, *Minnesota*, 2:237. Agent Galbraith felt that the problems in getting the annuities were related to a conspiracy within the Bureau of Indian Affairs to discredit his administration. There is evidence that political friends pressured Indian superintendent Clark W. Thompson to delay the payment in order to increase the indebtedness of Indians to traders. See Galbraith to Thompson, July 19, August 6, 1862, C. B. Hensley, a Mankato journalist, to Thompson, May 20, 1862, and D. L. Hew to Thompson, August 13, 1862—all in Thompson Papers, MHS; Galbraith to Henry B. Whipple, May 31, 1862, Whipple Papers, MHS.

5. Sheehan, Diary, August 4-13, 1862. Galbraith, a political appointee, was inexperienced, arrogant, and a "hard drinker"; some of his contemporaries, including Little Crow and Folwell, considered him responsible in part for the uprising. Lucius F. Hubbard and Return I. Holcombe, *Minnesota in Three Centuries*, 3:292 (St. Paul, 1908); Meyer, *History of the Santee Sioux*, 110.

6. Galbraith to Thompson, January 27, 1863, in 38 Congress, 1 session, *House Executive Documents*, no. 1, p. 387, 406 (serial 1182); Hubbard and Holcombe, *Minnesota in Three Centuries*, 3:285; Return I. Holcombe, "Chief Big Eagle's Story of the Sioux Outbreak of 1862," in *Minnesota Historical Collections*, 6:387 (1894).

7. Barton, *John P. Williamson*, 47-51.

8. Folwell to Dr. A. W. Daniels, February 29, 1919, Folwell Papers, MHS.

9. Folwell to Barton, September 25, 1920, May 9, 1922, and Barton to Folwell, May 21, 1922, Folwell Papers. For more on Folwell's early analysis of the event, see "Memorandum," March 28, 1919, Folwell Papers. Barton's response is attached to Folwell's September 25, 1920, letter.

10. Folwell to Robertson, August 4, 1922, Robertson to Folwell, August 8, 1922, and Robertson to George Allanson, November 28, 1922—all in Folwell Papers.

11. Folwell to Daniels, February 20, 1919, Daniels to Folwell, undated, Folwell to Allanson, November 13, 1922, Allanson to Folwell, November 15, 1922, Robertson to Allanson, November 28, 1922—all in Folwell Papers.

12. Jesse Williamson to Folwell, September 2, 1922, Thomas C. Williamson to Folwell, September 23, 1922, John B. Williamson to Folwell, undated but attached to Folwell's letter

of September 28, 1922, and Folwell to Allanson, December 12, 1922—all in Folwell Papers; Folwell, *Minnesota,* 2:232, 233.

13. Folwell, *Minnesota,* 2:233. Other historians have concluded that the killings at Acton sparked the war.

14. Williamson to S. B. Treat, August 25, 1862, ABDFM Papers.

15. Galbraith, in 38 Congress, 1 session, *House Executive Documents,* no. 1, p. 390. See also Williamson to Satterlee, July 25, 1917, Satterlee Papers, MHS.

16. Sheehan, Diary, July 2–25, 1862; Galbraith, in 38 Congress, 1 session, *House Executive Documents,* no. 1, p. 390; Galbraith to Thompson, July 19, 26, 1862, Thompson Papers. See also Hubbard and Holcombe, *Minnesota in Three Centuries,* 3:289–298; Lucius F. Hubbard, "Narrative of the Fifth Regiment," in *Minnesota in the Civil and Indian Wars, 1861–1865,* 2:243–248 (St. Paul, 1890); Sheehan deposition, September 11, 1901, in "Evidence for Defendant," 270–283, *The Sisseton and Wahpeton Bands of Sioux Indians* vs. *the United States,* Court of Claims, Docket no. 22,524.

17. Sheehan, Diary, August 4–8, 1862; Sheehan deposition, 271, Court of Claims, Docket no. 22,254.

18. Sheehan, Diary, August 4–8, 1862; Sheehan deposition, 271, Court of Claims, Docket no. 22,254; Hubbard and Holcombe, *Minnesota in Three Centuries,* 3:296; Galbraith, in 38 Congress, 1 session, *House Executive Documents,* no. 1, p. 388–390. On Quinn, see *St. Paul Pioneer and Democrat,* August 15, 1862.

19. Riggs, "The Dakota Bread Riot," in *St. Paul Daily Press,* August 20, 1862; Riggs, *Mary and I: Forty Years with the Sioux,* 175 (Minneapolis, 1969). Hubbard and Holcombe are incorrect in dating Riggs's arrival at the agency as August 7.

20. Sheehan, Diary, August 6–8, 1862; Galbraith, in 38 Congress, 1 session, *House Executive Documents,* no. 1, p. 387–390.

21. Sheehan deposition, 274, Court of Claims, Docket no. 22,254; Barton, *John P. Williamson,* 48.

22. Galbraith's letter is quoted in Hew to Thompson, August 13, 1862, Thompson Papers. The agent obviously wrote during the troubles at Yellow Medicine; he described "4,500 Indians who are troublesome as hell itself—it is enough to drive a man crazy."

23. Wakefield, *Six Weeks,* 10. Hubbard and Holcombe's report tends to confirm Wakefield's accuracy. They describe a confrontation in June during which Andrew Myrick told a group of Dakota: "you will come to me and beg for meat and flour . . . and I will not let you have a thing. You and your wives and children may starve, or eat grass, or your own filth." *Minnesota in Three Centuries,* 3:286.

24. Minnesota, *Executive Documents,* 1862, p. 444; Riggs, "Memoir of Hon. Jos. W. Lynd," and Holcombe, "Chief Big Eagle's Story," both in *Minnesota Historical Collections,* 3:114 (1880), 6:390. A burial detachment, including Nathan Myrick, found Andrew with "an arrow in his arm and an old burned scythe thrust through him." Major E. A. C. Hatch to his sister, September 24, 1862, Hatch Papers, MHS. Stuffing an enemy's mouth has a long history. German traveler Johann G. Kohl, writing in 1855, noted this and reported that "The Sioux . . . stuffed a white man through the mouth with soil . . . snarling: 'Eat dirt, you landthief!' " Kohl, *Reisen im Nordwesten der Vereinigten Staaten,* 255 (2nd ed., New York, 1857).

25. See Wa-pa-sha's testimony, in *Papers Relating to Talks and Councils Held with the Indians in Dakota and Montana Territories in the Years 1866–1869,* 91 (Washington, D. C., 1910); Holcombe, in *Minnesota Historical Collections,* 6:387; Sheehan's deposition, 274, Court of Claims, Docket no. 22,254.

Anti-Germanism in Minnesota Schools, 1917–1919

La Vern J. Rippley

At the outbreak of World War I, President Woodrow Wilson rallied the American people by assuring them it was the "war to end all wars" and the "war to make the world safe for democracy." The hope of making the world safe for democracy badly faltered at home in Minnesota as wartime creates an atmosphere where loyalty and patriotism may threaten or override constitutional safeguards. The establishment of the Minnesota Commission of Public Safety within days of the U.S. declaration of war created an institution with sweeping powers to define and enforce loyalty as the commissioners saw fit. LaVern J. Rippley concentrates on the Commission's anti-German efforts, especially in the area of education.

In a nation at war so concerned with being "100% American" that sauerkraut was renamed "liberty cabbage" and hamburger called "liberty sausage," and in a state with Germans as its largest ethnic group, the Commission found many opportunities for intervention. The Commission insisted on English-only instruction and sought to root out "German sympathizers" in the schools. Public schools, as well as private and parochial, were all suspect and possibly subject to the Commission's review. Tolerance was not a virtue in the heated atmosphere of wartime America.

Of all the cases handled by the Minnesota Commission of Public Safety during its brief official life, more than 56 per cent concerned members of the state's German population. The seven-man commission, which some historians have called dictatorial and fascist, was "an interim agency" designed to take swift and decisive action toward "suppressing disloyal outbreaks and possible disturbances of order in communities where the German element was predominant" during World War I.[1]

The Minnesota commission, modeled in a limited way on the National Council of Defense created by Congress three days after United States' entry into World War I, was the first such state agency established in the nation. On April 10, 1917, only four days after the declaration of war, the Minnesota senate voted unanimously to create the commission. The lower house followed suit four days later with only two dissenting votes; Governor Joseph A. A. Burnquist signed the bill into law; and on April 23 the Minnesota Commission of Public Safety met for the first time.[2]

Empowered to perform "all acts and things necessary or proper so that the military, civil, and industrial resources of the state may be most efficiently applied toward maintenance of the defense of the state and nation, and toward the successful prosecution of such war," the commission could do explicitly almost anything. It could seize or condemn property, require anyone to appear before it or its agents, demand that district courts issue subpoenas, examine the conduct of public officials, and advise the governor on actions against such officials.[3]

The commission was headed by Governor Burnquist and Attorney General Lyndon A. Smith, a banker from Montevideo, who were ex officio members. The other members, all appointed by the governor, were Charles H. March, a lawyer and for a time vice-chairman, from Litchfield; John Lind of New Ulm, a three-term United States congressman (1887–93), and a past governor (1898–1900); John F. McGee, a former Minneapolis judge and attorney for the Chicago Great Western Railway; Charles W. Ames, general manager of the West Publishing Company which printed lawbooks; and Anton C. Weiss, a conservative Democrat and publisher of the *Duluth Herald*. John S. Pardee was chosen as secretary and Ambrose Tighe, the man who had drafted the enabling act for the legislature, as counsel. Commissioners served without salary and at the pleasure of the governor.[4]

The commission addressed itself to problems in a wide area and issued 59 specific orders. These concerned such war-related subjects as food production, marketing, labor and industrial peace, iron-ore output, fuel, the welfare of soldiers, prevention of waste, forest fires, and the price of milk. Each week the agency processed an average of 18 sacks of mail and answered 300 letters; it mailed more than 21,000 pieces of German-language literature to persons on its address lists. Over 700 state newspapers received from the commission English or foreign-language materials about the war and the efforts to win it, and between September 8, 1917, and December 28, 1918, the government body published and distributed its own official weekly newspaper, *Minnesota in the War*.

Frightened by pro-German sympathizers among the German element in Minnesota when the draft was initiated and the national guard mobilized, the Minnesota commission created its own army. Order No. 3 authorized seven Home Guard battalions, six of which were organized by July, 1917, with headquarters in St. Paul, Duluth, Virginia, Winona, Mankato, and Faribault. One year later there were 21 battalions. According to the order, "only able-bodied men between the ages of 31 and 52 inclusive, will be enlisted when it is shown that they are probably exempt from service in the Federal Army."[5]

These neighborhood soldiers trained somewhat regularly throughout the year and in September, 1918, held the first encampment for the motor division. One historian has argued that "The very organization of the home guard so dampened the ardor of German sympathizers that no overt acts of opposition took place and disloyal sentiments rarely found expression." As the socialist weekly, the Minneapolis *New Times,* predicted on April 14, 1917, the commission was at once able to "Prussianize Minnesota and establish here that military autocracy which we are supposed to be fighting in our war with Germany."[6]

Scholars and critics have long questioned the necessity of a body like the Commission of Public Safety. Many, including some of its backers, judged the commission to be unconstitutional. The best rationale for its autonomy and dictatorial status was written by Ambrose Tighe, who clinched his argument with an analogy to the Minnesota Health Act of 1883 which provided that in the event of an epidemic, a board of health "shall . . . do and provide all such acts, matters and things as may be necessary for mitigating or preventing the spread of any such disease." Minnesota residents with ancestral homes in the nations with which the United States was now at war were potentially "such a disease."[7]

The authors of the agency's final report, which spanned its official life from April 23, 1917, to December 31, 1918, justified its existence by explaining that nearly a quarter of the state's 2,000,000 residents were either German born or of German-Austrian parentage. They pointed out that there were "many sections . . . where the English language newspapers did not circulate, and where a foreign tongue was the medium of communication of church and school, in the home and in business relations." The commission's defenders argued further that although great numbers of foreign-born Minnesotans, including those of German blood, favored United States participation in the war, there were

> many in Minnesota in 1917 who were not loyal in this sense. Some of them were traitors deserving of their fate which followed. . . . The public danger came when the anti-war feeling assumed the shape of concerted and public propaganda, and it assumed this shape here in the spring and summer of 1917. The Minnesota men who were disloyal in the sense above defined then formed a constituency of considerable size and there appeared leaders and spokesmen to organize them and give expression to their opinions. Misinterpreting the constitutional guaranty of freedom of speech and of the press, these leaders thought . . . that even in war times, they could properly oppose the government's policies in speech and writings.[8]

Among these leaders, the commissioners believed were pacifists who organized a nationwide antiwar campaign; pro-German sympathizers who were conspicuous in the Minnesota River Valley and during the New Ulm antidraft rallies of July, 1917; and socialists and politicians of the Nonpartisan League stamp who pandered to the treasonable sentiment in the population. One pacifist group that offended the commissioners was the nationally based People's Council for Democracy and Terms of Peace. Organized in New York during May, 1917, the council had gained notoriety for its role in drafting the St. Louis platform of the Socialist party, which branded the declaration of war by the United States a crime. Opposed to conscription and any interference with the personal liberties of American citizens, the People's Council had an ardent following, particularly among Minnesota's German-stock population. According to the commission's final report, the city of Minneapolis was selected as the most suitable place in the nation for the council's first national convention. "The polyglot population of this state and section was looked upon as a promising soil by the powers of sedition, and, moreover, the then mayor of Minneapolis had assured them of a most hospitable welcome and all needed protection."[9]

Planned for the first week in September, 1917, preparations for the convention received wide publicity. Special trains were chartered to bring leaders from the east to Minneapolis, and delegations were expected from many other parts of the nation. In the words of the commission, "The projected meeting was regarded not only as an overt action of sedition, but also a blot upon the good name of the city." Vexed by the pacifist outpourings in the press and by repeated assurances of Minneapolis's Socialist mayor, Thomas Van Lear, Governor Burnquist wired the sheriff of Hennepin County ordering "that the holding of said convention and meetings within the county of Hennepin or elsewhere in the state of Minnesota be and the same is hereby prohibited."[10]

Other leaders whom the commission feared were German sympathizers in the Minnesota River Valley. On the evening of July 25, 1917, under the auspices of the People's Council, a meeting of 8,000 to 10,000 people was held in New Ulm's Turner Park, preceded by a parade through the streets of the city. Acting as marshal was County Auditor Louis G. Vogel, who subsequently mounted a platform adorned with American flags. There he was joined by Dr. Louis A. Fritsche, who served both as mayor of New Ulm and as vice-president of the German American Alliance, the leading such organization in the nation; city attorney Albert Pfaender; Captain Albert Steinhauser, publisher of several German-language newspapers; and several others—including a local merchant and two faculty members of Dr. Martin Luther College, all of whom delivered speeches.[11]

The speeches as interpreted by the commission contended that war in defense of the nation was legitimate only on home soil; that congress should be petitioned to send no American soldiers to European battlefields; and that everybody should join the People's Council on Democracy and Peace in order to bring about a constitutional amendment requiring a referendum for the declaration of war. The commission described the rally's purpose: "With a cunning, but futile effort to observe the letter of the law, while outraging its spirit, the speakers advised the drafted men to submit to the draft in form, expressed doubt as to whether they could, under the constitution, be required to serve abroad, . . . and criticised the war as unworthy of popular support."

The commission took stern steps against the officials of this Brown County community. They were removed from office, and the commission also brought pressure on the state bar association to disbar Pfaender and on the state medical association to revoke Fritsche's license to practice. Simultaneously, it induced the board of regents to remove another participant, Adolph Ackermann, as president of Dr. Martin Luther College after 24 years of service. Captain Steinhauser, a veteran of two American wars, was expelled by the Minnesota Editorial Association, and the American Legion of Mankato attempted to have his pension canceled. John F. McGee presumably spoke for his fellow commissioners when he said to Pfaender, "You're a traitor and ought to be stood up against a wall and shot."[12]

Among political leaders whom the commission opposed were those associated with the Nonpartisan League and with Wisconsin's Senator Robert M. La Follette. Nor was the academic world immune to the agency's power. Such was the case for Dr. William A. Schaper, the American-born son of a German immigrant, who was summarily dismissed from the University of Minnesota by its board of regents. Schaper was informed on the afternoon of September 13, 1917, that he was to appear at a meeting of the regents that day and answer all questions put to him. Minutes after the interrogation began, Schaper was asked to resign as professor and chairman of the political science department. Since he refused to do so, he received a telegram the same evening from the regents terminating his relationship with the university. (In spite of this shabby treatment, Schaper, upon his death in 1955, bequeathed $10,000 of his estate to the University of Minnesota.)[13]

A little-known facet of the Minnesota Commission of Public Safety's involvement with the German element in Minnesota concerned the use of German in the schools. It was the language much more than the country of origin which made German-speaking Americans the butt of suspicion and harassment. Whether the foreign-born citizens were from Switzerland, eastern France, Germany proper, Austria, or perhaps from the German-speaking colonies of southern Russia was of little consequence to the vengeful critics of 1917.[14]

The commission left no doubt that it intended to create "One Country, One Flag, One People and One Speech." Little effort was made to prevent the languages of allied and neutral, as well as alien, countries from coming under the ban. Since the most widespread non-English language commonly used in Minnesota schools during World War I was German, however, the commission was understandably disturbed. As early as May 21, 1917, Commissioner Ames interviewed Irish-born Archbishop John Ireland of St. Paul about the advisability of eliminating German as a vehicle of instruction in Catholic schools. The archbishop urged caution, and thus the matter was tabled by the commission.[15]

There the German-language school question lay until the September 12, 1917, meeting in which the Minnesota superintendent of education, Carl Gustav Schulz, with commission approval, recommended a committee to investigate the teaching of German in the public schools. (This action did not extend to the private schools, which were considered beyond the jurisdiction of the state superintendent.) Advising that the study of German should not be suspended, Superintendent Schulz was authorized to appoint an eight-person committee to examine the German textbooks used in Minnesota. Reports from 350 elementary and secondary schools and from county superintendents listed the German texts in use, and from these the committee compiled 270 titles to investigate and determine which were "prejudicial to the interests of the United States, or contrary to those ideals of democracy which every liberty-loving nation wished to inculcate in the hearts of the young." Five categories of material were carefully scrutinized: (1) pictures or insignia of the imperial family or the military; (2) the principle of "might makes right"; (3) German propaganda; (4) material eliciting admiration for German life; and (5) German patriotic poems.[16]

While the textbook committee was at work, Superintendent Schulz assembled further data and on November 6, 1917, informed the commission that during 1914–15 German had been taught as a subject in 198 of the state's 221 high schools. A later survey of Stearns County in 1915 showed that 100 public, one-room schoolhouses used German for most of the day's instruction, while ten used Norwegian and two Polish. But this was only the proverbial tip of the iceberg; the real problem lay in the private sector where in 1917 Schulz counted 307 parochial schools with a total enrollment of 38,853 pupils. Among these private institutions, less than one-third (94) were using English exclusively as the medium of instruction; nearly two-thirds (195) spoke German primarily, with occasional periods when the vehicle of instruction was English. A mere handful of schools—ten Polish, four French, and one each in Norwegian, Dutch, Danish, and Czech—represented all the other non-English languages in the state.[17]

Superintendent Schulz was nevertheless reserved. Advising the commission that drastic action against these 195 schools was not warranted by the statistical evidence alone, he apparently slowed action by the commission. Instead of closing the schools, the agency resolved on November 20, 1917, "that school boards, principals and teachers be urged, as a patriotic duty, to require the use of the English language as the exclusive medium of instruction in all schools in the state of Minnesota, and to discontinue and prohibit the use of all foreign languages in such schools, except as a medium for the study of those languages themselves or as a medium of religious instruction." The following April 30,

1918, the commission tightened the language screws indirectly with an order "that no person who is not a citizen of the United States shall be qualified to serve as a teacher in any public, private, or parochial school, or in any normal school in which teachers for these schools are trained." To its credit, however, the commission never took the ultimate step of closing the German schools, private or public.

Meanwhile the textbook committee, using the criteria listed above, had concluded its evaluation of the 270 titles used to teach German in the public schools. After several meetings with the committee, Superintendent Schulz told the commission on November 13 that 47 books had "a distinct German atmosphere" and 17 of these were "obnoxious to the public interest." The longest list included 128 titles of a "literature type," most of them "untainted by modern Prussian ideas"; the final group consisted of 46 volumes of stories that were judged mostly unobjectionable. Commissioner Ames summarized:

> At this period in our national life, when the line is drawn so plainly between the Prussian ideal and the American ideal, it is clearly wrong and dangerous to permit instruction in the German language to awake, in the impressionable minds of our children, admiration and sympathy for the Prussian system of thought and government, and for the Hohenzollern family, the arch-enemies of mankind. For this reason, the curriculum of our public schools should be purged of all German text books which expert examination shows to be tainted with these false doctrines. There can be no question that some of these school books have been deliberately prepared as a part of the infamous German propaganda in the United States.[18]

Upon the recommendation of Ames, the commission adopted the report and asked the textbook committee to reduce its findings to a "'white list' of unobjectionable books, from which school boards may safely make their selections." At a final session on November 23–24, 1917, the committee complied Group A with 22 objectionable books and Group B with 238 titles which were unobjectionable except for a few incidentals—frequently the cover design. Ames remarked on the committee's common sense in not purging two patriotic German songs, "Deutschland über Alles" and "Die Wacht am Rhein," both written long ago with other purposes in mind. Ames urged that teachers employ these songs to point out how they had become the watchwords of a "Teutonic world empire which had drenched the world with blood," thus exemplifying the "full significance of the Prussianizing of German thought." Cautioning that there may have been other books not examined by the committee which should have been placed with Group A, the state education department published and distributed both lists.

In the manuscript version of the report, books by Paul V. Bacon were singled out for special condemnation—particularly one entitled *Im Vaterland*.

A close examination to understand what made this book anathema reveals pictures of the imperial family on three pages, and on two pages, with dialogue about the German army, are pictures of a parade and some German officers in a guardhouse. The entire book describes episodes of an American nephew's visit to his uncle in Germany to learn about life in that nation. There was precious little glorification of German life. For example, the nephew finds that he cannot visit a German classroom and remarks that in America such visits were common practice. The pictured classroom is not complimentary to the German stereotype of discipline. When discussing the military, the uncle tells about his mandatory year in the army but comments that "it was uninteresting. The soldiers usually spend their time in a camp, undergo strict discipline, get simple, though enough, food to eat, learn how to handle a rifle, have target practice and hear a lot about the methods of making war." Innocuous as this may seem, Commissioner Ames nevertheless wrote in the unpublished version of the report: "They are so evidently prepared as a part of the German propaganda that I think that every German book written or edited by Paul V. Bacon might properly be banned from the schools on general principles."[19]

Some contemporary German teachers in the Minneapolis public schools were puzzled by the proscription of the Bacon book. One group pointed out to the Board of Education that *Im Vaterland* "was a book written by an American, having a two-fold purpose, that of furnishing easy German reading for beginners and to give a knowledge and atmosphere of German life and feeling." Nevertheless, they agreed to cooperate fully with the Safety Commission.[20]

Sometimes the question of German in the schools was not simply left to the commission but was debated hotly in local chambers, on the streets, and in meetings of boards of education. In Minneapolis, the state's largest school system, for example, the question of the German language was argued at a special meeting of the city board of education. To accommodate representatives of the Parent-Teachers Association and the citizenry, the meeting was called for Saturday, September 12, 1917, at 10 A.M.[21]

Interestingly enough, school board member Henry Deutsch, after first announcing his German birth, launched a vituperative tirade against Germany. "I doubt that there has been a single movement made . . . or authorized or approved by the German Government, or anybody connected with it—and particularly those who have been tied up with its educational departments—that has ever lost sight of, for one instant, the ultimate . . . of elevating the German Autocracy to the highest pinnacle of admiration and adoration. . . . If we could get the motives back of even these text books, we would find that it was promoted with that same predominant idea of German supremacy."

With more equilibrium, board member David F. Swenson pleaded for tolerance. "I believe we should not require . . . a teacher of the German language, who is perhaps herself German born, or of German parentage . . . to be loud or violently open in her expression of loyalty. What we need to expect in such a case is, that if she still has feelings of sympathy and can not help it, she suppress those feelings as far as school-room instruction is concerned." But Deutsch shot back, "We should not have subjects of the German Emperor employed in our school, and teaching our children and drawing money paid by tax payers of this country."

Representatives of the PTA and several citizens lined up about equally on both sides of the German language question. Referring to *Im Vaterland,* one said: "I have not the slightest doubt but that Mr. Paul V. Bacon was paid a large bonus out of the German treasury for getting that book into the American schools." Another, admitting he could not read German, commented nevertheless: "I see in this book quite a demonstration of swords; quite an array of Military formation." A third argued more logically that "it would be a great mistake to take a hasty step and abolish the teaching of German. . . . If we should be at war for ten or fifteen or even twenty years, all the more reason that we should have as much insight as possible, and be able to read German and follow them in the method in which they take themselves and the rest of the world." Other citizens astutely observed that the material in the books ought to have been taught 20 years ago so that in 1914 Americans would have had a better understanding of the intentions of the German government.

In the end, surprisingly, the Minneapolis Board of Education, upon the recommendation of Superintendent Bennett B. Jackson, passed a resolution that school authorities keep the German language matter under strict surveillance but did not vote to eliminate either its own list of textbooks or the teaching of German as such. Only member Alex G. Bainbridge thought the board should at least temporarily halt the teaching of German in Minneapolis.

Precedents had been set in other states. Iowa, South Dakota, and Missouri, for example, took stringent measures against the use of the German language. The Minnesota Public Safety Commission never went that far. Instead of a prohibitive order, it passed a resolution on November 20, 1917, in which school administrations and teachers were urged to require the use of English as the exclusive medium of instruction. There may not have been much difference between the *de jure* and *de facto* results (namely, the disappearance of bilingualism from American life), but at least in this one respect Minnesota was not the most repressive of the state councils.[22]

The textbook issue generated only moderate correspondence after the list of banned books was distributed late in 1917. Consequently, the commission in March, 1918, sent a questionnaire to all schools to find out what action had been taken. Commissioner Ames, apparently under the assumption that the distribution of Groups A and B lists was having little effect, recommended on Mary 26,

1918, approval of an order "prohibiting outright the use of foreign languages as a medium of instruction in all schools in Minnesota after a date fixed by the commission," probably at the opening of the fall term. But the matter was tabled until the results of the questionnaire could be received. These arrived on May 17, 1918, showing that 93 of the 551 schools which had been using texts in Group A had discarded the books; 30 schools had eliminated the objectionable parts; 25 had voluntarily discontinued German; and 34 planned to eliminate it after the close of the school year. Presumably the rest of the schools had already been safely operating with books listed on Group B. Satisfied with these results, the commission repeatedly delayed the Ames proposal for an outright ban of German from the schools. A newly drafted proposal submitted by Superintendent Schulz was repeatedly postponed. As a result no tougher anti-German language resolution was forthcoming from the Minnesota Public Safety Commission.[23]

During the academic year 1917–18 the commission received many letters urging the elimination of the German schools, the language, or both. Most of them originated within the state, but some were from without. The foreign editor of a Wisconsin newspaper, for example, suggested that "German language study should be deferred because of the danger that children are liable to, from the insidious propaganda which German teachers are known to have carried on."[24]

From the cross section of incidents with which the commission dealt, many were school related. The Minnesota Education Association, for example, urged inspection and supervision of all state and parochial schools to assure that all elementary instruction "be in the American language," and presumably looked to the commission for implementation of the resolution. Early in 1918, citizens of New Auburn banded together into a "Loyal Service League" whose intended service was elimination of the German language schools. To the state commission they sent a "factual" resolution which asserted: (1) that the German parochial schools bar patriotism; (2) that such schools are under the domination of the German ministers in the communities and that they "are proger-man [*sic*] to the core: and "espouse the cause of Kaiserism . . . in a secret and cowardly manner which makes it all the harder to neutralize"; (3) that pupils in the German parochial schools were not taught to revere the flag; (4) that these schools fostered "Little Germanies" and therefore the Loyal Service League wanted all of them to use English and come under closer surveillance.[25]

Aided by the National Council of Defense, the Minnesota commission went to great lengths to generate patriotism. Rather overzealous in this category were the Teachers' Patriotic Leagues which by March, 1918, existed in 50 Minnesota counties. Each teacher in these counties was directed to organize Little Citizens' Leagues, which officially enrolled over 60,000 Minnesota children under the auspices of the public schools.

But loyalty leagues among the teachers and pupils were never fully adequate without the special investigating agent in the field. In March, for instance,
N. I. Lowry was dispatched by the commission to assess an anti-German student strike at Elk River. In his report Lowry wrote: "The trouble seems to have
started over the use of banned German text books in the schools. The students
refused to study the German language at all and had requested that they be
given a half year's credit and permission to drop the study of the language. This
idea was opposed by the School Board as well as the faculty. There were 56
striking students." Closer scrutiny reveals that local politics was a more serious factor than German textbooks. A certain Frank White had organized the
student strike as a way of getting back at Andrew Davis, the commission's
director of safety in Sherburne County and also a member of the school board.
White accused Davis of tepidity toward Liberty Bonds, but when Lowry appeared on behalf of the state commission, Davis hastened to reassure him that
the students had returned to their classes.[26]

Other schools had larger problems with German sympathizers in the classroom. Accusations were made in April, 1918, against Irene Bremer, a teacher in
School District 9 of Wabash County near Lake City. In the Bremer case, pupils
aged 11, 12, and 15 charged in an affidavit that Miss Bremer had said, "Germany
is the greatest country in the world." Allegedly she also claimed "Every country but England is ready to sign the peace treaty." Affiants attested that Miss
Bremer had permitted the children in her school to argue whether President
Wilson or the Kaiser were the better man. School board member Elmer Nygren
signed an affidavit that he would not allow his six-year-old child to learn from
this pro-German teacher. Another parent described how Irene Bremer had
taken a Red Cross pin from a boy who had paid for it, giving it to another of
German parentage who had not paid for it nor even assisted in the sale of Thrift
Stamps.[27]

The safety commission referred the sworn testimony to Superintendent
Schulz, who (although Miss Bremer had meantime resigned) laid down four
stipulations: (1) Miss Bremer's certificate to teach in the state be suspended;
(2) she attend Winona Normal School for six weeks and give evidence of her
loyalty to the president and her instructors, upon which her certification would
be reinstated; (3) thereafter she was to teach patriotism and loyalty and support the war aims in school; and (4) upon complaint, her certificate was subject to revocation permanently. In the Bremer case, as many times before, Carl
Schulz was a voice of moderation: "I do not feel her offence warrants the permanent revocation of her certificate for the period of war."

If charges against individual teachers were at times exaggerated, so were
the continuing allegations about German textbooks. On July 31, 1918, the *Winona
Republican-Herald* ran large headlines declaring: "GERMAN TEXTBOOK TEACH-
ING GERMAN PROPAGANDA IS FOUND IN WINONA PUBLIC SCHOOLS." Sub-

headlines continued, "Prof. J. M. Holzinger Denounces Volume and Writes to Minnesota Public Safety Commission—Urges Investigation of All Textbooks and Elimination of Dangerous Matter." Apparently the German and Polish stronghold of Winona and its newspapers had not studied the commission's German textbook list of the previous December. Without reference to the commission's A and B lists, Holzinger found a particular book by Philip Schuyler Allen, an associate professor of German at the University of Chicago, to be "well written and . . . excellent in literary technique. The propaganda is all the more dangerous because of the fact that it is so unobtrusive and apparently innocent." Aroused Winona citizens called for action. "Let the board of education order an immediate investigation of the textbooks now in use here and rigidly exclude everything that is not pre-eminently pro-American," wrote one. "Let parochial schools fall in line and do the same thing. Clean up the text books before the schools reopen a month hence." Endorsing this call to arms, the Winona paper affirmed that "the schools of Menominee, Michigan, excluded all German books. The students gathered the discarded volumes together and burned them publicly at a great patriotic demonstration."[28]

Fortunately Minnesotans were never obliged to burn their books publicly, but the hysteria over the German language in the schools came within inches of barbarism. One Ottertail citizen wrote to the commission that the largest ethnic group in his area were the Germans. "They have started a school of their own beside their church about a mile and a half from town. Before the war they had school in their 'private german' school house for three or four months, which almost ruined the American public school. Now they propose to have a school by the Germans and for the germans during the whole school year thus the American school will be almost killed. . . . I stand for America first last & all the time. But it would be a blessing to us few Americans in and around Ottertail if this German school could be knocked in the head."[29]

With comparable zeal, the mayor of Stillwater wrote to the commission, "I wish to bring to your attention the fact that in our city we still have two schools where German is the principal language being taught." The mayor's attention had been drawn to the city's German schools by an incident in which a local mother blamed the deficient performance of her young son in the public system on the language. She wrote to his public school teacher, "I have considered the matter and come to the conclusion that I would take him out of the public school and send him to German school." It is not known how this and many similar cases were eventually resolved, but it can be assumed that all of them were somehow painful.[30]

If the oppressed looked for quick relief after the armistice had been signed on November 11, 1918, they were disappointed, for the Minnesota commission kept up its pace to the end of its existence. One instance occurred in December when

Dr. O. E. Strickler of New Ulm wanted to donate $1,000 to the local board of education to establish the "Emilie Strickler-Doehne Memorial Fund," the proceeds of which were to be used "for the purpose of stimulating the study of modern languages." Defenders of the proposal noted that the money would be used for the teaching of Spanish. Swiftly opponents of foreign languages in the schools rose to the attack. A former mayor of St. Paul, Daniel W. Lawler, wrote to Commissioner McGee, asserting that he had "considerable knowledge about the extent of German propaganda in all the South American countries.... Chile is practically a German annex. My attention was struck by the unexplained circumstance that a poor man of well-known German sympathies living in such a hotbed of treason as New Ulm should cold turkey donate a thousand dollars apparently for altruistic purposes. If there is anything in the belief that Germany looks far ahead especially in establishing commercial supremacy, it would be a very good investment for it to train Americans in Spanish and have them represent Germany in South American countries." In the face of such opposition, Dr. Strickler relinquished his support for foreign languages and stipulated instead that the fund's earnings be used to purchase books of fiction. Only then was the New Ulm Board of Education authorized by the commission to accept the donation.[31]

Even after the Public Safety Commission ceased activities, complaints kept arriving. Typical was a letter from Pope County regarding the German school at Villard. As it had done many times before, the department of education responded, "This office has no authority or control over private schools. Our law permits such schools to operate without any particular restrictions. The only existing restriction is the order of the Safety Commission recommending that English be used as the medium of instruction in all schools, both public and private, except their religious instruction, or instruction in some foreign language."[32]

With Germany defeated and the German language in Minnesota schools routed, the Minnesota Commission of Public Safety had lost much of its *raison d'être*. It met only a few times after December 15, 1918, and when the legislature convened in January, 1919, it did not extend the life of the agency. On February 4, 1919, therefore, the powerful, highly efficient body rescinded its orders except those providing for the Home Guard and for peace officers.[33]

Ambrose Tighe had argued that not even the signs of rebellion or sedition were necessary for the commission to take action. Directives pertaining to the German language and those who spoke it, therefore, were considered preventive measures rather than remedial. It was a classic case of the state claiming rights that it held to be vastly superior to the rights of individuals guaranteed under the Constitution. The fact that the nation was at war was presumed by the members of the commission to be a circumstance that abrogated the rights of individuals. According to the final report: "The Commission . . . aimed . . . to make malefactors generally realize that many things which in peace times would be insignificant were serious in war times."

The members of the agency did not "regard the Constitution as so delicate a document that its pages will be soiled or torn by a little rough usage, while battles are raging." Tighe believed the commission's only weakness to be "its departure from the principle of constitutional government." Governor Burnquist, writing in 1924, explained the public safety agency in a mater-of-fact way without justification. He expressed gratitude that 200,000 aliens had been registered by the commission and that naturalization was given a boost, but he offered no evaluation of the civil rights that the commission may have violated. After the war, the governor never retracted his firm belief that the German language was an unfit tongue for an American citizen. Strongly supportive of Americanization programs in Minnesota, Burnquist maintained that "No one should have a right to make a living in this country, or exercise the electoral franchise in this state, unless he is willing to learn its language."[34]

In most matters, including the eradication of the German language from Minnesota, the Commission of Public Safety was highly efficient. Of the $1,000,000 appropriated for it, only $260,000 were spent, largely because its staff was composed of nonpaid volunteers and because it operated out of only four rooms in the State Capitol. In food and fuel conservation, price control, and waste avoidance, the commission advanced the war effort. In its attempt to purge the International Workers of the World and their drive for unionization, the commission no doubt overreacted. And the commission erred badly in judging leaders of the Nonpartisan League treasonous and its speakers, such as Wisconsin's Senator La Follette, seditious. After all, the league was at that very time in political control of North Dakota, which cooperated completely with the federal government's war aims.[35]

On balance, a few individuals tempered the commission's drive against the German language, notably Superintendent Schulz, a son of Swedish immigrants, and Swedish-born Commissioner John Lind, who resigned from his post in January, 1918, in protest over the necktie-party tactics of Commissioner McGee. Thus, there were three Swedes, including Governor Burnquist, at the heart of power—two of whom were on the side of moderation in dealing with the German language question as it was orchestrated by the Commission of Public Safety in Minnesota.

In the final analysis, however, the German language question in Minnesota was never viewed on its own merits. The language served as a focal point of a larger, more disguised animosity. Most instances of trouble over the German language in the schools were caused by nativist elements in the society, trying desperately to assert their control over education; in the process they believed it necessary to kill the German language because it was a major factor rigidly separating the private from the public schools.[36]

In many of the Catholic parochial schools of Minnesota the German language had long been under attack by Archbishop John Ireland of St. Paul. His plans for Americanization of the Catholic schools of Minnesota began in 1891 and persisted, though in muted form, until his death on September 25, 1918. Similarly, in Catholic Stearns County, Austrian-born Bishop Josef F. Busch, who might have been friendly toward the German language, had served as a secretary and personal friend of Archbishop Ireland and was wholly sympathetic to the distinguished churchman's views. Consequently he ordered that English replace German in the local schools, arguing, as had Ireland, "if the foreign-born Catholics of this district neglect to have their children learn English, the Catholic Church will be charged with fostering hyphenism or un-Americanism." The people of Stearns County tried to operate German public schools, but Busch ordered them to build English parochial schools.[37]

Frequently business competition was interwoven with the language question and resulted in anti-German pressure. It was all too easy for non-German competitors to exploit the Public Safety Commission's suspicions. Contrary to what might be assumed, it was often the better educated who were the most anti-German and who knew best how to manipulate skillfully the forces of the commission against the German element for their own advantage. Thus Brown County merchants, bankers, and lawyers were instrumental in the denunciation of the New Ulm officials. Newspaper publishers and doctors sometimes joined clergymen in agitating against their competitive German neighbors. Younger pastors, be they Lutheran or Catholic, were sometimes less than comfortable with the German language and welcomed the commission's anti-Germanism as the lever they needed to pry their elderly faithful away from their mother tongue. Irish Catholics, under the guise of obedience to their bishops, gladly campaigned to Americanize Minnesota's German Catholics. Streaking through all of this behavior was a sense of loyalty and patriotism that had become canonized by the reality of war. Patriotism, epitomized by the sanctimonious dictum "right or wrong, my country," was easily marshaled by the commission among the majority citizen groups of Minnesotans. But minority groups as well as individuals found no protection under the commission's umbrella, especially if they spoke the alien German language.

It is ironic that in 1980 the Congress of the United States struggled to understand the implications of a report filed by the Presidential Commission on Foreign Languages in America. The report bemoaned the lack of interest in non-English language study, but nowhere did it plumb the complicated depths of the foreign-language debacle that swept the nation under the banner of loyalty and dedicated Americanism during 1917–18.[38] Insight into this darker side of the nation's psyche might result from a hard look at Minnesota's Commission of Public Safety and its behavior toward Germans in Minnesota.

NOTES

From Minnesota History *47 (Spring, 1981).*

1. Minnesota Commission of Public Safety (CPS), *Report,* 29 (St. Paul, [1919]), hereafter cited as CPS, *Report;* William W. Folwell, *A History of Minnesota,* 3:556–575 (Reprint ed., St. Paul, 1969). See also Charles S. Ward, "The Minnesota Commission of Public Safety in World War One: Its Formation and Activities," unpublished master's thesis, University of Minnesota, 1965, copy in Minnesota Historical Society (MHS); Ora A. Hilton, "The Minnesota Commission of Public Safety in World War I, 1917–1919," in *Bulletin of the Oklahoma Agricultural and Mechanical College,* May 15, 1951, pp. 1–44.

2. United States, *Statutes at Large,* vol. 39, part 1, p. 650; Minnesota, *Session Laws,* 1917, Chapter 261. A dissenting vote was cast by Andrew O. Devold, Minneapolis; Minnesota, *House Journal,* 1917, p. 1712.

3. CPS, *Report,* 7, 55.

4. Here and below, see CPS, *Report,* 9, 28, 30; Hilton, in *Bulletin of Oklahoma,* p. 4. The commission's weekly bulletin is available in MHS. Lind resigned in protest of McGee's repressive attitudes. George M. Stephenson, *John Lind of Minnesota,* 335 (Minneapolis, 1935).

5. CPS, *Report,* 13, 75n; Franklin F. Holbrook and Livia Appel, *Minnesota in the War with Germany,* 2:30 (St. Paul, 1932); Folwell, *Minnesota,* 3:319. An extension of the Home Guard was the Motor Corps, a paramilitary civilian group of car owners, founded by Winfield R. Stephens, a Minneapolis car dealer. It had 143 officers and 2,440 men. Between 6,373 and 10,000 men served in the Home Guard.

6. *Minnesota in the War,* September 28, 1918, p. 5; Folwell, *Minnesota,* 3:318.

7. Ambrose Tighe, "The Legal Theory of the Minnesota 'Safety Commission' Act," in *Minnesota Law Review,* 3:12 (December, 1918); Carol Jenson, "Loyalty as a Political Weapon: The 1918 Campaign in Minnesota," in *Minnesota History,* 43:45 (Summer, 1972). A commission of public safety was first devised during the French Revolution when *Le Comité de salut publique* devoured "enemies of public safety" such as King Louis XVI, Marie Antoinette, Georges Jacques Danton, and thousands of others.

8. CPS, *Report,* 31, 32. Minnesota had a total foreign-stock population of 71.5 per cent in 1910; of this 24.9 per cent were German. United States, *Census,* 1910, *Population,* 56, 836, 919.

9. Holbrook and Appel, *Minnesota in the War with Germany,* 2:55; *Report of the First American Conference for Democracy and Era of Peace,* 7 (New York, 1917); CPS, *Report,* 33. On opposition in Minnesota see, for example, *New Ulm Review,* July 4, p. 8, July 25, p. 1, August 1, p. 1, August 29, p. 6, 1917, and July and August, 1917, issues of *New Ulm Volksblatt.* On the council, see Carl H. Chrislock, *The Progressive Era in Minnesota,* 1899–1918, 138 (St. Paul, 1971).

10. CPS, *Report,* 33, 34. A succinct account of the controversy is in Chrislock, *Progressive Era,* 138.

11. Here and below, see CPS, *Report,* 49–51.

12. A copy of the official indictment sent by the commission to Governor Burnquist, August 28, 1917, is in CPS Records, File 212, Miscellaneous Correspondence, Minnesota State Archives, MHS. See also *Minneapolis Morning Tribune,* July 26, 1917, p. 1; *New Ulm Review,* August 1, 1917, p. 1; Martin H. Steffel, "New Ulm and World War I," unpublished

master's thesis, Mankato State College, 1966; Charles Quimby, "German-Americans March in Protest: Don't Send Us to War against the Kaiser!" in *Review* (St. Cloud), July, 1975, pp. 16-18. On the Ackermann case, see "Indictment," addressed to trustees of the college, November 21, 1917; Tighe to trustees, January 2, 9, 24, 1918, G. E. Bergemann to Tighe, January 16, 30, 1918, all in File 136, Ambrose Tighe Correspondence, CPS Records.

13. On opposition to the Nonpartisan League, see, for example, Chrislock, *Progressive Era*, 152, 162, 169, 173; Jenson, in *Minnesota History*, 43:43-57; Willis H. Raff, "Coercion and Freedom in a War Situation," unpublished Ph.D. thesis, University of Minnesota, 1957, copy in MHS. On the Schaper case, see University of Minnesota Board of Regents, *Minutes*, September 13, 1917, p. 29; other documents may be found in William W. Folwell Papers and Guy Stanton Ford Papers, University Archives, University of Minnesota.

14. See, for example, La Vern J. Rippley, "Xenophobia and the Russian-German Experience," in American Historical Society of Germans from Russia, *Workpaper No. 18*, September, 1975, pp. 6-11, and Rippley, "American Milk Cows for Germany: A Sequel," in *North Dakota History*, Summer, 1977, pp. 15-23.

15. *Minnesota in the War*, December 1, 1917, p. 1; CPS, Minutes, May 21, 1917, p. 47, Minnesota State Archives, MHS. Ireland's attitude is somewhat surprising because he had vigorously opposed German-language schools during the Cahensly controversy in the late nineteenth century and in his Faribault Plan in the 1890s. See La Vern J. Rippley, *The German-Americans*, 121 (Boston, 176).

16. On the textbook committee, see original typescript in File 213, German Textbooks, CPS Records; CPS, *Report of Special Committee on German Text Books Used in Public Schools of Minnesota*, 3 (St. Paul, 1917). The report was written by Commissioner Ames. On the career and background of Schulz, see biographical sketch in Theodore Christianson, *Minnesota: The Land of Sky-Tinted Waters. A History of the State and Its People*, 4:589 (Chicago, 1935). For existing laws on the use of non-English languages in schools, see Minnesota, *Laws Relating to the Public School System*, 46 (St. Paul, 1901).

17. Here and below, see E. M. Phillips, *Report of the High School Inspector*, 14 (Minneapolis, 1917); William L. Cofell, "The Motives of German Immigration," in Clarence A. Glasrud, ed., *A Heritage Deferred: The German-Americans in Minnesota*, 120 (Moorhead, 1981); CPS, *Report*, 23. More information on the resolution is in *Minnesota in the War*, December 1, 1917, p.1.

18. Here and below, see CPS, *Report on German Text Books*, 5, 6, 7.

19. File 213, in CPS Records, MHS; Paul V. Bacon, *Im Vaterland*, 3, 9, 77, 79 (Boston, 1910). Bacon, a Harvard graduate, joined his father's publishing house in 1913, became editor-in-chief, and stayed with the firm until 1947.

20. Hermine R. Koenig, R. J. Schulz, and Susan Heffernan to Minneapolis Board of Education, September 15, 1917, in File 184, Department of Education, CPS Records. Biographical data obtained from Bacon's publisher indicates he had no strong affinity for Germany but rather careful scholarship "To make sure that the book . . . is a faithful picture of German life."

21. Here and four paragraphs below, see *Minneapolis Morning Tribune*, September 15, 16, 1917, both on p. 1; and minutes of the meeting, copy in File 184, CPS Records.

22. CPS, *Report*, 162.

23. CPS, *Report*, 162; C. G. Schulz to H. W. Libby, June 28, 1918, and the questionnaires are in File 184, CPS Records.

24. F. Perry Olds to CPS, February 5, 1918, in File 184, CPS Records.

25. Here and below, see *St. Paul Dispatch*, November 3, 1917, p. 3; L. W. Grace to CPS, January 23, 1918, in File 68, C. W. Ames Correspondence, and File 184, both in CPS

Records. On the Loyalty League in schools, see *Minnesota in the War,* January 26, 1918, p. 7; *Glencoe Enterprise,* January 24, 31, 1918, pp. 4, 6, respectively.

26. N. I. Lowry to H. W. Libby, March 13, 1918, in File 184, CPS Records. On anti-German eruptions that were largely unrelated to nationality, see Sister John Christine Wolkerstorfer, "Persecution in St. Paul—The Germans in World War I," in *Ramsey County History,* Fall/Winter, 1976, pp. 3–13, and "Nativism in Minnesota in World War I: A Comparative Study of Ramsey, Stearns, and Brown Counties," unpublished Ph.D. thesis, University of Minnesota, 1973, copy in MHS.

27. Here and below, see Schulz to Libby, June 28, 1918; Schulz to H. V. Frick, May 27, 1918; Libby to Schulz, June 13, 1918, all in File 184, CPS Records. The incident seems never to have been covered by local newspapers. The general climate of opinion in the area expressed in the *Standard* (Wabasha), November 28, 1917, p. 2, called for exclusive use of English in schools.

28. Philip S. Allen, *German Life: A Cultural Reader for the First Year* (New York, 1914).

29. Arthur Madsen to CPS, August 4, 1918, in File 184, CPS Records.

30. J. R. Kolliner to CPS, October 2, 1918, in File 184, CPS Records.

31. Lawler to McGee, December 21, 1918, and to CPS, December 31, 1918, both in File 211, N. I. Lowry Correspondence, CPS Records.

32. C. F. Angell to CPS, January 18, 1919, and P. C. Tonning to Angell, January 23, 1919, both in File 184, CPS Records.

33. Here and below, see CPS, *Report,* 30, 142; Tighe, in *Minnesota Law Review,* 3:13.

34. CPS, *Report,* 31; Tighe to Lind, February 13, 1918, quoted in Hilton, *Bulletin of Oklahoma,* 41n; Joseph A. A. Burnquist, ed., *Minnesota and Its People,* 2:200 (Chicago, 1935); Christianson, *Minnesota,* 2:403.

35. CPS, *Report,* 9; CPS, Minutes, September, 1917, p. 175.

36. New Ulm was a case in point with a fairly homogeneous German population that was divided almost equally among Catholics, Lutherans, and free-thinking Turners. See Noel Iverson, *Germania, U.S.A.: Social Change in New Ulm, Minnesota* (Minneapolis, 1966).

37. On Ireland's plans, see James M. Reardon, *The Catholic Church in the Diocese of St. Paul,* 291–299 (St. Paul, 1952); *My Message* (St. Cloud diocesan newspaper), August, 1916.

38. Barbara B. Burn, "The President's Commission on Foreign Language and International Studies: Its Origin and Work," in *Modern Language Journal,* 64:7–57 (Spring, 1980).

A Minnesota Couple's World War II Letters

John S. Sonnen

What Tom Brokaw has dubbed "the greatest generation" was made up of individuals, each with his or her own piece of the historical record. John Sonnen's military service was from March 1944 through March 1946 (the period which included D-Day in June 1944 through the end of the war in 1945). He was stationed in Georgia, Texas, and then overseas, mainly in Germany, as the war came to a close and in the months following the surrender. His letters provide a regular portrait of his war experience. His wife Georgiana's letters from St. Paul provide a Minnesota context for the same period.

This article, written by John Sonnen, describes the dilemma and confusion that he and his wife faced about what to do with all the letters they had written to each other during the war. Forty-one years had passed since the last letter had been mailed, received, and read. What to save, how to save, why save anything were just some of their questions. Were their letters that meaningful—to them over forty years later, or for that matter, to anyone else, like other family members or scholars?

Late in the autumn of 1987, while engaged in the vexing annual chore of bringing some semblance of order to the congested contents of the cramped attic of our modest home, Georgiana and I decided it was show-down time regarding the final disposition of accumulated memorabilia. Stuff we had bumped into, stumbled over, and shunted about in that slant-ceilinged, tucked-away space for the forty-eight years of our marriage. Most of it was mine.

There were two cartons of 78 RPM records from the 1920s and 1930s, a seventy-seven-copy collection of original *Life* magazines, an antique shotgun from my grandfather's days on the Minnesota frontier, a German army rifle and Luger pistol that were surrendered to me on the Westphalian plain the first week of April 1945. Our children, long gone from under this same roof, would be given one more opportunity to claim these artifacts. If refused, off the items would go to the first interested collector, historical society, or library. However, also stashed away with this unwanted memorabilia were "those letters—as in our annual question, "What shall we do about *those letters* we wrote to each other during World War II?"

There were hundreds and hundreds of them. We wrote almost every day throughout the two miserable years we were apart: March 27, 1944, to March 27, 1946. Contained in a heavy corrugated carton with a substantial cover, they had been serving as a platform for our boxes of records. Letters of mine were in their original mailing envelopes, which Georgiana had kept in three groupings: those I wrote from basic training (Camp Stewart, Georgia), from advanced training (Fort Bliss, Texas), and from overseas (Europe). Letters from her were more jumbled because I would squirrel them away in foot lockers, duffel bags, or knapsacks. The first lot I brought home in August 1944 when furloughed after basic training. The next arrived in an army-ordered shipment of personal effects when I was alerted for overseas duty a few months later. The balance came home in March 1946. Now here they were, more than forty years later, confronting us once again and awaiting a final reckoning. What to do? Keep them another year? Throw them out?

"What do you think?" Georgiana asked.

"I—well, I just don't know. They'll have to go some day. I suppose it might as well be now."

"Tell you what," I was told. "Take them down to your den. That's where they belong anyway—with those snapshots and maps you brought home from the war. Then, as a winter project you can peruse them. Maybe by springtime a decision will come easier."

I carried the carton down to my den.

After the holidays, when winter really set in, I started that project. The first task was to assemble the letters in chronological order. While arranging the ones from overseas, a small magazine clipping fell from the folds of a letter dated April 2, 1945. That would have been, I told myself, nine days after my combat intelligence squad had stormed across the lower Rhine River in the U.S. Ninth Army's final assault against Germany. Now why in blue blazes, I wondered, would I have been snipping out a magazine item to mail home during such turbulent days? I read the clipping.

It was printed in small type on thin, lightweight paper, for it came from an overseas G.I. digest of the *New Yorker* magazine. Cut from the "Talk of the Town" pages, the item announced, "Psychiatrists and rehabilitation experts are busy setting the stage for the returning veteran." It reported that these professionals all agreed that when he gets home, "the fighting man will require special handling." After listing some of the abnormalities the experts expected, the writer (would it have been E. B. White?) observed, "The rehabilitation people are frightening thousands of girls with these warnings and unfitting them to be the wives of returning soldiers. Girls are receiving so many instructions about pulling a man through the postwar marital adjustment period that they are going to be something of a domestic problem themselves." The advice to wives who had husbands in the war was simply to relax. "It's all right to mix the old warrior a drink," the columnist wrote, "but our advice is to mix yourself one first—you probably need it quite as much as he does."

Finished with the clipping, I turned to the letter, searching for my reason for slipping it in. I found it in the last paragraph: "The enclosed item from my overseas *New Yorker* is sent along for a laugh. We'll be so busy just having fun and loving each other that I doubt if either of us will give 'rehabilitation' a thought!"

How true that was! Five years after my army discharge, our first-born son, who was eighteen months old when I enlisted, had two sisters and a brother. Shaking off memories of the verbal lambastings I suffered from my mother and mother-in-law for taking such a fast-lane, procreant route back to civilian life, I returned to the letter. Its opening paragraph piqued my interest further: "Dearest: Our same nanny goat came again this evening to poke its head in our front gate, and it seemed to ask the same question: 'Where is my master?' Each night it gets a bit more friendly and each night it smells a little worse."

The letter had six other paragraphs, but nowhere was there a further explanation of that evening visitor. Searching through a few previous days' letters, I found the answer at the end of one dated March 30: "Another day has passed. The nights fall awfully fast, but they are not so noisy anymore. There is a wooly old sheep peering in the front gate at me now. It seems confused and lost. The poor thing is no doubt wondering what has happened to all the people who always looked out for him (her?). Now it is ambling down the road wondering and wandering. I see things like this all the time, making me more anxious than ever for peace and a normal world in which to live."

A letter dated March 26, two days after our Rhine River crossing at Wesel, jogged loose more dormant memories of those hectic days. "We are set up in a rather fine German home furnished with modern furniture. It was abandoned in a hurry. . . . I found clothes piled in a wash tub ready to be laundered, sliced bread set on the kitchen table ready to be served, linens, bedding, clothes and dishes—all in their accustomed places awaiting daily use."

The brick house, located just east of a smashed village we had found our way through, was in a countryside setting. It had three bedrooms. In its front yard, a bit of a formal garden arrangement was set off from the road by a wrought-iron fence. In back of the house were a small barn, a chicken coop, several fruit trees, and a large garden plot, tilled and awaiting its spring planting. Greening acreage and meadowland lay beyond.

Contributing to the great pleasantness of the place, beside the fact that it was undamaged, were its beds with white sheets and its chicken coop, accommodating four hens and a rooster. The chickens came and went as they pleased until Marshall, my squad's self-appointed chef, locked them in the coop. On his off-duty hours he would capture chickens wandering nearby and add them to our flock. Thus he was assured of a fairly stable inventory from which to choose a fried, roasted, or stewed dinner. Good laying hens, however, were spared. He depended on them for the fresh eggs that always livened up our C-ration breakfasts. The resourcefulness of Pete, another member of our four-man crew, became evident early one evening when he managed to make friends with a sad, bellowing cow out in the meadow and succeeded in milking her. Marshall was jubilant. The next morning we were treated to the best pancake breakfast I had had since leaving England. Fresh milk blended much, much better than water with our G.I. dehydrated pancake mix!

These were experiences never mentioned in any letter, for once any mail-censoring officer let the word out that our observation post (O.P.) was living "high on the hog," we would have had to field questions regarding our tending-to-business attitude. I dared not take the chance.

Going through the letters, I found little evidence of censor snipping. My first one home from England had two or three holes in it, but that is understandable. Crossing the Atlantic from New York to Scotland's Firth of Clyde in five December days aboard that great, fast, unescorted liner, *Queen Mary,* in the company of 14,999 other military personnel proved a bit heady for my pen. So I learned. There were enough experiences to tell that would not give the censor fits. We O.P. soldiers—while carrying out duties far beyond the gun batteries and headquarters—had a rather freelance type of existence. Our days and nights were bound to be eventful. A four-page letter to Georgiana on March 18, 1945, reminded me of one such experience in Holland.

We had been ordered out into the Dutch lowlands well east of Venlo, very near the German border. Throughout the day we were engaged in our usual activity of scouting and transmitting early-warning alarms of enemy aircraft and buzz bombs, a kind of pilotless aircraft. We were also expected to report on any civilians in the area. Coming upon a few tending their farms gave us concern. Andy, our squad's prime radio operator and at eighteen, the youngest, spit out this mature observation: "These stoic Dutchmen! Look at 'em! No goddamn war is going to disrupt their springtime duties to their land!"

One such family—an elderly couple, their son, and his wife—gave us shelter from the cold, raw, drizzly night in a storage area that led to the pump and laundry room at the rear of their house. We were worn out from our day's activity. After setting up four-hour guard stints, three of us folded into our bedrolls by nine o'clock. Two hours later I was awakened by the commotion of the elderly farmer, holding an oil lamp over his head, picking his way between us to get to the pump room. I awoke enough to keep an eye on him until he departed with a pitcher of water. A few minutes later he and his son returned for more water. The old fellow, while holding his oil lamp in one hand, gestured wildly at me with two fingers of the other, as his son feverishly pumped water into a very large pitcher. I let them use my flashlight, for which they were most grateful. Then, as they rushed out with the water, some key words in the son's excited Dutch fell back on my ears. His wife must be having a baby! Within a few minutes they were back for more water. The old man with more smiles and chuckles and still waving two fingers, the son now a bit calmer and deliberately speaking slower so I would understand. His wife had given birth to twins—a boy and a girl! The next morning the proud father invited us in to see his new family. My letter recounted:

> Darling you should have seen them! The two filled the small crib (built for one) completely, and this tickled the proud father more than anything. "Ya! Ya!" he laughed while spreading his arms wide over the crib. "Full— gross full!" We all laughed, even the mother lying in bed seemingly very healthy. We broke out some of our concentrated cereal rations and brewed some hot porridge for her. Later in the day we'll give her some bouillon.
>
> But the war goes on. . . . As yet I have not had any mail since leaving England, but one of these days it should find me. Don't worry about me. Things could always be worse. . . .
>
> All my love, John

Perusal of "those letters," while reviving memories of my soldiering days, did much to emphasize what suffering, disrupted lives loved ones back home were enduring. For everyone, it was the lousiest of times.

In 1944 when I left home and our family's grocery business for army duty, I was thirty-one years old. My father, then seventy, took leave of his retirement days' pleasures of gardening and enjoying his northern Minnesota lake home to supervise the business until my return. Six years earlier, when Georgiana's parents announced our engagement, he had raised my salary to $125 a month and granted me a junior partnership in the firm: C. J. Sonnen Co.-Groceries & Meats. He also offered to sell me a house he owned in the same neighborhood as our store: Merriam Park in St. Paul. Georgiana was ecstatic, I was happy, he was pleased. "Maybe," he said, "this will help compensate for your leaving college to help out at the store."

"Oh, Dad," Georgiana quipped, "think how I'm compensated for whispering my telephone number to John the night I met him in Carl's drug store!" Carl, one of my many cousins, was managing A. H. Sonnen-Pharmacy, his father's store at 574 Rice Street. During the late 1920s and through the 1930s it was a haunt for the young and restless as well as the old and lonesome. That whispered happening occurred one evening during the winter of 1936–37. After Carl introduced us, we both, out of deference to her evening date, feigned little interest. I, bending over by the soda-fountain chair she was sitting on, mumbled my question while fiddling with my overshoe zippers. She slowly whispered the answer, as I scratched the numbers on the lining of one of the boots. The die was cast.

We were married June 27, 1939. Sixty-five days later Germany invaded Poland. Two years later Japan bombed Pearl Harbor. Our first born, a strapping eight-pound boy we named Stuart, arrived on August 8, 1942. I thought: What a wretched world to present to a first-born son.

Early in 1944, while I was finishing basic training in Georgia, Georgiana and our toddler did quite well, but the temper of the times eventually dictated a change in living arrangements. Loneliness, economics, plus urgings by her parents and sister to come "back home" (a physical move of only two and one-half miles) finally prevailed. Then came Georgiana's task of renting out our furnished home. She struggled through procuring and interpreting the proper rent-control forms before suffering through the screening of dozens of possible tenants. The packing and moving of clothing, blankets, linens, personal valuables, and our son's junior furniture followed. She was good enough to leave unwritten all the sad and aggravating happenings the uprooting from our once-happy household caused, but on occasion the message got through. An excerpt from a five-page letter to me at Fort Bliss on October 1, 1944, her twenty-ninth birthday: "We're getting along pretty well, but quite frequently Stuart gets the family nervous. Many things irk them and vice versa. . . . It's a difficult adjustment for all concerned. I've been warned by other girls in the same position and I try awfully hard to say nothing."

Two weeks later she wrote of further disappointments: "Dad informed me last night in strong tones that I can't go to work while I live here. The kid is too difficult for mother to take care of. My hoped-for office career has gone poof! This will be a long war indeed. I intend to see how far I can get with him about doing *any* type of voluntary service."

I suspect that, during those weeks of adjustment, my letters did little to relieve the family's anxieties about me. On arriving at Fort Bliss, I was assigned to a veteran antiaircraft mobile battalion returning from the Aleutian Islands for a twenty-two week retraining cycle. Destined for another overseas mission, the men were in their eighteenth week and suffering through a schedule of maneuvers in the desert outwash area of the Franklin Mountains north of El Paso and the fort. Life in the desert, though educational, was not fun.

> It gets awfully hot in the middle of the day but late at night it cools off about 2 A.M. becoming almost an unbearable cold temperature. . . . We sleep right on the sand. Over me I had two blankets and my shelter half (pup-tent) rolling myself in them like a shroud. The only clothes removed are my leggings and shoes. . . . You should hear these Aleutian island vets kick and moan about Texas! They insist Attu was heaven compared to this desert "hell-hole." If they are having trouble getting through this—I cannot imagine where I will end up!

I should not have fretted over their aggravations. As events unfolded I ended up quite all right. Once out of the desert and back in camp, the intelligence-section sergeant informed me that I was "officially on their team." Now there were hours of training at the aircraft operation room, plotting incoming and outgoing air traffic at nearby Biggs Field; there were lengthy classes in aircraft target recognition; there were the usual inspections, standing of retreats, orientation classes, and "overnights" at the firing ranges. To me, fresh out of basic training, the schedule seemed far from taxing. To the Aleutian vets at my side, however, the program was an abomination.

Through the last autumn days of 1944, before our battalion shipped out, my letters recorded activities in preparing for, then suffering through, grueling Inspector General examinations.[1] Letters from Georgiana continued being newsy and comforting, but occasionally sad and worrisome paragraphs slipped in, exposing some fears. On November 5, 1944, after we had visited via long-distance telephone for the wartime allowable duration of three minutes, she wrote:

> The entire morning I waited for your call and I was so happy, but just to hear you say "Hello Georgie" tore my heart out. I'm more lonely now than I've ever been and so disgusted with myself for being that way. My folks said I sounded like I was talking to a stranger instead of my husband, but if I let myself go I know exactly what would happen. Thus, I have a strong fortification built all around my heart. No emotion can come in and none can go out. . . . I can't reconcile myself to the fact that you're going overseas. I fight it out within myself a hundred times a day. . . . How long this war has to go on. . . . I'm terrified enough while you're being trained, with you overseas—well, it's indescribable.

I did my best to put her at ease. I wrote that being fortified with her love and having that love actually living in the person of our son, Stuart, put all thoughts of danger out of my mind. I told her that our battalion would probably be assigned to protecting railroad junctions or marshaling yards miles back in the rear areas, "and rear areas today are safer than crossing University Avenue. Here's a kiss: X—X. Now stop worrying!"

As cavalier as I was about my battalion's future, there were days and nights a few months later when I wished I were back in St. Paul crossing University Avenue. Detailing such experiences, because of common sense and censoring, was taboo, but general phrases dealing with location and well-being were allowed. A V-mail note of March 8, 1945, is an example:

> I am now somewhere in Germany. Don't let this excite or disturb you too much, but I know you'll feel better knowing rather than wondering. My feelings are very mixed. I am excited, scared and very tired. This idea of now being the news rather than wondering what the news is, well—it's

disquieting. That news should be all good from now on because I am in the 9[2] Army.[2] I love you very much. It's the only feeling stronger tonight than fatigue.

Letters from home, when they reached me during those harrowing early months of 1945, came spasmodically in batches and in no sequence whatsoever. One with a cancellation date of December 23, 1944, for instance, found me on February 22. Letters I sent during that time carry postmarks two weeks later than the dates inside. Everyone, at home and abroad, was wondering what loved ones were putting up with at the given moment. Everyone lived on stale news. For example, the V-mail of March 8 reached Georgiana on March 22, while she was writing her daily letter to me. This is the third paragraph from her letter, which I received on April 5:

> Darling! A letter from you! I've been calling everybody and telling them to watch that 9[2] Army. All those knots in my tummy are loosening. I'm so glad you're not in the southern sectors for fear of that expected "bloody mountainous fighting" we've been told to expect. If it's any consolation—we all are extremely proud of you. For this V-mail written March 8[2]—what a relief it has brought!

On the day she wrote, I doubt if I was harboring such great relief, but by the time I read her reaction the worst was behind me. Since leaving Holland and our Dutch twins, we made three or four ordered moves along the west bank of the Rhine. I particularly remember the village of Orsoy, directly across the river from the Ruhr industrial area, because it was there that I saw my first jet plane: a converted JuU-88 screaming in low over the river, laying floating mines. In midafternoon of May 24 our group was recalled to headquarters battalion. By the coordinates transmitted we knew it was north of us, across from the town of Wesel. We found our comrades dug in along the shore below the west bank.

The battalion's mission was to provide antiaircraft cover for the Ninth Army bridgehead at Wesel. The city, a trans-Rhine communication center, had a peacetime population of twenty-four thousand—just slightly less than Winona. There, however, the similarity ended. Unlike the Mississippi River, which seems to spread around and meander into back bays and inlets as it finds its way past Winona, the Rhine at Wesel was a determined force rushing by the town's high bank in a deep and clear-cut channel. The scene reminded me more of the topography at New Ulm on the Minnesota River. Seen through my field binoculars, Wesel, like New Ulm, developed on three terraced levels rising from the river.

After being briefed we serviced our jeep, trailer, and weapons and drew C-rations for a week. Then, because night had fallen, we were told to dig in and leave at first light for our new assignment—the high countryside twenty miles east of Wesel. Because of nightfall, combat engineers had put restrictions on the pontoon bridge completed late that afternoon. In the morning, with priority orders in hand, we were in line at the bridge's shoreline take-off point.

"O.P. guys, eh?" an engineer M.P. said as he read the orders. "O.K. You're light. We'll swing you in between the half-track and Sherman tank over there— just to break the weight load. Maintain fifty-foot intervals. And for chrissake don't kill your engine! Ever been aboard a pontoon crossing?"

"Back on the Roer," I answered. "But that was just after the front moved on."

"Yeh. Well, you sure are in it now! O.K. Here we go. Good luck."

We took our position behind the half-track, and after it got fifty feet out on the bridge we started our crossing. Andy shouted at me: "John, how much does a Sherman tank weigh?"

"Slightly over thirty-seven tons," I called back.

"Oh, my God!" he exclaimed. "Why did I ever ask that question?"

The velocity of the rushing Rhine underneath us and the scream of outgoing artillery overhead were my concern. I was worrying about how securely the engineers had anchored the pontoons and how long a range the field artillery had calculated for the barrages. After all our assigned area was only twenty miles east of Wesel. As we neared the last section of the pontoon bridge, I had to concentrate on other matters.

The half-track ahead of us, upon reaching the shoreline, was directed off to our left. We were waved onto a meshed metal apron stretched across the beach leading to a rutted trail that climbed the bank at an oblique angle. The town was a shambles. We slow-geared our way up to, then beyond, the business section, which was on the second level above the river. Winding our way up through rubble, we got to the town's third level, suddenly coming upon a cemetery. Ravaged by the previous night's artillery barrage, the small, consecrated acreage had the appearance of some macabre state set—a ghoulish scene of unearthed corpses flung helter-skelter out of shattered coffins. The bodies lay in grotesque, unshapely positions among, over, and under blasted, upended headstones and tangled remnants of the cemetery's wrought-iron fencing. It was awful. It became one of those tucked-away memories. I recalled the scene, however, while engaged in genealogical research in the 1980s. My paternal great-grandfather's final resting place was the town cemetery of Duisberg on the Rhine—just fourteen miles upstream from Wesel.

Following that unforgettable assault crossing, my letter of April 5, 1945, hints at my real feelings. Inserted in the letter was a clipping from the *Stars & Stripes,* the daily newspaper of U.S. Armed Forces in the European theater of operations. This clipping was a concise reprint of General Dwight D. Eisenhower's April 3 Order of the Day, only the fourth issued since D-Day. He praised the Ninth and First U.S. armies for "yesterday's magnificent feat of arms" and declared that the encirclement of the Ruhr "will bring the war more rapidly to a close." My one-sentence comment about it was: "All of us get depressed, exasperated, worn out and into a plain don't-give-a-damn mood, but recognition from our Theater commander fills us with new spirit."

The letter then shifts to how "pressing business" during the previous night's radio transmissions led to hilarious situations involving a delightful fellow at another observation post, nicknamed "Tall-in-the-Saddle"—he was from New Mexico. Two weeks passed before Georgiana received the letter, and it pretty well confirmed the feelings she had of where I was and what I had been doing. In her answering letter, which I received in the middle of May, she wrote, "That letter on April 5th, the day you had so much fun with 'Tall-in-the-Saddle,' and (do you remember?) the one year anniversary of your leaving St. Paul.... I want you to go on laughing and having fun, but everything seems so mixed up. You are shielding me from the bad spots aren't you?"

Through those weeks of April 1945, my letters relate the changes taking place as we moved eastward toward the Elbe River. With the collapse of the Third Reich, mobile antiaircraft battalions such as ours were assigned policing and transportation missions. The battalion's rolling stock became a provisional trucking company. Observation post personnel served as police-patrol teams and checkpoint operators. O.P. noncommissioned officer (non-coms), if not on police duty, were chauffeuring commanders of truck convoys moving Displaced Persons (DPs) to railheads of camps.

As the tempo and tenor of those 1945 spring days changed for me, so did they for Georgiana. After V-E Day her letters take on a less worrisome tone. On May 9 she wrote, "We celebrated your victory on Monday as the authentic day and Tuesday as the official day! ... around town there was nothing hilarious or boisterous, not even like the Saturday nights of yore.... The best ever though, was an agreement of the Twin Cities that all bars would be closed. Lo and behold, St. Paul double-crossed Minneapolis and remained open. Good! Good!" Her letter then went on telling of farewell parties for Eleanor, a lifelong friend who was marrying a Navy man, and the trousseau-shopping arguments the women got into. "I've seen to it that she will have comphy?? clothes, and for my choices Ed will thank me.... We must have behaved badly in the stores ... she'd lean to conservative styles and prices. I would go the opposite. We'd exchange words. Who won? Guess. She has a screaming swim suit with several voluptuous dresses. Ed sent the money with warnings to buy glamorously. And did I!"

When I read the letter I thought to myself: Is this the College of St. Catherine girl I married and the mother of my son? What has God—and the war—wrought? The next surprise was her announcement that she was working afternoon hours at my family's grocery store. She would be away from her parents' home only during our son's nap time. Evidently, she had negotiated her way through her father's objections. She wrote, "The work is very interesting, but, Lordy, how is it possible to keep all the details clear in one's head? Let's get a farm so you only have to make hay and children. . . . This grocery work, at times, gives me the urge to start reeling like a ballerina."

Judging by my letters those April and May days of 1945, I too had my "reeling" urges. Checkpoint incidents, policing problems, and convoy-trip experiences all demanded that one be a sociologist rather than a soldier. Everywhere there were refugees plus confused and surrendering Germans. At one checkpoint a one-horse wagon with four unarmed, bareheaded Nazi officers and three refugees aboard was being shepherded along by two nuns. Because of the heavy flow of refugee traffic, I quickly checked them out, casually mentioning to Andy that the nuns were in charge.

"Well, by God!" he stormed. "This war has deteriorated into a hell of a condition when they let damn enemy officers wagon through the countryside under the charge of nuns!"

A late April letter tells of a three-year-old Russian boy clinging to me at a DP camp and then four adults almost crushing my ribs with hugs when I related the news of their armies encircling Berlin: "The Russians are marvelous people. . . . It is not too difficult to talk to them. A confused and cluttered German seems to help, and gestures plus sand drawings solve some of the more complex statements."

My chauffeuring duties that memorable month of May included an assignment to a brigade captain ordered to search out and inspect a rumored German airplane assembly plant in our sector. We found the plant but no assembled planes. A letter from May 22 tells about a two-day convoy trip covering more than seven hundred miles of Germany, moving 1,500 Russian DPs one way, then 1,330 French and 250 Belgians another way. All went to railheads to board trains (boxcars) for their countries.

But all was not drudgery. A letter on May 28 details the experience of a trip to the Elbe. An O.P. friend, Bob Mahen ("Tall-in-the-Saddle"), had permission to visit his brother Carl, who was with an antiaircraft unit on the Elbe. Through some off-the-record finagling, I got to go along. In February Carl had been wounded but had been discharged from the hospital in Paris on May 1. We found him quartered with a gun battery in the town of Gardelegen, thirty miles west of the river. For the brothers it was a joyous reunion, and all of us, including Carl's buddies and I, got caught up in an evening of wine and song.

The next morning, under Carl's guidance, the three of us drove to the Elbe River. I wanted to get some pictures of the damaged bridge beyond the village of Tagermunde. Through the blown-apart, tumbled-down wreckage of the bridge, engineers had built a narrow wooden walk—up, over, and through the wreckage—allowing at least a pedestrian crossing. It was the U.S. Army's farthest "Eastern Allowable Penetration" point. While we were up on the first planking, a Russian guard, from his post down in the middle of the wreckage, motioned vigorously for us to join him. We scurried down that rickety walkway and soon were shaking hands, laughingly conversing with gestures and my fractured high and low German while snapping pictures of him and us.

With the arrival of summer came the movement of all American troops into the southern sector of Germany. My letters of the first weeks of June originated from a variety of one-night stands, as the battalion meandered down into Bavaria. A letter dated June 8 from Landau on the Danube reports a new A.P.O. (mailing address) number and the news that the battalion is now in the Third Army. That letter, which Georgiana received ten days later, triggered mixed feelings in her: "If you were slated for the Japanese Empire at least I'd have you for 30 days. If it's definite you're occupational your folks and mine are happy. Seeing all the servicemen in town and listening to Ike's homecoming didn't help any today."

That letter did not find me until July 27. In the interim, we O.P. non-coms had been quite busy with delivering messages and chauffeuring not only battalions but also such units as military government and investigative staffs of the Counter Intelligence Corps and Office of Strategic Services. Through that summer my letters read like a travelog of battered western Europe. From the Austrian border in the Salzburg area: "Now I've seen some real mountains. It's amazing I've seen the Alps before the Rockies!" Then from the Oberammergau area: "Occasionally a real lake would appear, and this, plus the thick pine woods gave me a twinge of lonesomeness for our cabin up at Trout Lake." As expected, I found a sad paragraph in my letter of June 27, 1945—our sixth wedding anniversary—sent from Luxembourg, where I had gone on a mission.

> I shall probably drag myself through the day wondering more than ever just when it will be that I will again be in your arms. The minutes will struggle into hours and the hours will somehow, over a thousand obstacles, make themselves into the day. And suddenly our sixth anniversary will be gone—our second one apart from each other. I hope to God it will be our last separated one.

And it was.

There remained, however, a separation of nine more months through which we anguished our way trying to maintain an optimistic, cheery attitude. It was not easy. Two or three times during July my letters noted that the battalion's status remained as Cat. II (category 2: bound for the Pacific). What sustained both of us was my thought in one letter of a "great possibility of a 30 day furlough at home before being sent on to the Pacific, but what month (Sept., Oct., Nov.) remains unknown." On August 1 Georgiana was cheered by the delivery of four of my letters that were three and four weeks old. In her three-page answer that day, there is a melancholy tone in her description of "lots of G.I.'s in the store with their mothers or wives to pick out special food they've done without while overseas. We have no news of you later than July 15, so maybe—I'm just dreaming again."

On that first day of August 1945, Georgiana and I appear to have been enveloped in the same melancholy mood, for while she was writing me that Wednesday evening, I, in my own time zone, seven or eight hours earlier, had apologized for the shortness of my letters "because there's nothing to write about except the continuous odor of manure in this village, my inactivity and horrible heart-tearing rumors of our battalion not getting home this year." What sparked the similarity of our moods that same day could well have been thoughts of our son's approaching fourth birthday on August 8. Thankfully, the immediacy of these melancholy moods, whether indicated or openly confessed, was gone by the time we received each other's letter. Weeks would have passed, as well as yesterday's dispositions. It was the golden age before direct dialing. Even as I wrote another blue note on August 7 the *Enola Gay* B-29 had returned to base on Tinian Island after completing its mission over Hiroshima. By the time Georgiana received my letter, it was V-J Day and the war was over.

The V-J Day letter I wrote the night of August 15 is a pack of seven pages that overweighed its airmail envelope and arrived with six cents postage due. At the letter's end I put the question that would be on all of our minds: "When do we get out? Well, you and everyone at home know as much about it as we do. If you could see the thousands of 85 or higher pointers still over here you would understand who must be moved first. It looks like a long, tough sweat for my 49 point rank."[3]

In her V-J Day letter to me that day, Georgiana reported, "Stuart got to see all there was to see of Victory Day, but nothing was as impressive as the little kids in the block. They formed a parade of their own, and with regret, I took him out of the ranks to see mediocre sights downtown!"

Ten days later, upon receiving my first postwar letter, she wrote further reflections of that memorable V-J Day. This time all the bars were closed—in both cities! There was "lots of laughing and shouting, but everyone knew somebody who was never coming home. . . . At first I thought it was just me," she wrote. "Then the next day at the store everybody said they felt that way. It must have been universal."

She informed me that she had not, as yet, "filled the car's tank with gasoline. Now that rationing is over it doesn't seem to dwindle away so fast! I read in the paper that a man went one better on 'fill 'er up' command at a station. He called out: 'Splash 'er over!' Another motorist had a fill and the tank, not used to the weight, dropped off."

The euphoric mood of V-J Day was enhanced for me on August 17, when I received temporary duty at two hotels in Berchtesgaden that the U.S. Army had taken over to serve as rest and relaxation centers. I had, to say the least, a plush assignment. All I had to do was drive my jeep on errands for the hotel staff and perform small supply and marketing runs for the chef. Judging by my letter home announcing the assignment, the best percs were "no guard duty, no reveille, no aggravating detail duty and—thank God!—no more manure-filled streets of Waging village! The war is certainly over!"

During the remaining months of 1945 our letters, while still newsy accounts of our day's happenings, tend to reflect more and more what was really gnawing at us—War Department vacillations in carrying out discharge plans. Every third or fourth letter through those months contains a comment or two about some rumor, rumble, or argument concerning the latest "point spread" between duty-bound and home-bound G.I.s. On September 21 I wrote: "Whenever soldiers meet the conversation is 'points' along with Congress's pending action regarding two year men and fathers." Then in next day's letter I report: "According to today's news I again have 49 points. This point system is getting laughable. Up, down, in and out we go!"

From Georgiana came worrisome questions and wondering comments that were prevailing on the home front. October 17: "We read and hear much about the E.T.O. men with 44 points being replaced after the first of the year. Haven't you heard that?" October 19: "Does that softly whispered change of 50 points discharge by December mean anything to us?" November 9: "G.I.s with 45 points and over are being discharged in the U.S. Will you tell me why so much legislation has been put across to soothe the brows of those 'unfortunate' ones who have never been overseas?" December 16: "There has been a complete blackout as to change in point scores from the War Department. That's no help! As an added attraction hardly any mail is getting through. I should get first prize for grumbling, shouldn't I?"

What she wrote about the mail was factual, but nominating herself for the grumbling award was erroneous. Nobody could outgrumble the G.I. combat veteran. What had contributed to the foul-up of our personal mail delivery was the deactivation of the battalion that had brought me overseas. Then, from October on, the unit I was transferred into had four A.P.O. address changes. In addition, I was sent on assignments in five different localities: Berchtesgaden and Munich, Germany; and Salzburg, Wels, and Linz, Austria.

With the dawn of 1946 our worries and frustrations escalated almost into despair with the War Department's devastating announcement that the point system of discharging would be abandoned. Deployment and discharge would be accomplished "only at the Army's pleasure." At the time I was on duty in the security section of the Transportation Corps at Linz. When the *Stars & Stripes* broke the story on January 5, tempers of the thousands of G.I.s billeted in the city rose almost to flashpoint. Tempers were short not only about the point-system abandonment, but also Secretary of War Robert Patterson's admitted ignorance of the system and how it worked. Every "pipeline-bound" soldier was a bundle of nerves awaiting the *Stars & Stripes* of the day. In one letter I reported, "And when the paper hits the street murmurs and vocal abuse crescendo into roars as we read another asinine statement by some character in supposedly responsible position. For example: General Collins, Public Relations officer of the General Staff: 'There are few, if any men who are left in Europe that ever heard a shot fired in this war!'"

That irrational action by the War Department not only alienated we moldering warriors overseas but was also most distressing to loved ones awaiting us at home. "All the announcements coming from the War Department about demobilization have me frightened no end," Georgiana wrote. A later letter of hers pronounced, "It's getting impossible to wait for War Department announcements, letters or word from you if you are needed or not in Europe. And wouldn't this last hurdle be the most confused one!"

During the last days of January my letters, however, exhibit a growing conviction that within a few weeks my forty-nine points would qualify me for discharge. Throughout the month, despite all the nerve-wracking press releases from posturing officials and misguided editorialists back home insisting that deployment was "now at too rapid a pace," men with fifty-two to fifty-five points continued to be transferred into home-bound units. In a January 22 letter I mentioned that "if I were in Italy I'd be on my way home or, at least ready to ship. Maybe V-Me Day is pretty close at that." Then there is my January 31 letter:

> I met a new "stateside" replacement last night. He's a new kid that came up from Salzburg as currier from headquarters. We have over a hundred such replacements and more due in. The outfit will soon be a "young" unit. My day for transferring must be getting close. Yesterday the battalion executive officer offered me a couple of promotions *if* I would sign up for 60 or 90 more days. It's nice to know that I had the privilege of refusing.

It was February 8, 1946, that the long-awaited news of my "particular day of transferring" burst upon me. Orders were that on the following Thursday— February 14—I would be transferred into the Eighty-third Division, which was scheduled to sail early in March. How absolutely appropriate, I thought, to start the journey home to my love on St. Valentine's Day!

By February 16 I was in the pipeline with dozens of other home-bound soldiers from the Linz area. Trucked up into the small resort village of Bad Aussee in Austria's highland and lake district southeast of Salzburg, we remained packed inside two or three local inns of that snow-engulfed village for a week. There was no incoming mail, for on my last day in Linz, post-office forwarding cards had been filed. Georgiana would be getting back her letters—to be followed shortly, we trusted, by her husband. The last dispatch, the end-most communication in our collection of 1,116 letters, is a Western Union NLT cable night letter dated March 2, 1946. BUY THAT BEEF ROAST AM NOW IN LEHAVRE SHOULD SAIL WITHIN TEN DAYS ALL MY LOVE—JOHN

Thus it ended—my winter project of perusing our wartime letters: 1,116 of them unfolded, read, refolded. Sorted, bundled, accompanied by forty-five pages of notes on legal-pad paper and now assembled into four conveniently sized boxes, properly labeled. They rest atop a low-legged console table in my den. It is early spring of 1988. Ringing in my ears is Georgiana's premise: "Maybe by springtime a decision will come easier."

It does not. I am no longer noncommittal about the letters. We should keep them. Georgiana insists hers should be thrown away—only mine should be saved. This is ludicrous. The collection becomes meaningless, I tell her, if one-half of the whole is destroyed. The argumentative banter continues until all we do is agree to disagree. Through the spring days of 1988 I conclude that, because the letters are out of the attic, no longer a part of its tucked-away jumble, now arranged and cataloged in sensible order, the major condition of "doing something about them" has been met. I will hold the collection in my den, and on occasion, when the signs are right and moods in sync, reopen the subject about its final disposition.

But it was not to be. As spring evolved into summer Georgiana's health began to deteriorate, and for the next eighteen months the battle was fought to save her from that most insidious of all diseases—cancer. The matter of our letters never again was raised. She died on the Sunday evening of December 3, 1989. Down in my den our wartime letter collection remains neatly boxed and undisturbed. The same cannot be written about my memories or emotions.[4]

NOTES
From Minnesota History 53 *(Summer, 1992)*.

1. These were the U.S. Army's system of thorough inspections and oral examinations targeted at units scheduled for overseas duty.

2. A subliminal reference, no doubt, to assure those at home that I was still functioning in the U.S. Army despite our assignment to the British Twenty-first Army Group commanded by Field Marshal Bernard L. Montgomery.

3. The War Department's discharge plan was a flexible system of points gained by time in service, time overseas, battle zones experienced, age, and dependents. Point value fluctuated as political winds back home kept changing directions.

4. The author has donated the correspondence to the Minnesota Historical Society.

TECHNOLOGY & INDUSTRY

A Pioneer Businessman:
The Letters of Wenzel Petran

EDITED BY CARLTON C. QUALEY

> *The 1840s represented the high tide of Manifest Destiny. The*
> *Mexican War (1846–48) secured the Southwest, Texas, Utah, and*
> *California. The middle of the country, once viewed as a "natural"*
> *boundary of civilization, now needed to be settled, in part to justify*
> *a railroad to the Pacific. At the same time, new immigrants were*
> *flooding in from Europe, especially the Irish fleeing the potato*
> *famine and Germans the failed revolution in 1848.*
>
> > *Among the German immigrants arriving in 1849 was young*
> *Wenzel Petran. By 1855 he had left New York, started a family, and*
> *moved to St. Anthony in Minnesota Territory. The letters he sent his*
> *aunt and uncle back in Tetschen describe his successful business*
> *ventures in Minnesota. They also contain his observations of the*
> *Panic of 1857, the controversy over Kansas and Minnesota statehood,*
> *and the Civil War and the Dakota Conflict of 1862.*

INTRODUCTION

Much of the literature of immigration is marked by the stereotype of the
poverty and hardship of agricultural pioneering. An exception to this pattern
is the career of a young German immigrant named Wenzel Petran, who dis-
embarked from a steamboat at St. Paul in the late spring of 1855, accompanied
by his wife and three young children. Petran had already been a resident of the
United States for six years; he arrived with several hundred dollars in his
pocket and promptly established himself in the merchandise business in St.
Anthony. The story of Wenzel Petran is told in a series of letters, now in the
possession of the Minnesota Historical Society, written to relatives in Germany
over a period of four decades. The following selections from the correspondence describe his life in St. Anthony and Minneapolis during the years from
the mid-fifties until just after the Civil War. The letters have been translated by
Jacob Reiner.

Petran was raised in middle-class circumstances in the city of Tetschen
(later Cieszyn), in the much contested border region of Germany, Poland,

Slovakia, and Moravia. Because of his father's early death and his mother's re-
marriage, he was brought up by an uncle and aunt, Johann and Theresia Pompe.
The Pompes were a well-to-do family and, until it became apparent that Wenzel would not return from America, they expected to make him the heir to their
business and property holdings. Perhaps because of this relationship, Petran's
letters to them are rich in details of economic life, which give them particular
interest for students of Minnesota history.

In 1849, for reasons which may only be speculated about, Wenzel Petran left
Tetschen and began a journey to the United States. In August of that year he
sent to his aunt and uncle a letter which described his crossing of the Atlantic
in the three-masted sailing vessel "Rio Grande" along with 135 other immigrants and his trip by steamboat to Albany and by railroad to Buffalo. At Buffalo
he left his companions and struck off on a walking trip through the northwest
corner of New York State which took him to Niagara Falls and thence to Lockport, a town on the Erie Canal.

Despite Petran's limited knowledge of the English language, he found employment within a few hours of his arrival with a Lockport firm that sold dry
goods and groceries. Subsequent letters over the next few years described how
well he was getting on, business conditions generally, his investments in land,
his marriage, and the birth of his first child.

Then, on July 18, 1855, he wrote to his aunt and uncle from St. Anthony, Minnesota. His letters carry on the story from this point.

                              *   *   *

In the hope that you have received my letter of last April enclosing the pictures,
I am keeping my promise to write to you about my journey and my present
place of residence. Gripped, like many thousands of others, by the fever to seek
happiness in the Far West, I decided early this year to go there. I sold all my
property and belongings except the most essential and left with my family on
May 3. I sold my land for $900, receiving $200 in cash and the balance to be
paid in four yearly installments. My other property I sold mostly against notes
dated October 1, 1855, at one per cent interest. Thus I took with me about $650
in cash. My notes and debentures for the land I left behind with my wife's
brother-in-law. Our farewell from my wife's parents was a very painful one,
and made us actually regret our decision. My wife often longs to return, as she
has always lived near her friends, but she consoles herself with the hope that
she may be able to visit her friends in about a year.

Laden with good wishes for a happy journey and for our future welfare, we
left Lockport on May 3, on the railroad. Our journey took us after a day and a
night to Detroit, the principal city of Michigan, on Lake Erie. We traveled on
the recently completed railroad along the north shore of Lake Erie, through

the English province (Canada). After one night's rest we continued our journey on the railroad through the states of Michigan and Illinois. Chicago lies on Lake Michigan and is a large commercial city of 100,000 inhabitants.[1] However, it lies rather low and therefore is dirty and unhealthy. As it was our intention to go to the state of Iowa, we took one of the eleven trains that go out of Chicago. The train cuts across the state in a southwesterly direction and ends at Rock Island on the Mississippi. After arriving at Rock Island, not an important city, we crossed over the river to Davenport, Iowa. I wanted to go from here into the interior of the state, but this could be done only by wagon transportation, and it was already so warm that I could imagine how hot the summers must be. After three days' delay, I decided to go up the river to Minnesota, where St. Paul, the principal city, is situated on the Mississippi. We therefore embarked in Davenport on a steamer bound for St. Paul (four hundred miles from Davenport) and arrived after a six-day journey. The trip up the river would have been a very pleasant one; on such a large steamer one lives as comfortably as in a house; every family has its own room, and the table was very well supplied. However, since our sojourn in Davenport, I had been troubled with diarrhea, which did not leave me until three weeks later. Also there were many cases of Cholera on the steamer and in southern cities along the Mississippi. The shores of the Mississippi afford the traveler a view of many romantically beautiful districts and growing cities. It is the largest river of North America, cutting through the country from north to south, and has its source in Canada, north of the United States. It runs through Minnesota, touches in its course the borders of Iowa, Illinois, and Missouri, and continues on through the southern slave states, where it empties into the sea at New Orleans.

Only four years ago, St. Paul, like St. Anthony (nine miles from St. Paul), was a place of few houses. Now it has around ten thousand inhabitants, and is the seat of government of Minnesota. It is situated one hundred miles southwest of Lake Superior and about two thousand miles from New York. Upon arriving in St. Paul, I lodged my family in a boarding house and went to several places looking for openings, but could find none, as so many thousands of others had arrived this spring. I made my way on foot into the interior, where I looked up an acquaintance from Lockport, who lived thirty-five miles from St. Paul on a farm. On my return trip I passed through St. Anthony, where I again looked for an opening and succeeded in finding a shop, which I rented for one year for $146. As soon as I have got my money together, I wish to buy myself a lot, as real property here soon increases in value. Two or three years ago, one could buy lots on the best streets for three hundred dollars, but now they ask a thousand and get it too. I opened my business here on June 18, after buying my stock in St. Paul. It consists of groceries, hardware, and farmers' supplies. As soon as I get my money in the fall, I want to go to Chicago or St. Louis, the best markets of the West, to buy my supply for the winter, as one can buy much cheaper there. St. Paul is the end point for shipping on the Mississippi, as the river farther up is too shallow for heavy boats. Recently a boat was built which came here for the first time on July 6, and the inhabitants of St. Anthony were extremely happy that it really could be done with the water at such a low level.[2]

St. Anthony is delightfully located on the Mississippi, which here forms a beautiful falls seventeen feet high. A fine suspension bridge over the river has just been completed. It has approximately six thousand inhabitants. Business here is somewhat at a standstill, as with the low water level, timber cannot be floated down the river, and consequently no building can be done, which deprives several thousand persons of employment.

Minnesota is not yet a state; it is now classed as a territory. It has a very healthy climate, beautiful country and natural scenery, and with its clean, fresh air it reminds me strongly of the northern part of Germany. It has good well water, many rivers and small lakes, which are all fed by springs, and are full of fish. The railroads have not yet come here, although one is expected from Iowa or Illinois within the next two years. Fruit is not grown here as yet, but must be brought from below.

There is still much good government land here, of which every man may take 160 acres if he builds a cabin on it, lives there and cultivates the land. However, after several years, until [when] it is measured, he must pay $1.25 per acre. This would be a good place for speculation in real property, as the land is rapidly being populated. As money is not so plentiful here as in the eastern states, high rates are paid, twenty-five dollars to forty dollars per hundred being very common.

My dear friends, I greet you most heartily in the name of my family, and hope with all my heart that this letter will find you in good health and happy spirits. As for us, we are well, and will be quite well satisfied until [when] we get our own ground under our feet.

*   *   *

When Petran wrote to his aunt and uncle two and a half years later, his stationery was illustrated with an engraving of the village of St. Anthony, on which he had marked the location of his house. Among a variety of other matters, Petran comments on the effects of the Panic of 1857, which had a severely depressing impact on the economy of Minnesota Territory. The letter is dated January 30, 1858.

I received your welcome letter of August 30, 1857, and notice with pleasure that you are all well. You mention that traveling is connected with my business and you consider that burdensome, but it is the opposite from that. One counts it a pleasure here (although taken as a whole, it is more dangerous here than in

Europe) to make a trip twice a year. Traveling here is much more common than in Germany, both as regards private as well as business people. The American people are lovers of travel, the whole mass of them.

My house and ground seem expensive, but the ground is valuable as it is in the business district.[3] A distance from town, one can buy a building site 65 feet wide and 160 feet long for $100. My place just now is worth $100 the front foot. I have 25 feet on the front street and it extends 110 feet back to the next street where the hotel stands. The main street is adapted for business only and not many families dwell there. Most of them choose homesteads for building places; these are much bigger and cheaper. I am, at the present, still living over my store. I am, however, considering finding a suitable place in a nearby town. This town named Minneapolis has a very attractive situation and very beautiful buildings for a new city.

Since March the 5, I have bought three building lots here in St. Anthony and two in Minneapolis that are more suitable for business than for living quarters. These two places together cost me $2,800. I bought these places fairly cheap and would have been able to sell them for a good profit, but there is still a chance of an increase in valuation as new cities are populated quickly and real estate is rising in value.

After I sent the last letter to you, I went as usual to Chicago in '56 to buy merchandise. I only had $2,300 with me, but bought $6,500 worth of merchandise. Naturally the balance is on two, three, and five-month credit. I have had considerable business this fall and winter, because there was so much money in circulation. I pay my debts promptly and have made a nice profit.

Last spring ('57) I did not go to buy but ordered my merchandise for the summer trade. Throughout the whole summer, trade was not as lively as it had been before. There seemed to be a decrease in the amount of money. In the fall, it seemed to get worse, and I arranged my merchandise accordingly and did not even look at those things that were not absolutely necessary, and I had very good results. Then in the month of October, 1,459 private banks, that issue all the notes which circulate as money, defaulted on half of the payments and so most of the notes were worthless. Although at one time I had hundreds of dollars worth of notes, I lost on none of them as I had handed all questionable notes out in good time.

Following this, trade was practically stopped for a time and trades people who depended on credit (without capital) were in distress, being broken to pieces like thin wood, because they could not sell their merchandise quickly enough. As for me, the panic of which you have surely read and heard, which extended from America to England, France, Germany, and especially to Hamburg, found me in good condition. This was because I saw how trade was going and did not put my money into merchandise but loaned $1,500 of my capital on good land mortgages to different companies up to twelve per cent per month.

Several at three per cent, but most at four per cent per month. This will seem strange to you, but it is the usual amount of interest paid here. Even in New York, where the usual amount paid is seven per cent, they loaned out money from three to ten per cent per month.

It is not to be expected that business enterprises can stand another revolution like it, which caused many of the factories to let their employees go; which left thousands of people breadless, especially in the great cities. Many of the rich in New York who before lived like princes, have lost everything during this crisis and are now almost at the end of their resources. The amount of money squandered for luxuries and so forth for which the Americans are famous is the cause of the downfall.

Since the month of December, much gold is coming in from California (where the late crisis made no impression). This comes twice a month by steamship to New York. These shipments sometimes amounted to two millions to different establishments. By the end of December, the banks of New York had twenty-six millions of gold in their vaults, but still there is much distrust among the bankers and business people and so no use was made of it. Lately, the factories have taken their workers back again, and it is to be expected that by spring there will be more activity in trade and factories. Also the banks that had ceased making payments are now making payments again.

A great help to the poor was the fact that we had a very mild winter here in Minnesota. For the greater part we had sleigh roads and wonderful clear weather, the best I have ever experienced. And then too, we had a big crop in the United States. Grain and fruit in the north; sugar and cotton in the south. Living commodities therefore are cheap. In the western states wheat costs forty-five cents a bushel; corn, twenty-five cents, and potatoes fifteen cents per bushel. In our territory, living commodities are somewhat more expensive, because it is a new land and farming is still at its beginning, and besides this, the grasshoppers did much damage last summer, especially to the Mississippi River country. They came in great swarms. In the month of July in the summer of '56, they came and laid their eggs and in the spring of '57 they hatched out in millions. After they had consumed everything and had grown up, they arose in clouds and took their way southwards where they still are, coming down in Texas and Kansas. This plague has set many new farmers back in their farming, as they have lost everything. Many of these are new immigrants from Germany.

Fruit does not grow at all as yet in our territory, although we bring many apples from the eastern states. We have a kind of berries that grow in a swampy meadow on big quantities. These berries are like the German berries called [*name not given in translation*] in color and taste but are much larger. These berries are called cranberries and are cooked with sugar and make a good and wholesome food. In the last two years they have been very plentiful and many thousands of bushels were gathered by the farmers, bought by the trades people, and shipped out from [*to*] the East, as they grow in very few states.

Big quantities of wild game such as venison, rabbits, pheasants were brought in during the fall and winter. For the last two months, I have had hardly any other meat than venison, as at the beginning of the winter this meat is very fat and tender. There are also wolves and bears here, but they keep their distance from the settlements. One never hears of any calamities along that line.

The outstanding commodity that we ship from this territory is lumber. In the Northwest we have immense pine forests. The trees are felled in the winter time and are dragged by ox teams to the neighboring rivers that run into the Mississippi, and in the spring they are transported to the southern states where there is no lumber. In St. Anthony and Minneapolis we have saw mills (part of them operate with water power, others with steam) that cut our immense quantity of lumber that is used everywhere in the surrounding territory and shipped southwards on the river. Lumber is the usual material used for building in a new country, because it is the cheapest and the fastest building material one can get. Brick is still very expensive here, eight dollars per thousand. In the East it is from four to five dollars per thousand. We have a good many stones (nice limestones) but they cost considerably because of wages and shipping rates. Limestone and bricklayers are paid very well, higher here than in the East. Bricklayers are paid from $2.25 to 3.00 a day; carpenters from 2.00 to 2.50; day laborers 1.50 per day without board. These prices should become lower, however, in a few more years.

Our territory will probably be accepted into full statehood by Congress in Washington this winter. Each territory has to have a population of eighty thousand inhabitants and must adopt a constitution as to whether it wants to be a free state or a slave state. This then must be presented to Congress. With us there is no idea of a slave state as in the territory of Kansas, which is south of Missouri, which is settled by people from the North and the South, both of whom want to win the question for their party.[4] The last two years have brought much confusion, disagreement, struggle, and bloodshed to that section. More recently it seemed as though it would become a free state anyway, although the South put forth much effort to win it over.

Utah is a more or less separated territory on the Salt Sea not far from the Rocky Mountains inhabited by some people who are called Mormons. They have their own religion. These Mormons have ten to fifty wives each according to the number they are able to support. Their high priests, as they call their rulers, have the most. They have lived there since 1845, after they had been driven out from the states of Illinois and Missouri. Brigham Young is their governor and high priest. This Young contributes one-half of his proceeds in order to be in closer contact with God and so receive direct revelations. His people are upset of late, as the government has attempted to send them a new governor and other officials. They are now in confederation with the wild Indians of the Far West and are enemies to all who are not of their religion. This they have announced recently and they urged the Indians to rob and murder an immigrant train that was going from the eastern states over the Great Plains and the Rocky Mountains to California.[5] Hundreds of men, women, and children fell victims to their vengeance. The wagons, horses, and cattle were taken away, but the bodies were left to be devoured by the wolves. The government at Washington has tried previously to this to maintain a different governor and officials, but it was not safe living down there and they had to return.

Last October, the government tried anew to send a governor accompanied by two thousand soldiers. The Mormons heard that the soldiers were coming, prepared to make opposition, blocking all small passages with cannon and burned the grass everywhere. The military has gained considerably since October, but in spite of that the Mormons took seventy private wagons that were not accompanied by militia and destroyed them. They were driving a herd, two thirds of which starved because of lack of grass. The military has had to cease its operations for the winter and make their winter quarters in tents.

So as not to try your patience any more reading this long letter, I will close making these comments on things and inform you that my family is happy and well. Our boy, now over five years old, comes in very helpful in many things and is quite willing to do so. Although we always speak German to our children, they don't learn the language because they mix with the neighbor children with whom they always talk English, which I regret very much because both languages are very essential. I have been coming in contact also with the Bohemian language. For the last nine years some of them have immigrated from near Prague to a town about ten miles from here and I come in contact with them.

*   *   *

In the following years Petran sent a number of letters to his family, mostly about personal matters. Johann Pompe died in the spring of 1858 and Petran wrote a letter of condolence to his aunt. It and other correspondence mention the birth of a fourth child, a girl, and of another son, who died in early infancy. Business was "a little more lively," he noted in 1859.

On May 8, 1862, Petran wrote a long letter to a family friend, Joseph Steinhauser, in which he described the effects of the Civil War on business conditions and business ethics.

New Orleans was recently captured by the northerners. They now have most of the important places on the Atlantic. On the Mississippi, they made their way almost as far as Memphis in Tennessee. At Corinth in Tennessee, eight miles east of Memphis, the two armies face each other and a slaughter is expected almost any hour. The northerners and the southerners each have about 100,000 men. During the last slaughter at Pittsburg Landing (a few miles from where they are now) the northerners lost 13,763 men in dead, wounded, and captives, without any result.

Our national debt by July, 1862, will amount to about six hundred million and should the war last, the amount will be much greater. Contractors became millionaires, and there are officers, the smallest and the greatest, who cheat as long as they have a chance. Their patriotism is much talked of, but in reality there are no signs of it. It is hard to imagine the swindling that comes out in war. Often the highest officers take part. It is hard to imagine how bad it is and surely you could not find it to such a degree in any other part of the world. It shows that there are Americans with no moral character, who will sacrifice everything for the gain of money.

If the South should be conquered, as is to be expected, there will not be the friendly union that is looked for. The South has always disliked the North and now more than ever. There are to be seen many examples, how they have poisoned and murdered the northern troops whenever there is an opportunity. If conquered, it will do no good in the long run.

It is clear that when there are large expenses, there must be a large income. They tax therefore everything possible to be taxed in order to pay the interest on the debt. Like everything else is unsettled times, there is not much business enterprise, in the investment of capital. Therefore, as can be imagined, industry and trade are very dull and earnings are small. My earnings in the last year were fairly good, but I have too much landed property which is worth little now and taxes are higher.

*   *   *

When Wenzel Petran next wrote to his aunt, on February 2, 1863, he had moved to Minneapolis. His letter describes his house and garden, as well as making further comment on the Civil War and giving a brief description of the Dakota War.

It is a long time since I have written to you and therefore I must ask your pardon. I was very much occupied all summer building a house which is now about ready. I had contracted a cough through a cold in November, 1861, and the house that I occupied in connection with the store in St. Anthony always had water in the cellar, which made the whole house damp and unhealthy.

As, because of the war, all goods became very high-priced and there was little to be gained, and as St. Anthony continued to decrease in business and the place across the Mississippi called Minneapolis is increasing in business and being a nicer city, I built myself a private dwelling and have given up business for the present. I rented my store December 1, 1862, and moved into a house where I could be more comfortable than over the store.[6]

The lot on which I built is 65 feet wide and 155 feet long, which gives me a nice garden around the house. It is located on one of the best streets. It cost me, when I bought it five years back, $1,200, but is now worth only $800, as landed property has fallen greatly in price since that time.

My house is 20 feet wide, 30 feet long, with three rooms upstairs and three rooms downstairs, with a kitchen built on to it, 15 feet wide and 20 feet long, and with cellar and cistern under it. Behind the kitchen there is a wood shed 15 feet in width and length. At the end of the garden, I have a barn 16 feet wide and 24 feet long with a stall built in for a cow, which I lately bought. The house and the barn this far have cost me a little more than $900.

As I do not plan to go into business until I have got over my cough, I bought a horse and buggy last summer, so that I can go out every day in the fresh air, and in the fall I go hunting. The summers are very pleasant here, also the winter has been very nice thus far. We have had sleighing for only two weeks.

My six children all had the measles in December, but are all well now. My wife also is well, and I hope that you are comfortable and well in your old age.

The war in this country is doing terrible damage wherever it is raging. Whole communities are being destroyed and burned, and hundreds of thousands of people are losing their lives, and it is impossible to see the end yet as both sides are more bitter than formerly. Even though we are far from the scene, we feel the effects, as everything is very costly, except what one raises here: meat, flour, and vegetables. Taxes are also considerably higher and will stay high as the government's debt is already two thousand [hundred] millions.

The Indians that live on the borders of this state did considerable damage last fall. All of a sudden, in August, they began to attack the remote settlers, plundering, murdering, and burning up things. Those who got away with their lives had to leave everything and flee. About five hundred people lost their lives and many women and children were carried away captive by the Indians. The militia was sent out against them, and many of them were killed, but many of the Indians were captured and thirty-eight of these were hung. The war against the Indians is not ended yet, as nothing can be done in the unsettled part of the country. In our community, there is nothing to be feared any more, even though in the disturbance many of the farmers came to town to be safe.

*   *   *

Theresia Pompe died in 1866 and after her death Petran directed his letters to his sister Anna (Mrs. Joseph Liebsch). In January, 1867, he reported a marked improvement in economic conditions after the war. Minneapolis was thriving; mills and factories were being built and two railroads had been constructed. Petran himself had reopened his business at a new location in Minneapolis. His property, he boasted, was worth "considerably more" than the family business and lands in Germany.

A short letter written April 1, 1869, summarizes his situation at the end of the decade.

I have received your good letter of about a year ago, and also the Tetschen newspaper. I should have answered you long ago, and always meant to do so, but on account of the strenuous life here and of business, everything that does not absolutely have to be done is neglected.

The family consists now of seven children. My wife has been troubled with a chronic sickness for quite a while, and can go out of the house very little. I intend to keep a horse next summer so that I can take her out into the fresh air. The children are well. My oldest boy being sixteen years of age, and the youngest two and a half years.

Business has been very good since I started, until last July. But on July 12, 1868, my store burned down. My loss was about $3,500 to $4,000, of which I received $1,500 insurance. I started to build immediately on the same ground, and finished on December 1, 1868. I have now a better and larger place, built of brick, which is very comfortable and in which I can handle more goods. By and by I am going to go entirely into the wholesale business, whereas now I am both in retail and wholesale.

The main business in Minneapolis is the handling of wheat and since the same is very cheap now, there is little gold in circulation, which is also to be expected.

As long as one is in business one has to attend it all the time, for it cannot be left to others.

*   *   *

Although Petran continued his letters to his sister during the next two decades, his correspondence was devoted almost entirely to personal matters. His wife died of tuberculosis in 1874, and he himself suffered increasingly from poor health. Because of a lung condition he could no longer stand the cold winters of Minnesota. In 1876 or 1877 he gave up his wholesale firm and spent the cold months traveling in the warmer climate of California and the southern states. He died in 1891 in Jacksonville, Florida.

NOTES

From Minnesota History *39 (Summer, 1964).*

1. Here and in the succeeding paragraphs Petran's figures for population and mileage are not entirely accurate. The population of Chicago was about eighty thousand in 1855. St. Paul lies about 150 miles from Lake Superior and 1,300 railroad miles from New York. (In 1855 the distance by rail would have been somewhat greater.) The population of St. Paul was about five thousand and that of St. Anthony three thousand in 1855, and, of course, the Mississippi rises in Minnesota, not Canada. *Chicago City Directory and Business Advertiser*, 1855; J. Fletcher Williams, *A History of the City of St. Paul*, 359 (St. Paul, 1876); *St. Anthony Express*, January 13, 1855.

2. Petran probably refers to the "Falls City," a steamboat owned by a group of Minneapolitans who were anxious to promote navigation between Minneapolis and the lower river. Its trip represented one of a number of unsuccessful attempts to challenge St. Paul's pre-eminence as a river port. For more information on this subject see Lucile M. Kane, "Rivalry for a River: The Twin Cities and the Mississippi," in *Minnesota History*, 37:309–323 (December, 1961).

3. The store stood on Main Street near the Suspension Bridge (which was located at about the site of the present Hennepin Avenue Bridge), according to the *Commercial Advertiser and Directory for St. Anthony and Minneapolis* of 1859.

4. Petran's civics and geography were both somewhat awry. Kansas is, of course, west of Missouri, and there was no hard and fast population requirement for statehood.

5. The reference is probably to the Mountain Meadows Massacre of September, 1857. A band of Mormons with some Indian allies murdered 120 immigrants who were passing through Utah on their way to California. The massacre was incident to the so-called Mormon War, a guerrilla action that the Mormons waged against a force of 2,500 troops sent by President Buchanan to assert federal authority in Utah Territory. The first Mormons had reached Utah in 1847. Ray Allen Billington, *The Far Western Frontier*, 1830–1860, p. 214–217 (New York, 1956).

6. The Petran house was located on First Street North, between the present Second and Third avenues. The store was on the same street, in the block north of Hennepin Avenue. *Merwin's Directory of Minneapolis and St. Anthony*, 1861.

The Historic and Geographic Importance of Railroads in Minnesota

RICHARD V. FRANCAVIGLIA

After the Civil War, railroads became the main agent—and symbol—of American progress. They created towns and farms along their routes; they linked the country into one national market. Railroads represented the first American example of big business and developed new forms of corporate organization by connecting distant markets and sources of raw materials. Railroads even reorganized time in the United States as they required the country to be divided into four time zones for determining train schedules.

As railroads replaced river transportation, they also profoundly influenced local growth and development, especially for potential farming communities in western Minnesota and for logging camps and mining company towns in northern Minnesota. Richard Francaviglia analyzes the development of railroads in Minnesota by comparing eastern and western states, transcontinental and granger roads, and studying such settlement patterns as the both-side or one-side-of-the-track towns.

A new era began in Minnesota in 1862 when the state's first train made its initial run between St. Paul and St. Anthony. Symbolically, the first locomotive, the "William Crooks," arrived in Minnesota in 1861 by steamboat over the historic and well-traveled Mississippi River corridor. By the time the first railroad began operating within its boundaries, Minnesota had become a state, and its population exceeded 150,000. Fort Snelling had guarded the northwestern frontier for almost half a century. Cities like Stillwater, St. Paul, and St. Anthony were well settled and growing, and the gross framework of the state's present settlement pattern was established. Settlement was river-oriented, with population concentrations on the margins of the rich farming and lumbering hinterland that stretched to the west and northwest. By the time of the first railroad, then, some towns and settled areas were more than a generation old— albeit a rude, frontier generation. And for more than a decade after the introduction of the railroad, rivers such as the Mississippi and the Minnesota remained the major transportation corridors. Although the rural population began to spread out on the upland-till plains, market centers invariably remained on the rivers.

The railroad, however, soon challenged—successfully—the formerly undisputed reign of the riverboat in Minnesota, and the steel-rail epoch, as John R. Borchert has called it, rapidly emerged.[1] The new mode of transportation quickly began to shape urban and rural life, providing new opportunities and orientations for Minnesota settlers.

By the 1870s—a short decade after its introduction to Minnesota—the railroad had caught up with agricultural settlement. Railroads and settlement complemented each other during these years. Not only were railroads built to serve farm populations, but farmers, at the same time, located in accordance with projected or anticipated railroad construction.[2]

Soon after railroads reached the far edge of the westward-moving settlement, however, they passed it. Grading roadbeds and hammering spikes with a frenzy, railroad companies pushed out onto the uncultivated plains of western Minnesota in the 1870s. The high point of rail building on virgin land came in the 1880s, as railroads virtually plotted the course of empire. They no longer threaded their way through previously settled territory but, instead, now essentially dictated where both farmland and towns would be located, because lands close to railroads were simply worth much more than those farther away. By the 1880s, as well, railroad companies became the major promoters of farm and town sites from western Minnesota far into the Dakotas. New towns acquired a predictable uniformity, huddled as they were behind their railroad depots and below their tall grain elevators. Even town names took on a new character. Indian and "back-home" names became less common than easy-to-pronounce names of railroad men and dynamic businessmen. Examples: Staples, Tracy, and Aldrich.[3]

One might think of Minnesota, therefore, as having three major zones of settlement: one that was pre-railroad, one that developed simultaneously with the railroad, and one that was settled after—and usually because of—the railroad. This may make Minnesota unique among the states. It is neither a western nor an eastern state; it is both.

Southeastern Minnesota was part of the river frontier and was settled in the steamboat era, much like the land to the east. Stillwater, I would venture to say, is quite like towns on the Ohio River. Its setting, layout, and architecture have an eastern flavor. Its main street, like that of so many other river towns, parallels the river, in this case the St. Croix.

By contrast, such western Minnesota towns as Marshall and Worthington fit into a different category. Laid out in broad checkerboard squares, they grew from the prairie and took on a character distinct from that of river towns. Their main streets parallel the railroad, the most important element of their morphology, and the towns' orientations are linear. At one time Minnesota prairie settlements like Sleepy Eye and Waseca were on the western railroad frontier away from lush river valleys. They had difficulty acquiring wood and water, and blizzards swept across them as unimpeded as though the scene were farther west. Architecturally, too, these towns had a western flavor. It is appropriate that George B. Abdill's popular book, *Rails West* (New York, 1960), begins its narrative in Minnesota. The story of laying track and keeping lines open in western Minnesota reads like robust western history, pure and simple. And it is.

That Minnesota is both an eastern and western state can also be seen by looking at the types of railroads that serve it. Aside from the iron-range roads and a few short transfer lines, Minnesota's railroads fall into two distinct classes: the western transcontinentals and the granger, or midland, roads. The transcontinentals gave Minnesota its westward, prairie orientation and made the Twin Cities (as they still are) a nodal point for the northern Great Plains. Generating an exchange of ideas, people, and goods, the westward-looking railroads united Minnesota with the Pacific Northwest. Even railroad names reflected that unity. The Great Northern (now Burlington Northern), Northern Pacific (now also Burlington Northern), and the Chicago, Milwaukee, St. Paul, and Pacific were giants that linked East and West.

The grander roads, on the other hand, had a different relationship with Minnesota. The Chicago Great Western, the Illinois Central, the Chicago, Burlington, and Quincy (now Burlington Northern), the Chicago and North Western, and the old Minneapolis and St. Louis lines all reached Minnesota by the turn of the century, but they usually were the northernmost tentacles of well-established Midwest systems. They connected Minnesota with midland cities such as Omaha, Nebraska; Des Moines, Iowa; St. Louis, Missouri; and Rock Island, Illinois, rather than passing through the North Star state on their way elsewhere. At the margin of two major regions—the midwestern corn belt and the western wheat country—the Twin Cities were tied to the new wheat frontier by the westward continentals while they were linked to the already settled and tamed agricultural Midwest by the granger roads.

Numerous articles and theses written on Minnesota's evolving railroad pattern implicitly or explicitly acknowledge the primary role that railroads played in the settlement of Minnesota.[4] Economic historians have noted the importance of railroads in the distribution of trade items and farm goods. Social historians have maintained that antirailroad sentiment was the spark that gave life to the National Grange and other farmers' unions that were formed for cooperative opposition to what they considered to be the unfair monopolistic practices of the early railroads.

As a geographer, however, I miss the story of the actual visual and morphological impact of the railroad on specific kinds of places, especially towns and cities. To state, for instance, that Staples is a railroad town on the former Northern Pacific only whets my curiosity. Just what is there about Staples that makes it a railroad town? Was it laid out differently from non-railroad towns?

Did the Northern Pacific have a say in what the town would look like? Did the presence of the railroad have any ecological effects on urban growth other than those deliberately sought by the railroad company?

It must have. Towns that sprang up along railroads reveal striking geographic similarities. This is not surprising, however, when one realizes that railroads employed land survey companies which platted towns and gave them everything from their orientation on the land to their street names (like Atlantic and Pacific streets). Most small towns, too, are situated on one side of the railroad tracks, which often mark one "side" or "edge" of town. The Clay County railroad village of Sabin (population: 251) provides a classic example of the hundreds of towns in Minnesota and the Dakotas which exhibit this asymmetrical layout. In fact, perhaps 70 per cent of small towns are built upon only one side of the tracks.[5] There also are indications that the larger they grow the more likely they are to spread to both sides of the tracks—except in cases where they are river-front towns or lakeside towns.

How do we account for the one-side-of-the-track small town? There are several possibilities. First, railroad surveys may literally have dictated town morphology. Since the railroads usually were given alternate sections of land, they may have built towns on the side they owned simply to increase the real estate value of their property. The territory across the tracks would then remain private farmland. Yet railroads were by no means always laid out on section lines, since slavish adherence to a rectangular grid would present topographical problems. First and foremost, surveyors took account of variables such as gradient, curvature, and marshy land. (How they adjusted rail lines to topographic feature in a state with more than 10,000 lakes is another interesting story.)

In the beginning various companies sometimes plotted townsites. Although we know that some of them were independent, some worked with railroads, and some were an essential function of a railroad's early operations, we clearly need more information about the relationship between early railroad surveys and town surveys. Legal matters, too, should be studies: just what did townspeople have to say about where the railroad went?

This and other questions bring to mind another theory, ecological in approach and at the same time imbedded in folklore. It postulates that the railroad had the effect of a cultural-ecological barrier on town life. Let us say, for example, that a particular town was laid out on one side of the tracks for convenience—to avoid numerous grade crossings. The railroad depot, one of the first structures in town, was built on the town side for the safety of passengers. They did not have to cross any tracks to board trains. A depot's front door faced the tracks, and its rear was toward town.

Businesses naturally sprang up on Main Street, which ran either parallel or away from the tracks, but not across them. Industries and warehouse structures such as grain elevators naturally located along the tracks. (Even today one can determine the location of the railroad in a town with about 100 per cent accuracy by looking for the grain elevator.

As the town grew, it expanded out in directions away from or along the tracks—but not at first across them. Crossing the railroad was, of course, dangerous. But even more significantly, trains were frequently stopped for switching or to take on water and coal in towns, and thus they would delay anyone wishing to cross the rails in the days long before the no-more-than-five-minute limit on blocking crossings. Only after the town reached a certain size would people find inconvenient the distance between the central business district and the residential zone, which had developed on just one side of the tracks. Then townspeople would deliberately expand building construction across the tracks. Since retail locations are very slow to change in many towns, an inertia would develop, and new building across the tracks would probably not be the existing higher-class retail services but, rather, bulk dealers and establishments such as taverns. Houses built across the tracks, too, would probably not be those of the wealthy but, instead, of lower-class workers. The folk concept, then, of "the other side of the tracks" might have a factual base. Some sociological studies of small towns tend to substantiate this theory, but its validity as a generalization still lacks proof and needs more research.

People commonly talk about railroads as a problem. Railroad tracks are, for one thing, difficult to cross in many places. For example, the Minnesota State Planning Agency recently noted that in Braham, Minnesota, "the Great Northern railroad tracks . . . present a traffic and pedestrian cross-movement problem."[6] Even though, mechanically speaking, today's automobiles are easily maneuvered and controlled, hundreds of people are still killed every year in grade-crossing mishaps. Railroads, then, are psychological barriers, and town planners as well as local folk recognize this.

Railroads may be social barriers, too. In Sleepy Eye, for example, the Chicago and North Western tracks divide the town between the Catholic "north side" and the primarily Protestant "south side." Tension exists between these two sectors which have separate school systems. Occasional inter-high school brawls have reportedly occurred. Of course, religious differences express themselves in local politics, too. South side residents have stated that a proposed city swimming pool was voted down by the Catholic north side because the pool would have been located across the tracks on the south side of town. That the railroad is a localized socio-economic barrier in Sleepy Eye or any other place is not, however, proven. Perhaps the relationship is constant but dependent on the individual railroad company traversing the town, on county and local laws, and other variables.

One cannot deny, however, that railroads have been important factors in Minnesota settlement pattern. In terms of sheer mass, in fact, Minnesota's railroads are significant elements in the contemporary landscape and land-use patterns. Minnesota has about 12,000 miles of railroad track. About 65 per cent (7,800 miles) is what we might call main-line track—"high iron" (heavier, higher, and stronger), with heavy traffic and modern signal systems. Only about 5 per cent (610 miles) remains in branch lines—those spur-type operations which link main-line points to smaller towns in the agricultural or mining hinterland. The branch-line figure, once much larger, reflects the waning future of the marginal line which once was a county's or town's vital link with the outside world. In another two decades the branch line probably will be gone.

Of Minnesota's 12,000 miles of track, 30 per cent, or about 3,400 miles, is in railroad yards—areas of numerous parallel tracks where freight cars are stored, classified, and shuffled to make trains. This type of railroad property comprises a surprisingly large portion of urban areas. Fully 8 per cent of the built-up St. Paul area, about 5 per cent of Minneapolis, and some 8 per cent of Duluth consist of railroad yards. Even in smaller cities like Owatonna and Mankato about 4 or 5 per cent of the built-up land is in railroad yards and tracks. The percentages are disproportionately larger in towns like Staples, where important railroad yards and shops account for 16 per cent of the built-up area within the town limits. Land-use maps alone, not to mention payrolls, reveal the importance of the railroad in what are traditionally called "railroad towns." In Staples, to use that town again as an example, the former Northern Pacific yard is fully one-third the size of the built-up area of the town and its environs.

But railroading, like other industries, is consolidating itself. And when a railroad greatly reduces its operations at a particular place, not only are large numbers of workers laid off but also vast land areas, temporarily at least, are abandoned. Conservative estimates would indicate that several hundred miles of tracks will be abandoned in Minnesota by 1990. Railroad mergers such as the formation of the Burlington Northern from several companies are expected further to accelerate abandonment of tracks and facilities, since there is duplication on several lines. Other railroads, too, will doubtless part with redundant or simply unprofitable lines in the future.

The concept of abandonment is a basic part of the impact of the railroad in Minnesota; since large portions of urban areas and even small towns are taken up by railroad tracks, abandonment often makes available high-potential land. In the Twin Cities, for example, a Burlington Northern plan for yard development may free hundreds of acres of industrial land. Even in smaller towns, abandoned rail corridors may be used for industrial development, parks, or parking lots. At one time, for instance, much of Staples' economy depended on the Northern Pacific. The several hundred employees needed in the 1920s, however, have been replaced by only several dozen in Staples, and much of the land in and around the railroad yard is no longer used. Remaining railroad structures, such as roundhouses and shops, might conceivably be converted to community uses. Similarly, community use has been recommended for the old Great Northern roundhouse at Breckenridge, Minnesota.[7]

Railroads had, and still continue to have, a tremendous impact on Minnesota. At one time merely peripheral to the state's river and oxcart transportation system, railroads soon came to dominate Minnesota's settlement pattern. By 1885 there was no important area in the state that developed without a very close relationship to the railroad.

Conditions have changed drastically in the half-century since 1920, and in a sense the study of railroads in Minnesota is one of relict features. Yet, since so much of our settlement pattern was part and parcel of railroad planning, we may benefit by a better understanding of the ways in which decisions made almost a century ago still affect the lives of both rural and urban "settlers" today.

NOTES
From Minnesota History 43 *(Summer, 1972)*.

1. John R. Borchert, "American Metropolitan Evolution," in *Geographical Review*, 57:307 (July, 1967).

2. Harold A. Meeks, "Railroad Expansion and Agricultural Settlement in Minnesota, 1860–1910," in *Proceedings of the Minnesota Academy of Sciences*, 27:27–28 (1959); Ralph H. Brown, *Historical Geography of the United States*, 342–344 (New York, 1948).

3. Brown, *Historical Geography*, 342–344.

4. See, for example, Richard Prosser, *Rails to the North Star* (Minneapolis, 1966), and Harold A. Meeks, "The Growth of Minnesota Railroads," unpublished master's thesis, 1957. A copy is on file in the Geography Department at the University of Minnesota.

5. This figure is based on a survey of 100 small towns in Minnesota and the Dakotas taken by the author.

6. Nason, Wehrman, Knight, and Chapman, *Village of Braham, Minnesota: Comprehensive Plan*, 11 (Minneapolis, 1970).

7. Community Planning and Design Associates, *Breckenridge, Minnesota, Downtown Development Plan*, community discussion map (Minneapolis, 1968).

The Technology that Launched a City

ALISON WATTS

*In the period following the Civil War, there was tremendous growth in
American industry. This growth was driven by many factors, including
an increasingly national transportation network of railroads, a large
and growing workforce, abundant raw materials, ambitious entrepreneurs, and continuous technological innovations. Minnesota's economic
prosperity immediately following the Civil War was based on logging,
mining, and agriculture, what William Lass in* Minnesota: A History
*has referred to as "Minnesota's three frontiers." The next step for Min-
nesota's economic development was to find ways to turn crops into
market products, such as wheat into flour. Flour mills opened in St.
Anthony before statehood in 1858; however, as Alison Watts explains,
it was technological innovations (such as the middlings purifier) carried out by Cadwallader C. Washburn in the 1870s that revolutionized
flour milling in Minneapolis and made it the leading flour producer
in the nation until the 1930s.*

During the 1870s and 1880s several significant scientific and technological innovations were made to flour mills in Minneapolis. These developments greatly
improved flour manufacturing and propelled the city into becoming the nation's leading flour producer. The middlings purifier, the gradual-reduction
process, and the Berhns Millstone Exhaust System were the most important
innovations during this time period. These three inventions, adopted by local
flour millers, had great economic and social significance for both Minneapolis
and the state of Minnesota. The evolution from Minnesota's first grist mills in
the 1850s to the cutting-edge technology implemented by the 1880s, and the
impact that this evolution had on different industries, are very important to the
history of the state and the overall growth of the flour-milling industry.

According to one historian, "A fortuitous set of circumstances allowed Minnesota and especially Minneapolis millers to be at the very center of change
and to build for themselves a powerful industry which would dominate American and world flour milling for the next half-century." One of the most important factors contributing to flour milling in Minneapolis was the water

power supplied by St. Anthony Falls. The falls have been described as the "first and enduring impetus to the growth of Minneapolis." Since the falls, situated on the Mississippi River, featured level banks and a great volume of water, the U.S. government built the first grist mill there in 1823. This mill supplied soldiers stationed at Fort Snelling with fresh flour; however, the bread was unsatisfactory and Minnesota developed a bad reputation for flour production that would last until the millers made technological improvements.[1]

Minnesota's flour-milling business remained very modest throughout the first half of the nineteenth century. Mills produced flour for lumbermen who worked the sawmills and for immigrants who arrived around the 1840s. These mills were unsuccessful and often failed since millers were using methods that had not changed for hundreds of years. Minnesota pioneers had adopted the old grist-mill pattern from the East Coast. The grist mills operated when water was poured over a wheel that turned a pair of large stones by way of a simple gearing system. The millstones were set close together and run at high speeds to produce as much meal as possible from a single grinding. This process, known as "low-grinding," produced acceptable flour from winter wheat, the staple cereal of eastern mills, but did not produce favorable results from the spring wheat grown in Minnesota. How millers responded to the problem of grinding spring wheat would affect not only the future success of flour production in Minneapolis but also the development of the city.[2]

Spring wheat was hard, red, and the only kind that could grow in Minnesota's climate. The softer winter wheat, which was milled into the desirable white flour with great success in the East, was preferred and worth much more than spring wheat. According to the Chicago Exchange, flour made from spring wheat sold for about a dollar less per barrel than the winter variety before 1870. There were many problems with milling spring wheat under the old grist-mill process. Winter wheat had a soft gluten layer, and its outer bran coat, which tended to stay whole throughout the grinding process, could be sifted out of the flour. Spring wheat had a more brittle bran husk, which shattered into fine particles that discolored, darkened, and speckled the flour. The moisture from the bran shortened the storage life of the flour, and the heat from the process impaired its quality. Consumers also complained that the oily interior of the spring wheat kernel (the endosperm) caused the flour to turn rancid. Spring wheat did, however, have a high gluten content, the nutritious wheat substance that gives dough elasticity. But the glutenous layer was too hard to be pulverized in a single grinding, so it was instead granulated into "middlings," which were sifted out of the flour. Hence, the most nutritious element and the ingredient that made baked goods rise was removed, resulting in inferior flour. Millers realized that they had to find a way to grind the gluten and endosperm together but also eliminate the bran. In order to do this, they would need to improve their milling methods. These difficulties in milling hard spring wheat

served as a catalyst for Minneapolis millers to search for scientific and technological innovations that would improve their situation.[3]

Technological improvements introduced in the 1870s made Minnesota the
largest flour producer in the country and provided the foundation for the development of the city of Minneapolis. The area's success in flour milling was
attributed to "a technological revolution . . . [that] made spring wheat flour the
most desired of all such products, putting Minnesota and its millers in a fortunate position to serve the industry and giving Minnesota a name as 'the great
spring wheat state.'" The tremendous milling expansion made Minneapolis
flour the "most profitable product in the industry." The most important of these
refinements were the middlings purifier, the gradual-reduction process, and
the Berhns exhaust system.[4]

The man who is largely responsible for the technological revolution and the
importance of flour milling in Minneapolis is Cadwallader C. Washburn. He
established one of the largest milling companies, solved product transportation problems, and found a wide market for the distribution of his product.
Washburn's capital and business acumen, along with his ambition to lead the
way in the development of the new technology, resulted in a revolutionized
flour-milling industry. Washburn is spoken of as the father of modern milling
in America because of his "flair for technological innovation that was to transform the entire American milling industry." Confronted with the problem of
satisfactorily grinding spring wheat and determined to succeed in his milling
ventures, Washburn generously financed many experiments involved with the
milling revolution. A company booklet for children said that "Washburn-
Crosby Company's experts have searched the world over for the latest and
most improved methods, have studied scientific processes and applied this
study and research to the construction and equipment of their enormous plant."
According to business historian Don Larson, the Washburn family was "instrumental in pioneering several revolutionary changes in the U.S. flour
milling industry, refinements of which were adopted by mills throughout the
world."[5]

"A great flouring mill is a wonderful aggregation of delicate and ingenious mechanical processes," a magazine article once stated. If this is true, many great
flour mills were developed as a result of new technology. One of these mechanical processes was the middlings purifier. The middlings purifier cannot
be called the invention of any one experimenter. Instead, it came about as a result of contributions by many people. The middlings purifier was first invented
in about 1860 by the Frenchman Joseph Perrigault, but the machine was greatly
improved upon by Edmund La Croix under the direction of Washburn. George
Christian, who worked for Washburn in 1870, had tried to experiment with the

idea of a middlings purifier but needed help. He soon hired the La Croix brothers, French engineers who were also familiar with the purifiers that had been used experimentally in France since the 1860s. Christian and the La Croix brothers worked together in secret, and in 1871 the machine was installed in the Washburn B mill. One milling historian describes, in a simplified form, how the machine worked: "The wheat kernel passed through millstones set just high enough to break it up, cracking the hard center and separating the bran." He continues, "This meal was fed into the purifier on a vibrating sieve. Air blasts and suctions removed the light bran; larger and heavier impurities remained on the sieve, and the now-purified, white middlings passed through . . . [and were] put back through the millstones and reduced to flour." George T. Smith, who also worked for Washburn, continued perfecting the machine by devising an automatic traveling brush to keep the sifting cloth clean, putting air currents under more complete control, and developing a method that partially graded middlings. This machine became known as the middlings purifier and was to propel the flour-milling industry into a revolution of methods and machines.[6]

Washburn also contributed to another very important improvement in flour mills. In most mills at this time, sandstone millstones or the more advanced porcelain rollers were still being used to crush the wheat. This made milling difficult since sandstones were costly and time consuming to replace, and as they wore down, a fine grit would become mixed with the flour. Porcelain rollers tended to chip, wear unevenly, and produce an awful noise. Washburn was determined to overcome this difficulty and employed William de la Barre to help him complete the revolution in milling techniques.[7]

De la Barre was an Austrian engineer who became an important figure in Minneapolis flour milling. He was familiar with some of the new European ideas but not with any technological details. Washburn decided to send de la Barre to Hungary in search of this new technology. The Hungarians were very secretive about their processes, and de la Barre had to disguise himself in order to take notes on their machinery. Soon after, de la Barre began planning new machinery to be installed in the Washburn A mill. The new machinery, based on the "Hungarian method," included interspaced steel rollers, which ground wheat into different grades of flour. In an advertisement from the time period, the new technique is called "improved because it requires less power, has greater capacity, and produces better results than the old style gradual reduction." This new gradual-reduction method soon completely replaced grist stones because the steel rollers could do more work with less power, lasted much longer, and yielded more flour. The innovation also prevented heat discoloration, minimized the crushing of the bran husk that speckled the flour, and utilized equipment that was easier to maintain than millstones or porcelain rollers.

The new technology designed by La Croix and de la Barre was imple-mented in Washburn's largest and most impressive mill, the A. This mill was thought to symbolize the dominance of flour in Minneapolis and the city's drive toward milling supremacy. But it only stood for four years before one of the city's most devastating tragedies took place. On the morning of May 2, 1878, the Washburn A mill exploded, killing 18 workers, destroying six other nearby mills, a railhouse, and several other stores—and stunning the entire city. There was a question whether Minneapolis would recover from the blow and con-tinue on its path of milling dominance or "whether the explosion would mark the point at which the industry so important to the city lost its impetus for growth." This situation "brought scientists from all parts of these United States, as well as Europe, for the purpose of investigating and ascertaining, if possi-ble, the causes which should produce such a terrible calamity." The cause was air combined with very fine flour dust, which could explode if ignited by a stray spark from a pair of millstones, for example. "Ironically," one source said, "the explosion and subsequent rebuilding allowed Washburn and others the op-portunity to install the latest technology in their new buildings, thus propelling Minneapolis into nationwide dominance of the industry." According to another source, there would be no more explosions in Minneapolis: "Science and tech-nology went to work upon the problem of their cause and cure."[8]

Once the cause was discovered, Washburn and associates went to work re-building his empire, only this time he installed the gradual-reduction method and steel rollers in all of his mills. A safer ventilation system that drastically re-duced the amount of flour dust in the air, called the Berhns Millstone Exhaust System, was also introduced by de la Barre, a former Berhns company agent, as a way to prevent future catastrophes. The milling revolution was finally com-plete. The development of the middlings purifier, the gradual-reduction method with steel rollers, and the Berhns exhaust system now enabled Minneapolis to product flour faster, more safely, and more efficiently.[9]

The immediate and extended impact of the new technology was incredible. The improvements made over this time period "should not be seen as discrete developments, but together as a response to milling difficulties, and as a revo-lutionary synthesis born and nurtured first in Minnesota but soon spreading through mills everywhere," according to milling historian Robert M. Frame. Spring wheat became much more valuable than winter. More nutritious and yielding 12 percent more bread per given amount, it became recognized as high quality—the best in the world. By the 1880s the new technology was in com-mon use all over Minneapolis and the milling revolution was complete. Wash-burn had, by "championing the development of new techniques transformed a trade into a science." The milling revolution "wrote finis to the primitive practices that had endured for centuries and opened the modern chapter." In the end, the milling revolution was described as "the combined brains of many men, working on the practical application of an already established principle, produc[ing] a machine which revolutionized milling...and profoundly affected the economy of the Midwest."[10]

The expansion of the flour-milling industry after the development of the new technology was miraculous. Not only were 17 huge flour mills built between 1870 and 1880, but Minnesota flour prices also rose from $.50 profit per barrel in 1871 to $4.50 in 1874. Minnesota flour output rose from 850,000 barrels in 1875 to 7 million barrels in 1889. In 1880 Minneapolis replaced St. Louis as the nation's leading flour producer. Sawmills had all but disappeared from the falls areas by 1889, and Washburn's three brands of flour took gold, silver, and bronze medals at the Millers' International Exhibition in 1880, a testimony to the impact of the new flour-mill technology on both the city and the state.[11]

The scientific developments also influenced the perception of Minneapolis. One magazine claimed, "It is a pleasure to become acquainted with a city that owes its growth and prosperity to the manufacture of a good, honest article and to the earnest efforts to improve the quality of that article so as to make it the best of its kind to be found in the markets of the world. Such a city is Minneapolis." The source went on to say that the development of Minneapolis "from an obscure village to a handsome, busy, energetic town is...chiefly [due] to its flour-mills." Minneapolis developed around its flour mills. "As the St. Anthony Falls industrial district grew, so did the city of Minneapolis," another source said. In 1860 the population of Minneapolis was 5,809; by 1885 it had grown to 129,200. Technological advances in flour milling clearly led to the growth and development of Minneapolis.[12]

Flour milling affected other aspects of Minneapolis, as well. Many marketing schemes were developed as a result of the booming industry. In 1876 the Minneapolis Millers Association was formed to establish pricing rules and to buy and distribute wheat to mills. The Minneapolis Chamber of Commerce was formed in 1881 by merchants who bought wheat for eastern mills and soon took over the Millers Association. Consolidation of flour milling took place as giant corporations such as Pillsbury-Washburn and Washburn-Crosby (General Mills) were established.[13]

Minneapolis millers also greatly affected transportation in the state. Since the millers were forced to depend on railroads in Chicago, they sought alternative shipping methods. At first, Lake Superior provided a route to the East, but this passage could only be used in the summer. In 1873 Governor Israel Washburn of Maine (Cadwallader's brother) suggested the development of a new train system. This line would free Minneapolis from Chicago dominance, provide a shorter route to the Atlantic Coast, and open rich territory in surrounding states. This suggestion resulted in the success of the Soo Line, which was completed in 1888 and exported more flour than any other railroad during this period. Minneapolis millers also contributed to other railroad projects that would improve their sales. As one historian said, "In the growth of the Twin Cities as a railroad center, the Minneapolis milling business was a prominent factor; and in the cases of the Soo line and the Minneapolis and St. Louis, the millers had a dominant part . . . and benefited directly by their success."[14]

There are still more ways in which the development of new milling technology impacted the city of Minneapolis. "When an industry develops to the size and importance of Minneapolis flour milling," one source said, "it is bound to affect, in some degree, almost all the other industries of the city." Some examples are the bag and barrel factories that took hold during the 1870s (Minneapolis led the nation in bag production); the manufacturing of milling machinery; and the production of biscuits, crackers, and breakfast cereal by firms such as the Pettijohn California Breakfast Food Company, established in 1893 (later absorbed by Quaker Oats), and the Cream of Wheat company, which located in Minneapolis in 1897. Due to the many mill hazards, artificial limbs became a homegrown industry, with six local manufacturers of prostheses competing for business.[15]

The owners of flour mills also contributed to society by holding large amounts of stock in banks and railroads, and they played a prominent role in religious, social, charitable, and cultural organizations. To serve the growing community, stores, schools, churches, and a hotel were built, and hundreds of laborers and professionals moved in. By 1880 doctors, bankers, lawyers, teachers, merchants, and others were drawn to the thriving community. Minneapolis had evolved into a cultured and prominent city as a direct result of the technological developments in the flour-milling industry.[16]

Minneapolis reigned as the nation's leading flour producer until 1930. Soon after, many of the prominent companies left the Minneapolis area for places like Buffalo, New York, and many of the mills that had once had all the cutting-edge technology were demolished. Some of the old mills, like the rebuilt Washburn A, have stood in ruins for the last 30 years or so. But there is a new movement to restore this area and turn the old mills into a small community. The community will have condos and shops but will focus around Mill Ruins Park—a memorial to Minneapolis's roots in flour-milling—and a major museum about the history of the area.[17]

The effects of the innovations made to flour milling during the 1870s are startling. Spurred by the inefficiency of old grist-mill methods, Minneapolis millers, influenced by European engineers, were able to implement three very important technological innovations to flour milling. The middlings purifier, the gradual-reduction method, and the Berhns exhaust system impacted the way millers marketed grain, influenced railroads, and served as a catalyst for the growth of Minneapolis. These developments are significant not only for the city where they originated but for the entire world, since the methods were used everywhere. It is important to remember how the city of Minneapolis was impacted by the motivation of the millers and how, in turn, their technological innovations have influenced flour milling the world over since the 1870s.

NOTES
From Minnesota History 57 *(Summer, 2000).*

1. Robert M. Frame III, "The Progressive Millers: A Cultural and Intellectual Portrait of the Flour Milling Industry, 1870–1930" (Ph.D. diss., University of Minnesota, 1980), 38; Eugene V. Smalley, "The Flour-Mills of Minneapolis," *Century Magazine* 32 (May 1886): 38; William R. Fieldhouse, "History of the Flour Milling Industry of Minneapolis" (master's thesis, University of Minnesota, 1916), 1–2; Robert M. Frame III, "Millers to the World: Minnesota's Nineteenth-Century Water Power Flour Mills," report, 1977, p. 15, copy in Minnesota Historical Society Library, St. Paul.

2. "Historical Sketch of the Great Minneapolis Water Power," *Northwestern Miller,* Aug. 22, 1879, p. 121; James Gray, *Business Without Boundary: The Story of General Mills* (Minneapolis: University of Minnesota Press, 1954), 17; Joseph Hart, "The Lost City," *City Pages* (Minneapolis), June 11, 1997, p. 17; *Saint Anthony Falls Rediscovered* (Minneapolis: Minneapolis Riverfront Development Coordination Board, 1980), 36.

3. Gray, *Business,* 17; William E. Lass, *Minnesota: A History* (New York: W. W. Norton, 1977), 133; *Saint Anthony Falls Rediscovered,* 36; Frame, "Progressive Millers," 40; Lucile M. Kane, *The Falls of St. Anthony: The Waterfall that Built Minneapolis* (1966; reprint, St. Paul: Minnesota Historical Society Press, 1987), 105.

4. Gray, *Business,* 4; *Saint Anthony Falls Rediscovered,* 35.

5. Gray, *Business,* 5; Lass, *Minnesota,* 133; Smalley, "Flour-Mills," 41; *Saint Anthony Falls Rediscovered,* 51; *Wheat and Flour Primer* (Minneapolis: Washburn-Crosby Co., n.d.), 9; Don W. Larson, *Land of the Giants: A History of Minnesota Business* (Minneapolis: Dorn Books, 1979), 66.

6. Smalley, "Flour-Mills," 42, 45; Gray, *Business,* 19; Lass, *Minnesota,* 134; Frame, "Progressive Millers," 51; "The Early History of New Process Milling—IV," *Northwestern Miller,* Sept. 14, 1883, p. 248.

7. Here and below, Lass, *Minnesota,* 135–36; Larson, *Land of Giants,* 67; Gray, *Business,* 21–22; William C. Edgar, *Medal of Gold: A Story of Industrial Achievement* (Minneapolis: Bellman, 1925), 106; advertisement, *Northwestern Miller,* Sept. 7, 1883, p. 231; Kane, *Falls of St. Anthony,* 105.

8. Kane, *Falls of St. Anthony,* 102, 103; Lucile M. Kane and Alan Ominsky, *Twin Cities: A Pictorial History of Saint Paul and Minneapolis* (St. Paul: Minnesota Historical Society Press, 1983), 46; R. J. Taylor, *The Washburn Mill: A Complete Solution of the Mysterious Causes of the Blowing Up of the Washburn Mill* (Galesburg, Ill.: Galesburg Printing, 1880), 1; S. F. Peckham, "The Dust Explosions at Minneapolis, May 2, 1878, and Other Explosions," pamphlet, reprinted from *Chemical Engineer,* Mar., Apr., May 1908, p. 7; Robert M. Frame III, "The Minneapolis Horror: The Great Mill Explosion of 1878," *Old Mill News* 6 (Jan. 1981): 9; Smalley, "Flour-Mills," 42.

9. *Saint Anthony Falls Rediscovered,* 52; Larson, *Land of Giants,* 68.

10. Frame, "Progressive Millers," 38; Kane, *Falls of St. Anthony,* 105; Lass, *Minnesota,* 134; Smalley, "Flour-Mills," 37; Gray, *Business,* 17, 19, 24.

11. *Saint Anthony Falls Rediscovered,* 35; Gray, *Business,* 20, 28, 36; Kane and Ominsky, *Twin Cities,* 46; Kane, *Falls of St. Anthony,* 115.

12. Smalley, "Four-Mills," 37, 38; Hart, "Lost City," 18.

13. Kane, *Falls of St. Anthony,* 101; Charles B. Kuhlmann, "The Influence of the Minneapolis Flour Mills Upon the Economic Development of Minnesota and the Northwest," *Minnesota History* 6 (June 1925): 148; Kane and Ominsky, *Twin Cities,* 81.

14. Gray, *Business,* 27–28; Kuhlmann, "Influence," 145–46.

15. Kuhlmann, "Influence," 151–52; Hart, "Lost City," 20.

16. Kane, *Falls of St. Anthony,* 98–99.

17. Victor G. Pickett and Roland S. Vaire, *The Decline of Northwestern Flour Milling,* Studies in Economics and Business, no. 5 (Minneapolis: University of Minnesota Press, Jan. 1933), 16; Hart, "Lost City," 16.

WOMEN

Farmers, Warriors, Traders:
A Fresh Look at Ojibwe Women

PRISCILLA K. BUFFALOHEAD

American history as well as Minnesota history has been enriched in re-cent decades by the work of feminist scholars who have asked new ques-tions about old topics. What were the roles of women in society, their contributions, their opportunities? Should women in history be more than just the token recognition of an Abigail Adams, a Susan B. Anthony, a Pocahontas, or a "Betty Crocker"?

As Priscilla Buffalohead points out, the history of women in tribal societies has been even more neglected, perhaps because they seem more of the past, rather than the present or future. Questions of gender equal-ity may also be answered differently based on whether the society in question is stratified or egalitarian in cultural traditions. Buffalohead thoughtfully examines women's roles in a particular tribal hunting so-ciety, that of the Ojibwe Indian people, using their culture and history based on her careful examination of primary and secondary source materials over a two hundred and fifty-year period up to the early twentieth century. She argues that Ojibwe women played key roles as farmers, traders, and occasionally even as warriors.

Until recently in American history the only women from native or tribal cul-tures who mattered were those whose influences on past events were too im-portant to ignore or those whose lives provided anecdotal filler in historical scenes both great and small, in which men were the primary actors. While this orientation is beginning to change as a result of a growing interest in the his-tory of women, contributions of women in tribal cultures remains a much neg-lected field of study. This neglect may stem from a general ignorance of histori-ans and other scholars, an ignorance fostered by the unquestioned acceptance of ethnocentric notions that modern America somehow represents the pinna-cle of civilization and that tribal cultures are but relics of an ancient age. Un-fortunately, all too many feminist scholars wear the same ethnocentric blind-ers as their male counterparts, viewing the study of the history of tribal women as valuable only insofar as it illuminates the origins of sexism in human society.

199

Whether they realize it or not, feminist scholars dealing with the history of
Euro-American women become caught up in issues of sex equality precisely
because they belong to what has always been a class-stratified society characterized by unequal access to power, prestige, and privilege. Many tribal societies, on the other hand, stem from egalitarian cultural traditions. These traditions are concerned less with equality of the sexes and more with the dignity
of individuals and with their inherent right—whether they be women, men, or
children—to make their own choices and decisions. Clearly, then, issues associated with the status of women in stratified societies may be somewhat different from those in egalitarian societies. With these differences in mind, we
can compare the two if we treat egalitarian societies as viable alternative systems rather than as relics of an ancient past.

To understand the dimensions of women's status in the historical culture of
the Ojibwe Indian people of Minnesota and the neighboring upper Great Lakes
region, a critical evaluation of the information provided in primary and secondary historical sources is absolutely necessary. These sources, spanning the
period from the mid-seventeenth to the early twentieth centuries, were written
for the most part by men who represented the successive colonialist regimes
of France, Great Britain, and America. Taken together, these sources provide
biased and often contradictory images of native women as well as valuable insights into their lives. In much of the literature two pictures of Ojibwe women
can be found—one portraying them as drudges and slaves to men, the other depicting them in a far more dynamic role in the political, economic, and social
life of their communities. The difficult task of sorting out these images and arriving at some semblance of truth demands not only an understanding of the
major trends in Western thought about women, but also a thorough acquaintance with the history and culture of the Ojibwe people.

In the mid-seventeenth century, French explorers and missionaries described at least some of the ancestors of the Ojibwe as living in a large fishing
village at the rapids of the St. Mary's River near what is now Sault Ste. Marie,
Michigan. These early accounts spoke of a people who lived in harmony with
the cycle of the seasons. Summer village life depended on fishing, hunting game,
gathering wild plant foods, and planting small fields of corn. In late fall and
winter, village residents dispersed into smaller family or band units to pursue
large game and to trap or snare fur-bearing animals. While early sources were
silent on the specialized harvests of maple sap and wild rice, these resources
played a major role in Ojibwe economic life in later years.[1]

In the eighteenth century, with the exception of those who moved into
southern Ontario and the Lower Peninsula of Michigan, the Ojibwe migrated
westward. Some established villages along the north shore of Lake Superior
and eventually moved into the interior of northern Ontario, Manitoba, and

Saskatchewan. The main body, however, migrated along the southern shore of the lake, establishing villages at Keeweenaw and Chequamegon bays on the upper peninsulas of Michigan and Wisconsin, respectively. This group eventually moved into the interior of northern Wisconsin, Minnesota, and, by the nineteenth century, the eastern fringes of North Dakota. Despite an unsettled period of migration and intermittent warfare with the Fox and Minnesota Dakota, traditional Ojibwe economic life remained remarkably intact. While intensifying their search for fur-bearing animals to trade for European manufactured goods, the Ojibwe continued to make a living by hunting, fishing, gathering, and corn planting.[2]

Scattered references in the historical record on the role of women in the Ojibwe subsistence economy noted with some frequency that women did a great deal of the hard and heavy work. Some observers began to fashion an image of the women as burden bearers, drudges, and virtual slaves to men, doing much of the work but being barred from participation in the seemingly more important and flamboyant world of male hunters, chiefs, and warriors. This image is fostered in the published work of the Reverend Peter Jones, a Missauga Ojibwe and Christian missionary to his people in western Ontario during the mid-nineteenth century. "In accordance with the custom of all pagan nations," he stated, "the Indian men look upon their women as an inferior race of beings, created for their use and convenience. They therefore tend to treat them as menials, and impose on them all the drudgeries of a savage life, such as making the wigwam, providing fuel, planting and hoeing the Indian corn or maize, fetching the venison and bear's meat from the woods where the man shot it: in short, all the hard work falls upon the women; so that it may be truly said of them, that they are the slaves of their husbands."[3]

While these comments may accurately describe a portion of women's many economic roles, they greatly distort the status of women in the traditional Ojibwe culture. This image might be taken more seriously were it not that nineteenth-century writers very frequently made this kind of statement about women from a wide variety of American Indian cultures. Even among the Iroquois of New York, where women traditionally had the right to nominate and recall civil chiefs in political affairs, to manage and direct the lives of their families, to divorce, and to determine how many children they would raise, the nineteenth-century ethnologist Lewis Henry Morgan concluded that they occupied a position inferior to men because they worked very hard planting and harvesting extensive fields of corn and the men showed them no deference.[4]

American Indian women appeared exploited to many nineteenth-century writers if only because their ideal of woman, fostered by the privileged classes of Europe and America, was a frail, dependent person in need of protection. These writers may not have known consciously that their image was based upon the premise that women should be shown deference precisely because they were biological and intellectual inferiors of men. Other writers may also have deliberately promoted the notion that native women were exploited and mistreated to justify policies forcing Indians to adopt the religion and life style of Euro-American society.[5] Laden with the bias of the superiority of their own culture's traditions, observers failed to comprehend the full range of women's economic roles, the extent to which Ojibwe women managed and directed their own activities, and perhaps most importantly, the extent to which women held ownership and distribution rights to the things they produced and processed. It is only when women's duties are seen in relation to women's rights that the over-all status of women in Ojibwe history can be understood. That men in Ojibwe and other tribal cultures did not show their women deference did not in itself mean that they saw women as inferior beings.

Like many if not most cultures throughout the world, the Ojibwe believed that certain tasks were more appropriate for men and others for women. Hunting and trapping, for example, were ideally the male domain, and first-kill feasts honored only boys for their role as hunters. Gathering wild plant foods and gardening, on the other hand, belonged to the female domain. Yet to a large extent, domains overlapped, so that women and men often worked together, having separate duties in the same general activity. In canoe building, for example, men fashioned the frame of the birch-bark canoe and made the paddles while the women sewed bark to the frame with spruce roots and applied the pitch or gum to the sewn areas to create a watertight vessel.[6]

Thus, while an activity might be defined as male or female dominated, in actuality women and men worked side by side in mutually dependent roles. Even hunting, particularly the winter hunt, invariably included women because "women's work" was an essential part of it. Women built the lodges, spotted the game, butchered the meat; they processed the hides to be fashioned into clothing and footwear and the furs to be either trade items or robes and bedding, and dried the meat for future use.[7]

Women dominated the activities associated with the specialized harvests of maple sap and wild rice and the gathering of other wild plant foods. The trader, Alexander Henry the elder, who in 1763 lived for a time with an Ojibwe family in northern Michigan, provided one of the earliest descriptions of the maple-sap harvest. In his journal Henry discussed the extent to which families depended upon this seasonal resource for survival. He also left no doubt that the harvest was a female responsibility. "Arrived here," he noted, "we turned our attention to sugar-making, the management of which . . . belongs to the women." Likewise William Whipple Warren, the nineteenth-century Ojibwe historian, described the wild-rice harvest as women's work. "Their hard work . . . again commences in the autumn, when wild rice which abounds in many of the northern lakes, becomes ripe and fit to gather. Then, for a month or more, they are busied in laying in a winter supply."[8]

Women also managed the planting and harvesting of small fields of corn, pumpkins, and squash. In the late nineteenth century American government agents and missionaries pursued a uniform policy of making farmers out of all Indian people. Ojibwe women, who still assumed the major responsibility for planting and harvesting the gardens, then added stockraising to their provider skills. Government agents may have been surprised at times that many of the women readily accepted some white concepts of farming. In 1916, one issue of the *Red Lake News* reported, "Sophia Chaboyea deserves a great deal of credit for her activities in farming. She now has four milch cows, and finds a ready market for all the milk she gets. She also cares for three horses, four hogs, and about forty chickens. During the summer she farms . . . five acres of land and puts up all the hay for the stock. It would be encouraging if a number of 'around town men' would pattern after her and get busy."[9]

Both sexes shared in fishing, which at certain seasons of the year was as important as hunting in the Ojibwe round of subsistence. Each, however, appears to have had specialized fishing techniques. Men used the hook and line, spears, and dip nets while the women fished with nets. Observers in the nineteenth century portrayed women as responsible for bringing in the bulk of the fish that were used over the long winter months. The women made their own fish nets out of nettle stalk fiber and, in later years, out of twine they obtained from traders.[10]

Women's labor figured prominently in the process of transforming raw food and other resources into valued goods. The women butchered, roasted, and dried the game, waterfowl, and fish. They dried wild plant foods, made sap into maple sugar, and dried and stored corn and wild rice for future needs. Women also did most of the cooking that took place in and around the lodge. They decided when to cook and what portions each family member would receive. They cooked cooperatively for communal feasts and served the food.[11]

While male hunters provided the animal hides used in clothing, the women tanned the hides and sewed dresses, shirts, leggings, and moccasins for their families. They fashioned furs into blankets and used rabbit fur in cradleboards and in the interior of children's moccasins. The women were in fact innovators, blending traditional clothing concepts with new materials. They customarily used shells, porcupine quills, and paint to ornament clothing. When European trade goods were introduced, however, the women gradually added the use of trader's cloth, blankets, and glass or porcelain beads to create new styles of dress. The final products of women's labor, including food and manufactured goods, were important economic resources, essential not only in family life but also in trade and for gift exchanges among families, bands, and tribal groups.[12]

Women clearly managed and directed their own activities. The men who helped did not oversee the women but played assisting roles. In rare descriptions of women's labor, the workers hardly acted as if they were "virtual slaves." Henry Rowe Schoolcraft, the Indian agent at Sault Ste. Marie during the 1820s and 1830s, described corn planting in the following manner: "In the spring the cornfield is planted by her [the hunter's wife] and youngsters in a vein of gaity and frolic. It is done in a few hours, and taken care of in the same spirit. It is perfectly voluntary labour and she would not be scolded for omitting it." Schoolcraft described the late summer harvest as accompanied with the same festive atmosphere.[13]

Although it appears Ojibwe women were not coerced by men to perform much of the hard and heavy work of making a living, it might still be argued that they were exploited if the men maintained the ownership and distribution rights over whatever women produced. These rights are difficult to ascertain from primary source materials, but the journals kept by some fur traders in the Great Lakes area suggest that women came in to trade nearly as often as men. Traders frequently negotiated directly with Ojibwe women for their wattap (used in repairing canoes), wild rice, and maple sugar. Schoolcraft, writing about the corn harvest, provided further evidence of the rights of women over their own produce: "A good Indian housewife deems this a part of her prerogative, and prides herself to have a store of corn to exercise her hospitality . . . in the entertainment of lodge guests."[14]

Even in the male-dominated spheres of hunting and trapping where women only processed material, it appears that they may have had some ownership and distribution rights. Documentation of these rights is crucial to an understanding of women's status in hunting societies. Some leading anthropologists have concluded that, because game was the group's most valuable resource, men as the hunters and distributors had methods of gaining community prestige not available to women.[15]

Evidence among the Ojibwe suggests that women not only "fetched the venison and bear's meat from the woods" but also had a voice in determining who would receive the divided portions. In the late seventeenth century the French official Nicolas Perrot spoke of a custom common among the Great Lakes tribes whereby a young hunter brought his kill back to the lodge of his mother-in-law. She in turn distributed the meat, giving a large portion to the hunter's mother. Again in the mid-nineteenth century, the German writer Johann Kohl reported that at Chequamegon Bay, "His [the hunter's] feeling of honour insists that he must first of all consult with his wife how the deer is to be divided among his neighbours and friends." And in households of more than one wife he noted: "The hunter also entrusts the game he has killed to her [the first wife] for distribution."[16]

Fur traders occasionally mentioned having to negotiate directly with Ojibwe women to obtain the sought-after processed furs. Near his Pembina post in north-western Minnesota early in the nineteenth century, Alexander Henry the younger reported, "I went to the upper part of the Tongue river to meet a band of Indians returning from hunting beaver, and fought several battles with the women to get their furs from them. . . . I was vexed at having been obligated to fight with the women." These intriguing fragments of information provided some evidence that women who processed resources had some ownership rights as well.[17]

In assessing women's status, the ownership and distribution rights they claimed to food and other resources should not be underestimated, particularly in a tribal culture such as the Ojibwe where generous giving and sharing of valued goods was a major means of spreading one's influence. To the extent that these rights were recognized, Ojibwe women seem far less exploited than, for example, women factory workers in a capitalist economic system.

In the seasonal round of family life, women were primarily responsible for building the lodges. Female family members often worked together to construct a winter wigwam. They cut saplings from the woods to form the lodge frame, covered it with rolled sheets of birch bark sewn together and with woven rush mats made anew each fall. Together, the women could construct a comfortable and inviting winter dwelling in a matter of a few hours. They not only built the lodges but were also considered to be the owners of the lodge and managers of the activities that took place in and around it. Schoolcraft spoke of women as household heads when he noted, "The lodge itself, with all its arrangements, is the precinct of the rule and government of the wife. She assigns each member, his or her ordinary place to sleep and put their effects. . . . The husband has no voice in the matter. . . . The lodge is her precinct, the forest his."[18]

In the flow of family life, the ideal of mutual respect dominated the relationship between the sexes. As mothers, women assumed the full responsibility for their infant children until they were weaned. The mother determined when weaning should take place, and as the Ojibwe believed in practicing sexual abstinence until children were weaned, the mother had some right to decide how many children she would bear. Statistics regarding family size are very sketchy until the late nineteenth century, but the available evidence suggests that two or three children constituted an average family. A high infant mortality rate, a lower fertility rate, longer periods of sexual abstinence, and the option of abortion may have contributed to this relatively small family size.[19]

As children grew older, fathers played an active role in caring for and raising sons, while mothers took the responsibility for raising daughters. Grandparents, who frequently lived in the lodge of their daughter or nearby, also
were active in raising their grandchildren, sometimes shouldering the entire
responsibility. Grandmothers were especially important as caretakers of infants and small children when parents were busy at other tasks. That this practice has some antiquity in Ojibwe history is reflected in legends and stories of
children living in the lodge of their grandparents.[20]

Marriage ties bound family groups together. The data on Ojibwe marriage
practices, however, do not fit neatly into the structural model of society for-
mulated by the French anthropologist, Claude Lévi-Strauss, who proposed a
male-controlled exchange system in which women are considered as "objects"
or "gifts" to be traded upon marriage. Among the Ojibwe, mothers and grandmothers, playing key roles as "exchangers," frequently orchestrated first marriage arrangements for sons and daughters. John Tanner, a white captive who
spent much of his youth and adult life with an Ojibwe band whose territory
included portions of northwestern Minnesota, became aware of the authority
of women in marriage exchange when he attempted to find a wife on his own
and was reprimanded by his foster mother. He recalled that "It was not the
business of young men to bring home their wives. Here, said I, is our mother,
whose business it is to find wives for us when we want them."[21]

The idea that marriage is an exchange of women also assumes that it is invariably women who leave the parental household to live with their husband's
kin. In some cases young women did move to the locality of their husband's
male relatives upon marriage. The custom considered preferable, however, was
for the new husband to live with his wife's parents for two or more years.
Called bride service, this custom was practiced among the Minnesota Ojibwe
and neighboring groups at least until the mid-nineteenth century and probably later. While reasons for this preference are not explicitly stated, the resultant practice did afford the new wife's parents an opportunity to watch over
their new son-in-law to insure that he would become a good hunter, husband,
and father. Observance of bride service also gave the young wife an opportunity to be close to her own female kin upon the birth of her first child.[22]

Evidence concerning the extent to which young women had a say in first
marriages that were arranged for them is conflicting at best. These women
were not, however, bound by custom to accept the fate of a lifelong bad marriage. Women, as well as men, had the option of divorce, and the primary
sources indicate that they exercised it. If, for example, a first husband proved
to be a poor hunter, if he showed cruelty, or if he took another wife not to her
liking, the wife could leave and marry again. The second or third marriage
partner was more likely to be of the wife's own choosing.[23]

The obligations of a wife toward her husband's kin group and vice versa were most apparent in customs surrounding the death of a spouse. The widow observed a year of mourning. She allowed her hair to hang straight, she wore old clothes, and she carried a spirit bundle with her, which she referred to as her husband. Into this bundle she put any new item she acquired over the year; at the proper time, the deceased husband's relatives took the bundle from her, distributed the contents among their kin, and dressed her in new clothes symbolizing her freedom to marry again. In the event of the death of a wife, the husband carried a smaller spirit bundle and also observed a year of mourning.[24]

It has generally been assumed, at least by most twentieth-century scholars, popular novelists, and movie makers, that beyond the household level band and village affairs were invariably in the hands of male leaders or chief. This point of view ignores the fact that leadership had a wide variety of contexts in the yearly round of Ojibwe life. Groups to be governed could be as small as a single family or berry-picking party or as large as intertribal war parties or the people who came together for village ceremonials. In general, men led male-oriented pursuits such as the hunt or a war party, while women leaders supervised activities within the female domain. There were occasions, however, when elderly women were chosen as spokespersons for hunting bands. These women managed the products of the hunt and negotiated deals with the traders.[25]

Secondly, the argument that only men were the leaders or chiefs in Ojibwe history ignores the ample evidence in the historic record that suggests agents from the colonial regimes of France, Great Britain, and America actively interfered with the traditional, more flexible leadership system of the Ojibwe, creating male chiefs when they needed them to serve the economic and political interests of each regime.[26]

Finally, intriguing bits and pieces of information which have been virtually ignored by twentieth-century scholars offer the possibility that women village chiefs appeared with more frequency in eastern North America than had previously been assumed. And as late as the nineteenth century, United States government sources named three Ojibwe women as recognized leaders or chiefs of their bands: "The head chief of the Pillagers, Flatmouth, has for several years resided in Canada, his sister, Ruth Flatmouth is in her brother's absence the acknowledged Queen, or leader of the Pillagers; two other women of hereditary right acted as leaders of their respective bands, and at the request of the chiefs were permitted to sign the agreements." In 1889 government negotiators apparently felt compelled to explain to Congress why women were permitted to sign official agreements. Women leaders appear not to have been a problem for the Ojibwe but rather for the members of European American society.[27]

In addition to leadership roles in political affairs, women held other specialized status positions in Ojibwe history. Among the medico-religious specialists, medicine women played a prominent role. They not only treated illness in general but also served the special medical needs of other women, particularly at childbirth. Medicine women were not just midwives, as most adult women knew how to assist in labor. They were called in when complications arose and were paid for their services as specialists. Medicine women were also consulted by women who wished to induce abortion or prevent a miscarriage. In the latter case, one medicine woman mixed certain herbs with lint and had her patient stand over the smoldering mixture. Knowledge of this cure came "to my sister and me from my mother, and she received it from her grandmother. . . . Since no one but my sister and I have this knowledge, and we won't live much longer, it will die when we go; it belongs to our family."[28]

Direct historical evidence points to another specialized role played by a woman: that of prophet or shaman. In a small oval-shaped lodge, the prophet of the shaking tent could predict the future and determine the location of lost objects or missing persons by communicating with his or her guardian spirits. Blue Robed Cloud, who lived at Chequamegon Bay early in the nineteenth century, was such a prophet. She acquired her power in a youthful vision quest coincident with her first menstruation. In subsequent years, she used her gift of power to help her people find game in times of great need. After her first success, she recalled to Schoolcraft in later years, "My reputation was established by this success, and I was afterwards noted . . . in the art of a medicine woman, and sung the songs which I have given to you."[29]

As war captives, women played specialized roles in intertribal matters of war and peace. Those who had been taken as young girls and had eventually married into the enemy group were called upon to act as message carriers and peace mediators. Ojibwe historian Warren mentioned one such woman who became the favorite wife of a Yankton Dakota chief. According to oral traditions, Shappa, head chief of the Yankton Dakota, sent his Ojibwe wife on a "fleet horse" and with his "peace pipe" to arrange a peace between his people and the Ojibwe of the Pembina band. The image of women as peacemakers between tribal groups appears in the oral traditions of other Ojibwe bands as well.[30]

Oral tradition and primary sources provide evidence that some women became honored warriors, although men dominated that status position among the Ojibwe. An account collected by Schoolcraft, for example, speaks of an unnamed woman who demonstrated unusual courage on the path of war against Iroquois enemies. In the mid-nineteenth century, another woman warrior, whose name has been translated as Hanging Cloud Woman, of the Lac Courte Oreilles band in Wisconsin, became something of a legend among her people, according to three historical accounts. Hanging Cloud Woman was apparently a favorite daughter of her father. As a young woman, she accompanied him and her brother on a hunting expedition, where they were attacked by a war party of Dakota. One account suggests that after her father was killed she pretended to be dead long enough to satisfy enemy suspicions. Then she grasped her father's gun and pursued the fleeing Dakota. In the months that followed her successful warrior exploits, she was honored in many Ojibwe lodges throughout the surrounding territory. This woman warrior eventually married, and at one point in her life found herself with two husbands. Apparently she assumed that a first husband had been killed in the Civil War and married another man, only to find out later that her first husband was alive. Hanging Cloud Woman ended her very long career as a housekeeper for a local lumber baron and died in 1919.[31]

All too brief and scattered references to other such women among the Ojibwe point to the possibility that this position was institutionalized, that there was a patterned, community-recognized way of becoming a woman warrior. Warrior women, for example, exhibited common life histories: youthful vision quests which pointed them in the direction of a career that crossed gender categories; parental and community recognition of their superior athletic skills; and delayed marriage. Taken together, this information suggests that the Ojibwe maintained culturally recognized channels that women could use to enter male-dominated domains.

In exploring women's status in hunting societies beyond fleeting impressions and commonly accepted stereotypes, a new image of Ojibwe women begins to emerge. This image speaks of dynamic and resourceful women whose contributions encompassed traditionally defined female roles and reached beyond them into nearly every facet of life. Women were in a very real sense economic providers. They worked alone and in groups to construct the lodges, collect the firewood, make the clothing, and produce a substantial portion of the food supply. Credit for these contributions has for too long been hidden in the sources because historians and ethnologists presumed women's work to be supplementary and secondary to the primary hunting role of men. Furthermore, continued references to women's ownership and distribution rights, to their products, and to their strong voice in determining how male-acquired resources should be distributed suggest that the products of women's work were appreciated by the Ojibwe themselves.

Ojibwe oral tradition emphasized the distinctiveness of the sexes, and child-rearing practices stressed sex separation in work roles, dress, and mannerisms. While the ideal of sex separation ordered the work world and social life into mutually dependent spheres, some women were able to make unique contributions in male-dominated areas with seeming ease. Repeated clues in the primary historical sources resolve this apparent contradiction. Taken together, they describe the Ojibwe as an egalitarian society, a society that placed a premium value on individuality. Women as well as men could step outside the boundaries of traditional sex role assignments and, as individuals, make group-respected choices.[32]

Perhaps the over-all status of women in Ojibwe history and the quality of the relationship between the sexes are best summarized by the scientist-explorer, Joseph Nicollet, who nearly 150 years ago as a guest in Ojibwe lodges of northern Minnesota observed that family life was "not a matter of one sex having power over the other" but a matter of mutual respect.[33]

NOTES

From Minnesota History 48 *(Summer, 1983).*

1. Emma H. Blair, ed., *The Indian Tribes of the Upper Mississippi Valley and Region of the Great Lakes,* 1:109, 275–277 (Cleveland, 1911); Reuben G. Thwaites, ed., "Travels and Explorations of the Jesuit Missionaries in New France, 1610–1791," in *Jesuit Relations and Allied Documents: Iroquois, Ottawas, Lower Canada,* 54:129–133 (Cleveland, 1899); Albert E. Jenks, "Wild Rice Gatherers of the Upper Lakes," in Bureau of American Ethnology (BAE), *19th Annual Report,* part 2, p. 1013–1137 (Washington, D.C., 1898).

2. Blair, ed., *Indian Tribes,* 1:275–277; Ojibwe Curriculum Committee, *The Land of the Ojibwe,* 4, 5, 8–11 (Minnesota Historical Society, *The Ojibwe: A History Resource Unit*—St. Paul, 1973).

3. Jones, *History of the Ojibway Indians,* 60 (London, 1861). The same argument can be found in Joseph Gilfillan, "The Ojibways in Minnesota," in *Minnesota Historical Collections,* 9:58, 83 (St. Paul, 1901) and William W. Warren, *History of the Ojibway Nation,* 265 (Reprint ed., Minneapolis, 1957).

4. Judith K. Brown, "Iroquois Women: An Ethnohistoric Note," in Rayna Reiter, ed., *Toward an Anthropology of Women,* 237, 239–241 (New York, 1975).

5. For a description of nineteenth-century attitudes, see Peter N. Carroll and David W. Noble, *The Free and the Unfree: A New History of the United States,* 161 (New York, 1977).

6. Frances Densmore, *Chippewa Customs,* 121 (Reprint ed., St. Paul, 1979); Thomas L. McKenney, *Sketches of a Tour to the Lakes,* 319 (Reprint ed., Minneapolis, 1959).

7. Alexander Henry, *Travels and Adventures in Canada and the Indian Territories Between the Years of 1760 and 1776,* 201 (New York, 1809); Densmore, *Chippewa Customs,* 121.

8. Henry, *Travels and Adventures,* 68–70, 149; Warren, *History of the Ojibway Nation,* 186, 265.

9. *Red Lake News,* April 1, 1916, p. 1.

10. Thwaites, ed., in *Jesuit Relations,* 54:129–133; Blair, ed., *Indian Tribes,* 1:275; Densmore, *Chippewa Customs,* 154; Gilfillan, in *Minnesota Historical Collections,* 9:80.

11. Densmore, *Chippewa Customs,* 28, 29, 39–44, 123, 128.

12. Densmore, *Chippewa Customs,* 30–33; Carrie A. Lyford, *The Crafts of the Ojibwa,* 129 (Office of Indian Affairs, *Indian Handicrafts Publication No. 5*—Phoenix, Ariz., 1943). For descriptions of women whose clothing blended traditional and new elements, see also McKenney, *Sketches of a Tour,* 182, 255, 315.

13. Schoolcraft, *Archives of Aboriginal Knowledge,* 2:63 (Philadelphia, 1860).

14. Michel Curot, "A Wisconsin Fur Trader's Journal, 1803–04," in Reuben G. Thwaites, ed., *Collections of the State Historical Society of Wisconsin,* 20:423, 427–429, 436, 437 (Madison, 1911); Schoolcraft, *The Indian in His Wigwam or Characteristics of the Red Race of America,* 179 (Buffalo, N.Y., 1848).

15. Ernestine Friedl, *Women and Men: An Anthropologist's View,* 21, 22 (New York, 1975).

16. Blair, ed., *Indian Tribes,* 1:69; Kohl, *Kitchi-Gami, Wanderings Round Lake Superior,* 70, 111 (Reprint ed., Minneapolis, 1956).

17. Elliott Coues, ed., *New Light on the Early History of the Greater Northwest: The Manuscript Journals of Alexander Henry and of David Thompson,* 1:239, 240 (Reprint ed., Minneapolis, 1865); Curot, in *Collections of . . . Wisconsin,* 20:412, 423, 427, 429, 436, 441, 462.

18. Schoolcraft, *Indian in His Wigwam,* 73.

19. Densmore, *Chippewa Customs,* 48, 51; Schoolcraft, *Indian in His Wigwam,* 73; Martha Coleman Bray, ed., *The Journals of Joseph N. Nicollet: A Scientist on the Mississippi Headwaters with Notes on Indian Life,* 253 (St. Paul, 1970); Sister M. Inez Hilger, "Chippewa Child Life and Its Cultural Background," in BAE, *Bulletin,* 146:3, 10 (Washington, D.C., 1951). For descriptions of Ojibwe families of varying sizes, see also Schoolcraft, *Personal Memoirs of a Residence of Thirty Years with the Indian Tribes on the American Frontiers,* 248, 250, 303, 376, 380, 446 (Reprint ed., New York, 1978); McKenney, *Sketches of a Tour,* 255, 259.

20. Basil Johnston, *Ojibway Heritage,* 34–38, 69 (New York, 1976); Hilger, in BAE, *Bulletin,* 146:56, 57, 168.

21. Edwin James, ed., *A Narrative of the Captivity and Adventures of John Tanner,* 94 (Reprint ed., Minneapolis, 1956). See also Lévi-Strauss, *The Elementary Structures of Kinship* (Boston, 1969), especially 481, 496.

22. Blair, ed., *Indian Tribes,* 1:69; Schoolcraft, *Indian in His Wigwam,* 72; Densmore, *Chippewa Customs,* 73.

23. Hilger, in BAE, *Bulletin,* 146:161–163.

24. Blair, ed., *Indian Tribes,* 1:70; McKenney, *Sketches of a Tour,* 292; Densmore, *Chippewa Customs,* 78; Hilger, in BAE, *Bulletin,* 146:86; Kohl, *Kitchi-Gami,* 111.

25. Harold Hickerson, ed., "The Journal of Charles Jean Baptiste Chaboillez, 1797–98," in *Ethnohistory,* 6:275, 299 (Summer, 1959); James, ed., *John Tanner,* 15. For more on images of Indians in popular media see Raymond W. Stedman, *Shadows of the Indian: Stereotypes in American Culture* (Norman, Okla., 1982).

26. Arthur J. Ray, *Indians in the Fur Trade: Their Role as Trappers, Hunters and Middlemen in the Lands Southwest of Hudson Bay, 1660–1870,* 139 (Toronto, 1974); McKenney, *Sketches of a Tour,* 460; Schoolcraft, *Personal Memoirs,* 244, 250; Kohl, *Kitchi-Gami,* 66.

27. Christian F. Feest, "Virginia Algonquians," in Bruce G. Trigger, ed., *Northeast,* 261 (William C. Sturtevant, ed., *Handbook of North American Indians,* vol. 15—Washington, D.C., 1978); Reuben G. Thwaites, ed., "The French Regime in Wisconsin—III," in *Collections of the State Historical Society of Wisconsin,* 18:41 (Madison, 1908); William Henry Egle, ed., *Notes and Queries, Historical and Genealogical Chiefly Relating to Interior Pennsylvania,* 2:432–434, 460 (Reprint of 1st and 2nd series, Harrisburg, Pa., 1895); John Greer Varner and Jeanette Johnson Varner, eds., *The Florida of the Inca,* 297–326 (Austin, Tex., 1980); United States, 51 Congress, 1 session, *House Executive Documents,* no. 247, p. 26 (Washington, D.C., 1890—serial 2747).

28. Hilger, in BAE, *Bulletin,* 146:10–13.

29. Schoolcraft, *Indian in His Wigwam,* 169–173.

30. Warren, *History of the Ojibway Nation,* 358.

31. Schoolcraft, *Indian in His Wigwam,* 130–133; Kohl, *Kitchi-Gami,* 125; Richard E. Morse, "The Chippewas of Lake Superior," in *Collections of the State Historical Society of Wisconsin,* 3:349 (Madison, 1857); William W. Bartlett, *History, Traditions and Adventure*

in the Chippewa Valley, 65 (Chippewa Falls, Wis., 1929); Benjamin G. Armstrong, *Early Life Among the Indians,* 199–202 (Ashland, Wis., 1892).

32. Blair, ed., *Indian Tribes,* 1:136; Jonathan Carver, *Travels through the Interior Parts of North America in the Years 1766, 1767, and 1768,* 257 (London, 1778); Johnston, *Ojibway Heritage,* 61–63.

33. Bray, ed., *Journals of Joseph N. Nicollet,* 188.

In or Out of the Historical Kitchen?:
Minnesota Rural Women

GLENDA RILEY

*The development of a market economy in rural Minnesota during the
last decades of the nineteenth century changed farming and rural life.
Glenda Riley discusses how the new market economy, defined as "an economic system where supply and demand determine what goods are produced and the methods of production," altered the lives of rural women
in Minnesota.*

*Before the coming of a market economy, women worked in their
homes. Using letters and reminiscences of pioneer women living in Minnesota, Riley describes their usual tasks such as making candles and
soap, making cloth and clothes, hauling water to wash clothes, and cooking with open fireplaces or primitive stoves. They also usually had farm
chores like tending chickens, pigs, and cows. Often the women also tried
to generate a little extra income for their families by selling butter and
eggs. These early settlers also lived in a world with possible Indian intruders, frequent guests, and scarce raw materials. Nature was often
threatening with storms, blizzards, and grasshopper devastation. Using
rural Minnesota as a case study, Riley demonstrates how the lives and
activities of rural women changed with the economic developments of
the late nineteenth century.*

Whether categorized as women's history or rural history, the study of women
in the American West is not only alive and well, but is extremely robust and
vital. Its practitioners are numerous and its literature exceedingly rich. Yet one
troubling question increasingly demands attention: should the history of western women be recounted in a way that is as scholarly and "objective" as possible, or should it be presented in a manner that reflects and advances contemporary feminism?

Often, scholars of the first persuasion place women within the historical
kitchen while scholars of the second prefer to emphasize women's resistance
to, and rejection of, the kitchen. Sometimes the two sides engage in sincere,
collegial dialogue, but too often one side is disparaging and disrespectful of the

other. It is the intent of this essay to illuminate this scholarly conflict by establishing a case study of Minnesota women before and after the emergence of the market economy and to explore how each interpretive viewpoint might explain the alterations that that economy wrought in women's lives.

There is little doubt that the market economy created a wide range of modifications in Minnesota women's lives. This economic system, in which supply and demand determine what goods are produced as well as the methods of production, modified women's work loads, type and amount of work, equipment used, range and number of customers, and attitudes toward their work and leisure time.[1]

Before the market economy developed in any given region of Minnesota, women worked as domestic artisans in their homes, which also served as their workplaces or factories. The technology available to them ranged from basic to downright primitive. As a result, early rural women's writings overflow with details about whitewashing cabin walls, making medicines and treating the ill, making candles and soap, processing foods, cooking in open fireplaces or on small stoves, making cloth and clothing, and washing clothes "on the board." A Steele County woman remembered, for example, that her mother made shoes with uppers of thick cloth and soles cut from the tops of worn-out boots. She also dyed and braided straw for summer hats, spun yarn and knitted socks, and sewed clothes by hand for ten people. Most of this work was done during the evening by the light of a candle, but despite the difficult working conditions, she also made hide gloves to sell for extra cash.[2]

This combination of domestic and market production was not unusual. Mary E. Carpenter, who lived on a farm near Rochester, wrote to her cousin that she had gotten up at four in the morning to prepare breakfast. After breakfast, she "skimmed milk, churned . . . did a large washing, baked 6 loaves of bread, & seven punkin [sic] pies . . . put on the irons & did the ironing got supper &c—besides washing all the dishes, making the beds." In the same letter, she told of making 100 pounds of butter in June and selling "28 doz of eggs at 10 cts a doz" later in the summer. She proudly, and expansively, added that her butter-and-egg money had paid for "everything that her family had.[3]

These early rural women in Minnesota frequently performed their domestic and market chores under great pressure. For instance, they were often distressed by Indians who silently stared in their windows at them while they worked, or begged for food and medicine, or forcefully seized food from limited supplies. In 1862 a Hutchinson woman wrote that Indians had ransacked her house. In common parlance of the time, which was later immortalized by television westerns, she added that Indians were "skulking all around," even though white men with rifles had caused several of them "to bite the dust."[4]

In addition to Indian intruders, early rural women also had many invited and uninvited guests, for inns and hotels were crude or nonexistent. One Leon settler complained that the demands of frequent guests left her little time to write a letter or two home. A Forest River woman said that they had so much company, mostly travelers and homeseekers, that their house was widely known as "Sanborn Stopping Place."[5]

Women's work was also difficult because raw materials were scarce. Mary Burns, an inventive woman living near Ely Lake in 1892, created one "company" chair by embroidering burlap for its cover. She also made pillows by filling gunny sacks with pine needles; she ground coffee by putting "roasted berries into a strong cloth bag, taking it to a rock outside and pounding it to the right degree of fineness." She told her friends and family back east about her strange new life in letters that she wrote on thin sheets of birch.[6]

These women also had to cope with a volatile and destructive environment that frequently interrupted their lives and work with hailstorms, blizzards, and grasshopper plagues. Storms killed more than one woman's chickens and pigs and sometimes threatened, or killed, her children and menfolks as well. "Hoppers," as grasshoppers were known, not only devastated fields and gardens, but entered homes, eating furniture, curtains, clothing, and precious stocks of food. According to a Hawley woman, one swarm was so dense that it "obscured the sun." The despair that women felt after experiencing nature's devastation was best expressed by Mary Carpenter, who, during the mid-1870s, was living on a farm near Marshall. When she lost a baby, she attributed it to "worriment," depression, and "irregular diet" that resulted from recent damage to the Carpenter farm by natural disasters.[7]

Except for the fortunate few who employed help, women who lived in rural towns also performed demanding and exhausting domestic labor during the premarket years. They often kept chickens, or even pigs and cows, carried their family's supply of water from wells a street or two away, and washed "on the board." Nor were early rural towns far ahead of farms in technological "improvements" or social opportunities. During the early 1860s, for example, one woman characterized the town of St. Anthony, now Minneapolis, as a "very quiet village" in a "sleepy condition."[8]

In the years that predated the market economy, women held a variety of attitudes toward their work. Most saw their homes and families as their primary responsibility. Britania Livingston described her husband as "the man I came west with to take care of." Another loyally followed a husband filled with wanderlust from region to region, although she had buried four children along the way. She complained that, "If we would only light somewheres is what I say. . . . We always movin[*sic*]." Alice Claggett Evans remembered that rural society was organized simply: "The mothers bore children, the fathers broke the prairie."[9]

A significant number of these early rural Minnesotans looked upon their domestic work loads with distaste. Mary Carpenter complained about the "monotony of her chores" and the ever-present problem of finding wood on the prairie. She saw her straw-burning stove as a demanding demon, for someone, often she, had to sit by and feed it straw. And Britania Livingston became so discouraged that she saw failure everywhere she looked. She literally made herself sick by dwelling upon the failure of women to "make the best of their means." To her, these women had become "mere verbs—'to be, to do, and to suffer.'"[10]

Others, however, were positive about their work. In 1876 one 45-year-old woman had her tenth baby the morning that the threshing crew was to arrive. She cheerfully sat up in bed and peeled potatoes for the threshers' dinner. Still, Mary Burns takes the prize for optimism. She lived in an 11-by-13-foot log cabin, had only "three heavy tin pails" to cook in, and soon discovered that her bread pan completely filled the oven of her "doll-house sort of stove." Yet she wrote about her happy home and proclaimed that her "simple housekeeping" was like "taking part in a fascinating play of make-believe."[11]

It is difficult to determine ways in which the work of ethnic and black women of this era was clearly different or unique. The writings of ethnic women do indicate that they clung to Old World customs including language, religion, holiday celebrations, clothing, and special foods. And some mentioned doing heavy field work.[12] But similar generalizations cannot be made abaout black women's work because their documents are few.[13] It does appear, however, that the farm acted as a great leveler or acculturator, for, despite race or ethnic origins, women had to adjust quickly to the way work was done in their new locales if their families were to survive.

As the market economy reached various parts of Minnesota, it unquestionably brought many changes, and some improvements, to the lives of rural women. For one thing, women now labored in larger, better-equipped homes/workplaces. Still, their work loads changed more in nature than in amount. Women spent hours each day trimming wicks and cleaning kerosene lamps instead of devoting time to collecting tallow and making candles. They employed treadle-powered sewing machines to make clothing that was becoming increasingly complicated in style. One woman near Jordan explained that although her grandmother had spun thread on a spinning wheel and sewed clothes by hand, her mother worked on a sewing machine beginning in 1886. But a St. Cloud woman of the era remarked that it now took 12 yards of material and numerous ruffles and tucks to make an acceptable dress.[14] Growing numbers of women also washed clothes in washing machines but had to turn the agitators by hand and carry clean water to the machines and dirty water from them, because they lacked such support technology as indoor plumbing and electricity.

Agnes Kolshorn remembered clothes-washing days on the family farm near Red Wing during the 1880s and 1890s with great clarity. The washing equipment included: "the bench for the two wooden tubs, wash boards, the washing machine, the wringer to be clamped onto the tubs or the machine, the copper wash boiler, wooden clothes pins, clothes line ... clothes basket, pails and bottle bluing." She recalled that she heartily disliked the task of carrying water from the cistern to the stove to be heated and then to the washing machine and detested the job of removing frozen clothes from the line during the winter. She added that on the day after washing, women ironed the clothes with flatirons heated on the stove. Her family owned the latest technology in flatirons: each had a separate handle, clamped onto it before it was lifted from the stove.[15]

A Lenox woman remembered that her grandfather frequently purchased a variety of household "inventions" to ease her grandmother's heavy domestic chores. During the early 1890s he brought home a dishwashing machine composed of "one large sink, two tubs, and cranks and cogs and levers and inside works and a mop." To operate this wondrous device, a woman loaded dishes in the rack, closed the lid, turned a crank that churned the water and cleaned the dishes, and then transferred the dishes to the second tub for rinsing. Copious amounts of water had to be heated on the stove and carried to and from the tubs. This dishwasher created so much extra work that its new owner decided to wash dishes by hand in the larger tub, using the little mop. Her husband eventually carried away the smaller tub to use as a footbath.[16]

After the development of the market economy, women continued to produce domestic goods for sale. In fact, their work load often expanded, for the opportunity existed to sell in greater quantities to a larger market. During the closing decades of the nineteenth century, farm woman Lydia Sprague Scott sold butter, milk, and eggs to numerous customers in nearby Mankato. The Kolshorn women also made extra butter and collected eggs to sell in town. Agnes remembered the "exacting, time consuming task" that culminated in packing butter into two- or five-pound earthenware jars to be transported to Red Wing.[17]

Even after the Kolshorn family moved into Red Wing themselves in 1901, women's work continued to be difficult and tedious. Because their house lacked indoor plumbing, the women carried water from an outdoor cistern equipped with a hand-operated pump or from a well located in a nearby street. They got their milk from a married son who kept a cow in town. And the Kolshorn family emptied the drip pan of their new icebox several times a day and depended upon an iceman in a horse-drawn wagon to make deliveries several days each week.[18]

In some ways, of course, the market economy created definite improvements in women's domestic work. As soon as a region became settled and the economy began to develop, hotels and inns sprang up to house travelers and an abundant supply of raw materials became available. As early as the 1850s the pages of the *Minnesota Pioneer* advertised exotic foodstuffs like oysters at "$1.00 a quart for family use," a real treat for former New Englanders. Another advertisement announced that steamships from New York and Europe had just brought a stock of the latest American, French, and English dry goods and invited the "ladies of St. Paul, St. Anthony, and vicinity" to examine them. Women's account books and diaries indicate that many took advantage of the increasing availability of goods. During the 1880s Lydia Scott noted purchases of calico, velvet, thread, buttons, lace and braid edging, hats, shoes, a parasol, a fan, and a corset.[19]

Unlike rural women during premarket days who cherished their slim supplies of books and magazines, Minnesotans of the postmarket era had available an extensive supply of reading matter and household information. Books ranged from *Home Influence, Women's Friendship,* and *Mothers Recompensed* to *Buckeye Cookery and Practical Housekeeping.* The latter book, published in Minneapolis, dedicated its recipes and household hints "To Those Plucky Housewives who master their work instead of allowing it to master them."[20]

Another notable change, documented in gazetteers, city directories, and newspaper advertisements, was the increasing numbers of rural women who sought paid employment outside their homes. Although they usually worked as domestics, nursemaids, and in the needle trades, some women entered professions as teachers, nurses, doctors, and at least one as a minister. After 1870 more information became available regarding employed women in Minnesota, for the United States Census stopped categorizing women as "Not Gainfully Employed" and asked about their paid employment. In that year, 10,860 Minnesota women (both rural and urban) worked as compared with 121,797 men; in 1890, the census reported 65,625 women worked as compared with 403,461 men; and in 1910 there were 145,605 women working and 689,847 men.[21]

In most jobs and professions, the shift toward paid employment was accelerated, rather than created, by the emergence of the market economy, for women had worked for pay very early. As a case in point, rural women were among the first teachers in virtually every area of Minnesota. Anecdotal evidence indicates that they often established a settlement's first school in their homes. Students paid fees, brought their own books, and in the first such venture in Rochester, supplied their own seats.[22] When communities erected log or frame schoolhouses, women taught in them as well.

By 1870, when the census began to list teachers by gender, women outnumbered men. In Minnesota there were 1,294 female teachers (both rural and urban) compared to 460 men; in 1890 there were 7,371 women teachers as opposed to 2,085 men; and in 1910 there were 17,078 women and 2,452 men.[23]

Women entered other fields principally after the emergence of the market economy. For instance, a growing number began to write about domestic matters, travel, and other nonpolitical topics for newspapers and magazines during the late nineteenth century. In 1870 there were no female journalists in Minnesota but 77 males. In 1890, however, there were 16 female (both rural and urban) and 550 male journalists. And 20 years later, 100 women worked as journalists (including editors and reporters), while 753 men did so. Women who were correspondents for newspapers or authors of sketches, stories, and essays for newspapers and journals frequently used pen names to protect their privacy and their reputations. During the late nineteenth and early twentieth centuries, for example, one widely read Sauk Rapids woman used the name Minnie Mary Lee.[24]

During the postmarket years women's thinking about their work and lives began to show marked changes from earlier eras. Homes and families were still the focus of their lives, and many women insisted that they enjoyed managing farm homes. By the late nineteenth century, however, most rural women believed that their talents should be exercised outside, as well as inside, their domestic sphere. Rural women had a long tradition of helping neighbors and friends, occasionally through organized groups. But they increasingly believed that it was their responsibility to create and improve societal amenities and supplement the inadequate efforts of men. As one Dundas woman poetically phrased it: "Those men believed they built that church, point it out with pride, nor realized it was the [Ladies'] Aid who really stemmed the tide."[25]

As a result of their expanded role, Minnesota women became involved in the club movement of the late nineteenth century and were active in a remarkable variety of service organizations. During the early 1870s, for example, Jewish women living in and around St. Paul formed the Hebrew Ladies' Benevolent Society to provide food and other supplies to Jewish families in need. In 1877 the Minnesota chapter of the Women's Christian Temperance Union (WCTU) was organized. Soon such locals as the Scandinavian Young Women's Christian Temperance Union sprang up as well. Other associations were cultural groups, such as the Schubert Club, which sponsored musical performances. In 1895 Margaret Jane Evans Huntington became the first president of the newly formed Minnesota Federation of Women's Clubs.[26]

Rural women also became more interested in furthering their own educations, in part to take advantage of the new opportunities offered by the enlarged economy. In June, 1875, Helen Ely of Winona was heralded as the first woman to graduate from a four-year program at what is now the University of Minnesota.[27]

Women's rights also excited far more discussion than in premarket days. Rather than asking for equal jobs and equal pay, women believed that increased power lay in the right to vote. In 1870 Governor Horace Austin estimated that three-fifths of Minnesota's population was of foreign birth and opposed to woman suffrage—they are "hostile to the measure to a man"—yet many women worked on behalf of the cause. They also attempted to break down gender segregation in Minnesota politics in other ways. One instance is that of Susie Stageberg, long-term president of the Red Wing WCTU, who during the 1920s ran for Minnesota secretary of state on the Farmer-Labor ticket.[28]

There is no doubt that the changes that took place around the turn of the century are significant and deserving of further study. But they also raise an extremely important philosophic issue: how should academic and public historians interpret these alterations? How should they present modifications to students, readers, or visitors to museums, living history farms, and other historical sites?[29] What is the lesson to be derived from Minnesota rural women's history?

At the moment, many historians are divided concerning the answer to these questions. They clearly disagree regarding the method and purpose of historical interpretation. One group insists that researchers accept rural women's words as absolute truth: that is, as reasonably accurate representations of the way they saw things at the time, or the way they chose to remember their lives as they aged. These historians would probably agree that we cannot know the actual past but can only know the virtual past through written sources, artifacts, and other bits of evidence. Because we can only know the past through such material, researchers must interpret the sources as accurately as possible. Of course, all historians have biases, but a researcher can recognize them and strive for a degree of faithfulness to available source materials. If we do not try to achieve such scholarly rigor, the argument goes, and we let a feminist perspective, for example, take control, then rural women's history becomes a handmaiden of sorts to feminism.[30]

A historian holding this point of view, who attempted to follow Minnesota rural women's writings rather closely, might conclude that, although nineteenth-century women occasionally held jobs thought unacceptable, most worked at jobs that were in some way an extension of their domestic function and focus. Despite increasing numbers of working women, conceptions of proper paid jobs expanded little. The idea that women's work was supplemental to the breadwinner's income existed in the workplace as well as in the home. Women were seen as different from men, whether they were domestic or paid workers.[31] Even as they came to dominate the profession of teaching, they were seen as earning supplemental income and were thus routinely paid less than men.

The danger in this approach is the possibility of overlooking some key point, some insightful generalization, that might bring light to our understanding of the past. By adhering closely to women's sources, we may fail to implement a useful approach, such as a feminist perspective, that could result in insights, while helping the cause of contemporary feminism along its way.

Other historians argue for a different approach to the source materials. This school of thought draws another conclusion from the idea that we can know only the virtual, rather than the actual, past. Its proponents argue that because we cannot know the literal truth about the past, we can, indeed we must, interpret the past in light of current issues and understandings. We must read the past from the perspective of today's needs and concerns. In this view, rural women's history is a useful and logical handmaiden to feminism.[32]

Historians who accepted this approach might conclude that postmarket rural wives began to earn significant amounts of money that gave them increased power in the family; that rural women were knocking down the psychological walls of their homes by seeking employment and forming associations; and that such actions showed that they were chafing against their workloads.[33] And, by focusing on women who performed heavy farm labor, worked at a "man's" job, or got involved in politics, historians can present far better role models to women and men of the late twentieth century than by emphasizing women's domestic side.

One danger in this approach is the possibility of devaluing rural women's domestic labor. If men's work becomes the normative standard against which we judge the worth of women's work, do we not demean the historical kitchen? Although it is tempting to want to advance the feminist cause by focusing upon evidence of women breaking gender-oriented bonds, it is important to avoid the unintended result of devaluing women's domestic work.

Despite the pitfalls, proponents of each side seem absolutely convinced that their way is the only way. At a recent conference, I heard a speaker inform his audience that if historians were not interpreting the past in light of present issues and concerns, they were not doing history. I also heard another historian express his rage after the session was over. What I did not hear was anyone exploring whether there might be room for both approaches.

Clearly, it is increasingly a burning question whether our historical past will serve a comparatively abstract scholarship or assist a contemporary cause such as feminism. Should scholars call it as they see it only from the sources available to them? Or should they enlarge our understanding of the past by applying current perspectives? Or is there yet another choice: can historians who espouse different approaches learn to coexist and derive value from each other's interpretations?

NOTES

From Minnesota History *52 (Summer, 1990)*.

1. A recent definition of market economy characterized it as "an economic system in which decisions about the allocation of resources and production are made on the basis of prices generated by voluntary exchanges between producers, consumers, workers and owners of *factors of production*." Market economies "also involve a system of private ownership of the means of production (i.e., they are 'capitalist' or 'free enterprise' economies)"; David Pearce, ed., *The MIT Dictionary of Modern Economics*, 3rd ed. (Cambridge, Mass.: MIT Press, 1986), 263–264.

This article is based on a keynote speech made to the annual meeting of the Minnesota Historical Society in November, 1989.

2. Julia K. S. Hibbard, "Reminiscences, 1856–68," undated, and Kathryn Stover Hicks Moody, "Territorial Days in Minnesota," 1960, both at Minnesota Historical Society (MHS) manuscripts department; unless otherwise noted, all papers cited in this article are originals or copies available in MHS. See also Catharine Bissell Ely, Diary, 1835–1839, Edmund F. Ely and Family Papers, one of the earliest accounts of Minnesota rural women's work, although the diary focuses on child care after the birth of Ely's first child.

3. Carpenter to "Dear Cousin Laura," Aug. 18, 1871, in Mary E. Lovell Carpenter and Family Papers. For more on this woman, see Sara Brooks Sundberg, "A Farm Woman on the Minnesota Prairie: The Letters of Mary E. Carpenter," *Minnesota History* 51 (Spring, 1989):186–193.

4. Rebecca McAlmond Sumner, Diary, 1862. See also Arnold Fladager, "Memoir of My Mother," 1927, and Helena Carlson Vigen, "Reminiscences," 1921. On the New Ulm massacre, see Hibbard, "Reminiscences"; Moody, "Territorial Days"; Marion Louisa Sloan, "Reminiscences and Genealogical Data," 1926, 1936, 1937.

5. Sylvia Macomber Carpenter to "Dear Aunt" [Ellen S. Brooks in Portland, Michigan], 1863, Carpenter Family Papers; Harriet Sanborn, "Life Story," undated.

6. Mary Lyon Burns, "The Bright Side of Homesteading," 1923, p. 13–14.

7. Minnesota American Mothers Committee Inc. (MAMC), comp., Biographies Project, 1975, "Johanna Tatley"; Carpenter to "Dear Cousin Lucy," July 9, 1874, Carpenter Papers. See also Annette Atkins, *Harvest of Grief: Grasshopper Plagues and Public Assistance in Minnesota, 1873–1878* (St. Paul: MHS Press, 1984).

8. Abby Fuller Abbe, account of an 1854 trip, undated, and clippings, Abby Abbe Fuller and Family Papers; for quotations see Charlotte Ouisconsin Van Cleve, *"Three Score Years and Ten": Life-Long Memories of Fort Snelling, Minnesota, and Other Parts of the West* (Minneapolis: Harrison and Smith, 1888), 161.

9. Britania J. Livingston, "Notes on Pioneer Life," Dec. 22, 1929, p. 2, 3, quoted in Meridel Le Sueur, *North Star Country* (New York: Duell, Sloan & Pearce, 1945), 118; Alice Claggett Evans, "Some Reminiscences of Pioneer Days in Lura Township," undated. Another woman who followed her husband from region to region was Abby Bucklin, "Just Indians," undated.

10. Carpenter to "Dear Cousin Lovell," Mar. 26, 1887, Carpenter Papers, and Livingston, "Notes."

11. Moody, "Territorial Days"; Burns, "Bright Side of Homesteading," 14. Looking back, another woman thought that she had been happy before she had all the modern "conveniences"; Ida T. Skordahl, "Reminiscences," undated.

12. For a discussion of ethnic and black settlers, see June Drenning Holmquist, ed., *They Chose Minnesota: A Survey of the State's Ethnic Groups* (St. Paul: MHS Press, 1981). For a Swedish woman who kept up traditional ways, see "Marie Sonander Rice" and for a Norwegian woman who did field work and other heavy farm labor, see "Bertha Martinson Sonsteby," both in MAMC, Biographies Project. That ethnic women did field work and native-born women did not is borne out by Joan M. Jensen, *With These Hands: Women Working on the Land* (Old Westbury, N.Y.: Feminist Press, 1981), 32–34, and Jon Gjerde, *From Peasants to Farmers: The Migration from Balestrand, Norway, to the Upper Middle West* (Cambridge: Cambridge University Press, 1985), 34–36, 66–69, 168–169, 192–201, 235. The work of ethnic women is also found in Theodore C. Blegen, ed., "Immigrant Women and the American Frontier: Three Early 'America Letters,'" *Norwegian-American Historical*

Association Studies and Records, Vol. 4-5 (Northfield: Norwegian-American Historical Association, 1930), 14-29.

13. Sources identified to date on black Minnesotans include "Charley Jackson—He Walked Freedom's Long Road," *St. Paul Pioneer Press,* Feb. 12, 1968, clipping in Mattie V. Rhodes and Family Papers; Anna Ramsey to "My Darling Children," Mar. 31, 1876, and to "My Dear Daughter," June 27, Dec. 8, 1875, Feb. 2, 1876) about her black servant Martha), Alexander Ramsey and Family Papers; Patricia C. Harpole, ed., "The Black Community in Territorial St. Anthony: A Memoir," *Minnesota History* 49 (Summer, 1984): 42-55; "Pilgrim Baptist Church, A Brief Resume," ca. 1977, Pilgrim Baptist Church, Ladies Aid Society Records; and David Vassar Taylor, "The Blacks," in Holmquist, ed., *They Chose Minnesota,* 73-91.

14. Emily Veblen Olsen, "Memoirs," 1941, describes improved housing. In order to see the continuing domestic focus of women before and after the market economy, it is helpful to compare women's writings to those of Minnesota men. Unlike his wife, Edmund Ely, for example, seldom mentions his young daughter; Edmund F. Ely, Diary, 1838-1839. Another man advised his brother in 1858 to keep his wife "in oven wood & tea & there wont be much trouble." He added, "be carful [*sic*] & not let her get your pants on for if you do it will make a fus [*sic*] in the family." Rufus W. Payne to "Dear Brother," Dec. 12, 1858, R. W. Payne and Family letters. Other similar and interesting sources are E. Grahame Paul, "Reminiscences of English Settlements in Iowa and Minnesota," 1880; Charles V. Kegley, interview, Dec. 31, 1934, describes taking up land near Lydia; and Claude E. Simmonds, "George Davies, Wright County Pioneer," 1946, detailing settlement in Minnesota, especially near Lake Pulaski; Lucia B. Johnson, "Memoir," Aug. 28, 1963; Gertrude B. Vandergon, "Our Pioneer Days in Minnesota," 1940-41.

15. Agnes Mary Kolshorn, "Kolshorn Family History," 1983, quotation in supplement to Part 1, "Laundry"; for more on washing on the board, see Vandergon, "Pioneer Days."

16. Dorothy St. Arnold, "Family Reminiscences," part 1, p. 4 [1926].

17. Lydia M. Sprague Scott, Diary, 1878-1910, and Kolshorn, "Family History."

18. Kolshorn, "Family History." Keeping animals in early towns was not uncommon; one retired farm couple in Northfield during the 1880s kept not only a cow, but a horse and pig as well, while the Fuller sisters kept chickens in St. Paul. See Olsen, "Memoirs"; Sarah Fuller to "Dear Lizzy," June 12, 1852, in clippings, Fuller Papers.

19. *Minnesota Pioneer,* May 2, Oct. 24, 1850; Scott, Diary.

20. Clara Rieger Berens to "Dear Mama," Oct. 12, 1878, commented that other rural women were well read. Abby Fuller Abbe frequently spoke of reading, attending lectures about authors and their works, and told of a subscription club for *Godey's Lady's Magazine;* clippings, Fuller Papers; *Minnesota Pioneer,* May 19, 1849, June 26, 1851; *Buckeye Cookery and Practical Housekeeping* (reprint ed., St. Paul: MHS Press, 1988).

21. United States, *Census, Population: 1870,* 1:670; *1890,* part 2, p. 302; *1910,* 4:111. For the story of a hotel maid in Renville, see Louisa Wanner, Diary, 1903-04, in Elizabeth Hampsten, comp., *To All Inquiring Friends: Letters, Diaries and Essays in North Dakota, 1880-1910* (Grand Forks: University of North Dakota, 1979), 275-283. For the presence of milliners, seamstresses, and needleworkers, see, for example, *Minnesota Pioneer,* Feb. 5, 1852. For an account of a seamstress, see Abbie T. Griffin, Diary, 1882-85; of a tailor and seamstress, see Daisy Barncard Schmidt, "History of the Jacob Zed Barncard Family, 1817-1960"; of a dressmaker, see Bernice P. Jenkins, "Life of Jennie Atwood Pratt," 1949. For an account of several teachers, one of whom was also a part-time milliner, see Hattie Augusta Roberts Eaton, "Reminiscences," ca. 1934. The minister was Josephine Lapham;

see Susan B. Anthony Letter to "Dear Friend" (Josephine Lapham), June 22, 1868. On women doctors, see Winton U. Solberg, "Martha G. Ripley: Pioneer Doctor and Social Reformer," *Minnesota History* 39 (Spring, 1964): 1–17; Nellie N. Barsness, "Highlights in Career of Women Physicians in Pioneer Minnesota," 1947.

22. Advocates of women as teachers stressed their capacity for affection and maternal instincts, qualities that would create greater rapport with students than would be possible or proper for "the other sex," as men were often called during the nineteenth century. See Kathryn Kish Sklar, *Catharine Beecher: A Study in American Domesticity* (New York: Norton, 1976), 113–115, 168–183; Polly Welts Kaufman, "A Wider Field of Usefulness: Pioneer Women Teachers in the West, 1848–1854," *Journal of the West* 21 (April, 1982): 16–25, and *Women Teachers on the Frontier* (New Haven: Yale University Press, 1984); Sloan, "Reminiscences"; Maude Baumann Arney, "Earliest History of School District Number 64," undated, in M. B. Arney Papers. For a Swedish woman who moved her family to the loft so that a school and its teacher could occupy the lower level of their home, see MAMC, Biographies Project, "Mor Hetteen."

23. U. S., *Census, Population:* 1870, 1:677, 689; 1890, part 2, p. 319; 1910, 4:123.

24. U. S., *Census, Population:* 1870, 1:675, 687; 1890, part 2, p. 319; 1910, 4:120–121. On Minnie Mary Lee, see Henry S. Wood, "A Woman of the Frontier," undated.

25. On women's enjoyment of farm work, see Johnson, "Memoir." A description of a women's group to help settlers is found in Bucklin, "Just Indians." On an early church relief group, see Marine Sewing Society Minute Book, 1857, First Congregational Church, Marine, Minn., Papers. Another early group, which claimed to be the state's oldest philanthropic organization, was the Woman's Christian Association of Minneapolis, Minutes, 1866–67, in WCAM Records, 1866–1980. The Civil War spurred the formation of a number of other such groups; see "Pioneers of Mankato, Minnesota," typescript of interviews, ca. 1943. Quotes from Helen E. Howie, "The Historical Background of the Dundas Methodist Church," 1955, p. 5. For another ladies' aid society, see First Universalist Church, Minneapolis, Bylaws, 1878.

26. Described in Hebrew Ladies' Benevolent Society, St. Paul, Minutes, 1891–99. For a Jewish woman's account of life in Dubuque and St. Paul, see Florence Shuman Sher, "Reminiscences," 1976. For the Minnesota WCTU, see Minutes, 1866–67, Minnesota Women's Christian Temperance Union Records, 1866–1983. For the Scandinavian WCTU, see Minute Book, 1885, Scandinavian Young Women's Christian Temperance Union of Minneapolis, Minnesota, Papers; for a Minnesota temperance colony, see "Story of the National Colony," ca. 1943. On the Schubert Club 1882–1962," 1963. For accounts of a few of the numerous other women's clubs, see "The Woman's Club, Fergus Falls, 1897–1925," undated, in Elmer E. Adams and Family Papers, and Mrs. E. L. Lowe, "Short Sketches of Several Clubs in Anoka Co.," 1927; "Some Special Dates and Events, 1954," in Minnesota Federation of Women's Club Records; Alvin Guttag, "Mrs. Margaret Jane Evans Huntington"; *St. Paul Pioneer Press,* Oct. 18, 1925, sec. 6, p. 8. See also MAMC, Biographies Project, "Mrs. Anna Partridge."

27. Ely's graduation is reported in *Winona Daily Republican,* June 9, 1875, clipping in Orrin Fruit Smith and Family Papers. Another example of a woman who attended college (Carleton) is Olsen, "Memoirs." A few educated women went on to become college instructors, including Matilda Jane Wilkin of St. Anthony, who became an instructor at the University of Minnesota, and Margaret Huntington, who became the Lady Principal, or Dean of Women, at Carleton College; see Wilkin, "Autobiographical Sketch," 1923, and Guttag, "Mrs. Huntington."

28. Horace Austin to "My dear Madam" [Mrs. W. C. Dodge], Mar. 14, 1870, in Horace Austin and Family Papers. Accounts of two suffrage workers are found in Sloan, "Reminiscences," and Eugenia B. Farmer, "A Voice from the Civil War," 1918; Susie W. Stageberg Papers and MAMC, Biographies Project, "Susie W. Stageberg of Red Wing."

29. For a discussion of interpretation in public history facilities, see Michael Wallace, "Visiting the Past: History Museums in the United States," in Susan P. Benson, Stephen Briers, and Roy Rosenzweig, eds., *Presenting the Past: Essays on History and the Public* (Philadelphia: Temple University Press, 1986), 137–161.

30. Donald Ostrowski, "The Historian and the Virtual Past," *The Historian* 51 (Feb., 1989): 201–220; Jeffrey B. Russell, "History and Truth," *The Historian* 50 (Nov. 1987): 3–13. See also Gene Wise, *American Historical Explanations: A Strategy for Grounded Inquiry* (Revised ed., Minneapolis: University of Minnesota Press, 1980).

31. One woman even masqueraded as a man in order to get a more remunerative job to support her two children; Kathryn A. O'Connell, "A Lanesboro Report of 1864," 1965, in Julia F. R. Underhill Papers. For other recent descriptions of gender separation, see John Mack Faragher, *Sugar Creek: Life on the Illinois Prairie* (New Haven: Yale University Press, 1986); Deborah Fink, *Open Country, Iowa: Rural Women, Tradition and Change* (Albany: SUNY Press, 1986); Glenda Riley, *The Female Frontier: A Comparative Perspective of Women of the Prairie and on the Plains* (Lawrence: University Press at Kansas, 1988); and Carolyn E. Sachs, *The Invisible Farmers: Women in Agricultural Production* (Totawa, N.J.: Rowman & Allenheld, 1983).

32. See Russell, "History and Truth," 5–11. For an example of the clashing of the "objective" version and a "feminist" version of a past event in Minnesota history, see Thomas A. Woods, "Varying Versions of the Real: Toward a Socially Responsible Public History," *Minnesota History* 51 (Spring, 1989): 178–185.

33. For the argument that gender roles were followed less often than usually thought, see Anne B. Webb, "Forgotten Persephones: Women Farmers on the Frontier," *Minnesota History* 50 (Winter, 1986): 134–148. See also Nancy Grey Osterud, "'She Helped Me Hay It as Good as a Man'; Relations among Women and Men in an Agricultural Community," in Carol Groneman and Mary Beth Norton, eds., *"To Toil the Livelong Day": America's Women at Work, 1780–1980* (Ithaca: Cornell University Press, 1987), 87–97.

Organizing for the Vote:
The Minnesota's Woman Suffrage Movement

Barbara Stuhler

> By the end of the nineteenth century, women's suffrage took on a new
> immediacy, but there were also many divisive issues associated with
> it. A growing anti-suffrage movement included women as well as men.
> Some argued that suffrage challenged that old idea of separate spheres,
> but others countered that women could clean up society just as they
> had previously run their households. Women raised the question of
> why men, including immigrants and blacks, all had the franchise
> while educated, white women did not; thus, the suffrage movement
> had to deal with issues of race and class as well as gender. African
> American women found themselves excluded from the mainstream
> of the movement in part because of the white Northern leadership's
> fear of offending Southern white women. The best method also became
> a subject of debate: should the franchise be secured state by state or by
> a constitutional amendment which would only require ratification
> by three-fourths of the states?

More than two centuries ago the Declaration of Independence extolled the
equality of men and assigned to them—but not to women—certain inalienable
rights. From that time onward, individual women protested this partial citizenship, but their protests did not bear fruit for nearly a century and a half,
when they finally won the right to vote. Now, in 1995, Americans celebrate the
seventy-fifth anniversary of the ratification of the Nineteenth Amendment.

The campaign for woman suffrage began in 1848 when a group of five women,
led by Lucretia Mott and Elizabeth Cady Stanton, called the first women's
rights convention in Seneca Falls, New York. The most contentious debate centered on a resolution stating that "it is the duty of the women of this country
to secure to themselves their sacred right to the elective franchise."[1] Seventy-
two years later, women gained voices and votes in governments under whose
laws they were obliged to live.

Minnesota women were involved from the very beginning in the long suffrage
struggle. These first-generation suffragists sought to win the vote by amending

state constitutions. Lacking any organizational structure, women relied primarily on rhetoric to persuade citizens to sign petitions urging state legislators to support suffrage amendments. With the establishment of two national suffrage associations in 1869, followed by the sporadic formation of state and national groups, waxed and waned. In the 1890s, four western states achieved suffrage, but efforts elsewhere were frustrated by obdurate opposition from a variety of sources.

By the early 1900s, organizational efforts proved to be more effective. For one thing, traveling and communicating had become easier. Women had also acquired education and experience through the study groups and women's clubs that flourished after the Civil War. More worldly and informed, they had learned how to manage organizations. (Lucretia Mott's husband, James, had presided at the landmark Seneca Falls convention because women simply had no experience running meetings.)[2]

As the movement progressed into the twentieth century, second-generation suffragists across the country stood determined to bring the campaign to a successful conclusion. In Minnesota eight women, beginning with Sarah Burger Stearns and ending with Clara Hampson Ueland, personified the evolution and tactics of the suffrage campaign.

Minnesota's early supporters of suffrage had included some of the state's best-known women. In the 1850s Harriet Bishop, St. Paul's first public-school teacher, had spoken of women's responsibilities beyond the confines of the home. In 1858 St. Cloud's crusading journalist, Jane Grey Swisshelm, had observed that "a woman *ought* to meddle in politics," and Dr. Mary J. Colburn had lectured in her village of Champlin on the "Rights and Wrongs of Women."[3]

By the 1860s the Minnesota legislature was besieged with petitions from disparate "friends-of-equality" groups who pressed for the enfranchisement of women. On one occasion in 1868, when a recommendation "to amend the constitution by striking out the word 'male' as a requisite for voting or holding office" reached the floor of the House of Representatives, it was greeted with laughter and quickly tabled. Such was the mindset of Minnesota legislators. By 1875, however, male voters approved a constitutional amendment enacted by the legislature giving women the right to vote in school elections. Two years later, male voters turned down an amendment allowing women to vote on the "whiskey question." In session after session, Minnesota's legislators defeated efforts to extend voting rights either to tax-paying women or to all women in municipal elections and on temperance issues.[4]

The fundamental reason for denying women the vote was the presumption that politics was not their work. The demand for the vote subverted the widely held notion that a woman's place was in the home; it fell to men to bear the burden of the public domain, a burden that many men (and some women) thought inappropriate for women. People of this persuasion feared that suffrage would replace male authority with female autonomy, change women's role within the family structure from subordinate to equal, and open the door for women to move from the domestic sphere into the public arena.[5]

In addition to these anxieties about family values, other political concerns prompted male decision makers (and men in general) to oppose suffrage. Despite the reassurances of Southern women to the contrary, lawmakers in the South feared that suffrage would jeopardize white supremacy. In eastern states such as Massachusetts, the male hierarchy of the Catholic church opposed woman suffrage and actively led the opposition. In midwestern states such as Minnesota and Wisconsin, where brewers and liquor interests occupied a preeminent economic position, wets feared the temperance inclinations of women.[6]

Women did not form their own suffrage organizations until 1869, when the Fifteenth Amendment enfranchised African American men but excluded women. Disagreements over what was called "the Negro's hour" severed the abolitionist-suffragist alliance. Women who had relied on antislavery groups to support suffrage now had to promote their own cause. More accepting of the "Negro's hour," Lucy Stone and her husband, Henry Blackwell, formed the American Woman Suffrage Association. Angry about women's exclusion, Susan B. Anthony and Elizabeth Cady Stanton created the more militant National Woman's Suffrage Association. The passage of time and the influence of younger suffragists brought about the merger in 1890 of the two groups into the National American Woman Suffrage Association (NAWSA).[7]

In Minnesota in 1869, Sarah Burger Stearns and Mary Colburn formed independent suffrage societies in Rochester and Champlin. Other local organizations also sprang up, mostly in the southeastern area of the state. Not until 1881 did 14 women—including Harriet Bishop, Sarah Stearns, and Julia B. Nelson—meet in Hastings to establish the Minnesota Woman Suffrage Association (MWSA). Membership grew to 124 in the first year and doubled in the second, probably representing individuals who lived in communities without local societies. The MWSA's strategy was to increase its membership and influence by sustaining existing societies and establishing new auxiliaries. These auxiliaries deferred to the MWSA for leadership at the legislature and responded as requested with letters, petitions, and attendance at gatherings.[8]

Elected as first president of the MWSA was Sarah Burger Stearns. Born in New York City in 1836, she grew up in Ann Arbor and Cleveland, where she attended a suffrage convention at the age of 14. Following her graduation from a state normal school in Ypsilanti, Michigan, and her marriage to Ozara P. Stearns, she taught in a young ladies' seminary. During the Civil War she enlisted as an active worker in the North's Sanitary Commission while her husband joined the Union army. Commission women performed a variety of tasks, raising $30 million for food, uniforms, and medical supplies and competing with men for army contracts to manufacture military clothing. From these experiences, as historian Theodora Penny Martin observed, "Thousands of American women found sanction for work outside the home, discovered for the first time the satisfaction of formally organized cooperative achievement that arises from success in new endeavors, and were imbued with a sense of self-respect for the part they had played in a cause of larger purpose."[9]

In 1866, the Stearnses moved from Michigan to Rochester, Minnesota, and on to Duluth in 1872. There Sarah organized her second suffrage society, the Duluth Woman Suffrage Circle, and served as its president from 1881 to 1893. Active in the Unitarian church, she also supported temperance and served as a school-board member for three years. The energetic Stearns also founded, as she described it, "a home for women needing a place of rest and training for self-help and self-protection," perhaps the state's first battered women's shelter.[10]

As the first president of the MWSA, Stearns established a pattern of leadership that relied primarily on speeches and petitions to shape public opinion. Her political acumen was evident in her role in the adoption of the school suffrage amendment submitted to voters in 1875. "No effort was made," as Stearns remarked, to "agitate the question, lest more should be effected in rousing the opposition than in the educating the masses . . . between the passage of the bill and the election in November." Hoping to gain "the votes of the intelligent men of the state," she requested support from the editor of the state's leading newspaper, the *St. Paul Pioneer Press*, just before the election. He obliged, responding that he "had quite forgotten such an amendment had been proposed." Stearns and company had earlier persuaded the political parties to print their ballots with the wording, "For the amendment of Article VII relating to electors—Yes." Historian William Watts Folwell later wrote, "Opposers were thus obliged to unbutton their coats, get out their glasses, fumble for a pencil, and cross out 'yes' and write 'no.'" The amendment passed by a vote of 24,340 to 19,468.[11]

Characterized in one newspaper article as "a power in the young community [Duluth] as well as in the state of Minnesota," Stearns was also said to have "possessed the tenacity of purpose, the dogged persistence of the true reformer; no discouragements, rebuffs nor ingratitude seemed to downhearten her or swerve her from what she considered right." At a time when suffragists were dismissed, ridiculed, and mocked, they had to be made of stern stuff. Stearns passed that test (or perhaps lived up to her name). She organized local and state societies, orchestrated the first legislative success for suffrage, and bombarded the state legislature with petitions (in 1881 one urging woman suffrage on temperance issues contained 31,228 names representing every county in the state). She possessed a charismatic personality, invaluable in the early days of the suffrage campaign for attracting support. Stearns remained active until 1894 when her husband's illness took them to California. She chaired the

Los Angeles Suffrage League in 1900 and worked until her death in 1904 on behalf of the cause.[12]

Dr. Martha Ripley, a resident of Minneapolis, succeeded Stearns and served as president of the Minnesota Woman Suffrage Association from 1883 to 1889.[13] Trained in medicine in Boston, she was close to Lucy Stone and Henry Blackwell and was probably instrumental in bringing the prestigious convention of the American Woman Suffrage Association to the city of Minneapolis in 1885.

In 1890, Julia Bullard Nelson of Red Wing, who had served as MWSA vicepresident with Stearns, became president, bringing to the state organization public-speaking skills and links to the growing universe of women activists. Born in High Ridge, Connecticut, in 1842, Julia Bullard and her family arrived in Minnesota in 1857. She attended Hamline University (then in Red Wing) and taught in Connecticut and Minnesota for six years. In 1866 Julia B. (as she was called) married Ole Nelson, a Hamline classmate. Within two years, their young son died, and then Ole died, possibly from malaria contracted during the Civil War. Nelson found herself alone but not daunted.[14]

Nine months later, she set forth on a new adventure: teaching in freedmen's schools in Texas. An interval in Minnesota, prompted by her mother's ill health, found Nelson organizing and lecturing on behalf of the Woman's Christian Temperance Union (WCTU), which Frances Willard had transformed from a single-minded anti-saloon crusade to a women's all-purpose organization with suffrage high among its priorities. After an interval teaching African American students, this time in Tennessee, Julia B. returned again to Minnesota in 1881 and attended the MWSA organizational meeting in Hastings. The lure of teaching drew her once more to Tennessee, but the issues of temperance and suffrage stayed foremost in her mind. She spent a spring vacation at a national suffrage convention in Washington, D.C., and was in the delegation that addressed the House Judiciary Committee on February 29, 1886. After speaking about salary inequities between male and female teachers, Nelson concluded, "If it [the law] puts woman down as an inferior, she will surely be regarded as such. . . . If I am capable of preparing citizens, I am capable of possessing the rights of a citizen myself. I ask you to remove the barriers which restrain women from equal opportunities and privileges with men."[15]

In 1888 Julia B. returned to Minnesota to stay. In the period of her presidency of the state association (1890–96), she also served as superintendent of franchise for the WCTU. In linking the two organizations, she enhanced their work for suffrage. Nelson made an essential contribution in securing, as she reported, "thousands of signatures to the petitions for the franchise" that were sent to every legislative session, where she could be found pleading, prodding, and peddling propaganda. She took advantage of the fact that the WCTU, as she believed, was "better organized" than the MWSA and provided an opera-tional base with a much broader member network and the means to publicize the cause.[16]

Dependable, energetic, and articulate, Julia B. had worked for the National American Woman Suffrage Association over the years as a paid lecturer. In 1913 she attended her last national suffrage convention and was a member of the delegation that called on President Woodrow Wilson seeking his support for votes for women. She died a year later but not before one last suffrage tour in North Dakota. In 1917 when a Woman Citizen's Building was erected on the Minnesota state fairgrounds as a permanent suffrage headquarters, Julia B.'s legacy of $100 to the MWSA was used to build a memorial fireplace in her honor. It was a fitting tribute to the many suffrage fires lit by Nelson's leadership for more than 20 years.[17]

Like Stearns and Nelson, Ethel Edgerton Hurd, born in 1845, had been a schoolteacher after her graduation from Knox College in Illinois. Marriage to a railroad man took her to Kansas, where she became active in the suffrage movement, and then to Minnesota in the 1880s. Following her husband's death, she earned a medical degree in 1897 from the University of Minnesota and practiced medicine in partnership with her daughter, Annah. Hurd was a mainstay of the Political Equality Club of Minneapolis, founded in or after 1868 and the largest and most enduring of local suffrage societies. She twice served as president, the second time for its final six years. In one breathtaking sentence she provided a vivid description of their efforts:

> We have written letters, letters of protest, letters of gratitude, pleading letters, licked postage stamps, traveled miles and miles with petitions, given out thousands and thousands of sheets of literature, joined in public parades, in fact we have done all the drudgery consequent upon the forwarding of a great reform; we have done all this year after year, month after month, day in and day out with no thought of self or fame, or recompense; we have given voluntarily and freely of our incomes, our time, our energy, asking no return save one, the granting of the privilege for which we struggled.

Hurd helped to broaden the suffrage base in Minnesota by founding the Scandinavian Woman Suffrage Association in 1907 and the Workers' Equal Suffrage League in 1909. She also served as a director and officer of the MWSA for more than 20 years (1898–1919).[18]

Even though Hurd's involvement extended well into the twentieth century, she possessed the characteristics of the earlier generation of suffragists, many of whom were professional women. Because they dared to be physicians, ministers, or attorneys, they were scorned and often described as sexless spinsters—even if they were not. If they were at times somber as they went about their business, it was with good reason. Younger suffragists regarded Hurd as one of the old "war horses" because she remained committed to the conservative tactics of the earlier generation, but she applauded and accepted the new leadership styles of women such as Clara Ueland, seeing in that leadership the prospects for victory. The more radical confrontational approach of other Minnesotans such as Emily Haskell Bright and Bertha Berglin Moller, however, were not acceptable to Hurd, a suffragist of the old school.[19]

Exemplifying the tactics and experiencing the frustrations of the movement's early years, Stearns, Nelson, and Hurd also bore the brunt of public outrage, rejection, and ridicule that was especially intense in the early suffrage period. Of the three, Hurd was the only one who lived to see the day of victory on August 26, 1920.

In 1914, just 45 years after the schism that emerged in the aftermath of the Fifteenth Amendment, a second division of the suffrage house took place. A group of young suffragists, chafing at the slow pace of progress, took charge of NAWSA's somnolent congressional committee and brought it to life with daring initiatives such as parades, street speaking, and other noisy and notable activities. Uneasy with each other's company, the two NAWSA factions split, the younger women departing to form the Congressional Union for Woman Suffrage. In 1916 the same group of young leaders formed the Woman's Party to represent female voters in the 12 enfranchised states. A year later the party and the union came together as the National Woman's Party (NWP).[20]

The NWP broke with suffrage tradition by engaging in partisan politics. It campaigned against all Democratic candidates in suffrage states and picketed the White House and the Capitol to protest the continuing refusal by the president and the Congress to recognize women's right to vote. Such unconventional behavior seemed counterproductive to NAWSA suffrage leaders, who were trying to win the approval and votes of decision makers. When the picketers were forcibly fed following arrests, imprisonment, and hunger strikes, public sympathies swung their way. Those who suffered these indignities received NWP prison pins fashioned as badges of honor for having been "jailed for freedom"[21]

The division between the NAWSA and the NWP represented a classic case of disagreement over the most effective means to accomplish a common purpose. In this case, however, division proved to be not weakness but strength. The NAWSA and its state affiliates provided political organization and pressure, and their contributions on the home front during World War I (working for the Red Cross, promoting food conservation, and the like) helped to win the support of President Wilson and sway public opinion to their side. Although there were moments when relations between the two organizations were strained over tactics and claims for primacy, both parties realized, as

Clara Ueland once wrote, "The main thing, and really the only thing, is that the work is nearly finished."[22]

Some Minnesota women, attracted by the newer organization's verve and vitality, left the MWSA and joined forces with the Congressional Union or National Woman's Party. Both Emily Bright and Bertha Moller, coming from very different backgrounds, followed this course. (Ueland, too, had been an early supporter of the Congressional Union, testifying before the U.S. House Judiciary Committee on its behalf in December 1915 and giving it credit for animating the MWSA. The adverse reactions of influential Minnesotans to the picketing, however, prompted Ueland to temper her enthusiasm.) The fact that leaders like Bright and Moller served both organizations valiantly and enthusiastically may explain why the division was civil and led to success.

Emily Haskell Bright's interest in suffrage had been piqued as a young girl in Evanston, Illinois, when her mother took her to hear Susan B. Anthony, an occasion she described as having a great influence on her life. Emily married Alfred Bright in Milwaukee in 1887. He spent most of his career in Minneapolis as head of the Soo Line's legal department and always supported suffrage even though Ella Pennington, the wife of his boss, was head of the Minneapolis Association Opposed to Woman Suffrage.[23]

With Bright's children nearly grown by 1911, she began her active life in the suffrage movement. Her dynamic leadership as president of the Political Equality Club of Minneapolis (serving between Ethel Hurd's two terms) attracted an influx of new members, thereby broadening the base of suffrage supporters. She became president of the MWSA in 1913, but the death of one of her children in the fall of 1914 caused her to decline another term. She later returned to the MWSA board of directors and also joined the National Woman's Party. Bright served as a member of the party's national advisory committee, and while never imprisoned, she proudly wore a prison pin to protest Wilson's continuing recalcitrance on the issue of suffrage. A newspaper article praised her "tact, executive ability and sterling worth" that "distinguished her as one of the few real leaders of the suffrage movement in this country."[24]

Bertha Berglin Moller, born in Sweden in 1888 and reared in Rush City, attended the Duluth Normal School and, like many suffrage women, began her career as a teacher. She came by her suffrage interest naturally, given her Swedish heritage and its enlightened attitude about women. Two of her uncles were Swedish parliamentarians and authors of legislation for women's rights. Berglin married Charles Frederick Moller in 1910 and in 1916 began organizing throughout Minnesota for the MWSA. Impressed by Moller's skills, president Clara Ueland appointed her to the board of directors and assigned her the responsibility of making sure that the Minnesota congressional delegation voted for the federal amendment. (In 1919, with Moller gone to the NWP, Ueland took on those congressional duties, and the delegation gave the amendment its unanimous support.)[25]

Impatient with what appeared to her to be plodding progress in the national organization (and, by implication, in Minnesota), Moller after 1917 invested her energies in the activities of the National Woman's Party. She served as secretary (1918–19) of the Minnesota branch, but her most notable efforts stemmed from her demonstrations at the White House and the Capitol. She was arrested 11 times and served two short jail sentences in Washington, D. C., leading a hunger strike on one of those occasions. Moller is credited with persuading James M. Cox, the Democratic Party's presidential nominee in 1920, to help with the ratification drive for the Nineteenth Amendment in Tennessee. That same year, she led suffrage delegations from every state to lobby the Republican nominee, Warren G. Harding.[26]

St. Paul suffrage organizations never flourished to the same degree as they did in Minneapolis until Emily Gilman Noyes stepped into a leadership role. Born in New York in 1854, she moved to Minnesota when she married Charles Phelps Noyes. Emily came from a family steeped in idealism. Her father had risked his life during riots in Alton, Illinois, to shelter a radical abolitionist publisher.[27]

Thanks to the prosperity of Noyes Bros. and Cutler, a wholesale drug business, Emily had time for community work. In 1912 she helped organize the Woman's Welfare League, which quickly became St. Paul's most influential force for suffrage. This organization's stated purposes were to protect the interests of women, to enlarge their opportunities in business and the professions, to examine the impact of industrial and social conditions on women and the family, and "as a necessary means to these ends to strive to procure for women the rights of full citizenship." National suffrage leaders encouraged state leaders to increase their political leverage by organizing suffrage units in congressional districts, counties, and legislative districts, and Noyes, who served as the league's first president, proved to be eminently successful. As one contemporary said, she was "always in the advance guard of thought and action." A vice-president of the MWSA as well, she brought the suffrage movement in St. Paul into the twentieth century by dint of her organizing skills and political acuity. Noyes was recognized for her achievements by being named honorary president of the Ramsey County Suffrage Association and its successor, the Ramsey County League of Women Voters. In 1930, shortly before her death, she was one of six Minnesota women named to the honor roll of the National League of Women Voters at its convention in Louisville, Kentucky.[28]

Another important St. Paul activist was Nellie Griswold, an African American born in Nashville, Tennessee, in 1874. She and her family moved to St. Paul in 1883, and eight years later she graduated from Central High School. In 1893, she married William Trevanne Francis, whom she had met when they both worked at the Great Northern Railroad. Francis served as president of the Baptist Missionary Circle, corresponding secretary of the Tri-State Women's Baptist Convention, and president of the Pilgrim Baptist Church Pipe Organ Association.[29]

In 1914 Francis founded and assumed the presidency of the Everywoman Suffrage Club, an organization whose post-suffrage goals included promoting "political and economic equality and social justice to the Negro, cooperation between white and colored women and men, training of local colored women leaders and fostering the recognition of Negroes who have achieved success." She devoted her energies to other causes as well, joining the Woman's Welfare League, the Urban League, and the National Association for the Advancement of Colored People (her husband had been instrumental in organizing the local branches) and serving as president of the Minnesota State Federation of Colored Women. These associations and activities suggest the accuracy of Clara Ueland's observation that Francis's "ruling motive" was to "help her race." When young African American women would not gain access to St. Paul business schools, Francis, who had been a stenographer, held evening shorthand classes in her home. In 1921, after a lynching in Duluth, she wrote and helped persuade the Minnesota legislature to pass the first antilynching law in the United States.[30]

Francis brought color, conviction, and courage to the suffrage movement in Minnesota. She organized African American women in support of suffrage, recognizing that all women should join in securing the right to vote. Clara Ueland described Nellie Francis as a "star" whose "spirit is a flame" as she spoke and organized in the interests of her race and her sex. Francis left Minnesota in 1927 to accompany her husband to his new post as U.S. minister to Liberia. After his death two years later, she returned to family and friends in Nashville, where she died in 1969.[31]

It was Clara Ueland who directed the final act of the suffrage movement in Minnesota. Like women leaders in other states who had acquired education and experience in making things happen, she was an articulate spokeswoman whose style was more managerial than charismatic.

The nine-year-old Clara Hampson, in the company of her widowed mother and older brother, moved to Minnesota from Ohio in 1869. Despite her poverty, she did very well in school and learned—probably in reaction to her dependent mother—to be self-reliant and creative. Like many suffragists, she embarked on a teaching career. While still in high school she had met Andreas Ueland, a Norwegian immigrant, at a young-people's literary society. They were married 10 years later in 1885. Life proceeded conventionally. Clara had children, and Andreas, a probate judge at the time of their marriage, opened his own law office in Minneapolis and soon prospered.[32]

Clara first ventured outside the home by joining the Peripatetics in 1893. This club—which still exists—was one of the numerous study groups offering middle-class women a means to inform themselves on a wide range of topics, usually relating to literature, the arts, and history. Moving from study to action, Ueland inspired the founding of the Minneapolis Kindergarten Association, which promoted the formation of kindergartens and a training program for teachers. With the integration of kindergartens into the Minneapolis public school system in 1905, the organization disbanded, and the training school was handed off to its proprietor, who established and directed for 48 years the famous Miss Wood's School.[33]

In 1907 Ueland helped organize the Woman's Club of Minneapolis. Five years later she withdrew from the board because she had other things on her mind—suffrage for one. In 1913 Ueland organized the Equal Suffrage Association of Minneapolis to energize and politicize the local movement. In the spring of 1914, she orchestrated a parade of nearly 2,000 suffrage supporters in Minneapolis—an event that had a dramatic impact on changing attitudes and perceptions about women who wanted the right to vote. Later that same year, Ueland was elected president of the Minnesota Woman Suffrage Association.[34]

What a difference a leader can make! Following a succession of four presidents in four years and the organizational disarray suggested by that turnover, Ueland came to office with a considered set of priorities: to hire and support an efficient organizer; to magnify the association's clout by organizing in political districts; and to assign specific responsibilities to each board member. She was determined to improve the operations of the MWSA and to transform the suffrage organizations throughout the state into highly sophisticated mechanisms of persuasion pressure, and action. In the five years of her presidency, she achieved her original objectives and more. By 1919, and, a year later in a special session, Minnesota became the fifteenth state to ratify the Nineteenth Amendment.[35]

Ueland built her leadership with all kinds of support systems, appointing efficient staff in the office and in the field, attracting knowledgeable and energetic volunteers as directors, securing an adequate financial base, increasing political knowhow, recruiting experienced women for press work and public relations, and presiding over the growing sense of comradeship among suffragists who believed that their goal was in sight. She was highly regarded not just by suffrage colleagues but by legislators, journalists, businessmen and women, and political leaders, all of whom recognized that her many talents, coupled with a generous and caring spirit, made her one of the most remarkable women of Minnesota.[36]

Sarah Burger Stearns, Julia B. Nelson, Ethel Hurd, Emily Bright, Bertha Moller, Emily Noyes, Nellie Francis, and Clara Ueland: These extraordinary women, each with her own style and in her own milieu, guided the Minnesota suffrage campaign or influenced it in some significant way. The struggle for suffrage in Minnesota began as a stumbling overture lacking any form of sustained support except great enthusiasm, commitment, and hard work on the part of a few good women. It evolved to a more diverse organizational structure led by women with highly refined managerial and political skills. Clara Ueland's presidency was a fitting finale to a cause whose time was long overdue.

NOTES

From Minnesota History *54 (Fall, 1995).*

1. Anne Firor Scott and Andrew MacKay Scott, *One Half the People: The Fight for Woman Suffrage* (Philadelphia: Lippincott, 1975; reprint, Urbana: University of Illinois Press, 1982), 59.

2. Eleanor Flexner, *Century of Struggle: The Woman's Rights Movement in the United States* (Cambridge: Belknap Press of Harvard University Press, 1959), 75.

3. Jane Grey Swisshelm, *Crusader and Feminist: Letters of Jane Grey Swisshelm, 1858–1865*, ed. Arthur J. Larsen (St. Paul: Minnesota Historical Society, 1934), 34n; Elizabeth Cady Stanton et al., *History of Woman Suffrage* (Rochester, N.Y.: Susan B. Anthony, 1886), 3:650, 651.

4. Stanton et al., *History* 3:651; Minnesota, House of Representatives, *Journal* (hereafter *House Journal*, 1868, p. 47, 1875, p. 210; Minnesota Secretary of State, *Legislative Manual*, 1985–86, p. 44. For these defeats, see, for example, *House Journal*, 1877, p. 327, 431–32, 1895, p. 161, 203, 221, 1897, p. 378, 560; *Senate Journal*, 1877, p. 352, 439, 1895, p. 508, 749; *Legislative Manual*, 1985–86, p. 44.

5. Theodora P. Martin, *The Sound of Our Own Voices: Women's Study Clubs, 1860–1910* (Boston: Beacon Press, 1987), 21; Ellen C. DuBois, *Feminism and Suffrage: The Emergence of an Independent Women's Movement in America, 1848–1869* (Ithaca: Cornell University Press, 1978), 46–47; Flexner, *Century of Struggle,* 75–76.

6. Aileen S. Kraditor, *The Ideas of the Woman Suffrage Movement, 1890–1920* (Garden City, N.Y.: Doubleday & Company, 1971), 12–26, 141, 167; Flexner, *Century of Struggle,* 271, 296–98.

7. Quote from abolitionist Wendell Phillips in DuBois, *Feminism and Suffrage,* 59; Steven M. Buechler, *Women's Movements in the United States: Woman Suffrage, Equal Rights, and Beyond* (New Brunswick, N.J.: Rutgers University Press, 1990), 56–57.

8. Stanton et al., *History* 3:651, 657.

9. Stanton et al., *History* 3:657n; Sarah Burger Stearns entry, Minnesota Biography files, Minnesota Historical Society (MHS), St. Paul; Martin, *Sound of Our Own Voices,* 16.

10. Stanton et al., *History* 3:650.

11. Stanton et al., *History* 3:652–53; William Watts Folwell, *A History of Minnesota,* rev. ed. (St. Paul: MHS, 1969), 4:334; *Legislative Manual*, 1985–86, p. 44.

12. Mrs. W. S. Woodbridge, "Tells Lifework of Duluth's Pioneer Clubwoman and Suffragist," unidentified clipping, Northeast Minnesota Historical Center, Duluth; *House Journal*, 1881, p. 181; *Senate Journal*, 1881, p. 58, 229; *Duluth News Tribune*, Jan. 26, 1904, p. 4.

13. Stanton et al., *History* 3:657; Ethel Edgerton Hurd, *Woman Suffrage in Minnesota: A Record of Activities in Its Behalf since 1847* (Minneapolis: Minnesota Woman Suffrage Assn., 1916), p. 17, says 1888 but Nelson in Elizabeth Cady Stanton et al., *History of Woman Suffrage* (Rochester, N.Y.: Susan B. Anthony, 1902), 4:772, says 1889.

14. Julia Wiech Lief, "A Woman of Purpose: Julia B. Nelson," *Minnesota History* 47 (Winter 1981): 303–04.

15. Lief, "Woman of Purpose," 304–07; Stanton et al., *History* 4:79.

16. Stanton et al., *History* 4:773.

17. Hurd, *Woman Suffrage in Minnesota*, 29; Ueland to [?], Aug. 29, 1917, Minnesota Woman Suffrage Association (MWSA) Records, microfilm edition, R[oll]2, F[rame]728, MHS; woman suffrage material, 1915–19, Luth and Nanny M. Jaeger Papers, MHS; Lief, "Woman of Purpose," 314; Barbara Stuhler, *Gentle Warriors: Clara Ueland and the Minnesota Struggle for Woman Suffrage* (St. Paul: MHS Press, 1995), 157–58.

18. Hurd, *Woman Suffrage in Minnesota*, 10, credits Stearns with founding the Woman Suffrage Club of Minneapolis (later renamed the Political Equality Club) between 1868 and 1883. Early records of the organization were lost when a fire burned the residence of the secretary; Ethel Edgerton Hurd, "A Brief History of the Minneapolis Political Equality Club," Apr. 15, 1921, p. 1, 23, Political Equality Club of Minneapolis Papers, MHS.

19. Ethel Hurd to Anna Howard Shaw, Nov. 2, 1909, MWSA Records, R1 F75; Elisabeth Griffith, *In Her Own Right: The Life of Elizabeth Cady Stanton* (New York: Oxford University Press, 1984), 197–99.

20. Inez Haynes Irwin, *The Story of the Woman's Party* (New York: Harcourt, Brace and Co., 1921), 27; Stuhler, *Gentle Warriors*, 132, 138.

21. The phrase is from Doris Stevens's book, *Jailed for Freedom: American Women Win the Vote,* ed. Carol O'Hare (Troutdale, Ore: New Sage Press, 1995).

22. Clara Ueland to Jessie E. Scott, Aug. 25, 1919, MWSA Records R7, F173.

23. Brenda Ueland, "Clara Ueland of Minnesota" (privately published, 1967), 261, copy in MHS collections. Bright's birth and death dates are unknown, although she was probably born in the 1860s; MWSA Records R17, F261.

24. Minutes, Oct. 2, 19, 1914, Political Equality Club of Minneapolis Papers; Clara Ueland to Dear Secretary, R1, F211, and undated clipping, MWSA Records R17, F723.

25. Bertha Moller entry, Minnesota Biography files; Clara Ueland to Bertha Moller, Oct. 4, 1916, MWSA Records, R2, F243.

26. Mary Dillon Foster, comp., *Who's Who among Minnesota Women: A History of Woman's Work in Minnesota from Pioneer Days to Date* (privately published, 1924), 219.

27. *St. Paul Pioneer Press,* Sept. 10, 1930, p. 1; Rhoda Gilman to author, Apr. 1994.

28. Foster, *Who's Who,* 358; *Minnesota Woman Voter,* Jan. 1930, p. 3.

29. Judy Yaeger Jones, "Nellie F. Griswold Francis," in *Women of Minnesota: Biographies and Sources* (St. Paul: Women's History Month, 1991), 12.

30. Nellie Griswold Francis entry, Minnesota Biography files; B. Ueland, "Clara Ueland," 399; Arthur B. McWatt, "St. Paul's Resourceful African American Community," *Ramsey County History* 26 (Spring 1991): 5; Earl Spangler, *The Negro in Minnesota* (Minneapolis: T. S. Denison and Co., 1961), 100–03. Like most African Americans of the period, both Nellie and W. T. Francis were active in Republican Party affairs; Foster, *Who's Who,* 101.

31. B. Ueland, "Clara Ueland," 399; Jones, "Nellie F. Griswold Francis," 15. In 1920, only 8,809 African Americans resided in Minnesota, 0.4 percent of the total population of 2,387,125; United States, *Census,* 1920, *Population* 3:19.

32. Stuhler, *Gentle Warriors,* 35–44.

33. Martin, *Sound of Our Own Voices,* 81; Marguerite N. Bell, *With Banners: A Biography of Stella Louise Wood* (St. Paul: Macalester College Press, 1954), 47–48.

34. B. Ueland, "Clara Ueland," 243–44; Minutes, 33rd annual convention, Oct. 16–17, 1914, pt. 1, p. 1, 3, 14.

35. Executive board minutes, May 5, 1915, MWSA Records R14, F603; *Senate and House Journal,* Extra Session, 1919, p. 1, 13.

36. For more on Ueland, see Stuhler, *Gentle Warriors.* Ueland and Dr. Martha Ripley are the only two women recognized for their achievements with plaques in the state capitol or on its grounds.

POLITICS & LAW

The Origin of Minnesota's Nonpartisan Legislature

CHARLES R. ADRIAN

The early twentieth century was known as the Progressive Era, a period of sweeping reforms that sought to make American democracy more responsive to and representative of its citizens. Political reforms introduced during this period included initiative, referendum, and recall, primary elections to determine candidates for the general elections, municipal home rule and the city manager form of government, direct popular election of U.S. Senators, and women's suffrage. Muckrakers fueled the movement by documenting corruption, mismanagement, and incompetence from statehouses to packinghouses.

Minnesota's political environment was not spared. Lincoln Steffens, one of the leading muckrakers, devoted a whole chapter to corruption in Minneapolis in his book, The Shame of the Cities. *Changing the Minnesota state legislature from partisan to nonpartisan in 1913 is often cited as a reflection of the spirit of the Progressive Movement. However, Charles Adrian describes the development of a nonpartisan legislature in Minnesota as more a "political accident," possibly an unexpected result of struggles between wets and drys over the liquor question.*

In 1973, after this piece was first published, Minnesota ended its sixty-year experiment with a nonpartisan state legislature. By then, for many Minnesotans, "liberal" and "conservative" labels for nonpartisan legislators seemed mere aliases for Democrat and Republican.

Only two states—Minnesota and Nebraska—select their legislators on a ballot without party designations. Minnesota's unusual arrangement dates from 1913 and is largely the result of a political accident—of a series of events strongly resembling a comedy of errors. Nebraska acquired its nonpartisan legislature more than two decades later, in 1934, when that state's lawmaking branch was completely reorganized.

In 1913, like most of the rest of the United States, Minnesota was affected by a reform movement in state and local government—a movement that spread the concept of "efficiency and economy" to national as well as state government. It was inspired by the successful example of the business corporation and by general disgust for the low moral standards that marked much political party activity about the turn of the century. Muckrakers had been exposing politicians, and as a result party prestige was very low.

The movement toward political reform, which reached its peak in the second decade of the twentieth century, urged such innovations as the primary election, proportional representation, a shorter ballot, concentration of responsibility in state administrative structure, the unicameral legislature, council-manager and commission government in cities, the initiative, referendum, and recall, and the nonpartisan election of certain public officials. Some reformers urged that judges and city and county officials should be chosen on a nonpartisan ballot. A few extremists went so far as to propose the use of nonpartisan elections in selecting all state officials.

When the thirty-eighth Minnesota legislature met in January, 1913, probably not a single member suspected that before the session ended the state would have a lawmaking body chosen without party designation. It was generally assumed that debate during the session would center about county option on the liquor question, industrial accident insurance, the desirability of the initiative, referendum, and recall, and the nonpartisan election of county officials.

Minnesota reformers had precedents for the nonpartisan ballot in electing county officials. Not only had California recently furnished an example, but the year before Minnesota itself had also applied the nonpartisan principle to county superintendents of schools, officers of first-class cities, and state judges. Laws passed in 1912 by a special legislative session called by Governor A. O. Eberhart provided for the Minnesota changes. Five other states had previously removed the party label from their judicial ballots, and the move to "purify" this branch of government was in full swing. In four years, twelve states had adopted the plan.[1]

The nonpartisan principle was then extended to other areas of government. Reformers argued that local officials should be businesslike administrators, since there was no Republican way to gravel a road and no Democratic way to lay a sewer. California made all its district, county, township, judicial, school, and city officials nonpartisan. Other states considered extending the plan to the state superintendent of public instruction, university regents, local school officials, and city and village officials.

In 1913 Minnesota's political atmosphere was marked by many discordant elements, and was further complicated by the wet-dry issue that transcended party lines. The Republicans, who were rapidly becoming known as the dry party, were in complete command of all three branches of the state government.

In the organization of the 1913 legislature, the Senate was guided by Lieutenant Governor J. A. A. Burnquist of St. Paul, a dry Republican. After a close fight among the Republican elements, Henry Rines of Mora was chosen as the

Republican candidate for speaker of the House. He was not a radical prohibitionist, but favored county option and pursued a middle-of-the-road policy. His solid reputation for honesty made him a natural choice for presiding officer—a man acceptable both to the drys and to the progressive Republicans.[2] This was an important asset in a period when the drys were regularly split between the county optionists, who favored leaving the liquor question to the voters of each county, and the prohibitionists, who would settle for no less than a completely dry state, and therefore opposed county option. When a vote was taken on the speakership, it resulted in 101 for Rines and 19 for Frank E. Minnette, a Democrat.

On February 7, 1913, Senator Julius E. Haycraft of Madelia, a progressive Republican who was chairman of the Senate elections committee, introduced a bill to extend the nonpartisan provisions of the 1912 primary election act to include all judges and all city and county officers. He was convinced that the plan was sound and progressive, and the general feeling seemed to be that, although important and powerful party regulars opposed it, the bill was almost certain to pass.[3]

When the Haycraft bill reached the floor of the Senate on February 13, it was attacked from several angles by Senate leaders. F. A. Duxbury of Caledonia immediately introduced an amendment to eliminate the provision regarding all county officers except superintendents of schools. Joining him in the opposition was Senator A. J. Rockne of Goodhue County, a conservative and a long-time leader both in the Senate and in the Republican party. Rockne argued that political parties were necessary to the American system of government. The party system, he said, was anchored in the local community. Its elimination would destroy the roots of an important American institution. The Republicans, entrenched in all branches of state government and powerful also in county and city government, had nothing to gain from a change in the party system. The Rockne group had little choice but to fight the bill on the Senate floor, since progressives controlled the elections committee. The Duxbury amendment, however, was voted down 34 to 20.

Backed by thirteen conservative party regulars, including Duxbury and George H. Sullivan of Stillwater, Rockne then conceived the idea that the proposal could be killed by adding members of the legislature to the list of nonpartisan officers. After conferring with Speaker Rines and being assured that the House would kill any such provision in its elections committee, on February 27, the Rockne group, represented by Frank Clague, proposed an amendment calling for the nonpartisan election of legislators.[4]

The proposal caught the Senate by surprise. Battle lines that had been forming slowly were altered and reinforced, for the bill now affected every member of the legislature. Senator Haycraft, as the author of the original bill, let it be known that he had not contemplated including state officers and that he was opposed to the altered plan. He, too, hurried to the speaker of the House, and received assurance that the bill would not pass if it included legislators, or that it would be so changed that a conference committee would become deadlocked over it.

In the Senate, progressives who had looked with favor upon the Haycraft bill were obliged to reconsider their position in the light of the maneuvers of the conservatives. Confusion seemed general. Regulars assumed that the Republicans favored the proposal. Some progressives evidently assumed that if a little medicine was good for the body politic, a lot of medicine should improve it. Other senators apparently felt that a vote for the bill would find favor with the voters at home. Besides, it was common knowledge that the bill was to be killed in the House. The Senate was more concerned with the bill's main proposal, which was intended to revise the primary law passed in 1912. Consequently, the Clague amendment passed by a vote of 35 to 22 almost without discussion, although only 21 senators actually favored the proposal. With only a few of the Rockne group opposing it, the amended bill was passed 53 to 8, and was then sent to the House.[5]

Senate file 412 was given a first reading in the House on March 1, 1913, and was referred to the elections committee, where it remained for nearly three weeks. During this period, the political significance of the bill received real consideration, and lobbyists went to work. Seeing the Republican party, which nearly always controlled the legislature, securely in the hands of the drys, the liquor and brewery interests quietly began to work for the bill in its Senate form. Lacking a majority in either house, the wets resorted to an ancient propaganda technique in order to advance the cause of the bill. Through Democratic Senator John Moonan and Republican Representatives G. W. Brown and H. H. Dunn, former speaker of the House, the wets let it be understood that they opposed any type of nonpartisanship, since only the drys could benefit from abolishing parties. Many drys rose to the bait.

Rural legislators, feeling that the proposal to put county elections on a nonpartisan basis was sure to win, feared that the whole burden of local political organization and support would fall on them. Unhappy at the thought of assuming this thankless task alone, many decided that a nonpartisan legislature would be a simple solution for their problem. City members had still another reason for becoming interested in the novel and unexpected Clague amendment. They had been troubled in recent elections by the growing popularity of the Socialist party in the poorer sections of large cities. Since the bill provided that only the names of the two candidates who received the largest votes in the fall primary could appear on the election ballots, city members thought this would be a way to get rid of the Socialist threat.

Still another group of representatives who became interested in the new plan were those who favored Theodore Roosevelt's Progressive party, which the legislature was considering legalizing. If this were to happen, the "Bull Moose" Republicans would be faced at the next election with the difficult decision of whether to run as Progressives or Republicans. In a legislature elected without party designation, this problem could be avoided. The bill appealed to still others as a *de facto* recognition of the breakdown of party lines that occurred in the previous session.[6]

Speaker Rines and Representative N. J. Holmberg, Republican chairman of the elections committee, led the opposition to the bill. They believed that the measure would destroy the vitality of political parties, which they regarded as necessary since they provided the opportunity for a "natural cleavage" on questions of public policy. They also argued that state officers would not be able to carry out party policy with a nonpartisan legislature.[7]

Some minority party members, apparently fearful of losing their identity, opposed the bill. The legislature contained a Populist, a Prohibitionist, and a Public Ownership member. Among them, only the Prohibitionist, Representative George H. Voxland, favored nonpartisanship. Some drys opposed the bill because they were skeptical of the wets' argument that Prohibitionist candidates would no longer draw votes away from dry Republicans if the nonpartisan bill were enacted. Apparently it occurred to some legislators who favored county option that they were entrenched within the larger of the major parties, and could make the state dry without altering the traditional legislative arrangement.

The elections committee reported the bill out on March 20 with the unanimous recommendation that it should pass after being amended to exclude from the nonpartisan ballot members of the legislature and all county officers except superintendents of schools. This was the form of the bill that had been promised Senator Rockne and his group, but the elimination of county officials was not acceptable to the progressive followers of Senator Haycraft.

The effects of lobbying and propaganda were fully evident when the bill was taken up by the House on a special order on March 27. During the debate, Republican Representative G. W. Brown of Glencoe moved to restore county officers and members of the legislature to the list of nonpartisan positions. According to the *St. Paul Pioneer Press* of March 28, Brown asserted that no partisan issues had been raised in the current session, and he assured his colleagues that none would be. Representative W. I. Nolan, a leader among House Republicans, made a substitute motion that only county officers be reinserted. This move would have restored the bill to its original form, but the amendment was defeated by an overwhelming 74 to 84 vote.[8]

According to the *Minneapolis Journal* of March 28, Representative G. B. Bjornson of Minneota, who favored making all state officers nonpartisan, held that such positions were not political in nature. "The governor," he explained, "is the state's official traveling lecturer." Representative Charles N. Orr of St. Paul pointed out that the Senate had extended nonpartisanship to the legislature in an effort to kill the bill, and that the action had not been sincere. He warned the House that affirmative action would not support the genuine attitude of a majority of senators. Representative Albert Pfaender of New Ulm, a Democrat, thought the Senate version of the bill excellent, but feared that nonpartisanship might be extended to the governorship.

When a vote was taken, the Brown amendment prevailed 71 to 39. Thirty-seven Republicans, one Democrat (Henry Steen, a wet), and one Public Ownership member voted against the measure.[9] Opposition came from progressives like Speaker Rines and Charles A. Lindbergh, as well as from conservatives such as W. I. Norton and C. E. Stone. Republican leaders, convinced that nonpartisanship would greatly weaken the party, voted against the amendment. Negative votes were recorded by R. C. Dunn, Thomas Frankson, Nolan, Norton, and Rines.

The bill, which also contained numerous amendments to the primary election act of 1912, was adopted by a final vote of 94 to 17 on March 27, 1913. Die-hard opposition came from the Public Ownership member, a Democrat, and fifteen Republicans, all but one of whom were drys.

Apparently the relative merits and demerits of a nonpartisan legislature never were considered either on the floor of the House or in private discussions while the bill was under consideration. Voting seems to have been motivated purely by questions of political expediency. Eighteen wet Democrats supported the bill, while one opposed it. Most Republican wets favored it as did a large number of drys, including the Prohibitionist. The efforts of the beverage lobby seem to have been successful.

On March 28, C. H. Warner, a Republican, moved for reconsideration, but the proposal lost 63 to 47. In support of the motion, Nolan claimed that liquor groups had approved the nonpartisan measure and that this alone should be enough to warrant reconsideration.[10] The *Willmar Tribune* of April 2 reported that "the brewery interests, and their representatives, were beside themselves with delight when the House ... decided to retain this [nonpartisan] feature in the primary election law."

The bill was not yet law, however. Under an act of 1912, the date for the election was set in September. The Senate version of the Haycraft bill proposed to change the time to June, while the House bill suggested October. This discrepancy probably reflected an effort to create a deadlock between the two houses.[11]

A conference committee appointed on March 29 was deliberately "stacked" against nonpartisanship by Lieutenant Governor Burnquist and Speaker Rines.[12] When it did not report promptly, a political writer for the wet Democratic *St. Cloud Daily Times,* in an article published belatedly on April 18, commented: "Though passed by both houses over a week ago the nonpartisan primary bill is still a long ways from being a law. A conference committee composed of members of both houses has it in charge, and . . . they are out to either kill it or make it so obnoxious that neither house will adopt the changes proposed. The objectionable feature is the nonpartisan idea as applied to the election of members of the house and senate and which the house leaders, after giving their sanction, woke up to the fact, or rather they charged it, that unfriendly interests had put one over on them. They are trying to get back now by proposing that the nonpartisan idea be extended to state officers, which would include the governor. This simply means that the bill will never become a law."

Just what the conference committee wanted to do is not certain. According to the *St. Paul Pioneer Press* of April 12, committee members searched unsuccessfully for a precedent in Minnesota legislative history that would allow them to add completely new material to a deadlocked measure. It seems improbable that they believed they could add the state executive officers to the nonpartisan ballot and thus force both houses to reject the bill.

After stalling as long as possible, on April 11 the committee finally reported that its members were unable to agree on the scope of its authority. Specifically, they did not know if they could strike out the provisions concerning the nonpartisan legislature. N. J. Holmberg, one of the House managers, moved that the committee be allowed to consider this question. H. H. Dunn, leader of the wet Republicans, moved that the House committeemen be instructed to confer on only one difference between the House and Senate bills—the date for the primary election. The *Minneapolis Journal* reported on April 12 that G. W. Brown criticized the committee for attempting to say it knew what the House wanted better than did the House itself. The Dunn motion carried, but by a vote of only 64 to 47. This represented eight more negative votes than had been cast against the crucial Brown amendment to override the recommendations of the House elections committee. The changes of heart took place among dry Republicans, who became doubtful as a result of the interest taken in the bill by brewery representatives.[13]

Opposition to nonpartisanship then abruptly collapsed. After a brief meeting of the committee, Senator Haycraft announced that he remained opposed to a nonpartisan legislature, but that he was willing to go along with the majority. When the report of the committee was heard in the House, light attendance forced proponents of the bill to engage in hasty parliamentary maneuvering. The roll call on the adoption of the conference report lacked an absolute majority, with a vote of 48 to 32, and a motion to reconsider had to be made to keep the report alive. On the following Wednesday, April 16, after the dry Republicans had twice tried unsuccessfully to adjourn the House, the bill was repassed, 64 to 48.[14]

The Senate adopted the conference committee's report 36 to 15.[15] Among those who voted in the negative were six senators who had joined in the scheme to inject the legislature into the bill and who had opposed Senate passage earlier. Many confirmed opponents of the bill, including Rockne, found it expedient to support it.

Some senators saw fit to explain their votes. Among them was Senator Edward Rustad of Wheaton, who said that although he opposed the nonpartisan legislative principle, he found the June primary date so desirable that he voted for the bill. Senator George H. Sullivan of Stillwater explained that there were no longer any party lines anyway, since the state convention had been abolished. One might, he felt, just as well vote for a nonpartisan legislature and abolish party lines in name as well as in fact. The bill was signed by the governor without comment on April 19, 1913.

The Minnesota legislature had become nonpartisan without a single word of debate on the merits of the question. The proposal had been introduced without thought or intention that it ever would become law. Wet sponsorship of the bill had been entirely spontaneous and was based upon simple political expediency. The wets hoped that nonpartisanship would help break the strength of the Republican caucus in the legislature and disorganize the forces demanding county option. Subtly, the drys had been influenced to think that they, too, could gain politically by supporting the bill. To add to the confusion, the opposition consisted of both progressive and extremely conservative Republicans. The progressives felt that nonpartisanship on the local level was desirable, but deplored its extension to the legislature. Conservative Republicans thought the plan would destroy party organization.

According to the Red Wing Daily Republican of March 31, a nonpartisan legislature "was a suggestion so new and so radical that even the members who voted for it hardly realized what a revolutionary change" they were proposing. In fact, there is no evidence that any legislator expected the new arrangement to cause important problems of organization or to change executive-legislative relationships and responsibility. A few were concerned lest it weaken party strength needed for more important state and national offices. Other provisions seem to have been the determining factors in the final passage.[16]

Contemporary newspaper reports indicate a lack of interest in the new law, as well as of any realization that its application would involve important problems. Many rural papers did not even bother to comment. Country editors who did offer opinions seemed chiefly concerned with the probability that the new law would "hamstring" local party organization. The metropolitan dailies were not enthusiastic about the change. The Minneapolis Journal gave the plan tentative approval, although its chief political observer was skeptical and never approved nonpartisanship. The St. Paul Pioneer Press opposed the change.

Preoccupied with the prohibition issue, the *Red Wing Daily Republican* of April 26 merely noted casually that "a great change was brought about." On April 24 the *Fergus Falls Daily Journal* stated that county officials seemed pleased that henceforth they would be elected on a nonpartisan ticket. The paper suggested that the new system would be worthwhile if only because it would save money by reducing the size of the ballot. After considering the change in the light of the 1912 election, the editor suggested that the nonpartisan feature might well be extended to the office of governor. "Men are elected to office, not parties," read the editorial. "The official state ballot should not recognize any party organization."[17]

The *St. Cloud Daily Times* of March 3, looking toward the passage of the bill, was nostalgic concerning the party system. "Truly the day of political parties is passing away," it said. On March 7 the same newspaper reported that Stearns County officials generally favored the nonpartisan bill on the local level, but felt that it might be detrimental in state and national politics. They proved poor prophets, however, in predicting that the bill would result in shorter official lives, in increased competition for offices, and in the total elimination of party lines in offices elected without party designation. Others thought the plan would work to the advantage of a candidate active in a party, since he would get the support not only of his party but of independents as well.

A hidden danger in the new plan was suggested by the editor of the *Caledonia Journal* when he wrote: "The legislature seems to be determined to so amend the election laws that candidates for the legislature must run on a non-partisan ticket. It is a mistake. Extravagance is rampant now, and when we get a non-partisan Legislature it will be still worse. There will be no minority to watch over the extravagance of the majority." The *Anoka Union* also expressed disapproval. "A non-partisan ticket finds no favor with the Union," commented the editor. "It believes in party organizations, and particularly the old Republican party. . . . If a non-partisan ticket for county officers does not work out any better than the non-partisan judiciary ticket did last election, it will prove a gigantic failure."[18]

The *St. Peter Free Press* suggested that the new system "means a concentration of political power in a comparatively few people." Opinion was more favorable, however, in Fairmont. "Thank the Lord and the Legislature, hereafter a good and deserving man will not have to wear the brand 'Republican' in order to get a county office or be elected to the Legislature in Minnesota," wrote the editor of the *Sentinel*.[19]

Of all newspapermen, the *Minneapolis Journal's* veteran observer Charles B. Cheney proved the wisest. After the Senate added the legislature to the primary election bill, he commented on March 1: "Nonpartisan nominations in local government are sound in principle and work well in practice. But the case is very different with legislative nominations. The Minnesota plan throws the door open to nominations of the liquor and other interests. They find it easy to juggle the contests, once these have degenerated into mere personal struggles."

On March 28, Cheney demonstrated that he had a more truthful crystal ball than did the brewery lobbyists. The final result, he said, "might properly fool the liquor interests. The law would also wipe out the prohibition factor which has divided the temperance forces in many legislative districts. With nothing but the temperance issue involved and the temperance forces united, the demand for county option would very likely be able to make gains in several districts." That is exactly what happened in the election of 1914.

A *Journal* editorial of March 29, however, expressed a different view. It concluded that "the Legislature has dropped the party distinction" because through the adoption of the primary and "other changes," party lines had been all but obliterated and there was no longer a responsible party in the state. The writer expected that there would be some self-seekers, some one-idea men, a scramble for places, and an outcropping of personal platforms. He expressed the opinion that because of weakness in numbers, the Democrats had tended to make secret bargains, "horse-trading" rather than serving as an alert opposition. This the *Journal* writer thought unfortunate, concluding that "A nonpartisan legislature could hardly be worse."

The *St. Paul Pioneer Press* of April 15 expressed orthodox political theory in an editorial that asserted that "The Legislators would do well to consider carefully whether it is desirable to extend the nonpartisan feature to legislative and other state officials. There is no doubt about getting rid of party politics in local affairs. . . . But there is grave doubt if such should be the case in state and national affairs," it continued. "The best check against authority is a vigorous and well organized opposition. One party will keep another up to its duty."

A writer in the official journal of American political science took note of the change in Minnesota politics as follows: "It may be seriously doubted . . . whether the nonpartisan movement is not overreaching itself when it invades the field of political offices as it does for the first time in Minnesota."[20]

The lone enthusiastic comment seems to have come from the muckraking C. J. Buell, an ardent prohibitionist, who wrote: "It is to be hoped, that the time is near when men will be chosen for public positions in state and city, village and county, upon their honesty and fitness instead of how they line up on national issues that have no necessary relation to state and local affairs."[21]

Less than a week after the bill passed, a group of prominent attorneys who were active Republicans publicly announced that the bill creating the nonpartisan legislature was, in their opinion, unconstitutional. They argued that the act violated Article IV, Section 27, of the Minnesota Constitution, since it embraced more than one subject and that subject was not expressed in the title. The new law, in truth, was a fairly extensive revision of the Primary Elections Act of 1912, and it actually amended sections of the *Revised Laws* other than those listed in its title. The attorneys said that the act had not been adopted in a strictly constitutional fashion, and urged someone to test it by filing for office on a partisan basis. No one made such a move, however—probably because both the wets and the drys expected to gain from the law in the 1914 election.

Consequently the legality of the nonpartisan legislature was never tested in the courts. The state supreme court upheld the nonpartisan ballot for judicial nominations and elections, but the court decided that the case did not apply to the part of the law that concerned the legislature.[22] Although the origin of Minnesota's nonpartisan legislature can be traced to an accident resulting from a series of political maneuvers, at mid-century the state is still electing its lawmakers on a nonpartisan ticket under the provisions of the act of 1913.

NOTES
From Minnesota History *33 (Winter, 1952).*

1. The nonpartisan judicial movement died almost as suddenly as it began. Many states abandoned the plan after a few years. Since it was adopted by Nevada in 1923, no new states have tried it.

2. The term "progressive" as used in this article refers merely to the branch of the Republican party that supported the general principles of Theodore Roosevelt, as well as other moderate reform proposals. The progressives were opposed by the conservatives, standpatters, or regulars—all fairly synonymous terms.

3. For the text of the Haycraft bill see Minnesota Legislature, Thirty-eighth Session, 1913. Senate File 412.

4. *Minneapolis Journal,* February 27, 1913.

5. For the progress of Senate File 412 through the Senate see Minnesota, *Senate Journal,* 1913, p. 251, 288–290, 337–344, 472–475, 494–500, 513–515, 1055, 1409, 1681.

6. For summaries of the attitudes of various groups see the *Red Wing Daily Republican,* March 31, 1913; the *Willmar Tribune,* April 2, 1913; and the metropolitan dailies, especially Charles B. Cheney's report in the *Minneapolis Journal,* March 28, 1913.

7. Interview with Henry Rines, August, 1949.

8. For the progress of Senate File 412 through the House, see Minnesota, *House Journal,* 1913, p. 626, 1028, 1166–1170, 1193, 1214.

9. The Republicans included thirty-four drys and three wets, as indicated by the vote on the county option bill of 1913.

10. *Minneapolis Journal,* March 28, 1913.

11. *Fergus Falls Daily Journal,* March 29, 1913; *St. Paul Pioneer Press,* March 28, 1913; *Minneapolis Journal,* March 29, 1913.

12. Interview with Henry Rines, August, 1949.

13. *House Journal,* 1913, p. 1621–1623; *Willmar Tribune,* April 16, 1913; *St. Cloud Daily Times,* April 18, 1913; *Red Wing Daily Republican,* March 31, 1913.

14. *House Journal,* 1913, p. 1745.

15. *Senate Journal,* 1913, p. 1409.

16. *Red Wing Daily Republican,* March 31, 1913. The enactment was a surprise not only to the state at large, but to "most of the members responsible for its enactment into law,"

according to Robert E. Cushman. See his "Non-partisan Nominations and Elections," in the American Academy of Political and Social Science, *Annals*, 106:90 (March, 1923).

17. *Willmar Tribune*, April 9, 23, 1913.

18. *Caledonia Journal*, quoted in the *St. Paul Pioneer Press*, April 18, 1913; *Anoka Union*, quoted in the *St. Cloud Daily Times*, February 6, 1913.

19. *St. Peter Free Press*, quoted in the *St. Cloud Daily Times*, February 7, 1913; *Fairmont Sentinel*, quoted in the *St. Paul Pioneer Press*, April 24, 1913.

20. Victor J. West, "Legislation of 1913 Affecting Nominations and Elections," in *American Political Science Review*, 7:439 (August, 1914).

21. C. J. Buell, *The Minnesota Legislature of* 1913, 13 (St. Paul, 1914).

22. State *ex rel.* Nordin *v.* Erickson, in 119 *Minnesota Reports*, 152 (St. Paul, 1913).

The Minnesota Gag Law
and the Fourteenth Amendment

JOHN E. HARTMANN

On June 13, 1971, the New York Times *began publishing the Pentagon papers, the massive secret history of America's role in Southeast Asia for more than twenty-five years. After only three daily installments had been published, the Nixon Justice Department obtained a temporary restraining order and moved quickly to obtain a permanent injunction. The case went through the entire federal judicial system in less than three weeks, and on June 30, 1971, the United States Supreme Court ruled in* New York Times Co. v. United States *by a vote of six to three that the First Amendment to the U.S. Constitution guaranteeing a free press overrode the legal considerations raised by the government.*

The justices based their decision on the principle of "no prior restraint on expression" set down as a precedent after a Supreme Court case decided forty years earlier: Near v. Minnesota (1931) *by a vote of five to four. The following article by John Hartmann presents the background of that landmark Minnesota case that would lead to the continued publication of the Pentagon papers decades later. The article also presents Minnesota legend Governor Floyd B. Olson in a slightly different light as the Hennepin County Attorney using Minnesota's 1925 public nuisance law in his efforts to silence newspapers like Jay Near's in the 1920s.*

On June 1, 1931, the Supreme Court of the United States handed down a decision which, according to one authority, represented "the climax of a striking evolution in our Constitutional law whereby freedom of speech and press is at last effectively 'nationalized.'" In this decision, rendered in the case of Near v. Minnesota, the court for the first time used "the guarantee of liberty in the Fourteenth Amendment . . . to completely obliterate a state law."[1]

The law in question, which had been enacted by the Minnesota legislature in 1925, declared certain types of publications a nuisance and provided for injunctions to prevent their circulation. Of this Minnesota measure—the first to provide for actual suppression of the public press since the passage of the Alien and Sedition Acts in 1798—Supreme Court Justice Brandeis was reported to have remarked: "It is difficult to see how one can have a free press and the protection it affords a democratic community without the privilege this act seeks to limit."[2]

The origins of the Minnesota "gag law" are obscure. Some claim that it was sponsored by a legislator intent on silencing an editor who was attacking him, and that the editor died before the law could be applied to his particular publication.[3] The bill was initiated in the Minnesota Senate by Freling H. Stevens, a Minneapolis attorney whose firm included his brother and his two sons. He was serving his second term as state senator, and politically he was a Progressive-Republican. When the bill was introduced on March 27, 1925, as Senate File 1181, it did not cause a furor. In routine manner, it was referred to the committee on general legislation, which reported it out the following day without recommendation, and it was then placed on the general orders of business. On April 7, 1925, it came to a vote before the Senate and passed without dissent. Stevens himself did not vote on the final passage. The bill was then sent to the House, and on April 16, 1925, was passed by a vote of eighty-two to twenty-two. Governor Theodore Christianson signed it into law along with a large number of minor end-of-session bills. Thus the act which within a few years was to become a subject of national concern passed quietly into the Minnesota statute books. The Minneapolis newspapers, particularly the *Minneapolis Tribune*, which gave excellent coverage to the daily sessions of the legislature, did not report on its passage.[4]

The new law was defined in its preamble as "An act declaring a nuisance, the business . . . of regularly or customarily producing, publishing, or circulating an obscene, lewd, and lascivious newspaper, magazine, or other periodical, or a malicious, scandalous, and defamatory newspaper, magazine, or other periodical and providing for injunction and other proceedings." It provided that the county attorney or, in his absence, the attorney general or any citizen acting in behalf of the county attorney, might institute proceedings in district court for a temporary restraining order against any periodical which in the mind of the complainant violated the provisions of the act. The district court was then empowered to issue a temporary restraining order if it so desired. In any case, a summons would be served on the accused publisher, who would have the privilege of answering the charges or demurring. The case would be tried before the district court judge, who would either rule in favor of the defense or grant a permanent injunction, by which, in the language of the law, "such nuisance may be wholly abated." Failure to comply with the order of the court would involve contempt and would be punishable by a fine of a thousand dollars or a year in the county jail.[5]

There were in the 1920s literally hundreds of small weekly newspapers, many of which imitated and elaborated the techniques developed by Hearst and other publishers in the late 1880s and branded by Pulitzer as "yellow journalism." No grist was too offensive to the public taste to be avoided by this type of scandal mill. The reporting which filled its pages usually involved crime, sex and sexual perversion, attacks on minority religious and racial groups, grossly exaggerated accounts of malfeasance by public officials, and scandals revolving about prominent private citizens. Some publishers went beyond the sensationalism that was intended to increase circulation and indulged in extortion and blackmail.[6]

The procedures followed by an extorting editor are well known. Fabricating a story out of whole cloth or greatly exaggerating a tale involving some truth, he approached his victim with advance copy and intimated that the story could be suppressed for a consideration. The victim, usually a prominent individual, could either meet the demands of the extortionist or suffer the consequences of unfavorable publicity. If he made the latter choice, he might sue for libel. In such a suit, however, the plaintiff bears the burden of proving that the published facts are untrue. Few people care to have their personal affairs aired in a courtroom. Under some circumstances, the mere occurrence of a trial can damage the reputation and earning capacity of an individual, while he is deterred by the cost of initiating legal action. Thus many people are vulnerable to an extortionist. Blackmail differs from extortion only in that the blackmailer is actually in possession of some fact his victim wishes suppressed.[7]

Public officials frequently have been singled out for attack by the sensational press. The nature of their position makes them especially vulnerable to unfavorable publicity, and though an official may be innocent of any malfeasance, a continuous barrage of charges inevitably casts some doubt on his honesty. A fine but definite line exists between attempts by the legitimate press to expose corruption and the sensational charges of the scandal sheet. Rarely indeed has a conviction arisen out of accusations made by journals of the latter type, while on occasion they have been linked with criminal organizations or interests.

Of the scandal sheets established in the 1920s, many expired within a few weeks. Those surviving often moved from address to address, appearing at irregular intervals under varying editorships. The lives of such editors were often as shifting and unstable as their papers. In following the career of one such individual it was discovered that, over a period of nine years, the city directory listed him only five times, in each instance at a different address. A man might edit several papers in rapid succession, only to turn up a short time later on the staff of an erstwhile competitor.[8]

One such elusive personality was Howard A. Guilford, who in 1913 founded a paper in St. Paul called the *Reporter*. Little is known of his earlier life. He was born in 1888, probably in Massachusetts, since he refers to his family there and was buried in that state. In a privately published book of memoirs he alludes to a reading knowledge of "Mr. Blackstone," indicating some acquaintance with the law, but Guilford sheds no further light on his life before arriving in Minnesota at the age of twenty-five.[9]

Unfortunately, no copy of the St. Paul *Reporter* is preserved, but according to Guilford the paper accused the St. Paul chief of police, Martin J. Flanagan, of negligence in failing to pursue known criminals. Soon after its appearance on January 17, 1913, Guilford was arrested on a counterfeiting charge, but was subsequently released. This marked the beginning of a lengthy police record, which extended from 1913 to 1927. In 1914 he was arrested on a charge of carrying a concealed weapon, and acquitted; he was convicted of libel in 1918, and fined a hundred dollars; he was tried for extortion in 1920, and acquitted. In his book Guilford mentions three other occasions when a county attorney sought an indictment on charges of libel or extortion, but in each case the grand jury failed to indict him.[10]

Meanwhile, the *Reporter* appeared sporadically in 1913 and 1914. Beginning in 1915, the paper was published in Minneapolis under the name of the *Twin City Reporter* and it became a regular weekly. For a short time in 1915 Guilford attempted to issue it daily, but this attempt was unsuccessful, and he soon returned to a weekly schedule.

Each issue of the *Twin City Reporter* followed a set pattern; sex, attacks on public officials and prominent private citizens, and vicious baiting of minority groups were its major subjects. Three- or four-inch headlines, revealing a new sex scandal, screamed from every opening page. Some samples are: "Smooth Minneapolis Doctor with Woman in Saint Paul Hotel," or "White Slaver Plying Trade: Well Known Local Man Is Ruining Women and Living off Their Earnings." The lead lines and reporting conformed to the same style. The second feature story each week singled out a public official for "exposure" on charges which might include graft, failure to prosecute known criminals, or being in league with them.[11] Crimes most frequently cited were prostitution and gambling. Minority groups were attacked indiscriminately. The Salvation Army was accused of misappropriating the funds it collected and of preying on the poor it professed to serve. The Roman Catholic church was an almost weekly victim. Its adherents were referred to as "papists" or "Romish," and its clergy were accused of sexual irregularities. National or racial minorities were invariably referred to in common or derogatory terms—Chinese were "chinks," Italians, "dagoes," Negroes, "dinges," and so forth.

In the *Twin City Reporter* of December 22, 1916, the name of the editor was changed from Guilford to Jay M. Near. Early in 1920, Near's name was replaced by that of John D. ("Jack") Bevans. He continued as editor until Edward J. Morgan took charge in August, 1921, and the latter's name remained on the masthead through November 25, 1927. The same general style that had marked the paper since its founding continued throughout the entire thirteen years of the publication's existence.[12]

In 1917, the *Twin City Reporter* lost its mailing privileges. Under the federal Espionage Act of 1917 the postmaster general of the United States was authorized to rescind second-class mailing privileges of any publication which contained material inimical to the war effort. By criticizing the president and the war effort, and violently opposing the European food aid program, the *Reporter* probably incurred the displeasure of the postmaster general. The paper took no notice of the loss in its own pages.[13]

Little is known of the activities of Near and Guilford in the early 1920s. Guilford filed for mayor of Minneapolis in 1918 and was defeated. At about this time his wife instituted a suit for divorce. Ironically, the man who had for several years entertained the public with scandals involving infidelity and adultery, lost his own wife on these very charges. Near, who was born in Fort Atkinson, Iowa, in 1874, was married, and had a daughter living in California. When he first went to Minneapolis and what he did there prior to his connection with the *Twin City Reporter* is not known. According to Guilford, Near became the innocent victim of his erstwhile partner, Bevans, who was blackmailing people without Near's knowledge. When Near learned of this, he left the newspaper, and his name did not again appear before the public until 1927.[14]

In that year, Near and Guilford combined forces to bring out a new weekly called the *Saturday Press*. Guilford thus described its launching: "In August of 1927, J. M. Near, my former partner and later editor of the *Twin City Reporter*, returned to Minneapolis from the Pacific Coast. He looked me up and suggested that we enter the weekly newspaper game together. I gave the matter some thought . . . and finally told Near that I would join him with one understanding—that never a word of a sex nature would appear in the columns of our paper."[15]

The first issue of the *Saturday Press* appeared on September 24, 1927. The announcement on its first page stated that "The names of the publishers of this journal of ultra-intellectual epics are not unknown to readers of the Twin Cities and the Northwest. Unfortunately we are both former editors of a local scandal sheet, a distinction which we regret. We at least have the satisfaction of knowing that no blackmail ever dirtied our hands although we are aware that the taint of blackmail sullies our reputations."[16] The statement went on to declare that the paper would expose crime and corruption in high places and wage war on the *Twin City Reporter*. The *Saturday Press*, it announced, was about to embark on a crusade to clean up the city. That Minneapolis stood in need of reform was common knowledge; throughout the 1920s it had a reputation as one of the nation's chronically corrupt cities.[17]

In the same issue of the *Press,* Near claimed that he and his partner were marked for extinction if they dared to produce their paper: "Word has been passed to Mr. Guilford and myself within the last week that if we persisted in our exposé of conditions as they are in this city we would be 'bumped off'. Just a minute, boys, before you start something you can't finish. . . . We are going through, and if anything happens to either of us the stage is set so that within twenty-four hours old Sir John Law will begin stuffing Stillwater Penitentiary full of certain gentlemen."[18] Three days later, on September 27, Guilford was shot. In the company of his sister-in-law, he left his home in the Minneapolis suburb of Robbinsdale by automobile. He was followed by another vehicle, whose occupants forced his car off the road and fired into it a volley of shots. Guilford sustained bullet wounds in his abdomen and thigh, and was hospitalized for several weeks.[19]

Contrary to the predictions in the *Saturday Press,* no prison terms resulted from the Guilford shooting. Two men, Harry Jaffa and Paul Gottlieb, were apprehended by the police and identified by Guilford as his assailants, but he refused to press charges against them and they were subsequently released. Near, left to carry on alone, declared in the issue of October 1, "If the ochre hearted rodents who fired those shots into the defenseless body of my buddy thought for a moment that they were ending the fight against gang rule in the city they were mistaken."

The first public official to be attacked by the *Saturday Press* was Frank W. Brunskill, the Minneapolis chief of police, who, according to the issue of October 8, promptly "took upon his brawny shoulders the burden of suppressing this publication on news stands and other news agencies operating in the city." The following week Near continued to harass Brunskill, proclaiming in his lead article that "the Chief is banning this publication on news stands and other news agencies operating in the city." The following week Near continued to harass Brunskill, proclaiming in his lead article that "the Chief in banning this paper from news stands definitely aligns himself with gangland and violates the law he is sworn to uphold."[20]

Soon the vituperations against Brunskill extended to Mayor George E. Leach of Minneapolis and County Attorney Floyd B. Olson of Hennepin County. On November 5 Near queried, "Why is it that the Chief of Police has not been asked to resign by the Mayor, or his indictment sought by the County Attorney?" Two weeks later, on November 19, the feature story in the *Saturday Press* announced that "Mayor Leach suspends patrolman for tagging Mayor's car," and asked, "Is Leach immune from the law Bill Jones is forced to obey"

Following the line of their previous publications, Near and Guilford soon found a minority group to attack—on this occasion, the Jews. Writing on November 12, Near asserted, "There have been too many men in this city who have been taking orders from Jew gangsters, therefore we have Jew gangsters practically ruling Minneapolis. It is Jew thugs who have 'pulled' practically every robbery in this city."

Guilford, while still in the hospital, wrote an article criticizing once again the county attorney. Published on November 19, it accused Olson of failing to prosecute criminals and added this warning: "Now go ahead and run for Governor again, Floyd, and you'll find that what you took to be a chip on my shoulder is really a tomahawk."

Olson responded three days later by bringing action in Hennepin County District Court under the gag law of 1925. Declaring that the *Saturday Press* was a nuisance as there defined, he filed a complaint and asked relief in a temporary restraining order, which the court granted. The attorneys for Near and Guilford demurred. It was hardly possible for them to answer the complaint, since the *Saturday Press* was clearly scandalous and defamatory. By demurring, however, they contended that the Minnesota statute was unconstitutional, and this contention formed the basis for their defense. When the hearing was held before Judge Mathias Baldwin on December 19, the demurrer was overruled. In a memorandum, the judge asserted that, since freedom of the press is so sacred a liberty, the case should be certified immediately to the Minnesota Supreme Court. While the decision of this tribunal was awaited, Near and Guilford were restrained from publishing.[21]

In their appeal, the publishers based their case on three main premises. They argued that liberty of the press, as guaranteed in Article 1, Section 3, of the Minnesota State Constitution, was being violated; contended that the hearing had denied them the right to a trial by jury; and held that the 1925 statute was an arbitrary and unreasonable invasion of liberty, as set forth in the due process clause of the Fourteenth Amendment.

On May 25, 1928, when the court handed down its decision, one justice abstained, while Chief Justice Samuel B. Wilson joined three associate justices in ruling against Near and Guilford.[22] They decided that by the definition of the law of 1925, a newspaper business conducted in violation of the act was classified as a public nuisance, and that a court of equity had the power to enjoin and thereby abate public nuisances. It held further that the law was a legitimate exercise of the state police power. The chief justice said, "There can be no doubt that the police powers include all regulation designed to promote the public convenience, happiness, welfare, and prosperity... and extend to all matters of health, safety, and morals.... It is the prerogative of the Legislature to determine not only what the public interest requires but also the measures to protect that interest." He went on to say that the court must be very cautious in reviewing legislative acts, and in all cases of doubt, the benefit of that doubt should be with the legislature.

The chief justice next turned his attention to libel. Libel law alone, he pointed out, was not sufficient to protect racial and other minority groups that were being defamed or attacked. Who, the judge asked, is going to bring suit when no particular individual is the target of such attacks? Clearly, the abatement of such attacks was the aim of the legislature in enacting the law. Considering the problem presented by the language of the Minnesota Constitution, Justice Wilson said, "In Minnesota no agency can hush the sincere and honest voice of the press; but our Constitution was never intended to protect malice, scandal, and defamation, when untrue or published without justifiable ends." He further pointed out that while the state Constitution guarantees freedom of assembly, it does not thereby countenance illegal assemblies, such as riots, nor does it deny the state power to prevent them.

The remaining contentions of Near and Guilford were quickly dealt with. The due process clause of the Fourteenth Amendment was never intended to limit the subjects on which the police powers of the state might be exerted lawfully. Since this was an equitable proceeding, no jury was required.

The case was remanded back to the district court, where Judge Baldwin then issued a permanent injunction, by the terms of which the partners were perpetually prohibited from publishing any paper called the *Saturday Press,* or that paper under any other name.[23] Near and Guilford were out of business.

With the issuing of the permanent injunction, publishers outside the state became aware for the first time of the Minnesota law. They quickly came to the conclusion that a law of this nature was a genuine threat to the freedom of the press. Large metropolitan newspapers of the highest repute felt it their duty to investigate and expose irregularities in public office. Statutes similar to the Minnesota law, if enacted in their communities, could be used as effective muzzles on any newspaper that offended public officials. A storm of protest soon arose.

The first major newspaper to support Near was the *Chicago Tribune.* Whether he invited its intervention, or the paper acted on its own initiative, is not certain. It is known, however, that the *Tribune's* attorneys soon entered the case, and in conjunction with the lawyers already representing Near and Guilford, prepared an appeal from the permanent injunction to the Minnesota Supreme Court. The Chicago paper's publisher, Colonel Robert R. McCormick, was known as a champion of freedom of the press. In 1920 the *Tribune* had been sued for libel by the city of Chicago, which asked damages totaling ten million dollars because the paper published a series of articles charging that the municipality was bankrupt, insolvent, and so corruptly administered that its streets were not properly cleaned and its laws not efficiently enforced.[24] Chicago contended that the articles were untrue and libelous, and that their appearance had damaged the city's credit. The trial was a long one and was carried on appeal to the Illinois Supreme Court, where it was finally decided in favor of the *Tribune.*

Speaking about the case later, McCormick said, "Consequently we embarked upon the most extensive study of municipal law and the law of freedom of the press that has ever been undertaken. The results of our studies were embodied in the argument in the State of Illinois and led to the opinion, first of the Circuit Court of Cook County, of the Supreme Court [of Illinois] that a city may not sue a newspaper for libel. . . . While the information was fresh in our minds our attention was drawn to a case where acting under a statute of that state [*Minnesota*], the District [*County*] Attorney had filed an information, pernicious instrument for political persecution, against a newspaper alleging that it was a scandalous newspaper. A Chancellor of that state, after a very short hearing had enjoined further publication of the paper and the Supreme Court affirmed that decision. Therefore we took immediate steps to carry the case to the Supreme Court of the United States with the financial assistance and moral support of the American Newspaper Publishers Association."[25]

While the second appeal to the Minnesota Supreme Court was pending, the nation's press became articulate on the subject of the *Saturday Press* case. The *Cleveland Plain Dealer* decided that "The case is one of vast importance. It far overshadows the specific wrong committed against an obscure and unimportant weekly publication in Minnesota. It concerns the fundamental rights of free speech and free press."[26]

McCormick himself turned to his editorial columns to attack the Minnesota law. Classing Minnesota with the notorious "Monkey States," he contended that "Minnesota joins hands with Tennessee and, of the two states, Minnesota may justly claim to be more ridiculous. After all, it is less than one hundred years since intelligent men discarded the traditional biological notions found in the Bible. It is nearly three hundred years since John Milton stated that argument for free speech and free press and Milton was by no means the first champion of enlightenment in this field."[27] The more circumspect *New York Times* branded the Minnesota statute "A Vicious Law," and asserted that "A Soviet Commissar, one of the police bureaucrats who ruled Russia before the Revolution, or an oriental despot, could have no greater power than this. For not only are property rights destroyed, but the source of public information is blocked or cut off."[28] Not quite certain how it stood on the Minnesota law, but recognizing a need for housecleaning, the *Christian Science Monitor* observed, "The [Minnesota Supreme] Court's decision should impress on them [*publishers*] the need to work within their societies and with their publications for higher professional standards. Such efforts might obviate the necessity for new laws elsewhere."[29]

During the waning days of April, 1929, the American Newspaper Publishers Association met, and McCormick, as chairman of its committee on free press, had this to report: "The [*Minnesota*] Statute is tyrannical, despotic, unAmerican, and oppressive. . . . Whenever a grafting minority desires to remain in power or to prevent exposure of wrong doing it has a ready weapon at hand with which to cover up iniquity and suppress attempts to expose it." On the basis of McCormick's report, the association adopted the following resolution: "Now therefore be it resolved by the American Newspaper Publisher's Association that said statute is one of the gravest assaults upon the liberties of the people that has been attempted since the adoption of The Constitution, and is inherently dangerous to the Republican form of Government; and be it further resolved that the members of The Association cooperate in all respects to secure repeal of said statute and of any statute similarly directed against the right of free utterance."[30]

Meanwhile, the Minnesota legislature was in session. That body was well aware of the unfavorable national publicity that the state was receiving, and it was inevitable that it should devote some discussion to the "nuisance law," as it was coming to be known. Representative Ralph R. Davis of Breckenridge introduced into the House a repeal bill that was referred to the committee on general legislation. After deliberation, the committee submitted a majority report recommending indefinite postponement and a minority report favorable to passage. The author of the repeal attempt moved on the floor that the minority report be accepted. This motion was defeated by a vote of eighty-seven to thirty. The legislature was not yet ready to reconsider its actions; Minnesotans in general did not seem overly concerned; and the *Minneapolis Tribune*, reporting the failure of the repeal measure, did so without comment.[31]

Finally, on December 20, 1929, The Minnesota Supreme Court ruled on the second appeal. The case was now being carried in Near's name only, Guilford having withdrawn from the litigation. The contentions of the attorneys were basically those used in the first case. One new argument only was added. It contended that, in being prevented from earning his daily living, Near had been deprived of his property without due process of law, as defined in the Fourteenth Amendment. This argument sought to capitalize on the court's presumed concern with property and the individual's economic rights.

Speaking for the same majority as in the first case, Chief Justice Wilson handed down a terse and pointed opinion. An evil existed, the court asserted, which was inimical to the public and which the legislature intended to remedy. No claim had been advanced that the *Saturday Press* was not precisely what it was charged with being—namely, a business which regularly and customarily devoted itself to malicious, scandalous, and defamatory matter. In regard to the original arguments, the chief justice stood on the reasoning presented in his first decision. He then quickly disposed of the property argument presented by counsel for Near, saying, "We see no reason however for defendants to construe the judgment as restricting them from operating a newspaper in harmony with the public welfare to which we all must yield. The case has been tried. The allegations of this complaint have been found to be true. Though this is an equity action defendants have in no way indicated any desire to conduct their business in the usual and legitimate manner."[32]

Minnesota had spoken with finality. The only course of action remaining for Near was an appeal to the United States Supreme Court. Accordingly, with McCormick no doubt bearing most of the cost, arrangements were made for arguing the case in Washington before the nation's highest court.

The Minnesota decision once more stimulated a national outcry. An editorial entitled "A Dangerous Reprisal," in the *New York Times* of December 24, 1929, reads as follows: "For the passage of such a law and its sympathetic reception by the courts, the blame must be left on the doorstep of the sensational press. To such jackals of journalism, no morsel is inedible. Decent newspapers everywhere sympathize with the public resentment which takes form in laws such as that passed in Minnesota . . . [but] if the Minnesota law were commonly enacted, newspapers would be at the mercy of the courts, sometimes with personal spite to gratify or political purposes to achieve; the cure is worse than the malady." The *Literary Digest* was more succinct. In its issue of February 1, 1930, it declared "War on the Minnesota Gag Law," contending that "freedom of the press in Minnesota is reduced to about the freedom of a straight jacket."

While the case was pending before the United States Supreme Court, the Minnesota legislature met for its 1931 session. In the three years elapsing after the first action in Hennepin County District Court, Floyd Olson had been elevated from the office of county attorney to that of governor. As chief executive he once more faced the issue of the gag law. In his inaugural message he called for its repeal, declaring, "The cases in which the law was used were proper exercises of the operation of the law, but I believe that the possibilities for abuse make it an unwise law. The freedom of speech and the press should remain inviolate, and any law which constitutes an entering wedge into that inviolability is unsafe."[33]

Once more Representative Davis introduced a repeal measure in the House. Referred this time to the committee on printing and publishing, the bill was reported favorably, and on February 4, 1931, it passed the House by a majority of sixty-eight to fifty-eight. It was, however, killed by a determined minority in the Senate. There the committee on general legislation reported the bill without recommendation, and accordingly the measure was placed on general orders. Three days before the end of the session, a motion was made to bring the bill to a vote by placing it on a special order of business. Although this motion received a majority vote of thirty-eight to twenty-three, it failed to draw the two-thirds necessary for suspension of the rules. Thus the second attempt to repeal the gag law died.[34]

The fate of the case before the Supreme Court was by no means certain. Since 1833, judicial precedent had held that the Bill of Rights did not apply to the states, but served only to limit the federal government.[35] According to this doctrine, the states were limited only by such rights and freedoms as were set forth in their own constitutions, to be interpreted by state courts.

The framers of the Fourteenth Amendment had intended to apply the protections of the Bill of Rights to individuals, and to guard those rights against state interference. The amendment declared that no state was to abridge the privileges and immunities of any citizen, or to deprive him of life, liberty, or property without due process of law, or to deny to any person the equal protection of the laws. While the intent of the framers was to erect a barrier between the citizen and the state government, the courts had not interpreted the Fourteenth Amendment in this manner. Through a series of decisions from 1870 to 1920, the United States Supreme Court had used the wording of the Fourteenth Amendment to protect business from arbitrary and unreasonable state interference, but had done little to protect the liberties of the individual citizen.

In 1925, the Supreme Court had admitted, for the first time, that the word "liberty" in the Fourteenth Amendment might be used to guarantee to the individual the fundamental rights contained in the federal Bill of Rights and to overrule state legislation which interfered with those rights. Although in this instance the Court had upheld a New York law which seemingly abridged freedom of speech, the way was opened to apply the Fourteenth Amendment to state legislation infringing upon such freedom.[36] Two years later the Court interpreted the word "liberty" in the Fourteenth Amendment as protecting an individual. In this case the Court did not overrule the state law, but it did hold that the law, as applied to the appellant, deprived him of his liberty in violation of the Fourteenth Amendment.[37] Two weeks before handing down the Near decision, in the case of Stromberg v. California, the Court invalidated a state law as unconstitutional, holding that the statute deprived an individual of the right of freedom of speech without due process of law.[38]

On June 1, 1931, in a five to four decision, with Chief Justice Hughes and Justices Brandeis, Holmes, Roberts, and Stone comprising the majority, the Court invalidated the Minnesota statute and decided in favor of Near.[39] Speaking for the majority, the chief justice said, "This statute for the suppression as a public nuisance of a newspaper or periodical is unusual, if not unique, and raises questions of grave importance transcending the local interests involved in the particular action." The opinion pointed out that such liberty is not an absolute right, and a state may punish its abuse, but here the Court must cut through the mere details of procedure and must have concern for the substance and not the form; the statute must be tested by its operation and effect.

In meeting the question of whether a statute authorizing proceedings in restraint of publication is consistent with the historic ideas of liberty of the press, the chief justice quoted at length from Blackstone and raised the issue of previous restraint. According to Hughes, a man is responsible for the utterances he makes. Whether in words or in print, he can be called for his errors and tried for libel or slander. It is not the intention of liberty of speech or press to provide immunity from such proceedings. Prior restraint, however, is effective censorship, and from colonial times on, it has been the intention of Americans to prevent such censorship from being effected. The Court could not, he concluded, countenance such previous restraint.

Hughes then turned to the problem raised by the *Saturday Press*. "The administration of government had become more complex," he noted. "The opportunities for malfeasance and corruption have multiplied, crime has grown to serious proportions and the danger of its protection by unfaithful officials and of the impairment of the fundamental security of life and property by criminal alliances and official neglect emphasizes the need of a vigilant and courageous press, especially in the great cities. The fact that liberty of press can be abused by miscreant purveyors of scandal does not make less necessary the immunity of the press from previous restraint in dealing with official misconduct. Subsequent punishment for such abuses as may exist is the appropriate remedy."

The four conservative judges, Butler, VanDevanter, Sutherland, and McReynolds, did not concur in this opinion. In a dissent written by Justice Butler, who was himself from Minnesota, they took vigorous issue with it. Butler concluded that "The decision of the Court in this case declares Minnesota and every other state powerless to restrain by legislative action the business of publishing and circulating . . . malicious and defamatory periodicals. It gives freedom of the press a meaning and scope not heretofore recognized and construes liberty in the due process clause of the Fourteenth Amendment to put upon the states a federal restriction that is without precedent."

Butler based most of his dissent upon the facts of the particular case rather than upon the legal issue. He pointed out again that Near was doing precisely what the law was intended to prevent, and that Near was, by his own admission, tainted with blackmail. He quoted at length from the malicious articles appearing in the *Saturday Press*. He argued that the federal court should not reverse the judgment of the Minnesota Supreme Court on the mere basis that in some other case the law might be misapplied.

To sum up, Butler concluded, "The doctrine that measures, such as the one before us, are invalid because they operate as previous restraint to infringe the freedom of the press, exposes the peace and good order of every community and the business and private affairs of every individual to the constant and protracted false and malicious assaults of any insolvent publisher who may have the purpose and sufficient capacity to construct and put into effect a scheme or program for oppression, blackmail, or extortion." His main argument, that the decision would render the states powerless, is an extreme statement.

Hughes pointed out that the states and private citizens have recourse to all laws governing libel, and every publisher is responsible under these laws. Hughes, in essence, said that the Minnesota statute allowed the shutting down of a publication for what it might say. That, he felt, is censorship and is not constitutional.[40]

Shortly after the Supreme Court decision, Near resumed publication of the *Saturday Press*. The few extant issues printed after June, 1931, indicate that Near had lost his old editorial fire. The tone of the paper is strangely subdued. Near's attacks on public officials are less virulent, and the chief object of his wrath is the Communist party. The signing of his editorials as "The Old Man" is perhaps a more subtle indication of the change.

Guilford launched a new publication, the *Pink Sheet*, late in 1931 or early in 1932. It was, according to the motto on its masthead, "Published weekly in the interest of fair play for the under dog." Within a year it was apparently out of business and its editor was back with the *Saturday Press*. His career came to an abrupt end on September 6, 1934, when he was shot to death near his Minneapolis home by unknown and unapprehended gunmen. He was driving his automobile and had slowed down to make a turn. Another vehicle drew abreast and a shotgun was fired at close range at Guilford's head. He died instantly, and his car, out of control, continued across the street and smashed into a tree. The murder vehicle moved on without anyone noticing its license number.[41]

McCormick, true to his friends, lashed out at Minnesota authorities and Governor Olson. Reviewing the circumstances of the case, he pointed out that, shortly before his death, Guilford had announced he would begin a series of radio talks that would reveal "the whole story of Floyd Olson's connection with the Twin Cities underworld." Commenting pointedly that Minneapolis police had made no arrests as a result of the killing, McCormick implied that Olson was encouraging and assisting gangland in the elimination of any who dared to expose it. He concluded, "We can only believe that murder was used by public authorities and the underworld to coerce the freedom of the press after unconstitutional law had failed."[42]

Olson, who was dying of cancer in a hospital at the time of McCormick's attack, retorted by jeering at him as a self-styled champion of the free press and noting that "dozens of papers have been suppressed because of economic views expressed without one word from Bertie. It is only when a scandal sheet has difficulty that Bertie comes to the rescue. That is because he is the owner of the world's leading scandal sheet."[43]

Near, whose name was enshrined in the historic Supreme Court decision, died peacefully on April 18, 1936.[44] The last issue of the *Saturday Press* located by the writer was published after his death under the editorship of F. E. Wion on June 27, 1936. The exact dates of the demise of the *Twin City Reporter* and the *Saturday Press* are unknown, for they did not again appear in the regular news.

Near and Guilford inadvertently stimulated an important interpretation of American constitutional law. As the *Cleveland Plain Dealer* pointed out, few were concerned with the suppression of an obscure weekly in Minnesota, but many were concerned with the graver issues involved.[45] With the Stromberg and Near cases, the Supreme Court embarked upon a Constitutional interpretation that broadens the application of the Bill of Rights and guarantees the individual's liberties against interference at any level of government.

NOTES

From Minnesota History 37 *(December, 1960).*

1. Robert E. Cushman and Robert F. Cushman, *Cases in Constitutional Law,* 698 (New York, 1958); Merlo J. Pusey, *Charles Evans Hughes,* 2:720 (New York, 1951).

2. *American Law Review,* 58:614 (July–August, 1924); *New York Times,* January 31, 1931, sec. 1, p. 6, col. 3.

3. James R. Mock, *Censorship, 1917,* 223 (Princeton, New Jersey, 1941); *New York Times,* January 12, 1930, sec. 1, p. 26, col. 4; Marion D. Shutter, ed., *History of Minneapolis,* 3:616 (Chicago, 1923); Minnesota, *Legislative Manual,* 1925, p. 682.

4. Minnesota, *Senate Journal,* 1925, p. 990; *House Journal,* 1925, p. 1463. Since the journals of the state legislature do not contain records of debate, it is impossible to reconstruct discussion of the bill while it was under consideration. Presumably the measure was not debated extensively.

5. Minnesota, *Laws,* 1925, p. 358.

6. Lamar T. Beman, *Censorship of Speech and Press,* 198–205 (New York, 1930); Ernest W. Mandeville, "Gutter Literature," in *New Republic,* 45:350 (February 17, 1926); N. W. Ayer and Son, *American Newspaper Annual and Directory,* 1920–29. Ayer does not list all newspapers, since some were so ephemeral that they appeared and went out of business before their existence could be recorded.

7. These crimes are usually difficult to prove in court. Professor George Vold of the department of sociology in the University of Minnesota, who has served on crime commissions and is an instructor in criminology, aided the writer in preparing this description.

8. See J. M. Near in *Minneapolis City Directory,* 1927–36. The *Saturday Press,* published in Minneapolis, listed four different addresses from 1933 to 1936.

9. Howard A. Guilford, *A Tale of Two Cities: Memoirs of Sixteen Years Behind a Pencil,* 6–8, 13, 50 (Robbinsdale, 1929); *Minneapolis Tribune,* September 9, 1934, sec. 1, p. 4, col. 1.

10. *Minneapolis Tribune,* September 27, 1927, sec. 1, p. 2, col. 5; Guilford, *Tale of Two Cities,* 7–15, 82–91.

11. Guilford, *Tale of Two Cities,* 31–33; *Twin City Reporter,* August 17, 1914, October 8, 1915. The only known file of this paper, covering the years 1914 to 1927, is owned by the Minnesota Historical Society.

12. See issues of the *Twin City Reporter* for 1915, 1916, and 1917. The most virulent anti-Catholicism seems to be contemporary with the appearance of Jay M. Near on its editorial staff. He later published at least two pamphlets enlarging upon scandals involving Catholic clergy.

13. Mock, *Censorship*, 1917, 145. The loss of second-class mailing privileges—a preferentially low rate—practically precludes the use of the mails to any publication. Since the act did not require the postmaster general to file formal charges, his precise reasons for rescinding the privileges of the *Twin City Reporter* are unknown. Ultimately a newspaper restricted under the Espionage Act brought suit against the United States. The Supreme Court upheld this section of the act, ruling that control of the mails was clearly within the power of Congress. See Milwaukee Publishing Company *v.* Burleson, 255 *United States Supreme Court Reports* 407 (1921).

14. Guilford, *Tale of Two Cities*, 57, 63, 70; *Minneapolis Tribune*, April 19, 1936, sec. 2, p. 3, col. 1.

15. Guilford, *Tale of Two Cities*, 129.

16. *Saturday Press*, September 24, 1927. Texts of nine issues of the *Saturday Press* which appeared prior to its suppression are among the papers and briefs filed in connection with Near *v.* Minnesota, 283 *United States* 697 (1931). A few issues of the paper, dating from the early 1930s, are in the collection of the Minnesota Historical Society.

17. George H. Mayer, *The Political Career of Floyd B. Olson*, 14 (Minneapolis, 1951).

18. *Saturday Press*, September 24, 1927.

19. *Minneapolis Tribune*, September 27, 1927.

20. *Saturday Press*, October 15, 1927.

21. The proceedings of the district court may be found among the briefs filed in connection with 283 *United States* 697.

22. Olson *v.* Guilford, 174, *Minnesota Supreme Court Reports* 457–463 (1928).

23. See briefs filed with 283 *United States* 697.

24. See Robert R. McCormick, *The Freedom of the Press*, 42–45 (New York, 1936); *What American Editors Said About the Ten Million Dollar Libel Suit* (Chicago, 1923). The latter work, published by the Chicago Tribune Company, summarizes press comment on the trial and provides a bibliography.

25. Robert R. McCormick, *The Case for the Freedom of the Press*, 17–19 (1933). McCormick's facts are somewhat in error here. He first entered the Near case when it was appealed to the Minnesota Supreme Court for the second time, a year before the American Newspaper Publishers Association joined his effort. See Philip Kinsley, *Liberty and the Press: A History of the Chicago Tribune's Fight to Preserve a Free Press for the American People*, 4 (Chicago, 1944).

26. Quoted in Beman, *Censorship of Speech and Press*, 326.

27. *Chicago Tribune*, March 28, 1929, sec. 1, p. 14, col. 2. McCormick here refers to the Scopes trial of 1925 in Tennessee.

28. *New York Times*, April 26, 1929, sec. 1, p. 24, col. 3.

29. *Christian Science Monitor*, August 8, 1929, sec. 1, p. 14, col. 1.

30. American Newspaper Publishers Association, *Proceedings*, 1929, p. 73.

31. Minnesota, *House Journal*, 1929, p. 735; *Minneapolis Tribune*, March 27, 1929, sec. 1, p. 9, col. 5.

32. 179 *Minnesota* 41 (1929).

33. Floyd B. Olson, *Inaugural Message to the Legislature of Minnesota*, 11 (St. Paul, 1931).

34. Minnesota, *House Journal*, 1931, p. 74, 153, 216; *Senate Journal*, 1931, p. 50, 894, 1157.

35. Barron *v.* Baltimore, 7 *Peters* 233 (1833).

36. Gitlow *v.* New York, 268 *United States* 652 (1925).

37. Fiske *v.* Kansas, 274 *United States* 359 (1931).

38. Stromberg *v.* California, 283 *United States* 380 (1927).

39. 283 *United States* 697.

40. 283 *United States* 697–737.

41. *Minneapolis Tribune,* September 7, 1934. The only known example of the *Pink Sheet* is the issue of June 17, 1932, in the Minnesota Historical Society's collection.

42. McCormick, *Freedom of the Press,* 99, 108.

43. Mayer, *Floyd B. Olson,* 224.

44. *Minneapolis Tribune,* April 19, 1936, sec. 2, p. 3, col. 1.

45. Chief Justice Hughes's attitude toward the Near case is analyzed by Merlo J. Pusey in an article in Alllson Dunham and Philip D. Kurland, eds., *Mr. Justice,* 167 (Chicago, 1956). For Hughes, "there was no question that freedom from such arbitrary restraints" as the Minnesota statute had laid on newspapers "was included in the liberty protected by the due process clause of the Fourteenth Amendment," writes Mr. Pusey. "Nor was he shaken by the evidence indicating that the paper that had been suppressed was a miserable little scandal sheet. He spoke for a great principle, and that principle may now be regarded as firmly established in American law."

The Democratic-Farmer-Labor Party Schism of 1948

G. Theodore Mitau

As the presidential election of 1948 approached, the Democratic party was in disarray. Without the candidacy of Franklin Roosevelt for the first time in sixteen years, the party was factionalizing. The Democrats' disarray at the national level was reflected in Minnesota—with the further complication that the state democratic party was the Democratic-Farmer-Labor party (DFL) reflecting the merger of the Democrats and the Farmer-Laborites in 1944. The 1920s and 1930s had seen the rise and ascendancy of the Farmer-Labor Party. However, after the election of Republican Harold Stassen as governor in 1938 and charges of corruption and Communist infiltration in the party, the Farmer-Labor Party began its six-year decline ending in the DFL merger.

By 1948 the "Farmer-Labor" faction, led by former governor Elmer Benson, was revived by the possible presidential candidacy of Henry Wallace, FDR's second vice president. The more moderate Democrats supported President Truman and pursued anti-Communism abroad, as defined by Truman's foreign policy, and liberalism at home, including civil rights.

G. Theodore Mitau clearly documents how 1948 marked the rise of Mayor Hubert H. Humphrey to national prominence by his handling of the party schism, his speech to the Democratic National Convention endorsing a civil rights plank in the party platform, and his subsequent election to the U.S. Senate that November. In hindsight, we know that 1948 also launched the political careers of Eugene J. McCarthy, Orville L. Freeman, Walter F. Mondale, Eugenie M. Anderson, and Donald M. Fraser.

Behind the lively events of the Democratic-Farmer-Labor party schism of 1948 a long and complex background of political protest can be traced. As one writer has put it, Minnesota "through most of its history has shown symptoms of political schizophrenia. On the one hand, it was the staid dowager, as reliably Republican as its down-East Yankee sisters; on the other, it had skittish moments during which it produced a brood of third parties or helped raise the radical offspring of its neighbors"[1] Especially in periods of economic depression, voices of agrarian and urban protest, often discordant and intense, have risen from the mining pits of the Mesabi Range, from the slaughterhouses and railroad shops of the cities, and from the debt-ridden farms of the Red River Valley to find expression in the platforms and conventions of Minnesota's third and minor parties. Through the Anti-Monopolists and the Greenback party of the 1870s, and the Nonpartisan League and the Farmer-Labor party of the present century, this tradition of protest has continued to exert pressure on state politics.

Thus the fervor for social justice and economic opportunity has long had organizational expression in Minnesota, even though success in national elections has been rare and erratic. Along with other Midwestern states, Minnesota witnessed the well-known patterns of protest, genuinely active, rich in condemnation of the railroads, monopolies, and Wall Street, and proud of the righteous blasts from such "tribunes of the people" as Ignatius Donnelly, A. C. Townley, Magnus Johnson, and Floyd B. Olson. The quest for success at the polls, which would translate platform and program into actual public policy, caused leaders of the Populist movement to experiment with various types of political tactics. At times it led them to support a major party contestant, such as John A. Johnson, who ran for governor on the Democratic ticket in 1904, and Charles A. Lindbergh, Sr., candidate for the Republican nomination for governor in the primaries of 1918; at other times it led them to advocate fusion with emerging national parties, as in 1912 and 1924; and in other campaigns, like that of 1892, all fusion attempts were spurned and Donnelly was called upon to head a state Populist ticket as that party's candidate for governor. During the dark, unhappy days of the depression in the 1930s the voices of protest rose to a crescendo. In their commitment to left-wing radicalism, the Farmer-Labor platforms of that period are perhaps unmatched by those of any other American party which has been successful at the polls.[2] Those were, of course, bitter times, and the remedies proposed by the Farmer-Labor administration and party leaders were sharp and dogmatic curatives for deeply felt economic ills, offering many a strange combination of Marxism, agrarian egalitarianism, and Utopianism.

But even in the perilous 1930s, when the party had the popular Governor Olson to argue on its behalf, Farmer-Labor policies seemed to have reached the limits of their acceptability. Olson's legislative program encountered major modification, some features incurring intense hostility and some meeting with outright defeat. This happened, moreover, in sessions like those of 1933 and 1937, when Olson's party had control of the lower house of the legislature. Then in 1938 the electoral fortunes of Farmer-Labor protest reached a new low. Governor Elmer Benson was swept out of office by Harold Stassen, the relatively unknown county attorney from South St. Paul, after a campaign that stressed charges of administrative incompetence, corruption, and blindness to

Communist infiltration. The wave of popular indignation left Benson with a mere 387,263 votes to the amazing and overwhelming total of 678,839 for the Republican party's nominee.[3]

The Farmer-labor party lost its one-time broad popular support, according to one scholar, largely because it could not combat the undermining used by internal quarreling factions, and because it failed to provide necessary policy direction through executive and legislative leadership. The same writer concludes his analysis of the "great debacle of 1938" with the observation that "the next six years were to see the final disintegration of the Farmer-Labor party, culminating in its virtual extinction when it was fused with the Democratic party in the Democratic-Farmer-Labor party"; and he describes "the fusion of 1944" as "simply the requiem for a death that had occurred in 1938."[4]

What, in retrospect, can be inferred from these events? Minnesota's eleven electoral votes never have and probably never will determine the balance of presidential fortunes. Nevertheless, traditions of protest politics make Minnesota a most fascinating laboratory for the study of political dynamics of agrarian and labor discontent. Most populist movements have been motivated by an urge to broaden the base of socio-political and economic privilege through such state interventions as a particular grievance seemed to demand. What these movements lacked in the doctrinaire qualities of a European pattern of challenge was counterbalanced by the American tradition of practical and selective state intervention.[5]

Most of this protest, then, was genuine, necessary, creative. Especially relevant in a study of the fortunes of the protest tradition after the Democratic-Farmer-Labor fusion of 1944, however, is the fact that some of the protest lacked these qualities. Largely through union infiltration, the long arm of the Third Internationale seemed at times to reach all the way to the North Star State when efforts to exploit real grievances and to confuse, disrupt, and subvert the democratic processes were made in Minnesota. An early example of a truly dramatic clash within the ranks of the Farmer-Labor movement took place between the doctrinaire and highly disciplined forces of left-wing Marxism and the indigenous and reformist forces of Midwest progressivism in 1924. At that time such noted leaders as Samuel Gompers and Robert La Follette warned their followers not to attend a convention in St. Paul, predicting political suicide for those who took part in it.[6] The fusion of the Democratic and Farmer-Labor parties in 1944 did not, and perhaps could not, eliminate this numerically small, but quite vociferous, segment of left-wing Marxist radicals. As a matter of fact, the very presence of some of these radicals within the ranks of the Farmer-Laborites had caused many old-line Democrats and independents to oppose earlier attempts at fusion.

The attitude of the Democratic party—and more particularly its so-called liberal New Deal wing—toward the political far left presented a major ideological problem not only for Minnesotans but also for the nation as a whole. The problem was intensified after the Congressional elections of 1946. Two mutually antagonistic groups crystallized into organizations by the spring of 1947. On the left, the Progressive Citizens of America emerged from a fusion of the National Citizens Political Action Committee and the Independent Citizens Committee of the Arts, Sciences and Professions. On the right appeared the Americans for Democratic Action.

With spokesmen like Henry A. Wallace for the left and such well-known New Dealers as Leon Henderson, Chester Bowles, Mrs. Franklin D. Roosevelt, and Franklin D. Roosevelt Jr., on the right, the issues soon became clearly drawn. The right-wing "non-Communist liberal" Americans for Democratic Action supported the Marshall Plan and President Truman's Greco-Turkish aid program; the Progressive Citizens of America held these to be unwarranted circumventions of the United Nations, conceived in support of European forces of reaction and fascism.[7] Whereas the Americans for Democratic Action approved most of Truman's domestic, security, and defense measures, the Progressive Citizens of America considered them entirely inadequate halfway measures of a party which was doing little better than the Republicans. This clash of ideology and policy, debated at great length throughout the nation and in Congress, was personified locally by Mayor Hubert Humphrey of Minneapolis, a national leader of the Americans for Democratic Action, Orville Olson, chairman of the Independent Voters of Minnesota, and Ex-governor Elmer Benson, a leading figure in the Progressive Citizens of America.

Wallace himself left the national Democratic party after a now famous declaration on December 29, 1947, in which he denounced Truman and his program. Nevertheless, Benson and his Minnesota friends apparently decided early in 1948 that it would be politically wiser to work through the Democratic-Farmer-Labor party than to revert to the more traditional pattern of third-party politics. Speaking in Chicago at the second annual convention of the Progressive Citizens of America, the former Minnesota governor declared, "if we retain control of the Democratic-Farmer Labor party at the state convention, Wallace will be the nominee and we will present him at the national Democratic convention. . . . If President Truman runs in Minnesota, he'll have to run as an independent, or however he wants to label it."[8]

Thus plans were made to push Wallace in Minnesota not as a third-party candidate, but as a regular Democratic-Farmer-Labor nominee whose name would go on the party ballot after his faction had captured the state party machinery. When the Democratic-Farmer-Labor state central committee met on February 20, the battle for control of the precincts began to take shape. The

Humphrey-led right wing asserted its three to one lead over the Benson faction by appointing exclusively from its own ranks the steering committee that was to make arrangements for the precinct caucuses and the county and state conventions.[9]

The hostility that the left wing felt for Mayor Humphrey and his followers is expressed in an editorial in the *Minnesota Leader,* then the organ of the pro-Wallace Democratic-Farmer-Labor Association. "Your association," it reads, "with the unsavory Americans for Democratic Action, created nationally to serve as liberal window dressing for the Wall Streeters and militarists behind Truman and created in Minnesota as a haven for reactionary elements in the Democratic and Farmer Labor parties, is another indication of the character of your associations." It also accused the Minneapolis mayor of "close and friendly relations" with the Cowles press and General Mills, and of conducting a "reactionary" administration of city affairs; and it told the mayor that "by your associations and your record you have ruined any chance of your being an acceptable progressive candidate in the 1948 elections."[10] In the same paper the state chairwoman of the Democratic-Farmer-Labor Association charged Humphrey with the disruption of the Democratic-Farmer-Labor party in the 1944 and 1946 elections, with disloyalty to the party chairman, with red-baiting, and with giving support to Churchill's foreign policy.

The leaders of the right wing answered in the *Minnesota Outlook,* where they published this indictment of the Wallace-Benson faction: "We are convinced that if the DFL is to win support, it must remove from positions of leadership all those who have represented or who have otherwise aided and abetted the program and tactics of the Communist party which believes—not in progress towards a free world—but in the reaction of totalitarianism and suppression of individual freedom."[11]

A bitterly contested battle of the two factions was to develop in the ranks of the Minnesota Democratic-Farmer-Labor party in the spring of 1948. The party workers who were preparing for caucuses and conventions knew that the survival of their respective factions was at stake. The right wing made a strong offensive move on April 18, when its steering committee, under the leadership of Mayor Humphrey and the present governor, Orville Freeman, announced that Wallace's third-party supporters were disqualified from taking part in the regular Democratic-Farmer-Labor sessions. All county chairmen who identified themselves with Wallace were asked to turn their credentials over to the next ranking Democratic-Farmer-Labor leader. In the meantime the state chairman for the Wallace group countered this right-wing declaration by telling two thousand Wallace fans who met in the St. Paul Auditorium that "regardless of 'talk' about keeping them out," they were, in fact, "legally entitled to participate in all DFL caucuses and should do so en masse."

As the factional fight grew in intensity, charges and countercharges raised Democratic-Farmer-Labor tempers to the boiling point. Mayor Humphrey was quoted as saying that the third-party movement was part of a deliberate international pattern to confuse honest liberals and to hobble the functioning of democracy; that it was being used to serve the purposes of the Russian police state; and that, although most Minnesotans in the Wallace movement were non-Communist, Communists and party-line followers in all states were seeking with religious fanaticism to promote a third party as part of Moscow's strategy to split Americans into ineffectual groups fighting among themselves.[12]

Wallace supporters, in the meantime, continued to attack the Marshall Plan, Truman's cold-war strategy, universal military training, and the "reactionary nature" of domestic legislation passed by the Eightieth Congress. Theirs, they claimed, was a fight for peace through supporting Wallace as an independent candidate. Wallace himself was quoted as saying at Albuquerque that the Communists "support me because I say we can have peace with Russia." He further clarified his position by stating: "I will not repudiate any support which comes to me on the basis of interest in peace. The Communists are interested in peace because they want a successful socialist experiment in Russia."[13]

The factional battle reached its first significant parliamentary stage in the precinct caucuses of April 30. Aside from the customary citizenship and residence requirements, all that is needed for participation in such a caucus under Minnesota law is the assurance of a past vote (with the secret ballot precluding any external verification) or the promise of future affiliation with the party which is holding the caucus. When the results of these caucuses were finally tabulated, the right wing claimed a clear numerical majority throughout the state. This claim was loudly protested by leaders of the Wallace-Benson faction. After the county conventions of May 14, the right wing claimed still another victory, pointing out that only 161 of 402 state convention delegates had faced any contest at all, and that out of 76 county delegations, 59 were definitely anti-Wallace, 5 probably pro-Wallace, 4 uncertain, and 8 contested.[14]

On May 23, members of the Wallace-Benson faction, which was still very active, telegraphed Harold Barker, state chairman of the Democratic-Farmer-Labor party, demanding that its delegates be allowed to participate in the state convention called for June 12 and 13 at Brainerd. Unless this demand was granted, they said, they would call their own convention in Minneapolis and would repudiate the Brainerd convention as illegal and irregular. While the delegates were assembling at Brainerd, a temporary preconvention committee on credentials submitted a report giving a clear majority to the right wing. It showed that of 402 authorized delegates, 216 had been uncontested. Of the latter, 186 actually were present and ready to vote on the seating of the delegation.[15] The committee arrived at these figures even before contested delegations from Hennepin, Ramsey, St. Louis, and other counties were seated. The Brainerd convention was to serve as a "political court of last appeal" at which the results of the bitter struggle between the right and left wings were finally determined.

One left-wing leader, Orville Olson, protested the convention's opening proceedings and denounced what he felt to be its unlawful and arbitrary conduct of business. A member of the incoming Hennepin County right-wing delegation replied by branding the Wallace "fringe" as "the Communist party in action, a movement of revolutionary character," by asserting that the "Wallace movement is not a third party in the true American sense [and by] inferring that it is serving the interests of Moscow." Whereupon the convention voted "with an almost unanimous roar' to seat the right-wingers from Hennepin County.

The Wallace leaders thereupon held a hasty conference and decided to use the microphone in calling for a rump convention. When they were "greeted by loud laughter and derisive cries," five of the group gathered on the sidewalk in front of the convention hall and solemnly held a meeting, with Francis M. Smith of St. Paul acting as chairman. He appointed a secretary to keep minutes, declared the meeting a rump convention of the Democratic-Farmer-Labor party, and then adjourned it to the American Federation of Labor Temple in Minneapolis, where a gathering of the left-wing faction was already in session.[16]

According to leaders of this group, five hundred delegates from fifth-one counties assembled for the Minneapolis convention. They listened eagerly as Benson termed the "program of Marshall, Forrestal, Dulles, Vandenberg and Co. the most gigantic international swindle of all time . . . intended to suppress common people in every part of the world."[17] The convention then organized itself into the Progressive Democratic-Farmer-Labor League and endorsed James M. Shields of Minneapolis for the United States Senate and Walter Johnson of New York Mills for governor. In addition, five nominees were named for the national House of Representatives, eleven presidential electors pledged to Wallace were agreed upon, and delegates were chosen to attend the convention of the Progressive party in Philadelphia in July. As a final offensive stroke, the Minneapolis convention promptly presented its slate of presidential electors to the Minnesota secretary of state, claiming that since its group represented the true Democratic-Farmer-Labor ruling body, it was entitled to have its name placed on the ballot pursuant to the provisions of the Minnesota election code.[18]

Attorneys for the right-wing Brainerd convention then prepared a petition urging the Minnesota state supreme court to order the secretary of state, as the respondent, to reject the slate of the Minneapolis group as false and fraudulent and to substitute that of the petitioners as the true and legal one of the Democratic-Farmer-Labor party of Minnesota. The secretary of state, speaking through the attorney-general, insisted that he had no facilities or authority to investigate or determine the truth or falsity of the conflicting representations, and asked the court to ascertain the facts and determine what course of action he should take with respect to accepting one or the other of the two certificates.[19]

If certain factional and legal complexities which have no direct bearing upon the problem under discussion are overlooked, the case of the Democratic-Farmer-Labor state central committee, right wing, and others *v.* Mike Holm, secretary of state, raised and answered three fundamental questions: First, are the qualifications of members of a legally called political delegate convention subject to judicial determination and review? Second, is the legality of such a convention's actions affected by improper floor decisions? Third, does such an allegedly illegal action entitle disaffected members to withdraw from a convention, to terminate its legal life by so doing, and to resuscitate in a newly assembled convention such former authority as did exist?[20]

On September 2, 1948, the Minnesota supreme court handed down a unanimous decision in favor of the second slate, the Brainerd right-wing convention thus receiving negative answers to the three main questions raised. In support of its decision the court advanced two considerations: First, with regard to judicial review of the actions of political conventions, "In factional controversies within a political party where there is involved no controlling statute or clear right based on statute law, the courts will not assume jurisdiction, but will leave the matter for determination within the party organization." Second, in the absence of a controlling statute, "a political convention is the judge of the election, qualifications, and returns of its own members." Such a convention is not a select body requiring "the presence of a majority of all persons entitled to participate in order to constitute a quorum for the transaction of business and, if that convention is regularly called, those who actually assemble constitute a 'quorum,' and a majority of those voting is competent to transact business.... The withdrawal of either a majority or minority from a political convention does not affect the right of those remaining to proceed with the business of the convention, and those withdrawing cannot claim to be the legal party convention."[21]

The Minnesota court accepted the following proposition: "As elections belong to the political branch of the government, the courts will not be astute in seeking to find ground for interference, but will seek rather to maintain the integrity and independence of the several departments of the government by leaving questions as to party policy, the regularity of conventions, the nomination of candidates, and the constitution, powers, and proceedings of committees, to be determined by the tribunals of the party." This clearly reaffirmed the position that the Minnesota supreme court had taken earlier to the effect that "a political party, absent statutory restraints, makes its own reasonable rules for self-government."[22]

The language of the court leaves little doubt that it was the intent of the Minnesota judiciary so to construe applicable statutes that the affairs of party conventions, if correctly convened, are to be placed squarely in the hands of their duly elected delegates. Theirs, and not the judiciary's, is the responsibility for conducting the business of the party fairly and soundly. Legal theory at this point found itself in complete harmony with the well-established democratic principle that political power should always be centered in those whose actions are subject at least theoretically to popular scrutiny and accountability. And this faith in popular sovereignty was destined to be reinforced and mathematically underscored by the results of the primary election of September, 1948, when the right-wing nominees were victorious in all the important contests except that in the Seventh Congressional District. Even more significant were the results of the final election in November, which saw President Truman, then heading the Democratic-Farmer-Labor party ticket, garner 692,966 votes to the mere 27,866 cast in Minnesota for the Progressive party's candidate, Henry A. Wallace.[23] The successful right-wing struggle for control in the precincts, and in county, district, and state conventions provided President Truman with the type of major party instrumentality without which Minnesota's eleven electoral votes might well have gone to the Republican nominee. Not only the president's Minnesota victory, but Mayor Humphrey's election to the Senate and the addition of three Democratic-Farmer-Labor representatives to Congress, were hailed by right-wing leaders as direct results of the 1948 party struggle.

The outcome of the Democratic-Farmer-Labor party schism of 1948—showing as it does that the will of the majority can be made to prevail over the concerted efforts of even a better disciplined, numerically small, but closely knit party segment—served to reaffirm faith in the vitality of the major party system. Most assuredly, lack of vigilance there as in other political activities can rob a free people of its treasured political heritage, should they ever grow weary of freedom or supinely take their liberties for granted. The intensity of the 1948 factional struggle within the Democratic-Farmer-Labor party and the resulting schism well illustrate vigilance and a willingness to do battle for the sake of political conscience.

NOTES
From Minnesota History 34 (Spring, 1955).

1. Donald F. Warner, "Prelude to Populism," in Minnesota History, 32:129 (September, 1951).

2. On Governor Johnson's many progressive recommendations to the Minnesota leg-

islature during his administration, see William W. Folwell, *A History of Minnesota*, 3:286–289 (St. Paul, 1926). See also Theodore Saloutos and John D. Hicks, *Agricultural Discontent in the Middle West*, 187 (Madison, 1951); Hicks, *The Populist Revolt*, 258 (Minneapolis, 1931); and George H. Mayer, *The Political Career of Floyd B. Olson*, 171 (Minneapolis, 1951).

3. Minnesota, *Legislative Manual*, 1953, p. 333.

4. Arthur Naftalin, "The Farmer Labor Party in Minnesota," 382, an unpublished doctor's thesis submitted at the University of Minnesota in 1945.

5. Currin V. Shields, "The American Tradition of Empirical Collectivism," in *American Political Science Review*, 44:104–121 (March, 1952).

6. Mayer, *Floyd B. Olson*, 182–222; Saloutos and Hicks, *Agricultural Discontent*, 358. On left-wing radicalism in Minnesota after 1917, see O. A. Hilton, "The Minnesota Commission of Public Safety in World War I," in Oklahoma Agricultural and Mechanical College, *Bulletins*, 48:1–44 (Stillwater, Okla., 1951).

7. William B. Hesseltine, *The Rise and Fall of Third Parties*, 87 (Washington, 1948).

8. *St. Paul Pioneer Press*, January 17, February 22, 1948.

9. *Pioneer Press*, January 28, February 8, 20, 1948.

10. *Minnesota Leader*, February, 1948.

11. *Minnesota Outlook*, February 18, 1948.

12. *Pioneer Press*, April 19, 29, 1948. The latter issue quotes Philip Murray of the CIO as stating that "The Communist party is directly responsible for the organization of a third party in the United States."

13. *Pioneer Press*, June 4, 1948.

14. *Pioneer Press*, May 20, 1948; *Minneapolis Star*, May 14, 1948. The attitude toward a third party of national leaders, including Mrs. Roosevelt and J. H. McGrath, Democratic national committee chairman, is expressed in the *Pioneer Press* for April 30. For the law relating to precinct caucuses, see Minnesota, *Statutes*, 1953, ch. 202.14.

15. *Pioneer Press*, May 23, 1948; "Brief for Petitioners," in 227 *Minnesota*, 52.

16. 227 *Minnesota*, 52, 54; L. D. Parlin, in the *Pioneer Press*, June 13, 1948.

17. See Carl Henneman, in the *Pioneer Press*, June 13, 14, 1948.

18. *Minneapolis Star*, June 14, 1948.

19. 227 *Minnesota*, 52.

20. 227 *Minnesota*, 52; 33 *North Western Reporter*, 831 (second series, 1948).

21. 33 *North Western Reporter*, 831.

22. 29 *Corpus Juris Secundum*, Elections, section 88; case of Emil E. Holmes *v.* Mike Holm, in 217 *Minnesota*, 264.

23. *Legislative Manual*, 1953, p. 165, 335. In the seventh district, James M. Youngdale, who was endorsed by the left wing, won by a vote of 6,452 to 5,958 for the right-wing candidate, Roy F. Burt.

LABOR

Revolt of the "Timber Beasts": IWW Lumber Strike in Minnesota

JOHN E. HAYNES

By 1900 only a very small percentage of the labor force was unionized; there were deep divisions within the "movement" as to whom to include: skilled and unskilled, male and female, white and black, ethnic groups. The work force was also constantly shifting and many workers did not consider themselves part of a "permanent" labor force, thus they saw less relevance in organizing, instead searching for a "better run" logging camp, for example. With a steady supply of immigrants arriving in the country looking for work, employers usually could find scab replacements. The corporate forces against the movement had vast resources and power and usually had the support of local, state, and national authorities who might send in troops to restore order and protect company property.

One ideology seeking a more just order for both capitalists and workers was socialism. Some radical socialists led by "Big Bill" Haywood of the Western Federation of Miners founded the International Workers of the World or IWW ("Wobblies") in Chicago in 1905. By 1916 the Wobblies were working in northern Minnesota after the Mesabi iron miners in Virginia walked out. The strike was soon over but a union was established. Local Wobbly organizers persevered, the most colorful and militant being Jack Beaton, who planned agitation at the Virginia and Rainy Lake Lumber Company by the mill workers. A precipitous strike occurred there at the end of December, and Beaton realized any chance of success might depend on a total shutdown of the whole lumber industry.

Given the living and working conditions for the lumberjacks that John Haynes describes in this essay, the "Timber Beasts" did not need "foreign agitators" to realize they were being exploited. The worker turnover in the Virginia and Rainy Lake Company was 74 men a day! Thus when the call went out for a walkout on Monday, January 1, 1917, many lumberjacks walked. However, employers reacted swiftly, newspapers hysterically described terrorist attacks by the strikers (though

none was ever proved), and the company subsidized deputies, paying
them three times what the jacks generally earned, to break the strike.
When local farmers did not wish to be the company's gunmen, the com-
pany recruited aliens in Twin Cities bars and pool halls.

The brawny lumberjack who tells tall tales, fells giant trees, wears checkered shirts, and loves flapjacks is familiar in American folklore. This romantic image, though based partly on fact, glosses over dark and frightful features of the lumberjack's life that in 1917 prompted Minnesota's sons of Paul Bunyan to down their saws and axes and walk out of their camps. Led by the Industrial Workers of the World (IWW), a radical labor group advocating industrial unions and the overthrow of capitalism through strikes, sabotage, and eventual revolution, the jacks' strike for a time paralyzed the lumber industry of northern Minnesota. The resolution of that strike helped redefine the boundaries of permissible political and economic dissent in Minnesota, virtually erased the specter of strong IWW influence on the iron range, and served as a precedent for the state's treatment of dissenters during World War I.[1]

The inciter of the strike, the IWW, was a national organization formed in Chicago in 1905 by western socialists and miners. The IWW made few inroads into the lumber industry of the Great Lakes states during the first ten years of its existence. A lumber workers' local was active in Deer River, Minnesota, by 1910, and "Wobblies" (as IWW members were popularly called) became involved in free-speech fights in 1911 and 1912, but it was the actions of mine workers at Virginia, Minnesota, that first awakened the lumber workers of the area to the power of united action.[2]

The spark for the lumberjacks' 1917 strike was ignited in Virginia, a city of more than 10,000 people, in the summer of 1916 when Mesabi Range iron miners spontaneously walked off their jobs in protest against the contract wage system, long hours, and private mine police. Caught unprepared, the IWW tardily established headquarters for an energetic task force at Virginia to try to unite the unorganized miners into a viable strike force. The miners were forced to return to work by September, however, because of insufficient funds and repressive police actions against their leaders. Salvaged from the defeat was an organization known as Metal Mine Workers' Industrial Union No. 490. Local 490 continued to hold the allegiance of some 2,000 miners out of the 10,000 to 15,000 who struck.

Active in sustaining the fervor of this organization, the largest Wobbly group in northern Minnesota, was Charles Jacobson, long-time resident of Virginia and secretary-treasurer of Local 490, whose offices were located in Virginia's Finnish Socialist Opera. An intelligent, quiet, young miner, Jacobson possessed considerable ability and common sense under pressure. His subtle humor never left him, even in times of crisis, and his keen sense of the IWW's fragile position on the range acted as a restraint on more militant Wobblies.

Of opposite temperament was a fellow Wobbly organizer named Jack Beaton who also operated out of the Socialist Opera in Virginia. Reveling in the nickname "Timber Beast" (abusive slang for "lumberjack"), Beaton epitomized the colorful, romantic tradition of the IWW. Dressed in a many-colored Mackinaw and tall leather boots, Beaton affected a belligerent proletarianism. A swashbuckler who usually carried a revolver in his hip pocket, he was never averse to flaunting his armed status. Beaton maintained a studied irreverence for the sensibilities of middle-class society and never passed up an opportunity to *épater le bourgeois* with his fire-eating rhetoric. A lumberjack himself for many years in Wisconsin, Beaton knew intimately the life of the lumber workers. His open manner, raw humor, and celebration of their life style made him an immediate leader among them.

Less concerned with tactics and timing than fellow-organizer Jacobson, Beaton and several other militants turned after September to the 1,200 employees of the Virginia and Rainy Lake Lumber Company's giant sawmill as fertile ground for union agitation. Here they precipitated the event that led directly to the lumberjack walkout.

The Virginia and Rainy Lake Lumber Company was a concern combining the northern Minnesota interests of the Weyerhaeusers, the extensive Minnesota and Wisconsin holdings of the Edward Hines Lumber Company, and the giant Virginia mils of the Cook and O'Brien Company. The Virginia and Rainy Lake plant was the largest white pine mill in the world as well as one of the "most modern and complete." The grounds covered perhaps fifteen square miles, and the plant produced an average of one million board feet of lumber a day on a 24-hour, seven-day-week schedule.[3]

Mill workers received between $2.50 and $3.00 a day for a 12-hour day and seven-day week. This daily wage was about 25 per cent below what sawmill workers in the Pacific Northwest, already organized by the IWW, received for the same work. If one ignores the number of hours worked, the mill pay compared favorably with that of most industrial laborers in 1916. The latter, however, earned as much in a 50- to 55-hour week as the Virginia mill workers did in an 84-hour week. In an easily seen comparison, the mill workers could note that common labor employed by the City of Virginia received $2.75 a day for an eight-hour day, six-day week and were spared the health and social costs of such a schedule.[4]

Many mill workers were Finnish in origin, and the gospel of industrial unionism was not altogether new to them. Socialism had always been acceptable to a strong minority of Finns in northern Minnesota, and Finnish socialist halls, which often served as centers of communal life, existed in most iron range villages. In 1913–14 most of the Finnish socialist locals on the range had split from the Socialist party and joined the Industrial Workers of the World. The strong Finnish participation in the Wobbly-led iron range strike foreshadowed the support that many hundreds of Finnish workers at the Virginia and Rainy Lake mill gave Beaton and the IWW organization there throughout the sawmill strike and the allied lumberjack strike. Many of the workers, in fact, were blacklisted iron miners from the Mesabi Range strike of the previous summer.[5]

Throughout the fall of 1916 Beaton and several others discussed conditions with mill workers and made the point that a union of industrial workers could force management to listen to the workers' grievances. Patience and careful organization were never "Timber Beast" Beaton's strong points, however, and when five nationally prominent IWW leaders of the Mesabi strike were released from a strike-connected murder charge in a "deal" with the authorities in early December, Beaton's determination for a confrontation intensified. The arrangement, which left several rank-and-file miners to plead guilty to manslaughter charges, prompted Wobblies and others to voice accusations of a sellout. Infuriated that the IWW appeared to be compromising itself in this way, Beaton lost all restraint in his agitation among the mill workers. Without the steadying influence of an experienced organizer, the mill employees soon worked themselves into a highly emotional state that could be satisfied only by immediate action.[6]

On Sunday, December 24, 1916, several scores of mill workers met with Beaton at the Socialist Opera to draw up a set of demands. They asked for a flat 25 cents per day raise for all workers, an eight-hour Saturday night and Sunday day shift, no Sunday night work, a shift change every week, and no reprisals for union activities. The workers then elected a committee of six to present the demands two days later to the Virginia and Rainy Lake Lumber Company management along with an ultimatum demanding a reasonable response by noon on Wednesday, December 27, or the mill workers would go on strike.[7]

At this juncture, Jacobson intervened. Experienced in bargaining tactics and more realistic than Beaton about the strength of Wobbly organization in the mill, Jacobson argued that an immediate strike would be disastrous. He also telegraphed the details of the situation to William D. ("Big Bill") Haywood, IWW general secretary in Chicago. A veteran organizer and a founder and prime mover of the IWW, Haywood immediately wired back that "a successful strike at the present time in the Virginia mills would be hopeless. Must wait until better organized. Continue with organization work."[8]

The warnings were useless. The committee, with Beaton as spokesman, went as planned to the plant offices on December 26 to confront Chester R. Rogers, superintendent of manufacturing for the Virginia and Rainy Lake Company. Beaton presented the demands and emphasized the group's intention to strike if it failed to receive a reasonable reply. Rogers in turn demanded to know by what right Beaton gave him this ultimatum. Beaton retorted that the committee asked him to speak and showed the superintendent his IWW organizer's commission from Haywood. Rogers's reply was earthy: "I wouldn't piss on Bill Haywood. And I can piss a good bit." Understandably taking this as a negative answer, the "Timber Beast" turned and left.[9]

Rogers's antagonism toward the Wobblies was more than a businessman's calculated hostility to union economic muscle. The superintendent regarded the IWW not only as a menace to his production costs but also as a threat to American society. He later testified before a legislative committee investigating the affair that Wobblies were "foreign agitators" whose only interest was to "make trouble for everybody, people with homes." He expressed contempt for his workers, too. "You can drive them like cattle," he asserted and added that IWW agitators had them "hypnotized." To him the solution to labor discontent was simple: "They ought to pass a law when a foreign agitator comes into a community, to run him out."[10]

When Wednesday noon passed with no word from Rogers or the company general manager, Samuel J. Cusson, Beaton called a strike meeting at the Socialist Opera. That night some 700 mill workers quickly shouted through a strike resolution. At dawn on Thursday, December 28, several hundred pickets waited at the gates of the huge Virginia and Rainy Lake Company plant. A majority of the 1,200 workers struck—perhaps as many as a thousand. One of the plant's two main sawmills immediately shut down. The other was crippled and able to continue only intermittent production.[11]

The sudden strike at the Virginia sawmill placed the larger IWW organization in a difficult position. The outcome of the earlier Mesabi strike had shown that, with time and the help of public authorities, the company could and would gather a new crew to operate the mill and wait out the strikers. But the Wobblies knew of at least one alternative that might force management to meet their demands—quick, total shutdown of the entire lumbering industry. If the loggers quit the woods in a sympathetic strike, the sawmills would be silent despite any scab crew that might be gathered. Such a move, though, directly conflicted with the long-range strategy recently agreed upon by the national IWW.

Since its founding in 1905, the IWW had relied upon street speaking, propagandizing, and seizing leadership of spontaneous strikes to further its syndicalist goals. The result was that the IWW remained small but famous, or infamous, across the nation for radical militancy and involvement in sometimes bloody, but always dramatic, strikes. These strikes, with few exceptions, ended in defeat.

It was in 1915 that a new IWW branch, Agricultural Workers Organization (AWO) 499, altered Wobbly tactics drastically. It repudiated soapboxing and guerrilla methods and quietly sent "job delegates" into the midwestern grain belt to organize migratory laborers. Radical propaganda was soft-pedaled and immediate bread-and-butter goals emphasized in an attempt to transform the IWW from an essentially propagandistic league into a powerful economic force. Through a series of small, well-organized strikes in 1916, and aided by wartime grain demands of European countries, the AWO won unprecedented wage increases for harvest hands. Members poured into the IWW through the AWO, whose membership was close to 20,000 by the end of 1916.[12]

When the 1916 harvest season ended, the national AWO headquarters in Minneapolis, for a time located at 254–256 Hennepin Avenue, dispatched dozens of job delegates to lumber camps in northern Minnesota. Some worked as lumberjacks; others became cooks and blacksmiths. All quietly spread the Wobbly gospel of labor solidarity and radical unionism. By December, the *Daily Virginian* reported that company foremen in many camps were finding stickers with the IWW slogan, "One Big Union," pasted on bunkhouses and cook shanties. Foremen attempted to eliminate Wobbly organizers but had little success. The job delegates worked discreetly and never hesitated to tear up their red membership cards or to disavow connection with the IWW if questioned by a foreman.[13]

The IWW branch at Bemidji furnished the literature and office services for the job delegates. Wobbly locals in Virginia, Duluth, Gemmell, and Minneapolis, recruiting areas for camp labor, also contributed to the drive. These locals continued to conduct their traditional propaganda activities, but now the propaganda functioned as preparation for the actual organizing on the job.

The AWO job delegates worked slowly, hoping only to spread union sentiment among lumberjacks during the 1916–17 logging season. It would be a year, the Wobblies calculated, before they would have gained enough knowledge of lumberjacks' problems and won enough support to ask the loggers to strike. A sympathy strike in support of the mill workers, they feared, would abort these plans and test the job delegate system before it was ready.

Lumber company managers were equally skeptical about a potential lumberjack strike. Beaton had threatened to close down the lumber camps when the IWW mill workers first put their demands to Rogers, but the superintendent had laughed off the warning. Commercial papers such as the *Daily Virginian* and the *Duluth News Tribune* ridiculed Beaton's statement, and the latter featured the opinion of a Virginia and Rainy Lake Company official that the idea of a loggers' strike was a "joke."[14]

Prospects of a major IWW walkout were enhanced, however, by the working and living conditions of the lumberjacks. Typically, jacks lived in rough-cut lumber shanties. A bunkhouse 30 feet by 80 feet by 11 feet would house anywhere from 60 to 90 men in rows of double-decked wooden bunks lining each wall. Each individual bed with its mattress of loose straw slept two men. Each jack received two or three woolen blankets from the camp (sheets were unknown). The turnover was so high that four or five men might easily use the same blankets each season. Virtually all the beds, blankets, and men were infested with lice. In 1914 inspectors from the State Department of Labor and Industries observed that "the conditions under which the men were housed . . . made it impossible for men to keep their bodies free from vermin."[15]

Bunkhouses were ventilated only by doors at each end and one or two small skylights in the roof. One or perhaps two iron stoves, kept fired all night, provided heat. The poor ventilation compounded sanitary problems. The men worked 11-hour days in the cold northern Minnesota winter and generally wore two or three sets of underwear in addition to their outer garments. The combination of wet snow and hard labor soaked the jacks' clothes every day, but the men were without washing facilities either for themselves or what they wore. Since most of them put on all the clothing they owned (one old jack observed about the typical logger: "When his coat is buttoned his trunk is locked"), dozens of sets of wet-from-sweat clothes hung near the stove every night to dry for the next day. The steam from the clothing joined the stench of tightly packed, unwashed bodies in the bunkhouse, prompting one Wobbly to comment that "the bunk houses in which the lumber jacks sleep are enough to gag a skunk."[16]

Toilet facilities were primitive in the extreme. Privies were no more than shallow, open pits with a roof and some poles for seats. Excrement was only rarely treated with lime or even covered with dirt. State inspectors repeatedly and despairingly observed that "there seem to prevail an idea that toilet facilities in a camp are superfluous."[17]

Safety precautions were ignored, too. Engaged in strenuous manual labor with lethal tools in frigid weather, lumberjacks had an extremely high accident rate. Although immediate first aid was therefore the jacks' greatest medical need, a survey of logging camps several years before the strike revealed that "in none . . . were there any facilities for giving first aid to the injured."[18] Testimony before a legislative committee in 1917 disclosed that nothing had changed in the intervening years.

For all its investigations the state had no authority to improve these conditions. In its 1913–14 biennial report, Minnesota Department of Labor and Industries pleaded for jurisdiction. It quoted two of its inspectors who concluded after visiting a typical camp: "Both of us regretted that we did not have the authority to order all the men out of the camp and burn the place to the ground." Requests for regulation of sanitation in lumber camps were repeated, vainly, in the biennial reports of 1915–16 and 1917–18.[19]

"As a community," economist and author Rexford G. Tugwell wrote, "a lumber camp is a sad travesty at best." The camps where the men spent the logging season of three to six months consisted of a few bunkhouses, the cook shanty, some equipment sheds, and the foreman's quarters. Six days a week the men were awakened in the dark to give them time to eat and to reach the cutting area as the sun came up. After dark they returned for supper, a few free hours, and then a fatigued sleep in the lousy beds and foul air of the bunkhouses. There were no recreational facilities other than drinking the liquor the company commissary sometimes stocked and playing cards or a guitar the men might have brought with them. Most of the camps were completely isolated, so even a Sunday trip into town was rare. And, of course, the camps were without women.[20]

Because of these conditions the lumberjack was constantly on the move. He would return to the camps only after the fall harvest or when the open-pit mines of the Mesabi closed for the winter. Few lumberjacks could stand one camp for very long. They would quit, relax in a brief spree in the nearest sizable town, and move on to a new camp rumored to have more tolerable conditions. Therefore the Virginia and Rainy Lake Company employed a total of more than 22,000 men during one logging season, although it accommodated only about 2,000 workers in its camps at any one time. The turnover of workers averaged 74 a day or a completely new crew each month.[21]

Lumber companies were clearly concerned only with the jacks' muscle, not their well-being. Social welfare and church organizations had not as yet displayed any concern for the loggers. When the workers came out of the woods most townspeople avoided them. They were "timber beasts," foul men in filthy clothing who had no place in respectable society. After weeks of the monotony of camp life many loggers made straight for the bars and brothels. There, at least, the "beasts" and their money found welcome.

The IWW was perhaps the first organization to express interest in the welfare of the lumberjack. In the bunkhouses during the fall of 1916, job delegates began talking to small groups about the power of "One Big Union," patiently attempting to break through the jacks' apathy and suspicion. The job delegates told them others were responsible for their wretched conditions. Rather than search for that rare gem, the decent camp, the jacks could organize and force their employers to improve the camps.

At the same time lumberjacks were being welcomed in IWW halls, such as Virginia's Socialist Opera, in towns near the lumber camps. Offered a back room to sleep in, coffee off the stove, and friendly conversation, the jacks were again asked to consider the notions expressed by the job delegates in the camps. They heard about a new tomorrow when there would be "One Big Union" and a lumberjack would walk with dignity and live in comfort. The success of the IWW centers where loggers could "escape the torture of forever being indecently kicked about" was considerable.[22]

With only a few months of concerted and disciplined effort behind them, AWO 400 job delegates had no plans to bring the jacks into any conflict in the

1916–17 season. But the Wobbly spirit of uncompromising militancy ran deep in passionate souls like "Timber Beast" Beaton, and his insistence forced Charles Jacobson's hand. The secretary-treasurer of the mine workers' union reluctantly committed the Wobblies to the strike venture.

On December 27, the day when Superintendent Rogers declined to answer the mill workers' demands, Jacobson and Beaton organized a "flying squad" of a dozen IWW militants to carry word of the proposed strike to the camps. Early on December 28, the first day of the mill strike, several hundred workers gathered at the Virginia and Rainy Lake plant gates while the flying squad headed north to International Falls. Most of the company's camps lay on logging railroads off the present-day Canadian National Railway Company line. Communications from Virginia to IWW branch secretary Nels Madison in Bemidji sent another hastily organized flying squad north from Bemidji to the predominantly International Lumber Company camps along the line to International Falls (now operated by the Northern Pacific Railway Company). As soon as the squads were dispatched, Beaton left for Wisconsin. He had done some organizing there and hoped to persuade Wisconsin and perhaps even Michigan jacks to strike with those in Minnesota.[23]

When men of the flying squads reached a camp they sought out AWO job delegates, told them of the plans, and spelled out the demands agreed upon by IWW members familiar with camp conditions: a $10 per month pay increase, a nine-hour day, clean bedding and sanitary food, cleaning of bunkhouses twice a week, and no discrimination against union employees.[24] Three lumberjacks were to submit these demands to the camp foreman, who would almost certainly refuse to consider them.

The workers were then called together in the bunkhouses where the organizers reported to them on the mill strike and appealed for their help in the form of a walkout on Monday, January 1, 1917. Quickly the flying squad passed on to new camps while the job delegates continued agitation and attempted to rouse the men to strike. Lumberjacks were generally inarticulate, silent men, and for perhaps the first time in their lives they were being asked to make a collective decision. It is difficult to say what arguments raged in the crowded bunkhouses among men torn between the prospect of striking a blow for a better life and the suspicion that they were being used just as the company, barkeeps, cheap hotels, and brothels had used them. Factors in their decision probably included frustration, boredom, idealism, intimidation, and even fear of being left in the minority.

As the Wobblies passed through the camps the foreman, of course, immediately notified company officials and they in turn telephoned the county sheriffs. But the sheriffs were unable to gather deputies and reach the lumber camps before Monday. By then they were too late.

Early Monday morning the first lumberjacks in the camps farthest up the logging railroads packed their gear and walked out. Going south along the rail line, they were joined by workers from camps closer in. A thousand lumberjacks came out of the woods on the first day. Another thousand emerged on Tuesday, and hundreds more straggled in every day during the rest of the week. Trains were filled with lumberjacks riding into International Falls, Bemidji, Gemmell, and Virginia. Figures are difficult to verify, but more than a thousand of the strikers came from half a dozen Virginia and Rainy Lake Company camps. Another thousand struck from nine camps of the International Lumber Company (ILC).[25]

Local press coverage to the contrary, the first few days of the strike were surprisingly successful. One of the nation's largest lumber plants was almost completely shut down at Virginia, and International Lumber's sawmill at International Falls was also crippled by a partial walkout of mill workers. Both companies ceased all logging operations. A number of smaller companies and independent loggers were also shut down in northern Minnesota, but logging operations in central Minnesota were relatively unaffected.[26]

Employers, though caught off guard, responded swiftly to the strike. Soon after the committee of mill workers left his office on December 26, Superintendent Rogers hired a large group of guards for the Virginia plant. At Rogers's request, Sheriff John R. Meining of St. Louis County obligingly deputized the guards even though they were paid, equipped, and directed by the Virginia and Rainy Lake Company. For good measure the sheriff deputized Rogers and put him in charge of the deputies.

Rogers also telegraphed other company mills around the state and obtained enough skilled sawyers and filers to keep one of the plant's two main mills in partial operation.[27] The plant lay inside the Virginia city limits, so Rogers's deputies lacked authority over pickets who stayed off company property and within the city streets. Virginia police cooperated with Rogers, however. On the first day of the strike they dispersed the picket line and pushed the men back to a point three blocks from the plant gates. They also arrested six pickets for distributing "flaring red bills." When the police were informed in court the next day that there was no law against distributing handbills in Virginia, the city council soon corrected this oversight by banning any handbill distribution as constituting an "unsightly appearance."[28]

Rather than wait for the new ordinance, however, the Virginia police found that imagination and a sympathetic judge sufficed to make existing laws work for arrests. Six leaders of pickets were jailed on charges of disturbing the peace, intimidation, and distribution of IWW literature. One Wobbly, Leo Ahlgren, was sentenced to pay a fine of $100 or to serve 90 days on the work farm for "intimidating" an unidentified complainant with the statement, "You better not go to work." Two others were fined $100 or given 60 days for taking part "in a disturbance of the public peace by speaking . . . the following words [*sic*], to wit, 'Scab.'"[29]

Fifty-three strikers, labeled by local newspapers as a "rebel gang," were arrested on January 1, 1917, and sentenced for allegedly taking over a bunkhouse in Camp 41 near Cusson, Minnesota. There they reportedly slept in bunks not assigned to them, ordered themselves fed, intimidated nonstriking workers, and ran the cook out of camp. It apparently was of little concern to authorities that the arrested strikers were transported for eight hours in one unheated boxcar and in some cases nearly froze to death, or that no one could identify the men or testify to the tardily-arrived-at charges. In mid-January another 40 men, charged with obstructing the sidewalk in front of the Virginia and Rainy Lake Company employment office in Duluth and with distributing handbills about the strike, were similarly arrested and sentenced.[30]

The reaction of the local press to the lumberjacks' strike was close to hysterical. On January 1, for example, the *Daily Virginian* ran the headline, "Armed Squads of IWW's Drive Lumberjacks Out of Camps," over a report that described the "reign of terrorism" and "gun attacks" conducted by Wobblies who were "looting the camps" and would stop at "nothing short of arson and murder." The *Minneapolis Tribune* repeated all this and added well-poisoning and horse-crippling to the list of IWW acts. These charges were repeated many times by company officials, hostile legislators, county sheriffs, and a management-oriented press, although not a single specific instance of any of the accusations could ever be documented. No one, during the strike or in the investigation that followed, could be found who witnessed any burning, looting, shooting, or even threatening use of firearms. No victims were identified or came forward. No one was ever tried for these crimes for the reason that they probably never were committed.[31]

Terrorist charges served as an effective smoke screen for lumber company officials and cooperating lawmen while they moved to break the strike. The sheriffs of St. Louis, Carlton, Beltrami, Itasca, and Koochiching counties swore in hundreds of deputies in the first days of the strike. Most of the striking camps were in St. Louis and Koochiching counties, but deputies were dispatched to the other counties to prevent organizers from spreading the strike. These deputies operated under direct orders of lumber company officials—not without some logic, since the companies paid most of the deputies' salaries. They received $2.00 a day, to which the companies added another $3.00 and board. At best, a lumberjack received a total wage of $1.50 a day and board.

Among farmers in Koochiching County the feeling against the lumber companies, particularly the International Lumber Company, was so strong that Sheriff Thomas P. White was unable to swear in local men. Consequently, International's employment office in Minneapolis scoured Twin Cities poolrooms and bars for gunmen. Among those selected and sent north were non-citizens and minors whom Sheriff White then illegally swore in as deputies. So little attention was paid to the background of those who carried a gun and a badge that White and the company hired and swore in two spies from the Minneapolis IWW office.[32]

In Koochiching County Sheriff White personally led a posse to the IWW hall at Gemmell where many striking jacks of the ILC had gathered. White cleared the hall and locked it, arrested every Wobbly leader he could find, and told the striking workers to return to the camps or leave town. After a week or so White released those he had arrested because they could not be charged with any statutory crimes, but in that time the leaderless jacks had scattered to Bemidji and points south, losing all cohesion and organization.

Sheriff White displayed a peculiar sense of public responsibility and political morality. He hired his deputies through the International Lumber Company, which paid more than half of each salary. At the direction of the company president, Edward W. Backus, White swore in ILC foremen as deputies and placed them in charge of the seventy-odd deputies patrolling the county during the strike. Nevertheless, in the previous election White had run on a strong anti-lumber company platform, publicly denouncing the alliance of county officials with Backus. When an amazed legislative investigating committee inquired how he had run on an anti-ILC platform in light of his later behavior, White frankly answered: "It was easier. If they [*Koochiching citizens*] had suspected you were a Backus man, you couldn't be elected." At a time when it was open scandal that Backus corrupted Koochiching officials to gain low tax assessments on lumber land and employed cutting policies which eroded farm land, White confessed that he had been "unable to find out" why Koochiching citizens would not elect a Backus man. He repeated all the charges of Wobbly terrorism but could not name a single victim or perpetrator or even a place where the acts were supposed to have occurred.[33]

After the Gemmell raid, Sheriff White left James McAndrews in charge of deputies stationed there and in the camps nearby. McAndrews was an ILC foreman who possessed special talents as a Wobbly hunter. It seemed that McAndrews could always tell a member of the IWW, as he said, "by his looks." When a camp came down with diarrhea, apparently because a cook failed to wash dishes properly, and a horse in another camp suddenly frothed at the mouth and died, McAndrews recognized the long arm of the Industrial Workers of the World. Any spoken criticism of the International Lumber Company heard by foreman McAndrews led to swift discharge, because "everyone that made any trouble in the camp, I think . . . they were IWWs, and nothing else." Sharing Rogers's opinion that aliens were the main source of trouble and that most workers were of a low sort, McAndrews regularly termed them "vermin."

In his zeal to smoke out Wobblies, McAndrews authorized the opening of federal mail by recruited deputies to check for subversive sympathies.[34]

The suppressive actions of White and his deputies in Gemmell and in the woods destroyed the cohesion of the strike against the International Lumber Company in the area of International Falls. Learning a lesson from the previous summer's mining strike in which workers lost the battle but salvaged a powerful trouble-making organization, Local 490, authorities took steps this time to break the back of the IWW movement itself.

The mining village of Eveleth led the way, adopting the simple expedient of banishing Wobblies. Disregarding statutory authority and constitutional liberties, Eveleth ordered all active IWW members to leave town or face arrest. The strategy, directed by Police Chief Robert Mitten, was successful. The Eveleth branch of the mine workers' union disintegrated as its leaders either left or were jailed.[35]

Following suit on January 2, the day after the lumberjacks struck and just about a week after the mills closed down, the police and fire commission of Virginia met in extraordinary session. It classified all Wobbly militants as "undesirables" and ordered them to leave town by 4:00 P.M. the next day or face arrest. This was enough for many IWW lumberjacks. They boarded trains for Duluth and the Twin Cities.[36]

IWW organizers and mill strike leaders who defied the banishment order were promptly jailed on charges such as loitering or vagrancy. Those who promised to leave Virginia were released while those who refused received stiff fines up to $100 as well as several months in jail. The leadership and discipline the job delegates exercised over the lumberjacks were already weakened by the dispersal of the men when they came out of the camps. The banishment order began destroying what unity remained.

A special target of the banishment order was Charles Jacobson. He could hardly be termed an outside agitator, however. He had been a resident of Virginia for 26 of his 28 years and was a family man and a property owner. As a full-time paid employee of Local 490, Jacobson avoided arrest on vagrancy charges. But the Virginia police were resourceful. Late in the afternoon of January 4, 1917, Jacobson sat in his office in the Socialist Opera, working on the account books of the mine workers' union. Owen Gately, Virginia chief of police, walked in and arrested him for "lurking and lying in wait with intent to do mischief," terms of an ordinance—found on many statute books today—designed to allow police to control street solicitation by prostitutes. The judge allowed this questionable extension of the law and handed Jacobson a $100 fine or 90 days in jail.[37]

Another miner, Richard Mattson, took over Jacobson's position as the union leader served his sentence. Mattson also ignored orders to leave town by

4:00 P.M. on January 13 and on January 15 was arrested and convicted under the ordinance regulating street-walking. By the middle of January virtually every IWW organizer or militant was either in exile or in jail. Then on January 16, whatever substance there was to Jack Beaton's fantasy of a general Great Lakes states lumber strike vanished when the "Timber Beast" was arrested and jailed on a concealed weapons charge in Park Falls, Wisconsin.[38]

Most of the Minnesota press fully approved the illegal but highly effective expulsion policy. The *Duluth News Tribune* congratulated Virginia on its banishments and commented, in reference to their manifest illegality, that for Wobblies "to claim rights under the laws they defy, under the constitution they war upon, and the flag they deny, is absurd." Editorially, the *Minneapolis Tribune* agreed that sympathizers with the IWW should be denied constitutional liberties. Adding its enthusiastic endorsement, the *International Falls Press* proudly noted that local police were adopting the banishment policy. Aside from various labor union journals and such left-leaning papers as the *Mesaba Ore and Hibbing News,* very few papers took issue with the methods used to suppress the IWW in northern Minnesota. The *St. Paul Dispatch,* although not usually sympathetic to labor, was one of the few journals with a sizable circulation to condemn as unconstitutional and undemocratic the suppressions in Virginia.[39]

IWW organization on the range was effectively destroyed. The job delegate system exercised enough leadership to get the men out of the woods, but when the jacks found that the IWW could provide only meager strike relief funds, hundreds were forced to hop freight trains for Duluth and the Twin Cities to find other jobs. With the strike leaders jailed or exiled, those who had gathered at the IWW halls in Gemmell, International Falls, Bemidji, and Virginia drifted away in various directions.[40]

The mill workers returned to their jobs in the last week of January. The lumberjacks held on a bit longer and neither the Virginia and Rainy Lake Company nor the International Lumber Company was able to reopen logging operations until February. What remained of the Wobbly lumber strike leadership gathered in Duluth. On February 1 the leaders called off the strike, claiming a partial victory by way of improved conditions.[41]

Most companies did attend to their camps better after the strike. The ILC bought new blankets for the men and raised slightly the base pay. The quality of food seems to have been improved, too, in most camps. In 1917 the Virginia and Rainy Lake Company spent nearly 20 per cent more per man for food than earlier. Wartime price inflation accounted for part, but not most, of the increase.[42]

The Wobbly Metal Mine Workers' Union Local 490 disappeared as the IWW was driven from overt activity on the Mesabi. The IWW promised to return to the camps and the mines, but before it could launch another offensive the nation entered World War I.

Minnesota, along with twenty-one other western states and two territories most affected by radical activities, passed a criminal syndicalism law in 1917 making it illegal to advocate "crime, sabotage, (. . . *malicious damage or injury to the property of an employer by an employe*) violence or other unlawful methods of terrorism as a means of accomplishing industrial or political ends." In September, 1917, Minnesota became the first state to convict anyone under such a law when Jesse Dunning, a lumberjack and former secretary of the IWW local at Bemidji, was convicted of publicly displaying books teaching sabotage. A bill making a fund of $50,000 available for immediate action against labor and radical activities only narrowly failed to pass the Minnesota legislature, but talk continued about alleged intimacies between the Wobblies and the Kaiser or the Bolsheviks.[43]

Federal prosecution for antiwar activities placed the IWW strictly on the defensive. On the iron range agitation continued among die-hard Finnish Wobblies who conducted minor demonstrations during and immediately after World War I. But the wartime Minnesota Public Safety Commission had thoroughly infiltrated the organization and frustrated it at every turn.[44] Techniques developed to suppress the IWW in northern Minnesota were later extended to pacifists, war dissenters, and members of the Nonpartisan League who faced official prosecution for their beliefs and activities.[45]

NOTES
From Minnesota History *42 (Spring, 1971).*

1. The history of Minnesota's lumberjacks has not been immune to romantic treatment. See, for example, Wright T. Orcutt, "The Minnesota Lumberjacks," in *Minnesota History,* 6:3-19 (March, 1925). On the miners' strike, see Neil Betten, "Riot, Revolution, Repression in the Iron Range Strike of 1916," in *Minnesota History,* 41:82-94 (Summer, 1968).

2. George B. Engberg, "Collective Bargaining in the Lumber Industry of the Upper Great Lakes States," in *Agricultural History,* 24:208 (October, 1950).

3. Duane W. Eichholz, "Virginia and Rainy Lake Logging Company," 4, term thesis, University of Minnesota at Duluth, 1959, in the Minnesota Historical Society; Charlotte Todes, *Labor and Lumber,* 54-58, 64-65 (New York, 1931); Agnes M. Larson, *History of the White Pine Industry in Minnesota,* 400 (quote), (Minneapolis, 1949); Ralph W. Hidy, Frank E. Hill, and Allan Nevins, *Timber and Men: The Weyerhaeuser Story,* 195-196 (New York, 1963).

4. Paul H. Douglas, *Real Wages in the United States,* 1890-1926, 205, 383, 636 (Boston, 1930); U.S. Bureau of Labor Statistics Bulletin No. 604, p. 468, 472 (1934); *Daily Virginian,* December 26, 1916, p. 1.

5. Interview (1948) with Frank H. Gillmor, superintendent of logging for the Virginia and Rainy Lake Lumber Company, by Lucile Kane, in the Gillmor Papers, in the Minnesota Historical Society; Hyman Berman, "Education for Work and Labor Solidarity: The Immigrant Miners and Radicalism on the Mesabi Range," 18-25, 30-32, 36-58, unpublished paper in the Minnesota Historical Society.

6. On the "deal," see Betten, in *Minnesota History*, 41:89–90.

7. In 1917 the Minnesota legislature held extensive hearings on IWW activity. The IWW was allowed to subpoena and cross-examine witnesses, as were attorneys for the employers. For stenographic records of the hearings, see Minnesota House of Representatives, Committee of Labor and Labor Legislation, Hearings, "Labor Troubles in Northern Minnesota, January 30, 1917," in the John Lind Papers, in the Minnesota Historical Society. Hearing references will hereafter be noted as "testimony of _____." Testimony of Charles Jacobson, p. 214–223; handbill of demands read into the committee records, p. 86–87, both in Lind Papers.

8. *Daily Virginian*, December 26, 1916, p. 1; testimony of Charles Jacobson; testimony of Archie Sinclair, IWW job delegate, p. 139–149; *Duluth News Tribune*, December 28, 1916, p. 5 (quote).

9. Testimony of Chester R. Rogers, p. 306–321. The quote is on p. 309.

10. Testimony of Rogers, p. 310, 313 (quotes).

11. *Duluth News Tribune*, December 28, 1916, p. 1–2; *Daily Virginian*, December 28, 1916, p. 1; *Mesaba Ore and Hibbing News*, December 30, 1916, p. I.

12. Minutes of the Founding Conference of Agricultural Workers' Organization 400, in the Edwin Wilbur Latchem Papers, in the Minnesota Historical Society; Philip S. Foner, *History of the Labor Movement in the United States*, 4:473–485 (New York, 1965); Philip Taft, "The IWW in the Grain Belt," in *Labor History*, 1:53–67 (Winter, 1960); "The Militant Harvest Workers," in *International Socialist Review*, 17:229 (October, 1916).

13. *Daily Virginian*, December 16, 1916, p. 1; testimony of James McAndrews, lumber company foreman and deputy sheriff of Beltrami County prior to the strike seems to have revealed most of the job delegates in the Bemidji area and probably explains the failure of jacks there to strike with the others. See testimony of Andrew Johnson, sheriff of Beltrami County, p. 958–988.

14. *Daily Virginian*, December 26, p. 1, December 29, p. 1, December 30, 1916, p. 1; *Duluth News Tribune*, December 29, p. 5, December 30, 1916, p. 1.

15. Testimony of Albert Nelson, strikebreaker for the International Lumber Company, p. 1297–1312; testimony of Jay Hall, ILC strikebreaker, 1278–1296; testimony of William Peterson, IWW job delegate, p. 196–211; testimony of Archie Sinclair, p. 139–149; testimony of Horace W. Wood, independent lumber contractor, p. 110–122, all in Lind Papers: Arthur Boose, "The Lumber Jack," in *International Socialist Review*, 12:414–416 (January, 1916); Minnesota Department of Labor and Industries, *Fourteenth Biennial Report*, 1913–14, p. 195–199. The quote is on p. 198. Four years later the department noted that conditions it reported in 1913–14 had deteriorated. See *Sixteenth Biennial Report*, 1917–18, p. 117.

16. Testimony of Jay Hall; *Sixteenth Biennial Report*, p. 117; Boose, in *International Socialist Review*, 14:414 (quote).

17. *Sixteenth Biennial Report*, p. 117.

18. *Fourteenth Biennial Report*, p. 196.

19. *Fourteenth Biennial Report*, p. 198 (quote); testimony of James McAndrews, p. 403–435.

20. Rexford G. Tugwell, "The Casual of the Woods," in *Survey*, 44:472, 473 (quote), 474 (July 3, 1920). Tugwell was speaking specifically of Pacific Northwest lumber camps just hit by IWW strikes.

21. 1916 Account Books for Logging Operations, Virginia and Rainy Lake Co., in the Gillmor Papers.

22. Rexford G. Tugwell, Letter to the Editor, in *Survey*, 44:641–642 (quote) (August 16, 1920).

23. *Daily Virginian,* December 28, 1916, p. 1; Harrison George, "Hitting the Trail in the Lumber Camps," in *International Socialist Review,* 17:454-457 (February, 1917); *Duluth News Tribune,* December 31, 1916, p. 8.

24. Testimony of A. W. ("Slim") Thorne, IWW job delegate, p. 2-73. The demands were printed in the *Minneapolis Tribune,* January 3, 1917, p. 1.

25. Testimony of A. W. Thorne, of Albert Nelson, of Jay Hall, and of Frank H. Gillmor, p. 264-306, all in Lind Papers.

26. Testimony of Edward W. Backus, p. 1221-1267; testimony of Frank H. Gillmor; 1917 Account Books for Logging Operations, Virginia and Rainy Lake Co.; *Daily Virginian,* January 9, 1917, p. 1.

27. *Daily Virginian,* December 27, p. 1, December 28, 1916, p. 1.

28. *Daily Virginian,* December 29, 1916, p. 1, January 8, 1917, p. 1; *Duluth News Tribune,* December 29, 1916, p. 5 (quote).

29. Testimony of Sigmund M. Slonin, IWW attorney, p. 82 (first quotes), 83 ("scab" quote).

30. Testimony of Sigmund M. Slonin, p. 81, 89-92.

31. Almost any issue of the *Daily Virginian,* the *Duluth News Tribune,* and the *Minneapolis Tribune* for the first weeks of January, 1917, covered the strike hysterically. There were few exceptions to the lurid press treatment. The *Mesaba Ore and Hibbing News* and the *Labor World,* the journal of the Duluth Central Labor Union (AFL), reported the strike without dramatics and were editorially sympathetic to the strikers but not to the IWW.

32. Testimony of Sheriff John R. Meining, 801-843; of Sheriff H. W. McKennon of Carlton County, 988-1005; of Andrew Johnson; of Sheriff Charles Gunderson of Itasca County, 436-481; of Sheriff Thomas P. White, 352-403; of R. L. Buck, IWW member and deputy, 162-187; of James Sorenson, IWW member and deputy, 188-196.

33. Testimony of Thomas P. White, p. 387 (quote); testimony of Edward W. Backus.

34. Testimony of James McAndrews, p. 403-435 (quotes are on p. 417, 422, 430).

35. *Eveleth News,* January 4, 1917, p. 3.

36. *Daily Virginian,* January 3, 1917, p. 1; *Duluth News Tribune,* January 3, 1917, p. 5 (quote).

37. *Daily Virginian,* January 4, p. 1, January 5, p. 1, January 10, p. 4, January 11, p. 1, January 13, 1917, p. 1 (quote).

38. *Duluth News Tribune,* January 17, 1917, p. 6; *Daily Virginian,* January 15; p. 1, January 18, p. 1, January 19, 1917, p. 5.

39. *Duluth News Tribune,* January 4, 1917, p. 6; *Minneapolis Tribune,* January 18, 1917, p. 16; *International Falls Press,* January 4, 1917, p. 4; *Labor World,* January 13, p. 4, reprinting editorials from the *St. Paul Dispatch; Mesaba Ore and Hibbing News,* January 6, 1917, p. 1.

40. *Daily Virginian,* January 3, 1917, p. 1; *Minneapolis Tribune,* January 17, 1917, p. 1.

41. *Industrial Worker* (Chicago), February 10, 1917, p. 1.

42. Testimony of Edward W. Backus, of Frank H. Gillmor, of Chester R. Rogers, of Albert Nelson; 1917 Account Books.

43. Eldridge F. Dowell, *A History of Criminal Syndicalism Legislation in the United States,* 4-43, 147 (Baltimore, 1939); Minnesota, *Session Laws,* 1917, p. 311 (quote); Engberg, in *Agricultural History,* 24:210; *Minneapolis Tribune,* January 12, p. 5, March 25, 1917, p. 8; *Daily Virginian,* January 25, 1917, p. 1.

44. See such items as spy reports, Public Safety Commission reports, and memoranda in the John Lind Papers.

45. See Robert Morland, *Political Prairie Fire: The Nonpartisan League,* 1915-1922 (Minneapolis, 1955).

Father Haas and the
Minneapolis Truckers' Strike of 1934

THOMAS E. BLANTZ, C.S.C.

*After 1933 and the inauguration of President Franklin D. Roosevelt,
the American labor movement finally had a friend in the White House.
In Roosevelt's first one hundred days, fifteen New Deal programs were
proposed and passed to provide recovery, reform, and relief during the
Great Depression. Businesses were to accept a blanket code guaranteeing a minimum wage, maximum work week, and elimination of child
labor, as well as acknowledge workers' rights to form unions and engage
in collective bargaining. These codes, however, were without enforcement mechanisms; thus, Roosevelt's support for labor did not mean
unions and bargaining were at all guaranteed.*

*By late spring of 1934, a truckers' dispute led to bloodshed and class
warfare in Minneapolis. Reverend Thomas E. Blantz details the critical
mediation efforts of Father Haas, as he dealt with both sets of "official"
negotiators, the people behind them, and the governor. Though the costs
of that summer of tension and violence in Minneapolis were high—four
people died, many more were injured, thousands of dollars were spent—
through the skilled efforts of Father Haas, the workers were guaranteed
the right to organize and engage in collective bargaining. It was a turning point in Minnesota and American labor history.*

Father Francis J. Haas, a seminary professor of ethics and economics, was one
of the New Deal's best known and most successful labor mediators in the turbulent 1930s. Born in Racine, Wisconsin, in 1889, he was ordained a Catholic
priest in 1913. He received a doctorate in sociology in 1922 from the Catholic
University of America, studying under such liberal Catholic social thinkers as
John A. Ryan, William Kerby, and John O'Grady. In 1931, after several years on
the faculty of St. Francis Seminary in Milwaukee, Wisconsin, Father Haas was
appointed director of the National Catholic School of Social Service, a graduate school of social work for Catholic young women, in Washington, D.C.

In June, 1933, President Franklin D. Roosevelt named Father Haas to the
Labor Advisory Board of the National Recovery Administration. Four months

later he joined William Green, president of the American Federation of Labor, and John L. Lewis, president of the United Mine Workers, as a labor representative on the National Labor Board headed by Senator Robert F. Wagner of New York.[1] By the time this board gave way to the more powerful National Labor Relations Board in June, 1934, Father Haas had been instrumental in mediating or arbitrating more than 125 industrial disputes. That month the *Milwaukee Journal* called him one of the Department of Labor's "chief conciliators," and to the *Northwestern Chronicle,* a Catholic weekly, he was "the ace of federal peacemakers." Consequently, when the violent strike by truckers erupted in Minneapolis in that summer of 1934, it was not surprising that Washington officials assigned Father Haas, a Midwesterner and an experienced mediator, as chief federal conciliator.[2]

To many observers, the Minneapolis strike was much more than a labor dispute; it approached class warfare.[3] Thirty years before, a small group of bankers and business executives had organized the Citizens Alliance—"a mysterious organization with no known membership but immense power and resources," according to one reporter—primarily to preserve freedom of individual bargaining and the open shop throughout the city. Over the next couple of decades the Alliance established its own employment agency, set up its own craft schools (to obviate the need for union training), and reportedly hired its own corps of industrial spies. The organization's anti-union policies were remarkably successful. When wages across the country increased 11 per cent in the 1920s, they rose only 2 per cent in Minneapolis; for several years the Alliance was able to force the open shop even on the powerful American Federation of Labor building trades; and in 1934 the Alliance could boast that it had defeated every major strike in the city since the end of World War I. Minneapolis in the early 1930s was known across the nation as a "one hundred per cent open-shop town" and "the worst scab town in the Northwest."[4]

In the Minneapolis labor movement, however, the Citizens Alliance found a worthy opponent. Railroad workers, mill hands, and immigrant day laborers joined the Industrial Workers of the World, the Nonpartisan League, and the Farmer-Labor party in efforts to better their lot. Socialism seemed particularly attractive to the Scandinavian peoples of the upper Middle West—the Finnish Federation was allied with the Socialist party as early as 1904—and in Minnesota Socialism seemed more radical than elsewhere.[5] When the Socialist party split after World War I, the Minnesota branch followed the Third International, and when Communism itself divided in 1928, the Minnesota party joined the Trotskyites on the left. Many leaders of the American Federation of Labor in Minneapolis—Farrell Dobbs, William S. Brown, Carl Skoglund, and Vincent, Grant, and Miles Dunne—had Socialist, and in some cases Trotskyite, sympathies. When Floyd B. Olson of the Farmer-Labor party captured the governorship in the early 1930s, insisting "I am not a Liberal, but what I want to be—a radical," thousands of discontented mill and factory workers were determined to redress the wrongs of nearly half a century and overturn the power of the Citizens Alliance.[6]

The coming of the New Deal and the passage of the National Industrial Recovery Act in 1933 drew the battle lines tighter. The Citizens Alliance refused to relax its opposition to organized labor, despite the collective bargaining guarantees of the act's Section 7a. The only difficulty with the president's Recovery Act, Charles L. Pillsbury, Munsingwear Company executive, suggested, was that "labor leaders have interpreted it to mean that collective bargaining can come only through belonging to a union." Alliance leader Albert W. Strong added: "I can conceive of dealing with a conservative and responsible labor leader, but certainly not with any of the AF of L leaders in Minneapolis."[7]

But Section 7a and the economic upswing of late 1933 had given the workers greater confidence, too. In February, 1934, the newly organized Local 574 of the General Drivers and Helpers Union called a strike against Minneapolis coal dealers. Caught by surprise in the middle of a harsh Minnesota winter, the companies capitulated to the union's demands.[8] By April 1 the union numbered over two thousand members and felt strong enough to threaten all the city's trucking interests with a general strike. To the employers' bargaining committee on April 30 the union leaders presented their demands—union recognition, seniority rights, and higher wages—and when these were rejected, they called a strike for May 15. This first city-wide strike lasted eleven days and was both violent and successful. Pickets halted all commercial trucks and common carriers except those transporting ice, milk, and coal. From large factories to corner groceries, all business was hurt. The city was closed "as tight as a bull's eye in flytime," the strikers boasted. "They had the town tied up tight," the sheriff later admitted. "Not a truck could move in Minneapolis."[9]

On May 19 local officials recruited and deputized a citizens' army to help convoy trucks through the city, and two days later the new "recruits" clashed with strikers in what became known as the "Battle of Deputies Run." Business executives with badges were no match for truck drivers with baseball bats. Before local police could intervene, two deputies were killed and scores from both sides were injured. Class hatred had boiled to the surface in Minneapolis.

On May 21 the Regional Labor Board in St. Paul assumed jurisdiction over the case, a federal mediator was rushed in from Washington, and after five days of almost around-the-clock negotiations a compromise was finally reached on May 26. By the terms of the agreement the strike was to be called off at once, all strikers were to be reinstated without discrimination, hours of work were to be regulated by NRA code provisions, arbitration machinery was established to determine wage rates in case joint negotiations did not bring agreement, and Local 574 was recognized as bargaining agent wherever it commanded a majority of the workers. Although the war was far from over, the union had clearly won the first battle.[10]

The compromise of May 26, however, had been possible only because one of the main points in dispute was left unsettled. Leaders of Local 574 had claimed jurisdiction over all "inside workers" (primarily warehouse employees) besides their truck drivers and helpers, but the companies would not agree. The Regional Labor Board's consent order of May 31 was intentionally vague: "The term 'employees' as used herein shall include truck drivers and helpers, and such other persons as are ordinarily engaged in trucking operations of the business or the individual employer."[11] Union leaders immediately requested an official interpretation of this agreement, and on July 7 the Regional Labor Board declared that, although inside workers did not fall within the union's jurisdiction, the board "recommends that all workers of the firms involved who were on strike should be dealt with on the bases as are provided in the consent order of May 31." The industry of course found the recommendation unacceptable, and the union voted to strike again on July 16. A day later Lloyd Garrison, chairman of the newly constituted National Labor Relations Board, asked Father Haas to fly to Minneapolis to take charge of the government's mediation efforts.[12]

Father Haas arrived in Minneapolis early on July 18 and spent the rest of the first day conferring with Federal Conciliator Eugene H. Dunnigan who had been helping with negotiations since late June. On the following day Haas submitted the first of many compromise proposals to each side. According to this proposal, all strikers would be reinstated and minimum wages of fifty-five cents an hour for drivers and forty-five cents for helpers and inside workers would be established for one year. The strategy behind this suggestion was obvious. Haas realized that the Employers' Advisory Committee and the union bargainers were still hopelessly deadlocked on the question of the union's jurisdiction over the inside workers, and he therefore wanted to bypass that central issue. If the parties could agree on temporary wage rates, collective bargaining could be delayed a full year and with it the determination of the proper representation of the inside workers. The employers, however, rejected the proposal, insisting that it already implied union jurisdiction over the inside workers. Representation was clearly the crucial issue. "Father Haas and I believe," Dunnigan wrote that evening, "that just as soon as we have the question of representation smoothed out, we won't experience difficulty in bringing both sides into agreement."[13]

By Friday morning, July 20, Father Haas was confident of an early agreement. "I am sanguine that we are going to settle this strike without much more delay," he had remarked after Thursday's conferences, and negotiations the following morning progressed well.[14] This optimistic mood was suddenly shattered that afternoon when violence broke out. A crowd of pickets and by-standers had been milling around in the 90-degree-plus heat of summer, when shortly after noon a delivery truck, convoyed by approximately twenty police cars, began to make its way toward one of the local retail stores. The strikers had earlier permitted a truck carrying hospital supplies to pass unmolested, but this second truck, transferring fresh vegetables, was obviously not heading toward the hospital. As the truck approached Third Street, ten or more pickets in an open truck moved to intercept it. They were followed by other strikers on foot and a crowd of onlookers. After a brief scuffle the more than fifty police-men opened fire on the unarmed pickets. In an unequal battle that lasted only a few minutes, two strikers were killed and more than sixty wounded. The work-ers insisted that this "Battle of Bloody Friday" had been a deliberate trap and that the police had opened fire without provocation. Others blamed the union leadership, insisting that union headquarters had been informed of the con-voy and had ordered the unsuspecting workers into the area in a deliberate effort to provoke the shooting. Whatever the explanation, the police's assertion that they had fired only in self-defense was largely discredited when it was re-vealed later that forty-eight of the wounded had been shot in the back.[15]

To Father Haas the incident was both disheartening and inexcusable. On the day after his arrival in Minneapolis he had asked Chief of Police Michael J. Johannes to maintain a truce and to desist from convoying trucks during the early stages of the negotiations. The priest insisted that this assurance had been given. He noted in his diary, however, that the employers had met with Johannes that same evening and, by emphasizing "liberty of the streets," had convinced him to furnish the convoy on Friday.[16]

"We were progressing nicely," Father Haas recalled later. "It was because of the negotiations that we asked the chief not to convoy any trucks. He promised us he would not. We got an awfully bad setback as a result of Friday's violence. Aside from the tragedy, developments definitely have postponed any attempts for immediate settlement." Governor Olson concurred. "I dislike to become in-volved in a dispute with a public official," he asserted, "but there is no question but that Mr. Johannes . . . promised Father Haas and me that he would not con-voy any trucks until Saturday evening." After this outbreak of violence, Com-missioner Dunnigan urged a declaration of martial law, but Olson and Father Haas both felt that negotiations could continue more calmly under a voluntary truce.[17]

The negotiations had undoubtedly suffered "an awfully bad setback." Union officials were discredited in the eyes of those who believed that the incident had been deliberately provoked in order to precipitate open class warfare. The employers, confident of the sympathies of Mayor A. G. ("Buzz") Bainbridge and Johannes, renewed their determination to break the strike and, if possible, Local 574 with it. The workers themselves were no less determined. Soup kitchens were opened for the pickets, farmers donated produce to feed strikers and their families, and "women's auxiliaries" were set up to care for the wounded. On the night of the shooting union leaders organized a march on city hall and many embittered workers threatened to lynch both the mayor and the chief of police. Alarmed citizens across the country feared that Minneapolis was on the brink of civil war.[18]

Although the atmosphere was clearly not conducive to calm negotiations, Father Haas met with the employer representatives on the day following the shooting. The companies indicated a willingness to reinstate some of the strikers and to recognize the union's jurisdiction over inside workers in twenty-two of the more than one hundred fifty firms involved. On the other issues, however, they would not compromise: they refused to admit the union's jurisdiction over the other companies' warehouse employees, and they insisted that the wage dispute be submitted to the Regional Labor Board in St. Paul for arbitration.[19] The workers by this time had repudiated any intervention by the Regional Labor Board because they felt its official interpretation of the earlier agreement on July 7 had favored the employers. On July 23 Father Haas and Dunnigan suggested a compromise settlement calling for arbitration of wages and secret elections to determine employee representation, but the union rejected the first provision and the employers turned down the second.[20]

With negotiations thus completely deadlocked, stronger measures seemed necessary. The two mediators, consequently, broke off discussions and, with the assistance of Olson and Bainbridge, began to draft a new proposal, which the governor promised to support with the full authority of his office. This "Haas-Dunnigan plan" was submitted to each party at noon on July 25. According to its provisions the strike was to be called off immediately, all workers were to be reinstated, union elections were to be conducted by the Regional Labor Board, negotiations on wages and hours were to be undertaken as soon as employee representation was determined, and, if no agreement was reached, wage levels were to be established by a five-man board of arbitration. Wages, however, could not be set below minimums of 52½ cents an hour for drivers and 42½ cents an hour for other workers. Lloyd Garrison of the National Labor Relations Board in Washington had at first opposed this minimum wage provision, but Olson had insisted and Garrison finally agreed. Olson accompanied the release of this Haas-Dunnigan plan with the announcement that, unless both sides accepted the proposal by noon the following day, he would declare martial law and permit trucks to move throughout the city only with special military licenses.[21]

The governor hoped his threat of martial law would prompt the employers to accept the Haas-Dunnigan proposal since trucks could no longer be convoyed by local police sympathetic to the companies. As expected, President

William S. Brown of Local 574 immediately notified the mediators that "by overwhelming majority in a secret ballot Local Union 574 accepts your proposal of July 25, 1934, to settle the strike." The governor's strategy failed, however, when the Employers' Committee accepted the plan only with modifications, Haas insisted, "nullified their acceptance."[22] Haas continued to meet with the employers to urge their agreement to the proposal without reservations, but to no avail. The Haas-Dunnigan plan, the employers claimed, would leave "the issue and the methods of the present strike wide open for repetition in the future." Therefore, in keeping with his earlier announcement, Olson on July 26 placed the city under martial law.[23]

Very little progress was made during the next ten days. On July 30 the two mediators submitted an amended version of the Haas-Dunnigan plan to the disputing parties, but once again the employers rejected it. Just before dawn on August 1 the National Guard raided union headquarters at 215 Eighth Street South, allegedly because pickets had assembled in violation of martial law. Fifty-five union members, including leaders William Brown and Vincent and Miles Dunne, were imprisoned in a temporary military stockade at the state fairgrounds.[24]

On the following day the Employers' Advisory Committee submitted its own terms to Father Haas and Dunnigan: minimum wages of fifty cents an hour for drivers and forty cents for helpers, the reinstatement of strikers not involved in the violence of July 20, and secret elections to determine jurisdiction over the inside workers. Father Haas suggested certain revisions more favorable to the workers, and when the committee declined these the union rejected the whole proposal.[25] On August 3, under severe criticism for the recent attack on union headquarters, the National Guard raided the offices of the Citizens Alliance in the Builders' Exchange. The Alliance had apparently been forewarned, however, and few incriminating documents were discovered. Olson later announced what most observers already knew or suspected: "The evidence seized corroborates my charge that the Citizens' Alliance dominates and controls the Employers' Advisory Committee, and that it maintains . . . stool pigeons . . . in . . . labor unions."[26]

On Sunday, August 5, Olson played his final card. He announced that, effective that midnight, no trucks would be permitted on city streets except those owned or operated by employers subscribing to the Haas-Dunnigan plan of July 25. The governor took this step partly to recapture the waning support of the workers. Under military permits issued since July 26, city trucking had returned to 65 per cent of prestrike volume, and union leaders vehemently accused the governor of thus using the National Guard to aid the employers. The Farmer-Labor administration, William Brown declared, was "the best strike-breaking force our union has ever gone up against."[27] Neither Father Haas nor Dunnigan had recommended this further step by the governor. "Olson intended putting his order into effect midnight last Friday." Dunnigan wrote on Monday, "but Haas and I persuaded him not to do so. We made the same effort Sunday night but he declined to yield." The mediators were not discouraged, however. "Haas and I worked on case from nine o'clock Sunday morning until three o'clock Monday morning," Dunnigan continued on August 6, "and it now begins to look as though our efforts to bring about a settlement is [*sic*] in sight." After eighteen hours of conferences, the commissioner's meaning was clearer than his syntax.[28]

The following ten days were undoubtedly the most difficult of the whole strike for Father Haas. In an attempt to nullify Olson's directive of August 5, the Employers' Committee petitioned the U.S. District Court the following day for an injunction to force the governor to suspend martial law. Father Haas feared the worst. "It if is granted," he wrote a friend in Washington, "I dread to think of the violence and bloodshed that will follow." Olson argued the case personally on August 9, insisting that the employers' rights had not been abridged and warning the judges of the violence that would be unleashed if the troops were removed. After five days marked by uncertainty and almost no progress in strike negotiations, the court, on August 11, decided in favor of the governor, although the judges criticized him for his handling of the situation.[29]

On August 13, two days after the federal injunction was denied, Father Haas took the very controversial step of bypassing the union negotiators and presenting an employer proposal directly to a rank-and-file Strike Committee of One Hundred. The workers not only rejected the companies' plan, chiefly for its clause denying union jurisdiction over all inside workers, but also bitterly criticized Haas's conduct. "All my life I have been a follower of the Church," one worker declared, "and I say it's a crying shame when a man wearing the cloth of the Church as you do stands up before his brother workers and attempts to swindle them into acceptance of such a sell-out as you are giving us." The strikers' bulletin, the *Organizer*, declared that the mediators "thought they could put over the rotten settlement if they got a chance at the rank-and-file." Herbert Solow, in a letter to the *Nation* six weeks later, stated that Haas had first tried "to put something over on the strikers," and then "... a moral and almost physical wreck, withdrew his endorsement of the scheme he had urged the strikers to adopt."[30]

Such criticism seems unjustified. Even after four weeks of negotiations the Employers' Committee still refused to meet jointly with the union officials, and consequently all communication between the two was carried on through the federal mediators. By this time Father Haas may have been willing to bypass the negotiators on both sides in an almost desperate effort to break the deadlock. The *Organizer*, moreover, although critical of Father Haas's appeal to the rank and file, carefully noted that he had not given the employers' plan his endorsement, but this point was apparently overlooked by other critics.[31] Finally, Father Haas's diary indicates that he agreed to this step only on recommendation of Reconstruction Finance Corporation officials who by this time were beginning to play a decisive role in the strike negotiations. Father Haas agreed to bypass the union negotiators and appeal to the rank-and-file committee only because he was bypassing the Employers' Committee also and was appealing, with RFC cooperation, directly to the leaders of the Citizens Alliance.[32]

The federal mediators had been in contact with the Reconstruction Finance Corporation since late July. On July 26 Father Haas had notified Washington that "the Citizens Alliance dominates the employers by the threat of cutting off bank credit." Many of the Alliance leaders were bank executives who had little personal interest in the trucking dispute but who were determined to see the union defeated and the open shop preserved in Minneapolis. The same bank executives, a member of the NLRB staff reported to Father Haas on July 28, were indebted to the RFC for more than $25,000,000, and the mediators immediately sought ways to bring the influence of the RFC into the negotiations.[33] On August 8 President Roosevelt visited Rochester, Minnesota, to take part in ceremonies honoring Doctors William and Charles Mayo, and Olson discussed the Minneapolis situation there with the president. Roosevelt immediately contacted Jesse Jones of the RFC, and Jones then telephoned Father Haas.[34] Jones revealed that at least part of that multimillion-dollar loan might be recalled from Minneapolis because the collateral on which it was based had shrunk in value since the strike began, and he suggested that Father Haas meet with the bank executives that afternoon. The priest realized that the negotiations could now turn very unpleasant and he advocated extreme caution and secrecy. "Suggest no news release giving details in present status of controversy," he wired the NLRB as talks with the RFC began.[35]

In the week following Roosevelt's visit to Minnesota, Father Haas kept in daily telephone contact with Jones in Washington and with local RFC officials in Minneapolis. All this time the employers' position was becoming more and more difficult. On August 11 the District Court in St. Paul denied their request for an injunction, and two days later the rank-and-file committee angrily rejected the settlement proposal they offered through Father Haas. As leading Minneapolis bankers—the chief financiers of the employers' resistance—became more concerned over the safety of their government loans, members of the Employers' Committee began searching for an acceptable compromise. On August 15 they notified Father Haas that they were willing to permit employee elections in all 166 firms if the National Labor Relations Board in Washington would recommend them. Union leaders immediately agreed to this proposal, and Father Haas requested the NLRB that evening to send a special representative to Minneapolis to conduct the elections. The strikes' first major breakthrough had occurred.[36]

Father Haas, convinced that union elections alone could not solve the dispute, continued to work behind the scenes with Jones to reach a full settlement. On August 16, the day P. A. Donoghue of the NLRB left Washington to conduct the Minneapolis elections, Father Haas had a particularly stormy session with several leading bankers of the Citizens Alliance. Jones had suggested that he "knock their heads together," and apparently he did. One bank executive, according to Father Haas's notes, was "furious." He heatedly denounced the "politics in this thing," threatened to call a mass meeting of citizens to demand the recall of "you two," and then slammed the receiver with a "Damn!"[37]

Disagreeable as such sessions were, however, they were bringing the controversy closer to a settlement. At 6:00 P.M. on August 18 Father Haas again spoke with Jones by telephone, and Jones immediately contacted Albert Strong, the "prime force in the Citizens' Alliance." At 9:00 A.M. Strong phoned the NLRB's Donoghue and asked for a conference the following day. When Donoghue met with Strong and the Employer's Committee on August 19, the employers finally agreed to rehire all strikers without discrimination and to accept arbitration of wages above basic minimums demanded by the union. That evening Donoghue and Father Haas worked until long past midnight drafting the final agreement, and on August 20 the union accepted it by an overwhelming vote. The companies agreed to the proposal by a vote of 155 to 3 the following day. After thirty-six days of violence and controversy, peace was finally restored.[38]

The final agreement, in the words of Olson, was "practically an acceptance of the Haas-Dunnigan proposal." The strike was to be called off immediately, all strikers were to be reinstated in order of seniority, elections were to be conducted in all firms by the Regional Labor Board, and collective bargaining was to begin as soon as representatives were chosen. The agreement differed from the Haas-Dunnigan plan only on the question of wages. Both plans provided for arbitration of wages if no agreement could be reached through collective bargaining, but the final settlement established minimum wages of fifty cents an hour for drivers and forty cents for others, while the Haas-Dunnigan plan had provided minimums 2½ cents higher.[39]

Reaction to the strike settlement was generally favorable. The *Organizer* of August 22 ran a one-word main headline: "VICTORY!" Union leader Vincent Dunne considered the settlement "substantially what we have fought for and bled for since the beginning of the strike." His brother Grant agreed: "We did not get all we thought we ought to have, but the union is recognized, it is now well established and—what is better—the machinery of arbitration is established whereby disputes ought to be settled without trouble." Although the employers themselves declined to comment, the conservative *Minneapolis Journal* called the agreement "a fair compromise." "There is, in fact," the paper added, "very little difference between the final settlement and the employers' proposal of July 25, nine days after the strike began." (This was not quite accurate since on July 25 the employers had rejected any minimum wage provisions as well as the reinstatement of strikers involved in the earlier violence and union elections in many of the 166 firms.) The feelings of the rank and file were indicated by a twelve-hour celebration that broke out as soon as the final agreement was announced.[40]

Father Haas could be justly proud of his part in the settlement. The strike had lasted thirty-six days and had cost the city an estimated $50,000,000. Bank clearings during the strike were down $3,000,000 a day, approximately $5,000,000 was lost in wages, and the maintenance of the National Guard had cost the taxpayers over $300,000.[41] The violence that erupted left four persons dead and scores injured.

Perhaps Father Haas had done more than help settle a strike and restore order to a city after five weeks of bitter industrial dispute. To him a strike was not necessarily evil, not simply something to settle. "A strike is like an operation," he frequently remarked. "Of course it is not a good thing in itself. But when there is a diseased condition in an industry a strike may be necessary. The refusal of an employer to deal with a union, low wages and long hours are diseases in an industry. Very often the strike is the only way to remove these evils, and under these conditions it is wholly justified."[42]

Minneapolis in 1934 was undoubtedly afflicted by serious disease. For more than fifty years the city's economy had been dominated by a small aristocracy of bankers and industrialists. The rights of workers had been denied, collective bargaining had been a sham, wage and hour standards were among the lowest in the country, and the city seethed with class hatred. In the violent strike of 1934 the city's deep-rooted disease was brought into the open, and in the settlement of August 21 the first steps of relief were provided. Reasonable standards of wages and hours were established, grievance machinery was set up, and the right of collective bargaining was explicitly recognized. Even more important, the power of the Citizens Alliance was broken, the nonunion shop was overthrown, and the right of workers to organize unions of their own choice was guaranteed. Minneapolis never again had a strike as violent, nor did it need one. The strike settlement that August left the city healthier than it had been for decades, and major credit for this agreement was due to the patience, perseverance, and mediation skill of Father Haas.[43]

NOTES
From Minnesota History 42 *(Spring, 1970).*

1. The National Labor Board of August 5, 1933, was composed of labor representatives Leo Wolman, Green, and Lewis, along with industrial representatives Gerard Swope, Walter Teagle, and Louis Kirstein. Senator Wagner was public representative as well as chairman. Father Haas and Major George Berry were added to the board on October 6, 1933.

2. *Milwaukee Journal*, June 28, 1934; *Northwestern Chronicle*, September 8, 1934, p. 4.

3. Among the most useful published accounts of the strike are: George H. Mayer, *The Political Career of Floyd B. Olson*, 184-222 (Minneapolis, 1951); Charles Rumford Walker, *American City*, 79-183 (New York, 1937); Sam Romer, "Five Minutes That Changed the Face of Minneapolis," *Minneapolis Sunday Tribune*, July 19, 1964, p. 10A; Arthur M. Schlesinger Jr., *The Coming of the New Deal*, 387-389 (Boston, 1958); Eric Sevareid, *Not So Wild a Dream*, 58 (New York, 1946); Herbert Solow, "War in Minneapolis," in *Nation*, 139:160 (August 8, 1934); Selden Rodman, "A Letter from Minnesota," in *New Republic*, 80:10-12 (August 15, 1934); Anne Ross, "Minnesota Sets Some Precedents," in *New Republic*, 80:121-123 (September 12, 1934); William F. Dunne and Morris Childs, *Permanent Counter-Revolution: The Role of the Trotzkyites in the Minneapolis Strikes* (New York, 1934); "Twin Cities," in *Fortune*, April, 1936, p. 112; and "Unionism Wins in Minneapolis," in *Nation*, 139:274 (September 5, 1934).

4. Solow, in *Nation*, August 8, 1934, p. 161 (first quote); Walker, *American City*, 85-86 (last two quotes), 87, 185-193. See also Mayer, *Olson*, 184; Romer, in *Minneapolis Tribune*, July 19, 1964; Schlesinger, *New Deal*, 386.

5. *The American Labor Year Book*, 1916, 94-150 (New York, 1916) gives an indication of the strength of the Socialist movement in Minnesota in the years before World War I. See also Robert F. Hoxie, "The Rising Tide of Socialism: A Study," in *Journal of Political Economy*, 19:609-631 (October, 1911), and Walker, *American City*, 46-58.

6. Anne Ross, "Labor Unity in Minneapolis," in *New Republic*, 79:284-286 (July 25, 1934); Dunne and Childs, *Permanent Counter-Revolution*, 3-7; Walker, *American City*, 46-58, 90, 160; Sevareid, *Not So Wild a Dream*, 57; Philip Taft, *Organized Labor in American History*, 445 (New York, 1964); Maurice Goldbloom and others, *Strikes Under the New Deal*, 55 (New York, n.d.); Mayer, *Olson*, 17-56, 187, 203-205; and Herbert Lefkovitz, "Olson: Radical and Proud of It," in *Review of Reviews*, May, 1935, p. 36 (quote).

7. Mayer, *Olson*, 189 (first quote); Schlesinger, *New Deal*, 386 (second quote).

8. For the February strike, see Mayer, *Olson*, 188, and Walker, *American City*, 90.

9. For the first quote, see Solow, in *Nation*, August 8, 1934, p. 160, and Schlesinger, *New Deal*, 387. The second quote is from Walker, *American City*, 98. For the May strike, see Walker's account on pages 93-128; Mayer, *Olson*, 192-201; and Dunne and Childs, *Permanent Counter-Revolution*.

10. *New York Times*, May 27, 1934, p. 25.

11. "Docket No. 77; Minneapolis General Drivers and Helpers Union Local No. 574 v. Minneapolis Employers of Truck Drivers and Helpers." A copy of this order is in the large Haas collection (hereafter cited as Haas Papers) in the archives of the Catholic University of America.

12. E. H. Dunnigan, "Preliminary Report of Commissioner of Conciliation, July 7, 1934," in records of the National Labor Relations Board, Case No. 38 (new series), National Archives Record Group (hereafter cited NARG) 25. With the expiration of the National Labor Board in late June, Father Haas remained in Washington as an adviser to the new National Labor Relations Board.

13. A copy of the proposal, dated July 19, 1934, is in the Haas Papers, as is Employers' Advisory Council to Haas, July 20, 1934; Dunnigan to Hugh Kerwin, director of conciliation, July 19, 1934 (quote), NARG 25.

14. *Minneapolis Journal,* July 19, 1934, p. 1. *The Washington Star* of July 21, 1934, declared that "hardly an hour before the outbreak, Rev. Francis Haas . . . had expressed optimism over the outlook for settlement."

15. *Minneapolis Journal,* July 21, 1934, p. 1; *Organizer,* July 21, 1934, p. 1; Meridel Le Sueur, "What Happens in a Strike," in *American Mercury,* 33:329-335 (November, 1934); Mayer, *Olson,* 207-211; Romer, in *Minneapolis Tribune,* July 19, 1964; and Walker, *American City,* 155-183.

16. Haas Diary (quote), July 19, 1934, Haas Papers. See also Walker, *American City,* 169.

17. *Minneapolis Journal,* July 21 (Haas quote), July 22, p. 2 (Olson quote), 1934; "Memorandum," July 20, 1934, NART 25.

18. Meridel Le Sueur, *North Star Country,* 289-297 (New York, 1945); Mayer, *Olson,* 210; Solow, in *Nation,* August 8, 1934; Lefkovitz, in *Review of Reviews,* May, 1935, p. 36.

19. Haas Diary, July 21, 1934, Haas Papers. A "Summary" of events (hereafter referred to as Summary), drafted by Haas, Dunnigan, and P. A. Donoghue of the NLRB on August 28, 1934, is in NARG 25.

20. A copy of the proposal, dated July 23, 1934, is in the Haas Papers. The same envelope contains replies of the Employers' Committee and of President Brown of Local 574. See also *Organizer,* July 24, 1934, p. 1.

21. Haas Diary, July 23-25, 1934, Haas Papers. The same collection includes a copy of the Haas-Dunnigan plan, which also is spelled out in *Minneapolis Tribune,* July 26, 1934, p. 1, and *Minneapolis Journal,* July 26, 1934, p. 2. See also Mayer, *Olson,* 211.

22. Brown's reply is in the Haas Papers. It is dated July 26, 1934, and consequently union members may have known when they voted that the employers had already rejected the plan. See also *Organizer,* July 26, 1934, p. 1. Haas's remark is from his Diary, July 26, 1934, also in the Haas Papers.

23. Letters of Haas and Dunnigan to the Employers' Committee and the committee's reply, all dated July 27, 1934, are in the Haas Papers. The employers' quote is from the *Minneapolis Journal,* July 26, 1934, p. 2.

24. A copy of the amended proposal and the employers' reply, a letter from Joseph R. Cochran of the Employers' Papers. For accounts of the raid, see the Haas Diary for August 1, 1934; Walker, *American City,* 207; *Organizer,* August 1, 1934; *Minneapolis Tribune,* August 1, 1934, p. 1.

25. Cochran to Haas, August 2; Haas to Cochran, August 2; Cochran to Haas, August 3; and Haas to Cochran, August 5, 1934, all in Haas Papers.

26. Walker, *American City,* 212 (quote); Mayer, *Olson,* 217; *Minneapolis Tribune,* August 4, 1934, p. 1.

27. Olson to Adjutant General Ellard A. Walsh, executive order no. 7, August 5, 1934, copy in Haas Papers; *Organizer,* August 1, 1934, p. 2 (Brown quote).

28. Dunnigan to Hugh Kerwin, August 6, 1934, in records of the U.S. Conciliation Service, Case No. 176/1539, NARG 280; Haas Diary, August 5-7, 1934, Haas Papers.

29. Haas to Agnes Regan, August 6, 1934 (quote), Haas Papers; Mayer, *Olson,* 217-219.

30. Walker, *American City,* 218 (first quote); *Organizer,* August 14, 1934, p. 1; 139:352 (September 26, 1934). A copy of the employer proposal is in NARG 25. It also is in *Minneapolis Journal,* August 14, 1934, p. 1.

31. *Organizer,* August 14, 1934, p. 1. During the meeting with the Strike Committee of One Hundred, this paper pointed out, Father Haas "was pale as a ghost and sweating." For

further criticism of the priest, see Walker, *American City,* 217, and Art Preis, *Labor's Giant Step,* 30 (New York, 1964). John W. Edelman of the American Federation of Hosiery Workers defended Father Haas against Solow's criticism in *Nation,* 139:271 (September 5, 1934): "We have found this priest a real liberal on economic issues and one of the last men in this country who would attempt to trick or deceive a group of labor unionists. . . . I, for one, resent this sort of loosely worded and unsupported attack on one of the few persons in this country who are willing to make real sacrifices of time and effort in the cause of peace in industry."

32. Haas Diary, August 11, 1934, Haas Papers.

33. Memorandum, July 26, 1934, NARG 25; NLRB to Haas, July 28, 1934, Haas Papers; Haas Diary, July 26 to August 8, 1934.

34. Haas Diary, August 8, 1934; a memorandum of a member of the NLRB staff, August 8, 1934, summarizing telephone conversation with Haas, NARG 25; Mayer, *Olson,* 218.

35. Haas to NLRB, August 7, 1934, NARG 25.

36. Cochran to Haas, August 15, 1934, Haas papers; Haas Diary, August 15, 1934; Memorandum, August 14, 1934, NARG 25.

37. Haas Diary, August 16, 1934.

38. "Twin Cities," in *Fortune,* April, 1936, p. 112 (quote about Strong); Haas Diary, August 18-19, 1934; *Minneapolis Journal,* August 22, 1934, p. 1; *Minneapolis Tribune,* August 22, 1934, p. 1. Both newspapers for that date include a chronology of the strike, and there is an outline of events from July 8 to August 22, 1934, in the Haas Papers.

39. *St. Paul Dispatch,* August 22, 1934, p. 4 (Olson quote); *Minneapolis Journal,* August 22, 1934, p. 1; *Minneapolis Tribune,* August 22, p. 1, and August 23, p. 1, 1934.

40. Walker, *American City,* 218 (Vincent Dunne quote); *Minneapolis Journal,* August 22, p. 2 (Grant Dunne quote), August 23, p. 14, 1934.

41. *St. Paul Dispatch,* August 22, 1934, p. 1; *Minneapolis Journal,* August 22, 1934, p. 1.

42. Quoted in the *Toledo Catholic Chronicle,* July 23, 1937; from a clipping in the Haas Papers. See also Haas, *Rights and Wrongs in Industry,* 30 (New York, 1933) and *The American Labor Movement,* 23 (New York, 1937).

43. Father Haas returned to Minneapolis in 1937 to help settle the strike of 700 workers of the Minneapolis General Electric Company. In all, he was credited with taking part in the settlement of more than 1,500 strikes. In October, 1943, he resigned as chairman of the government's Fair Employment Practices Committee and the next month was installed as bishop of the Grand Rapids (Michigan) Roman Catholic diocese. He died August 29, 1953. E. H. Dunnigan, his colleague in mediating the 1934 strike, suffered a stroke in October, 1934, and died the following December.

Labor, Politics, and African American Identity in Minneapolis, 1930–1950

JENNIFER DELTON

While the usual perception of unions and the labor movement is that of enhancing power and strength through numbers, for African Americans in Minneapolis it could also mean increased individual significance and possibly expanded participation in the political arena. The labor movement became a vehicle for organizing blacks and then integrating them into the city's mainstream political and economic life, although they remained a very small minority in terms of population.

The New Deal programs created by the Roosevelt Administration to cope with the Great Depression provided jobs for the unemployed, including some blacks. Before the 1930s most unions did not have black members, but by 1935 the Congress of Industrial Organizations (CIO) was calling for integration in its unions and worked with the Farmer-Labor party and black leaders in Minneapolis to achieve this goal. Jennifer Delton explores the relationship between union leadership and expanded political participation in the political arena for African Americans in Minneapolis, using the personal stories of Brutus Cassius, Albert Allen, Nellie Stone Johnson, and Cecil Newman.

When Anthony Brutus Cassius walked into Minneapolis's Midland National Bank in the fall of 1949 to borrow $10,000, he was greeted with skepticism and laughter. Like most banks, Midland considered black borrowers to be a poor risk and normally refused them loans. After a few minutes alone with the bank president, however, Cassius secured the money he requested for buying a restaurant. What convinced the bank president to take the risk? As Cassius tells the story, it was the fact that he had been a union leader. He recalls that the president told him: "I believe you'll make it. Everybody else that's in the labor movement'll make it and I like your style." As a black man, Cassius was perceived as a racial category, but as a union leader he became an ambitious individual.[1]

In the labor movement of the 1930s and 1940s, black Minnesotans like Cassius achieved status and individual autonomy in a world that had denied them both. A new generation of black leaders, typified by *Minneapolis Spokesman* editor Cecil Newman, translated their experiences in the labor movement into political power, urging ordinary black Minnesotans to organize themselves as a political force. African American participation in the labor movement was both the outcome of a long struggle for civil rights in Minnesota, built on earlier legislative victories, and also the beginning of a new kind of activism that linked the political power of organized black people to a liberal, New Deal agenda of full employment and economic justice. Black Minnesotans such as Cassius, Albert L. Allen Jr., Nellie Stone Johnson, and Cecil Newman saw the labor movement as a way to integrate themselves into mainstream economic and political life in a state where they were truly a minority.

The most important fact about the African American population in Minnesota was its small size. The 1910 census counted just 7,084 blacks in a population of more than two million. While Detroit's black population increased sixfold and Cleveland's threefold during World War I, the Twin Cities saw only a 50 percent increase. By 1940, 4,646 African Americans lived in Minneapolis, 0.9 percent of the total population, while 4,139 lived in St. Paul, 1.5 percent of that city's population. Between 1940 and 1950, Minnesota's African American population rose to 14,022, a 41 percent increase, but still only 0.5 percent of the total.[2]

As elsewhere, African Americans in Minnesota suffered discrimination. Despite antidiscrimination laws, many restaurants and clubs refused them service, swimming pools were segregated, and restrictive covenants barred them from most neighborhoods. The most pervasive form of discrimination in Minnesota was economic: white employers simply refused to hire African Americans. The few jobs open to blacks were primarily in service industries and on railroads.[3]

Racial violence was rare, but not unknown. In 1920 three black circus workers were lynched in Duluth. Only three members of the white mob were convicted (for rioting). In 1931 Arthur Lee moved into an all-white Minneapolis neighborhood, and a mob of 4,000 besieged and stoned his home for four days. Civic leaders diffused the situation by convincing Lee to sell his house (although he apparently stayed). Later that year, citizens in Anoka threatened to lynch a black man, who was taken to Minneapolis for safety.[4]

African Americans fought discrimination and violence in the courts and through newly founded civil rights organizations. In 1890 John Q. Adams and Frederick McGhee helped found the National Afro-American League with Booker T. Washington. McGhee later helped W. E. B. Du Bois and others organize the Niagara Movement, an alternative to Washington's accommodationist philosophy. Attorney Frank Wheaton won a seat in the state legislature in 1898 and authored a law banning discrimination in bars. Chapters of the National Association for the Advancement of Colored People (NAACP) were begun in St. Paul and Minneapolis in 1913 and 1914. The NAACP fought housing discrimination, the identification of race in crime reporting, and the screening of *Birth of a Nation* in 1915. In 1917 lawyer J. Louis Ervin won an acquittal for a black man accused of murdering a white man. Duluth founded an NAACP branch in 1920 after the lynching. Settlement houses helped blacks deal with the effects of discrimination: St. Paul's Welcome Hall Community Center (1916) and Hallie Q. Brown House (1929) and Minneapolis's Phyllis Wheatley House (1924) provided limited health and welfare services for the unemployed.[5]

The St. Paul Urban League, founded in 1923 to address the problem of unemployment, was perhaps the most active black organization in Minnesota. Before World War I, African Americans seeking employment in St. Paul consulted S. E. Hall or his brother O. C. Hall, two barbers who cultivated relationships with their white clients to secure jobs for black workers. By 1923, however, newcomers to the state overwhelmed the barbers' capacity to find work for the newcomers. After months of negotiation with the Chamber of Commerce and promises by black leaders to curb the further influx of southern migrants, St. Paul's black leaders finally got the Urban League off the ground. The new organization concentrated on convincing Twin Cities employers to adopt hiring and promotion policies for blacks. St. Paul's Ford Automobile assembly plant, Minneapolis Moline, and Northland Greyhound lines were among the companies that agreed to hire and maintain ten black workers. The League also sponsored population surveys, race-relations research, and educational services, including job-interview and health-improvement classes. As a result of their success, Urban League leaders became the main spokespeople for the Twin Cities black communities.[6]

While black leaders in the Urban League, in churches, and in the settlement houses provided some challenge to racism in the years before the Great Depression, they were less successful in rousing ordinary black Minnesotans to activism on their own behalf. The small size of the population made it difficult to sustain mass protest organizations, but class issues were also at play. The consciously interracial Urban League was made up of white philanthropists and entrepreneurs and a small group of black professionals and businessmen. It worked closely with white capitalists and civic leaders to secure jobs for black workers, but it offered little to integrate them into mainstream political life. Similarly, settlement houses provided essential services but gave African Americans no public presence. Legal victories cleared obstacles to integration but did not in themselves bring black Minnesotans forward. The interracial NAACP, which in other cities sowed seeds of mass activism, was constantly short of members. Not until the mid-1930s did ordinary black Twin Citians discover the kind of political relevance and clout lacking in these earlier forms of activism. They would find it in the labor movement.

Black Minnesotans had good reasons for not embracing the labor movement before the 1930s. Although a few blacks—most notably Charles E. James, who organized shoe workers' locals and served three terms as president of the St. Paul Trades and Labor Assembly—joined unions, most unions barred blacks from membership. (In turn, this was a primary reason listed by employers for not hiring African American workers.) The Urban League's negotiation with white employers to secure jobs further exacerbated conflicts between black workers and white unionists. The New Deal, however, changed the terms of racial politics and made the labor movement a viable avenue for black political participation, nationally and in Minnesota.[7]

The New Deal was a hodgepodge of federal programs designed to relieve the effects of the depression and mend the economy. In Minnesota, New Deal jobs programs widened the activities of the black settlement houses and integrated them into a growing network of state and federal social services. Programs such as the Civil Works Administration (CWA), Public Works Administration, National Youth Administration, and Work Projects Administration (WPA) provided funds for daycare centers, libraries, and educational activities at the houses. These programs found jobs for the unemployed, in many cases jobs formerly off-limits to blacks. Among the 72 positions secured for black workers through the CWA in 1934, for example, were the first black nurse, hospital file clerk, and bookbinder. CWA projects also hired blacks as skating instructors, librarians, and housing surveyors. WPA projects hired semiskilled construction workers. Settlement-house workers expressed hope that these New Deal programs would open previously closed employment areas and "go a long way in conquering prejudice." Instances of racial prejudice in New Deal programs brought immediate protest and organization.[8]

The New Deal not only changed traditional employment patterns in the Twin Cities, but it also helped give labor unions political and economic legitimacy. Section 7a of the National Industrial Recovery Act (1933) and the Wagner Act (1935) protected unions and workers from employers. When grateful unionists became loyal Democratic Party constituents, they gained a voice in politics and, in turn, made American politics more attuned to economic-justice issues.[9]

The most significant new organization to emerge during this period was the Congress of Industrial Organizations (CIO). Recognizing that racial and ethnic divisions were the most serious impediments to strong industrial unions, CIO organizers campaigned extensively to teach workers how employers pitted ethnic and racial groups against each other. The CIO also began to integrate its unions, most successfully in Chicago and Detroit. In Minnesota, radicals in the Farmer-Labor Party and black leaders joined forces with the new CIO unions to begin education about integration.[10]

The first integrated union in Minnesota, however, was not a CIO union, but an American Federation of Labor (AFL) trade union of miscellaneous hotel workers: Local 665 of the Hotel and Restaurant Employees International Union. Started at a picnic in 1935 sponsored by either a Bulgarian-Macedonian or Swedish workers' club, the local had been discussed for a long time among its organizers: George Naumoff, a Greek socialist and elevator operator at the Minneapolis Athletic club; Swan Assarson, a Swedish socialist; Bob Kelly, a local communist and bellhop at Minneapolis's Curtis Hotel; and Anthony Brutus Cassius, a waiter and head of the all-black waiters union at the Curtis Hotel. These leaders of existing unions wanted to organize the miscellaneous hotel workers—elevator operators, maids, and receptionists, many of whom were black, most of whom were women—in order to strengthen their own unions' bargaining power with hotel management. Cassius's waiters union was already involved in suing the Curtis Hotel for equal wages with white waiters at other hotels. In order to carry out its threat of a complete shutdown, the union needed support from the vast body of unorganized miscellaneous workers. After the picnic, Naumoff enlisted Albert Allen, the Athletic Club's athletic coordinator, and Nellie A. Stone (later Nellie Stone Johnson), a service-elevator operator at the club, to recruit black members for the new union. Cassius, Allen, and Stone represented a broad diversity of motivations and ideologies that would come to inform African American labor activism.[11]

Cassius had gotten involved in organizing unions after discovering that white waiters at other hotels made about $50 a month more than the black waiters at the Curtis. Rebuffed by the Hotel and Restaurant Workers Union, which did not accept black workers, he organized Local 614 of the Hotel and Restaurant Waiters' Union, an all-black local chartered by the Hotel and Restaurant Employees International (AFL) in 1930. As head of Local 614, Cassius sued the Curtis Hotel, demanding not only equal pay with white waiters at other hotels, but back wages as well. The hotel scoffed at the idea of his black local finding support among white unions to strike, but Cassius cultivated the support of the Teamsters, the most powerful union in the city after 1934, and secured as attorneys for the suit two left-wing labor activists, Ralph Helstein and Douglas Hall. Helstein and Hall publicized the plight of the tiny black local and introduced Cassius to members of other unions in order to garner support for a possible strike. In 1940 they eventually won their case against the Curtis without striking and attained a $13,000 wage increase (on a par with white workers' wages), and $3,500 in back wages.[12]

While fighting 614's long battle, Cassius became involved in the labor movement and local politics. He manned soup kitchens during the 1934 Teamsters' truckers strike, served as a delegate to the 1936 Farmer-Labor convention, socialized at the Bulgarian-Macedonian Workers Club on Third Avenue, and registered black voters. Cassius also helped build Local 665, which was crucial to the waiters' eventual victory against the Curtis Hotel. He recalls meeting daily for coffee with Bob Kelly, a Curtis bellboy, at a nearby Greek sweet shop and discussing how to organize the ethnically and racially diverse workers.[13]

For Cassius, the idea of organizing into unions represented progress and educated thinking, a way to rise above menial labor and fulfill one's individual potential; the labor movement provided opportunity for educated blacks to be leaders, not peons. As a waiter, Cassius was just another subservient black man, but as a union leader he was a powerful individual who took on Curtis Hotel executives and won. While his scraps with the Curtis management repeatedly cost him his job and even brought FBI harassment, these challenges only strengthened his identity as a successful union leader. As he noted proudly, just about everyone in the labor movement was questioned by the FBI (and the Central Labor Union always got him his job back). In his 1981 recollections, he highlighted his central role in events by contrasting himself with the passive, clannish waiters he wanted to organize:

> I thought, "This can't be right, we working here 'cause our faces are black for $17 a month." So I attempted to organize, which was very difficult because black people were afraid of organizations. The only organizations that they knew anything about was the churches and a few lodges, and it was awful hard to sell it to them. But through persistence and effort and having a few blacks in the Curtis Hotel who had finished high school [I] was able to talk to them and get some kind of understanding.[14]

As part of the labor movement, Cassius saw himself as a mover of history, defying the passive destiny to which he felt his racial identity bound him. In relating his story, Cassius inserted himself personally into labor history. He shared a YMCA room with the Reuthers. He was in San Francisco when Harry Bridges was indicted for throwing a bomb. He heard Samuel Gompers speak. In a statement that conflated the labor movement's success with his own, Cassius recalled: "I had the potential, if I'd stayed in the labor movement, of being a great man, a big man in it anyway."[15]

When Cassius left the labor movement in the late 1940s to open the Cassius Club Cafe with his brother, his connections to the labor movement proved key to his business success. In a battle against City Hall for a liquor license, his experiences and friends in labor helped him skirt the pitfalls of city politics.

When the fight against City Hall depleted his bankroll, his labor experience helped him get a loan from Midland Bank.[16]

Albert L. Allen Jr., one of the principal organizers and president of Local 665, shared Cassius's desire to transcend a narrow racial identity, and, like Cassius, he did so by becoming a labor leader. Ironically, Allen recalled that, at the time, he regarded himself as "anti-union" and a strict "individualist," who believed fervently in climbing to the top by sheer ability. In his 1981 oral history, Allen remembered that as a star tennis player in high school, he was treated as "an individual," but off the tennis court he became "one of those, well, there was a derogatory term, but I would say here it was a 'Negro.'" When Allen went to work at the Minneapolis Athletic Club in the 1930s, he tried to recapture that nonracialized individual identity. Working his way up to a prominent position as the athletic coordinator, he arranged strategic tennis and handball matches between executives, potential clients, and buyers. This made him feel integral to the wheelings and dealings of the high-powered business world. Other black employees looked up to him as someone who had escaped the confines of pre-scribed black work.[17]

It would be as a labor leader, however, that Allen felt the most empowered. His prominent position in the athletic club prompted organizer Swan Assarson to approach him about helping unionize the miscellaneous hotel workers in 1934. When Allen reluctantly attended a meeting, he was discomfited by the dark room and "foreign-born" unionists, and he recalled thinking that there was "no power here." But because the organizers had identified him as a man other black workers looked up to, he agreed to help on the condition that blacks "come in just as individuals" like everyone else.

In his oral history Allen claimed that he remained ambivalent about the labor movement until the day a boss who learned about Allen's new role re-marked that he had always thought Allen was smarter than the foreign-born troublemakers. This, he recalls, galvanized him to accept the labor movement. His was no epiphany about solidarity but, rather, a desire to show his boss that he was a force to be reckoned with and smarter than the other workers. Unlike Cassius, Allen remained in the labor movement, and he subsequently organized and was president of Local 3015 of the Clerical Workers Union at the Minneapolis airport. He served as president of the Minneapolis NAACP from 1946 to 1949 and was a member of the Minneapolis Fair Employment Practices Committee in the early 1950s. Like Cassius, he attributed his success in life to the labor movement and the opportunity it gave him to be an individual.

Another original Local 665 organizer, Nellie Stone Johnson went a step further and explicitly linked her new sense of personal power to the political arena. Unlike Cassius and Allen, who saw the labor movement in terms of their own

success, Johnson saw it as labor historians like to see it: as a collectivist struggle for economic security and racial justice.[18]

Born in 1904, Johnson arrived in Minneapolis in 1925, found work as an elevator operator at the Minneapolis Athletic Club, and helped organize Local
665. She marched in the rallies and strikes that enveloped the Twin Cities in
the 1930s. She attended education programs sponsored by the trade-union
movement, traveling to Chicago for seminars and workshops. There she met
other organization activists. The union paid for classes at the University of Minnesota, where she became involved with the Communist Party and attended
its seminars and rallies.

As a unionist, Johnson worked in the Farmer-Labor Association (FLA), the
"educational" wing of the Farmer-Labor Party that endorsed, funded, and campaigned for candidates. Here Johnson discovered not only that she enjoyed
planning political campaigns and framing issues, but that politics offered a
genuine avenue for social and economic change. The Minneapolis labor movement controlled the Farmer-Labor Party after 1938, largely through the FLA,
making organized labor's goals of full employment, health insurance, job security, and affordable housing relevant in state politics. As an involved member
of her union and the FLA, Johnson saw her issues and candidates become part
of the political mainstream. When black civil rights emerged as a social issue
during World War II, Johnson was one of the activists who tied it to the liberal
goal of full employment and thrust it into the political arena.[19]

In 1945 Johnson entered politics herself by running successfully for a seat
on the Minneapolis Library Board. She recalls that Hubert Humphrey, who
was campaigning for mayor, encouraged her to run because she would be Minneapolis's first black elected official and would speak for labor and equality
"from experience." According to Johnson, she campaigned alongside Humphrey,
each benefiting the other. Most of her campaign support came from the academic community, and Johnson regrets that more rank and file did not join in.
Significantly, the *Minneapolis Tribune*'s list of city candidates did not include
her photograph, as it did most of the other candidates, although it did list her
union credentials and labor endorsement. She won the seat by a large margin,
not as a lone black pioneer but as a representative of a viable political force—
the unions and the DFL.[20]

After her six-year stint on the library board, Johnson decided to return to
being a behind-the-scenes, grass-roots activist. Unlike Cassius and Allen, she
eschewed leadership positions in the labor movement. It was as though by remaining part of the rank and file, she kept the labor movement genuine for
herself.[21]

As a ground-level political activist, Johnson transcended the ideological and
factional struggles that tore the labor movement apart in the late 1940s. Had
she been a paid union organizer or an elected official, she would have had to

take positions on these issues. Instead, her relative anonymity allowed her to work all sides of the fence in pursuit of her political goals: jobs and economic security. An AFL union member, she nonetheless ran off strike sheets for the CIO. ("Oh, if [AFL president] Bill Green had caught up to us at the time, he'd have excommunicated us, gosh.") Despite her links to the Communist Party, she adored anti-Communist Hubert Humphrey, personally and for his political agenda of a full-employment welfare state. In the 1948 election, while the Progressive and DFL Parties tore each other down, Johnson worked for both; she wanted Hubert Humphrey to win, but she wanted him, and the Democratic Party, to incorporate the values and agenda of the Progressive Party. She saw this as simple pragmatism, and she prided herself on this kind of political savvy. After the election, she quit the Progressive Party and dedicated herself to working within the Democratic Party. She later opened a small tailoring shop in Minneapolis and focused her political efforts on trying to build a multiracial, labor-oriented Democratic Party.[22]

The recollections of Cassius, Allen, and Johnson reveal that they saw the labor movement as an integrating force that pulled the isolated black community into the political and social mainstream. Other black unionists in the Twin Cities labor movement, including Maceo Littlejohn, who in 1938 led the drive with Hector Vassar and Maceo Finney to organize Local 516 of the Dining Car Employees Union, Frank Boyd of the Brotherhood of Sleeping Car Porters, and Frank Alsup, who helped organize the South St. Paul meat-packing plants for the CIO in the late 1930s, had similar notions.[23]

In trying to convince black citizens of the benefits of unionization, these leaders became deeply involved with black organizations around the city, mainly the Urban Leagues, churches, and settlement houses. Their presence transformed and revived these organizations. Maceo Littlejohn held the first mass meeting of the Joint Labor Negro Council at Wheatley House in March 1940. There, the leader of the Ames Lodge of Elks spoke on his difficulties in obtaining a job at the Speed-O-Lac Paint Company. Cassius frequently worked evenings for the Urban League with no pay after finishing his shift and lectured at Wheatley House about why black workers should join unions. Frank Boyd's union activities got him thrown off the deacon's board at Pilgrim Baptist church, but he continued as an active member, which, Nellie Stone Johnson remembered, enhanced his reputation as a unionist and a Baptist.[24]

By 1938 Minnesota's Urban Leagues and settlement houses recognized the labor movement as an important component in the struggle for racial justice. At the 1938 meeting of the National Federation of Settlements, social workers from Wheatley House heard the director of Chicago's Hull House affirm the role of labor in their own work: "Those of us who have advocated Social Security and other reforms must bow our heads in recognition that none of our proposals became law until organized labor backed them." This particular speech was excerpted for Wheatley staff, along with a four-point plan to work with the labor movement. Social workers invited black and white labor activists to settlement houses, and representatives from the Southern Tenant Farmer's Union, the Trotskyist wing of the Teamsters, the CIO, the Minneapolis Central Labor Union, the Farmer-Labor Party, and others spoke at the houses in the late 1930s. Wheatley House sponsored a weekly forum devoted to world events and national political and economic issues. Organized in part by Selma Seestrom, a white, left-wing Farmer-Laborite, the Forum, as it was called, sponsored debates about the Negro and Communism, the Negro and the labor movement, Pan-Africanism, the Spanish Civil War, Ethiopia, and race relations in America. Participants recall that the Forum was a place where individuals from different sectors of the black community came together to discuss and debate racial problems in the city. According to a 1945 Minnesota survey, blacks were clearly moving into unions, with 109 unions reporting 646 black members and 54,334 white members.[25]

The influence of the labor movement in settlement houses, the Urban Leagues, and the Twin Cities in general contributed to the perception that black citizens had to form their own organizations in order to gain participation in public life. The labor movement demonstrated what could be accomplished when apparently powerless individuals united to improve their situation, but more importantly it suggested that black leaders need no longer depend simply on the largesse of rich white employers. It is no coincidence that the new leaders most insistent on organizing as blacks came out of the labor movement.

No one more effectively articulated the benefits of an independent black interest group than the Pullman-porter-turned-newspaper-editor, Cecil E. Newman. Born in Kansas City, Missouri, in 1903, Newman moved to Minnesota as a child, worked as a bellhop and a porter, and wrote for the *Twin Cities Herald*. In 1934 he began publishing the *Minneapolis Spokesman* out of a barbershop in southeast Minneapolis. Other black newspapers had floundered, but Newman quickly made his paper a main source for news about the Twin Cities black communities for both black and white readers. While reporting the news, he also used the paper to foster black citizens' full participation in industrial, civic, and political life.[26]

Like Nellie Stone Johnson, Newman focused on jobs and employment issues. Unlike Johnson, however, who believed that the labor movement was the best place to fight for better jobs, Newman saw the political arena as key. It was a small difference and one of emphasis, since Newman also recognized the value of the labor movement and Johnson the importance of politics. Newman's philosophy was consistent with many 1930s black activists and intellectuals, who recognized that the New Deal had strengthened the federal government and legitimized the labor movement, thereby changing the terms of black political organization. Complacency and dependence on white largesse were no longer necessary.[27]

Using the tactics and issues of the labor movement, Newman sought to make the Twin Cities' tiny black population into a viable political force. In the mid-1930s he organized a boycott of the local brewing industry, whose all-white unions kept out black workers. In 1935 he also helped organize picketing against Barney's Cafe for discrimination against black patrons, forcing it to hire a black counter person. He exhorted his black readers to organize in some way, any way; "'Let's Form a Club' Slogan of the Hour," one 1940 headline declared, suggesting that the clubs would then form a federation to win jobs from establishments patronized by blacks. Another headline announced the slogan of the Minneapolis Council of Negro Organizations: "Every Minneapolis Negro in Some Organization in 1941." Much of the *Spokesman*'s main news was about new groups such as the Cosmopolitan Club, the revitalized Minneapolis NAACP, and a slew of interracial labor-civil rights committees. The paper reported diligently on the groups' aims, meetings, and achievements, urging Twin Cities blacks to participate and scolding those who did not.[28]

Under Newman the *Minneapolis Spokesman* attacked the community's complacency, isolation, and middle-class pretension. While organized blacks in Chicago, Detroit, and New York were taking advantage of 1930s political and economic changes to fight for racial justice, blacks in the Twin Cities seemed more content with their lot, Newman observed. He blamed the black elite, who had presented themselves as the "thinking" or "better element of Negroes." These older, comfortable families with their ice-cream socials and silver tea sets refused to participate in the larger movement for racial equality sweeping the nation. *Spokesman* columnist Nell Dodson Russell skewered the middle-class elite's obsession with respectability and acceptance of rhetorical bones tossed their way by white politicians: "All a candidate has to do is mutter something about 13,000,000 Negroes, 'Democracy,' and getting us out of the kitchen; and from then he can ease by on the reputation of being the greatest liberal since good old Abe, God rest his soul!" The alternative to relying on white beneficence, Dodson urged, was "organizing ourselves into a solid unified political bloc and pressure group that will have them all losing sleep."[29]

To create this voting bloc, Newman advocated new, class-inclusive black organizations that would bring together the old families with the newer generation of workers. Blacks, he wrote in 1940, should "stick together, the professionals rubbing elbows with the workers." The groups would also be boldly integrationist, seeking white allies, not benefactors. They would be less stodgy and more confrontational. In particular Newman celebrated organizations that downplayed the social and fraternal aspects of clubs and instead stressed political activism—the new, multiracial Cosmopolitan Club at the University of Minnesota, for example. In response, readers affirmed his message, one urging an "All Negro Day," where blacks of all classes would stop fighting and work together.[30]

Was the older generation as complacent as the younger generation painted it to be? After all, black elites such as the Hall brothers and the Hickmans participated in the new organizations. The *Twin Cities Observer,* edited by Republican Milton G. Williams, targeted an older, more genteel readership and seems at first glance to affirm Newman's assumptions. It was preoccupied with guest lists and church news. It periodically called for race purges of "men and women of ill-repute." On the other hand, the *Observer* also reported diligently on national and international political events and boasted that it had the Northwest's only black correspondent in Russia. It reported on events in Africa and other colonized areas, a feature absent from the *Spokesman.* Like the *Spokesman,* the *Observer* followed and encouraged the formation of new groups, with the noticeable difference being that the *Observer* paid more attention to all-black cooperatives and all-black organizations than the *Spokesman,* which celebrated interracial organizations. Politically, the *Observer* followed Republican Party politics, while the *Spokesman* tended toward the New Deal wing of the Democratic Party, but both editors recognized that black interests transcended party affiliation. Finally, readership of the two papers overlapped, and many readers wrote letters to both. In sum, the older elite was not nearly as complacent or parochial as Cecil Newman and the younger generation drew it, but its continued obsession with respectability made it an easy foil for activists trying to create a clear alternative to "traditional" middle-class leadership.[31]

When World War II revived white interest in racial justice, Newman lost no time in alerting Twin Cities black communities to the possibilities for change. No longer need they be merely supportive observers of struggles going on in New York, Chicago, and Dixie. Newman's paper buzzed with local and national stories about the Fair Employment Practices Committee (FEPC), local black soldiers abroad, the fight for a "double victory" over racism and fascism, and American wartime propaganda about interracial unity. The *Spokesman*'s pages divulged that black Minnesotans were participating as delegates and organizers in national groups such as the Democratic and Republican Parties, the CIO, and Washington's new bureaucracies. Clarence Mitchell resigned from the St. Paul Urban League to take a position with the Office of Production Management. Frank Boyd and Nellie Stone Johnson served on the committee that merged the state's Farmer-Labor and Democratic Parties in 1944. St. Paul native Mildred Vernon went to work for the War Department in Washington, where she refused to join a committee to select separate black and white Miss Valentines. Black organizations took part in A. Phillip Randolph's March on Washington Movement, which demanded an equal chance for wartime jobs and desegregation of the armed forces, and Randolph came to the Twin Cities to galvanize support for a permanent FEPC.[32]

Newman believed that the most important issues to come out of the war were fair employment and jobs. Randolph's successful threat of direct action had forced President Franklin Roosevelt in 1941 to create by executive order the FEPC, which forbade discrimination in defense industries. After the war, liberals and civil rights activists made the struggle for a permanent FEPC part of a broad program of federally insured prosperity and social security.

Not merely an issue for blacks, creation of a permanent FEPC was now part of a national liberal agenda to reform the Democratic Party and strengthen the federal government. This meant that black activists who engaged in the struggle were an integral part of something larger than "Negro rights," and their activism was important. As Newman stressed in his paper, blacks were no longer wards defined by skin color, but players in a tumultuous political arena. As activists and voters they could shape their world and their fates.

Newman frequently reminded readers, white and black, of black voters' growing political influence in national elections. Since the war had begun, two million black Americans had migrated out of the South, where they could not vote, and resettled in northern cities, where they could. Black voters' potential influence lay not in their numbers, he argued, but in their "strategic diffusion in the balance-of-power and marginal states" whose electoral votes were essential to the winning candidate. While Newman understood that Minnesota was not one of these key states, he drew on national excitement about the growing black vote to invigorate local participation in political coalitions with a stake in a strong federal government. First among them was the labor movement.[33]

Newman articulated black citizens' interest in a strong federal government. He monitored congressional attempts to dismantle federally controlled agencies, noting any potential transfer of power away from the executive branch to the southern-dominated Congress. "The only time when Negroes north or south get any real benefit from federal funds is when Uncle Sam administers such funds himself," he wrote in 1949. He lambasted Republican Party conservatives who joined with southern Democrats to prevent legislation empowering the federal government. He followed the Republicans' attempts to shut down the Office of Price Administration (OPA) and condemned the antilabor Taft-Hartley Act throughout 1947. Newman's antipathy toward the Republican Party was based not on its record on black civil rights, which in any case was stronger than the Democrats', but rather on Republicans' opposition to a strong federal government.[34]

By urging black Minnesotans to be political actors, Newman hoped to create a more even balance between black leaders and white industrial and political elites. The personal challenge this created was illustrated in Newman's relationship with businessman Charles Lilley Horn. President of the Federal Cartridge Corporation, Horn hired 1,000 black workers at the start of the war. Newman wrote an article titled "Experiment in Industrial Democracy" about this event for the National Urban League's *Opportunity* in 1944. The article described how Horn, the first paid subscriber to the *Spokesman*, was one of the few Twin Cities manufacturers to comply with the president's order barring discrimination. Horn had contacted Newman about finding black workers, and Newman suggested using the Urban League, which was set up for exactly these kinds of placements.[35]

On one level, Newman's mediating efforts resemble barber O. C. Hall's earlier attempts at soliciting jobs for black migrants. Newman was quick to differentiate his ties with Horn, a conservative Republican opposed to big government, from past practices, however. For Newman the important thing was that the federal government stood behind him. Furthermore, Newman wrote, Horn wasn't engaged in any "maudlin sympathy of the Negro" but hired them on the premise that "Negro workers are citizens and thereby entitled to all of the rights and privileges of taxpayers—which include the right to work and earn a living." Unlike earlier leaders, then, Newman could urge blacks to look to Washington rather than to individuals for economic change.[36]

Newman's relationship with another member of the white elite, Minneapolis mayor and later Senator Hubert Humphrey, was less complicated. Humphrey shared Newman's commitment to the political principles of inclusion, cross-class organization, and a strong, socially responsible federal government. Their relationship was based on friendship and shared ideals, but it was also based on political opportunism. Newman used his connections to Humphrey to sustain his leadership among Twin Cities African Americans, while Humphrey leaned on Newman for black support in local political skirmishes within the labor movement and the newly created Democratic-Farmer-Labor Party.[37] For Newman, however, this was a far cry from the old one-sided relationship between black leaders and white politicians. For a variety of complicated reasons, Humphrey and his allies in the labor movement needed and wanted black citizens' support for their liberal agenda. Humphrey's solicitation of Newman's endorsements and favors acknowledged that black citizens in Minnesota were finally relevant.

Whether or not this political relevance would deliver the material improvements promised by the labor movement is open to debate. What is striking, however, about African Americans' involvement in the Minneapolis labor movement is less the achievement of economic or racial justice than the excitement of newfound political possibilities. African Americans successfully used the labor movement to make themselves independent actors in the political arena, becoming part of a larger public that they ultimately transformed.

NOTES
From Minnesota History 57 *(Winter, 2001–02).*

1. Anthony Brutus Cassius, interview by Carl Ross, Dec. 1, 1981, transcript, p. 13–14, 20th Century Radicalism in Minnesota Project (hereinafter, Radicalism Project), Minnesota Historical Society Library (MHS), St. Paul.

2. United States, *Census,* 1950, vol. 2, pt. 23, p. 44, table 14; Governor's Commission on Interracial Relations, *The Negro Worker in Minnesota* (St. Paul, 1945), 3; Earl Spangler, *The Negro in Minnesota* (Minneapolis: T. S. Denison, 1961), 90–95; David V. Taylor, "The Blacks," in *They Chose Minnesota: A Survey of the State's Ethnic Groups,* ed. June D. Holmquist (St. Paul: Minnesota Historical Society, 1981), 80–83.

3. Spangler, *Negro,* 107; Governor's Commission, *Negro Worker,* 21, citing studies based on 1936 relief rolls. See also David V. Taylor, "John Adams and *The Western Appeal:* Advocates of the Protest Tradition" (master's thesis, University of Nebraska, 1971); oral history interviews, Minnesota Black History Project, 1970–75, MHS Library. For descriptions of Minnesota's black communities, see S. Edward Hall, interview by David Taylor, Dec. 19, 1970, Minnesota Black History Project; Evelyn Fairbanks, *Days of Rondo* (St. Paul: Minnesota Historical Society Press, 1990); Anna Arnold Hedgman, *The Trumpet Sounds* (New York: Holt, Rinehart and Winston, 1964); Eula Taylor, "Growing Up in Minnesota," *Ramsey County History* 27 (Winter 1992–93): 4; Randall Kenan, *Walking on Water: Black American Lives at the Turn of the Twenty-First Century* (New York: Knopf, 1999), 165–200.

4. See Michael Fedo, *The Lynchings in Duluth* (1979; reprint, St. Paul: Minnesota Historical Society Press, 2000); *The Crisis,* 38 [40](October 1931): 337–39; *Minneapolis Star,* Sept. 7, 1931; *Minneapolis Tribune,* July 15, 16, 17, 1931.

5. Spangler, *Negro,* 71. David Taylor argues that John Q. Adams, the editor of the *Western Appeal,* made St. Paul a thriving black intellectual center, attracting leaders like Du Bois, Washington, and William Trotter; see David Taylor, "Booker T. Washington and *The Western Appeal,*" unpublished manuscript, David Taylor Papers, MHS Library. For more on settlement houses, see Alice S. Onqué, "History of the Hallie Q. Brown House" (master's thesis, University of Minnesota), 1959, and "Phyllis Wheatley House, 1924–1934," tenth anniversary booklet, box 1, Phyllis Wheatley Community Center records, MHS Library. See also NAACP, St. Paul Branch, minutes and related records, 1904, 1905, 1934–42, both MHS Library.

6. Hall interview, Dec. 19, 1970; S. Edward Hall, interview by Ethel Ray Nance, May 28, 1974, transcript, MHS Library; Governor's Commission, *Negro Worker,* 21–22. Black leaders and white employers conspired to keep migrants out of the Twin Cities by advertising that no jobs were available. See Spangler, *Negro,* 67, citing interview with Cecil Newman and J. Louis Ervin. On the Urban League, see Whitney Young, "History of the St. Paul Urban League" (master's thesis, University of Minnesota, 1947); and Spangler, *Negro,* 105.

7. Young, "Urban League," 39; Governor's Commission, *Negro Worker,* 33–34; Dave Riehle, "When Labor Knew a Man Named Charles James," *St. Paul Union Advocate,* Labor History series, www.workdayminnesota.org; *St. Paul and Minneapolis Appeal,* Sept. 22, 1923.

8. Phyllis Wheatley House, Annual Report, 1933–34, box 1, Wheatley Center records, MHS; *Minneapolis Spokesman,* Jan. 19, 1940; Onqué, "Hallie Q. Brown," 40.

9. On the dynamic relationship among unions, the New Deal, and politics, see Lizabeth Cohen, *Making a New Deal: Industrial Workers in Chicago,* 1919–1939 (New York: Cambridge University Press, 1990) and David Plotke, *Building a Democratic Political Order* (New York: Cambridge University Press, 1996).

10. For examples of the Minnesota labor movement's interest in organizing African American workers, see the *St. Paul Union Advocate* throughout the 1930s.

11. According to Johnson, out of the union's eventual 1,300–1,400 members, 800–900 were women. One of the union's first victories was equal pay for women; Nellie Stone Johnson, interview by Carl Ross, Nov. 17, 1981, transcript, p. 7–8, Radicalism Project. Ross interviewed Cassius, Allen, and Johnson in 1981–82 as part of a Local #665 series, now part of the Radicalism Project.

12. *Minneapolis Spokesman,* Mar. 1, 1940; A. B. Cassius to Central Labor Union, Mar. 8, 1940, Central Labor Union of Minneapolis Papers, MHS Library. According to the Minnesota Negro Council, however, in 1933 black waiters at the Curtis earned $18 a month, and "after several wage negotiations in 1938, the men now receive $62.50 per month with other favorable stipulations"; *News and Reviews,* May 22, 1930. The *Minneapolis Spokesman,* Aug. 8, 1940, reported Cassius as saying that Negro waiters' wages jumped from $21 to $86 per month.

Helstein later became president of the United Packinghouse workers, CIO, while Hall became involved with the left wing of the DFL Party.

13. Cassius interview, 7.

14. Cassius interview, 3, 13.

15. Cassius interview, 29.

16. Cassius interview, 13–14. On his battle against City Hall, see also *Minneapolis Spokesman,* June–Aug. 1947; *Minneapolis Tribune,* July–Aug. 1947.

17. Here and two paragraphs below, Albert Allen, interview by Carl Ross, June 17, 1981, transcript, p. 2, 10–12, Radicalism Project; Carl Ross, *Radicalism in Minnesota, 1900–1960: A Survey of Selected Sources* (St. Paul: Minnesota Historical Society Press, 1994), 35. See also Johnson interview, Nov. 17, 1981, p. 21.

18. Here and below, Johnson, interviews by Ross, transcripts, Nov. 17, 1981, and Mar. 1, 1988, Radicalism Project; Steve Perry, "The Good Fight: Nellie Stone Johnson's 70 Years in Minnesota Politics," *City Pages,* May 29, 1991. See also David Brauer, *Nellie Stone Johnson: The Life of an Activist* (St. Paul: Ruminator Books, 2000), and Kenan, *Walking on Water,* 183–88.

19. For a history, see Paul Holbo, "The Farmer-Labor Association: Minnesota's Party within a Party," *Minnesota History* 42 (Spring 1970): 301–09.

20. Brauer, *Johnson,* 129, 132; *Minneapolis Tribune,* May 13, 1945, p. 3L. No Humphrey biographers have mentioned this side-by-side campaigning.

21. Johnson interviews, Nov. 17, 1981, p. 9, and Mar. 1, 1988, p. 39.

22. Johnson interview, Mar. 1, 1988, p. 28.

23. Cassius interview, 17, 40; "Twentieth Anniversary of Joint Council Dining Car Employees' Union Local 516, July 15, 1958," MHS Library; Johnson interview, Mar. 1, 1988, p. 22. Littlejohn apparently approached the railroad brotherhoods first, but they refused to accept blacks into their unions, so he unionized with the hotel and restaurant workers instead.

24. *Minneapolis Spokesman,* Mar. 15, 1940; Johnson interview, Mar. 1, 1988, p. 6–7.

25. "Resume, National Federation of Settlements, Pittsburgh, June 1–5, 1938," and calendars, Wheatley Center records; Cassius interview, 35; Interracial Commission of Minnesota, *The Negro Worker's Progress in Minnesota: Report* ([St. Paul]: 1949), 56; Taylor, "Blacks," 90.

26. See L. I. Liepold, *Cecil Newman: Newspaper Publisher* (Minneapolis: Denison, 1967); Lois Richardson, "Twin Cities Spokesman," *Negro Digest,* July 1948, p. 66–70.

27. On black activism in the 1930s, see John Kirby, *Black Americans in the Roosevelt Era: Liberalism and Race* (Knoxville: University of Tennessee Press, 1980); Patricia Sullivan,

Days of Hope: Race and Democracy in the New Deal Era (Chapel Hill: University of North Carolina Press, 1996).

28. *Minneapolis Spokesman,* Feb. 14, 1941. On the brewery boycott, see *Minneapolis Spokesman,* Jan. 25, May 10, May 24, July 19, 1935. On Barney's Cafe picket, see *Minneapolis Spokesman,* July 5, 1935; *Twin Cities Herald,* July 6, 1935. On clubs, see *Minneapolis Spokesman,* Mar. 15, May 3, May 31, 1940.

29. *Minneapolis Spokesman,* Feb. 2, Mar. 15, 1940, Feb. 15, 1946.

30. *Minneapolis Spokesman,* Jan. 19, Mar. 15, 1940, Mar. 14, 1941.

31. *Twin Cities Observer,* May 4, 1945, and elsewhere.

32. *Minneapolis Spokesman,* Jan. 19, Mar. 15, 1940, Apr. 18, 1941, Apr. 14, 21, 1944, Jan. 18, Feb. 8, 1946.

33. Henry L. Moon, *Balance of Power: The Negro Vote* (Garden City: Doubleday, 1948), 198; *Minneapolis Spokesman,* Mar. 15, July 2, Oct. 15, 22, 1948.

34. *Minneapolis Spokesman,* July 26, 1940, Feb. 1, 8, 15, 1946, Aug. 29, Sept. 5, 1947, Aug. 6, 1948, Apr. 8, 1949. For example, see Newman reply to letter dated Mar. 24, 1948, regarding Ohio Senator Robert Taft's positions on the FEPC and big government; *Minneapolis Spokesman,* Apr. 2, 1948.

35. *Opportunity* 22 (Spring 1944): 52–56, 89.

36. *Opportunity* 22 (Spring 1944): 53. Horn also monitored the activities of radicals in the labor movement. See Charles Horn to Hjalmar Petersen, Nov. 21, 1946, Hjalmar Petersen Papers, MHS Library. See also correspondence between Horn and the state Republican Party, indicating Horn's monitoring of union newspapers, in Republican State Central Committee Papers, MHS.

37. On Humphrey and Newman, see Liepold, *Cecil Newman;* Timothy Thurber, *The Politics of Equality: Hubert H. Humphrey and the African-American Freedom Struggle* (New York: Columbia University Press, 1998), 38–39, 42–43; Jennifer Delton, "Forging a Northern Strategy: Civil Rights in Liberal Democratic Politics, 1940–1948" (Ph.D. diss., Princeton University, 1997).

RACE & ETHNICITY

Race and Segregation in St. Paul's Public Schools, 1846–1869

WILLIAM D. GREEN

Education, especially public education, has been valued since the early days of the American Republic. William Green discusses St. Paul's commitment to public education from 1846 to 1869 and its decision to segregate black school children by the mid-1850s even though the "white" public schools continued to include mixed race (Indian) children. After achieving territorial status in 1849, citizenship increasingly became tied to white male suffrage. As St. Paul's population grew, race lines became more distinct. Most white arrivals from the east came from states already practicing segregation in education; increasing black migration up the Mississippi fueled racist fears in St. Paul. However, after the Civil War, the movement for black suffrage grew as part of Reconstruction.

While Minnesotans voted down a state referendum in both 1865 and 1867, in 1868 black suffrage was passed in Minnesota, two years before the Fifteenth Amendment was ratified. By March of 1869, St. Paul's brief experiment with segregated education (definitely separate and not equal) was over, long before the 1896 Plessy v. Ferguson and 1954–55 Brown v. Board of Education decisions dealt with those issues nationally.

For early St. Paul residents, the city's venture into racially segregated schools was new. Before 1857, when the town's board of education first decided that black children should attend separate schools, it was not unusual to find them seated next to white, Indian, or racially mixed students. Thomas S. Williamson, a physician-missionary seeking a teacher for his St. Paul school, wrote in 1846 that the person "should be entirely free from prejudice on account of color, for among her scholars she might find not only English, French and Swiss, but Sioux and Chippewas, with some claiming kindred with the African Stock." Unlike other places in the antebellum North where blacks lived in rigid segregation, territorial Minnesota was a virtually integrated community. In 1849, in fact, the newly seated legislature guaranteed funding for public education without reference to skin color. Antiblack sentiment was probably impractical in a place where bitter winters made mere survival a challenge, where one's

335

success at farming and hunting was unpredictable, and where relationships with the native populations were uncertain.[1]

Racial intermingling had been commonplace in pre-territorial Minnesota. In 1837 schoolmaster Peter Garrioch recorded in his diary that his school at St. Peter's (Mendota) opened "on the heterogeneous system" and included students of "Negro extraction." Historian J. Fletcher Williams commented on St. Paul's "curious commingling of races, the old Scotch, English and French settlers having married with the Crees and Chippewas, and crossed and re-crossed until every shade of complexion, and a babel of tongues, was the re-sult." People of color clearly predominated in the community in 1845 when, Williams continued, "by far the largest proportion of the inhabitants were Canadian French, and Red River refugees and their descendants. There were only three or four purely American (white) families in the settlement. . . . English was probably not spoken in more than three or four families."[2]

Racial mixing and acceptance, however, began to decline after Minnesota attained territorial status. In the fall of 1849, the first legislature embarked on a series of measures that incrementally limited civic participation to white males only. First, the body restricted suffrage to white males. Subsequent en-actments used suffrage rights as the basis for such activities as serving as ju-rors and referees in civil law cases and holding village office. Race thus became a determinative factor in public life, and in this way the territory came to re-semble most of the northern states that chose to deny black residents their civil rights.[3]

The same legislators distinguished the new territory, however, when they enacted their "most important measure," one which declined to exclude black children from being educated with white students. The act to establish and maintain common schools provided for a fund "for the education of all the chil-dren and youth of the Territory," ages 4 to 21 years, and authorized a state tax of one-fourth of one percent, to be supplemented when necessary by a tax voted in each school district. In other words, this law required taxpayers to finance education for all children, including those whose parents were in the process of being disenfranchised.[4]

The author of the common-school bill was Canadian-born Martin McLeod. McLeod had been raised in the Red River settlement, where the majority of residents were of Catholic and mixed white-Indian heritage. Growing up in that community had taught McLeod that race was not a standard by which to judge character, but this set him apart from his fellow legislators. Most were white, Protestant, and Anglo-American from the Midwest and East, where laws discriminated against blacks. McLeod nevertheless succeeded in persuading a majority of his colleagues to adopt inclusionary language for public education.[5]

One factor in McLeod's success was likely the miniscule size of the territory's black community compared to the rapidly growing white population. Between 1849 and 1850 St. Paul's population increased from 840 to 1,294 while the number of black residents remained at 40.[6]

A second factor in McLeod's success was probably the popular belief that Minnesota's black population was not likely to increase. The majority of new white Minnesotans had come from areas of the Midwest that shared borders with slaveholding states. Back home they may have felt threatened by the widespread influx of fugitive slaves and free blacks. Although whites vastly outnumbered blacks everywhere, the percentage of growth in the black population in some states was greater than in the white population. Responding to constituent concerns, public officials and legislative committees enacted laws to discourage further black settlement. For example, a very important piece of business facing legislators even in racially tolerant Iowa, according to historian Robert Dykstra, was "devising a set of statutes to protect white Iowans from a numerically important in-migration of free blacks" from Missouri. Dykstra concludes: "Frontier enthusiasm for such laws was by no means limited to the southern-born and bred."[7]

Minnesota, on the other hand, was geographically insulated. None of the territory's neighbors was slaveholding. In the late 1840s and early 1850s no indications appear in legislative records, newspapers, or legislators' correspondence to suggest residents feared fugitive slaves and free black streaming into the very far northwesternmost corner of the nation.[8]

A third factor in legislator McLeod's success at engineering race-blind schools may have been the relatively positive opinion that Minnesotans—especially St. Paul's political and commercial elite—held of their black neighbors. Some feared more that St. Paul would acquire a "bad name" from the rowdy, single men that streamed into town in search of opportunity. In contrast, the tiny black population was stable. In the 1850 census a total of seven families—only one headed by a female—lived in St. Paul. Only one male household head was unemployed. The fifteen blacks not listed as heads appeared to have been servants in white households.[9]

Subsequent census data, which recorded the value of property, suggest that these early black residents reflected the economic diversity of a people who had not been excluded from mainstream society. Many black adults listed in the 1850 territorial census were literate. Living in every ward of St. Paul, they were relatively free of the stigma associated with being confined to racially identifiable neighborhoods. They were deemed, in short, a population "assimilable" into the culture of Anglo-American Minnesota. More like than unlike the native-born white population, they were "a useful class," observed St. Paul's *Minnesota Pioneer,* and good candidates for the sort of citizenship that public education promised to nurture. The paradox of treating black children as the educational equals of white children while denying their parents citizenship rights seems not yet to have bothered the city's Yankee elite.[10]

By January 1850, St. Paul had three schools, "now in full blast," that provided "ample means for the education of all the children in town." One school was located on Jackson Street below Sixth Street; another was in the basement of a Methodist church (constructed with materials provided by Jim Thompson, an early African-American resident); and the third was in the lecture room of Rev. Edward D. Neill, chaplain of the legislature and future superintendent of St. Paul's public schools. In total, 150 children attended integrated schools in racially and socioeconomically diverse wards. In the ensuing months, however, as increasing numbers of settlers moved into town, housing patterns reflecting class and ethnicity began to appear.[11]

Native-born easterners and midwesterners moved into wards across the town, but foreign-born settlers began concentrating in Lowertown, where Irish, Germans, Norwegians, Swedes, and Jews created what one historian has described as a "potpourri of merging ethnic boundaries and residential life." Lowertown was also where newly arrived blacks began settling, initiating a housing pattern that perhaps suggests white Minnesotans were defining them, too, as aliens. Residential enclaves grew as more poor immigrants arrived. Throughout the decade of the 1850s foreign-born laborers were less likely to achieve higher occupational status in St. Paul than native-born workers. Locked into this class structure, the new population found it increasingly difficult to secure employment and join the economic mainstream. On the bottom, groups competed for the available jobs.[12]

One manifestation of growing black economic distress may have been the marked increase in truancy among the school-age population, as well as the physical deterioration of schools. In 1852 the *St. Paul Pioneer* lambasted the town for allowing them to fall into disrepair:

> Truth compels us to say, that there is not a building in all Saint Paul, fit to be called a District school house. The only building known as such, is hardly fit for a horse stable. . . . All this in an opulent town, swarming with children, little untaught brats, swarming about the streets and along the levee, in utter idleness, like wharf rats.[13]

Concurrently, St. Paul's Catholics had formed their own schools, but their success was no more evident. One source noted in disgust, "Ragged school children ran about the streets" on the lower landing, where they committed vices ranging from "lying and profane swearing" to the "high calendar of crimes." In 1853 St. Paul's leaders attempted to revitalize formal public education by establishing Baldwin School, organized by Neill and named for Philadelphia philanthropist Mathew W. Baldwin, the principal donor to the building fund.

Some 71 pupils reportedly attended by January 1854. While there is no record of how many students, if any, were black, it matters little, since St. Paul was entering a new phase of race relations, one much less tolerant of black-white comity.[14]

By the mid-1850s, as national tensions over slavery and its extension into new territories heightened, more free blacks and fugitive slaves began migrating to Minnesota, settling almost exclusively in St. Paul. Their numbers remained tiny compared to the white settlers streaming in during the same period, but white prejudice against recent black arrivals, compounded by the cooling reception offered by St. Paul's established black residents, made assimilation difficult. Many white feared that the Mississippi River was becoming a conduit for blacks expelled or fleeing from the South who would become paupers or wards of the territory. In 1854 St. Paul legislators sponsored a bill intended to discourage black settlement. When the effort failed, John Day of St. Paul threatened a second bill that would have restricted black residency to St. Anthony and Minneapolis. Social customs and beliefs that had already segregated blacks elsewhere in the United States had now spread to Minnesota.[15]

Throughout the North, discriminatory "black laws" or "codes" had been enacted as early as 1807, principally to discourage the immigration of free blacks. Although residents of the Old Northwest and the border states were opposed to slavery, by midcentury they were also adamantly opposed to the residence of free blacks. As a historian of the period, Eugene Berwanger, observed, "Antislavery settlers from the border slave states unjustly considered the Negro, and not the slavery system, responsible for the conditions from which they had fled."[16]

Although some northern white schools admitted black children, especially before 1820, most states either excluded them or established separate schools. While Pennsylvania, New York, and Ohio extended public-school privileges to all, they required segregated facilities for black children whenever 20 or more could be accommodated. Even in New England, local school committees usually assigned black children to their own institutions. Newer states such as Indiana, Illinois, Michigan, and Iowa frequently excluded blacks from public education altogether. By 1850 nearly every northern community legally consigned black children to separate schools or denied them public education by custom and popular prejudice.[17]

Proposals to educate black children invariably aroused bitter controversy, particularly in the newer states. Admitting them into white schools, opponents maintained, would lead to violence and sabotage public education. Many whites asserted that blacks were incapable of learning, while others insisted that providing educational opportunities would further encourage black immigration and antagonize southern-born residents. Historian Leon Litwack, observed, "The possibility that Negro children would be mixed with white children in the same classroom aroused even greater fears and prejudices than those which consigned the Negro to an inferior place in the church, the theater, and the railroad car." Berwanger concluded, "In whichever section they had previously lived, the midwestern concept of society held no place for free Negroes."[18]

By 1856 black children in St. Paul who sought formal instruction were being discouraged from attending public schools, and antiblack sentiments appeared in editorials in the city's papers. Finally, in November 1857 the St. Paul Board of Education resolved to formally segregate St. Paul's black children. As reported in the *Weekly Pioneer and Democrat,* the new school policy read, "Whenever thirty pupils of African descent apply for instruction, the Secretary be authorized to employ a teacher for the same, with salary of thirty-five dollars per month."[19]

Requiring a minimum of 30 black pupils to establish a segregated school meant that no school would be established for less. While approximately 60 black school-age children lived in St. Paul, concentrated in the commercial area and Lowertown, less than 15 sought formal instruction with Moses Dixon, the appointed teacher, and St. Paul's first segregated school closed shortly after opening. By contrast, some 1,150 school-age children reportedly lived in St. Paul's three wards at this time. Although black children who sought formal instruction in predominantly white schools were not necessarily denied admission in the next two years, the few who sporadically attended public school caused much consternation among white townsfolk. In response, the St. Paul Board of Education reestablished in early 1859 a separate school for black children, but this time designated 15 pupils as the requisite number. The *St. Paul Minnesotian* reported the board's decision this way:

> The committee feel a deep interest in the education of children of African descent, and while they are sensible that the expense of educating so small a number of pupils of this description may seem large, they deem the subject of sufficient importance to require that some practical measures should be adopted for this purpose.... They would recommend that any school of children of African descent... that may be kept for three months with an average daily attendance of fifteen pupils between ages of five and twenty years, be received by the Board and its expenses defrayed as a public school.[20]

The city's formal commitment to providing adequate resources for the education of black children proved to be hollow. The new blacks-only facility was allowed to deteriorate; a teacher could not be retained. Student attendance fell. Within months after opening, the second school was disbanded. And now, unlike before, black children were actively—and on occasion officially—prevented from attending white schools. When Benjamin Drew, hired to head the city's schools, discovered in 1859 that a "quadroon" boy was attending a white school, he told the teacher that "she had done wrong to receive him as [the boy] would not be allowed to remain." The teacher responded, to no avail, that the mixed-race boy "is no darker than many Indians-mixed who are here."[21]

St. Paul's segregation efforts of 1857 and 1859 were paradoxes typical of the period: On one hand, racial mingling offended the sensibilities of white St. Paul. On the other, in accordance with the public-education credo "Teach youth, for men cannot be taught," St. Paulites believed it necessary to provide formal instruction to help black children become good members of society.[22]

Between 1860 and 1869, as more blacks moved into Minnesota, several efforts were made to organize schools for the children of "contraband," the term given to freed slaves who followed Union troops to the North. Anti-black sentiment in St. Paul reached a high point in 1863, when some 218 blacks, the largest single migration to the state, traveled upriver from St. Louis to St. Paul. White workers engaged in a labor dispute with the Galena Packet Company, believing that the men in the party had come to break their strike, harassed them at the dock until they departed for Fort Snelling.[23]

Black adults may have represented threats to low-skilled or unskilled white laborers, but it was black children who seemed to pose the worst threat by personifying the future of blacks in St. Paul. Accordingly, in August 1865 the school board "almost unanimously" passed a resolution challenging the racial mingling which had been "to some extent permitted" in the schools and again instructed the superintendent to provide "a suitable teacher and accomodations" for black children. It further resolved that "no children of African descent be thereafter admitted to any other public school." In October official notice was given that a "School for Colored Children" would open in Morrison's Building at Ninth and Jackson Streets (although furniture was not yet available). Classes would be led by a Miss Morrow, who would receive a monthly salary of $35 for teaching some 40 or 50 black school-age youth who reportedly resided in St. Paul at the beginning of the academic year of 1865–66.[24]

Soon after classes began, however, the board of education discovered "problems of maintaining and operating" the school. (No such problems apparently existed in the city's three established schools—Washington, Adams, and Jefferson—and one new German-English school, where a total of 1,241 students were enrolled.) In late 1867 the *St. Paul Daily Press* critically called attention to the "very dilapidated condition" of the building.

> The colored children of this city are excluded from the free schools which are located in convenient and comfortable buildings, well-supplied with maps, charts, blackboards, and the usual equipments of such institutions. . . . Some of the windows have been broken out, the plastering is

falling off and the keen air of winter will find entrance through many a crack and cranny. To keep out a part of the cold that would otherwise find entrance, the windows have been partly boarded up, so that while the benefit of increased warmth is attained, the disadvantage of a decrease in light has to be submitted to.[25]

In essence, the newspaper observed, the structure was incapable of providing adequate shelter for ill-clothed children against the harsh Minnesota winter. The paper then urged that funding and supplies "similar to that which is provided for the white schools" be made available. The plea fell on deaf ears, however, and the school limped on with windows filled in with pine boards, dim lighting, and decreasing attendance.[26]

Apparently it was the school's resilience that inspired the paper to observe in January 1868 that it was in "flourishing condition" and attended by an average of 20 students. By contrast, however, white students attended three elementary schools each valued at more than $8,000, a respectable sum for that day, and in the same year Franklin Elementary School was constructed at a cost of $16,969.65, including the site, furniture for 18 rooms, fence, and outbuildings. Although separate, Miss Morrow's rickety facility was clearly not equal.[27]

After the conclusion of the Civil War, national sentiment for extending suffrage to blacks began building slowly. In Minnesota statewide referenda failed in 1865 and 1867, but in November 1868 voters approved amending section one of article seven of the state constitution to extend full suffrage rights to black males and to Indians and mixed-bloods who "have adopted the customs and habits of civilization." Votes for and against tallied along party lines, with Republican voters supporting and Democratic voters opposing. Predating by two years national ratification of the Fifteenth Amendment to the U.S. Constitution, Minnesota distinguished itself as the only northern state to approve black suffrage by popular vote. In Democratic St. Paul, however, the largest city with the largest black population in Minnesota, referendum voters solidly opposed granting suffrage to blacks.[28]

In the face of the town's vote, Minnesota blacks converged on St. Paul for a victory convention on January 1, 1869, the sixth anniversary of Lincoln's Emancipation Proclamation. Marching through the streets, they stopped to express their gratitude at the homes of key officials, including that of Republican Mayor Jacob H. Stewart. (This victory, and the militant public display, may have mobilized local antiblack forces, for in the city elections that spring Stewart lost to Democrat James H. Maxfield, and Democrats who opposed black suffrage regained control of city government.)[29]

At the New Year's celebration, Republican Governor William R. Marshall proclaimed St. Paul's blacks to be legitimate Minnesota voters with these words: "In the name of forty thousand of the free electors of this commonwealth, I welcome you to liberty and equality before the law. In the name of the State of Minnesota, which has relieved itself of reproach of unjust discrimination against a class of its people, I welcome you to your political enfranchisement."[30] His words proved to be a rallying cry. Within a few months, Minnesota legislators took a logical next step.

A dozen years after St. Paul first endorsed separate black and white schools, Minnesotans challenged St. Paul's system. On Saturday, February 27, 1869, Republican state representative William H. C. Folsom of Taylors Falls sponsored Bill No. 198 in the legislature to amend section 39, title 1 of chapter 36 of the general statutes, "regarding education." Despite its cunningly understated name, the bill held major implications. It proposed to deprive school districts in incorporated towns of state school funds if the districts denied black children admission because of their race. If made into law, the bill would end school segregation in St. Paul, incorporated since 1849.[31]

Desegregating Minnesota's schools had been an ongoing matter of concern for Republicans. On January 10, 1865, members of the Golden Key Club, a literary society of black men in St. Paul, had filed a petition with the Republican-dominated house on behalf of black suffrage that stressed the need for better education to awaken in blacks "integrity and moral worth" as fine as in the most enlightened and intelligent whites. Legislators who supported the bill had also linked literacy and good citizenship. John Kellet, a persistent commentator in the *Mankato Union* who signed his articles with the initial "W," had challenged the legislature to extend civil rights to black Minnesotans, observing that blacks "never have had the advantages of an education. . . . They have for centuries been taught their inferiority and stupidity. But the day is dawning when they will show . . . that there is stamped upon their race the image of the same all wise God."[32]

With suffrage a reality and Folsom's bill pending, representatives John L. MacDonald of Shakopee and James J. Egan of St. Paul spoke against it, but to no avail. It passed the house with a large margin, won approval in the senate after lengthy discussion, and on March 4, 1869, was enacted into law. With the words, there shall be "no classification of scholars with reference to color, social position or nationality by any school trustees . . . without consent of parent or guardian," the state finally forced St. Paul to end segregation in its schools. Black children—many of whom were poor, illiterate, recent arrivals from the South—were legally free to share the city's educational facilities with white children.[33]

In St. Paul many voices expressed concern. The *St. Paul Daily Press* commented that black students "will have to take their chances in our already over-crowded schools." It continued, "The greatest difficulty will arise in classifying them, as even the full-grown colored boys will have to go into the lowest primary classes, and in rooms where the desks are arranged for children from six to ten years old."[34]

For white families with deeply held antiblack sentiments, the image of older black youth seated next to younger white children was profoundly unsettling. Perhaps because of the strength of these not-so-private prejudices, only 13 of St. Paul's black students enrolled in the spring of 1869. Prejudice, one historian has written, was surely "a strong deterrent in keeping many Negroes away from the schools they were legally entitled to enter." Six of these 13 attended Franklin Elementary, where they enjoyed the amenities that clearly did not exist at their former school.[35]

Without state action, segregation in St. Paul schools would likely have continued for a long time. Many whites maintained that desegregation was bad for black children because more had been enrolled in the black school than attended white schools after the law was passed. The *St. Paul Pioneer,* sharing the negative views of Superintendent of Schools John Mattocks and Mayor Maxfield, editorialized

> The fact stares us in the face that nearly all of the colored pupils in this city are deprived of the means of obtaining an education, through the public schools, by this law. . . . It was impertinent and worse than unnecessary in its inception, and is wholly wrong and injurious in the operation. . . . That is sufficient cause to warrant its repeal.[36]

The notion that desegregation deprived black children of an education is curious, although it is possible that some black parents agreed that their children would best be educated in all-black classrooms, removed from the hostility they anticipated in predominantly white schools. Moreover, the lowered enrollment may have been connected to some black parents' beliefs that education was pointless when they and their children would be kept on the lowest rungs of society. Whatever the reason, the low enrollment was taken as positive proof by opponents of the new desegregation policy.

In his address to the board of education on April 19, 1869, Maxfield expanded on this view when he insisted that black parents preferred separate school facilities and asked the legislature to cooperate. Calls by white citizens for separate schools persisted for years. As late as 1909, a committee of white parents appeared before the board of education to protest admission of black students to Mattocks School.[37]

Despite its resistance, the city soon felt the positive impact of suffrage and school desegregation. Flowering into social and political maturity by the mid-1870s, blacks formed a literary society, the forerunner of other cultural-improvement efforts. Several black newspapers began publication in the city, further exhibiting the importance of literacy. By the end of the century, despite persistent vestiges of de facto segregation, the community had made great strides. Many blacks entered colleges. They increased their participation in politics. This potential for success in Minnesota attracted other professionals from across the country, who became respected leaders in Minnesota's black and white communities.[38]

While full equality was still in the future, the school desegregation law of 1869 clearly set progress in motion. By 1896, when the concept of "separate but equal" schools was adjudged constitutional in *Plessy v. Ferguson,* St. Paul would not see its utility. To opinion makers, the *Pioneer Press* observed in 1896, *Plessy* was simply a "Jim Crow (railroad) car law," a Supreme Court decision springing from a southern law whose purpose was to manifest the southern way of life. Jim Crow practices existed in St. Paul in other arenas—restrictive covenants denied black ownership of homes in white neighborhoods, for example—but integrated public education was a way of life. St. Paul had officially made peace with the idea of black and white children learning together.[39]

NOTES

From Minnesota History *55 (Winter, 1996–97).*

1. Thomas S. Williamson to former Vermont Governor William Slade, Thomas Smith Williamson and Family papers, Minnesota Historical Society (MHS), St. Paul, quoted in J. Fletcher Williams, *A History of the City of St. Paul to 1875* (1876; reprint, St. Paul: MHS, 1983), 162–64.

2. George H. Gunn, "Peter Garrioch at St. Peter's, 1837," *Minnesota History* 20 (June 1939): 127–28; Williams, *History,* 305, 149.

3. David V. Taylor, "The Blacks," in *They Chose Minnesota: A Survey of the State's Ethnic Groups,* ed. June D. Holmquist (St. Paul: Minnesota Historical Society Press, 1981), 74; Minnesota Territory, *Laws,* 1849, p. 6, 1850, p. 53–54. The bills prohibiting blacks from being referees and from holding village offices are found in Minnesota Territory, *Revised Statutes,* 1851, p. 358–59, and 1854, p. 83, and Minnesota Territory, *House Journal,* 1854, p. 255. Section 5 of St. Paul's charter gave voting rights only to persons eligible "to vote for County or Territorial officers"; *St. Paul Weekly Minnesotian,* Mar. 11, 1854.

4. Minnesota Territory, *Laws,* 1849, p. 41–43; Minnesota Territory, *House Journal,* 1849, p. 68–70.

5. John H. Stevens, *Personal Recollections of Minnesota and Its People* (Minneapolis: Tribune Job Ptg. Co., 1890), 266.

6. Williams, *History,* 228, 266; Taylor, "Blacks," 73.

7. Eugene H. Berwanger, *The Frontier Against Slavery: Western Anti-Negro Prejudice and the Slavery Extension Controversy* (Urbana: University of Illinois Press, 1967), 31; Robert R. Dykstra, *Bright Radical Star: Black Freedom and White Supremacy on the Hawkeye Frontier* (Cambridge: Harvard University Press, 1993), 24.

8. *United States Census,* 1850, p. ix. See also Berwanger, *Frontier,* 30–59.

9. Williams, *History,* 364; Taylor, "Blacks," 73; Patricia C. Harpole and Mary D. Nagle, eds., *Minnesota Territorial Census,* 1850 (St. Paul: MHS, 1972), 37–70.

10. *United States Census,* 1857, Ramsey County entries, microfilm roll 4, MHS: Taylor,

"Blacks," 73, 74; David V. Taylor, "Pilgrim's Progress: Black St. Paul and the Making of an Urban Ghetto, 1870–1930" (Ph.D. diss., University of Minnesota, 1977), 21; Joseph Alexander, "Blacks in Minnesota: 1850–1870," unpublished manuscript, 1970, box 375, p. 13–16, Minnesota Ethnic History Project papers, MHS; Earl Spangler, *The Negro in Minnesota* (St. Paul: Dennison, 1961), 26; *St. Paul Minnesota Pioneer,* Sept. 30, 1852. Taylor questions the reported level of black literacy, since a number of the states of origin prohibited teaching blacks to read.

11. *Minnesota Chronicle and Register,* Jan. 6, 1850; Williams, *History,* 244–45; "Early School History in St. Paul," St. Paul Dept. of Education Staff Planning Committee, Apr. 9, 1956, p. 2, St. Paul Public Library.

12. Taylor, "Blacks" 76; *United States Census,* 1850, p. 1004–05; *United States Census,* 1857, Ramsey County entries; *United States Census,* 1860, *Population,* 262. See also Berwanger, *Frontier,* 34.

13. Here and below, *St. Paul Pioneer,* July 29, 1852.

14. Williams, *History,* 334, 347.

15. Taylor, "Blacks," 73, 75; *St. Paul Recorder,* Feb. 28, 1958, p. 3; James K. Benson, "New England of the West: The Emergence of the American Mind in Early St. Paul, Minnesota, 1849–1855 (master's thesis, University of Minnesota, 1970), 45–46; Minnesota Territory, *House Journal,* 1854, p. 258–59.

16. Berwanger, *Frontier,* 22, 112.

17. Leon F. Litwack, *North of Slavery: The Negro in the Free States, 1790–1860* (Chicago: University of Chicago Press, 1961), 114–15.

18. Litwack, *North of Slavery,* 72, 114; Berwanger, *Frontier,* 112.

19. *St. Paul Weekly Pioneer and Democrat,* Nov. 5, 1857; Spangler, *Negro,* 33–34.

20. *St. Paul Recorder,* Feb. 28, 1958, p. 3; Spangler, *Negro,* 34; "Early School History," 3, 12; Taylor, "Blacks," 76; *St. Paul Daily Minnesotian,* Feb. 17, 1859.

21. "Early School History," 12; *St. Paul Recorder,* Feb. 28, 1958, p. 3; Spangler, *Negro,* 34; Benjamin Drew, "Journal," Apr. 18, 1859, microfilm copy, MHS.

22. *St. Paul Daily Minnesotian,* Feb. 17, Mar. 9, 1859.

23. Taylor, "Blacks," 75.

24. *St. Paul Daily Press,* Aug. 10, Oct. 10, 1865; Spangler, *Negro,* 34.

25. *St. Paul Daily Pioneer,* Oct. 10, 1865, Sept. 6, 1867; *St. Paul Daily Press,* Nov. 30, 1867.

26. *St. Paul Daily Pioneer,* Oct. 10, 15, 1865, Sept. 6, 1867; *St. Paul Daily Press,* May 8, 1865, Nov. 30, 1867, Jan. 30, 1868.

27. *St. Paul Daily Press,* Jan. 30, 1868; "A Century of Service: St. Paul Public Schools," 1956, p. 3, copy in author's possession.

28. Minnesota, *General Laws,* 1868, p. 149–50; Gary Libman, "Minnesota and the Struggle for Black Suffrage, 1849–1870" (Ph.D. diss., University of Minnesota, 1972), 154–85; *United States Census,* 1870, *Population and Social Statistics,* 6–7, 40–41; *Legislative Manual,* 1869, p. 89.

29. *Proceedings of the Convention of Colored Citizens of the State of Minnesota* (St. Paul: Press Printing Co., 1869), 7–8, MHS; Williams, *History,* 433, 462.

30. *Proceedings,* 9–10.

31. Minnesota, *House Journal,* 1869, p. 244; Minnesota, *Laws,* 1849, p. 99.

32. *St. Paul Press,* Jan. 20, 27, Feb. 22, 1865; *Owatonna Gazette,* reprinted in *Chatfield Democrat,* Aug. 12, 1865; *Mankato Union,* Mar. 17, 24, 1865.

33. Taylor, "Blacks," 74; *St. Paul Weekly Press,* Mar. 1, 1869; Minnesota, *Laws,* 1869, p. 7.

34. *St. Paul Daily Press,* Mar. 14, 1869.

35. Spangler, *Negro,* 35; *St. Paul Daily Pioneer,* Apr. 13, 1869.

36. *St. Paul Daily Pioneer,* Apr. 13, 1869.

37. St. Paul Board of Education, "Minutes," Apr. 19, 1869, Sept. 1, 1909, quoted in Frank W. Cummings, "Segregated Education in St. Paul, Minnesota" (master's thesis, Macalester College, 1961), 36.

38. Taylor, "Blacks," 78–80. See also Kevin J. Golden, "The Independent Development of Civil Rights in Minnesota, 1849–1910," *William Mitchell Law Review* 17 (1991): 449, 456–60.

39. *St. Paul Pioneer Press,* May 19, 1896; Taylor, "Blacks," 81.

Indian Education and Bureaucracy: The School at Morris, 1887–1909

WILBERT H. AHERN

After the Civil War, the government sought to resolve conflicts with indigenous peoples through assimilation, grouping Native Americans on small, undesirable reservations and subjecting the children to indoctrination through "education." The model was Carlisle Indian School in Carlisle, Pennsylvania. Captain Henry Richard Pratt, the school's founder, stated his goal was to "kill the Indian in him and save the man." He believed assimilation would best be achieved with total immersion in "civilization"—cut hair, school uniforms, white names, strong discipline. Education would include some ability to read, write, and speak in English (speaking any words in native languages was severely punished), exposure to other academic areas like arithmetic and white history, training in manual labor for future employment, and conversion to Christianity.

Wilbert Ahern discusses the particular situation at the Indian school at Morris, Minnesota, first started by Mother Joseph and the Sisters of Mercy. While one of the goals of Indian education was clearly to Christianize the Indians, many of the Washington bureaucrats imagined this would be Protestant Christianity, which did not help the cause of Mother Joseph. A contemporary of the Pipestone Indian School in southwestern Minnesota, the school at Morris demonstrated the tensions and evolution of U.S. Indian education policy at the time.

Fifteen buildings sat empty on a wind-swept knoll in western Minnesota during the winter of 1910. Freshly planted trees and shrubs as well as the new brick facades on the two most substantial buildings gave the grounds an air of expectancy rather than abandonment. Yet both moods were appropriate. These buildings and the associated 292 acres of campus on the eastern edge of Morris in Stevens County were soon to become the University of Minnesota's West Central School of Agriculture and Experimental Station, a new venture in agricultural education. During the preceding two decades, they had served a different enterprise.

These buildings—the earliest dated back to the fall of 1887—had been constructed as the Morris Indian School. It did not last long. After 22 years, the federal government abandoned the school and the policies that created it, suggesting the stillbirth of a comprehensive national system of Indian education. In its score of years, however, the Morris Indian School reflected dramatic shifts in federal Indian policy and the role of education in that policy. Moreover, in the history of this school, one can see, writ small, implications of the emergence of the modern nation-state.

The dreams of Mother Mary Joseph Lynch and her companions in the Convent of Mercy at Morris gave birth to the first Indian school in Morris. Born in Ireland in 1826, Mother Joseph had joined the Sisters of Mercy at the age of 20. She had served with Florence Nightingale in the Crimean War and in 1860 came to America, where she established an industrial school in Brooklyn, New York, and taught in it for 15 years. She then led missions to Michigan and to Minnesota. Independence and determination marked her path. As T. S. Ansley, an inspector for the Department of Interior, observed: "Mother Joseph is a genuine speciman of an Old Country farm woman: a worker, a manager and a close calculator; one who works hard herself and expects everyone around her to do likewise."[1]

The Sisters of Mercy traveled to Morris in 1886 at the invitation of the local parish priest, Father Francis Watry. He wanted them to staff a parochial school, but they came because the Morris location brought them closer to the Indian children with whom they wished to work. The examples of the Benedictines at Collegeville and St. Joseph, the Franciscans at Clontarf, and the Sisters of St. Joseph of Carondelet at Graceville encouraged them to try blending education for white and Indian children. For the Sisters of Mercy, genteel education of prosperous young ladies never had the attraction that mission work for "benighted" Indian children held. Mother Joseph envisioned an industrial training school for Indian girls from 12 to 16 years of age. "More can be done for them at that age," she told the commissioner of Indian affairs.[2]

Her plan coincided with a dramatic shift in federal Indian policy. Even as the costly conquest of the tribes of the Great Plains moved ahead, Indian policy reformers grew influential. These self-styled "Friends of the Indian" advocated assimilation into American culture. The General Allotment Act of 1887 dramatically highlighted the move to destroy tribal relations, but the faith of the reformers in education had the most significant implications for the Office of Indian Affairs. Education had long received lip service from federal policymakers, and most treaties had committed the government to provide schools to the tribes. Beginning with the "peace policy" of President Ulysses S. Grant, however, the school evolved as the linchpin of Indian policy. By 1886 attendance in the Indian schools had more than tripled, and appropriations devoted for them were almost 50 times greater, growing from $37,597.31 in 1873 to $1,788,967.10 in 1886 (in constant 1873 dollars). [3]

The disparity between enrollment and appropriations underscored the difficulty of creating a federal system of education within little more than a decade. Not only the magnitude of the task but prevailing definitions of the role of government mandated that non-governmental agencies, mainly the churches, play an essential role in the first stages of the expansion of Indian education. In 1887 the various religious denominations still managed 35 percent of the Indian boarding schools through contracts with the federal government. The Roman Catholic church educated more Indian students than any other denomination and was responsible for all federally sponsored Indian schools in Minnesota. [4]

At Christmastime 1886, the Reverend Joseph A. Stephan, director of the Bureau of Catholic Indian Missions (BCIM), gave Mother Joseph some good news. She had received a contract for 12 students from the Sisseton and Rosebud agencies. With "a thousand thanks," Mother Joseph revealed a grander scheme. She immediately requested permission to expand enrollment to 50 and began plans to build an Indian school on the edge of Morris. [5]

Although her first trip to South Dakota in April, 1887, recruited only three young children, she enrolled 12 within a few months. South Dakota, however, was not the best source for students. The reservations at Pine Ridge and Rosebud were too far removed. Despite being located at Lake Traverse, only 60 miles west of Morris, the Sisseton-Wahpeton Sioux showed little enthusiasm for sending their children away from home. Both their growing disillusionment with the United States failure to recognize its obligations to them and their lengthy experience with missionary schools encouraged them to keep the schools for their children close to home. In this they had the support of their Indian agent who wished to fill the government school on the reservation. Moreover, those who wanted a Roman Catholic education found the school at Graceville more attractive since it was only half as far away as Morris. [6]

By 1889, however, Mother Joseph discovered an interested community in the Turtle Mountain Ojibwe of north-central North Dakota. The longtime presence of French traders among the Pembina Ojibwe had resulted in their almost universal conversion to Roman Catholicism. In addition, extraordinary poverty had struck these people by the late 1880s. Many of them were métis who had moved to the region following the failure of the second Riel rebellion of 1885 in Manitoba. This population growth came on the heels of a drastic reduction in the geographic boundaries of the reservation occasioned by an arbitrary federal action in 1882. Thus the prospect of sending children and orphans to a place where they would receive room and board as well as acceptable religious instruction must have been attractive to many of the parents and guardians. [7]

In any case, Turtle Mountain students became the mainstay of the school. They arrived in greater numbers than the government was willing to subsidize, stayed for the full terms, and even re-enrolled. To be sure, the sisters' paternalism alienated some of the parents and led to some complaints that they were keeping the children too long. Yet, relative to the subsequent history of the school, complaints were few. No record remains of disciplinary problems or runaways, two common signs of student resistance to the schools. Perhaps this was because Mother Joseph emphasized persuasion rather than coercion and allowed no corporal punishment of the students. The material conditions also were attractive. The food was above standard, with at least one meal per day including meat. By 1893 the dormitories were well ventilated, and each child had his or her own bed, wash basin, soap, and towels. The sisters had invested all their energy and resources into their program.[8]

The school had grown rapidly in five years and now offered a three-year course of study with a staff of 15. The 85 children spent half of their day in the classroom and the other half at work learning "industries." The boys worked in the fields and with the livestock under the supervision of a hired farmer. The girls were trained in cooking, laundry, sewing machine work, making clothes for the boys and themselves, knitting, crocheting, spinning, and weaving. The sisters had acquired 220 acres, which were in cultivation, and they rented 160 acres for hay. A new three-story dormitory and classroom building costing $9,000 was added to bring the capacity of the school to 150 students. Of the $13,110.80 operating budget, the federal subsidy provided $8,772.55 at the rate of 27 per student per quarter. The remainder of the income came from the proceeds of the farm and donations. By 1895 the staff included 24 sisters and a man hired to supervise the Indian boys. The student body of 103 was 13 more than the contract allowed, making it the largest contract Indian school in Minnesota. The students, primarily girls, were older than in other schools. Mother Joseph took pride in their work; samples of their stitchery appeared in the Atlanta Exposition of 1895.[9]

Visiting the school later in that year, James McLaughlin, a special agent for the Secretary of Interior and an experienced member of the Indian service, praised it and the work of the sisters. He concluded: "Everything pertaining to the school and its educational work is wisely and economically conducted with no extravagant notions inculcated, while the pupils manifest a cheerfulness and application in their classroom work and other duties in the respective departments that is remarkable." He went on to recommend that the courses of study be extended from three to five years.[10]

Within a year the school was closed. While this action stands in sharp contrast to the tone of the reports from Mother Joseph or Agent McLaughlin, the progress of the school had not been smooth. McLaughlin's visit there had even been occasioned by complaints. In fact, the statistics of its growth obscured several problems with which the staff constantly struggled. The final closing reflected but one of the problems—a change in the direction of federal policy toward contract schools.

To blame the end of Mother Joseph's dream on Protestant nativism, as some did, is too simple. To be sure, Protestant-Catholic tensions had long complicated American policy toward Indian peoples, but now at work were new forces unleashed by the emergence of a more interdependent, national society. Most relevant to the story of the Morris Indian School, this era inspired some to look toward a more comprehensive, integrated system of schooling, confident that it could incorporate diverse peoples into one nation. If natives had been the basic determinant of Indian policy, the Morris school should have disappeared in 1889 when Thomas Jefferson Morgan became commissioner of Indian affairs. A Baptist minister and educator whose confirmation as commissioner was fought by the BCIM from fear of his anti-Catholicism, Morgan actually awarded the Sisters of Mercy their largest contracts at Morris. His advocacy of education as the basis for Indian policy overrode his qualms about some sectarian schools.[11]

Morgan came into the office with faith that a comprehensive system of schooling for Indians, as for the nation's children as a whole, was the key to civilization and progress. He unveiled his plan at the annual fall meeting of the Lake Mohonk, New York, Conference of the Friends of the Indian. The central component of his system was the grammar school, a boarding school where the greatest number of children would be from 10 to 15 years old. They would be taught the meaning of citizenship, the importance of work, diligence, and thrift, and the value of Christian civilization, as well as the academic studies "ordinarily pursued in similar white schools." As he described the location and plant of such institutions, the appropriateness of the Morris school became apparent: "The schools should be located in the midst of a farming community, remote from reservations, and in the vicinity of railroads and some thriving village or city. The students would thus be free from the great downpull of the camp, and be able to mingle with the civilized people that surround them, and to participate in their civilization. . . . The plant required for a grammar school should include suitable dormitories, school buildings, and shops, and a farm with all needed appointments."[12]

The only way in which the Sisters of Mercy school did not fit was in its sectarian nature. Morgan declared, as one of his general principles, that the "system should be conformed, so far as practicable, to the common-school system now universally adopted in all the States. It should be non-partisan, *non-sectarian*." Yet the phrase, "so far as practicable," was important. He would need an annual appropriation of $3,102,500 to maintain the operation of such a program for the 36,000 school-age Indian children. On top of that would come the cost of construction and maintenance. The 1889 appropriation for Indian education, however, which was higher than ever before and an increase of 14 percent over the previous year, stood only at $1,348,015.

To abandon contracts with the sectarian schools in the face of those budgetary realities would have meant not simply a standstill but a drastic reduction because of the loss of school buildings and inexpensive faculty. Rather than cancel contracts with such schools, therefore, Morgan expanded them. For the short run, at least, he was more interested in bringing schools to more children than in assuring their nonsectarian, let alone their non-Roman Catholic, nature. Thus the Morris Indian school blossomed during the early 1890s.[13]

By 1895, however, the contract system was eroding. In that fiscal year, Congress began reducing the appropriations that could go to sectarian schools. These cutbacks accompanied a depression-born reduction in the over-all appropriations that aggravated the loss to these institutions.[14]

Mother Joseph and her Sisters absorbed successive reductions of 10 and then 15 students in 1894 and 1895, respectively. The 1895 retrenchment placed their school in a precarious financial position. They had built and struggled to maintain a plant with a capacity for 150 students. Twenty-five sisters now taught there. The limits to the income from the farm, even in a good year, and from the subsidies for only 65 students would push them deeper into debt. Yet Mother Joseph was committed to continuing. Special Agent McLaughlin's inspection of the school in November, 1895, gave her hope. Not only did he call for an expansion of the course of study, but he also recommended that it be one of the last contract schools to have its contracts reduced. Instead, the Office of Indian Affairs canceled all contracts with the school as of July 1, 1896.[15]

This action reflected no dissatisfaction with features peculiar to the Morris school or its staff. In 1896 Congress declared it "to be the settled policy of the Government to hereafter make no appropriation whatever for education in any sectarian school." Some mission schools located on reservations where no government schools existed were allowed to continue, albeit with a reduced subsidy. No Catholic nonreservation boarding schools received further contracts. The commissioner of Indian affairs tersely explained the policy shift. When government nonreservation schools were available, sectarian institutions required federal dollars for travel expenses as well as subsidies. To eliminate them saved the most money.[16]

Unstated, however, was the larger rationale behind congressional action that could be traced back to the sentiments articulated by Morgan and other "Friends of the Indian." Fearful of "a distended society," these reformers became more insistent on the separation of church and state. The force behind this action was more than anti-Catholicism. The government must give no aid to forces for diversity such as sectarian schools. The schools must, instead, be a force for homogenizing a population frightening to Victorian Americans in its heterogeneity.[17]

Another expression of this trend was the call for expertise. As government schools took the place of mission schools, professionally trained teachers were to replace missionaries and clerics. Inspector Ansley's criticism of a sister at the Morris school for having a brogue so thick as to be incomprehensible was neither simply anti-Catholic nor picayune. It represented a concern that foreign-born teachers, unless demonstrably assimilated in terms of language and education, could not inculcate American civilization. The struggle for including the staff of Indian schools under civil service regulations reflected an effort to have a trained American corps of teachers.[18]

By 1896, then, a public system of Indian education emerged that had no place for the Sisters of Mercy. Yet to portray the bureaucratization as a smooth evolution would obscure some important dimensions of the Morris Indian School and of the transformation of Indian education. Sectarian opposition in Congress, as well as procedural inefficiencies within the Office of Indian Affairs (OAI), obstructed both the implementation of a rational system and the work of the Sisters of Mercy.

The difficulties appeared most clearly in finances. Partisan wrangles in Congress slowed down the schedule of budget increases called for by the advocates of an educational system. The actual payments of subsidies twice created a severe problem. In 1890 disagreement over the general appropriation bill caused the subsidies to be late. The payment for the July-September, 1890, term did not arrive until February 16, 1891, a delay that could not have come at a worse time for the Morris school. A hailstorm the previous summer destroyed most of its crop, and a severe winter both added to expenses and prevented the sisters from visiting parishes to make collections on behalf of the schools. On top of this, the addition of a $9,000 building had expanded their debt. By early February Mother Joseph feared that the sisters and the school would succumb to their creditors. A short-term loan of $500 from the BCIM and understanding creditors allowed the school to survive. Yet the sisters' record of indebtedness, coupled with the tightening of credit in 1893, made them even less prepared to weather the delay in contracts that occurred in that year. Only a good harvest allowed them to survive.[19]

These delays in subsidy payments were unusual and reflected moments of exceptional parsimony on the part of Congress. A more consistent sign of federal penny-pinching came in travel expenses. The government was supposed to reimburse the school for the cost of travel incurred in bringing and returning students from home to school. Receiving reimbursements was a constant problem for Mother Joseph. Until she received money in advance, she delayed in sending students home. This angered Indian parents and students but was

apparently fully acceptable to the OIA. Indeed, the delay in these reimbursements was compatible with the federal office's effort to keep children separated
from their homes. The correspondence suggests, however, that, especially during the mid-1890s, austerity rather than policy was the paramount factor. For
the long run, the bitterness of parents and students was probably a more important consequence than the frustration experienced by Mother Joseph and
the BCIM.[20]

The fledgling bureaucrats stumbled also in student enrollment. The Office
of Indian Affairs attempted to distribute educational resources more efficiently
by specifying the reservations from which the schools could secure students.
But how exactly to assign the reservations? To the government, geographic
proximity and community need, as measured by expressions of interest by
Indians or their agents, were decisive factors. When Commissioner Morgan further rationalized the system, he added the new ingredient of level of educational achievement. To contract schools interest was more important than
proximity. A related factor, of course, was the influence of the particular religious denomination on the reservation. As a recitation of these factors should
suggest, the designation of eligible recruitment areas was crucial to the survival
of the schools. The contracts, after all, provided subsidies only for those students actually enrolled.

For Mother Joseph, a struggle to achieve access to favorable communities
began with the first contract in 1887 and continued until 1896. While it would
seem that both the government and the schools would be interested in continuity in contracts, practice did not reflect this. For whatever reasons, the Office
of Indian Affairs made several changes in contracts over the years. Mother
Joseph sought to counteract this disruption by clinging to a clause that allowed
students already enrolled to continue. The composition of the student body in
1896, when the school was closed, testified to the success of her approach. Although all contracts after 1891 disallowed recruitment of students from Turtle
Mountain, almost all of the students sent home in 1896 were from the North
Dakota reservation.[21]

A recital of the difficulties the Sisters of Mercy encountered gives force to
Mother Joseph's claim that her group was engaged in Indian education because
of love and a sense of mission. To fill the gap between federal subsidies and the
cost of educating the students, the sisters exhausted not only their energy but
also their capital. Thus, the frustrations that came from working with a federal
agency struggling to rationalize itself were not enough to cause Mother Joseph
to welcome the termination of her ties to the OIA.

The cancellation of the contracts for the Morris school shocked Mother
Joseph. Upon receipt of the notice of termination from the OIA, she wrote to
Father Stephan at the Catholic bureau, "What to do we do not know. We have

expended over $25,000 and have a lovely place. We have no school but this . . . and will have nothing to do now. . . . I feel wretched to have to send away seventy-three children. . . . I hope our Lord will keep me in *my mind* for I never before had such a disappointment."[22]

The shift in federal policy had indeed left Mother Joseph with few alternatives. Without any source of revenue, these autonomous Sisters of Mercy could not continue their work in Indian education. While her religion disqualified her from affiliation with a national system, Mother Joseph's parochialism in regard to the church reduced the aid from that quarter. She did not work well with either the area bishop or the BCIM. Both her independent spirit and her Irishness in a predominantly German archdiocese had led the vicariate to provide neither financial nor moral support from early on in her work. Her disinclination to bow her will or to cede the deed for the school to the BCIM sapped the enthusiasm with which its director would fight on her behalf. The bureau would not provide the revenues to allow the school to continue.[23]

The bureau staff did assist Mother Joseph in achieving her only alternative, the sale of the school to the federal government. Sectarian schools, despite a steady decline following Morgan's move toward a wholly federal system, still had a significant enrollment. The 10 whose contracts were terminated had enrolled more than 600 students in the previous year. With encouragement from the BCIM, the federal Indian Office decided to buy five nonreservation mission schools and continue their work. The Morris school was the only one of the five located in Minnesota.[24]

The transition from contract to government school was an uneasy one because of the congressional decision to implement immediately what had begun as a gradual revision in policy. Launching of the government school required completion of the sale and staffing of a program. Three elements complicated the sale. First, the Sisters of Mercy and the government began with very different estimates of the value of the property—$30,000 and $15,000, respectively. Not surprisingly, the government's estimate prevailed. The only potential customer was the OIA. At the urging of the BCIM, Mother Joseph finally accepted the government offer. A second complicating element was the confusion in titles to Mother Joseph's property because of outstanding mortgages. Her inclination "to make debts" meant that the proceeds of the sale at the government's price went almost entirely to her creditors. Finally, the state legislature had to authorize the sale of land within its boundaries to the federal government.[25]

Upon deciding to buy the school in mid-November, Daniel M. Browning, the recently appointed commissioner of Indian affairs, first met the staffing question by offering the superintendency to Mother Joseph. Pleased that his lobbying had discovered a way to continue a Roman Catholic presence in Indian education, Father E. H. Fitzgerald of the BCIM urged Mother Joseph to accept. Yet his satisfaction was shortlived. By mid-December, Commissioner Browning had instead offered the position to William H. Johnson, then superintendent of a reservation boarding school at the Quapaw Agency, Missouri. Apparently the OIA had intended to hire the Sisters of Mercy only as a transition faculty. In evaluating the school's potential as a federal school, Inspector William Moss had recommended against keeping the sisters as staff. "They have failed in judgment, business management, and are not educators, but nurses," he wrote.[26]

That evaluation might have reflected a bias against the sisters in particular and Catholics in general. Moss had earned the suspicion of the BCIM, but the terms in which he made his criticism were significant. They were not "educators." Where Congress was concerned about the separation of church and state, the Indian Office wanted a professional staff. Operating essentially in the tradition of Morgan, Superintendent of Indian Schools William N. Hailmann believed that a professional education, preferably normal school training, was a prerequisite for a school superintendent. This observation is not to deny that nativism was at work in this time of transition but rather to point out the harmony between the movement toward a trained staff and the removal of the "foreign" sectarian influence. Despite 50 years of experience, Mother Joseph was not an educator![27]

Mother Joseph and seven of the sisters remained in Morris during that bleak winter. Their discovery, first made in the columns of a St. Paul newspaper, that someone else had been hired to superintend the federal school set the tone for the season. The absence of income or any local credit left them close to starvation. Finally Superintendent Johnson's arrival at the end of January brought lease payments for the school. Over the next month he negotiated the purchase from the sisters of the supplies and equipment useful for the school. In the spring the sisters left for Oregon to assume new missions of mercy. Philanthropy gave way to professionalism at Morris.[28]

Johnson began his new duties with enthusiasm. Although the transition involved some unpleasant surprises—no students were present, buildings and grounds had deteriorated, and he had to phase out the nearby St. Paul's Indian School at Clontarf—he had good reasons for optimism. It was a new era. The acting commissioner of Indian affairs endorsed Johnson's plans to improve the industrial education component at Morris and promised an appropriation for remodeling and the construction of new buildings.[29]

The Morris civic leaders followed the transition with enthusiasm and gave support where they could. Perhaps because of her "inclination to make debts," but also because of the opposition of the parish priest, Mother Joseph had found little encouragement in the local community. In contrast, the local newspaper interviewed Johnson upon his arrival and continued with optimistic reports about the progress of the new school. Morris was coming out of the economic depression, and Main Street boosterism was on the rise. The community looked to the federal government's purchase of the school as a further guarantee for economic recovery. By the end of the summer Morris boosters had persuaded Senator Knute Nelson and Congressman Frank Eddy to visit the school, to meet with Johnson and local leaders, and, most important, to advocate appropriations for building renovation. Not only did the community receive Johnson and his plans well, but, he reported, they made the students generally welcome.[30]

By the beginning of 1898 the new era seemed well under way. Johnson's concern about finding students was realistic, but 95 Ojibwe from White Earth Agency were enrolled. The pending absorption of the Clontarf school into the Morris campus would increase the number of students while eliminating a nearby competitor. Johnson's argument that the merger would save $3,020 per annum without consideration of remodeling costs at Clontarf had persuaded the Indian Office to abandon that site. Meanwhile, remodeling of the buildings had begun and a full staff was assembling.[31]

The most obvious changes that occurred with the emergence of the federal stage of Indian education reflected increased resources. The physical plant developed rapidly. Soon after his arrival Johnson recommended the major renovation of two buildings, the construction of a new dormitory, a classroom building, a bathhouse, an independent water system, and the installation of steam heat and electricity. By 1905 these recommendations had been met. The brick buildings were augmented by a superintendent's residence, a separate laundry, and a barn. Early on the school purchased 160 acres of arable land close to the campus to allow the scope of agriculture that had been intended in the original purchase. Inspector John Charles described a modern and prosperous school in 1904.[32]

The increase in average size of staff from 13 to 16 was a less significant change than dramatic differences in personnel background, tenure, and definition of duties. The 14 individuals recruited for the first year of operation were all members of the federal Indian service. That common characteristic assured much less homogeneity than had membership in a religious order. The staff of seven men and seven women included two couples, a married woman, four single women, and five single men. For the first time the staff included Indians. Indeed, half of the staff were Indians—four women and three men, of whom none were teachers. Titles and salaries suggested a clear hierarchy that corresponded to training and also to race: superintendent, teachers, matron, seamstress, and laundress, of whom only the latter was Indian; then assistants for the last three titles, an assistant cook, two Indian assistants, and a watchman, all of whom were Indians. In subsequent years, more titles appeared—principal teacher, industrial teacher, kindergartner, clerk, carpenter, and engineer—

and some were held by Indian staff. During these years the staff experienced constant turnover.[33]

The curriculum continued to emphasize both the academic and the industrial, but, as the proliferation of titles suggests, the components of the curriculum became more defined and in parallel with the recommended course of study promulgated by Estelle Reel, the new federal superintendent of Indian schools. Called an industrial school, the Morris Indian School nevertheless began with a kindergarten program and offered academic instruction through the eighth grade. Whether or not the new teaching staff was better able than the sisters to meet the goal of linking classroom lessons and the world of the Indian students is impossible to determine. At least in the first years, the Morris superintendent agreed with the inspector that they were not fully meeting the more "progressive" model of education. Yet some new features were clearly present. The school regularly, if not annually, graduated students from the eighth grade and enabled them to pass the examination used in the Minnesota public schools. Music became an important feature of the school. By 1903 the staff included a bandmaster and full-time teacher of music. A William Morris Literary Society also was organized for the older students.[34]

While classwork occupied half of the student's day, "domestic or industrial work of a character suited to their age" filled out their program. As with the Sisters of Mercy this involved the girls in domestic and the boys in agricultural work. An emphasis on purely agricultural tasks for the boys had several advantages. It fit the mode of labor that dominated the region; it contributed an income that helped support the costs of the school; and it was in keeping with the OIA's predicting of the likely occupation of Indian students who returned to their home communities.[35]

The Morris school sought with mixed success to add training in other trades. Nonreservation boarding schools were intended to introduce vocations the students could pursue on the reservation or in non-Indian communities. Upon his arrival, Johnson concluded that the severity of the winters required some other industrial training to occupy the boys when weather made agricultural tasks impossible. Blacksmithing was inevitable, but he wished to add harness making as a compatible occupation much in demand in country or city. Before that program was instituted, the construction of new buildings opened up another possibility—carpentry. From 1899 to 1904, the faculty included a carpentry instructor, and the students worked on the campus buildings. When the campus was complete the staff re-introduced the idea of a harness-making shop.[36]

This pattern of limited diversification characterized most nonreservation boarding schools. A few students shared a rarer experience—outing—modeled after the eastern schools, Hampton and Carlisle. As a last step toward assimilating the Indian youth into white culture, those schools placed their students "out" on a farm or in an industry separate from the school during the summers. Seven boys at Morris had such an experience during the summer of 1898—five with farmers, one with a blacksmith, and one as a chore boy with the school's physician. The next record of such a program came in 1902. Now it was directed away from agricultural pursuits and no longer limited to the summer. One boy served as an apprentice in the blacksmith shop and another in the printing office.[37]

Industrial training for the girls reflected the assumption that they would be homemakers. Sewing, cooking, and laundry dominated. Emphasizing sewing, Mother Joseph had hoped to place at least some of her women students in a position to earn their own livelihood. Educators in the Indian service, however, increasingly stressed Indian women as forces for civilization. As Captain Richard Henry Pratt of Carlisle posed the question, "Of what avail is it that the man be hardworking and industrious, . . . if the wife, unskilled in cookery, unused to the needle, with no habits of order or neatness, makes what might be a cheerful, happy home only a wretched abode of filth and squalor?" Thus the core of industrial education for girls became "lessons in housekeeping."[38]

How did this curriculum affect the students who attended the Morris Indian School? Little evidence exists to answer this question. No records of alumni are available. The student records that do survive, however, allow some inferences. A few students did graduate, but most came to the school without the prior education that was expected. Nonreservation schools were supposed to enroll students who knew English and had been to the earliest grades. In 1902, however, 60 of the students at Morris were at the first-grade level. This breakdown in the system might explain part of the low rate of completion, but alienation was an important factor.[39]

Studies of Indian boarding schools in this era suggest that students both accommodated to and resisted their programs. Students who graduated reflected some level of accommodation. Despite the many assaults on their cultures, students did stay and learned the basic skills the school offered. Yet the records also suggest resistance. Discipline problems and running away from the school figured constantly in the annual reports.[40]

School was no longer the totally alien experience for the students that it had been for the previous generation; many of them had relatives or acquaintances who had gone to a federal Indian school. But, like other boarding schools, the Morris program alienated students not necessarily averse to learning to read and write. Only English was to be spoken; the curriculum emphasized the value of the white man's way and at least implicitly the evil of the child's home.

Nevertheless, the student body grew and became more diverse. From 1901 through 1908, average attendance stood close to 160 students, about 10 greater than the nominal capacity. During 1901–1902 a total of 202 students enrolled. Some continued to come from the Turtle Mountain area, but the Ojibwe reservations of northern Minnesota supplied most of the students. A further diversity came through connections of the school's Indian staff with other reservations. Thus, Hugh James, an Oneida assistant teacher, brought several students from his Wisconsin community. The average age of the students increased. Both the superintendents and the OIA inspectors agreed that more "full-blooded" students were coming—that is, students from traditional Indian homes.[41]

The shift to federal control, then, meant qualitative as well as quantitative change. More people moved in and out—students, staff, federal inspectors. More money came for construction and purchases. The school represented for the community the clearest presence of federal government and the advantages thereof. Indeed, the most striking change was the way it served the white population— the local community, the staff of the Indian service, and building contractors. To be sure, the students lived in better quarters, worked with more faculty, including Indians, and had a more advanced curriculum. Yet some problems continued, some new ones emerged, and it was the Indian students and staff members who bore the brunt of them. As the national system strengthened, the difficulties for Indian peoples increased.

In theory, the termination of nonreservation contract schools represented the increased rationality of a federal system of education. Morgan's plan for a hierarchically arranged system of schools had apparently come into being. The day schools and reservation boarding schools would prepare the students to enter the more advanced nonreservation boarding schools, which would complete the education for most students but send the talented and motivated on to advanced industrial schools, such as Carlisle, Hampton, or Haskell, or to normal schools or colleges. No longer would sectarian barriers stand between Morris and other Indian schools. Its staff could concentrate on educating its natural pool of recruits, not waste energies in seeking students.

Several factors, however, operated to obstruct the enrollment of students at Morris, and, more generally, to reveal continued contradictions within the system of Indian education. Indian parents continued to resist sending their children long distances to school if comparable institutions were available nearby. They especially balked at the tendency of the schools, and Morris in particular, to keep students over summer vacation. Continued parental resistance was less surprising than was the cooperation they received from agency officials.[42]

Some of this cooperation undoubtedly showed the influence of tribal members who served as the agents' intermediaries with their tribe. Their children most often fit the model of the students who had received some education and should now go to a more advanced school. Yet if they resisted, the agent was likely to support them. Charles Gardner was such a man on the White Earth reservation. An allottee and successful farmer, he agreed to enroll his children at the Morris school. When, to his surprise, they did not return for the summer vacation, he traveled to Morris to discover why. After an argument with Johnson, Gardner withdrew his children in the superintendent's absence and returned home with them. Johnson's inflamed attack on Gardner's action, including a call for his imprisonment, sparked effective opposition from Agent John H. Sutherland of White Earth. Not only did he commend Gardner's character, but he also charged Johnson with dishonesty for implying that the children would be allowed to return for the vacation and then refusing to do so. The Gardner children did not return to the Morris school.[43]

School superintendents on the reservation also resisted sending advanced students to nonreservation schools. When Morris was in the first year of transition, men such as Charles F. Pierce, school superintendent at the Oneida Agency in Wisconsin, challenged the claim of the Morris school to advanced status. As the school developed, reservation educators continued to resist. Not only did they wish to ensure that their schools be full, but they wanted to fill them with the best students. In contradiction to the OIA's guidelines, reservation educators wished to keep the older, more successful students to help the younger ones. Johnson lamented that the Morris school could secure only the incorrigibles or children with no previous schooling.[44]

The Indian Office paid little attention to these tensions within the system. In only one instance on record in connection with the Morris school did the commissioner reprimand an agent; this was because he billed the Morris school recruiter for lodging, board, and transportation and failed to report this to the OIA. Moreover, the office allowed parents some freedom in choosing schools for their children. The compulsory education law required uncoerced parental consent to enroll a student in a nonreservation school, but they could also choose between several nonreservation boarding schools.[45]

Despite these barriers to enrollment, a superintendent was judged by his ability to keep his school full. Johnson felt the pressure immediately, but his response only aggravated the problem. Gardner was not the only parent he misled about the duration of the stay at school. He refused to release children for vacation, fearful of losing them either to the call of traditional ways or to another school. He also contrived to extend his students' terms from three to five years without their agreement. Tribal leaders at Mille Lacs as well as at White Earth petitioned against his behavior. His encouragement of his Indian staff to bring back students from distant communities without insuring that they would not interfere with other schools earned him the enmity of other educators. Finally, he resorted to the ties that Mother Joseph had established in North Dakota. Less careful than she about assuring that the students from Turtle Mountain were indeed Indians, he fulfilled the prophecy of Inspector Moss that the only students who would come from long distances to attend Morris would be whites trying to pass as Indians in order to secure a free education. For this, and for some other reasons that will be explored below, the commissioner of Indian affairs fired Johnson in the summer of 1901[46]

Within a year the new superintendent, John B. Brown, managed to fill the school and keep it full. His style and the effectiveness of the school certainly had something to do with this success. But Brown was also frustrated in securing suitable students for a nonreservation school aspiring to offer advanced industrial training. Concerned about the future enrollment of the school, Brown expressed that concern in a way that revealed the preoccupation with authority that characterized Indian educators. The competition for students between elements of the school system, he observed, "creates the impression that the parents and children are conferring a great and personal favor on the representative and the school if the children are permitted to go." He wished to reduce the room to maneuver of these "dependent" people. Schools of the same type should have exclusive territories. Students would have some choice between types but would not be able to play off the schools against each other. The Indians must feel beholden to the educators, not vice versa.[47]

Federal superintendents, following Mother Joseph in the frantic quest for pupils, shared her fiscal anxieties. The Morris experience highlights the absence of a federal financial commitment to fulfill the dreams of Morgan and other advocates of education as the instrument for immediate assimilation. Beneath the surface prosperity of new buildings, austerity crippled the school's operation. When appropriations for Indian education dropped to a depression low in 1895, the individual school operated on a budget formula of $167 per capita. Ten years later that same formula existed despite a one-third increase in the cost of supplies. These statistics explain the constant lamentations in the correspondence of Morris school superintendents. They also reveal a growing tendency to equate efficiency with economy.[48]

No matter who was in charge of the school, such federal parsimony had repercussions on the quality of its operation. Johnson's refusal to send children home for vacations, which only aggravated his difficulty in securing students, had been based in large part on his desire to use as little money on transportation as possible. Available food and clothing necessarily deteriorated in quality. Extraordinary expenses met delays. In the midst of a typhoid epidemic, after one child had died and 37 were ill, Brown apologized to his superiors for the deficit caused by hiring the four nurses he needed. Raw sewage continued to be deposited yards from the campus for years before dollars were appropriated to construct an adequate sewer.[49]

At its best, industrial education contributed only haphazard subsistence to a school. Pedagogy took precedence over productivity. Hailmann and Reel, superintendents of Indian schools, recommended guidelines that involved formal instruction in industrialization. But the fiscal poverty contravened policy and reduced industrial education to menial chores. Reflecting his experience at another school, the Winnebago alumnus of Yale University, Henry Roe Cloud, attacked this form of miseducation: "The government should not use the labor of the students to reduce the running expenses of the different schools, but only where the aim is educational, to develop the Indian's efficiency and mastery of the trade.... I worked two years in turning a washing machine in a government school to reduce the running expenses of the institution. It did not take me long to learn how to run the machine and the rest of the two years I nursed a growing hatred for it. Such work is not educative." It may be surmised that Morris subjected its students to similar experiences under the motto, "learning by doing." At least a few parents expressed concern about their children spending too little time in class and too much time doing chores.[50]

In this fiscal climate what quality of faculty could be secured? Morgan and, subsequently, Supervisor Hailmann had stressed the necessity of providing salaries competitive with the public schools. Indeed, the isolated location of even some of the nonreservation schools such as Morris might have required more than average salaries to attract competent staff. While many teachers in federal Indian schools exhibited a near missionary dedication, Morgan and like-minded policymakers felt that a truly public and professional system should not depend upon such zeal. Yet the turnover in staff and the scandals and turmoil that characterized the early years of the federal stage of the Morris Indian School demonstrated the inadequate implementation, if also the wisdom, of this vision.[51]

Johnson and several staff members shared neither the zeal nor the moral tenor of Mother Joseph and her colleagues. Scandals growing out of petty rivalries and sexual improprieties among the staff and between the staff and students plagued the school under Johnson's leadership. Johnson himself was accused of raping two Indian students and engaging in adulterous relations with at least one of the staff. Despite his pleas of innocence, these charges added to other complaints against him led to his dismissal.[52]

Indian staff members contributed to the over-all turmoil at the school. They filed some of the complaints against Johnson, attacking his integrity and morality. These Indians, who had adapted to white culture to the point of accepting the value of education and Christianity, found Johnson's behavior to be unchristian and intolerable. Their complaints illustrated the tensions between Indian and white staff and the discomfort of white staff working with Indian peers.[53]

At first, the federal school at Morris seemed to be continuing a trend of Indian policy closely tied to the optimistic assimilationist thrust of Morgan and the "Friends of the Indian." Anxious to demonstrate the value of education and to hasten assimilation through the influence of educated Indians, the Office of Indian Affairs emphasized the hiring of "returned Indians." Among the early Indian staff at Morris were alumni of Carlisle and Hampton. Their status and salaries significantly improved by 1903. At that time they held five supervisory positions and had an average salary close to that of the white staff.[54]

Yet sentiment locally and at headquarters was moving in the opposite direction. Some sign of this had come in 1900. Johnson had temporarily staved off an exposure of his misdeeds by blaming the Indian staff for the strife. Inspector Charles H. Dickson of the OIA endorsed Johnson's credibility: "It has not been my practice to say aught against Indian employes. The policy of the Government in giving preference to Indians in appointments when qualified, is right and proper. With the full-bloods there is but little trouble, but with the mixed-bloods, it is an exception when they do not give more or less disturbance." In November, 1900, Commissioner William A. Jones accepted the recommendation that five of the Morris school Indian staff be fired and replaced, if possible with local white workers.[55]

The return of Indian staff after Johnson's departure and the increased responsibility of the positions by 1903 suggest that Johnson had manufactured the hostility towards Indians. His correspondence reveals an anti-Indian prejudice. Yet the alacrity with which Office of Indian Affairs inspectors and Jones believed Johnson was instructive. During the winter of 1904-05 another purge occurred. Five more Indian staff were dismissed for "objectionable . . . conduct." If this terse phrase from the *Annual Report* left much unexplained, the files contain such equally vague and unsubstantiated assessments as "lacking in discipline and . . . candor." That such explanations sufficed revealed a trend of increased suspicion of Indian employees by the Indian Office.[56]

This attitude was a corollary of a broader and more significant shift in the administration of Indian policy. Lessened confidence in Indian employees corresponded with a greater sense of the resilience of differences between Indians and whites. Policymakers' confidence that assimilation would rapidly occur diminished. With this came the racialistic pattern of thought that held mixed-bloods especially suspect. With it as well came changes in the educational system. The nonreservation boarding school, the conduit for rapid assimilation into white society, lost its central role.[57]

In 1901, even as he quoted figures documenting the impact of education on Indian students, Jones expressed his first skepticism about the nonreservation school. Such schools were obstacles to, not cultivators of, civilization, he argued. They encouraged dependence, not independence, and accustomed the students to a style of living impossible to maintain when they returned to the reservation. The student was indiscriminately drawn out from reservation homes, placed in relatively luxurious surroundings, all with no effort of his own. Wrote Jones: "Here he remains until his education is finished, when he is returned to his home—which by contrast must seem squalid indeed—to the parents whom his education must make it difficult to honor, and left to make his way against the ignorance and bigotry of his tribe. Is it any wonder he fails?"[58]

Morgan and Hailmann had been impressed by the successes of the "returned" students and saw them as ideal candidates for the Indian service. Despite the thrust of his statistics, Jones was less persuaded. He opposed hiring such students on the grounds that it furthered an unhealthy dependence on the government. He lacked confidence in the ability of Indian students to handle the demands of modern life.

The 1901 statement was only a harbinger of a shift in educational policy. Jones continued to downplay the nonreservation boarding school, calling it "an almshouse." The Morris school's difficulty with scarce resources and its treatment of Indian staff probably reflected the new influence. But on the surface these schools received continued support. In 1904 the 25 nonreservation schools comprised, in the commissioner's words, "the largest class of Indian schools in point of capacity and extensive equipment." Reformers at Lake Mohonk were not ready to abandon a comprehensive system of Indian education. Their influence remained compatible with congressmen's reluctance to abandon that component of Indian education that most directly benefited white communities in which they were placed.[59]

Francis E. Leupp, Theodore Roosevelt's appointee as commissioner of Indian affairs in 1905, accomplished the transformation of Indian educational policy. More than Jones, he had solid credentials as a "friend of the Indian," having served as the Washington lobbyist of the Indian Rights Association during the early 1890s. By 1907, however, he had little faith in the nonreservation school. He reiterated his immediate predecessor's concern that such boarding schools undercut self-reliance, also calling them "educational almshouses." At the same time, he offered an additional rationale. The issue of Indian education, he asserted, "pivots on the question whether we shall carry civilization to the Indian or carry the Indian to civilization, and the former seems to me infinitely the wiser plan. To plant our schools among the Indians means to bring the older members of the race within the sphere of influence of which every school is a centre."[60]

Initially, Leupp accompanied his critique with piecemeal reforms. New regulations prohibited nonreservation school personnel from visiting reservations to recruit students. Rules against enrolling youth under 14 in out-of-state boarding schools soon followed.[61]

These changes made more difficult Superintendent Brown's recruitment of students. The opening of a reservation boarding school at Wahpeton, North Dakota, also boded ill for the future of the Morris school. The new school was within 50 miles of Morris and that much closer to the Indian population. Moreover, its curriculum was identical to that of Morris. Enough rumors circulated about the closing of the Morris school that in August, 1908, Brown sent a letter to superintendents and agents reminding them that the school was still open. While informing Leupp of his action he also agreed that the nonreservation school idea had been overdone. Yet he argued that Morris's size and proximity to Indian communities should make it an exception. The main problem, in Brown's estimation, was that the schools were getting too big.[62]

If Leupp wished to reduce the role for such schools as Morris, what would become of them? His answer, first suggested in 1907, both reaffirmed his commitment to education and took into account the interest of congressmen within whose districts such schools were located. As a step toward connecting Indian education to white, state educational systems, Leupp would transfer these schools to state governments, saying: "here is a school plant of some value, in good order. It has industrial shops, a small farm, school-rooms, dormitories. We will make you a gift outright of the whole establishment if you will agree to continue it as an industrial school, and to put a proviso into its charter that for the next ensuing ninety-nine years any Indian who wishes an education there may have his tuition free."[63]

The Indian Appropriations Act of April 30, 1908, authorized Leupp to explore transfers with the governors of selected states. Morris was one of five schools to begin the experiment. Determined lobbying by Morris's state representative, Lewis C. Spooner, gained the support of United States Senator Moses E. Clapp, chairman of the committee on Indian affairs, who introduced a bill for the school's transfer from federal to state control on December 9, 1908. On March 3, 1909, Congress deeded the Morris school to the state of Minnesota on the condition "that Indian pupils shall at all times be admitted to such school free of charge for tuition and on terms of equality with white pupils."[64]

The Morris Indian School closed in early June, 1909. The townspeople who had welcomed the federal school now expressed no regrets about its demise. Rather, civic leaders were enthusiastic about a new school to serve the white citizens of the region. When it appeared that Governor John A. Johnson was balking at accepting the facility, Morris boosters, led by Spooner, entertained members of the legislature and administrators from the University of Minnesota to demonstrate the support for a regional school of agriculture as well as the potential of the campus and community.[65]

Their campaign was successful. The West Central School of Agriculture opened in the fall of 1910. For the next 50 years it offered a boarding school experience for white rural youth under the auspices of the University of Minnesota's Institute of Agriculture. Its staff also operated an agricultural experiment station that provided advice to farmers of the region on scientific agriculture.[66]

In retrospect, the closing of the school merits mixed reactions. An awareness of the ethnocentric assumptions behind Indian education at that time and the documentation of the problems that plagued the school suggest that its termination was timely. Even if one grants that some students gained skills of value to them and to their communities, the argument of the Indian Office that these skills could be gained more effectively closer to the students' homes is compelling.

The transfer in the school's mission occurred, however, in the context of a retreat from meeting treaty obligations to Indian peoples. The move from non-reservation schools was not a step toward giving Indian communities more control over their children's education. When Leupp spoke of the strengths of Indian cultures, he was not, after all, making a pluralistic approach. That strength was a problem, one that he hoped to overcome to some extent by placing more schools in Indian communities as outposts of civilization. But he did not expect totally to solve the problem. He held a more pessimistic view of the character and destiny of Indian peoples than did many of the "Friends of the Indian." While some at the Lake Mohonk conferences were beginning to challenge the injustices of too precipitous a withdrawal of the federal obligations, Leupp appeared to accept them as inevitable. In the area of schooling, his call for a reduction in advanced training was couched in terms of realism, but it coincided with a reduction in federal spending for Indian education.[67]

In particular, the transfer of schools such as Morris to state control effectively closed them to Indian students. The proviso for attendance of Indian students on free and equal terms, which Leupp suggested would satisfy "the sentimental needs," also reflected the fact that the school plant which had been built by funds appropriated on behalf of Indians was given free to the states. In fact, the proviso did appear to be more sentimental than real. During the 50 years of the West Central School of Agriculture, only two Indian youths attended.[68]

The brief history of the Morris Indian School, then, does disclose a rapid shift in white assumptions about and policies toward racial minorities and Indians in particular. In the early 1890s the fight to control Indian education was a part of the engrossing sectarian struggle within American society. By 1910, rather than fighting over providing such services, white Americans were eager to transfer even the educational resources from Indians to themselves. Yet this diminution of services to Indian peoples suggested as well a feature of the emerging liberal state. The bureaucratization of American society showed the increased power of those groups who looked to the national arena to meet their needs. Governmental agencies, despite their growing efficiency and rationality, would ill-serve locally oriented individuals. As the most place-oriented of American peoples, Indians experienced that neglect more rapidly and completely than other localists.

NOTES

From Minnesota History 49 *(Fall, 1984).*

1. The author is indebted to the graduate school and the Morris campus of the University of Minnesota for grant support and to the staffs of Record Group 75, National Archives, at Marquette University, and at the Rodney Briggs Library, Morris.

Ansley to Commissioner of Indian Affairs (CIA), March 17, 1892, Bureau of Indian Affairs (BIA), letters received, National Archives Record Group (NARG) 75, copy in the Morris Indian School Records, 1884–1909, West Central Minnesota History Center (WCMHC), Morris. This collection of duplicates of NARG 75 documents relating to the school will hereinafter be cited as MISR. Information about Mother Mary Joseph Lynch comes from the author's correspondence with the late Sister Cecilia M. Barry. R.S.M., historical researcher for the Sisters of Mercy, Omaha, Nebr., and from Mother Joseph's communications with the Office of Indian Affairs, Washington, D.C., and with the Bureau of Catholic Indian Missions (BCIM), whose archives are in the Marquette University Archives, Milwaukee, Wis., hereinafter cited as ABCIM. See especially Mother Joseph to Father Joseph A. Stephan, March 19, July 9, 1896, and Mother Joseph to the Reverend E. H. Fitzgerald, November 25, 1896, both in ABCIM.

2. Questionnaire, Assumption of Blessed Virgin Mary Church, Morris, in James A. Reardon Papers, Catholic Historical Society, St. Paul; *Morris Tribune,* March 5, 1885, September 19, 1947; Sue Irvin, "The Sisters of Mercy and Sectarian Indian Education," 3, unpublished manuscript, 1973, WCMHC; Mother Joseph to CIA, July [?], 1884, letters received, NARG 75; Sisters of Mercy to Commissioner Thomas J. Morgan, August 21, 1890, MISR; Mother Joseph to Father Stephan, March 24, 1887, ABCIM. The work of schools at Collegeville, St. Joseph, Clontarf, and Graceville, all in Minnesota, is reported in annual reports of the Commissioner of Indian Affairs (ARCIA) for this era.

3. Francis Paul Prucha, *American Indian Policy in Crisis: Christian Reformers and the Indian,* 1865–1900 (Norman, Okla., 1976) offers the most recent and comprehensive treatment of this stage of American Indian policy and the influence of the "Friends of the Indian." See also his valuable collection of primary sources, *Americanizing the American Indians: Writings by the "Friends of the Indian,"* 1880–1900 (Cambridge, Mass., 1973). Wilbert H. Ahern, "Assimilationist Racism: The Case of the 'Friends of the Indian,' " in *Journal of Ethnic Studies,* 4:23–32 (Summer, 1976), examines the central role of education in this phase. Paul Stuart, *The Indian Office,* 127 (Ann Arbor, Mich., 1978).

4. ARCIA, 50 Congress, 1 session, 1887–88, *House Executive Documents,* vol. 2, p. 13–17, 758, 799 (serial 2542). Francis Paul Prucha, *The Churches and the Indian Schools, 1888–1912* (Lincoln, Nebr., 1979), especially chapters 1–3, provides the most complete and balanced analysis of the role of the churches in Indian education and the controversies that arose from this.

5. Stephan to Mother Superior, Morris, December 22, 1886, and Mother Joseph to Stephan, December 27, 1886, both in ABCIM.

6. Stephan to Mother Superior, Morris, December 22, 1886, July 11, 1887, Mother

Joseph to Stephan, April 12, August 24, October 1, 1887, March 12, May 19, June 21, 28, September 19, 1888, Mother Joseph to Charles Lusk, September 8, 1888, all in ABCIM; Mother Joseph to Thomas J. Morgan, CIA, January 6, 1892, MISR; Roy W. Meyer, *History of the Santee Sioux: United States Indian Policy on Trial*, 198–219 (Lincoln, Nebr., 1967).

7. Mother Joseph to Lusk, September 8, 1888, to G. L. Willard, February 26, 1889, both in ABCIM. For more on the federal actions in 1882, see David P. Delorme, "History of the Turtle Mountain Band of Chippewa Indians," in *North Dakota History*, 22:121–134 (July, 1955).

8. Of the 101 students present in March, 1892, the average length of stay at the school was two and one-third years; in June, 1896, 16 of the students sent home had been in attendance in March, 1892. See Morris Indian School statement of attendance, March 31, 1892, and Mother Joseph to Daniel M. Browning, CIA, July 13, 1896, both in MISR. For Turtle Mountain community tensions over duration of students' terms and other matters, see Mother Joseph to Morgan, July 21, 1892, to CIA, July 6, 1893, May 1, 1894, February 16, 1896, to William N. Hailmann, January 28, 1895, all in MISR; James A. Cooper to CIA, April 16, June 26, 1890, Ansley to CIA, March 17, 1892, Mother Joseph to Downing [*Browning*], late April, 1893, James McLaughlin to Secretary of the Interior, November 25, 1895, all in MISR; Mother Joseph to Bureau of Catholic Indian Missions, [May, 1893], in ABCIM.

9. Morris Indian School annual report, July, 1892, Mother Joseph to Hailmann, January 28, 1895, to CIA, April 5, 1895, Browning to Mother Joseph, August 21, 1895, all in MISR; ARCIA, 53 Congress, 3 session, 1894–95, *House Executive Documents*, 501 (serial 3306).

10. McLaughlin to Secretary of the Interior, November 25, 1895, MISR.

11. Even Prucha's balanced treatment of the struggle between Morgan and the BCIM in his *Churches and the Indian Schools* fails to predict an increase in contracts while Morgan was commissioner. For a discussion of the emergence of an interdependent national society, see Robert Wiebe, *The Search for Order* (New York, 1967).

12. Here and below, Thomas J. Morgan, "Supplemental Report on Indian Education," in Prucha, ed., *Americanizing the American Indians*, 221–238, quotations from 231, 230, 234, 224 (emphasis added to "nonsectarian").

13. From 1889 to 1892 the budget allotment for Roman Catholic contract schools increased by 13.5 percent from $347,672 to $394,756. While this was less than the over-all increase for contract schools of 15.4 percent, the Catholic share of the 1892 budget was 64.5 percent. ARCIA, 53 Congress, 2 session, 1893–94, *House Executive Documents*, 19 (serial 3210).

14. Harry J. Sievers, "The Catholic Indian School Issue and the Presidential Election of 1892," in *Catholic Historical Review*, 38:129–155 (July, 1952); ARCIA, 54 Congress, 1 session, 1895–96, *House Documents*, 10 (serial 3382); *Reports for the Department of the Interior for* 1912, 214 (serial 6409); Frederick E. Hoxie, "The End of the Savage: Indian Policy in the United States Senate, 1880–1900," in *Chronicles of Oklahoma*, 55:157–190, especially 173, 175–179 (Summer, 1977), suggests that Democratic disinterest in Indian education was more important than their affinity to the contract school issue. While his conclusion that the 1890s saw a basic shift in Indian policy is important, the contradiction between the Democratic opposition to federal programs and the elimination of the nonfederal component of Indian education under the Cleveland administration needs more explanation.

15. CIA to Mother Joseph, August 10, 1894, July 2, 1896, Mother Joseph to Hailmann, June 19, 1895, all in MISR; McLaughlin to Secretary of the Interior, 1896, in ABCIM.

16. ARCIA, 54 Congress, 2 session, 1896–97, *House Documents,* no. 13, p. 14, 15–17 (serial 3489); Fitzgerald to Mother Joseph, July 8, 1896, ABCIM.

17. Daniel Walker Howe, "Victorian Culture in America," in Howe, ed., *Victorian American ica,* 3–28 (Philadelphia, 1976), and Prucha, *American Indian Policy,* chapter 5, support the interpretation in this paragraph. The analysis of congressional motivation has received too little attention.

18. Ansley to CIA, March 17, 1892, MISR.

19. Stephan to Superintendents, Catholic Indian Schools, August 4, 1890, St. Paul Industrial School Records, Catholic Historical Society; Mother Joseph to Stephan, December 1, 1890, February 4, 26, 28, 1891, December 5, 1893, all in ABCIM; Mother Joseph to Frank C. Armstrong, December 7, 1893, MISR.

20. Mother Joseph to Stephan, June 21, 1888, February 19, 1890, to Lusk, December 28, 1888, to Bishop M. Marty, December 31, 1891, all in ABCIM: Mother Joseph to CIA, August 24, September 9, 1892, August 20, 1894, CIA to Mother Joseph, September 17, 1892, John H. Waugh to CIA, July 16, 1892 (with enclosures), all in MISR.

21. George L. Willard to Mother Joseph, February 19, 26, March 12, November 20, 1889, Mother Joseph to Willard, April 6, 1889, Stephan to Morgan, February 13, 1891, all in ABCIM; Acting CIA to director, BCIM, Washington, D.C., November 29, 1890, Morgan to Mother Joseph, October 26, 1891, Mother Joseph to Browning, July 12, 1896, all in MISR.

22. Mother Joseph to Stephan, July 6, 1896, ABCIM.

23. Mother Joseph to Stephan, May 8, June 28, 1888, February 19, 1890, Stephan to Mother Joseph, March 29, 1890, to Edward Morrell, February 25, 1891, all in ABCIM; *Catholic Directory,* 1887, p. 355.

24. Mother Joseph to Stephan, June 1, July 6, 1896, to Fitzgerald, July 11, 1896, all in ABCIM; ARCIA, 1895, serial 3382, p. 10–12, 1896, serial 3489, p. 14–16; 55 Congress, 2 session, 1897–98, *House Executive Documents,* vol. 13, p. 7 (serial 3641).

25. Mother Joseph to Browning, June 1, 1896, MISR; Lusk to Archbishop John Ireland, September 18, 1896, Fitzgerald to Mother Joseph, July 11, October 18, November 12, 1896, Mother Joseph to Fitzgerald, October 21, 1896, and correspondence between Fitzgerald and Mother Joseph during the first six months of 1897 documenting the complications in the sales, all in ABCIM. Lusk of the BCIM was finally able to announce the completion of the sale in a letter to Mother Joseph, June 15, 1897, ABCIM.

26. Mother Joseph to Stephan, July 6, 1896, to Fitzgerald, August 4, November 21, December 1, 1896, Fitzgerald to Mother Joseph, November 21, 1896, assistant director, BCIM, to Browning, CIA, December 8, 1896, all in ABCIM; Mother Joseph to Browning, June 1, 1896, Browning to William H. Johnson, December 17, 1896, William Moss to CIA, August 15, 1896, all in MISR.

27. Lusk to Stephan, July 31, 1896, ABCIM, reveals the suspicion of Moss. Hailmann had fought for the inclusion of the Indian education staff under the civil service rules. For this and his concern for formal training as a requirement for teachers and superintendents, see his monograph, ARCIA, 1896, serial 3489, p. 347, and his *Education of the Indian,* 6–8, 14–16 (Albany, N.Y., 1900). The continuation of federal subsidies for Hampton and Lincoln institutes, both founded by Protestant denominations, fueled the conviction that antisectarianism was actually anti-Catholicism; Prucha, *Churches and the Indian Schools,* 33, 43.

28. Mother Joseph to Fitzgerald, January 15, 30, March 14, and n.d., 1897, all in ABCIM.

29. Johnson to CIA, February 9, 16, March 4, October 15, 1897, to Hailmann, September 7, 1897, Thomas P. Smith, acting CIA, to Johnson, February 16, 1897, all in MISR.

30. *Morris Tribune,* February 8, 17, April 7, May 12, July 7, August 4, September 22, 1897; editor J. A. Campbell to Knute Nelson, December 6, 1897, attached to Nelson to CIA, December 10, 1897, MISR; ARCIA, 55 Congress, 3 session, 1898–99, *Executive Documents,* 15:373 (serial 3757).

31. Johnson to Hailmann, September 7, November 29, 1897, to CIA, June 18, 1898, supervisor Thomas P. Smith to CIA, May 5, 1898, all in MISR; *Morris Tribune,* October 13, 1897.

32. ARCIA, 1899–1905, serials 3915, 4101, 4290, 4458, 4645, 4798, and 4959, respectively, report improvements in the sections devoted to the Morris school; Charles to CIA, February 25, 1904, MISR.

33. ARCIA, 1898, serial 3757, p. 652. Each annual report, 1898–1905, includes a listing by name of the staff of the school, including title, sex, race, and salary.

34. On the general curricular trends see Hailmann, *Education of the Indian,* 12, 16–18, and David W. Adams, "The Federal Indian Boarding School: A Study of Environment and Response, 1879–1918," chapter 4, Ph.D. thesis, Indiana University, 1975. Specific trends in the Morris school can be followed in the annual reports of the CIA, 1898–1906. For information on graduates see the reports and *Morris Sun,* July 15, 1909. Shortcomings in but also goals of the curriculum are revealed in Charles D. Rakestraw to CIA, October 8, 1899, J. Franklin House to CIA, May 19, 1902, John B. Brown to CIA, June 2, 1902, all in MISR.

35. Hailmann, *Education of the Indian,* 12; Adams, "Federal Indian Boarding School," 151–154.

36. ARCIA, 1899–1905; see especially 58 Congress, 2 session, 1903, *House Documents,* no. 5, p. 420 (serial 4625).

37. A. O. Wright to CIA, December 23, 1898, CIA to superintendent, Morris school, March 12, 1902, Brown to CIA, May 19, 1902, all in MISR.

38. Mother Joseph to CIA, October 11, 1892, to Hailmann, June 19, 1895, Brown to CIA, June 2, 1902, all in MISR; Adams, "Federal Indian Boarding School," 155, 156n.

39. ARCIA, 57 Congress, 1 session, 1901, *House Documents,* no. 5, p. 2–4 (serial 4290); House to CIA, November 8, 1902, MISR.

40. Adams, "Federal Indian Boarding School," chapters 5, 6, provides a valuable discussion of patterns of acquiescence and resistance.

41. Johnson to CIA, December 6, 1898, House to CIA, May 19, 1902, Brown to CIA, February 16, 1903, March 16, 1904, all in MISR.

42. Johnson to CIA, May 10, 1897, July 31, 1899, Chiefs of Mille Lacs Indians to CIA, June 20, 1899, all in MISR; Supervisor Hailmann's concern over the pattern of agent resistance is expressed in ARCIA, 1896, serial 3489, p. 351–354.

43. Johnson to CIA, June 27, 1898, John H. Sutherland to CIA, August 16, 1898, both in MISR.

44. Charles F. Pierce to CIA, November 19, 1898, Johnson to CIA, May 10, 1897, July 31, 1899, Brown to CIA, February 16, 1903, all in MISR.

45. Thomas P. Smith, acting CIA, to Robert M. Allen, White Earth agent, May 14, 1897, MISR. The limits to compulsory education as revised by Commissioner Browning (ARCIA, 1894, serial 3306, p. 6) still stood. The degree to which this law was enforced, however, needs study.

46. Johnson to CIA, June 1, 1898, Gus H. Beaulieu to CIA, June 10, 1899. Only after Johnson's dismissal did his recruitment of "non-Indians" become apparent; see Brown to CIA, November 19, 1901, June 2, 1902, House to CIA, May 19, 1902. Moss's prediction came in a letter to CIA, August 15, 1896. All the above correspondence is in MISR.

47. Brown to Commissioner Francis E. Leupp, January 24, 1906; see also the attached endorsement by J. A. Dortch, early February, 1906, MISR.

48. The general trend of appropriations for Indian education, 1878-1912, is revealed in ARCIA, 1895, serial 3382, p. 12; 58 Congress, 3 session, 1904, *House Documents*, no. 5, p. 446, 571 (serial 4798); *Reports of the Department of the Interior of 1912*, 2:214 (serial 6409).

49. Brown to CIA, October 23, 1904, MISR.

50. Adams, "Federal Indian Boarding Schools," 157-159; Mrs. J. R. Brown to Brown, December[?], 1907, MISR.

51. Morgan, "Supplemental Report on Indian Education," 224, and his "Supplemental Report of the Commissioner of Indian Affairs," ARCIA, 1890, 51 Congress, 2 session, *House Executive Documents*, 12:CXXXV-CXLV (serial 2841), 1896, p. 347, 358 (serial 3489).

52. Commissioner William A. Jones to Secretary of the Interior, July 30, 1901, MISR, summarized the charges against Johnson and recommended his dismissal. The original in letters received, Office of Indian Affairs, NARG 75, includes as an attachment the full brief of the charges against Johnson and his reply. The evidence of staff and student unrest appears as early as late winter 1899; Wright to CIA, April 14, 1899, Cornelius H. Wheelock, et al., to CIA, December 31, 1900, Edwin L. Chalcraft to CIA, February 11, 1901, Eugene MacComas to CIA, June 26, 29, 1901, all in MISR.

53. Wheelock, et al., to CIA, December 31, 1900, MISR.

54. ARCIA, 1896, serial 3489, p. 351-354, 1903, serial 4645, p. 570. White salaries averaged $586 a year in contrast to $508 for Indians. In 1899 the contrast had been $582 to 227.50, for reflecting the lower status positions then held by Indian staff.

55. Dickson to CIA, November 15, 1900, Jones to Johnson, November 24, 1900, Johnson to Jones, December 4, 1900, all in MISR. For an earlier expression of hostility to mixed-bloods, see Wright to CAI, April 14, 1899, MISR.

56. ARCIA, 59 Congress, 1 session, 1905, *House Documents*, 19:421 (serial 4959); Brown to CIA, February 28, 1906, MISR.

57. Hoxie, "Beyond Savagery," chapter 11 especially, characterizes the shift in assumptions as one from viewing Indians as "an exceptional people" to a "backward race."

58. Here and below, see ARCIA, 1901, serial 4290, p. 2-6, 39-41, 1896, serial 3489, p. 351-354; Hailmann, *Education of the Indian*, 27.

59. ARCIA, 1904, serial 4798, p. 32, 39.

60. Allan Nevins's sketch of Francis Leupp in Dumas Malone, ed., *Dictionary of American Biography*, 11:195 (New York, 1933); ARCIA, *Reports of the Department of the Interior for 1907*, 2:17-26 (serial 5296); Francis E. Leupp, *The Indian and His Problem*, 135-140 (New York, 1910).

61. ARCIA, *Reports of the Department of the Interior for 1908*, 2:17-22 (serial 5453); *Reports of the Department of the Interior for 1909*, 2:17 (serial 5747).

62. 57 Congress, 1 session, *House Report*, no. 2664 (serial 4407); ARCIA, 1907, serial 5296, p. 32; Brown to Superintendents and Agents of the Indian Service, August 15, 1908, to CIA, August 15, 1908, MISR.

63. Leupp to Brown, August 21, 1908, MISR; ARCIA, 1907, serial 5296, p. 17-26; Leupp, *Indian and His Problem*, 138-140.

64. Lewis C. Spooner to Leupp, July 10, 1907, May 26, 1908, Moses E. Clapp to Leupp, July 10, 1907, Leupp to Clapp, November 24, 1908, Charles F. Larrabee, acting CIA, to Spooner, July 6, 1908, all in MISR; *Congressional Record*, 60 Congress, 2 session, 1909, 43:67, 571; ARCIA, 1909, serial 5747, p. 22.

65. The governor's reluctance to accept the school is evidenced in Johnson to Larrabee, October 10, 1908, and to Robert G. Valentine, acting CIA, May 26, 1909, MISR. Johnson's attitude, combined with the failure of the Minnesota legislature to appropriate funds to operate the school in 1909, meant that the new school could not open until the fall of 1910. See also *Morris Sun,* especially May 4, 11, 25, April 8, 15, June 3, 10, 24, July 15, August 26, September 16, 1909.

66. Theodore H. Fenske, ed., "A History of the West Central School of Agriculture," in *The Moccasin,* vol. 50 (1963). This publication celebrated the school's 50th year with a history of the school and the West Central Experimental Station and also recognized the transformation of the campus from the WCSA to the University of Minnesota-Morris, a residential four-year liberal arts college.

67. Leupp, *Indian and His Problem,* 45, 110, 115–150. Earlier evidence of his racialism and yet commitment that policy should continue to indoctrinate the "American way of life" included his "Failure of the Educated American Indian," in *Appleton's Magazine,* 7:594–602 (May, 1906).

68. Fenske to Rodney Briggs, July 24, 1962, Records of the Office of the Provost, University of Minnesota-Morris Archives, Rodney Briggs Library.

Knute Nelson and the Immigration Question

Robert F. Zeidel

*The story of Norwegian immigrants in Minnesota in many ways repre-
sents the challenges faced by every ethnic group who comes to a new
place: what to retain from the old cultural heritage; how far to become
assimilated in order to be accepted. Every immigrant faced this dilemma,
but foreign-born citizens who became active in politics and the democratic process found these issues both personalized and public. Robert
Zeidel's article analyzes the life of Knute Nelson, a Civil War veteran,
the first Norwegian-born U.S. Congressman, a Minnesota governor, and
the first Scandinavian in the U.S. Senate, from the 1880s to his death in
1923. His long career depended on his creating and keeping a winning
coalition in Minnesota's Republican party of "Yankee" and Norwegian
voters in the late nineteenth and early twentieth century, when the immigration question was becoming increasingly difficult. Immigration
became embroiled in labor and urban conflicts and later in the anti-
immigrant hysteria and militant one-hundred-percent-Americanism
generated by American participation in World War I.*

The career of Minnesotan Knute Nelson, the first Norwegian immigrant to
serve in both the U.S. House of Representatives and the Senate, exemplifies the
personal dilemma that ethnicity has posed for foreign-born politicians. From
the 1880s to the 1920s, during Nelson's congressional tenure, millions of immigrants arrived in the United States. Minnesota attracted a significant number of immigrants, especially Germans, Scandinavians, British, and people
from the Russian and Austro-Hungarian Empires. The state's foreign-born
population ranged from 36 percent in 1890 to 20 percent in 1920, with a high
of 544,000 in 1910.[1]

Many Americans distrusted these newcomers, blaming them for a host of
socio-economic maladies and eventually demanding that the federal government reduce their numbers. This demand put ethnic politicians in the predicament of facing a contentious issue directly related to their own foreign birth.
Nelson tried to resolve this difficulty by endorsing restrictive legislation and,
at the same time, praising immigrant virtues, thereby striking an intriguing

balance between his Old Country identity and the majority's expectations in his adopted land.

Conditions during these years of Minnesota's often turbulent transition from a predominantly rural-agrarian state to an increasingly urban-industrial one help to explain the development of Nelson's seemingly contradictory stance. The excellent works of historian Carl H. Chrislock have captured the essence of these chaotic times and are particularly important for understanding Nelson. Chrislock has shown that the "political heterogeneity" of Minnesota's growing foreign-born population "prevented the organization of a solid immigrant voting block." This fragmentation necessitated coalition building with old-stock or native-born Americans. Biographers Millard L. Gieske and Steven J. Keillor have presented Knute Nelson as the embodiment of such a union, calling him a "Norwegian Yankee." Their fine work gives a richly detailed account of Nelson's life while ultimately assessing his era as a time of political failure. Examination of his response to the immigration question, however, shows his mastery of this especially difficult issue.[2]

As a Norwegian immigrant, the politically ascending Nelson no doubt identified with others of foreign birth who wished to improve their lot in America. They, in turn, could look to him as one of their own, as their spokesman. In 1892 John Lind, a Swedish immigrant and U.S. congressman from Minnesota, shared his thoughts on their common obligations: "Both of us are burdened to a certain extent not only with the responsibility of our individual success, but by reason of the peculiarity of our situation with maintaining and furthering the good name and fame of a great people in a strange land." Nelson's transplanted countrymen certainly expected nothing less as they supported him in his bids for elective office.[3]

Yet to succeed in public office, Nelson had both to maintain and transcend his ethnic heritage. He had to preserve his ties to fellow immigrants, especially Minnesota's large Norwegian American community, while at the same time demonstrating that he had assimilated mainstream American values. This balance was especially important in his statewide campaigns for governor and senator, which required broad-based support. Nelson met this challenge by successfully combining his innate ethnic appeal with evidence of an acquired native-born sensibility. Over the course of his career, this dichotomy served him well.

Its formation began with his own immigration and assimilation. Born in Evanger, Norway, seven-year-old Knute and his mother came to the United States in 1849, appropriately arriving in New York City on the Fourth of July. The newcomers moved on to Chicago and eventually to Dane County, Wisconsin. He subsequently studied at the nearby Albion Academy, a decidedly Yankee institution, taking time out to teach school in the predominantly Norwegian American township of Pleasant Springs. The classroom gave him an early opportunity to balance his Norwegian past and American present. He was "Old Country" enough to communicate with immigrant and first-generation children and enough of a "Yankee" to appeal to those with older American roots. During the Civil War, Nelson served in the Fourth Regiment Wisconsin Volunteer Infantry and was both wounded and held as a prisoner of war. At the close of hostilities he returned to Albion, graduating with a bachelor's degree. He thereafter trained for the bar but soon answered the siren call of public service.[4]

State government provided Nelson's political apprenticeship. He first served in the Wisconsin State Assembly, and after his 1871 move to Alexandria, Minnesota, he won election in 1874 to the state Senate. During the Civil War, he had changed his political affiliation to the Republican Party of Abraham Lincoln, abandoning the Democrats because he considered their behavior to be too frequently disloyal and antiwar. He thereafter championed Republicans as saviors of the Union and purveyors of sound fiscal policy and national prosperity. During his first Minnesota campaign, wherein he defeated Van Hoesen, a more experienced opponent, Nelson came across as the candidate who best could advance the region's material interests. This especially meant securing railroad connections. An editorial from the nearby *Fergus Falls Journal*, reprinted in Nelson's hometown *Alexandria Post*, described train service as being the difference between "wealth and poverty... happiness and misery."[5]

Nelson may have wished to concentrate on economic development and other related issues, but ethnic concerns quickly came to the forefront. While still in Wisconsin he had angered his more pious countrymen with his antagonism toward some Lutheran clergymen who advocated parochial, as opposed to public, schools. In Minnesota he lost his first bid for the U.S. Congress in 1876, largely due to the machinations of the state's old-stock Republican elite. In 1882 the creation of the new Fifth District, encompassing the predominantly immigrant regions of northern Minnesota, gave him a second opportunity. Attracting both ethnic and native-born support, Nelson prevailed in a tumultuous three-way race and became the first Norwegian immigrant in the U.S. House of Representatives. He won reelection twice before voluntarily stepping aside in 1889.[6]

Nelson's experiences in the House of Representatives served as a prelude to the more intense immigration-related debates of his later career. He supported an 1885 law to prohibit employers from hiring contract laborers overseas, but many Americans, including petitioners from Nelson's home state, wanted even greater restrictions. Some in Congress also had concluded that it was time to "close the gates." Californian Charles N. Felton made this perfectly clear to Nelson after the Minnesota representative made a seemingly innocuous reference to Norway's seafaring prowess. That small nation, Nelson asserted during debate on mail-steamship subsidies, was "one of the most successful" in terms of nautical accomplishment. Felton took exception to this statement, describing Norway's poor standard of living as "the cheap and the nasty." He then asked why one of Nelson's committees had not produced a bill "to prevent objectionable immigration." Nelson responded by accusing Felton of letting his typically West Coast hatred of the Chinese carry over to "everything else in the shape of a foreigner." This concluded their brief exchange, but it should have sent a clear warning to Nelson and other ethnic lawmakers: immigration was becoming a controversial and volatile issue.[7]

Minnesota's 1892 gubernatorial contest, Nelson's next campaign for public office, bore special witness to the difficulties faced by an ethnic candidate. Agrarian revolt, organized in support of the People's (Populist) Party, had attracted a significant Minnesota following, especially among wheat farmers in the state's northwest, home to many Norwegian Americans. Populist candidates included the firebrand Ignatius Donnelly. Republicans desperately wanted to beat back this rebellious challenge to their hegemony and maintain control of state government and its politically lucrative patronage. Hence they turned to Nelson, in part because he appeared as an orthodox contrast to the insurgent Donnelly. Even so, Nelson received subtle reminders of the need to avoid any hint of militant association or even sympathy. One writer expressed his certainty that "*Radical* Legislation in the Interests of the Granger or any other special clique would not meet with your approval." Such an admonition would have been well taken if Nelson had only been concerned with attracting staid Yankee voters, but he also had to contend with populism's appeal to Scandinavian-immigrant voters.[8]

The ethnic issue quickly surfaced. "No one questions Knute Nelson's stalwart Americanism," asserted R. C. Dunn, publisher of the *Princeton Union,* but some did disparage his ethnic background. "I am a straight Republican, but I can *never* vote for *you or any other man of foreign* descent for the high office [to which] you aspire," wrote one voter, who professed to be writing for thousands of like-minded men. The self-proclaimed patriot acknowledged that Nelson was smart and capable but maintained, "*America must be run by Americans.*" Elsewhere, rumors circulated about an organized effort to discredit Nelson on account of his foreign birth. "It is a shame," decried one backer, "that the native element acts that way, especially against men who have voted longer in this country than some of them had a vote . . . but when they cannot [use us], or we ask favors of them, we are d—d Dutchmen or Norwegians." Nelson's allies even worried that the violent labor dispute at the Carnegie Steel Works, halfway across the country, might somehow prejudice Minnesota's "straight American vote."[9]

To counter such xenophobia, Nelson's supporters played down his ethnicity, instead stressing such things as his Civil War military service. They quickly rebuked those who doubted Nelson's patriotism or asserted that his candidacy was simply a ploy to attract Norwegian voters to the Republican Party. The *Minneapolis Tribune* called him a "straight-forward and brainy citizen . . . an earnest and conscientious public servant." Frank F. Davis, the Hennepin County delegate who seconded Nelson's gubernatorial nomination at the state convention, went even further. Although born in a foreign land, the candidate's record clearly showed that he had "eliminated foreign thought, foreign custom and foreign prejudices from his nature." Nelson had become so "thoroughly American" that the party, by acclamation, had demanded his nomination.[10]

Their fear of a nativist or antiradical backlash notwithstanding, Nelson and his supporters realized that they needed the solid support of predominantly rural Scandinavians and other ethnic voters. Endorsements by foreign-language papers were deemed particularly important. Tams Bixby, secretary of the Republican State Central Committee, worked at securing endorsements or favorable coverage in the Norwegian- and Swedish-language press. He feared that the latter might prove to be more difficult, but other sources indicated broad Scandinavian support. Editors of the Norwegian-Danish daily *Nordvesten* and northern Minnesota's weekly *Scandia* enthusiastically backed his candidacy. The American Bible Society requested a biographical sketch for circulation in its periodicals appealing to Welsh communities.[11]

Organizers sought Nelson's presence at a host of ethnic gatherings, especially local fairs in counties with large numbers of foreign-born voters. Representatives of the Minneapolis Scandinavian Union League wanted the candidate's help in securing the University of Minnesota coliseum for a "gigantic mass-meeting of Scandinavians." When requesting his presence at the Freeborn County fair, a solicitor noted that Nelson's attendance would help in securing Norwegian American votes, many of which had gone to the People's Party ticket two years earlier. Bixby sent Nelson a map, asking him to identify the best places for making speeches in Norwegian and Swedish. "It is easy for a Yankee to be misled in this regard," he explained, "and if I do not get my pointers from a well posted Scandinavian it is very liable to be inaccurate."[12]

Nelson's candidacy succeeded in maintaining the traditional Minnesota-Republican coalition of native-born and Scandinavian voters. Norwegian Americans reported unbounded enthusiasm among their transplanted countrymen, with signs of their interest coming from as far away as Chicago. Having just returned from a visit, the *Nordvesten* editor reported that "'Scandinavians' everywhere is [sic] watching Minnesota and praying for your success." Others offered more specific responses. Reverend L. G. Almen suggested that Nelson's support for temperance measures would be attractive to Swedish and Norwegian Lutherans, and another correspondent asserted that few Scandinavians would vote for him unless he distanced himself from Governor William R. Merriam, the state's reputed Republican boss.[13]

In the election, Nelson eked out a narrow victory over his three People's, Prohibitionist, and Democratic challengers. Ironically, although voters selected him as the alternative to the obstreperous radical agrarianism of Donnelly, Nelson demonstrated great sympathy for embattled farmers, supporting measures to inspect grain elevators, build a state elevator at Duluth, and outlaw certain industrial trusts. Commentators have noted only slight divergence between Nelson and populist Sidney M. Owen, who opposed the governor's successful reelection bid in 1894. Nelson—Norwegian American, reformer, and trustworthy Republican standard bearer—had accomplished the difficult task of appealing to a diverse constituency.[14]

The issue of Nelson's ethnicity did not fade with his election. "Governor Nelson," asserted St. Paul's *North-Western Chronicle,* "seems to have persuaded himself that he has been elected the governor of Norway and Sweden instead of Minnesota." This charge stemmed from his visit to the 1893 Chicago world's fair. While there, Nelson failed to attend the dedication of the Minnesota Building but on the same day took part in a Norwegian liberty celebration. *Skandinaven,* a Chicago periodical, responded that Nelson's administration was "not open to charges of clannishness. It is, in fact, the most thoroughly American administration Minnesota has had for many years." The only legitimate charge was the disproportionately low patronage that had been doled out to Norwegian Americans. In a later speech at the fair, Nelson spoke of assimilation producing men and women "of one language and of one spirit, intensely and truly American."[15]

The public stump provided Governor Nelson with other opportunities to present his ethnic ideas. Amidst increasing demands for more stringent immigration restriction, including calls by his state party for the exclusion of all paupers, criminals, and "other dangerous and undesirable classes," Nelson responded with paeans to immigrant virtue. Minnesota had been settled by a mixture of American Anglo-Saxons, Teutons, and Scandinavians who had built up the state. Immigrants to Minnesota had received full rights soon after their arrival, and they generally had "made an honest use of the gift." In time, new elements would arrive and "assimilate and combine into one people," American in character and "a No. 1 hard specimen of humanity."[16]

In January 1895, when senators were still chosen by state legislatures rather than elected by popular vote, Minnesota lawmakers picked Nelson to succeed William D. Washburn and become the first Scandinavian American to serve in the U.S. Senate. Nelson's tenure, which lasted until his death in 1923, coincided with the nation's contentious effort to resolve the so-called immigration question. For the better part of four decades, amid increased popular agitation, Congress tried to develop an acceptable policy for regulating the quantity and quality of alien newcomers. Republican Party platforms, beginning in 1896, generally favored greater restriction. The Boston-based Immigration Restriction League, which carried on a nationwide campaign, listed Minnesota newspapers, trade unions, and farmers' associations as sympathetic to its cause. Letters from Minnesota organizations to various league leaders indicated sharp and seemingly irreconcilable differences among Nelson's constituents. The loss of support from either side could have scuttled his career. Yet outside pressures were only part of the senator's dilemma.[17]

The immigration debate affected foreign-born leaders personally, requiring them to formulate national policy that touched on their very essence. Biographers Gieske and Keillor have noted that Senator Nelson could never escape his youthful Fourth of July passage through Castle Garden, the pre-Ellis Island entry facility. Some immigrant congressmen, such as German-born Richard Barthold of Missouri and Bohemian-born Adolph Sabath of Illinois, distinguished themselves as ardent antirestrictionists, but Nelson took a different tack. Throughout his long career he succeeded in establishing a middle ground.[18]

This balance paid political dividends. During the years between statehood in 1858 and Nelson's death in 1923, Minnesota sent 15 immigrants to Congress, but most filled only a single two-year term. Irishman James Shields, Minnesota's only other foreign-born U.S. senator, served for one year, 1858–59. Until 1917, just three immigrant representatives, Swedes John Lind and Charles A. Lindbergh and Canadian James T. McCleary, served more than 4 years. Among those who spoke up on the issue, German-born Andrew R. Kiefer (in office from 1893 to 1897) typified immigrant congressmen in his opposition to any changes to existing admission requirements. Interestingly, Lind (1887–93) favored the literacy test, a controversial proposal that would require most adult immigrants be able to read and write some language, because he believed that it would ensure the admission of high-quality immigrants. Nelson agreed, but he did so in his usually balanced manner.[19]

In May and again in December 1896, during his first term as senator, Nelson endorsed the imposition of a literacy test. Such a provision, he averred, would be "entirely in harmony" with the particulars of American government, which necessitated an educated and intelligent electorate. Conversely, giving the vote to the ignorant, "like certain peoples of the Old World, especially in the Russian Empire, would be as dangerous as gunpowder in the hands of a child before a blazing fire." Restrictionists may have cheered such remarks, especially his denigration of eastern Europeans, but Nelson also went to great lengths to praise Europe's "intelligent working people," America's "most desirable" immigrants. This set him apart from most other restrictionists.[20]

Indeed, the senator used most of his long and detailed May speech to highlight the extent to which those of foreign birth had contributed to America's greatness. Describing them as farmers, tradesmen, and unskilled manual laborers, Nelson told how they had worked hard to clear America's forests and build its railroads. Rather than displacing those already on the job, they had occupied positions willingly given to them by native-born workers. Immigrants also had contributed to victories in the War for Independence and the War of the Rebellion. Along with democracy and an abundance of free land, Nelson asserted, America owed its success to the tide of European immigration.

Nelson also repudiated any connection between his views on immigration and those of the virulently anti-Catholic American Protective Association. The A.P.A., which likely had a considerable following in Minnesota, especially among Lutheran Scandinavian Americans, opposed the immigration of non-Protestants. At the time of Nelson's May 14 speech, news of the association's national convention was making the front page of Minnesota newspapers. Maryland Senator Charles H. Gibson, who spoke immediately before Nelson in May, accused literacy-test supporters of fronting for the association, and a later historian has noted that the A.P.A. had tried to encourage Nelson's gubernatorial candidacy among anti-Catholic Norwegians. Nelson railed against Gibson's accusation, saying that nothing "of an A.P.A. nature, or any opposition to the Catholic Church . . . ever entered my mind, and I do not think anything of the kind ever entered the minds of the [Senate immigration] committee."[21]

Nelson then articulated ethnological views far different from those of other literacy-test supporters. Although he used terminology such as *race* and *stock*, indicating at least tacit acceptance of the then-popular notion that ethnic groups represented unique biological types, he did not do so to vilify. Immigrants, he argued, supplied more than mere physical labor. They provided moral, physical, and intellectual additions to American society. As a result, its citizens, although English speaking, were more cosmopolitan, with more pronounced elements of strength and energy, more force and vigor, than the English. The British themselves were an amalgamation of several different races, and this, he said, had made their kingdom the mightiest nation on earth. America's vast immigration had produced an even stronger stock, and the future promised more of the same.

Here, the senator took great pains to refute those who wished to belittle the potential contributions of more recent arrivals. Earlier immigrants, from similar Germanic tribes, had responded almost intuitively to American political, moral, and intellectual conventions. While some now contended that the so-called new immigrants, those from southern and eastern Europe, lacked the qualities necessary for assimilation, Nelson dismissed such arguments as wholly unfounded. The tremendous achievements of each beleaguered nationality, which he described in detail, illustrated its attributes. "A strain of the irrepressible, hot, riotous blood of these nations of southern Europe," he declared, "may be productive of much good. It may infuse into our stolid and phlegmatic German blood an element of vim, force, and fire now absent."

Nelson concluded by refuting two of the most common restrictionist allegations. First, he denied that immigrants adversely affected the labor force. Contrary to the notion that they depressed wages, the influx of new workers prompted existing employees to seek more profitable and prestigious positions, he declared. Earlier immigrants were pushed up the employment ladder by new arrivals. Nelson next used figures compiled by Hastings H. Hart, secretary of the Minnesota Board of Corrections and Charities, to debunk claims that an undue number of the foreign born were criminals. Hart's calculations, adjusted to account for children—an overwhelmingly native-born and non-criminal class—showed that immigrants accounted for a smaller percentage of criminals than the native born in most northern and western states. Nelson attributed immigrant crimes to social and economic pressures. Foreigners usually arrived poor, and their impoverished condition forced them to live in urban slums, where some turned to crime to escape drudgery. Even so, these were the minority; many others arrived poor but worked hard to fulfill their intense desire to become good American citizens.

Nelson's remarks received extensive, favorable coverage. His hometown *Alexandria Post News* called his speech "an able defense of foreign immigration to this country. It has attracted very general attention, and all praise the address for its vigor, individuality and learning." The *Duluth News Tribune* praised the senator as being "more competent" than anyone else due to Minnesota's long-standing interest in immigration, to deliver such a "truthful and eloquent portrayal." By evidently ignoring his initial remarks calling for passage of the literacy test, St. Paul's *Weekly Globe* characterized the speech as being *against* additional immigration restriction.[22]

The Scandinavian American press also responded positively. By fortuitous coincidence, Nelson gave the speech only three days before Syttende Mai, the May 17 celebration of Norwegian independence. Editors conveyed favorable impressions of his remarks by incorporating them into coverage of the ethnic festivities. This made the speech part of a larger tribute to Norwegian culture and history on both sides of the Atlantic, even though the senator had not called any attention to his own ethnic group. Clearly, the editors focused on the praise that Nelson directed toward immigrants in general rather than his endorsement of restriction. As historian Keillor has noted, he "had it both ways."[23]

After considerable and often acrimonious discussion, Congress passed the literacy-test bill, but President Grover Cleveland vetoed it in 1897. This certainly did not resolve the issue. Restrictionists, including those from Minnesota, expressed disappointment and vowed to continue their crusade.[24] Nelson clearly had established himself as one of their number but not as a zealous xenophobic. He instead had adopted a unique stance, one that allowed him to support what can only be described as anti-immigrant legislation while concurrently heaping praise upon its intended object.

Nelson persisted in this vein. Speaking to the Norwegian Old Peoples' Home Society of Chicago in 1905, as Congress prepared to renew its immigration debate, he stressed the benefits of immigration. "Her doors have been wide open," he said of the United States, "and she has received us with a welcome hand." The immigrants, in turn, had supplied necessary manual labor, contributed to the national wealth, and then risen up the economic ranks. America had experienced no difficulty absorbing the newcomers, and they had rapidly and wholeheartedly adapted themselves to its customs and traditions. Of particular importance, they had taken advantage of the nation's public schools. The cumulative effects had resulted in the "physical and intellectual reinforcement" of America's citizenry.[25]

During 1906–07 the immigration question returned to the forefront of congressional debate, and Nelson reiterated his concern for securing "as good a class of immigrants as possible." He once again struck an intriguing balance, devoting almost all of his attention to the benefits of proper distribution. Too many of the newcomers colonized urban ghettoes, where they failed "to become Americanized as swiftly and to become as prosperous and in as good condition as those who go to the West." Nelson had seen this firsthand on a recent visit to New York City's East Side. Its inhabitants stood in bleak contrast to Minnesota's sturdy immigrant pioneers. Therefore, he hoped that his colleagues would support a plan to promote greater immigrant distribution. While Nelson's allusion to bygone sod-buster days may have been outdated, his remarks nonetheless provided yet another opportunity to commend immigrants' contributions to their new nation.[26]

Nelson subsequently admitted his own ambiguity on the matter of immigration. He had voted for three unsuccessful literacy-test bills, he told colleagues in 1916, but he was still not satisfied that the test was the best possible provision. One problem was the likelihood that it would exclude "thrifty, industrious" workers while leaving the door open to educated but worthless "sots." Nelson wished that he could conceive of a rule that would proscribe the "educated tramps—tramps who are filled with socialism, who are quasi anarchists, who come here to exploit the Government of the United States."[27]

Despite these concerns, Nelson still pledged to support the pending literacy-test bill because it was the fairest rule that Congress had yet devised for reducing immigration. Present conditions necessitated its enactment, he believed. He had hoped that more recently arrived southern and eastern Europeans— "good people"—would settle in Minnesota, which needed farm laborers. Unfortunately, they did not, thereby creating the need for greater restriction.

Congress finally passed the literacy test in 1917, but this did not close the immigration debate. The U.S. entry into World War I that year had what has been aptly described as a chilling effect on virtually all aspects of ethnic expression, producing demands for 100-percent loyalty among the foreign born and their progeny. Nelson himself, who for the first time faced direct election rather than legislative appointment under the new seventeenth Amendment, came in for scrutiny during the resultant "anti-hyphenate" frenzy, but the senator's diligent efforts to secure immigrant solidarity for the U.S. war effort clearly established his patriotic credentials. For example, he engineered the appointment of his friend and supporter, Nicolay A. Grevstad, as the Minnesota Commission of Public Safety's monitor of the foreign-language press. His job was to ensure that the various periodicals complied with the Sedition and Espionage Acts by avoiding disloyal sentiments and publishing patriotic material. Nelson also supported the conscription of aliens into the U.S. military. During the 1918 election his backers characterized a vote for him as a Scandinavian American's patriotic duty.[28]

At war's end, legislators returned their attention to the matter of restriction. Initial figures indicated that there would be considerable immigration from war-ravaged Europe. To stop the expected onrush, Congress enacted a draconian quota system, setting annual limits for each immigrant nationality at only 3 percent of its total number in the United States according to the 1910 federal census. Nelson made no public remarks on this new policy, but the final roll-call vote shows that he supported it. At the same time, he voted to defeat an even more severe alternative, which would have prohibited all immigration for two years.[29]

It is difficult to understand the rationale behind Nelson's support for the quotas. The passage of time may have altered his beliefs, making him less positive about immigrants. Some have suggested that preoccupation with family problems, specifically a homicide involving his son-in-law, may have clouded his judgment when it came to other issues. Although either is conceivable, evidence suggests that national conditions played the strongest role. The war's end had ushered in the Red Scare, creating an hysterically antiradical milieu. Nelson had long made clear his disdain for the immigrant "nihilist . . . anarchist, or any of those things." They were to be as enthusiastically condemned as the honest and hard-working man or woman was to be welcomed.[30]

In a letter to Nicolay Grevstad, Nelson disparaged radical tendencies even among his fellow Norwegian Americans, loathing their connection to the agrarian Nonpartisan League. The league's plan for state ownership of various agribusinesses had won the support of many of Minnesota's immigrant farmers, and their conduct dismayed Senator Nelson. "I hope I may live to see a change for the better. . . . I hope they may become more loyal and public spirited," he wrote. Nelson must have felt the same about other ethnic groups' perceived association with radical causes, which likely contributed to his support for the restrictive quotas. His contempt for the allegedly disgraceful would not necessarily conflict with his long held, favorable impressions of more upstanding newcomers.[31]

Knute Nelson died in 1923, just before quotas became the permanent foundation of American immigration policy. Over the course of his long career, Nelson's remarks placed him squarely within the restrictionist camp but not necessarily among those who feared America's immigrant influx. He did consider selective limitation to be a just and proper manner of national self-protection, yet he did not view the "teeming masses" as being inherently bad. He saw in them many positive qualities that would benefit their new society. This was the message that he had developed as a nascent politician on the Wisconsin and Minnesota frontiers and that he carried over to his years in the Senate.

Given this positive attitude, along with his own ethnicity, Nelson's support of restriction cannot be seen as nativism—the dislike of immigrants themselves. He instead connected his ideas about immigration policy with civic duty. New arrivals were expected to be positive and peaceful additions to the nation. Norwegian Americans, whom he considered "radicals by nature," provided an excellent example in that "their prosperity and the freedom of our Government has made them careful and conservative in public and national affairs."[32] He expected other foreign arrivals to behave in a similarly acceptable fashion. By supporting more stringent immigration restriction, Nelson showed his personal concern for preserving America's social order. At the same time, he couched his remarks in such a way as to pay homage to his own immigrant heritage along with that of many million fellow travelers.

Carl Chrislock used the poignant phrase "ethnicity challenged" to explain Norwegian American experiences during World War I. Knute Nelson, who much earlier had sought a career in American politics, had long faced that test. "There would now be no 'immigration problem' to settle," eulogized Wyoming Senator Francis E. Warren, speaking of his deceased Minnesota colleague, "if all who seek our shores and the benefits of our glorious land were made of the same stuff." Paradoxically, it was Norwegian American Nelson's mastery of the immigration question that helped to propel his rise to fame and ensured his long-term success.[33]

NOTES

From Minnesota History 56 (Summer, 1999).

1. United States Census, 1920, Population, 2:36; June D. Holmquist, ed., They Chose Minnesota: A Survey of the State's Ethnic Groups (St. Paul: Minnesota Historical Society Press, 1981), 1–3.

2. Carl H. Chrislock, *The Progressive Era in Minnesota, 1899–1918* (St. Paul: Minnesota Historical Society [MHS], 1971), 32, 33 (quotes)–36; Millard L. Gieske and Steven J. Keillor, *Norwegian Yankee: Knute Nelson and the Failure of American Politics, 1860–1923* (Northfield, Minn.: Norwegian-American Historical Assn., 1995). On failure, see Gieske and Keillor, xii–xiii.

3. Here and below, see, for example, John Lind to Nelson, Mar. 22, 1892, S. E. Olson to Nelson, Mar. 9, Apr. 12, 1892, and M. O. Hall to Nelson, Apr. 15, 1892—all Knute Nelson Papers, MHS, St. Paul.

4. Gieske and Keillor, *Norwegian Yankee,* 3, 10, 13–31, 34–54; Martin W. Odland, *The Life of Knute Nelson* (Minneapolis: Lund Press, 1926). Nelson's birth date is usually given as 1843, but a baptismal certificate filled out by his parson in 1923 gives the date as Feb. 2, 1842; see memorabilia folder, Nelson papers.

5. *Alexandria Post,* Aug. 21, 1874, p. 1; Gieske and Keillor, *Norwegian Yankee,* 48, 55–78.

6. Gieske and Keillor, *Norwegian Yankee,* 64–68, 97–119, 143–44; William W. Folwell, *A History of Minnesota* (St. Paul: MHS, 1969), 3:145–49. By 1889 Nelson apparently considered himself a failure as a congressman.

7. *Congressional Record,* 50th Cong., 1st sess., 1888, vol. 19, pt. 3: 2635, vol. 19, pt. 7: 6275–78.

8. Cal W. Kyte to Nelson, July 20, 1892, Nelson papers; Folwell, *Minnesota,* 3: 195–97; Carlton C. Qualey and Jon A. Gjerde, "The Norwegians," in *They Chose Minnesota,* 236–37; Carl H. Chrislock, "A Cycle in the History of Minnesota Republicanism," *Minnesota History* 39 (Fall 1964): 94–96. Chrislock refers to Nelson's political identity as "conservative liberalism."

9. Editorial by R. C. Dunn, *Minneapolis Journal,* Apr. 5, 1892, clipping; Charles Whitney to Nelson, June 9, 1892; Charles Kittelson to Nelson, July 9, 1892; William Bickel to Nelson, Aug. 18, 1892; C. A. Gilman[?] to Nelson, July 9, 1892—all Nelson papers. For full coverage of the election, see Gieske and Keillor, *Norwegian Yankee,* 145–71. Newspaper clippings are filed chronologically with correspondence in the Nelson papers.

10. Dunn editorial, *Minneapolis Journal,* Apr. 5, 1892; *Duluth Herald,* May 2, 1892; *Duluth News,* May 3, 1892; *Minneapolis Tribune,* Apr. 5, 1892; *St. Paul Pioneer Press,* July 29, 1892—all clippings in Nelson papers.

11. James A. Peterson to Nelson, May 20, 1892; Tams Bixby to Nelson, Aug. 16, 1892; Swan B. Molander to Nelson, Apr. 7, 1892; Søren Listoe to Nelson, Mar. 26, 1892; A. B. Lange to Nelson, June 16, 1892; Joshua T. Evans to Nelson, July 5, 1892—all Nelson papers. It is notable that support came from Listoe, who, 10 years earlier, had been a political foe; see Gieske and Keillor, *Norwegian Yankee,* 123, 398n46.

12. See, for example, P. W. Wildt to Nelson, May 23, 1892; Frank B. Fobes to Nelson, Aug. 20, 1892; F. L. Puffer to Nelson, Aug. 20, 1892; Bixby to Nelson, [1892, in "undated" folder]—all Nelson papers.

13. See, for example, Peter G. Peterson to Nelson, July 4, 1892; S. E. Olson to Nelson, July 9, 1892; C. O. Christianson to P. W[ildt], May 5, 1892; S. Listoe to Nelson, July 6, 1892; Charles Kittelson to Nelson, July 9, 1892; Rev. L. G. Almen to Nelson, July 17, 1892; H. G. Stordock to Nelson, Mar. 19, 1892—all Nelson papers.

14. Theodore C. Blegen, *Minnesota: A History of the State* (Minneapolis: University of Minnesota Press, 1963), 388–90; Chrislock, *Progressive Era,* 11–12. Historian George M. Stephenson contends that Nelson "played a shrewd game in his campaigns to ensnare the Scandinavian vote"; see "The John Lind Papers," *Minnesota History* 17 (June 1936): 161.

15. *Minneapolis Journal,* May 18, 1893; *North-Western Chronicle* (St. Paul), May 26,

1893; *Scandinaven,* quoted in *Scandia* supplement, May 27, 1893, *Daily Globe* (St. Paul), Oct. 14, 1893—all clippings, Nelson papers.

16. *St. Paul Pioneer Press,* July 12, 1894; transcript of Nelson's speech at the Redwood County Fair, in *Redwood Gazette,* Sept. 28, 1893—clippings, Nelson papers.

17. O. C. Gregg, superintendent, State Farmers Institute of Minnesota, to Prescott Hall, Immigration Restriction League, Dec. 10, 1897, Prescott Hall Papers, Houghton Library, Harvard University, Cambridge, Mass.; A. W. Gutridge, Associated Charities of St. Paul, to Joseph Lee, Immigration Restriction League, Joseph Lee Papers, Massachusetts Historical Society, Boston; *Endorsements of the Illiteracy Test,* Immigration Restriction League Publication No. 20 [ca. 1898], *Forcible Demand of the Press for the Further Restriction of Immigration,* League Publication No. 23 [ca. 1898–99], and *Digest of Immigration Statistics,* League Publication No. 30 [ca. 1901–02], all in Widener Library, Harvard University; Republican Party platforms, 1896, 1900, and 1912, in Edward Stanwood, *A History of the Presidency* (Boston: Houghton Mifflin, 1916), 1:536, 2:48, 252. On the politics of being chosen senator, see Gieske and Keillor, *Norwegian Yankee,* 199–220.

18. Gieske and Keillor, *Norwegian Yankee,* 136–37, 341. For background on the immigration debate, see John Higham, *Strangers in the Land: Patterns of American Nativism* (New York: Atheneum, 1978); on Sabath, see p. 303–04. On Barthold, see Robert F. Zeidel, "The Literacy Test for Immigrants: A Question of Progress" (Ph.D. diss., Marquette University, 1986), 85–91.

19. For a debate on the literacy test, see *Congressional Record,* 54th Cong., 2d sess., 1897, vol. 29, pt. 2: 1225–28; George M. Stephenson, *John Lind of Minnesota* (Minneapolis: University of Minnesota Press, 1935), 75–77. On Minnesota congressmen, see Bruce M. White et al., comps., *Minnesota Votes: Election Returns by County for Presidents, Senators, Congressmen, and Governors* (St. Paul: MHS, 1977), especially 222–23, 225.

20. Here and below, *Congressional Record,* 54th Cong., 1st sess. 1896, vol. 18, pt. 6: 5221–26, and 2d sess. 1896, vol. 29, pt. 1: 241–42.

21. Here and three paragraphs below, *Congressional Record,* 1896, vol. 28, pt. 6: 5221–26 (quotes, 5221, 5223). On the A.P.A. see, for example, *Duluth News Tribune,* May 15, 16, 1896, p. 1; *Minneapolis Times,* May 16, 17, 1896, p. 1; Lowell W. Soike, *Norwegian Americans and the Politics of Dissent, 1880–1924* (Northfield, Minn.: Norwegian-American Historical Assn., 1991), 56–62, 82–83. There is no evidence that Nelson embraced the A.P.A.'s message, and he did worry about a "Know Nothing" backlash.

22. *Alexandria Post News,* May 21, 1896, p. 4; *Duluth News Tribune,* May 18, 1896, p. 2; *Weekly Globe,* May 21, 1896, p. 2.

23. Steven J. Keillor, "Scandinavian Americans Seek a Usable Past: Scandinavian Experiences as Public Arguments for American Acts," paper presented at the Northern Great Plains History Conference, Bismarck, No. Dak., Oct. 1997, copy in author's possession. Keillor and others have suggested that Nelson "shrewdly" planned the timing of his speech, but this seems unlikely. The bill came out of committee in February, and Henry Cabot Lodge, its principal author, gave the inaugural endorsement speech on March 16. The Senate took no other action until Marylander Charles Gibson gave the first rebuttal on May 14; only then did Nelson take the floor. Given the bill's contentious nature, it is doubtful that Nelson could have influenced this timing for his own political gain. See *Congressional Record,* 54th Cong., 1st sess., 1896, vol. 28, pt. 2: 1827, vol. 28, pt. 3: 2817–20, vol. 28, pt. 6: 5213–20.

24. O. C. Gregg to Prescott Hall, Dec. 10, 1897, Hall papers.

25. Nelson, speech on Norwegian immigration delivered to the Ninth Annual Festival

of the Norwegian Old Peoples Home Society, Chicago, Apr. 13, 1905, typescript, quotes, p. 6, 8, Nelson papers.

26. *Congressional Record,* 59th Cong., 1st sess., 1906, vol. 40, pt. 8: 7284.

27. Here and below, *Congressional Record,* 64th Cong., 1st sess., 1916, vol. 53, pt. 13: 12,775–76.

28. Carl H. Chrislock, *Ethnicity Challenged: The Upper Midwest Norwegian-American Experience in World War I* (Northfield, Minn.: Norwegian-American Historical Assn., 1981), 24, 47, 68–70, 99–105. For detailed coverage of the commission, see Carl H. Chrislock, *Watchdog of Loyalty: The Minnesota Commission of Public Safety During World War I* (St. Paul: MHS Press, 1991).

29. *Congressional Record,* 67th Cong., 1st sess., 1921, vol. 61, pt. 1: 928–30, 968.

30. *Congressional Record,* 62d Cong., 2d sess., 1912, vol. 48, pt. 2: 1760; Chrislock, *Ethnicity Challenged,* 116, 163n106; Odland, *Knute Nelson,* 364–05.

31. Nelson to Grevstad, Oct. 21, 1920, quoted in Chrislock, *Ethnicity Challenged,* 116.

32. Nelson, Norwegian immigration speech, 20.

33. Francis E. Warren, "Memorial Address," in 68th Cong., *Memorial Addresses Delivered in the United States Senate in Memory of Knute Nelson, Late a Senator from Minnesota* (Washington, D.C.: Government Printing Office, 1925), 18.

"Gentiles Preferred":
Minneapolis Jews and Employment, 1920–1950

Laura E. Weber

Discrimination based on both race and ethnicity was a major problem for Jews in Minneapolis from the 1920s into the 1950s. Job discrimination was always a problem for new immigrants, most significantly during times of economic crisis, but even when the economy was rebounding after the Great Depression, Minneapolis Jews still read employment ads stating "Gentile" or "Gentiles Preferred." Laura E. Weber discusses and documents job discrimination for Jews in Minneapolis from the 1920s (when "100% Americanism" continued, even though World War I was over), through the 1930s and the Great Depression (even though Governor Floyd B. Olson, who had grown up in North Minneapolis, had Jewish friends, and spoke some Yiddish, promoted jobs for Jews in state government), and during the 1940s (even though the United States was at war with Nazi Germany). Weber traces changes in the 1950s to several factors: the election of Hubert H. Humphrey as mayor of Minneapolis; his creation of the Mayor's Council on Human Relations; other local groups' advocacy of equal economic opportunities; and changing national postwar attitudes toward religious and racial discrimination.

Minneapolis at the end of the twentieth century has the image of a liberal, progressive city. In the 1990s concerns about discrimination and racism focused on the African-American, Asian-American, American Indian, and Hispanic communities. No one thinks much about the Jews of greater Minneapolis who are, for the most part, economically comfortable, if not well off. Many are integrated into the economy as successful business owners, professionals, or corporate managers. But this benign situation has not always existed. Minneapolis has a dark past with respect to its attitude toward Jews and employment, a difficult era that lasted from the end of World War I until a number of years after the conclusion of World War II. Its peak occurred during the Great Depression.

Economic discrimination against Jews was a problem in virtually every United States metropolitan area during this period. It was acknowledged even at the time, however, that the problem was particularly virulent in Minneapolis, given its size and relatively small number of Jews. What were some of the historical factors that contributed to the economic discrimination against Jews in Minneapolis?

Jews were among the people who arrived in Minneapolis after its major industries were established. "Empire builders," ambitious men of Anglo-Saxon descent who moved to the Midwest after the Civil War, developed the sawmill, flour milling, and railroad industries upon which the city's growth was based. The rank-and-file Minnesota miner, lumberjack, farmer, or railroad worker, however, was more likely to be of Scandinavian or German origin or perhaps of Irish or French-Canadian descent. He had been attracted to the area by the economic opportunities created by the Anglo-Saxon entrepreneurs. The worlds of the industry owner and the worker who toiled for him did not mix.[1]

Jews from Germany were the first statistically significant of the group to settle in Minnesota, attracted first by the commercial opportunities in St. Paul, then Minneapolis, as that city grew. By 1880 it is estimated that 103 Jews lived in Minneapolis. (The total state population was 780,773.) St. Paul had two synagogues by the time the first one was established in Minneapolis in 1878.[2]

Unlike the German Jews who settled earlier in other midwestern towns and cities, those in Minneapolis apparently bypassed the peddler stage. They opened stores, using capital they had acquired from ventures in previous residences in eastern or southern communities. They sold clothing, dry goods, and general furnishings, supplying the needs of the lumberjacks from the north woods and workers in the other industries of the state. These merchants and their families lived a comfortable life in Minneapolis and were on good terms with their non-Jewish neighbors, whom they tried to emulate in external ways. These Jews wanted to take their place in the community, but they associated socially with each other.[3]

Eastern European Jews began to arrive in large numbers in Minneapolis (as in the rest of the country) during the 1880s, as a result of Russian programs in 1881 and rampant anti-Semitism and poor economic conditions in other countries. Most of those who traveled to Minneapolis at this time came alone, earning their livings as peddlers and sending for the rest of their families when they had enough money. The Eastern Europeans settled in neighborhoods with others of their nationality, distinct from the German Jews and each other. The Romanian Jews, for instance, settled in south Minneapolis in the vicinity of Franklin Avenue and Fifteenth Street. The Russians, Poles, and Lithuanians lived on the near north side, but each group had its own synagogue. The German Jews had, by 1915, moved from the central city neighborhood near their business establishments to the lakes district on the west side of town. By the time of the First World War, however, a number of conscious efforts by community leaders, as well as sociological forces and other events, helped break down the nationality barriers that had separated the city's Jews. One of these institutions was the Twin Cities-based Anglo-Jewish newspaper, the *American Jewish World,* founded in 1912.[4]

Few if any Jews in Minnesota participated in the major industries such as iron mining or flour milling in the early years, but a very few became grain merchants. Banking and the lumber industry were also closed to Jews, as to almost anyone not a part of the Anglo-Saxon elite. Areas where the early Jewish settlers did pioneer economically were in manufacturing specialty apparel such as furs and other types of winter clothing, paralleling the role Jews took in the garment industries of New York. Not until the early 1900s, when Minnesota's Jewish population grew from 6,000 in 1900 to 13,000 in 1910, did Jewish employment in garment and cigar factories become widespread. There, Jewish employers allowed their Orthodox employees to follow their religious practices by closing on Saturdays and Jewish holidays. However, Minneapolis did not have much to offer in the line of light manufacturing, which provided employment to Jews in other large cities. Jews in Minneapolis by the 1920s, for the most part, had to be self-employed, either as businessmen or professionals.[5]

The image of prosperity that colors recollections of the 1920s did not apply in large measure to Minneapolis or Minnesota. Agriculture never really shared in the boom that manufacturing and commerce enjoyed in the 1920s, and agriculture was the cornerstone of the state's economy. Farm machinery and improved methods, which were used to meet the increased demands caused by World War I, only contributed to overproduction when the war was over. Deflation of land values and decline in export markets in Europe also added to the farmers' woes. When farm areas suffered, Minneapolis, the market center, suffered as well.

Minneapolis's other economic mainstays also were in trouble by the 1920s. The once-strong lumber industry dwindled rapidly after 1910. The sawmill towns that sprang up during the lumber boom were left without an economic base, and they shrank or disappeared. Many of the residents descended on "the Cities" looking for work. The opening of the Panama Canal made it cheaper to ship a load of freight from Seattle to New York via canal, then west to the Midwest, than to send it by train from Seattle to the Midwest, shattering James J. Hill's dream of an empire based on rail freight throughout the Northwest. The great flour milling industry of Minneapolis began to move to Buffalo and the South, although financial control remained in the city. Even small and middle-sized businesses were affected, not only by the inevitable lessening of trade caused by the downturn in the main industries, but by the rise of national manufacturing companies, chain-store syndicates, and mail-order houses.[6]

The post–World War I years were marked by a continuation of the 100 percent Americanism brought on by the war, but without an external enemy, these xenophobic feelings were directed inward at recent immigrants and their families. The clamor to restrict immigration resulted in the quota system of 1924.

Historian John Higham wrote of this period: "The Jews faced a sustained agitation that singled them out from the other new immigrant groups blanketed by racial nativism—an agitation that reckoned them the most dangerous force undermining the nation."[7]

Nationally, job opportunities for Jews were narrow, and this first became obvious during the 1920s. Historian Leonard Dinnerstein wrote that Jews did not protest job discrimination nor feel it was unusual; rather, the immigrants and their children *expected* it because of their European experience. It would take two decades before organized protest would have an effect on the situation. A study of anti-Semitism in Minnesota from 1920 to 1960 claims that the end of World War I marked the beginning of almost total exclusion of Jews from participation in civic and social organizations in certain parts of the state. Jews began to find themselves discriminated against more intensely in employment, housing, and resort accommodations. These developments coincided with increased instances of anti-Semitic rhetoric among certain religious leaders.[8]

The local activity of Jewish hoodlums and gangsters in the 1920s also contributed to Minneapolitans' low opinion of Jews. Scandal sheets such as the *Saturday Press* and others that proliferated during this period ceaselessly examined the theme of links among Jewish gangsters, the police department, and the mayor. Even though their readership was not significant, constant battles to suppress and censor them kept the "rags" and their contents highly visible.[9]

Dr. Maurice H. Lefkovits, a rabbi who settled in Minneapolis after World War I and went on to become active in social-welfare agencies, described the state of the Minneapolis Jewish community in 1922. While it was healthy because of its strong religious, cultural, and social-welfare groups, Lefkovits wrote of its status in the larger community in depressing terms: "Minneapolis Jewry enjoys the painful distinction of being the lowest esteemed community in the land so far as the non-Jewish population of the city is concerned."[10]

Higher education as a means of upward mobility for the children of immigrants is a familiar story in American Judaism. Minneapolis residents were no exception. But a college degree in the hand of a Jewish man or woman in the 1920s did not necessarily mean that white-collar jobs were open to them. As a consequence of this discrimination, a large percentage of Jewish men became professionals or independent businessmen. But even as professionals, they faced forms of discrimination. By the mid-1920s they were restricted as to where they could practice. A quota system was enforced in some downtown office buildings, including the LaSalle, Syndicate, Physicians and Surgeons, Besse, and the Donaldson buildings. The Yates Building did not rent to Jews at all. Jewish physicians had difficulty finding hospital residencies, compelling the community to think of building its own hospital.[11]

Nationally, job opportunities for Jews continued to shrink through the 1920s. By the end of the decade, one source indicated that Jews were excluded from

90 percent of the general office jobs in New York City. In Minneapolis Jews did not work in factories as laborers (except some light industry such as garment, specialty manufacturing, and cigar making), nor were they permitted on a rung of the corporate ladder. They instead filled supplemental but necessary roles in the Minneapolis economy as small retailers, salespeople, or professionals.[12]

The first three years of the Great Depression hit Minneapolis no differently from the rest of the nation. The effect was somewhat moderated, however, by the facts that the local economy had been stagnant before 1929 and depended on consumer industries rather than heavy manufacturing. The full impact of the depression hit the Midwest by 1932, as it did in the rest of the nation. During the "winter of despair"—November, 1932 to March, 1933—the economy came to an almost complete halt.[13]

Times of economic panic usually create fertile ground in which seeds of fear and prejudice can grow. By the winter of 1932–33, about 68,500 people were reported jobless in Hennepin County. But having a job was no guarantee of economic security, as hourly wages—already low in Minneapolis—dropped in many industries and work weeks were cut. Some employers attempted to lower costs by utilizing wage-sex differentials, increasing the proportion of lower-paid women workers on the payroll, especially in the laundry and dry cleaning industry. In 1931, Abe Altrowitz, writing in the *American Jewish World*, said that societal dislocation caused by the Great Depression meant discrimination and prejudice were increasing appreciably.[14]

Rabbi C. David Matt wrote in a Rosh Hashana (Jewish New Year) review of Minneapolis in 1930: "It goes without saying that whenever economic conditions are not of the best the surest barometer and the greatest sufferer is the Jew. And since so much of Jewish energy and man-power is devoted to trade and business the strain of economic reverses is felt more heavily by the children of Israel."[15]

Politically, Minnesotans reacted early to the distress of the depression years when they elected Floyd B. Olson governor in 1930, the first on the Farmer-Labor ticket. The Jewish community of Minneapolis supported Olson from the beginning of his political career. Indeed, each knew the other well. One of Olson's biographers described his north Minneapolis boyhood home as "austere and quarrelsome" and said that Olson found the congenial family life he was seeking in the Jewish households of his neighborhood. He learned Jewish customs and the Yiddish language and even took part in religious services, acting as a "Shabbos goy," one who lights the candles on the Sabbath when religious Jews are forbidden to do any work. "They [the Jews] reciprocated with an affection, trust, and loyalty that grew almost fanatical when the mature Floyd went into politics." Several of his old Jewish friends were part of his administration and that of his elected successor, Elmer Benson. This situation prompted the charge in 1938 that the Farmer-Labor party was run by Jews, and the vicious anti-Semitic campaign of 1938 was perhaps the worst display of public Jew-hatred in Minnesota history.[16]

Floyd Olson's influence was a decisive factor in changing the long-standing bar against Jews working in state government, remembered Edward P. Schwartz, who participated in an oral history project on the Jewish immigrant experience in Minneapolis. The two or three years following the crash of 1929 were especially rough on the Jews, Schwartz said. The were "the last to get the jobs." Young men never had an opportunity to work in a bank or with the major railroads, and a young woman had no chance at all of working in any public institution or even for the government, he remembered. "The few people that were accepted in the post office and the state were so infinitesimal against the population that it isn't even worth accounting. . . . Maybe 10 or 12 kids got into city government and county government and state government [because they knew someone] until a man like Floyd Olson came along. . . . We saw the pattern, it was very clear, and as time progressed the only way out was to work your way out and that's what the average Jewish kid in this city did."[17]

Nathan M. Shapiro, another interviewee, remembered: "There weren't too many fields open to us in those days unless you had a good WASP name." Shapiro worked for a coreligionist at Max P. Snyder Cut-Rate Cigars in the late 1920s. By that time Jewish people in Minneapolis, as nationally, dominated the cigar business—both production and wholesale and retail sales. The lifting of Prohibition in 1933, first by allowing 3.2 beer, then, at year's end, all liquor, created an economic opportunity for Minneapolis Jews, according to Shapiro. Legal saloons had been shut down for many years and the market was wide open for all, because no one group was already entrenched. Like a great many Jews, Shapiro went into the 3.2 bar-restaurant business with his brother Monroe, whose nickname "Curly" provided the name for their venture. When all liquor was legalized, a number of prominent Jewish families went into the wholesale business. "Here was an opportunity for people who didn't have the opportunities that WASPs had, to go into a business and show what you could do," Shapiro said.[18]

But even this opportunity could be studded with prejudicial roadblocks. "When the country went wet," Cy Young, an executive from Northern States Power Company, located across the street from Curly's, offered to back an off-sale liquor store next door. But Young's banker from First National Bank, "a real anti-Semite from the old school—actually not much different from most of them around here in those days," did not want to give Young a loan "because we were Jews and shouldn't be trusted." With the insistence of Young, however, the loan went through and the venture expanded. Curly's Bar was sometimes called "the Stork Club of the Northwest" because of its excellent food and nationally known entertainment acts.

Minneapolis began to come out of the worst effects of the depression by 1936. Economic improvement was evident there in most categories by June, 1935, and in all areas by June, 1937. Improvement in economic conditions, however, did not bring about a decline in job discrimination and other forms of anti-Semitism in Minneapolis.[19] It was 1936 when William Dudley Pelley's Silver Shirts, a fascist hate group, first actively attempted to recruit members in the Twin Cities. The group made enough of an impact to become the subject of a six-part investigation in the *Minneapolis Journal* in September of that year. The reporter was Arnold Eric Sevareid, fresh from the University of Minnesota, much later to become famous as a network television newscaster. According to Sevareid's reports, the group claimed 6,000 members in Minnesota with 300,000 nationwide. One of the aims of the local group was to segregate all Jews in one city in Minnesota. "Anti-Semitism is the outstanding feature of the Silvershirts [*sic*]," Sevareid wrote.[20]

Some, like Edward Schwartz, looked back and saw Sevareid's series as one of the first public exposures of anti-Semitism in Minneapolis. "This was one of the worst Jew-hating communities in the world through the Thirties and into the Forties [and] if it weren't for the finger of publicity—fellows like Eric Sevareid and his remarkable series on the Silver Shirts—no attention would have been called to it."[21]

The issue surfaced again in 1938, causing more community tension the second time around. In July and August, organizers held three Silver Shirt meetings in Minneapolis. The first drew 350 people, but photos were taken of people exiting, a factor given in explaining the much smaller attendance (65) noted at the second meeting.[22]

Among those present at the first meeting were Dr. George Drake, a member of the Minneapolis School Board, and George K. Belden, automotive company head and president of the Associated Industries of Minneapolis, an employers' group. Rabbi Albert I. Gordon of Adath Jeshurun Synagogue in south Minneapolis immediately wrote a letter to the directors of Associated Industries asking for an explanation of Belden's presence at the meeting. Part of Gordon's letter tactfully and obliquely brought up the relation between the anti-Semitic aims of the Silver Shirts and the professed aims of the employers' association: "Inasmuch as the Associated Industries of Minneapolis is an employer organization that has as one of its professed aims the establishment of amicable relationships between all the classes and groups in this city, the presence of Mr. Belden . . . appears to be a true violation of the purpose and spirit of your organization and should, therefore, be regarded as utterly shameful."[23]

The reply to Gordon said that Belden attended as an individual and not as a representative of the Associated Industries, which as a group abhorred the Silver Shirts. Belden himself also responded to Gordon, saying that he accepted the invitation to the meeting out of curiosity and was "pretty much disgusted" with what he saw and would not attend again. He also trotted out the old cliché often used when someone is accused of discrimination: "I have always had the highest regard for the Jewish people of this community, among whom I have many close friends."[24]

Gordon also sent copies of his letter to Minneapolis's three daily news-papers—the *Star, Journal,* and *Tribune*—where it and the replies to it received front-page coverage. During the next week, letters to the editor blasting the Silver Shirts poured into these newspaper offices, as well as those of the *Minnesota Leader,* the *Minneapolis Labor Review,* and the *American Jewish World.* Editorials agreed with the letter writers. Fundamentalist ministers, led by Dr. William B. Riley of the First Baptist Church in Minneapolis, attempted to de-fend Belden and tried to insinuate that an attempt was made to deprive him of his constitutional right to attend any meeting he wished. This was not the first public stand of certain fundamentalists against the city's Jewish population. Earlier in the year George Mecklenburg, pastor of Wesley Methodist Episcopal Church, had been banned from the airwaves of radio station WTCN after giving an anti-Semitic radio lecture entitled "Who Runs Minneapolis." At the same time that Jews were having severe difficulties securing any kind of job at major corporations, utilities, and banks or as civil servants, Mecklenburg felt that the Jews controlled the city.[25]

As early as 1936 concerned community members had formed the Jewish Anti-Defamation Council of Minneapolis, an informal organization dedicated to investigating the city's profascist climate. Council members realized their need to become a permanent, formal body after the gubernatorial campaign of 1938. The group was renamed the Minnesota Jewish Council in May, 1939, and Samuel L. Scheiner was appointed executive director. (Except for two leaves of two years each, he continued in that role through 1974.) The name was changed again in the 1950s to the Jewish Community Relations Council (JCRC).[26]

In the late 1930s help-wanted ads could still be found in Minnesota news-papers stating "Gentile" or "Gentile preferred." Some Minneapolis Jews pas-sively accepted this discrimination by avoiding the Gentile-dominated mar-ketplace, either by becoming independent businessmen or self-employed professionals. Others tacitly accepted discrimination by attempting to "pass" as non-Jews, changing or lying about their names. But the Jews of Minneapo-lis also worked actively throughout the decade in an organized fashion to counteract job discrimination, both in the practical realm of trying to obtain jobs and also by fighting the attitudes that resulted in discrimination. As one means of response, Scheiner attempted to get the Duluth papers to use "State nationality" instead of the blatant preference. Even though the intention of the substitute phrase was still obvious, apparently the consolation was that sus-ceptible minds would not be exposed to and influenced by the bald truth.[27]

The main agent of this effort, however, was the Jewish Free Employment Bureau (JFEB), known after 1936 as the Jewish Employment Service (JES).

This organization existed before the Great Depression, but that cataclysm, coupled with a growing perception of widespread job discrimination against Jews in Minneapolis, led to a great expansion of its work. Begun as an aid to Eastern European immigrants at the turn of the century, the Jewish bureau was reestablished in 1927. Four years later, Dorothy D. Gordon, wife of Rabbi Albert Gordon, conducted a survey under the auspices of the Council of Jewish Women and the Jewish Family Welfare Association (JFWA) to determine whether conditions merited continuation of the service. It seems odd that it was deemed necessary to conduct a survey, for the JFWA knew well that unemployment was a problem among Jews in the city. In October of 1930 the *American Jewish World* reported that calls for help from the welfare association had never been greater. A large number of the people seeking help were unemployed and hoped for assistance in finding a job rather than direct financial aid. Many of the applicants were reported to be trained in factory, office, and other work and were willing to accept temporary or odd jobs. Furthermore, at the November, 1930, board of directors' meeting of the JFWA, Executive Secretary Anna F. Skolsky reported on 57 unemployed people and suggested that their names and qualifications be given to members of the board, many of whom were employers, and that a list of qualifications, without names, be published in the *American Jewish World*.[28]

The results of the 1931 survey indicated that discrimination, not merely economic depression, was causing some of the problem. Employment agencies were contacted, and eight responded. They revealed that employers who used their services—Jewish as well as Gentile—often qualified their needs with "Gentiles preferred." Between October, 1931, and January, 1932, researchers interviewed 96 employers to try to determine the causes of the discrimination. Some of the common responses were: Jews were too social with their own group and not courteous to others; Jews wanted raises in salary too soon and wanted jobs that did not require physical labor; fear of hiring too many Jews lest the business look "too Jewish"; Jews showed too much familiarity with those in authority; Jewish employees represented the danger of ultimate business competition; and Jews refused to take instructions readily and took off work on Jewish holidays. The survey uncovered some positive comments about Jewish workers too. Jewish employers had good things to say about employees who had shown unusual ability and character. Other attributes given by both Jewish and Gentile employers: Jews made good salespeople, were unusually good at technical details, adjusted easily to new tasks, were often loyal employees, and young women in particular were said to catch on quickly and work at high speed when necessary.[29]

The results of the survey convinced community leaders that an agency was still needed to place Jewish applicants. Consequently, a reorganization and expansion of the employment bureau occurred in October, 1931. A social worker,

Margaret S. Ginsberg, was named director. Her job was to make contacts with employers "with a view to elimination of the attitudes which result in rejection of applicants for jobs because they are Jews," and to find jobs for men and women, skilled and unskilled. Various city employment services claimed that they recognized the value of the new bureau and were willing to cooperate. A cynic might say this was because they were glad to have someone else deal with the problems of Jewish applicants.[30]

In early 1932 the *American Jewish World* reported on the types of applicants; males ranged from unskilled boys to tradesmen such as carpenters, tailors, upholsterers, and printers, and a small group of salesmen and accountants. The females were clustered in the categories of stenographer, bookkeeper, saleswoman, and factory help. The number of domestic workers and laborers was small, about 50 out of the 400 job seekers at that time. Margaret Ginsberg described the applicants as generally well groomed and well mannered. The bureau did a thorough investigation of each person's capabilities, school history, and employment records to see if the common criticisms of Jewish employees were warranted. Only two such cases were found.[31]

Ginsberg was particularly concerned about discrimination by Jewish employers. "If he shows no tolerance, what can be expected of the Gentile employer? . . . If we can induce Jewish employers to let our Jewish applicants apply for positions, we are breaking down certain taboos," she said. After interviewing employers during a five-week period following mid-October, 1931, the bureau began to receive requests for experienced workers in various trades. In November, 17 placements were made, four permanent.

Throughout the year, the *American Jewish World* publicized the employment bureau's placement record. In the first six months of 1932 there were 68 placements, 20 permanent, 42 temporary or seasonal, and six odd jobs. March was the best month with 15 jobs secured. June had the highest number of applicants—144—hopeful that the coming summer would bring seasonal work and temporary jobs filling in for vacationing workers, but only one permanent and nine temporary jobs were found.[32]

By the end of Ginsberg's first year, 635 employers were listed in the files of the agency and about 400 people had applied for jobs. After making this commendable beginning, Margaret Ginsberg resigned as director of the Jewish Free Employment Bureau, citing other interests to which she wished to devote her time.[33]

The bureau was not the only resource available. Unemployed Minneapolis Jews also looked to New Deal programs for relief. In May, 1933, the JFWA brought up the question of encouraging young men to enlist in the Civilian Conservation Corps: by October, 25 had joined and "very fine results were obtained with the young men and . . . all felt they were greatly benefited by the experience." The *American Jewish World*, meanwhile, ran articles pinning hopes for increasing job opportunities on the National Recovery Act (NRA). "The new codes demand more employees. Whatever your 'help' needs . . . call the Jewish Free Employment Bureau," said an article in August, 1933. The next month a story entitled "NRA Gives Impetus to Employment Bureau" claimed that "The inauguration of the 'Blue Eagle' campaign with its resulting expansion of business and industry has given impetus to the activities of the Jewish Free Employment Bureau." The ratio of job applicants to placements was given as 125 to 12 a month. Applicants ranged from "college graduates to scrub women."[34]

The Jewish Free Employment Bureau became part of the Jewish Family Welfare Association in early 1934, ending the joint management by the welfare association, B'nai Brith, and the Council of Jewish Women. One of the reasons for the change was that 1934 saw the beginning of government relief intended to help the unemployed and other needy people, thereby usurping the welfare association's direct relief function. "With the passing of the more acute phases of the Depression in 1933, and the assumption by public agencies of . . . basic needs . . . it was natural that our agency should turn its attention to the effects of the prolonged crisis upon the economic structure of our community," said Charles I. Cooper, who had succeeded Anna Skolsky as executive secretary of the JFWA in 1932.[35]

By May, 1934, a permanent manager for the employment bureau had been hired to replace Margaret Ginsberg. Belle W. Rauch was engaged for a trial period of six months at a salary of one hundred dollars a month. She was to remain with the bureau for the rest of the decade. A three-person employment committee to oversee the bureau was also appointed, chaired by Minneapolis lawyer J. Jesse Hyman. Hyman worked actively throughout 1934 in his new post. He organized a regular series of weekly meetings with Rauch, Cooper, and his committee. He arranged noontime sessions with Jewish businessmen to enlist their support for the JFEB. He also worked on plans to enlist the support of non-Jewish businessmen. The board of directors was extremely pleased with Hyman's "very businesslike and energetic activities," and later, for "splendid work done."[36]

The fruits of Hyman's, Rauch's, and Cooper's efforts were reported at the annual meeting of the JFWA and the Community Fund. From May 1 to December 31, 1934, the employment bureau had found 99 permanent and 203 temporary jobs. It had interviewed 170 Jewish employers, 144 non-Jewish employers, and 2,953 job applicants. Placing Jews in jobs was a task of educating employers, Jewish and non-Jewish, Rauch reported at the meeting. Although the educational process was difficult, definite progress had been made, as companies that had never hired a Jewish employee had now done so. Rauch's comments that she put herself in the employer's place and tried to send over the best possible candidate sounds merely like good business practice, but her next comment—that she told applicants that their prospective employers would judge other Jewish workers by their achievements—shows that even positive action to combat Jewish joblessness was a delicate, defensive operation.[37]

Hyman took advantage of the meeting to address the greatest problem his committee encountered—lack of cooperation by certain Jewish employers, several of whom were present: "It was naturally found that a greater acceptance of the problem and willingness to cooperate was shown by the Jewish employers, but unfortunately they as a whole do not make use of the bureau in a measure at all consistent with its opportunities to perform service. This lack of cooperation or forgetfulness—or call it what you will—is a serious handicap. And I could be quite scathing in my comments in this regard, and if made would affect a number of employers who are in this room at present."[38]

The report of these remarks in the *American Jewish World* brought a flood of applicants into the offices of the employment bureau during the following month, interpreting the criticism "as indication that jobs would be immediately available 'in abundance.'" Rauch commented, however, "It seems that all prospective employes read the criticism.... but I'm afraid the employers haven't read it." In February, 1935, the agency found 20 permanent jobs and 17 temporary ones. Hyman moved from Minneapolis soon afterward, and Jacob G. Cohen, president of a Minneapolis publishing firm, succeeded him as chairman in December.[39]

The year 1936 was a time of cataloguing and counting for the Minneapolis Jewish community. In spring a communal survey was done under the auspices of the Minneapolis Council of Social Agencies with the cooperation of the Minneapolis Federation for Jewish Service. Field work for the survey pointed up the need for authoritative date, so a population census, supervised by Charles Cooper, was conducted during summer.[40]

While the communal study did not include any detailed information about economic status or employment distribution, the census showed there were 16,260 Jews in Minneapolis or 3.5 percent of the city's 1930 total of 464,356. Almost 70 percent of the city's Jews lived on the north side (11,018), with two other areas of lesser concentration to the southwest. Most of the population consisted of Eastern European immigrants and their native-born children, but the immigrants had been in Minneapolis for quite a while—almost half of them for 25 years or more. Only 536 or 8.8 percent of the Jewish population had been in the United States for 15 years or less. In summary the communal survey report said "In many respects the Jewish community reflects the essential economic and social characteristics of Minneapolis, which is a commercial and distributing center, located in the heart of the 'Wheat Empire.' The Jews are largely engaged in small business, with no extremes of wealth. The depression affected the Jewish business man as it did his neighbor, but both came through the experience with less relative loss than was generally evident elsewhere. Although a minority group, the Jewish population has kept pace with the rest of the city in its concern for the general social welfare."[41]

The final report of the survey also gave a convenient summary of the work of the employment bureau through spring, 1936, noting that the JFEB was located across the street from the Minnesota State Employment Service, "whose services are available to Jewish applicants, although it is not used very extensively by them. Though no studies of anti-Jewish discrimination in employment are available, it is felt that discrimination exists and that the Jewish applicant can get a more sympathetic hearing at the Jewish Free Employment Bureau."[42]

The study showed 566 placements were made in 1935, of which 206 were permanent jobs. Among the 942 applicants women outnumbered men, 510 to 432. Of the jobs, 421 fell into six categories: sales (104); factory workers (90); general office assistants (75); stenographers (75); bookkeepers (45); and shipping clerks and stock boys (32). Other occupations where three or more jobs were found were housecleaners, laborers, automobile drivers, practical nurses, waitresses, carpenters, and upholsterers.

To aid its work, the JFEB began making contacts in earnest with both state and federal employment agencies. In March its offices were moved next to the State Annex on Second Avenue South, partly to facilitate greater cooperation. That same month, the bureau was renamed the Jewish Employment Service (JES). Committee chairman Cohen initiated a letter-writing campaign explaining the purpose of the service to area firms, which paid off with a big spring and summer. Workers for spring odd jobs and summer-vacation fill-ins were the greatest number being requested, unlike 1932 when these kinds of work never materialized. Even so, Rauch reported that the service could accommodate twice the number of odd jobs already filled. A serviceman's bonus paid to veterans in mid-June, 1936, by the federal government provided a boost to the work of the JES as well. Businessmen and merchants of Minneapolis hoped to lure the recipients in to spending their bonuses by sending direct-mail advertising. The ad blitz required stenographers, filing clerks, and "classifyers." "Many who have applied for work through the JES have already been given employment because of the bonus. Many more are available," asserted Rauch.[43]

Business was good at the JES for the remainder of 1936, due in part to the efforts of Cohen and Rauch to continue publicizing the service. The *American Jewish World* had begun printing small articles in 1935, advertising on behalf of individual applicants. A typical "article" read: "Salesman Wants Work:

Among the latest applicants at the Jewish Free Employment Bureau is a 35-year-old salesman, who has had experience in general merchandise and men's furnishings. For further information, call Mrs. Rauch." Such ad-articles continued throughout the decade on a regular basis.[44]

At the annual meeting of the Jewish Family Welfare Association held in February, 1938, Executive Secretary Cooper reported, "Our placement service records for 1937 the finding of 606 jobs; but 606 jobs speak volumes." Placement figures for 1939 included a breakdown by age. Positions were secured for 76 people under age 20 and 43 for those over age 40. Jobs for those ages 20 to 30 numbered 235 and for those 30 to 40 years old, 60. The total number of jobs found for those 414 individuals was 619. Jacob Cohen reported on some of the problems of the JES at the 1939 annual meeting: "Applications are taken from every member of the community, and the community looks for positions for children and relatives of members of this board, as well as for relief clients from the Jewish Welfare Association and the Department of Public Welfare.[45]

"It is a gruelling task that Mrs. Rauch . . . has to face every morning when she opens her office, and must go through, by the time she has completed her round of visits, consultations, and phone calls. It is a depressing piece of work, and great credit must be given to her for keeping up the spirit of optimism, as well as for placing as many individuals as she does during the year."

By the end of the decade and at the beginning of the 1940s, the immediate crisis turned from economic depression to war. Europe was already fighting, and the United States was anxiously watching developments there. The economy was given a boost when the United States began selling arms to the Allies. In the 1940 annual report of the JFWA, Jacob Cohen noted that while employment conditions in the United States had improved because of the defense industries, Minnesota had not benefited as few such plants were located in the state. He hoped that as work proceeded on defense contracts, subletting would eventually help Minnesota industries.[46]

Employment figures for 1940 were about the same as 1939, although the greatest number of persons were found temporary jobs. The number of employers working with the agency had increased by 6 percent, yet there was still a call, nine years after the first reorganization of the JES, for more cooperation from the Jewish community.

Also on the agenda for the employment committee in 1940 was a study of the effectiveness of public employment agencies and their degree of cooperation with the JES. There was concern that duplicate services might be offered. The committee was also considering investigating the problem of job discrimination for Jewish applicants. Later in the year, Cohen reported that his committee was undertaking a review of employment discrimination at some of the public utilities and large corporations. By June, 1941, the "improved industrial condition in the community" contributed to the large number of placements made during the month—77, of which 46 were permanent.[47]

The entrance of the United States into World War II in 1941 meant the end of the long-term depression. The needs of the war revitalized American industry in a way the New Deal could not. But it did not mean that anti-Semitism waned in the United States. Historian Dinnerstein noted that one national poll indicated that anti-Semitism in the U.S. "reached its zenith as World War II approached, declined somewhat during the conflagration and rose again immediately after the war ended." In Minneapolis, too, employment discrimination continued. Indeed, it was so persistent that in 1942 Samuel Scheiner wrote, "Employment discrimination work has taken at least three-fourths of my time. We have a full-time man hired for that purpose now." Attempts to boycott Jewish businesses and discrimination by certain insurance companies were other ways economic bias was practiced.[48]

Thus, poor economic conditions alone were not the sole cause of job discrimination. Underlying prejudice on the part of a significant number of Minneapolis citizens that continued during the "good" times of the 1940s was also a factor. Selden Menefee, a journalistic observer of the country during wartime as a representative of the Office of Public Opinion Research of Princeton University, wrote in 1943, "I found almost no evidence of anti-Semitism in the Northwest and West Central States. Except in Minneapolis, no one considered it to be a problem." Three years later in the book *Assignment: U.S.A.,* he reiterated, "Signs of militant anti-Semitism I found to be almost entirely lacking in the Middle West, as in the South and West—except for Minneapolis."[49]

Carey McWilliams's 1946 investigation of anti-Semitism in Minneapolis and lack of it in St. Paul coined a phrase that stuck to describe Minneapolis: "the capitol [*sic*] of anti-semitism in the United States." McWilliams pointed out that the most striking aspect of anti-Semitism in Minneapolis was the lack of significant Jewish participation in the dominant economic activities of the city, such as milling, lumber, transportation, banking, insurance, private utilities, and to a degree, department-store merchandising. This sounds no different from the situation in the 1920s, but actually community attitudes were gradually changing. Acts of discrimination were rarely overt after the war, as they had been in the late 1930s and early 1940s. Instead, they became more "discreet."[50]

Minneapolis Jews by 1946 had carved out influential niches in wholesale meat distribution, scrap iron, cleaning and laundry, jewelry, furniture, furs, theater operation, wholesale and retail liquor, dry goods and wearing apparel, grocery, produce, and drugs and cosmetics. They were somewhat active in manufacturing, but tended chiefly to wholesaling and jobbing. A few were involved in building and demolition. That year Minneapolis had 66 Jewish doctors,

56 dentists, 92 lawyers, and a few each of teachers, journalists, and social workers. A high proportion of the Jewish working population was described as white collar, involved in sales and office jobs.[51]

After the war, feelings of national unity and patriotism brought on by the defeat of fascism caused many to view discrimination against racial and religious minority groups as unacceptable, even un-American. And efforts of American Jewry to fight anti-Semitism began to pay off. No semblance of unity had existed among major American Jewish groups until 1943. By this date, these groups were attempting to use the social sciences to discern the causes of prejudice and develop a cure for it—and to use the legal system to try to eradicate it. The areas these groups focused on included discrimination in employment, education, and immigration.[52]

Attacks on anti-Semitism began coming from non-Jewish sources as well after the war, including two popular 1947 movies, *Crossfire* and *Gentleman's Agreement;* popular magazine articles and books; and scholarly studies. President Harry S Truman appointed blue-ribbon panels to investigate fair employment practices, higher education, and civil rights. After these groups cited examples of widespread prejudice in the country, Truman proposed a major civil rights bill in 1948.

Before the wartime Fair Employment Practices Commission (FEPC) expired on V-J Day, August 25, 1945, Representative Mary T. Norton of New Jersey had already introduced legislation in Congress to make it permanent. In Minnesota the Council for Fair Employment worked to pass the national FEPC bill and similar legislation on the state level. Minneapolis Jews strongly supported the permanent FEPC bill, as Aaron M. Litman, former Farmer-Labor party publicity director, aide to Congressman Magnus Johnson, and executive director of the Jewish Anti-Defamation Council from 1944 to 1946 said: "The Jews in Minneapolis prior to Pearl Harbor [felt], and unless a permanent FEPC bill is adopted, will again feel the sting of employment discrimination."[53]

Hubert H. Humphrey was elected mayor of Minneapolis in 1945 and created the Mayor's Council on Human Relations that same year. This action had come none too soon, according to Litman: "Minneapolis has lagged considerably in the formulation of councils for goodwill in furthering intergroup relations ... only within recent weeks, and as a result of approximately a year of pressures exerted upon conscientious Christians, have we taken steps to formulate sound organizations for intergroup relations under the call of the new mayor, Hubert Humphrey."

A "Mayor's Self-Study" was conducted in 1947, and the results were released in September, 1948. Its purpose was to collect opinions about various racial and religious groups from a representative cross-section of about 2,000 adult residents. The final study showed that 63 percent of all Minneapolis firms hired no blacks, Jews, or Japanese Americans; a qualified black was the most narrowly restricted in occupational choices. Substantiating this claim, a study initiated by the Federation of Women Teachers of Minneapolis found that job discrimination persisted in spite of a 1947 city ordinance that made it unlawful for a person to be denied employment because of race, creed, or color. The report indicated that many retail establishments would not hire a qualified member of certain religious and racial groups as sales or office personnel. As a result of this study, 20 local organizations, including the Urban League, National Association for the Advancement of Colored People, and League of Women Voters, formed the Joint Committee for Employment Opportunity (JCEO) in May, 1947.[54]

Forty-six organizations had joined the JCEO by the end of 1949. The committee had circulated a petition advocating equal opportunity for equal ability in employment, which garnered more than 10,000 signatures. It had initiated a series of "friendly conferences" with managers and heads of retail stores downtown to discuss employment patterns. "Almost without exception, conferences were fruitful and pleasant," said a report. Stickers reading "I should like to see racial and religious EQUALITY practiced in your entire employment policy," were sold for customers to paste on their billing statements. More than 26,000 stickers were purchased in 1948.[55]

Other local groups with aims similar to those of the Mayor's Council on Human Relations and the JCEO after World War II included the United Labor Committee of Minnesota for Human Rights, the Central Body of the Minneapolis Central Labor Union of the AFL, and the local chapter of the National Conference of Christians and Jews. Evidently, all this activity on behalf of intergroup relations, racial and religious tolerance, and antidiscrimination had some effects. In 1949 the National Conference of Christians and Jews cited Minneapolis for having done the most of all cities in the nation in the field of human relations. The mayor's council reported in 1952 that the problem of lack of appointment of Jewish physicians to hospital staffs had been eliminated. (Unmentioned in the report is the fact that the opening of Mt. Sinai Hospital in 1948 created a place where many Jewish physicians and other health professionals could practice.) Frank W. Fager, executive secretary of the mayor's council, said in 1952: "A number of years ago employers wouldn't even talk about changing their policies. There's a far different climate now. Business leaders who in 1946 wouldn't support the FEPC now are working actively in the field. The chamber of commerce is studying a program of education for top management in employing on merit alone."[56]

Minneapolis was a declining commercial center during the period from 1920 to 1950. Jews had been relative latecomers to the city, not arriving in large numbers until the turn of the century. Although other ethnic groups, including Scandinavians, Germans, and Irish, generally were not part of the economic or social elite, they were not denied job opportunities the way Jews were. By the end of the 1920s, Minneapolis Jews were restricted in their economic, social, and civic activities and lived, worked, and socialized among themselves.

In the 1930s the Jewish press began reporting job discrimination nationally. Jewish leaders attempted to call attention to the problem, and magazine articles and books written at the time also testify to its existence. Documentation of anti-Semitism relating to jobs and employment in Minnesota can be found in oral history testimonies of Jews describing Minneapolis during the Great Depression and in numerous places in the papers and records of Jewish groups, now in the collections of the Minnesota Historical Society. However, no scientific surveys were taken during the period to measure or document employment discrimination, nor did the 1936 Jewish community census ask any questions about economic status.

The hard fact remained that during the 1930s and into the 1940s, it was very difficult for Jews to get jobs in Minneapolis. The Jewish Free Employment Bureau (Jewish Employment Service), which was expanded in 1931 to fight job discrimination, could only place a fraction of its applicants over the course of the decade, but the work it did manage to accomplish was significant. Besides finding jobs for people who badly needed them, the employment bureau was a visible, active presence working to overcome stereotypes and to promote tolerance.

The war and postwar attitudes concerning racial and religious discrimination, brought about by the common national effort to defeat totalitarian and racist governments abroad, contributed to a change of attitude in Minneapolis as well. Things did not change overnight, but by the beginning of the 1950s attitudes about Jews and employment that had been matter-of-factly accepted in Minneapolis were becoming openly unacceptable. The fact that Jews of Minneapolis occupy a spectrum of occupational positions from corporate executive to secretary to postal clerk in the economy of the 1990s and the fact that young Jews in Minneapolis today would find the story told here as remote from their own experience as the Great Depression itself is a testament to that change.

NOTES

From Minnesota History *52 (Spring, 1991).*

1. Charles R. Walker, *American City: A Rank-and-File History* (New York: Farrar and Rinehart, 1937), 1–42.

2. Hyman Berman, "The Jews," in *They Chose Minnesota: A Survey of the State's Ethnic Groups,* ed. June D. Holmquist (St. Paul: Minnesota Historical Society [MHS] Press, 1981), 489–91; Albert I. Gordon, *Jews in Transition* (Minneapolis: University of Minnesota Press, 1949), 14; United States, *Census,* 1900, *Population,* 1:2.

3. Gordon, *Jews,* 14–15.

4. Gordon, *Jews,* 17–19, 30–42; Michael G. Rapp, "Samuel N. Deinard and the Unification of Jews in Minneapolis," *Minnesota History* 43 (Summer, 1973): 213.

5. Berman, "The Jews," 495-496; Herbert S. Rutman, "Defense and Development: A History of Minneapolis Jewry, 1930-1950 (Ph.D. diss., University of Minnesota, 1970), 10.

6. Walker, *American City*, 21-23.

7. John Higham, *Strangers in the Land: Patterns of American Nativism* (New York: Atheneum, 1977), 278.

8. Leonard Dinnerstein, "Anti-Semitism Exposed and Attacked, 1945-1950," *American Jewish History* 71 (Sept., 1981): 138; Michael G. Rapp, "An Historical Overview of Anti-Semitism in Minnesota, 1920-1960—With Particular Emphasis on Minneapolis and St. Paul" (Ph.D. diss., University of Minnesota, 1977), xix.

9. Fred W. Friendly, *Minnesota Rag: The Dramatic Story of the Landmark Supreme Court Case that Gave New Meaning to Freedom of the Press* (New York: Random House, 1981), 36-37, 40-43, 57-59.

10. Lefkovits quoted in Charles I. Cooper, "The Jews of Minneapolis and Their Christian Neighbors," *Jewish Social Studies* 7 (Jan., 1946): 32-33; *Minneapolis Star,* May 20, 1950, p. 3.

11. *American Jewish World* (hereafter *AJW*), Jan. 6, 1925, p. 8; Rapp, "Historical Overview," 25.

12. Higham, *Strangers in the Land,* 278, citing research by Heywood Broun and George Britt; Rapp, "Historical Overview," 28.

13. George D. Tselos, "The Minneapolis Labor Movement in the 1930s" (Ph.D. diss., University of Minnesota, 1970), 59; Rapp, "Historical Overview," 39; William E. Leuchtenberg, *Franklin D. Roosevelt and the New Deal* (New York: Harper and Row, 1963), 18-40.

14. Tselos, "Minneapolis Labor Movement," 65-67; *AJW,* Nov. 6, 1931, p. 11.

15. *AJW,* Sept. 19, 1930, p. 19.

16. George H. Mayer, *The Political Career of Floyd B. Olson* (reprint ed., St. Paul: MHS Press, 1987), 8. For more on this campaign, see Hyman Berman, "Political Anti-semitism in Minnesota during the Great Depression," *Jewish Social Studies* 38 (Summer-Fall, 1976): 247-264.

17. Edward P. Schwartz, tape-recorded interview with Rhoda G. Lewin, 1976, tape in MHS collections. The oral history project was the basis for Lewin's Ph.D. dissertation, "Some New Perspectives on the Jewish Immigrant Experience in Minneapolis: An Experiment in Oral History" (University of Minnesota, 1978).

18. Here and below, see Nathan M. Shapiro, tape-recorded interview with Rhoda Lewin, 1976, tape in MHS collections.

19. Cooper, "Jews of Minneapolis," 34; Tselos, "Minneapolis Labor Movement," 323.

20. *Minneapolis Journal,* Sept. 11, 1936, p. 1.

21. Schwartz interview.

22. *AJW,* Aug. 5, 1938, p. 1.

23. *Minneapolis Journal,* Aug. 4, 1938, p. 1, 2.

24. *Minneapolis Journal,* Aug. 4, 1938, p. 1, 2; *AJW,* Aug. 5, 1938, p. 3.

25. *AJW,* Aug. 12, May 13—both 1938, p. 1; Gordon, *Jews,* 50.

26. Inventory notebook, JCRC of Minnesota Papers, archives and manuscripts reading room, MHS.

27. Clippings from unidentified newspaper and S. L. Scheiner, Report, Jan. 2, 1940, JCRC Papers.

28. Gordon, *Jews,* 36; *AJW,* Jan. 8, 1932, p. 3, Oct. 24, 1930, p. 13; JFWA Board of Directors, Minutes, Nov. 19, 1930, Jewish Family and Children's Service (JFCS) Papers, MHS.

29. *AJW,* Jan. 8, 1932, p. 3.

30. *AJW,* Oct. 16, 1931, p. 2.

31. Here and below, see *AJW*, Jan. 8, 1932, p. 3.

32. *AJW*, July 22, 1932, p. 8. The paper actually claimed 69 jobs for the first six months, but the numbers tally to 68.

33. *AJW*, Sept. 23, 1932, p. 1.

34. JFWA Board, Minutes, May 10, Oct. 18, 1933, JFCS Papers; *AJW*, Aug. 25, Sept. 1—both 1933, p. 10.

35. *AJW*, May 18, 1934, p. 8; Report of Executive Secretary, Feb. 9, 1938, JFCS Papers.

36. JFWA Executive Committee, Minutes, May 15, Aug. 3, and JFWA Board, Minutes, May 9, Oct. 10—all 1934, JFCS Papers.

37. *AJW*, Feb. 1, 1935, p. 15.

38. *AJW*, Feb. 8, 1935, p. 5.

39. *AJW*, Mar. 8, 1935, p. 4; JFWA Board, Minutes, Dec. 11, 1935, JFCS Papers.

40. *AJW*, Aug. 28, 1936, p. 8; Sophia M. Robison, "The Jewish Population of Minneapolis, 1936," in *Jewish Population Studies*, ed. Sophia M. Robison (New York: Conference on Jewish Relations, 1943), 152.

41. [Minneapolis Council of Social Agencies], *Minneapolis Jewish Communal Survey* (Minneapolis, 1936), 3:1; Robison, Jewish Population of Minneapolis," 153–154.

42. Here and below, see [Minneapolis Council], *Minneapolis Jewish Communal Survey*, 1:11, 22–23.

43. JFWA Board, Minutes, Mar. 11, 1936; *AJW*, April 17, p. 12, May 15, p. 13, June 12, p. 11—all 1936.

44. *AJW*, Jan. 3, 1936, p. 13.

45. Here and below, see Report of the Executive Secretary at 28th Annual Meeting of JFWA, Feb. 9, 1938, p. 5, and Minutes of Annual Meeting of JFWA, Jan. 10, 1940, p. 4, both in JFCS Papers.

46. Here and below, see "Report of the Industrial Division of the Family Welfare Assn.," in Minutes of Annual Meeting of JFWA, Jan. 27, 1941, p. 5–6, JFCS Papers.

47. Memorandum of Sub-Committee Appointments (Preliminary), Sept. 25, 1940, and JFWA Board, Minutes, Dec. 11, 1940, June 25, 1941, p. 2—all in JFCS Papers. The minutes record 77 placements—"46 permanent and 36 temporary" [*sic*].

48. Dinnerstein, "Anti-Semitism," 134; Samuel L. Scheiner to Miles Goldberg, Sept. 29, 1942, JCRC Papers; Rapp, "Historical Overview," 41.

49. Selden Menefee, "What Americans Think," *The Nation*, May 27, 1943, p. 765, and *Assignment: U.S.A.* (New York: Reynal & Hitchcock, 1943), 101.

50. Carey McWilliams, "Minneapolis: The Curious Twin," *Common Ground*, Autumn, 1946, p. 61–62; Rapp, "Historical Overview," 179.

51. Cooper, "Jews of Minneapolis," 34–35.

52. Here and below, see Dinnerstein, "Anti-Semitism," 136–138, 142–144.

53. "Q and A About Permanent FEPC," pamphlet in Central Labor Union of Minneapolis and Hennepin County (CLU) Records, MHS; here and below, see Aaron Litman, "Civic Protection in Minneapolis," typewritten copy of speech, undated but filed under "Anti-Semitism 1946–52," JCRC Papers.

54. Gordon Connelly (general manager of field operations, National Opinion Research Center, University of Chicago) to George Phillips (CLU president), undated; memo to affiliated local unions from the CLU, April, 1947; Opal G. Gruner (chair of JCEO) to Phillips, Nov. 10, 1947; "History and Aims of the JCEO," Jan. 28, 1948; Phillips to J. Selmer Drage and Jean Robertson, Dec. 1, 1948—all in CLU Records.

55. JCEO, letter to presidents of its member organizations, 1948, CLU Records.

56. *Minneapolis Tribune*, May 4, 1952, Upper Midwest sec., p. 12.

MAKING HISTORY

Mirrored Identities:
The Moys of St. Paul

SHERRI GEBERT FULLER

During the course of her work as a project manager for museum collec-
tions at the Minnesota Historical Society, Sherri Gebert Fuller encoun-
tered a silver loving cup embellished with Chinese calligraphy and, two
days later, the business card of Moy Hee, the businessman to whom the
cup was presented. Starting from these two artifacts, Gebert Fuller
pieces together the story of a successful Chinese American businessman
who arrived in the United States after the Chinese Exclusion Act (and
therefore never became an American citizen), navigated federal bureau-
cracy to make several round trips to China, and, by the time of his acci-
dental death in 1921, had earned the respect of Twin Cities civic leaders
and the Chinese communities across the Midwest.

Objects can tell us many things if we know how to "read" them. An 1890s auto-
graph quilt, for example, documents the materials, designs, and embroidery
techniques common in its time. Beyond these tangibles, the quiltmakers' embroidered signatures can send the researcher on a more intriguing—and challenging—journey to learn more about the lives of individuals who would otherwise remain anonymous.

I began such a journey in 1992, when a silver loving cup was brought to my
attention while I was helping move the Minnesota Historical Society's three-
dimensional collections to the new Minnesota History Center in St. Paul. I was
surprised to learn from the object, embellished with Chinese calligraphy on
one side and English text on the other, that a "Chinese Public School" had existed in the St. Paul–Minneapolis area in 1921. A few days later, while assisting
a researcher, I found the business card of Moy Hee, the man to whom the loving cup had been presented. This synchronicity—two items coming to my attention within so short a time—motivated me to find out more about Moy Hee
and St. Paul's early Chinese American community.

In 1994 I started my research journey by looking at acquisition records associated with the loving cup. Along with four family photographs, it had been
donated to the Society by Judith Moy in 1923. Engravings on the trophy and a

handwritten note on the business card led me to Moy Hee's obituary and related newspaper articles. I continued to search for other resources as time permitted. Fellow staff members sent me book titles, articles, and newspaper clippings that served as reminders that the information I was looking for was out there—finding it would just require patient sleuthing.

For the next six years, I delved into church and school records, gleaned city directories, paged through theater programs, listened to oral histories, conducted interviews with members of the Chinese American community, read microfilmed probate records at the Ramsey County Courthouse, and, with the help of independent scholar Peggy Christoff, located Moy Hee's records in the Chinese exclusion files at the National Archives regional offices in Chicago and Seattle. From these strands of information emerged the story of a successful Chinese American businessman and his family who lived in St. Paul from 1901 to 1921.

Moy Ju Hee was born in 1865 in Gum Ping village in the Taishan area of Guangdong Province. It is estimated that 60 percent of the Chinese immigrants in the United States before World War II emigrated from this area in southern China, where food production could not support the population. Moy's family purportedly owned large tracts of land, and his mother, Jun Shee, had bound feet, a common sign of wealth in Chinese society at that time. Because of his family's economic status, Moy likely received an education in Confucianism, which emphasized moral rather than utilitarian training. Such teaching encouraged introspection, emulation of virtuous leaders, and the ability to remain balanced in the face of adversity. His education would serve him well when, in 1886, he decided to see what business opportunities awaited him in the United States.[1]

Leaving behind his widowed mother, his wife, Hom Shee, and daughter, Moy Foon Hai, 21-year-old Moy sailed west to San Francisco, where he managed Hong Yen Hong, a Chinese drug store. He soon ventured east to work with relatives in Oshkosh, Wisconsin, where a small population of Chinese had established a number of laundries, restaurants, and stores. Moy Hee first assisted his uncle at Hop Chong and Company and later became a partner in the Mee Lee Yuen Company, which specialized in teas and Chinese and Japanese goods. William Dichman, mayor of Oshkosh from 1891 to 1892, later told immigration officials that "during all the time Moy Hee was a resident of the city of Oshkosh, he conducted himself in a straight-forward and honest manner, becoming a Chinese gentleman. . . . He was energetic and attentive to his business, that of a Chinese merchant."[2]

In 1882, four years before Moy arrived in Oshkosh, the United States had passed the Chinese Exclusion Act, the first federal law to bar immigration on the basis of race and class. Nativist and political rhetoric on the West Coast, where Chinese settlers made up 10 percent of the California population, fueled this law. With the onset of a poor economy in 1873, Chinese laborers were blamed for unemployment, both locally and nationally. Rather than focusing on the roots of economic upheaval and how to resolve the problems, much of the country became caught up in a wave of Sinophobic emotion—even though Chinese immigrants represented only .002 percent of the U.S. population in 1880.[3]

The exclusion law prohibited skilled and unskilled Chinese laborers from entering the United States for ten years. Those laborers already in the country were allowed to remain but would not be readmitted if they left. Exempt from this law were teachers, students, merchants, government officials, and travelers—individuals such as Moy who could facilitate trade relations with China.[4]

Section 14 of the exclusion act also prevented naturalization of all Chinese immigrants residing in the United States. This not only kept them from participating in politics but severely restricted their ability to acculturate and be accepted into mainstream America.[5] Within these prohibitive parameters, individuals like Moy Hee made every effort to adapt to the United States to demonstrate their ability to be good "Americans."

Despite a marked decrease in the Chinese population on the West Coast between 1882 and 1891, the "Yellow Peril" question continued its impact upon the political sphere. Debate raged in the 52nd Congress, where Charles Felton of California stated that "races so dissimilar as the white and Asiatic could not exist together. One or the other must survive. This is the law of Nature."[6]

Fueled by this sentiment, Congress in 1892 called for the renewal of the exclusion act and greater resources to implement it. The amended Geary Act, "An Act to Prohibit the Coming of Chinese Persons Into the United States," made permanent the exclusion of all Chinese laborers. Those already living in the United States were now required to carry a certificate of residence with them at all times or risk immediate arrest and possible deportation.

To enforce the Geary Act, a new federal office was created in the Treasury Department—the Superintendent of Immigration (today's Immigration and Naturalization Service). This office's "Chinese inspectors" were charged with the responsibility of determining whether individuals had the right to immigrate or return to the United States.[7] These developments would directly affect Moy Hee and his family for the rest of their lives.

Chinese inspectors, who often got their jobs through patronage, were frequently anti-Chinese. Many used their positions for political gain. Assigned to ports of entry and metropolitan areas throughout the United States, including Minneapolis, they often lacked any kind of training to enforce the law consistently and fairly. This was especially detrimental, since the inspectors' public attitudes and actions often set the tone for the rest of country.[8]

Chinese exclusion files now in the National Archives provide excellent examples of just how much paperwork, redundancy, and bureaucracy quickly evolved to enforce the law. Exempt classes, including merchants such as Moy Hee, were still allowed to travel to and from China but had to work within a restrictive system. Merchants were required to provide information about their business and its value, to answer question after question about their families in China and the United States, and to provide testimonies from two "witnesses other than Chinese" who were familiar with their business. This paperwork had to be completed for each trip, and answers were often compared to previous application forms. Travel plans could be delayed or reentry denied if an inspector was not satisfied with the applicant's answers.[9]

A successful application gained the resident immigrant a certificate of identity, the only means to gain reentry into the United States. Between 1894 and 1921, Moy's merchant status allowed him to make five trips: four return trips to China and a business trip to Mexico. All of these journeys required the same amount of paperwork and questioning, despite Moy's local and national reputation as a leader and astute businessman.[10]

For example, in early 1920 he initiated paperwork to travel to Mexico with nephew Charley Toy, a Milwaukee businessman, to stake out a potential investment. A flurry of correspondence took place between Chinese inspectors in Minnesota and Texas after Moy submitted what appeared to be a simple request. He planned to return to the United States through the border city of Calexico, California, the same city from which he would depart for Mexico. The exclusion law, however, stated that Chinese could leave the U.S. from any location but could only return through one of 12 designated ports of entry. Moy would have to travel from Mexico by water to San Diego, the nearest designated port.[11]

Moy then asked his lawyer, Joel Mark Dickey, for help, and Dickey turned to Washington, D.C., for support. On March 30, 1920, immigration official Louis F. Post wrote to one of Minnesota's U.S. senators, Frank B. Kellogg, "In reply to your letter . . . I beg to state that the Department has this day issued instructions whereby the departure and re-entry of Moy Hee via Calexico, Cal., will be allowed, provided his status as a merchant has been satisfactorily established, as set forth in Mr. Dickey's letter to you." After four months of correspondence, a May 26, 1920, letter confirmed that Moy Hee successfully returned through Calexico, a rare triumph over the bureaucracy.[12]

Moy's visits to China combined family and business matters. While living in Oshkosh, he returned to China in 1894 and 1896 for extended visits. His family in Gum Ping village occupied a brick house consisting of one parlor, two sleeping rooms, one kitchen, and a hall. In addition to Moy Foon Hai, born before he first left for America, Moy eventually had four other children: two girls, Moy Quai Fong and Moy Son Woon, and two boys, Moy Hong Yik and Moy Tai Heung, who seem to have been born during and after these trips to China. Or, perhaps, they were not. The restrictions in the exclusion act led some merchants to claim more immediate family members than they actually had in order to create immigration slots for children of friends and family in China who would not otherwise be allowed into the U.S. While there is no conclusive evidence, events of later years hint that one or both of Moy Hee's boys were "paper sons."[13]

According to exclusion-file records, Moy's wife, Hom Shee, died in 1896, shortly after the birth of their youngest son, Moy Tai Heung. Moy's mother soon arranged for her 31-year-old son to marry Wong Shee from Canton province, a merchant's daughter with natural feet. After a traditional Chinese wedding on March 3, 1897, Moy Hee and Wong Shee remained in Canton for a short period before returning to Moy's village.

In 1898 Moy boarded a steamship with his new wife, second daughter, Moy Quai Fong, and oldest son, Moy Hong Yik, en route to the United States. Unaware of new requirements in the Geary Act, however, he lacked the proper paperwork from the American consul in China for his family to enter the U.S. Materials in his exclusion files reflect Moy Hee's attempts to round up support. For example, a "witness report" from a friend, Ole Oleson of Oshkosh, states: "Moy Hee is a good and respected citizen of this State and being so well and favorably known among the best citizens of our city, I would consider it a grievous wrong and heart-breaking hardship if the law of our country should tear this family asunder, to deprive these children of the benefits of a common school education, and to bar their return to their home here in Oshkosh."[14]

Bureaucracy prevailed, however, and Moy's family was rejected at Port Townsend, Washington, on August 15, 1898, after having traveled for more than 30 days in hopes of making Oshkosh their new home. Not until 1904 did Moy's wife join him in the United States. His plans to bring Moy Quai Fong and Moy Hong Yik that same year fell through; Quai Fong died shortly before, and the boy stayed in China.[15]

In 1901 Moy Hee moved from Oshkosh to St. Paul to manage Hui Xian Low (Gathering of Immortals Building), advertised as a "high-class Chinese Chop House," at 439 Jackson Street. The business was likely a collaboration with the Hum Gin family who had recently relocated to St. Paul from Duluth. Partnerships with friends and family served as important networks for Chinese immigrants, since job opportunities were limited. Such partnerships also helped raise capital for family-owned businesses, thus diminishing the need to rely on loans from Chinese associations located on the East and West Coasts of the United States.[16]

According to an advertisement in St. Paul's *Northwest Magazine*, the restaurant offered a "palatable YAO A MAN or some toothsome CHAW MIN" along with "first-class Chinese Merchandise of all descriptions and the Choicest Teas of direct importation." It appeared that Moy Hee was especially interested in luring theater attendees and guests at the Hotel Ryan, directly across the street from the restaurant, for he advertised frequently in local periodicals and brochures.[17]

In St. Paul, Moy Hee had discovered a small but growing Chinese community in the area extending from St. Peter to Sibley and Third to Seventh Streets. A few Chinese had settled in St. Paul as early as the 1870s, but most migrated later from the West Coast to escape discrimination, unfair taxes, and violence. Xenophobic attitudes severely restricted employment opportunities for Chinese throughout the United States, and Minnesota was no exception. By 1900 there were approximately 52 Chinese living in the St. Paul-Minneapolis area, all working in Chinese laundries, restaurants, or stores.[18]

In 1902 Moy Hee established a retail shop in St. Paul, Wing Wah Chong Merchandise Company, at 191 Eighth Street. Eight partners, all Moys, provided capital to start the new venture. Moy Hee initially invested $5,000, while the others contributed between $1,000 and $1,500 each. Moy Hee was responsible for purchasing merchandise, while his cousin, Moy S. James, also a recent transplant from Oshkosh, managed the store. The shop's location and partners changed several times in the next two decades. By 1917 Moy Hee had nine partners, one of them from Hibbing and one from China. Four full-time employees, likely family members—Yip Wei Yik, Moy Kee Gat, Moy Fung Gat, and Moy Guy Chong—assisted him with bookkeeping and sales. Each was paid a monthly salary of $40.[19]

The store's merchandise during its early years is not known, but 1921 Ramsey County probate records provide a picture of what was likely available under Moy's management. Wing Wah Chong specialized in silks, embroidered goods, rice, pottery, canned goods, groceries, and toys. To meet the needs of Chinese laundries, it carried ironing pads and bottles of Mrs. Stewart's bluing. By 1921 the store housed 247 jars of Chinese drugs (herbs) along with a wide variety of teas. A sampling of foods included 19 cans of sour bamboo, 5 jars of Chinese cheese, 35 cans of "cucumber bitter melon," 25 pounds of imported dried noodles, 40 pounds of Chinese dried vegetables, 2 cases of lily root, and 100 pounds each of thick and thin soy sauce.[20]

During an interview for his fourth return trip to China, Moy stated that his store made a profit of $17,000 in 1916. Considering that the Twin Cities Chinese population was approximately 300 by 1920, it is conceivable that Wing Wah Chong also provided goods to restaurants, stores, and laundries outside of the metropolitan area.[21] Using knowledge and experience gained from his work at Mee Lee Yuen in Oshkosh, Moy Hee likely prospered by supplying businesses throughout the region.

Besides providing local Chinese with goods from home, Wing Wah Chong may also have served as a gathering place where men could share news or get assistance with letter writing and translations. As historian Ronald Takaki pointed out in *Strangers from a Different Shore*, "A uniquely Chinese-American institution, the store was a center of life in the Chinese community.... There they escaped from the strangeness and fierceness of their everyday world."[22]

In addition to starting his own retail shop, Moy established Kwong Tung and Low Co. (Guangdong [Province] Building and Co.), a restaurant at 373 Robert Street in 1903. He would move his eatery one more time before finding his most opportune location at 413 Robert Street in 1908. A Star Theatre program from that same year listed his restaurant hours as 11:00 A.M. to 3:00 A.M., and a 1909 *St. Paul Shopping Guide* advertisement reminded readers that "Visitors should not fail to see this beautiful place, the most elegant in the Northwest."[23]

Moy also relied on partners to establish Kwong Tung Low. While no records were found to verify the names of his early partners, an August 10, 1918, interview in his exclusion files noted that Moy Yin, Moy Bing, and his son Moy Hong Yik each held a $1,000 share in the restaurant in addition to Moy Hee's $7,000 investment.[24]

Shortly after Kwong Tung Low was up and running, Moy established another restaurant at 255 First Avenue in Minneapolis. Shanghai Low (Shanghai Building) was managed by his cousin Moy S. James and, according to a 1904 *Minneapolis Journal* article, was a "first-class Chinese restaurant, catering only to the best class of patronage and run strictly on business principles."[25]

The decor of Moy's restaurants was similar to other Chinese eateries found in St. Paul and Minneapolis at the time. Their interiors were filled with elaborate mirrors, teakwood tables with marble tops, mahogany chairs, embroidered panels, Chinese carved arch partitions, and glass chandeliers.[26] These ornate and colorful interiors, an early marketing tool, attracted visitors looking for an "exotic" experience, a word often used by newspapers to describe Chinese culture and food.

In 1906 Moy Hee helped his cousin Moy James plan a Chinese New Year's celebration at Shanghai Low, where approximately 100 countrymen from throughout the Midwest joined in the festivities, complete with fireworks. A delightful description of the menu appeared in the January 21, 1906, issue of the *Minneapolis Journal*:

> The menu ... contains everything which the Mongolian heart can wish. The feast will begin with tea and li chee nuts. After this will come the soups.... the [whole] fish, Hen San Gui.... then Shue Bec Gap—baked young pigeon.... [and] Quong We Hae. This delicacy is made from the bones of chicken and other birds ground fine and made into sort of a paste.... While the banqueters are wielding their chop sticks an orchestra will render a few of the Chinese classics.... The majority of the Chinamen in town still have their native garb and about half have retained their cues [*sic*].

Photographs in Moy Hee's exclusion files show that he had adapted to western-style garb and hair as early as 1896.[27]

Moy's turn-of-the-century restaurants were part of a significant increase in the number of Chinese eateries across the country at the time. One individual who indirectly influenced this growth was Chinese envoy Li Hung Chang, who traveled to New York City in 1896 in hopes of improving relations between China and the United States. Reports of Li's visit piqued the curiosity of many New Yorkers and, as a result, thousands of people ventured to Chinatown for the first time to experience "exotic Chinese culture." Restaurant owners took advantage of this opportunity and advertised chop suey, a meal made by Li's personal chefs during his visit, as the envoy's favorite dish. As a result, chop suey became a familiar term to New Yorkers and helped spur the development of the Chinese American restaurant industry.[28]

In 1904, after living in St. Paul for three years, Moy again visited China. This time he used his merchant status to secure certificates of identity for both himself and his wife, Wong Shee. After returning to Vancouver, they traveled east by rail through Canada and entered the United States through Portal, North Dakota.[29] Wong Shee, who adopted the name Judith Moy, quickly became an integral player in Moy Hee's business and social interactions.

Judith Moy joined St. Paul's very small circle of merchants' wives including Bessie Moy (married to Moy Hee's cousin and partner Moy S. James) and Mrs. Hum Gin (married to another business partner). The relationship among these women likely was an important means of sharing information and ideas as they adjusted to their new lives. Had they remained in China, Confucian ideals and patriarchal expectations would have narrowly defined their roles and responsibilities. Life in the United States presented new opportunities, improved status, and more independence.

Forging a new life in a strange country could not have been easy for these women. According to a 1949 report to Minnesota Governor Luther W. Young-dahl, "Over thirty-five years ago a Chinese restaurateur brought his wife [to First Baptist Church on Wacouta Street] and asked that someone instruct her in the Bible and American social customs. Miss Alice Northrup was selected and she found her pupil willing and grateful." Church members established a Chinese Bible class in 1912, where teachers worked on a one-to-one basis with students. A photograph of this class from about 1914 shows Judith Moy in the center next to Alice Northrup, leading one to presume that it was Moy Hee who first requested help for his wife. The class continued with 30 members, including Bessie Moy and Mrs. Hum Gin, until 1917. It was here that Judith learned to speak and write in English.[30]

Female instructors in Bible classes often served as Chinese women's first role models for American social etiquette and dress. Many Chinese women in the United States converted to Christianity out of appreciation, since they lived in predominantly male communities. According to author Victoria Wong,

> In many ways Christianity drew Chinese women into Western society, legitimizing their community involvement. . . . In becoming active in their communities, the women broke from Chinese tradition, which idealized women as cloistered, uneducated, and dependent on their families and husbands. The Christian emphasis on women's organizations brought Chinese American women together for the first time in the context of gender, encouraging them to develop a stronger gender-based identity. It implied that they, as women, could contribute to social change in their communities.[31]

Judith became a member of First Baptist Church in 1914. In April 1917 the *St. Paul Pioneer Press* reported approvingly that she was "one of the prominent members of the Bible class. . . . She has the distinction of being the only Chinese woman in St. Paul who is a member of any church of the Christian faith." Her ability to write and speak English liberated her from the secluded life often experienced by merchants' wives in Minnesota in the early-twentieth century.[32]

Judith may also have benefited from the experiences of Liang May Seen, the first Chinese woman to settle in Minneapolis in 1892. Married to businessman Woo Yee Sing, Liang managed her own Minneapolis curio shop and was an important role model for Chinese women in the Twin Cities until her death in 1946. Her family often took the trolley east to St. Paul for Sunday afternoon visits with the Moys.[33]

Hee and Judith lived on the fourth floor above the 413 Robert Street restaurant. Their apartment decor was a balanced juxtaposition of eastern and western design including leather chairs, a cigar stand, four inlaid teak chairs with marble insets, and four inlaid teak flower stands. The space was also adorned with a large picture of the last emperor of China, as well as several small pictures and framed photographs on the wall.[34]

While the Moys did not have any children together, they did not live alone. Census records from 1920 show that they shared their apartment with six adult males and one adult female. Moy Hee was listed as the head of household in the rented building, an employer, and the proprietor of a chop suey restaurant. All of the other men were employed at Wing Wah Chong or Kwong Tung Low and Company. Of the seven lodgers, only one had been born in the United States; the rest had immigrated from China, including his two sons Hong Yik and Tai Heung and his daughter-in-law Gun Shee.[35]

Having established a retail shop and two restaurants within a few years of his arrival in the Twin Cities, Moy Hee was seen as an important business leader, both within and outside of the Chinese community. In the U. S., merchants commonly assumed leadership roles traditionally held by Chinese gentry and scholar-officials, who tended not to emigrate because China still offered them

opportunities for upward mobility.[36] Thus, Moy's education, wealth, and pro-
ficiency in two languages worked to his advantage.

Despite these advantages and the respect they brought, Moy also knew that
his business ventures and transnational family ties depended on his ability to
use the legal and social tools available to him. Dinners that he held for St. Paul
and Ramsey County officials, including Joel Dickey, his lawyer, reflect his
efforts to network with those who could best advise him. Moy understood that
his success in the United States depended on his resourcefulness to adapt to
and manage opportunities. Poised between the expectations of two countries,
Moy Hee discovered what it meant to be Chinese American.[37]

Moy quickly won favor with the St. Paul and Minneapolis newspapers. Articles featuring him were always complimentary, in contrast to the usual de-
piction of Chinese laborers as "heathen," "almond-eyed," and "celestials." As
author Sucheng Chan noted, "Throughout the nineteenth century, newspaper
reporters repeatedly praised the educated urbanity of Chinese merchants, often calling them gentlemen—in sharp contrast to the extremely derogatory
manner in which they depicted Chinese laborers. Undergirding this class prejudice was the fact that one of the chief concerns of U.S. foreign policy during
this period was expanding trade with China."[38]

Articles about Moy Hee began to appear in local newspapers as early as
1902 when the *Minneapolis Journal* described him as enjoying the "unique distinction of being a thirty-second degree Mason, capable of handing any white
man who enters his place high signs which mean much to some and are absolutely as unintelligible as 'Chinese' to others." The article enthusiastically
called him a "very bright and intelligent representative of his race . . . [who has]
neglected no opportunity to improve his mind."[39]

First-person accounts from Moy's contemporaries in the Chinese American
community are harder to come by. After many attempts to track down Moy descendants in the 1990s, only one individual was found who recalled Moy Hee.
Howard Woo (son of Liang May Seen and Woo Yee Sing of Minneapolis) remembered his family taking the trolley from downtown Minneapolis to visit
Moy Hee on the weekends in the 1910s. He recalled that Moy "took everything
seriously and was from the old school of thought. He was a big man in Chinese
circles and a very prominent family in St. Paul. He had long fingernails, which
was a sign of aristocrats, the significance being that he wasn't a laborer."[40]

In addition to his business and social entertaining, Moy Hee also took time
to host Chinese diplomats who traveled to Minnesota. In August 1911 Moy Bach
Hin, the Chinese consul at Portland, Oregon, and Quan Kai, special commissioner for the viceroy of Canton, were touring the country to make plans for
founding a national library in Canton. They stopped in St. Paul to look at the
state law and historical society libraries. Moy Hee's business card in the Minnesota Historical Society's collections, that seemingly ephemeral object that

helped launch this research journey, records this visit with its handwritten notation: "August 9, 1911 with Canton Commission." The official guests were invited to dine with a number of St. Paul Chinese at a chop suey restaurant—likely Moy S. James's Joy Ying Low at 440 Wabasha Street.[41]

Moy Hee also attended to family matters. In January 1906 he initiated paperwork to bring over his two sons, Moy Hong Yik, about 19 years old, and ten-year-old Moy Tai Heung. The two boys were allowed to enter the country as minors of a "bona fide domiciled" merchant under an exception made to the exclusion law by the U.S. Supreme Court. His sons finally arrived in St. Paul in December 1907.[42]

Once there, Hong Yik and Tai Heung received private instruction from a "lady teacher, who was paid $7 per week for several months." The oldest son then helped out with restaurant work, and Tai Heung attended public school. He did not live with his father but with a Mr. Watts who was paid $30 per month for board and washing. It is not known why Tai Heung only met with his family on Sundays. Perhaps he was a "paper son," or perhaps Moy Hee thought that the boy would benefit from immersion in American living. By about 1909 Heung was enrolled at Washington School at Eighth and Olive Streets in St. Paul. His teachers called him Henry and described him as "industrious, mannerly, and bright."

In the fall of 1910 his teacher, Ella C. O'Brien, sent him to the school nurse to check the visibly swollen glands in his neck. Although his illness was deemed not contagious, Tai Heung stopped attending school in hopes of improving his health. He was unsuccessfully treated in St. Paul, Milwaukee, and New Richmond, Wisconsin. Finally, Moy Hee asked his lawyer to prepare papers for his son's return to China, where he might find a lasting cure. Since Moy Hee wanted Hong Yik to accompany his younger brother, he asked lawyer Dickey how to proceed. Dickey, in turn, asked Charles Seaman, the Chinese inspector for Minneapolis, what kind of papers Hong Yik needed to gain readmission to the United States.

Seaman informed Dickey that the exclusion law would allow Hong Yik to accompany his brother to China but not to return to the United States. At 26, he was "no longer a minor, and therefore dependent upon his individual employment as to the legal status under the Chinese exclusion laws.... [He] is undoubtedly a laborer under the law.... and I therefore know of no papers ... which would permit his re-entry to the United States." Another travel companion, Moy Wing Art, likely a relative, was found to accompany Tai Heung to China.

As the Twin Cities' Chinese population grew to approximately 150 by the year 1910, tong members sought to establish a presence in Minnesota. Tongs were one branch of a complex hierarchical structure that evolved on the West Coast during the nineteenth century to provide assistance to Chinese communities often isolated from mainstream America. Local newspapers were eager to report on tong-related activities, since drug trafficking, blackmail, gambling, and prostitution were often associated with these groups from the mid-1800s until the 1920s.[43]

Alleged tong activity in the Twin Cities is documented as early as October 29, 1907, when the *Minneapolis Journal* initiated a series of articles about a raid at On Wong's store at 239 Fourth Avenue South in Minneapolis, sarcastically entitled "Innocent Chinks Smoking Tobacco." The articles, which ran through March 1908, covered the arrest and trial of 15 men and related gambling activity.[44]

Stories about tong activity continued to appear in the *Minneapolis Journal* from 1910 to 1912. The Hip Sing tong made headlines in 1912 when it allegedly tried to blackmail money from local Chinese businessmen. According to the *Journal,* "Two restaurant employees were told in a letter to furnish a certain Chinaman $100 each to go toward organizing a tong in Minneapolis." On that same day, the *St. Paul Pioneer Press* reported that "Many Minneapolis Chinese . . . are now paying tribute of from $3 to $15 a week." The *Journal* further stated that the Chinese community had asked Moy Hee and Moy James to meet with state officials to see what could be done to prevent the organization and incorporation of the Hip Sing tong in the Twin Cities. (Unfortunately, the newspapers did not report the results of this meeting.) While illegal tong activity likely remained in the Twin Cities throughout the 1910s, various sources suggested that the presence of respected Chinese elders and business partners Moy Hee, Moy James, and Hum Gin, known in Chinese circles as the "three musketeers," may have helped to minimize tong-related activities, at least in St. Paul.[45]

Meanwhile, back in China, Moy's youngest son, Tai Heung, had recovered. His grandmother then arranged for him to marry a young woman named Gun Shee in April 1917. Moy Hee and Judith returned to China to witness the wedding and see Moy's daughters Moy Foon Hai and Moy Son Woon, who had married and remained in China.[46]

A letter Judith sent to lawyer Joel Dickey from aboard the steamship *RMS Empress* just before it left Seattle prompted the *St. Paul Pioneer Press* to cover their trip. The article nicely summarized the complex weavings of Moy's life, noting that he was recognized by the Six Companies of California, an association of tongs, as being the "leading representative Chinaman in the States of North Dakota, South Dakota, and Minnesota." The newspaper noted that Moy gave four farewell banquets before leaving on his trip: one for the well-known citizens of St. Paul, two for fellow merchants, and one for laundrymen.[47]

The article also provided details about Moy's financial status, reporting that he took $40,000 in exchange with him: $10,000 for presents and banquets for his friends in China, and the rest for investments, possibly for purchasing rental properties. (Moy reportedly owned many buildings in China.) During their three-month visit, the Moys did not return to Gum Ping village but stayed in Hong Kong and Canton. American Chinese were no longer welcome in the home village, and Moy's mother and children joined him in Hong Kong.

Two years after their marriage, Tai Heung and Gun Shee departed for the United States. No longer minors by 1919, they were able to immigrate as students. Within one year, however, Tai Heung lost his exempt student status and, thus, his ability to travel to and from China, when he chose to work at his father's restaurant. His and Gun Shee's certificates of identity were canceled "in accordance with the provisions of subdivision 5, Rule 19."[48]

During his visits to China from the 1890s through the late 1910s, Moy Hee witnessed the ever-evolving and complex politics in his homeland. Unfair treaties with Western nations had resulted in fierce antiforeign riots in 1900 (the Boxer Rebellion) and, after thousands of people lost their lives, an army of troops from eight nations moved in to keep order. The Manchu (Ching) Dynasty, in power since 1644, abdicated in 1911. Despite Sun Yat Sen's efforts to establish a democratic Chinese republic, a decade of rule by rival warlords followed. When a weak Chinese government accepted concessions to Japan after World War I, nationalism soared, enabling Sun Yat Sen to revitalize the National People's Party, or Kuomintang (KMT).[49]

Support for the KMT in St. Paul was organized in early 1920. People met to learn of Sun Yat Sen's progress and raise money for his efforts. Moy Hee established a Chinese Nationalist League office on the second floor of Wing Wah Chong, where pictures of George Washington, Abraham Lincoln, and Woodrow Wilson decorated the walls. In February 1920 more than 100 representatives from Detroit, Milwaukee, Chicago, and Minneapolis attended a fund-raising dinner at Jim Moy's restaurant (he was no longer called Moy S. James in the local newspapers) at 440 Wabasha Street. Sam Wong, a "graduate of the Mechanic Arts High School," presided over the meeting. He emphasized the democratic ideals of the new Chinese Republic and also "urged Americanization among the Chinese, and especially among the young men," according to a newspaper account. Moy Hee, president of the local chapter of the Chinese Nationalist League of America, also encouraged attendees to adopt and practice American ways.[50]

This was the first and last known dinner held in St. Paul to support Sun Yat Sen's efforts. Most Chinese were not making enough money to provide for both the Kuomintang and families back home. Also, in 1921, the KMT collaborated with the Chinese Communist Party to end the division of China into military regions run by warlords and the exploitation by privileged powers such as Britain, France, the U. S., and Japan. The political powers and energies of China were moving in yet another new direction.[51]

Despite Moy Hee's attempts to encourage Americanization, there was little hope that he would ever become a U.S. citizen. According to historian Takaki, "Chinese in America had realized for a long time how their situation here was tied to developments in China. The very political weakness of the Chinese government conditioned their treatment here. . . . Unlike the Irish and other groups in Europe, Asian immigrants could not become mere individuals. Regardless of their personal merits, they sadly discovered they could not gain acceptance in the larger society. They were judged not by the content of their character but by their complexion." Not until 1943, long after Moy Hee's death, could Chinese seek American citizenship, thanks to China's role as an ally in World War II.[52]

During China's politically unsettled year of 1921, Moy Hee established the Chinese public school in St. Paul to which the engraved silver trophy in the Minnesota Historical Society bears mute witness. Since the trophy names Moy as "founder," one can guess that he provided the monetary support while handing over the responsibility of managing the school to others. Years later, the report to Governor Youngdahl claimed that Y. Y. Toy, owner of the Ambassador Restaurant at Fifth and St. Peter Streets in St. Paul, hired Dr. K. M. Chan, a graduate student at the University of Minnesota, to teach ten Chinese children the "Chinese language and the classics of Chinese literature." Most of the students were enrolled in the St. Paul public schools during the day and attended the Chinese school in the evening or on weekends.[53] The location or life of the school—or anything beyond these bare facts—has yet to be learned. Such a school would undoubtedly have served to bridge the generations of Chinese, encouraging acculturation in their new homeland while maintaining ties to family traditions in China.

The English text and Chinese calligraphy engraved on opposite faces of the loving cup are basically equivalent, reading, "Presented to Mr. Moy Hee, the Founder of the Chinese Public School, St. Paul and Minneapolis, by the pupils of 1921." The Chinese inscription, however, adds four central characters that translate as "Develop schools/Save the country," a common nationalist slogan during this time. Many Chinese in the United States dreamed that their children would return to China not only to support their troubled homeland but also to work in professions unattainable in the United States.[54]

Moy Hee's active social and business life came to an abrupt end at age 56 when he was struck and killed by an automobile at Ninth and St. Peter Streets on August 3, 1921. In traditional, patriarchal Chinese society, elder brothers of the deceased or the head of the family clan usually planned the burial ceremony, and, despite their accommodations to some American ways, the Moys had remained faithful to tradition. Thus Moy Toy, son of Moy's nephew Charley Toy of Milwaukee, traveled to St. Paul to arrange funeral details. The funeral was held at First Baptist Church, where Judith had been active since 1914. Reverend Edgar A. Valiant led the service, and Judge John W. Finehout and Dr. Kchew Chow, Moy's business secretary, added tributes. Testifying to Moy Hee's respected role in Chinese and American society, the west wing of the church was decorated with floral arrangements from several city banks, department stores, and the Chinese societies of St Paul, Minneapolis, Detroit, Chicago, Milwaukee, and Cleveland. According to local newspapers, the church was filled to capacity, Moy Hee's amazing ability to balance the expectations of two cultures was perhaps best summed up by the *St. Paul Pioneer Press:* "His phenomenal success in all business enterprises and his many friendships here and throughout the country are attributed to his genial personality, his staunch advocacy of American principles while he still maintained a love for his native land, and to his habitual readiness to take an interest in anything that would supersede the old order of things."[55]

After the service, friends and family joined the funeral procession, led by mounted police and the Minnesota State Band. The band played in front of the Chinese Nationalist League office on Ninth Street and then slowly made its way to Rice Street and University Avenue. A second band was in the middle of the 125-automobile procession, and thousands of persons lined the streets.

The final destination for the slow-moving cortege was Oakland Cemetery in St. Paul, where the casket was transferred to a small chapel for viewing. When the service was over, two young Chinese children carrying woven baskets distributed "candy of sorrow" and nickels. The candy was to take "the bitter taste of sorrow from the mouth," according to the *Pioneer Press,* and the money was "regarded as a personal expression of good will from the deceased." The newspaper described the event as a "blend of Chinese stoicism and Christian display." The body remained at the cemetery until June 1922 when Moy was returned to China and buried with traditional Chinese rites.

Upon her husband's death, Judith Moy petitioned Ramsey County to be allowed to administer the estate, which was estimated to be worth $40,000, according to local newspapers. Thus began two years of closing accounts with local banks, making rent and repair payments while keeping books and managing the store and restaurant, and inventorying personal and business-related property, court costs, and other expenses.[56]

Moy's obituary noted that Kwong Tung Low and Company had lent money to "no less than fifteen first cousins and ten nephews" in the Twin Cities. According to probate records, 55 individuals were indebted to him at the time of his death.[57] Moy had continued the practice of helping friends and relatives with employment and loans, just as his family had done for him years before in Oshkosh and St. Paul.

The restaurant continued to do well until winter moved in. Profits from February to August 1922 were meager, at best. On September 8, 1922, Judith advertised its sale in the *St. Paul Dispatch, Duluth Herald, Minneapolis Tribune,* and *Fargo Forum:* "Moy Hee's Kwong Tung Restaurant, 413 Robert Street, St. Paul, must be sold to highest bidder to close estate. Bids must be in by Sept. 16. Inspections and bids can be made at restaurant, 9 A.M. to 5 P.M. Address Judith Moy Hee, administratrix."[58]

Business transactions surrounding the sale of the restaurant created a stir among some members of the St. Paul-Minneapolis Chinese community. Large, red-lettered signs requesting that "whosoever taking over the business must notify us before you start it," signed by the On Leong tong, were displayed near the exterior of the building. An anonymous informant told one of the local newspapers that Moy Hee operated a lottery and often held drawings on Sunday mornings. After Moy's death, players were never able to collect their winnings. According to the On Leong, "Debts of honor against the Moy Hee estate must be settled in the Chinese way."[59]

Despite such threats, Judith continued working to settle the estate. In 1922 the restaurant was sold for $8,777.10 to Moy Gan Nai (Maurice Moy, perhaps a cousin), who had originally established a laundry in Chicago with his sons Bruce, Tom, and Hugh after fleeing China to escape execution following the 1910 revolution. In 1924 the restaurant name was changed to Port Arthur Café. It remained in business at 413 Robert Street until about 1957, when the building was razed to make way for an expanded Emporium department store.[60]

Moy Hee's retail business, Wing Wah Chong, was sold to Moy Fook Yuen for $1,500 in late November or early December 1922. By 1928 the name of the store had been changed to Kwong Chung and Company, and it was managed by Harry Yep. It remained in business at 13 West Ninth Street until the mid-1930s.[61]

It is interesting to note that neither of Moy's sons assumed responsibility for Kwong Tung Low or Wing Wah Chong, although both had worked in these businesses. According to traditional patriarchal structure, sons were first in line to inherit and run family businesses. Probate records also show that Judith informed the Ramsey County court that "the deceased left him surviving your petitioner and two children, whose names and ages are as follows: Gong Moy Fu Hau and Chin Moy Sing Wone, who reside in Sunning District Canton, China."[62]

Since sons Moy Hong Yik and Moy Tai Heung were Judith's stepchildren, why were they not listed in the records? Were they paper sons after all? While some Chinese merchants sold paper slots in order to make money, Moy Hee probably did not need to do this. The "sons," therefore, could have been nephews, cousins, or close acquaintances from his home village whom he was trying to help. Or perhaps they were his real sons, and information that would explain this mystery is still waiting to be found. Or perhaps it never will be. Neither Moy Hong Yik nor Moy Tai Heung are listed in the St. Paul or Minneapolis directories after 1924.

After the estate was settled, Judith purchased a house in White Bear Township and a three-room summer cottage, which she rented to summer vacationers and lodgers for $15 per month. She died in 1938, leaving behind the daughter she had adopted after her husband's death, Frances Marquez, a son-in-law, Manuel, and a grandson, Phillip. She is buried in St. John's Episcopal Cemetery, White Bear Lake.[63]

We do not know what motivated Judith Moy to donate the silver loving cup to the Minnesota Historical Society in 1923. Rediscovered almost 70 years later, this modest object served as a gateway to information about a Minnesota family whose lives mirrored the complex politics and growing pains of two very different cultures. While the wide range of sources that yielded information for this article may not reflect the actual voices of the Moy family, they do provide today's reader with a glimpse of evolving Chinese American identities in early twentieth-century St. Paul.

Thank you, Judith.

NOTES

From Minnesota History *57 (Winter, 2000–01).*

Research for this article was supported by the Charles E. Flandrau Research Leave Fund, Minnesota Historical Society. The author wishes to thank the following for their insight, contributions, and synergy: Joe Hart, Chen Zhang, John Moy, Tim Moy, Connie Moy, Wee Ying Moy, Helen Fong, Howard and Lolita Woo, Stanley and Marvel Chong, Judy Olsen, Erika Lee, Philip Choy, Susan Karren, and supportive family, friends, and colleagues.

1. File 20111, Moy Hee, in Chinese Case Files, District 10, St. Paul, Segregated Chinese Files, 1893–1942, Immigration and Naturalization Service, Record Group 85, National Archives and Records Administration (NARA)—Great Lakes Region, Chicago; Sarah Mason, "The Chinese," in *They Chose Minnesota: A Survey of the State's Ethnic Groups,* ed. June D. Holmquist (St. Paul: Minnesota Historical Society Press, 1981), 532; *St. Paul Pioneer Press,* Aug. 8, 1921, p. 10; portrait of Jun Shee, Minnesota Historical Society (MHS) Library, St. Paul. For more on Confucian teachings, see Arthur Waley, trans., *The Analects of Confucius* (New York: Vintage Books, 1938); Donald J. Munro, *The Concept of Man in Early China* (Stanford, CA: Stanford University Press, 1969).

2. File 20111, Moy Hee, NARA—Chicago; *Weekly Northwestern* (Oshkosh), Sept. 12, 1889, p. 5, Feb. 10, 1894, p. 7.

3. Philip P. Choy, Lorraine Dong, and Marlon K. Hom, eds., *Coming Man: 19th Century American Perceptions of the Chinese* (Seattle: University of Washington Press, 1994), 19.

4. Choy, Dong, and Hom, *Coming Man,* 169.

5. Qinsong Zhang, "The Origins of the Chinese Americanization Movement: Wong Chin Foo and the Chinese Equal Rights League," in *Claiming America: Constructing Chinese*

American Identities During the Exclusion Era, ed. K. Scott Wong and Sucheng Chan (Philadelphia: Temple University Press, 1998), 51.

6. Here and below, Charles J. McClain, *In Search of Equality: The Chinese Struggle Against Discrimination in Nineteenth-Century America* (Berkeley: University of California Press, 1994), 202–03. Minnesota Senator Cushman K. Davis's attitude was not as harsh; see his "Relations with China: Speech Delivered in the Senate of the United States, Nov. 2, 1893, on the Chinese Exclusion Legislation," copy in MHS Library.

7. McClain, *In Search of Equality,* 215.

8. Erika Lee, "Chinese Exclusion and Its Legacy for United States Immigration History," lecture, May 20, 1999, Immigration History Research Center, University of Minnesota, St. Paul.

9. McClain, *In Search of Equality,* 214–15.

10. File 20111, NARA—Chicago. See also *St. Paul Dispatch,* Aug. 5, 1921, p. 5; *St. Paul Pioneer Press,* Apr. 22, 1917, sec. 4, p. 8.

11. File 20111, NARA—Chicago. The designated ports were San Francisco and San Diego, CA; Portland, OR; Port Townsend and Sumas, WA; Malone, NY; Portal, ND; Richford, VT; and Boston, New York, New Orleans, and Tampa; Mary Roberts Coolidge, *Chinese Immigration* (New York: H. Holt, 1909), 279.

12. File 20111, NARA—Chicago.

13. Here and below, Mason, "Chinese," 536; file 20111, NARA—Chicago.

14. File 35450-2-2, Moy Hee, in Seattle District Chinese Exclusion Act Case Files, 1895-1943, Immigration and Naturalization Service, Record Group 85, NARA—Pacific Region, Seattle; file 20111, NARA—Chicago.

15. File 35450-2-2, NARA—Seattle.

16. *Northwest Magazine* 19 (Nov. 1901): 41; Albert Hum, interview by Sarah Mason, Nov. 18, 1980, and Stanley Chong, interview by Sarah Mason, Jan. 11, 1979, notes in Minnesota Ethnic History Project, Box 20, MHS Library. For more on Chinese associations, see Him Mark Lai, "Historical Development of the Chinese Consolidated Benevolent Association/Huiguan System," *Chinese America: History and Perspectives* 1 (1987): 13–51.

17. *Northwest Magazine* 19 (Nov. 1901): 41; *Star Theatre Program,* Apr. 26, 1908, p. 3, and *Auditorium, St. Paul, Program,* Jan. 1918, p. 44, pamphlet file, MHS Library; *St. Paul Shopping Guide,* Jan. 1909, p. 52, MHS Library.

18. Mason, "Chinese," 531–32.

19. File 35450-2-2, NARA—Seattle.

20. File 35450-2-2, NARA—Seattle; estate of Moy Hee, Nov. 23, 1921, Ramsey County Probate Records, Ramsey County Courthouse, St. Paul.

21. File 35450-2-2, NARA—Seattle; Mason, "Chinese," 531.

22. Ruthanne Lum McCunn, *Chinese American Portraits: Personal Histories, 1828-1988* (Seattle: University of Washington Press, 1996), 47; Ronald T. Takaki, *Strangers from a Different Shore: A History of Asian Americans* (New York: Penguin Books, 1990), 127–29.

23. *St. Paul City Directories,* 1903-21; *Star Theatre Program,* 3; *St. Paul Shopping Guide,* Jan. 1909, p. 52.

24. File 20111, NARA—Chicago.

25. *Minneapolis Journal,* Oct. 12, 1904, p. 7.

26. Estate of Moy Hee; Mason, "Chinese," 535.

27. *Minneapolis Journal,* Jan. 21, 1906, p. 12; file 35450-2-2, NARA—Seattle.

28. The number of Chinese restaurants in New York City increased from eight to more than 300 between 1880 and 1902; Renqui Yu, "Chop Suey: From Chinese Food to Chinese American Food," *Chinese America: History and Perspectives* 1 (1987): 92–95.

29. File 35450-2-3, Wong Shee, in Seattle District Chinese Exclusion Act Case Files, 1895-1943, NARA—Seattle.

30. Governor's Interracial Commission of Minnesota, *The Oriental in Minnesota: A Report to Governor Luther W. Youngdahl* (St. Paul, 1949), 24; [Norma Sommerdorf], *A Church in Lowertown: The First Baptist Church of Saint Paul* (St. Paul: Mason Publishing, 1975), 110; *St. Paul Pioneer Press*, Apr. 22, 1917, sec. 4, p. 8. This was not the first English class offered to Chinese immigrants in St. Paul. A similar class was organized as early as Nov. 1883 by the Young Men's Christian Association; *Minneapolis Tribune*, Nov. 18, 1884, p. 6.

31. Ginger Chih, "Immigration of Chinese Women to the U.S.A., 1900-1940" (master's thesis, Sarah Lawrence College, 1977), 34; Victoria Wong, "Square and Circle Club: Women in the Public Sphere," *Chinese America: History and Perspectives* 8 (1994): 136-37.

32. First Baptist Church Parish Records, 1851-1944, MHS Library; *St. Paul Pioneer Press*, Apr. 22, 1917, sec. 4, p. 8; Mason, "Chinese," 537.

33. Sarah Refo Mason, "Liang May Seen and the Early Chinese Community in Minneapolis," *Minnesota History* 54 (Spring 1995): 223-33; Howard Woo, Minneapolis, telephone interview by author, Feb. 28, 1994, copy of typed transcript in MHS museum collections accession file 6305.

34. Estate of Moy Hee.

35. United States, *Census, 1920, Population,* St. Paul, Ward 4, Precinct 2, enumeration district 38, sheet 10, microfilm roll 852, MHS Library.

36. Lai, "Chinese Consolidated Benevolent Association," 16.

37. *St. Paul Pioneer Press*, Apr. 22, 1917, sec. 4, p. 8.

38. See, for example, *St. Paul Daily Globe*, Apr. 13, 1879, p. 1; *Minneapolis Journal*, Oct. 27, 1918, p. 1; Sucheng Chan, "The Exclusion of Chinese Women, 1870-1943," *Chinese America: History and Perspectives* 8 (1994): 117.

39. *Minneapolis Journal*, Apr. 11, 1902, p. 3. No further information about Moy's involvement with the Masons has been found.

40. Woo interview.

41. *St. Paul Pioneer Press*, Aug. 9, 1911, p. 12, Aug. 10, p. 4.

42. Here and three paragraphs below, file 20111, NARA—Chicago. The case, *Mrs. Gue Lim v. U. S.*, 176 U.S. 459, is cited in Moy's file. Ages and dates cited on various documents in the file do not always add up correctly.

43. For an overview, see Lai, "Chinese Consolidated Benevolent Association"; Mason, "Chinese," 539. See also Joseph Hart, "The Tongs in Minneapolis: A Preliminary Exploration," directed research paper, Department of History, University of Minnesota, 1999, copy in author's possession.

44. *Minneapolis Journal*, Oct. 29, 1907, p. 6.

45. *Minneapolis Journal*, Nov. 9, 1912, p. 1; *St. Paul Pioneer Press*, Nov. 9, 1912, p. 2; Mason, "Chinese," 539; Governor's Interracial Commission, *Oriental in Minnesota*, 10. See also *St. Paul Pioneer Press*, Aug. 5, 1921, p. 1, and *St. Paul Daily News*, 1921, Aug. 5, p. 2, wherein lawyer Joel Dickey commented that Moy Hee was successful in keeping the tongs out of St. Paul.

46. File 20111, NARA—Chicago.

47. Here and below, *St. Paul Pioneer Press*, Apr. 22, 1917, sec. 4, p. 8; file 35450-2-2, NARA—Seattle.

48. File 20111, NARA—Chicago.

49. See Jonathan D. Spence, *The Gate of Heavenly Peace: The Chinese and Their Revolution, 1895-1980* (New York: Viking Penguin, 1982).

50. *St. Paul Dispatch*, Feb. 23, 1920, p. 14.

51. Ed Thom, interview by Sarah Mason, June 7, 1979, notes in Box 20, Minnesota Ethnic History Project; Spence, *Gate of Heavenly Peace.*

52. Takaki, *Strangers,* 268; *St. Paul Dispatch,* July 21, 1944, p. 16.

53. Governor's Interracial Commission, *Oriental in Minnesota,* 23.

54. Translation by Chen Zhang, Sept. 14, 1999, notes in accession file 6305, MHS; Gloria H. Chun, "Go West . . . to China": Chinese American Identity in the 1930s," in *Claiming America,* 173.

55. Here and two paragraphs below, *St. Paul Dispatch,* Aug. 5, 1921, p. 5, Aug. 9, 1921, p. 1; *St. Paul Pioneer Press,* Aug. 10, 1921, p. 5, Aug. 8, 1921, p. 10 (quote); estate of Moy Hee.

56. *St. Paul Pioneer Press,* Aug. 6, 1921, p. 10. Probate records show that the estate was actually valued at approximately $20,000; estate of Moy Hee. According to the Minneapolis city directories, Moy's other restaurant, Shanghai Low, was no longer in business by 1920.

57. *St. Paul Pioneer Press,* Aug. 8, 1921, p. 10; estate of Moy Hee.

58. Estate of Moy Hee; *Duluth Herald,* Sept. 8, 1922, classified sec., p. 31.

59. Unidentified newspaper clipping, ca. Oct. 1922, in file 20111, NARA—Chicago.

60. Estate of Moy Hee; John Moy, Eagan, interview by author, May 5, 1994, copy of typed transcript in accession file 6305. John, grandson of Maurice Moy, recalled Port Arthur having five or six cooks. During the St. Paul Winter Carnival parades, it was filled to capacity. Family members continued to live on the fourth floor, including Seong Moy, a contemporary artist whose paintings are in the MHS art collection and museums throughout the United States. John Moy also noted that Chinese Americans stationed at Fort Snelling during World War II frequented Port Arthur, by then run by his father, Hugh-Moy Wing Yip.

61. Estate of Moy Hee; *St. Paul City Directories,* 1923–36.

62. Estate of Moy Hee.

63. Estate of Judith Moy, Dec. 20, 1938, Ramsey County Probate Court, Ramsey County Courthouse, St. Paul; *St. Paul Dispatch,* Nov. 5, 1938, p. 10.

Walk a Century in My Shoes: Minnesota 1900–2000

ANNETTE ATKINS

On the eve of the twenty-first century, many historians grappled with ways of demonstrating the awe-inspiring technological advances of the previous one hundred years—the age of the automobile, the airplane, radio, television, nuclear weapons, computers, and the internet. Annette Atkins chose something more personal to examine: her feet. Or, more accurately, her shoes. How did her shoe collection, she wondered, differ from those of women in Minnesota at the turn of the twentieth century? Beginning with the three pairs of locally made shoes owned by Sarah Christie Stevens in 1900, Atkins follows changes in production, marketing, and sales of shoes. In so doing, she explores the twentieth century's impact on consumer attitudes and, in turn, reveals a bit about our shifting values and lifestyles.

My favorite shoes are flat, black tie shoes that remind me of Sister Francita, my seventh-grade teacher, and of Katherine Hepburn, my other fashion idol. My friends tease me because these shoes are so dowdy, but they're comfortable. They don't pinch my toes or slide off when I walk down stairs. I can run if I have to, and my feet stay dry. Most importantly, they're "me." I wonder what Sarah Jane Christie Stevens would have thought of them.

Sarah and her husband, William, farmed near the village of Good Thunder, 14 miles from Mankato, on the Chicago, Milwaukee, and St. Paul Railway line. In 1900 she was 56 years old and had lived in the state for the better part of three decades. Like a third of the population, she was foreign born, though not German or Scandinavian like a majority of Minnesota's immigrants, but Scottish by way of Ireland. Her father was a Scottish weaver working in Ireland when she was born in 1844 to her Scots-Irish mother. The next year the family emigrated to Wisconsin. With her father, stepmother, half brother, and three brothers Sarah moved on to Minnesota in the mid-1860s and lived there until her death in 1919. By the year 1900 she had been married for about 20 years and had four stepchildren, two daughters of her own, and a husband she clearly loved, even if she did call him Mr. Stevens to outsiders, including her brothers. He was 19 years older than she.[1]

Sarah faced the twentieth century full of memories of her own and Minnesota's past. She had witnessed the Civil War, the coming of the railroads, the rise of populism, and the creation of White Earth Reservation, as well as the recently concluded Spanish-American War. She watched the coming of the telephone, the bicycle, and the automobile, though she owned none of them, and a modern improvement most important to her: rural free delivery of the mail. She campaigned for prohibition of alcohol and suffrage for women. Minnesota granted women the vote on school-related matters in 1875, paving the way for Sarah's election as Blue Earth County's superintendent of schools in the 1890s. Although she died before Minnesota ratified the woman-suffrage amendment, she did live to see Prohibition. World War I, too. Her pantheon of famous Minnesotans would have included Ignatius Donnelly, Henry H. Sibley, Alexander Ramsey, Little Crow, and Archbishop John Ireland. John Lind, born in Sweden, was governor in 1900 but was defeated that November by Samuel R. Van Sant, a Civil War veteran. Knute Nelson from Norway, Minnesota's first foreign-born governor, and Cushman Kellogg Davis, another former governor, were her senators.

Sarah's village, Good Thunder, was named after a Dakota man who had converted to Episcopal Bishop Henry Whipple's Christianity and who, having aided whites during the Dakota War, was known to them as a "good Indian." She would not have had much contact with the Dakota, however, most of them having been removed to Nebraska in the 1860s. She would not have known many African Americans either. Of the state's 1.7 million residents, they comprised just under 5,000. About half lived in St. Paul. She might, though, have had contact with J. R. Wysong, one of only 200 Chinese in the state; he operated a steam laundry in Mankato.[2]

Sarah agonized over the safety of her brother, Sandy, who had joined the gold rush to Alaska in 1898 and hadn't yet returned in 1900. She regularly corresponded with her brother Tom, a Congregational minister, and his wife, Carmelite, who were working in Turkey. Her other brothers farmed, William near Winona and David, who raised sheep, in Montana.[3]

Her father had encouraged her brothers in their education and they had encouraged her. She was chronically in money trouble, and throughout her life she searched for schemes to make a little cash. She opened a doomed seamstress business, sold magazine subscriptions, taught school, sold garden produce. She suffered from the confinements of gender roles and rejoiced when her daughter entered medical school and then practiced medicine with her doctor husband first in Virginia, Minnesota, then in Minneapolis. I drive past what was once her daughter's house—at 2550 Dupont in Minneapolis—and try to imagine Sarah coming and going. I can almost see her.

I don't know if Sarah Christie Stevens had a favorite pair of shoes. In her thousands of letters—available for study in the library at the Minnesota History Center in St. Paul—she did not describe her shoes once, nor even a shopping expedition. Not worth her notice, but worth ours. Watches tell one kind of time, our shoes another, if only we know how to read them. They can tell us a lot about her, about her times. Comparing her shoes with our own, we can also learn a lot about the past 100 years in Minnesota.

If we presume that in her fashions Sarah Christie Stevens was like other rural, white women of her time and place, we can construct a virtual inventory of her closets. First, though, she probably didn't have a closet. Some late-nineteenth-century houses had built-in closets, but most had freestanding wardrobes instead. The storage of clothing—and shoes—didn't demand too much space, so a compact wooden clothing cupboard would do just fine. The 42-room James J. Hill house on Summit Avenue in St. Paul, built in 1891, had 10 family bedrooms, a dining-room table big enough to seat 22 for dinner, and lots of closets. Its design preceded the invention of hangers, however, so closets offered hooks and drawers, with no space beneath the clothes to kick—or carefully arrange—even a modest number of shoes. Nor were wardrobes practical for shoes. The front door opened several feet above the floor, so to store shoes you had to pick them up, drop them into the well of the wardrobe, and then in the morning lean over and fish them out again. More likely, Sarah didn't go to that trouble. Instead, she'd have pushed her shoes under the bed—it stood up high and had lots of room underneath.

The shoes she wore most often—her work boots—rarely made it inside the house. They stayed in the boot room or on the porch. Every farmhouse had an entryway where people dropped their wet, muddy outdoor shoes before going into the house. Mud and dirt must have been the nightmare of many a farm woman, and "take off those shoes," her mantra. In any case, it was easier to leave them, muddy, at the door than to clean them off only to go back outside an hour or so later and get them muddy again.

Nineteenth-century advice manuals may have designated the home as woman's proper sphere, but that wasn't a luxury available to most women, even if they wanted it. Sarah's sphere for a time had included teaching at Carleton College in Minnesota and Wheaton College in Illinois and supervising Blue Earth County's school system, but in 1900 it revolved around the daily demands of her and William's farm. She was a working woman by anyone's standards. In her 1902 journal she kept track of her summer produce. She raised, harvested, and then sold, canned, or otherwise preserved peas, lettuce, turnips, asparagus, radishes, carrots, parsnips, tomatoes, cabbage, onions, black raspberries, blackberries, currants, gooseberries, white currants, apples, grapes, celery, parsley, cucumbers, and plums. Like most midwestern farm women, she also raised and sold chickens and eggs. In April and May 1900 alone, she delivered 1,440 eggs to J. G. Graham's general store in Good Thunder. For this outdoor work she needed sturdy footwear.[4]

Many farm people of her day wore wooden shoes or clogs, the European work shoe for both women and men. Clogs are best for barn work such as shoveling or milking because they're comfortable and they raise the wearer a little above the muck. They were also cheap. With only a little practice, a farmer could make a decent enough clog since they didn't require exact sizing.

A century later clogs are big business. Rarely homemade, they come in dozens of colors. The Sven Clog Company in Chisago City, Minnesota, owned and run by Marie Carlsson, employs two other full-time and six part-time workers (all women), who turn out about 150 pairs per day. Cooks, doctors, and nurses are among the most loyal customers, plus women who like the comfortable peasant look and feel.[5]

Clogs in the nineteenth century also had that peasant look, but it was a look that some immigrants wanted to leave behind. Sarah talked about the Irish as "them" and Americans as "us." Because she was assimilated, she probably wore boots instead, though perhaps men's boots.[6]

Sarah's brothers and her husband, William, all wore boots most of the time. Men's dress boots came in several styles, but most work boots have looked virtually the same for 150 years. Rural men, factory men, mining men, milling and timbering men all wore five-eye, tie-up black leather boots. They were sturdy, if nothing else.

Many women needed sturdy footwear to work in, too, but there wasn't much commonly available in Sarah's day. The 1897 Sears and Roebuck catalog, from which you could buy everything from nails to underwear to farm equipment—all the most practical things—did not offer work boots for women. Oh, there were many styles of women's boots, all with pointed (surprisingly pointed) toes and heels. Both impractical and uncomfortable. The flat, slightly wider shoes—what Sears called Ladies' Common Sense Oxfords, for example—were the kind that Sarah would have put on to go into the house from the entryway.

So, Sarah had work shoes and indoor shoes. She also would have had "good" shoes: thin, kid-leather dress-up boots. It would be another decade before most women wore a lower-cut shoe. Boots would have served her for all the seasons—even if they didn't keep her feet warm in winter. When she and Mr. Stevens got dressed up, for going to the Good Thunder Baptist Church especially, they both put on high-topped boots. He tied his; she either tied or buttoned hers with the aid of a buttonhook. Their dress boots, like their work boots, clogs, and house shoes, looked remarkably alike in their styling and detailing, even in their pointed toes. Hers, though, were narrower and had higher heels, slightly more seductive that way.[7]

High heels have not always been the province of women. Until the French Revolution, aristocratic men all over Europe wore heels. Heels didn't denote gender, they denoted class. The republicanism of the French Revolution brought a leveling of shoes. Pointed toes and high heels were originally devised, and quite useful, for men on horseback. Cowboy boots still have them.

High heels have never caught on much among Minnesota men, but for all of the twentieth century the state's women have shared the national mania for high heels—not because they were useful, either. Podiatrists inveigh against them, declaring them as damaging to the feet as footbinding in China (where the ideal length for a woman's foot was three inches). Many women happily ignore the warnings.

Sarah, of course, wasn't wearing four-inch stiletto heels; those came 50 years later as part of the return to glamour and, some said, femininity, after World War II. They appeared in the mid-1950s along with Ozzie and Harriet and the Cleaver family (though not *on* Harriet or June). June, the mom in *Leave it to Beaver,* though, wore medium-high heels even to do the laundry. I suspect that Betty Crocker—the feminine personification of General Mills—stood at her kitchen counter in heels, too. She was just like that.

In Sarah's day and among women of her social circumstances, the heels on dress shoes were one-to-two inches high and only just visible beneath the skirts that, even for laboring women, nearly touched the floor. So, you might ask, why bother with pointed, narrow shoes? Perhaps for the same reason that most women today wear shoes that are too narrow, too small, and too often uncomfortable.[8]

If the Stevens's boots had come from Grimsrud Shoe Company in Minneapolis, William might have picked either the expensive boots at $2.50—black, with patent-leather toes, a "yellow rope edge," and laces through nine holes—or less expensive ones, at $1.75, same styling, made out of kangaroo hide. For women, Grimsrud offered 11-hole tie-up boots with a slightly pointed toe and a two-inch heel at $1.75 or a one-strap shoe with a bow, a more pointed "needle" toe, and the same high heel. The company did sell a "Comfort line" shoe for women, a slip-on with elasticized side gussets, but these were never intended for outdoor wear.[9]

These pairs—work boots, dress boots, and indoor shoes—would have made up Sarah's active shoe wardrobe, except, perhaps, for overshoes. Vulcanized rubber was developed in the late-nineteenth century, and among the thousands of uses to which it was put were various attempts to weatherize shoes. Overshoes were one of the early efforts.[10]

Some people may not be able to throw away their own shoes, but apparently their descendants can. Few examples of everyday shoes have been saved and donated to the Minnesota Historical Society. People do save and donate two other kinds: wedding and baby shoes. Beginning in the 1850s, many women were married wearing special shoes. Made of white kid leather or satin, they were used only once, then tucked away, soon to be joined by the baby shoes that were outgrown before they were worn out. Shoes are evocative. Like the song that zooms us back to the prom or the smell that recalls a long-forgotten kitchen, shoes summon powerful memories. In the 1940s, not content simply with saving shoes, more and more parents took to the more permanent preservation of baby shoes—bronzing them. My mother-in-law kept her only child's bronzed baby shoes on display with her best china in the corner glass cupboard for all of her life.

If Sarah had been born 50 years earlier or 50 years later, her shoes would have been completely different. She was standing in the middle of an industrial revolution in the making, selling, and meaning of shoes. It wasn't a revolution like the American Revolution, with a clear beginning, middle, and end. Its effects, however, have been at least as significant and have shaped everything from how and where people live to what they hope for, how many children they have, and what shoes they wear. Industrialization and its results, especially consumerism, have been in the twentieth century the most important shaper of Minnesota and Minnesota life.

Industrialization involves changes in four key relationships. First, the relationship between producer and consumer. A single worker making a single product for a particular person he knows decides to make an extra on speculation to sell to a stranger. This act breaks the bond between the maker and user and opens the door—and the imagination—to producing more products for more strangers, with the hope of increasing profits. Different industries took this step at different times. Textiles and guns preceded shoes; clothing and cigars followed. The timeline varied, but this basic idea was the same whether the thing was a chair, a hammer, a hat, a house, or a pair of shoes.

Second was a change in the relationship between the maker and the thing made. Where a single shoemaker once made a whole shoe, increasingly one person made one part of a shoe repeatedly, and someone else made another part. The worker's ability to do a task exactly as specified by another—so that all the pieces would fit together—became the most important qualification for the job. Many jobs still required skill—cutting out shoe uppers demanded experience and ability—but no one person was responsible for a particular shoe. This step streamlined the process, made it more efficient and profitable. It also routinized the work and, historian Daniel T. Rodgers argues, the workers and, in so doing, alienated them from their work. They became pieceworkers rather than shoemakers. Shoemakers had been proud and independent tradesmen organized into the Knights of St. Crispin. Workers in shoe factories were quick to organize and unionize, too.[11]

Third, the use of machines changed the nature of the thing produced. What had once been made by hand, with all of the variations that come from hand-work, could be made on a machine more precisely and consistently and, often, better. Things made more efficiently brought greater profit. The sewing machine and, more recently, the computer have revolutionized the shoemaking industry.

Finally, industrialization brought a change in the relationship between home and workplace. The introduction of machines made work more central-ized, made workplaces more permanent, and divided work and home more sharply. The shared economy of most preindustrial households had allocated productive and necessary labor and responsibilities to men and women. When industrialization took most paid labor out of the house—and with it, most men—his job came to be called "work" and hers something else. She did her work in the place increasingly identified in the nineteenth century as a refuge, while he was in the "workplace." Whatever her productive labor, he made the money in a world where cash was becoming increasingly important and in-creasingly the measure of a person's value. It was perhaps not coincidental that as this gender division widened, men's and women's shoes came to look less and less alike. By the 1910s, you could tell women from men simply by looking at their shoes.

Minnesota was in the midst of all these changes in 1900. Sarah stood on one side of them, and we stand on the other. These changes have made our worlds different, too.

The shift from home to factory and from hand to machine did not happen smoothly or all at once. In Sarah's day some Minnesotans still made their own shoes out of whatever was at hand: leather, birch bark, wood, old shoes, wool, cloth, yarn. A few itinerant shoemakers still traveled from door to door with their shoe forms and some pieces of leather. Many skilled boot and shoemak-ers were still at work, carrying out their traditional craft with apprentices and family members. Wherever Sarah had lived in Minnesota, she could have found shoemakers at work.

St. Cloud, for example, like Mankato, had 4 boot and shoemakers in 1900. Minneapolis and St. Paul each had 42. Biwabik had 2. Ely, Eveleth, and Chisholm each had 3. Duluth had 36. Their names are wonderfully suggestive of the cities' and state's ethnic diversity: Santino DeBernardi, P. A. Fredreksen, Adol-phus Gamache, J. B. Laframboise, Emmett O'Meara, Herman Olson, and A. J. Tallakson.[12] The shoemaking trade, however, was on the wane.

John Leisen, for example, in 1889–90 was one of St. Cloud's skilled cob-blers. He lived and made boots and shoes at 624 St. Germain Street. His three sons lived at home; Frank was a clerk at a bank, Michael and John Jr. both clerked in a dry goods store. Two other shoemakers plied their trade across the street: Mr. Biggerstaff at 627 and Mr. Schoemacher at 611. Leisen both made and sold shoes, so he was already producing for strangers. He certainly had at least a small sewing machine, but he still made the whole shoe largely by himself. He lived and worked in the same place.[13]

Into the 1890s, the State of Minnesota still held shoemaking to be a valuable skill. The Minnesota School for the Deaf and the Minnesota State Prison in St. Cloud taught students and inmates to make shoes to give them a useful life trade. But change was happening. By 1910 John Leisen was dead. His son Michael ran a shoe store—no shoemaking listed—at his father's address. His brother John Jr. had opened a "Dry Goods, Millinery and Ladies Garments" shop next door, at 620–622 St. Germain. Neither of them lived above or behind their stores but in nice houses some blocks away. In 1910 the Minnesota Bureau of Labor, Industries and Commerce stopped distinguishing between custom shoe work and shoe repair. By 1920 shoemaking as a category had disappeared entirely from the Minneapolis directory.

Minnesota in 1900 had 16 boot and shoe factories with 13 "proprietors" (owners or managers), 142 superintendents, and just over 2,000 wage earners. Ten years later 18 factories employed 285 proprietors and clerks and 2,664 wage earners.[14]

The three smallest factories employed only one to five workers. The custom shops employed, on average, one or two workers. (These types of businesses were different enough that the state and federal government both reported them as separate categories.) Since the smallest factories and the smallest custom shops were about the same size, the difference must have been in the processes employed—in the custom shops one person making one shoe; in the factories, piecework or one person making multiples of one part.

The largest factory, unidentified by name, employed 625 workers in more than 100 different jobs including cutting, outsole; cutting, insole; cementing; stitching; heel building; fastening eye on button stay; sanding; brushing; packing; seam lining; labeling; and trimming. But the census categorized most workers as "shoe makers, unclassified" or "machine operators, unclassified." Custom shops employed virtually no women; factories had labor forces nearly 40 percent female. Men more often did the cutting (higher paid) while women did the sewing (more "delicate"), the Minnesota Department of Labor reported.[15]

In 1900 shoemaking was Minnesota's tenth most important industry in value of output. One hundred years later shoemaking is so small a part of the state's manufacturing that it doesn't merit a separate category in the published records. The shift from home to small factory to larger factory to consolidated, even larger factory has characterized manufacturing growth (and farm growth) in Minnesota and in the United States in the twentieth century. The other major trend has been to move manufacturing south and then outside of the country. In 1900 Massachusetts was the largest producer of shoes in the United States; in 1997 it was Texas.[16]

In 1877 nearly half of the shoes sold in Mankato were made in Mankato. If Sarah had been born 100 years later and was 55 in the year 2000, she, like us, would probably not wear shoes made in Mankato, or in Minnesota, or even in the United States. My Sister Francita/Hepburn shoes are Rockports. That's an American company, but the shoes were manufactured in Brazil. All Red Wing brand shoes—headquartered in Minnesota—are made in the United States (mostly in Minnesota, with smaller plants in Missouri and North Carolina), but Red Wing is an exception. Most U.S. shoe companies like Minneapolis-based Minnetonka Moccasins Co., Inc., manufacture their shoes "off-shore" in order to reduce costs.[17]

In the 1950s, U.S. shoe manufacturers exported more shoes than they imported—4 million out and 3 million in. In the last 20 years domestic production of shoes has dropped from 500 million pairs to 188 million. In 1998 we imported seven times more shoes than we exported—36 million out and 1.4 billion in.[18]

In the mid-1990s more than 50 percent of the shoes in the United States were imported from China, 11 percent from Brazil, 8 percent from Indonesia. A growing new production area has been Vietnam, where wages average $.24 an hour, about $500 a year for a laborer. (American shoe workers earn about $9.40 per hour and their managers more than that.) A midlevel manager in Vietnam takes in about $150 per month. The chief executive and administrative staff salaries, however, continue to be paid on a U.S. scale. The CEO of Nike recently received about $3 million annually.[19]

Manufacturers in many industries have been squeezed by competition and lower labor costs outside of the United States. Until the 1970s, Minnesota's Iron Range thrived because of American steel production; mining there has nearly ceased, however, because, like my shoes, more and more steel is produced more cheaply in Brazil.

In 1900 about 6.5 percent of Minnesota's population was employed in manufacturing. A century later, the percentage is almost 20 percent and the nature of the manufacturing has changed radically.[20]

Driven by water power at the now unlikely looking St. Anthony Falls in the Mississippi River at Minneapolis, flour milling dominated the state's economy in 1900 and was Minnesota's most important contribution to the national economy. Flour milling went through essentially the same industrializing process as did shoemaking, only slightly earlier and propelled by improved technology that increased the quantity of wheat milled and the quality of flour produced. Minnesota's two largest and most successful mills were Pillsbury and Washburn-Crosby (the latter renamed General Mills in 1928). These two mills produced world-famous wheat (Gold Medal and Pillsbury's Best) that served an international market. They then diversified into dozens of foods (Bisquick, cake mixes, Burger King, Wheaties), then into dozens of nonfood industries, including WCCO radio, whose call letters come from Washburn-Crosby Company, still the best station in the state for announcing farm commodities prices and winter school closings.

In 1900, after flour milling, the state's ten largest manufacturing industries included lumber and timber products; slaughtering and meat packing; butter, cheese, and condensed milk; printing and publishing; foundry and machine-shop products; steam railroad car construction and repair; linseed oil; malt liquor; and, tenth in value of products produced, shoes and boots.[21]

In 1900 Minnesota was clearly an agricultural state—its people, its economy, and most of its major industries depended heavily on farming. The federal census reported that 40 percent of the state's gainfully occupied worked in agriculture. Nearly 70 percent of the population was rural, and about 20 percent lived in the Minneapolis-St. Paul area.[22]

One hundred years later only about 1 percent of the population is employed in agriculture and nearly 60 percent of all Minnesotans live in or near the Twin Cities. Agriculture still plays an important role in the state's economy—we're the nation's largest producer of sugar beets, sweet corn, and green peas and the second-largest producer of turkeys. (Jennie-O Foods in Willmar is currently the world's largest turkey processor, in 1999 producing 860 million pounds of turkey worth $500 million.) We're seventh nationally in wheat production. But Sarah's kind of farm is long gone. If Sarah and William were alive now, they could not have survived on their farm; it was too small, too diversified, too local.[23]

But new industries have emerged, especially since World War II. The fastest growing in the 1990s has been what the state calls "Instruments and Related Products," a category that includes precision scientific, technological, and health-related devices manufactured by, for example, Medtronic, Johnson Controls, and Control Data.[24]

Fifteen Fortune 500 companies are headquartered in Minnesota. Four are food related: producers General Mills and Hormel and distributors Supervalu and Nash Finch. The list also includes Dayton-Hudson and Best Buy (retail); 3M; Northwest Airlines; U.S. Bank; Lutheran Brotherhood and the St. Paul Companies (insurance); and United Healthcare Corporation. Honeywell, founded in 1888 as a maker of automatic thermostat controls and one of the state's largest industrial corporations, is merging with a New Jersey firm and moving its corporate headquarters.

These changes have transformed not only the economic but also the social and cultural landscape from Sarah's time to ours. Sarah would hardly recognize her Minnesota in 2000. It's not just that the buildings are taller or that there are so many more of them or that they're made more often out of steel and glass than brick and wood, but that their businesses function differently and by different principles. Fewer than one-fifth of Minnesotans in 1900 were involved in transportation and trade. Today, that many are employed in retail trade alone. Sarah's experience of buying shoes, already in the process of transformation, was far different from how we buy ours today.

In 1900 William's and Sarah's account books show that they spent $15.05 total on three new pairs of shoes and three pairs of overshoes (plus an additional $.40 on laces and polish), one each for William, Sarah, and a daughter. They didn't spend so little because they were poor. They weren't, and they would have taken offense at being thought hard up. They lived much as their neighbors and friends did, and it wasn't bad.[25]

If each of us spent as little as the Stevenses, American shoe manufacturers would long ago have gone out of business. Their success has depended on our willingness to buy. And we have. In the early 1990s we spent about $130 per person, and by the late 1990s more than $200 (in a period of low inflation). Americans spend about $24 per pair, but that's an average.

William and Sarah could have bought their shoes from the Sears and Roebuck catalog beginning in 1895. This wish book made available, especially to farm people, a broader range of goods than they could buy locally and often at slightly cheaper prices. The company worked hard to sever buyers' relationships with their local sellers. The friendly, folksy, and not slightly preachy language of the catalog belied the competitive edge that Richard Sears was so good at sharpening.[26]

The Stevenses could also have used one of the itinerant cobblers who still hauled his lasts from one farm to the next. He more often repaired shoes but could still make the occasional pair. Or, they could travel to one of the custom shoemakers in Mankato.

Or, they could go to a store that sold ready-made shoes. In Good Thunder four stores advertised shoes: J. M. Graham's General Mercantile, August T. Graft's, Henry Wiedenheft's General Store, or Albert Ziegler's shoe store. All four were family owned and run, and three of them were local general stores offering a little bit of everything.[27]

William and Sarah dealt at Graham's Mercantile for many of their needs. Among other things, the Stevenses in 1900 bought a wash tin, ribbon, gingham, linen, serge, percale, soap, crackers, pins, tea, pickles, oranges, cheese and butter, hairpins, a corset, starch, canning jars, a union suit, coffee, raisins, a jacket, a coat, a man's shirt, and gingersnaps. While at Graham's, they also sold eggs, potatoes, strawberries, and apples. They bought $128.51 in goods and collected $58.50 for those they sold.[28]

The Graham family was a fixture in Good Thunder. John and Loretta Graham were the town's first settlers in 1870, when they moved in upstairs over the store that they built. He was also the first postmaster and she the deputy postmaster. (I imagine that the post office was in the store, as well.) In 1878 the Grahams added a hotel and a dance hall. When the Bank of Good Thunder opened in 1893, John was one of its directors. Frank, their son, clerked in the store. Bertha and Louis, daughter and son, taught in the Good Thunder schools.[29]

All four of the town's general stores, however, were experiencing a revolution in retailing that mirrored the revolution in manufacturing. Competition, specialization, and standardization knocked at their doors and could not be ignored. The world of individual, personal service in a community was giving way to more specialized merchandising in a regional market. Graham's responded by getting out of the business. By 1908 it had closed its doors. John had become president of the bank. Loretta had been promoted to postmaster, and Bertha and Louis continued to teach. Frank had left town.

The Wiedenhefts dealt with the competition by going in the other direction. Henry's two sons took over and expanded the store. When Graham's closed, Sarah shifted her business to Wiedenheft Brothers. The store survived for at least another 30 years.[30]

By the end of the twentieth century all of those businesses were gone, and Good Thunder had dwindled in population from 650 to 500. There's no passenger railroad service, but it's quick work to drive to either Mankato or Minneapolis. The retail market is quite different than in Sarah's days. Local merchants have mostly been replaced by local branches of national stores—and in any case there aren't many shops at all. Good Thunder people have fewer choices locally but many, many more regionally and nationally.

Now, the people in Good Thunder, Minneapolis, and St. Cloud, as well as in Toledo, Ohio, and Sacramento, California, shop in one big market, and we all have hundreds of options for buying shoes. In any one of these places—or in dozens of others—we could look at the same range at Payless Shoes or Kmart or J. C. Penney. I happened to buy my favorite shoes at Dayton's in St. Cloud, but I could as well have bought them at Nordstrom's, which has the biggest shoe selection in the state, or at the Rockport store, both in the Mall of America; or off the internet. When I decided that these were great shoes and I had to have a second pair for when my first pair wore out, I went back to the St. Cloud Dayton's. They were sold out, but the saleswoman checked her computer and found pairs in Des Moines, Fargo, and Sioux Falls—did I want a pair mailed to me? I did.

I didn't go to Dayton's in the first place because of any personal connection. We don't have a reciprocal relationship where they buy my books and I buy their shoes. Nor did I expect to know the sales clerk or for her to remember me if she happened to be the person I'd dealt with before. Open about 70 hours a week, the store needs lots of full- and part-time staff to cover the shoe department alone. And that's what I want—convenient hours, efficient service, little or no waiting in line. Like many Minnesotans and Americans, I buy in an impersonal way that makes the clerk and me interchangeable parts.

Places like Dayton's sell only about 12 percent of the shoes that Americans buy. More—15 percent—are bought in shoe stores, Foot Locker or Kinney's, for example. About 30 percent are bought in discount stores; in Minnesota, that's often a Target.[31]

So, for Sarah, buying shoes was a relational act. For me it's a consumer act.

If we could make no other generalization about the twentieth century, we could safely say that it has seen the proliferation of "stuff" and the rise of consumerism: good dishes and everyday, five sets of sheets, 10 sets of towels, several televisions, telephones everywhere. More than just having all those things, we believe that we *need* them. I can't serve wine in a plastic milk glass, can I? Certainly not to guests. And, I can't serve milk to my nephew Jeffrey in a wine glass. New housing developments offer bigger and bigger houses—starter castles I've heard them called—just to hold all the stuff. People say all the time that they need more room; really, most of us need more storage space. The trend was evident in a 1930s house plan in the *Good Thunder News Herald* that showed a Dutch Colonial house with a special design feature: two more closets. Closet chaos—not enough room for everything, especially for shoes—drives people these days to professional closet organizers. Many businesswomen without closet space in their offices have transformed desk drawers or file cabinets into shoe-storage bins.[32]

Manufacturers make more and more things, and we, somehow, buy them. The Red Wing Shoe Company provides an excellent case in point. Founded in 1905, Red Wing Shoes started with big dreams and a modest factory building. From the beginning the owners applied modern industrial principles to their operation. They developed a combination of piecework and line work, mechanized when possible and hand worked as necessary, and initially produced 150 pairs of shoes in a 10-hour work day. With six work days a week, that's about 50,000 pairs annually. Red Wing did well, grew rapidly, and found its niche making primarily men's work boots. When the 1905 building reached capacity—500 pairs a day—the company expanded and in 1923 posted its first year of sales over $1 million. In 1999 sales reached about $300 million, and the company turned out about 9,000 pairs of shoes a day (nearly 3 million a year). Today Red Wing produces more shoes than all Minnesota shoe manufacturers combined did in 1900.[33]

And Red Wing is a small manufacturer. To put it into perspective, Nike, maker of athletic shoes, had sales in the neighborhood of $9.5 billion. Nike and all other athletic-shoe manufacturers make up only one-quarter of the shoe market. In the United States we consume about 1.6 billion pairs of shoes per year. In every year of the twentieth century, Americans have had a higher per-capita consumption of shoes than residents of any other country.[34]

Minnesotans spend more on shoes than do people from the West but less than people in New England and the South. Women buy more shoes than men. Adults more than children. African Americans and Hispanics more than whites. Wealthy people have more shoes—and more of most other kinds of stuff—than do other people, but a broader and broader range of the population also has more of everything than they once had. With industrialization, owning and the possibility of owning things has become more democratized.[35]

By some magic of averaging, one industry analyst determined that we have an annual consumption rate of about 6 pairs of shoes per person in the United States. That's a half-dozen pairs per year for every man, woman, and child. Linda O'Keefe, in *Shoes: A Celebration of Pumps, Sandals, Slippers, and More,* reports that the average American woman owns 30 pairs of shoes; the average man, 16.[36]

It's not as many as Imelda Marcos, whose 3,000 pairs became a metaphor for the misuse of the resources of the Philippine people. While writing this essay I've asked many people how many shoes they own. A few admitted right off that they owned a lot. "I kind of have a thing for shoes," they'll say. My hairdresser's brother-in-law has at least 400 pairs of shoes; several others admitted to having more than 100. In my family we've teased my sister Linda for years about how many pairs she owns—sling backs, thin-soled, platform, no toes, no backs, flats, heels, high heels, square toes, pointed (not many rounded, though), spangled, plain, black, tan, gold, white, eight shades of blue—you get the message. She keeps in her closet the shoes she's willing for her husband to know about. He was quite surprised that time he moved the bed and found 28 other pairs.

Most of us, however, answer modestly. Oh, I have two pairs or three, implying that only an idiot could own 30 pairs. A few people really do own only one or two, some by necessity, some out of principle, but most of us own more and don't quite want to admit it, partly because some people really do own only one pair. We don't want others to know how often we've succumbed to the temptation of shoes. Is our ambivalence about our excess a Minnesota or Scandinavian American phenomenon, this having a lot of things but being embarrassed about it? I certainly feel it as I contemplate my own shoe collection. So, how many do I have?

Fashion, of course, existed before the twentieth century, but industrialization, while increasing the supply, also brought down the prices of many goods, thus making more fashions and styles available to more people. Moreover, as shoe designer Manolo Blahnik declared, the shoe was born in the twentieth century as a fashion accessory. "Dress designers know that the right shoes are a crucial ingredient to a successful look."[37]

Having the right shoes—like having the right drinking glass—seems so important, somehow. I have five pairs of black heels: one quite low and new; one quite low, two years old, and uncomfortable, so I don't wear them much; one higher and also uncomfortable, but I love them and they're just right if I'm going to be sitting (concert or play or church shoes); plus one pair to wear with pants. There's also the pair I bought in the airport last year when the ones I had on suddenly looked a little too dowdy even for me. But I only wore them once—they didn't quite fit.

Fashions change, too. Shoe manufacturers spend millions of dollars every year on advertising designed to convince us to take off perfectly good, perhaps even hardly worn shoes and buy new ones. Even those of us who don't consider ourselves especially stylish are pulled along. I do have one pair of brown heels, in style two years ago, but they seem a little clunky now. They're not worn out, but I don't wear them either. (That's six pairs.)

Casual shoes. Comfort was not necessarily a characteristic of nineteenth-century handmade shoes. Making a shoe to measure often meant determining which of the shoemaker's several lasts, or forms, came the closest to the person's foot size. In addition, the shoemaker made no distinction between right and left shoes or feet. These "straights," as they were called, weren't replaced with "crookeds," that is, left and right shoes, until the mid-nineteenth century. Finally, as design historian Witold Rybczynski argues, comfort as a concept is a twentieth-century invention. Look at furniture, he urges us. Who would have sat in most pre-twentieth-century chairs seeking comfort? No one; it wasn't an option. Nineteenth-century shoes, similarly, were not made for comfort, particularly, and people didn't expect it.[38]

My dress shoes are certainly more comfortable than Sarah's, but I still wouldn't wear them except for dress. Instead, I have my flat black tie shoes (and their replacement safely stored on the top shelf of my closet). Rockport even calls its product "The Comfort Shoe." I have two pairs of clogs, the four-year-old synthetic ones that I slip on to run to get the newspaper and my newer Eddie Bauer wooden-soled ones (harder to run anywhere in). Since I'm not much of an athlete I also include in this category my so-called running shoes (the newer ones, for use in the gym, and the older ones, good for a walk around the lake), my Keds (what used to be called a tennis shoe), and my hiking boots. (That's 14 pairs.) Instead of an array of casual shoes, my husband, like many men, has simply opted for rubber-soled boat shoes.

Specialization has invaded the athletic-shoe industry—and many people's closets. Depending on how they spend their leisure time, even amateurs might have running, walking, and aerobic shoes as well as cross trainers. Other people have climbing shoes, swimming shoes, golf or bowling shoes, track shoes, biking shoes, cleats, ballet slippers, etc. You can't play baseball in ballet slippers, after all. Athletic shoes are also subject to fashion trends—new soles, lighter-weight synthetics, some special feature that makes us ran faster, jump higher, or protects our feet better. Americans buy more athletic shoes than any other kind, and a majority of Americans wear them almost every day.[39]

Then there are seasonal shoes: boots and sandals. When looking back on the nineteenth century, it's striking to think about Sarah's and other Minnesotans' willingness to be hot in the summer and cold in the winter. Not just that they had, by my standards, inadequate heating—a central stove in a Minnesota house leaves most of the rooms frigid, windows and floors frosted—and no air conditioning, but they also didn't much adapt their clothing to the seasons. Civil War soldiers, both North and South, fought year 'round in woolen uniforms. British soldiers in the Boer War in South Africa at the turn of the century wore lighter-weight khaki uniforms for the first time. Sarah and William wore some lighter fabrics in 1900, but many days she wore a long-sleeved, high-necked, to-the-floor dress and underneath it a camisole, corset, pantaloons, several petticoats, and long stockings. Sarah and William wore their boots winter and summer, except when they went barefoot, which was much more often than most of us do today. Farm kids at the turn of the century and later spent a lot of time without shoes. My dad remembers a day in about 1925 when his dad brought the wagon to fetch his barefoot kids home from school because it had snowed. Few parents today would consider sending their children to school shoeless, and most schools would not let them come in, either. Adults, too, rarely go without shoes except at home on the carpet.

Today, we change our clothes and our shoes with the weather. Boots for winter and sandals for summer (and more than one pair of each, dress and casual). And there's that one pair of orange (!) slinky, sexy sandals that I bought in 1974 and wore on the one day in my life that I pretended to be slinky and sexy. (Add another four.)

Most Minnesotans also own seasonal play shoes: ski boots (cross country or downhill or both) and ice skates and, increasingly, in-line skates. If Sarah Christie Stevens ice skated or skied or roller-skated, she attached runners or blades or wheels to her boots. If we're lucky, our ice skates are made by Reidell, the specialists just across the street from Red Wing Shoes, and our in-line skates by Rollerblade—the brand name—in Minneapolis.

Then there are the miscellaneous ones: the old pair that I garden in, the too-small penny loafers, now ten years old, that I leave in my office in case I wear boots to work but forget to bring shoes. I have a pair of Wellingtons somewhere (lost?). (How many does that add up to? More than I want to count.)

So, this is part of how we end up buying—and believing that we need—more than Sarah's three pairs of shoes: wanting the right shoe for the right occasion and segmenting our lives into more occasions.

Shoes, like goods generally, don't just serve a practical purpose; they have a meaning. If shoes were just shoes, pollsters wouldn't ask women what was their "favorite item of clothing to buy," and 6 out of 10 wouldn't answer "shoes." Nor would 6 out of 10 women tell another pollster that there's no such thing as too many shoes.[40]

Shoes cover our feet, but which shoes we choose express and convey something about ourselves. Because we can choose from such a huge range (shoe superstore Just for Feet stocks 5,000 different styles in each store and offers a free thirteenth pair to anyone who buys 12), our choices mean something. Manufacturers—and their ad agencies—understand this dynamic and sell us something more than shoes, too. Facing a mid-1990s slump in shoe sales, one shoemaking executive told his colleagues, "You have to give [consumers] an emotional reason to buy a product." Reebok told its shareholders in 1999, "We are not just a sneaker company," and Its charter declares that the company has a "fun, energetic culture" that is "relentlessly committed" to its customers' success. Nike declares that it wants to "establish and nurture relevant emotional ties with consumer segments." Rockport asserts that "freedom begins with comfort." "When you're comfortable with yourself, you can do anything. Rockport shoes are part of this movement. Insist on comfort in every aspect of your life."[41]

I've selected these at random. Other shoe manufacturers are also selling values in addition to shoes, just different values: beautiful, stylish, rebellious, sexy, responsible, economical, artistic, rugged, individualistic, manly, feminine. In the industrial revolution, things acquired meaning and came to represent and convey people's values, politics, and identity. We may not intend to demonstrate who we are by what we buy, but our things do have political, social, and emotional meanings.

In *The Theory of the Leisure Class* (1899) Thorstein Veblen critiqued the Gilded Age's extraordinary displays of what he called "conspicuous consumption." Veblen excoriated people for their flagrant use of "stuff" to demonstrate their class. Perhaps his response wasn't rooted in a particularly Minnesota consciousness, but *New Yorker* writer Adam Gopnik found it both "odd and apt that the three most eloquent satirists of American display in the first half of the twentieth century—Veblen, [F. Scott] Fitzgerald, and [Sinclair] Lewis—were all Minnesota boys abroad."[42]

Some people have long known about the relationship between things and identity, perhaps because they were forced into consciousness about it. From the 1750s to the 1830s, certainly, and as late as the 1840s, Dakota, Ojibwe, Euro-Americans, and mixed-blood people—women and men—in our region all wore moccasins most of the time. European fur traders may have arrived in European shoes but did not stay in them for long. The greater suitability of moccasins was immediately evident, and whites adapted. Moccasins were practical, comfortable, warm, dry, quiet, simple to make but possible to make beautiful.

The common footwear hints at a time when these people lived in overlapping and intersecting, sometimes even congenial, worlds. As the relationships changed with statehood and a string of disregarded promises, so did the shoes. First whites took off their moccasins, then pushed Indians to abandon them as well; they represented what increasingly came to be identified by whites—even those whites who had been part of it—as a less civilized time. When whites next set about "civilizing" Minnesota Indians in boarding schools, they cut the boys' hair, forbid the use of native languages, and took away their moccasins. School officials issued instead hard-soled, ill-fitting, leather boots that cut and blistered the feet. The students had to make do. Sometimes they were quite enterprising. A few cut off the soles and threw them away, then turned the leather uppers into quite crude, but entirely better and more comfortable, moccasins. Doing so was an act of both self-preservation and self-assertion. Whites and Indians both knew that shoes conveyed values. Many Native Americans continue to make and wear traditional moccasins, which continue to be items of comfort, beauty, and identity.[43]

Most of the rest of us have learned less harshly that our identity is implied by our choice of shoes. In her wonderful little book on shoes, O'Keefe argues that "shoes are the gateway to the psyche." Some people may never think about it consciously, but that doesn't negate the revealing power of the choices. A 16-year-old sets a different path for himself (and a different social circle) if he wears Doc Martens or Birkenstocks or wingtips. My friends would faint dead away if I showed up in three-inch heels or a pair of feathery mules. Obviously, shoes don't tell everything, but they can suggest a lot about a person.[44]

Similarly, shoes don't tell us everything about a state, but they're one way to its heart, to understanding it over this last 100 years, to thinking about industrialization and consumerism in our own lives—to thinking about changes over time. Industrialization has altered so much about us—how we live and where, with what expectations and desires, how we make our livings and with what sense of ourselves, and, even, what shoes we buy, where and how they were made, where we buy them, and what we want from them.

Sarah's Minnesota was rural, agricultural, and on its way to being the Minnesota that it has become. We do her an injustice if we romanticize her times (the good old days) or her (how could she have done all that work?). She was not essentially different from us. If she'd been given the choice, she probably would have owned more than three pairs of shoes. But she lived in a different world that offered her different choices. She couldn't have anticipated that we would one day live as we do now.

If Sarah had been born a hundred years later she would now be about my age. My memory bank holds Hubert Humphrey, Rudy Boschwitz, Walter Mondale, Dave Durenberger, Gene McCarthy, and Jesse Ventura; Edo De Waart and

Kirby Puckett and Bud Grant and Curt Carlson, Meridel Le Sueur, John Hassler, Patricia Hampl, and Phillip Brunelle.

I've watched the coming of snowmobiles and the internet, of cable television, videocassette recorders, and answering machines. I've been a beneficiary and a promoter of the breakdown of rigid gender roles and of a greater appreciation of many kinds of differences. I've witnessed turbulent controversies about taconite dumping into Lake Superior, abortion, motorized vehicles in the Boundary Waters Canoe Area Wilderness, Indian spear fishing on Mille Lacs, the Vietnam War.

My Minnesota is urban, industrial, and on its way to being yet again another Minnesota whose contours we can see no more clearly than Sarah could predict the century ahead of her. The industrial revolution is over, and we're standing in the early stages of another economic adjustment—post-industrialism—that will provoke other cultural earthquakes.

Our shoes don't tell us everything we need to know about those changes—or about the others that swirl around us. They do, however, walk us across the divide between Sarah's time and our own.

NOTES

From Minnesota History 56 *(Winter, 1999-2000).*

1. Sarah Christie Stevens's papers form a significant portion of the James Christie and Family Papers at the Minnesota Historical Society (MHS), St. Paul. See also Jean Christie, "'An Earnest Enthusiasm for Education': Sarah Christie Stevens, Schoolwoman," *Minnesota History* 48 (Summer 1983): 245-54.

2. United States, *Census,* 1900, Population, pt. 1, p. xx, cxx, 483, 544-45; *Mankato City Directory,* 1899-1900.

3. Here and below, see Christie Family papers.

4. See especially Barbara Welter, "Cult of True Womanhood, 1820-1860," *American Quarterly* 18 (1966): 151-74; Nancy F. Cott, *The Bonds of Womanhood: "Women's Sphere" in New England,* 1780-1835 (New Haven: Yale University Press, 1977); Carroll Smith Rosenberg, "The Female World of Love and Ritual: Relations between Women in Nineteenth-Century America," in Carroll Smith Rosenberg, *Disorderly Conduct: Visions of Gender in Victorian America* (New York: Oxford University Press, 1985), 53-76. See also Mary C. Neth, *Preserving the Family Farm: Women, Community, and the Foundations of Agribusiness in the Midwest,* 1900-1940 (Baltimore: Johns Hopkins University Press, 1995); Joan Jensen, *Promise to the Land: Essays on Rural Women* (Albuquerque: University of New Mexico Press, 1991); Nancy Grey Osterud, *Bonds of Community: The Lives of Farm Women in Nineteenth-Century New York* (Ithaca: Cornell University Press, 1991).

5. Marie Carlsson, telephone interview with author, July 8, 1999; *American Shoemaking Directory* (Cambridge, Mass.: Shoe Trades Publishing Co., 1995), 64-65. See also www.clogplace.com.

6. Patricia Williams, "From Folk to Fashion: Dress Adaptations of Norwegian Immigrant Women in the Midwest," in *Dress in American Culture,* ed. Patricia A. Cunningham and Susan Voso Lab (Bowling Green: Bowling Green State University, 1993), 95-108.

7. Minnesota apparently had no button manufacturers; Iowa, however, was the largest producer of buttons in the United States in 1890, with 53 companies that employed almost 2,000 people (one-quarter women). Wisconsin had nine. See U. S., *Census, 1900*, Manufactures, pt. 1, p. 90–98, 520.

8. *Washington Post*, May 12, 1998, p. Z12.

9. Grimsrud Shoe Co., *The Assistant* (Minneapolis [1890]), pamphlet, MHS Library.

10. Rubber also made the athletic-shoe industry possible. By 1920 records about shoes were divided into leather and rubber. By the 1990s people were buying more rubber-soled shoes than leather. Bureau of the Census, *Current Industrial Reports, Footware Production—1997*, table 1, www.census.gov/ftp/pub/industry/ma31a97.

11. Don D. Lescochier, *The Knights of St. Crispin, 1867–1874: A Study in the Industrial Causes of Trade Unionism* (Madison: University of Wisconsin Bulletin, May 1910), 25–37.

12. *St. Cloud City Directory*, 1888–89, 1899–1900; Watson & Co.'s Classified Business Directory of Minneapolis, St. Paul and Other Enterprising Cities of Minnesota and Wisconsin, 1899–1900; Davison's Minneapolis City Directory, 1920. By 1908 the number of shoemakers in Duluth had decreased slightly to 34, but only 12 from 1900 reappeared in the 1908 list. *R. L. Polk & Co.'s Duluth Directory*, 1900; R. L. Polk & Co.'s Range Towns Directory, 1907–08.

13. Here and below, *St. Cloud City Directory*, 1899–1900; John H. Ley's St. Cloud, Sauk Rapids, Waite Park, and Sartell City Directory, 1910; R. L. Polk & Co.'s Duluth Directory, 1920.

14. U. S., *Census, 1900*, Manufactures, pt. 1, U.S. by Industries, p. 92–97, and pt. 2, States and Territories, Minnesota, 441–61; U. S., *Thirteenth Census of the United States, Abstract . . . with Supplement for Minnesota,* 1910, p. 687; State of Minnesota, *Twelfth Biennial Report of the Bureau of Labor, Industries and Commerce of the State of Minnesota,* 1909–1910, p. 90.

15. *Twelfth Biennial Report,* 90, 420–21, 593–95. The factories followed a strict gender-role division of jobs, even when both women and men worked on machines.

16. Census, *Current Industrial Reports—Footwear,* table 1.

17. Minnetonka Moccasins introduced me to one characteristic of modern competitive industry—secrecy. A privately owned company, Minnetonka Moccasins does not publish much information about its internal life. The answers to basic questions—how many pairs of shoes do you produce, how many styles do you manufacture, how many employees do you have—can reveal information that could be damaging in the hands of competitors. Telephone interview with staff person, July 10, 1999.

18. *Market Direction Report 7.3: Footwear* (Chicago: Euromonitor International, 1996).

19. See http://adage.com/dataplace/archives/dp183.html.

20. U. S., *Census, 1900*, Manufactures, pt. 2, States and Territories, 441.

21. There are various ways to determine such a list; see U. S., *Thirteenth Census, Supplement,* 678, for the value of manufactured products. In 1910 the value of all flour products was about $140 million; of boots and shoes, almost $8 million.

22. U. S., *Census, 1900*, Population, pt. 1, p. xc.

23. *Star Tribune* (Minneapolis), July 18, 1999, D1.

24. Here and below, Minnesota Department of Trade and Economic Development, *Compare Minnesota: An Economic and Statistical Fact Book, 1998/1999* (St. Paul, 1998), tables 3.6, 3.10.

25. Here and below, Graham's account, 1900, Correspondence and Papers, box 20, Christie Family papers; Laurence Kieran, "Footwear Retailing in the USA," *Footwear Business International,* Dec. 1998, p. 30; *Market Direction Report 7.3: Footwear,* 7.

26. Boris Emmet and John E. Jeuck, *Catalogues and Counters: A History of Sears, Roebuck and Company* (Chicago: University of Chicago Press, 1950).

27. See miscellaneous 1900 issues of *Good Thunder Herald*. In 1900 most stores and businesses, including Sears and Roebuck, were known by the proprietor's name. A century later, some stores still carry a family name, either explicitly, such as Herberger's, or embedded, as in Wal-Mart. But, signaling the shift from personal to corporate, more store names are not people's names: Payless Shoes, Timbuktu, Land's End. In Minnesota, for example, Washburn-Crosby Milling Company became General Mills.

28. Graham's account, 1900, Christie Family papers.

29. Thomas Hughes, *History of Blue Earth County and Biographies of Its Leading Citizens* (Chicago: Middle West Publishing Co., [1909]), 263–65.

30. Sarah Stevens, Account Book, vol. 16, Christie Family papers. Wiedenheft Brothers was still running ads in the *Good Thunder Herald* in 1920.

31. *Market Direction Report 7.3: Footwear.*

32. *Good Thunder Herald,* Sept. 10, 1930; Norma Koetter, Anne Kaplan, Lori Jane Brandt Anderson, interviews with author, 1999.

33. Sara M. Schouweiler, *Fifty Years of Red Wing Shoes,* 1905-1955 (Red Wing: Ray Johnson Printing Co. [1956]); U. S., *Thirteenth Census, Supplement* 687, 691; *Shoemaking Directory,* 65. Shirley Perkins, Red Wing Shoes, kindly provided production and earnings figures.

34. See www.oregonlive.com/business/99/top50; Kieran, "Footwear Retailing," p. 30; U. S., *Statistical Abstract of the United States,* 1997, p. 754; National Shoe Manufacturers Association, "Facts and Figures on Footwear," pamphlet (New York, 1958), 54.

35. Marcia Mogelonsky, "Meet the Inner-City Shopper," *American Demographics* 20 (Dec. 1998): 38–41; Joan C. Courtless, "Trends in Apparel and Textiles," *Family Economics Review* 8 (1995): 23; *Market Direction Report 7.3,* 5.

36. Kieran, "Footwear Retailing," p. 30; U. S., *Statistical Abstract,* 1997, 754; Linda O'Keefe, *Shoes: A Celebration of Pumps, Sandals, Slippers, and More* (New York: Workman Publishers, 1996), 13.

37. Colin McDowell, *Shoes: Fashion and Fantasy* (London: Hudson and Thames, 1989), 7.

38. Witold Rybczynski, *Home: A Short History of an Idea* (New York: Viking, 1986).

39. Marcia Mogelonsky, "Best Foot Forward," *American Demographics* 18 (Mar. 1996): 10.

40. Karlyn Bowman, "American Fashion Embraces the Casual and the Comfortable," *Public Perspective* 8 (Aug.-Sept. 1997): 58–60.

41. "Industry Executives Call It as They See It," *Footwear News,* Jan. 1, 1996, p. 2–3; www.Reebok.com/annual report/ceo; nikepark.simplenet.com; www.rockport.com/comfort/main.

42. Adam Gopnik, "Display Cases," *The New Yorker,* Apr. 26–May 3, 1999, p. 176. Sarah Stevens may have known Thorstein Veblen, who was a decade younger, because she knew his older brother A. A. Veblen; "Description," Christie Family papers. See also Thorstein Veblen, *The Theory of the Leisure Class* (1899; reprint, New York: Penguin Books, 1994), 170–71. Nearly a century after Veblen, social critic Lewis Hyde offered an equally provocative analysis of Americans' attachment to things; see *The Gift: Imagination and the Erotic Life of Property* (New York: Random House, 1983).

43. Moccasins, like clogs, are also now big business in the United States, and in Minnesota particularly. Minnetonka Moccasins turns out dozens of styles for wearers throughout the world. Most have rubber soles and are often called boat shoes, but they share with traditional moccasins a comfortable fit and feel.

44. O'Keefe, *Shoes,* 13.

Searching for Florence

BENJAMIN FILENE

> *Often we are confronted by history unexpectedly—captivated by an item*
> *in an antique shop or surprised by a forgotten store of family letters in a*
> *relative's attic. For Benjamin Filene, an exhibit curator at the Minnesota*
> *Historical Society, it was the eyes of a little girl, identified only as Flor-*
> *ence Blood, photographed at her piano on February 25, 1912. Florence's*
> *photograph was one of hundreds Filene pored over while preparing the*
> *Minnesota music exhibit,* Sounds Good to Me, *but her eyes haunted him.*
> *He embarked on a minor odyssey of discovery, searching not only for the*
> *girl in the photo, but also for some tangible connection between our time*
> *and the living past.*

For me, it was the eyes. With her hand resting easily on the piano, the girl gives the camera a piercing look of pride and self-possession, with just a hint of defiance. That look stirred up deep feelings in me—about music, about daughters (especially prideful, self-possessed, occasionally defiant daughters), about reaching back for the past. I admit—and it became even more plain later, when I knew more—that I brought personal feelings to bear on the image. But this wasn't a time to be an "objective historian." This was a time to indulge, for a moment, the warm, vaguely melancholy feeling that comes from connecting to the past and to remember why I became a historian in the first place. And it was time to learn more.

All that was written on the back of the photograph was "Florence Blood seated at piano, Feb. 25, 1912," plus the call number assigned by the Minnesota Historical Society's library. The photo was one of hundreds that a team of us flipped through on an early winter afternoon in 1998; it is printed on page 411 of this book. The group was assigned to develop a new exhibit for the Society, *Sounds Good to Me: Music in Minnesota.* Two years before the opening date, we were starting to work in earnest. Until that point, "Sounds Good to Me" had been more a felicitous phrase than a meaningful title. Seeing Florence, though, brought it into focus for me. The exhibit should be about the feelings this girl had for music and the feelings I was having about the girl. It should be about how we all—in different ways, in different times, and in different places—weave music into our lives: sounds good to *me*.

Without telling the rest of the team, I order a print of the photograph, slide it into a frame, and put it on my piano at home. For several months, it sits there largely unexamined. Occasionally my four-year-old daughter, Eliza, notices it and asks if it is a picture of her. "No," I say, "it's someone who lived a long, long time ago." "You mean before I was born?" "Yes, before you were born." Is that all? Can the photograph become more than just a reservoir for the vaguely nostalgic feelings I'd imposed on it? Can Florence be found? One day, I begin the hunt.

The most obvious route dead-ends. Most objects in MHS's collections have donor files that tell how they came to the Society. But our photography curator, Bonnie Wilson, turns up no file on this image, just a record showing that the actual donation had been a $4'' \times 5''$ glass-plate negative, not a print. In the 1950s and '60s, shortly after the Society established its audio-visual library, it was not uncommon for people to donate a stack of glass negatives. The understaffed department might not have time to develop the images for a while, and donor records either were not created or did not itemize all of the images. The surprisingly precise name and date on Florence's photo likely were handwritten on the paper wrapper that held the negative when it was dropped off. Bonnie speculates that since the identification includes Florence's last name, the photograph was probably snapped by someone other than a family member (who would have written just "Florence")—perhaps an itinerant photographer or an amateur who owned a camera and took pictures for everyone on the block.

Regardless of the exact scenario, I can't call Florence's descendants and say, "Tell me about your grandmother." I turn back to the photo itself. Again I am struck by the clarity of the image. You can tell Florence dressed up for it—hair in a braid and a corkscrew curl with ribbons in the back, bracelets and a bead necklace, rings on fingers, shiny boots laced up tightly, cotton dress with nary a wrinkle. The room that holds the piano is not as fancy as some of the other turn-of-the-century parlors I've seen in photos. Sometimes you can hardly spot the instrument beneath the doilies, plants, statues, and bevy of family photographs. Florence's instrument looks to be covered with a tasseled cloth. There's a metronome on top in the center, a fern arrangement and vase on a table nearby, a framed painting (spaniels!) on the wall behind, and a flowered flue-cover on an adjacent wall. It's not a lavish set-up, I think, but certainly comfortable. I realize that the idea of a not-wealthy person dressing up to pose with a piano is part of what I find moving. With an air of idealism and hope, the photo places music in the center of Florence's life—as an avenue for personal and public expression, for feelings of self-worth and hopes for self-advancement.

Tantalizingly, you can read the titles of the music on Florence's piano: "Meet Me To-night in Dreamland" and "Moon Wind." Sheet music, I know from our exhibit research, was all the rage in this period. Pianos had become more affordable in the late 1800s, and their new owners wanted easy-to-play music for parlor sing-alongs. Colorful, single-sheet copies of popular songs became the stock in trade of a booming industry. Although the player piano and then the phonograph began appearing in middle-class homes in the 1890s, the sheet-music trade flourished until the 1930s, when it went into steep decline.

What would it have been like to sit in the parlor and hear Florence play? The question calls to mind an institution I'd read about, the Chatfield Brass Band Music Lending Library in southeastern Minnesota. Jim Perkins, a lawyer in Chatfield, had started a community brass band in 1969 and needed repertoire. He wrote to schools and bands, asking for old sheet music that wasn't being used. At first Perkins filed the donations in his attic in wooden cabinets he bought from the Mayo Clinic for $5.00. As more and more music came pouring in, he moved the collection to City Hall and then, in 1981, opened a 3,000-square-foot library. Today the collection has more than 100,000 songs, with another 500 boxes of music waiting to be catalogued.

I ask Ayesha Shariff, the researcher working on the music exhibit, to call Chatfield. "Moon Wind" doesn't ring a bell, but, yes, "Meet Me To-night in Dreamland" is in their collection. Ayesha orders a photocopy of the music and, with an eye toward reproducing it in the exhibit, asks about the color of the original sheet. A week later the copy comes—clearly legible, showing the same dramatically bonneted woman on the cover as appears on Florence's music. There is also a typewritten note: "I have cut off a corner of the cover of the sheet music we have so you can get an idea of the color." Egad! To the conservation-minded, this is akin to getting a thumb in the mail. But it does show clearly that the cover is pink with a yellow border and red script.

At home I put the music on my piano, a 1908 upright, not too different, probably, from Florence's. The music has a 1909 copyright along with a warning at the top of the inside page: "PLEASE NOTE:—Owing to the phenomenal and unprecedented success and sale of this beautiful song, there have been placed on the market, imitation 'Dreamland' songs with very similar titles. This song written and composed by LEO FRIEDMAN and BETH SLATER WHITSON is THE ORIGINAL song of this title AND WE CAN PROVE IT."

I start to play the song and immediately run into trouble. It's a waltz-time piece meant to be played "dreamily," according to the notation. But as the music moves along, with three-note chords in each hand, my rendition brings to mind a three-legged cow. I haven't taken a formal piano lesson in 20 years, but I do play for pleasure pretty regularly. Is this the "easy-to-play" music that historians have told me about? Could a young girl in 1912 really play this piece? Did someone else play it for her? Regardless, I'm impressed. Struggling along, I gain a new appreciation for the piano's place in people's lives a century ago. If songs like this were considered a dilution of the repertoire, then people must have had quite a degree of facility, and that, I know, requires many hours of practice.

After a second and third try, "Meet Me To-night" starts to come through a little more clearly for me, although still at a ridiculously slow tempo for a waltz. The tune is just as schmaltzy as the title would lead you to expect, and the lyrics follow suit: "Dreaming of you / that's all I do— / Night and day for you I'm pining, / And in your eyes, / blue as the skies / I can see the love-light softly shining." And the chorus: "Meet me to-night in Dreamland / Under the silv'ry moon / Meet me to-night in Dreamland / Where love's sweet roses bloom." (If you're curious, you can hear the tune on a player piano in the *Sounds Good to Me* exhibit.) I imagine young Florence singing these words. Could she deliver them without the edge of a smirk that we would feel obligated to add now? Probably. At her age, she was likely just starting to become preoccupied with this sort of sentiment.

But what age *was* Florence in the photo? I still know so little. I go down to the MHS library and begin looking at the 1912 city directories, alphabetical listings of people, their addresses, and occupations. Florence could have lived anywhere, but I start with Minneapolis and St. Paul. In those two directories alone, I count eleven Bloods, none of them Florences. As today, the directory doesn't list children. The census does, but the 1910 census has no index. You have to know the name and address of the person you're searching for; and, again, entries appear under the name of the head of the household. The 1920 census does have an index, but it seems unlikely that Florence would show up in it, eight years after she posed by her piano.

With the feeling of turning over the last stone, I listen as a reference librarian explains how the 1920 index works. Called Soundex, it's an arcane but, in its own way, beautifully simple system. The first step is to convert the last name you're searching for into a code. The first letter of the last name stays as is, but the remaining ones are assigned numbers from zero to six, except for vowels, which are ignored. If you run out of consonants, you add zeroes. (Today, drivers-license numbers start with Soundexes.) B-L-O-O-D becomes B430. This bureaucratic finagling has a practical, even noble, purpose. B430 leads to Blood, but it would also lead to Bloud or Blaud or Blode. Spelling variations introduced by a time-pressed or tin-eared census-taker or Ellis Island clerk cannot wash out the trail.

On microfilm, I flip through the pages of the Soundex, four handwritten 3″ × 5″ cards per screen. And there she is. Florence E. Blood. She appears under the entry for Hulda (yes, Hulda) Blood, whom I remember as one of the names in the St. Paul city directory. I had been searching for drops of information; suddenly I have a flood. Florence was 21 in 1920, so she was 13 when my photo was taken. She was born in Minnesota. Her mother, Hulda, was born in Sweden. Hulda, 42 in 1920, emigrated in 1888 (at age 10) and become an American citizen in 1893. Florence had a brother, Wallace, three years younger than she. The family of three lived at 666 Ottawa Avenue, just across the Mississippi River from downtown St. Paul.

I can't believe my good fortune. If Florence had married and changed her name before 1920, I wouldn't have found any of these morsels. From the Soundex card, I go to the census enumeration sheet itself. Following the handwritten list, I feel as if I'm walking down the street with the census-taker as he visits the Clarks at 660 Ottawa, the Silvers at 662, the McCarthys at 664, the Bloods at 666. The enumeration sheet tells me that the Bloods rent their home; that all three can read and write; that Hulda does not have a job; and that Florence does, as a clerk for the railroad. (Florence is all grown up!) Wallace is an electrician apprentice with the telephone company. Interestingly, Hulda appears as the head of the household, and she is listed as divorced, quite unusual for the early decades of the century.

With my new information, I can look for the Bloods in the 1910 census. I find them renting at 695 Ottawa. Hilda (yes, Hilda) is again identified as the head of household (again without a profession), but she is listed as married (for 13 years), not divorced. Her husband was apparently born in New York. Returning to the city directories, I find Hulda (yes, Hulda again) at 695 Ottawa from 1911 to 1914, around the corner at 322 West Page Street between 1915 and 1917, and then at 666 Ottawa from 1918 to 1921. I'm startled in the 1917 directory, for there Florence appears, clear as day, sharing the Page Street house with her mother. She was there all along; I just hadn't thought to check so far beyond the date of the photo. The listing identifies her as "clk G N Ry." I talk to two reference librarians before we figure it out: clerk, Great Northern Railway.

The 1917 directory also is the only one that lists Hulda as the "widow of Geo W." Widow? George W.? I backtrack and, yes, George W. appears, living in various addresses (but never with Hulda) and working for Blood and Thomas, which, according to the directory, is a downtown St. Paul firm that handles real estate loans and building contracts. George is listed in 1917, disappears in 1918, the year after Hulda is listed as a widow, but then resurfaces in 1919 and on into the 1920s, still in the real estate business! So was Hulda widowed or not? There was significant stigma attached to divorce in this period. Had Hulda told the city directory surveyor that she had been widowed to avoid uncomfortable questions? Had George moved out of town in 1917–18, prompting Hulda to imagine being rid of him once and for all? Or could she have lost touch with him for a while and presumed him dead? Once again, the historical record is as fallible as it is revealing—and revealing in its fallibility.

As for Florence, the trail abruptly dries up in the 1922 directory. Her mother has moved again, this time to South Smith Street, where, for the first time, she is listed with an occupation: seamstress. But Florence Blood appears nowhere in the 1922 volume, nor in directories for the rest of the decade. No doubt she got married, I figure. I learn that St. Paul's marriage records, wonderfully indexed, are housed in the Ramsey County courthouse, just down the hill from the Minnesota History Center. I'm buoyant as I walk through the doors of the Art Deco building, past the gigantic white onyx statue of the "Indian God of Peace," and into the marriage-record office. After I find Florence's married name, I'll use the directories to trace her and her family down to the present, interview her children, hear stories about how much music meant to their mother, maybe even see the family piano itself!

But Florence doesn't appear in the marriage index—not in 1921 or '22, or '23, or even up to 1930. I almost wish the indexes were less neat so that there would be room to consider other options. I trudge back to the History Center, sit in the microfilm room, and ponder my possibilities. There are few. Florence could have moved out of town or gotten married somewhere else entirely; if so, I will never find her. Or, gulp, she could have died.

The reference librarian tells me that, yes, the historical society has death records on microfilm. In contrast to the marriage records, they are organized chronologically with no index at all. Mainly to avoid admitting that my search is over, I begin paging through the death certificates for January 1922. Almost immediately, they make me feel even more down in the dumps than before. Baby Boy Brown—stillborn. Baby Girl Robbins—mycosarcoma of neck (urgent). Julia French Metcalf—cerebral softening. Fanny Claus—ruptured liver due to auto accident. Florence Grant—diabetes mellitus. Albert H. Neuenfeldt—organic heart. As I turn to each new record, I feel a queasy tension, hoping to find Florence but just as much hoping not to. I want to imagine her as the flashing-eyed girl in the photo, not reduced to an anatomical malfunction.

After 300 deaths in January 1922, I give up and, for the first time in this process, start to wonder about myself. What is going on here? Earlier, I had joked with a colleague that my search for the Bloods was a quest for a surrogate Minnesota family (Blood-lines, so to speak). Lacking local roots of my own (I grew up in North Carolina), I was adopting some. Now I wonder if there might be some truth to this theory. My wife and I moved to Minnesota in 1997 and have loved it from the start. We know, though, that we will always be easterners in a midwestern culture that accepts outsiders but does not exactly embrace them.

If the Bloods are supposed to be surrogate family members, though, they're proving to be more than standoffish. Have I reached the end of the line? Lacking documentary clues, I decide to return to physical evidence. I hop into my Chevy Nova and head for Ottawa Avenue.

All of the homes that Hulda, Florence, and Wallace lived in were within a few blocks of each other in a neighborhood called Cherokee Heights. Some of the houses of their era no longer exist, but as I drive slowly down the street, I see the one I had been hoping for: 695 Ottawa, where Florence lived in 1912 when her photograph was taken. No doubt the house looks different today than it did on that February day 88 years ago. The one-story place has green siding, a "Collie on Guard" sign, and, indeed, a collie looking at me amiably from behind a wire fence. In my mind, I subtract the front porch and side additions, and I'm struck by how small the house must have been when Hulda and her children rented it. What an act of optimism and determination it was for a divorced mother of two to bring a piano into this home! After briefly considering a knock on the door ("Hi, I have this photograph"), I drive home.

Cherokee Heights is in Ramsey County, but it's near the border of Dakota County. Somewhat dispiritedly, I decide to follow up on a long shot suggested by the Ramsey County marriage-license office. I drive 25 miles to Hastings to check if Florence by chance filed her marriage paperwork in the Dakota County courthouse. With the streamlined index system, it takes all of five minutes to bring Florence back to life once again. On March 11, 1921, in St. Paul, a Presbyterian minister married Florence Blood and Arnold S. Jensen. On the printed form, "Dakota" County is crossed out and "Ramsey" is handwritten above it. I walk out of the office with a secret smile.

Arnold S. Jensen, the 1921–22 St. Paul directories say, was a student in the Nichols Expert Business Office Training and Secretarial School. After that, neither he nor Florence are listed until 1930, when Arnold shows up as a clerk at the Great Northern Railway, the same position Florence had held a decade before. Florence herself has no job listing after 1921. In the 1940s, Arnold appears as supervisor at the State Railroad and Warehouse Commission. Arnold and Florence Jensen live on Margaret Street on St. Paul's east side, six or seven miles from where Florence grew up. By 1950 Florence is a widow. In 1956 she herself disappears from the directory.

Searching for further signs of Florence, I notice that Hulda Blood, at age 78, appears in the 1956 directory, living with her son Wallace at 305 West Annapolis, still in the same neighborhood where she had raised her children. Wallace is listed as a pressman at Brown and Bigelow, a printing factory, with a wife named Evelyn. Hulda no longer shows up in the directory after 1960. Evelyn is a widow by 1962 and last appears in 1978.

From the directories, I can't tell which Bloods or, certainly, Jensens, might be children of Wallace and Evelyn or Florence and Arnold, so I'm left with the last resort of the desperate genealogist, the cold phone call. It's going to be "Hi, I have this photograph" after all. Early on, I had looked at the list of 15 Bloods in the St. Paul phone book with a feeling of helplessness, but now one name stands out, an E. C. Blood at 330 W. Annapolis—intriguingly close to where Hulda lived with Wallace and Evelyn. With a deep breath, I dial the number and prepare to try to explain my pursuit of Florence Blood without frightening the person on the other end of the line.

"Know her?! I hated her guts!" The name Florence Blood certainly rings a bell with the woman who answered the phone. "You, you did?" I stammer. "Wh—Why?" "I kept her mother for 28 years. When I asked Florence to take her in, she threw me out of the house! When my husband died, she had to take her, but she put her in a nursing home the next year." Reeling, I grasp for the only solid information at hand: "Your husband? Could that be Wallace?" "Yes. Wallace."

Twenty years after the city directories had stopped listing her, 90-year-old Evelyn Blood—Florence's sister in law, Wallace's widow—is living on Annapolis Avenue. Talking with her, I begin to piece together the story of a family feud. "It was like the Martins and the Coys," says Evelyn, referring to a 1940s ballad opera based on the feuding Hatfields and McCoys. Some of the tension had to do with caring for Hulda who, Evelyn tells me, lived to be 102. Whatever the cause, Evelyn says, "Nobody liked each other." For their part, Wallace and Evelyn saw the Jensens as "a real odd outfit." Relations deteriorated to such an extent that Florence didn't attend her brother's funeral. And, yes, Florence had died in about 1986, thirty years after I'd lost track of her.

Despite her bitterness toward her sister-in-law, Evelyn is being open and generous with me. I venture that the historical society has a wonderful photograph of Florence as a girl. Could I show it to her sometime? "I don't want to see her if she is eight years old." "Well, it shows her sitting by a piano," I say. "She didn't know how play the piano. She wasn't that smart!"

I end the conversation by asking whether Florence had children. She had three, I learn: Delores, Richard, and Carol. Evelyn recalls that the daughters moved away but thinks Richard still lives in town, although she hasn't said a word to him in more than a decade.

I thank Evelyn profusely, hang up, and try to get my bearings. In some ways, my search has succeeded: I have spoken to someone who actually knew Florence and, in fact, had strong feelings about her! Plainly, though, there must be another side to this story. One doesn't interview the Martins but not the Coys. In the Twin Cities phone books, I count 25 Richard Jensens. (Why couldn't Florence have married into the Jabberwocky family?!) Over the next two days, I call them all. In itself, the process turns out to be a heartening gauge of the civic fabric. Twenty-five times I tell my tale, and each time the person on the other end listens and responds politely, sympathetically, encouragingly. "No, that's not my mother. But best of luck!" "Sorry, that's not us. We're from Iowa." After leaving messages on several answering machines, I start getting calls back. "Hello, this is Richard Jensen." My heart leaps. "I'm calling to let you know that my mother was not named Florence. She was Alice"—or Gladys, or

Doris. "Yes, my mother was named Florence," says Richard Jensen #14—but not, it turns out, the *right* Florence.

What more could I do to bring to life Florence Blood and that moment on February 25, 1912? Quite a lot, I suppose: mount a day-by-day newspaper microfilm search for Florence's obituary; enlist a piano expert to identify the model of Florence's instrument; search for the Presbyterian church that married Florence and Arnold; contact a genealogical society and enlist the aid of other Jensen buffs; consult the city's building records for 695 Ottawa Avenue; knock on doors in the Jensens' east side neighborhood; place an ad in the *St. Paul Pioneer Press.*

But no, it seems time to call it quits. Somehow, having a story with a beginning, a middle, and an end is satisfying, even if the story follows a very different arc than I had expected. In itself, the unpredictability has been instructive. An image is not always what it seems. Your daughters don't always turn out as adorable as they start out—at least in the eyes of their sisters-in-law. Evidence is not always evidence. History is an improvised tune that deviates willy-nilly from the printed score.

These pointed reminders, though, have done nothing to dissipate the spark of feeling that Florence Blood first elicited in me. If anything, the search for Florence has deepened my sense of her as a living presence. In its own way, this sense of humanity offers the most valuable lesson of all. History isn't about building airtight narratives. It's about searching for human connection. And when you find it, you know it.

From Minnesota History *57 (Fall, 2000).*

Contributors

CHARLES R. ADRIAN is a professor of political science at the University of California at Riverside. His books include *American Politics Reappraised: The Enchantment of Camelot Dispelled* (McGraw-Hill, 1974), *Governing Urban America* (McGraw-Hill, 1977), and *State and Local Politics* (Wadsworth, 1999).

WILBERT H. AHERN is the Morse-Alumni Distinguished Teaching Professor of History at the University of Minnesota, Morris. His articles documenting the history of Indian schools in Minnesota and the Dakotas have appeared in *Ethnohistory, Journal of Ethnic History,* and *Tribal College Journal.* His essay on the Morris School included in this collection received the Solon J. Buck Award for best article published in *Minnesota History* in 1984.

GARY CLAYTON ANDERSON is a professor of history at Texas A & M University and the author of several books including *Little Crow: Spokesman for the Sioux* (MHS, 1986) and *Kinsmen of Another Kind: Dakota White Relations in the Upper Mississippi Valley, 1650–1862* (MHS, 1997), and co-editor of *Through Dakota Eyes: Narrative Accounts of the Minnesota Indian War of 1862* (MHS, 1988).

ANNETTE ATKINS is a professor of history at Saint John's University in Collegeville, Minnesota, and author of *Harvest of Grief: Grasshopper Plagues and Public Assistance in Minnesota, 1873–78* (MHS, 1984) and *We Grew Up Together: Brothers and Sisters in Nineteenth-Century America* (Illinois, 2001). Her article, "Walk a Century in My Shoes," was the keynote of the Winter 1999–2000 special issue of *Minnesota History.*

RICHARD BARDON, M.D., was a prominent Duluth physician and a native of the Lake Superior country. He was president of the St. Louis County History Society and a frequent contributor to *Minnesota Medicine.*

THOMAS E. BLANTZ, C. S. C., is a professor of history at the University of Notre Dame. He is the author of *A Priest in Public Service: Francis J. Haas and the New*

Deal (Notre Dame, 1982) and *George N. Shuster: On the Side of Truth* (Notre Dame, 1993). His article "Father Haas and the Minneapolis Truckers' Strike of 1934" received the Solon J. Buck Award in 1970.

Solon J. Buck was superintendent of the Minnesota Historical Society from 1914 to 1931 and founding editor of *Minnesota History Bulletin* (later *Minnesota History*). His books included *The Granger Movement: A Study of Agricultural Organization and Its Political, Economic and Social Manifestations, 1870–1880* (Harvard, 1913), *The Agrarian Crusade: A Chronicle of the Farmer in Politics* (Yale, 1920), and *Stories of Early Minnesota* (Macmillan, 1925). He died in 1962. The award for the best article published each year in *Minnesota History* is named in his honor.

Priscilla K. Buffalohead is a lecturer at Augsburg College and educator for the Native American Indian Education Program in Anoka-Hennepin School District 11, for which she has authored the student booklets *Plants and Their Uses by the Chippewa Indian People* and contributed to *Ojibway Family Life in Minnesota.* Her article on Ojibwe women included in this collection received the Solon J. Buck Award in 1983.

Jennifer A. Delton is an assistant professor of history at Skidmore College and author of *Making Minnesota Liberal: Civil Rights and the Transformation of the Democratic Party* (Minnesota, 2002).

Benjamin Filene is an exhibit curator at the Minnesota Historical Society and author of *Romancing the Folk: Public Memory and American Roots Music* (North Carolina, 2000), winner of the ASCAP-Deems Taylor Award for outstanding print, broadcast, and news media coverage of music. "Searching for Florence" was cited as a notable essay of the year in *Best American Essays 1999*.

Richard V. Francaviglia is a professor of history at the University of Texas at Arlington, where he serves as director of the Center for Greater Southwestern Studies and the History of Cartography. His many books include *Main Street Revisited: Time, Space, and Image Building in Small-Town America* (Iowa, 1996), *From Sail to Steam: Four Centuries of Texas Maritime History, 1500–1900* (Texas, 1998), and *The Cast Iron Forest: A Natural and Cultural History of the North American Cross Timbers* (Texas, 2000).

Sherri Gebert Fuller is project manager for museum collections at the Minnesota Historical Society. Her essay, "Mirrored Identities: The Moys of St. Paul," received the Theodore C. Blegen Award for the best article published in *Minnesota History* by an MHS staff member in 2000.

RHODA R. GILMAN is the author of many books and articles on Minnesota history, including *The Red River Trails: Oxcart Routes between St. Paul and the Selkirk Settlement, 1820–1870* (MHS, 1979) and *The Story of Minnesota's Past* (MHS, 1992). She also co-edited the companion to this collection, *Selections from Minnesota History* (MHS, 1965). She is currently senior research fellow emerita at the Minnesota Historical Society.

WILLIAM D. GREEN is an associate professor of history at Augsburg College. He is a frequent contributor to *Minnesota History* and wrote the foreword to Michael Fedo's *The Lynchings in Duluth* (MHS, 2000). His article on segregation in St. Paul's public schools received the Solon J. Buck Award in 1997.

JOHN E. HARTMANN's article "The Minnesota Gag Law and the Fourteenth Amendment" received the Solon J. Buck Award for 1960.

JOHN E. HAYNES is the author of *Dubious Alliance: The Making of Minnesota's DFL Party* (Minnesota, 1984), *The American Communist Movement: Storming Heaven Itself* (Twayne, 1992), and *Red Scare or Red Menace?: American Communism and Anticommunism in the Cold War Era* (Ivan R. Dee, 1996). He is the twentieth-century political history specialist in the manuscript division at the Library of Congress. His essay included here received the Solon J. Buck Award for 1971.

EDWARD G. LONGACRE is the author of numerous articles and more than twenty books on the Civil War, including the Fletcher Pratt Prize-winning *The Cavalry at Gettysburg: A Tactical Study of Mounted Operations During the Civil War's Pivotal Campaign, 9 June–14 July 1863* (Nebraska, 1993), *Joshua Chamberlain: The Soldier and the Man* (Da Capo, 1999), and *William Dorsey Pender: Lee's Favorite Brigade Commander* (Da Capo, 2001). He currently resides in Newport News, Virginia.

G. THEODORE MITAU was a noted professor of political science at Macalester College for most of his teaching career and Chancellor of the Minnesota State University System from 1968 to 1976. His books included *Decade of Decision: The Supreme Court and the Constitutional Revolution, 1954–1964* (Scriber, 1967) and *Politics in Minnesota* (Minnesota, 1970). He died in 1979 at the age of fifty-nine. His article on the Democratic-Farmer-Labor Party received the Solon J. Buck Award in 1955.

BARBARA T. NEWCOMBE was the news librarian with the *Chicago Tribune* in its Washington, D.C., bureau when she researched her article on the treaty meetings of 1858. She subsequently became the electronic news librarian in the

Chicago office, where she worked until she retired. In 1997 she was awarded the Joseph F. Kwapil Memorial Award, the news division's highest honor, and co-authored *Paper Trails: A Guide to Public Records in California* (Center for Investigative Reporting, 1998). Her article in this collection was one of two that tied for the Solon J. Buck Award for best article published in *Minnesota History* in 1976.

GRACE LEE NUTE was curator of manuscripts and research associate at the Minnesota Historical Society for nearly forty years, during which time she also taught at Hamline University, the University of Minnesota, and Macalester College. Her books include *The Voyageur's Highway: Minnesota's Border Lake Land* (MHS, 1941), *Caesars of the Wilderness: Médard Chouart, Sieur des Groseilliers and Pierre Esprit Radisson, 1618–1710* (Appelton-Century, 1943; MHS, 1978), and *Rainy River Country: A Brief History of the Region Bordering Minnesota and Ontario* (MHS, 1950). She died in 1990 at the age of ninety-four.

CARLTON C. QUALEY was a long-time professor of history at Carleton College (1946–1970), author of several books, and the chief architect of the Minnesota Ethnic History Project that resulted in the book, *They Chose Minnesota*, published by the Minnesota Historical Society Press in 1981. His contribution to that project formed the basis for *Norwegians in Minnesota* (MHS, 2002). He died in 1988.

GLENDA RILEY is the Alexander M. Bracken Professor of History at Ball State University. Her numerous books include *Building and Breaking Families in the American West* (New Mexico, 1996), *Women and Nature: Saving the "Wild" West* (Nebraska, 1999), and *The Life and Legacy of Annie Oakley* (Oklahoma, 2000).

LaVERN J. RIPPLEY is professor and chairman of the German department at St. Olaf College in Northfield, Minnesota. His books include *The Immigrant Experience in Wisconsin* (Twayne, 1985), *German-Bohemians: The Quiet Immigrants* (St. Olaf, 1995), and *Noble Women, Restless Men* (St. Olaf, 1996).

JOHN S. SONNEN was a longtime member of the Minnesota Historical Society and a resident of St. Paul when his correspondence was published.

BARBARA STUHLER is a retired professor and administrator at the University of Minnesota. Her books include *Gentle Warriors: Clara Ueland and the Minnesota Struggle for Woman Suffrage* (MHS, 1995), *Women of Minnesota: Selected Biographical Essays,* co-edited with Gretchen Kreuter (MHS, 1998), and *A Bond of Learning: Changing Times and the New Century Clubs of St. Paul, 1887–2000* (Pogo Press, 2001).

ALISON WATTS is the youngest historian included in this collection. She was a sophomore in high school in 1999, when she participated in the annual History Day Program and was named the winner of the best senior division History Day paper on a Minnesota topic. The prize included publication of her paper in *Minnesota History*.

LAURA E. WEBER is the communications coordinator for the University of Minnesota General College. Her essay, "Gentiles Preferred," received the Solon J. Buck Award for 1992, and her thesis, on which the article is based, won the Harold Goldenberg Award for best paper on a Jewish topic. Another of her articles, "Wins and Losses: The National Register of Historic Places in Minnesota," published in *Minnesota History*, received the David Stanley Gebhard Award from the Society of Architectural Historians.

BRUCE M. WHITE is the author of numerous articles on Minnesota history. He is a contributor to *Where Two Worlds Meet: The Great Lakes Fur Trade* (MHS, 1982), *Making Minnesota Territory, 1849–1858* (MHS, 1999), and *Fish in the Lakes, Wild Rice, and Game in Abundance: Testimony on Behalf of Mille Lacs Ojibwe Hunting and Fishing Rights* (Michigan State, 2000). His article on gift giving in the fur trade received the Theodore C. Blegen Award in 1982, and his piece on Joseph Rolette, Jr., received the Solon J. Buck Award in 1999.

ROBERT ZEIDEL is a senior lecturer at the University of Wisconsin-Stout, where he was recently awarded a Professional Development Grant to pursue his research on anti-Semitism in United States immigration policy from 1910 to 1924. His previous work has appeared in *Minnesota History* and *North Dakota History*. He is a frequent presenter at the Northern Great Plains History Conference.

Index